GERMAN PHILOSOPHY AND
THE FIRST WORLD WAR

How did the First World War, the so-called Great War – widely seen on all sides as "the war to end all wars" – impact the development of German philosophy? Combining history and biography with astute philosophical and textual analysis, Nicolas de Warren addresses here the intellectual trajectories of ten significant wartime philosophers: Ernst Bloch, Martin Buber, Ernst Cassirer, Hermann Cohen, György Lukács, Martin Heidegger, Edmund Husserl, Franz Rosenzweig, Max Scheler, and Georg Simmel. In exploring their individual works written during and after the war, the author reveals how philosophical concepts and new forms of thinking were forged in response to this unprecedented catastrophe. In reassessing standardized narratives of German thought, the book deepens and enhances our understanding of the intimate and complex relationship between philosophy and violence by demonstrating how the 1914–18 conflict was a crucible for ways of thinking that still define us today.

NICOLAS DE WARREN is Professor of Philosophy and Jewish Studies at Pennsylvania State University. He is the author of *Husserl and the Promise of Time* (Cambridge University Press, 2010), *A Momentary Breathlessness in the Sadness of Time* (2018), and *Original Forgiveness* (2020).

GERMAN PHILOSOPHY AND THE FIRST WORLD WAR

NICOLAS DE WARREN

Pennsylvania State University

Shaftesbury Road, Cambridge CB2 8EA, United Kingdom

One Liberty Plaza, 20th Floor, New York, NY 10006, USA

477 Williamstown Road, Port Melbourne, VIC 3207, Australia

314–321, 3rd Floor, Plot 3, Splendor Forum, Jasola District Centre, New Delhi – 110025, India

103 Penang Road, #05–06/07, Visioncrest Commercial, Singapore 238467

Cambridge University Press is part of Cambridge University Press & Assessment, a department of the University of Cambridge.

We share the University's mission to contribute to society through the pursuit of education, learning and research at the highest international levels of excellence.

www.cambridge.org
Information on this title: www.cambridge.org/9781108437615

DOI: 10.1017/9781108526180

© Nicolas de Warren 2023

This publication is in copyright. Subject to statutory exception and to the provisions of relevant collective licensing agreements, no reproduction of any part may take place without the written permission of Cambridge University Press & Assessment.

First published 2023
First paperback edition 2025

A catalogue record for this publication is available from the British Library

ISBN 978-1-108-42349-6 Hardback
ISBN 978-1-108-43761-5 Paperback

Cambridge University Press & Assessment has no responsibility for the persistence or accuracy of URLs for external or third-party internet websites referred to in this publication and does not guarantee that any content on such websites is, or will remain, accurate or appropriate.

*An meine Heidelberger Freunde
Rick, Paul, Charlie, Rupert, Jan-Ivar, Jörg,
Christian, Albrecht, und Christina Marie*

Contents

Acknowledgments	*page* viii
Introduction: "What's the Seminar Got to Do with the War?"	1
1 The Genius of War, the Genius of Peace: Max Scheler's Demons	12
2 *Deutschtum und Judentum*: Hermann Cohen in the Time of the Nations	47
3 I and Thou: Martin Buber and Dialogical Creation	83
4 More than Life: Georg Simmel's Philosophical Testament	115
5 The Apocalypse of Hope: Ernst Bloch's Phenomenology of Utopic Spirit	153
6 The Road to Damascus in the Age of Capitalism: György Lukács and *History and Class Consciousness*	186
7 From Death into Life: Franz Rosenzweig's Redemptions	226
8 "A Journey around the World": Ernst Cassirer, Freedom in Ways of Worldmaking	272
9 Martin Heidegger and the Titanic Struggle over Being	312
10 The Tragedy of the Person: Edmund Husserl at War	367
Bibliography	401
Index	420

Acknowledgments

During the writing of this book, I benefited from advice, discussion, and ideas from friends and colleagues: Gérard Bensussan, Roland Breeur, Joseph Cohen, Sophie De Schaepdrijver, Stein De Cuyper, James Dodd, Kenneth Haynes, Ulrich Melle, Susan Neiman, Panos Theodorou, Thomas Vongehr, and Sam Willems. Michael Gubser and William Remley kindly read earlier versions of the manuscript and offered valuable comments. Years ago, I was fortunate to have been warmly received by Michael Hampe, whose inspiration has since never abated. My thanks as well from those days to Dominic Kaegi and Hans-Peter Schütt. I am particularly grateful to Hilary Gaskin for her patience and encouragement with the long-overdue completion of this book. This project was launched through a European Research Council Consolidator Grant, obtained in 2015 during my stint as Research Professor of Philosophy at the Husserl Archives, Higher Institute of Philosophy, KU Leuven. Unless otherwise indicated, all translations are mine.

Introduction
"What's the Seminar Got to Do with the War?"

In his autobiography, *Mein zwanzigstes Jahrhundert*, Ludwig Marcuse recalls:

> Toward the end of July, I encountered one of my respectable seminar colleagues, Hellmuth Falkenfeld, on Goethestrasse [in Freiburg]. He said, despairingly: "Have you heard what's happened?" I said, full of contempt and resignedly, "I know, Sarajevo." He said, "Not that, Rickert's seminar tomorrow is cancelled." I said, alarmed: "Is he sick?" He said, "No, because of the threatening war." I said, "What's the seminar got to do with the war?" He shrugged sadly.[1]

More than a century later, the broader implication of Marcuse's question – what has philosophy got to do with the war? – remains as alluring as ever, and has arguably become more challenging to answer given the sedimentation of established narratives, or lack thereof, that have long shaped our presumed understanding of the relation between European philosophy and – in George F. Kennan's oft-quoted expression – "the original catastrophe of the twentieth century." This question concerning the relation between the First World War and philosophical thought – and more generally, the relation between war and philosophy – does not only take the form of inquiring what philosophers did in the war (military service, observers from the home front, exiled in a foreign country), but of what philosophers intellectually did with the war, of how the war became a catalyst for their thinking, a theme of philosophical reflection, an opportunity for the renewed relevance of philosophy, or an obstacle to philosophical understanding. Of equal (and inseparable) significance is the question of what the war did to philosophers, of how the war impacted philosophical thinking, and, likewise, of how the role and image of the philosopher became affected, indeed afflicted, by the war. The aim of this book is to explore how there is

---

[1] L. Marcuse, *Mein zwanzigstes Jahrhundert* (Zurich: Diogenes, 1975), p. 30.

no simple or single answer to this tangle of questions, and that, more specifically, one cannot understand the formation of twentieth-century German philosophy – the focus of this study – without returning to the First World War in light of the twin questions: "What has philosophy got to do with the war?" and "What did the war do to philosophy?" Guided by these questions, *German Philosophy and the First World War* orchestrates a series of explorations of the paths taken by central figures in German philosophy in their reaction to, and experience of, the Great War (as it was then often called) in such a way that recognizes the complexity of the philosophical issues that animated their thinking, as well as the existential demands of wartime and its aftermath to which these thinkers responded in both word and deed.

Within weeks after the outbreak of hostilities in August 1914, the First World War was recognized from various philosophical perspectives as a world-historical event that would reveal, condemn, or decide the fate of the twentieth century. For many, the war promised release from the tedium and contradictions of an ever-advancing modernization of life; for others, it was anticipated with fright and foreboding; for yet others, it was welcomed as a fulfillment of revolutionary change and destructive renewal. Regardless of how the war's significance was perceived, none could then fathom the enduring ways in which European civilization – its values, forms of thought, social organization, and political orientations – would be transformed. As Henry James, residing in England, grasped lucidly in 1914:

> The plunge of civilization into this abyss of blood and darkness by the wanton feat of two infamous autocrats is a thing that so gives away the whole long age during which we have supposed the world to be, with whatever abatement, gradually bettering, that to have to take it all now for what the treacherous years were all the while really making for and *meaning* is too tragic for any words.[2]

And yet, words there were aplenty, especially from philosophers, whose loquaciousness during this time of war was historically unprecedented. The guns of August provoked a widespread engagement of philosophers in the principal belligerent nation within the wider spectrum of what Kurt Flasch insightfully calls the "spiritual mobilization" of intellectuals, university professors, artists, and writers.[3] Henri Bergson, Max Scheler, Bertrand Russell, and others took to arms by taking to their pens, for or against national cause and culture, for or against the war itself, for or

---

[2] Henry James, *Letters*, ed. P. Lubbock (London: Macmillan, 1920), p. 398. Letter of August 5, 1914.
[3] K. Flasch, *Die geistige Mobilmachung. Die deutschen Intellektuellen und der Erste Weltkrieg. Ein Versuch* (Berlin: Alexander Fest Verlag, 2000).

against established conceptions of philosophy. This catalyst for philosophical expression and engagement did not only gravitate around fathoming (or prophesizing) the meaning of the war (culturally, socially, historically, and philosophically); it reflected more pervasively a situation of philosophy *at* war, whether transfigured into the pursuit of war by other means or whether the war set in motion the transformation of philosophical thinking by other means. For many thinkers, the war was seen as in need of philosophical justification and conceptualization. For some, the war appeared as a force capable of bestowing or rejuvenating meaning in a world deemed to be empty of meaningfulness. For others, the war provided a stage for the awakening of philosophical thinking from its dogmatic slumber or skeptical resignation. And for still others, the war revealed the urgency of finding philosophically an exodus or exile from a cultural wasteland and the history of Western civilization with its legacy of endemic conflict. From a variety of approaches and angles, the war was an event that called into question the meaningfulness of it all. Whether for metaphysics, ethics, politics, culture, value, history, modern culture, social theory – indeed, the full range of philosophical concerns – the First World War was experienced as an original catastrophe of philosophical proportions.

What is immediately striking about the wartime invigoration of philosophical thinking across the European continent is its range and diversity, which cannot be reduced to simply being "about" the war inasmuch as the war was not understood as being simply "about" the war. No other European conflict before the First World War, and arguably no European conflict since, including the Second World War, witnessed such an intense and widespread impact in situ on philosophers. This veritable explosion of intellectual activity took on many forms, and was often specific to its institutional and cultural context, including the engagement of philosophical discourse in the war itself, extending from shrill justifications of a nation's war efforts to endorsements of military and political strategy (for example, the support for the implementation of unrestricted submarine warfare in Germany) to rarer instances of calls for pacifism (as with Bertrand Russell). This wartime mobilization of philosophy adopted and adapted a host of literary and rhetorical configurations: public speeches, university lectures, private notebooks, letters, pamphlets, monographs, newspaper editorials, and longer forms of gestation that would only come to fruition decades after the end of hostilities.

Philosophy, however, was not only mobilized in the service of the war. For the war (and its aftermath) provoked the mobilization of philosophy in its own service; namely, as a crucible for philosophical contestation and creativity. As a historical watershed, the war set the stage for the conceiving of "new thinking" and the composition of original philosophical works that have since become recognized and canonized as defining twentieth-century philosophy: Ludwig Wittgenstein's *Tractatus Logico-Philosophicus*, Franz Rosenzweig's *The Star of Redemption*, Martin Buber's *I and Thou*, Ernst Bloch's *The Spirit of Utopia*, and György Lukács' *History and Class Consciousness* – to name but a few. Aside from philosophical thinking at war, philosophical thinking became forged *in* war. Moreover, in addition to works written during the war and its volatile revolutionary aftermath, numerous original philosophical works composed during the 1920s and 1930s – Martin Heidegger's *Being and Time*, Ernst Cassirer's *The Philosophy of Symbolic Forms*, Henri Bergson's *Two Sources of Morality and Religion* – emerged in the wake of a war that, philosophically, culturally, and psychologically, was far from over and done with. Most famously, under the long shadow of the war's devastation, the 1920s and 1930s witnessed a parting of the ways in twentieth-century philosophy between "Analytic Philosophy" and "Continental Philosophy." Within the shattered intellectual landscape of the interwar years, there occurred, in fact, multiple partings of ways (and contrary to received wisdom, not just one), as one of the war's most profound and enduring legacies, arguably its most defining philosophical aftershock. Conjointly with the reconfiguration of philosophical movements and methods along fault lines of divide, there occurred as well during these turbulent interwar years the forgetting or exiting of philosophical ways of thinking that did not survive the aftermath of war. The eclipse of German-Jewish thinking and destruction of German-Jewish culture in the 1930s and 1940s, the collapse of the Austro-Hungarian space of philosophical thought, and the obliteration of Goethe's paramount significance for German thinkers are examples of how narratives of "the parting of ways" should include a history of forgetting and disappearance as the manifestation of historical violence upon philosophical memory. The historical consciousness of philosophy – the stories told and not told – was itself transformed, giving rise to different genealogies of modern philosophy and its underlying plot (secularization, the end of metaphysics, and so on), canonizations in the historiography of philosophy (the ascendency of Marx, Kierkegaard, and Nietzsche, for example), and movements that have since become entrenched in curricula and histories of twentieth-century philosophy (the Frankfurt School, phenomenology, and existentialism at the expense of Neo-Kantianism and British Hegelianism, for example). And lastly, in this all too brief aperçu, it was during the war and its aftermath that novel ways of speaking philosophically entered into circulation: "intentionality," "totality," "the other," "alterity," "the in-between," "dialogue," "state of affairs," "facticity," and other examples abound. All in all, not one aspect of twentieth-century European philosophy can be understood without inquiring "What has philosophy got to do with the war?" and "What did the war do to philosophy?"

*

It is therefore surprising that while the impact of the First World War on literature and the arts – and on culture, institutions, and values more generally – has been the subject of inquiry and interpretation, the question of whether and how the war induced a fundamental change in philosophical thinking remains relatively unexamined, often misunderstood, or simply taken for granted. Aside from a handful of specialized studies of individual philosophers and their biographies, the rare monograph, and an occasional collection of conference papers, the First World War's impact on European philosophy, during the years of conflagration and interwar years leading to the Second World War, has passed into a veritable historical as well as philosophical oblivion.

This forgetting of the war within philosophical memory can in part be accounted for by the controversial "war philosophy" mobilized during 1914–18, mainly but not exclusively in Germany (one thinks, for example, of Bergson's wartime writings, speeches, and diplomatic activity). Aside from a handful of minor studies of individual philosophers, predominantly Martin Heidegger, the few exceptions that have taken up German philosophy during the First World War, and in particular *Kriegsphilosophie*, in a more concerted fashion are (nearly) unanimous in their sweeping judgment that German philosophers during these years of conflict succumbed to "self-deceit" and "ideology."[4] Such a judgment is bolstered by the manner in which wartime intellectual support embraced its role as propaganda and, indeed, pioneered modern propaganda in a highly literate culture of mass media and robust political identification.[5] Max Scheler, Rudolf Eucken, Hermann Cohen, and others produced philosophical writings (books, public and university lectures, pamphlets, newspaper pieces) in support of the German war effort that are routinely dismissed as paradigmatically "unphilosophical." On such a judgment, these philosophers were swept away by the prevailing tides of

---

[4] H. Lübbe, *Politische Philosophie in Deutschland* (Munich: DTV, 1974); Sebastian Luft, "Germany's Metaphysical War: Reflections on War by Two Representatives of German Philosophy: Max Scheler and Paul Natorp," *Themenportal Erster Weltkrieg* (2007), www.erster-weltkrieg.clio-online.de; Peter Hoeres, *Krieg der Philosophen: Die deutsche und Britische Philosophie im Ersten Weltkrieg* (Paderborn: Ferdinand Schöningh Verlag, 2004).
[5] Extensively studied in H. Fries, *Die große Katharsis. Der Erste Weltkrieg in der Sicht deutscher Dichter und Gelehrter* (Konstanz: Verlag am Hockgraben, 1994); see also Flasch, *Die geistige Mobilmachung*.

nationalism and chauvinist prejudice. This argument for the collapse of philosophy into ideology extends to what is undoubtedly the most studied aspect of the impact of the war on philosophy, namely, the development of a German conservative revolution and reactionary modernism during the 1920s and 1930s in the writings of Heidegger and Carl Schmitt (among others). The long shadow of complex (and contentious) questions regarding these two German mandarins has arguably eclipsed the wider and more diverse impact of the war on philosophy during the interwar years, with the question remaining open whether the *Kriegsphilosophie* of the First World War is only to be seen as evidence of an absence of philosophy in a time of war.

There is a further reason for the paucity of research in and understanding of the relation between the First World War and European philosophy that reflects an entrenched conceit exemplified in *The Cambridge History of Philosophy 1870–1945*. This collection of essays on the development of philosophy from 1870 to 1945 is organized around the dividing marker of 1914–18, thus ascribing a decisive significance to the First World War. And yet, although it is acknowledged that the question of whether the war "induced a significant shift is addressed in English surprisingly rarely," and is "not a simple one," the editor concludes that the consequences of the war were "primarily external to the internal dialectic of philosophy." On this view, an answer to the question of whether "philosophy in any way internalized the experience of the war" must receive a "primarily negative response": The war did not "produce new understandings but rather called into question older ways of thinking […] *without providing replacements.*"[6] This claim, however, is implausible given the numerous attestations among "the who's who" of interwar thinking in search of a "new thinking," "the renewal of philosophy," and "another beginning for reflection." Whereas the war transformed poetry, literature, and the arts, philosophy would have remained internally unfazed. The strangeness of the amnesia expressed with such a claim can aptly be formulated with Kurt Flasch's contention: "While no one would dare to write an history of painting or literature in our century without reference to the First World War, German historians of philosophy have confirmed once again their monkish extraterritorial autonomy […] Post-War German historians of philosophy have forgotten the war."[7] A comparable forgetting of the war can be ascribed to historians of twentieth-century philosophy more generally.

---

[6] *The Cambridge History of Philosophy 1870–1945*, ed. T. Baldwin (Cambridge, UK: Cambridge University Press, 2012), p. 377 (my emphasis).
[7] Flasch, *Die geistige Mobilmachung*, p. 369.

However implausible, the claim (and conceit) that philosophy did not "internalize" the experience of war and "produce replacements" for old ways of thinking can nonetheless be seized as both an opportunity and a provocation to undertake a reframing of the question of whether and how the First World War induced any significant transformation in philosophical thought. Limiting itself to German philosophy, the aim of this book is to delineate and develop an original approach to this question (in fact, a tangle of questions) based on the guiding thought that the war's impact on philosophy does not have one general "meaning," "effect," or "significance," and thus does not admit of one *kind* of answer. Rather than assume a generic or generalized "answer," *German Philosophy and the First World War* seeks instead to examine the question of the war's impact on philosophical thinking *in the plural*, and, through this multifocal lens, critically to reassess the transformations of German philosophy during the First World War and its aftermath. In this respect, *German Philosophy and the First World War* is not an intellectual history of German philosophy nor a biographical study of German philosophers. The endeavor has not been to write a history painted in broad strokes and told in swift narratives of philosophical ideas. The aim is likewise neither to present a comprehensive historical-cultural account of *Kriegsphilosophie* nor to offer a sociology of knowledge for the wartime mobilization of German academic mandarins, although certain thinkers discussed in this book contributed to the phenomenon of *Kriegsphilosophie* (whether early or later in the war, or throughout the war).

The ambition here is at once broader and more nuanced, namely, to think about philosophy in the time of war, about how the war impacted German philosophers in their thinking as well as their personal attitudes (the two of which are inextricable). This ambition must necessarily fall short of any claim to exhaustiveness; many thinkers who could have been included – Walter Benjamin, Gershom Scholem, Karl Jaspers, Carl Schmitt, and Rudolf Eucken (to name but a few) – have been set aside due to considerations of space. *German Philosophy and the First World War* likewise excludes from consideration sociologists (with the exception of Georg Simmel), theologians, historians, and other intellectuals and artists, although many of these figures, such as Max Weber and Oswald Spengler, are discussed parenthetically. For reasons of space and, more importantly, historical-cultural context, other constraints have been imposed on the remit of this study: German-language thinkers of the Austro-Hungarian Empire (Ludwig Wittgenstein, Fritz Mauthner, and Sigmund Freud, for example) have been left aside (with the exception of György Lukács), as have members of the Vienna Circle, the origins of which, however, cannot be understood without the First World War.

German Philosophy and the First World War is organized around studies of Ernst Bloch, Martin Buber, Ernst Cassirer, Hermann Cohen, György Lukács, Martin Heidegger, Edmund Husserl, Franz Rosenzweig, Max Scheler, and Georg Simmel. This gallery of philosophical portraits is not fashioned into a unified image of "German thought" and parsed into a menu of different "movements," nor are they meant to be viewed as museum pieces of antiquarian curiosity. On the other hand, these portraits are not haphazardly or eclectically brought together without intersecting relations and resonances among the chapters of the book. A reader is invited to view these portraits as forming together a philosophical kaleidoscope; variable combinations of different portraits can be rotated to produce different overall images or gestalts of central themes running through various thinkers ("modernity," "secularization," and so on). The effort throughout these portraits is to exhibit and explore how these thinkers thought in different rhythms (at times in tune with the war, at other times out of tune) and at different speeds of intellectual innovation. Rather than a linear narrative connecting these portraits in a one-dimensional sequence, this gallery of portraits embodies Ernst Bloch's notion of "the simultaneity of non-simultaneity" as characterizing the temporality of modernity in which philosophical thought, in each of the cases studied here, sought to find, or lose, its way.

The thinkers here on view often moved in the same circles, wrote for the same venues, and reacted to one another's philosophical initiatives. Most substantially, of course, these thinkers experienced the war, and yet did not experience the war in the same manner, from the same place, and, crucially, with the same experience of its unfolding and impact on their philosophical thinking. The kaleidoscopic composition of *German Philosophy and the First World War* moves at variable speeds and configurations through a shared space of concerns, with overlaps that reappear (or disappear) through different registers of significance and implication. In this manner, this kaleidoscopic topography allows for complex resonances and dissonances to emerge across a plurality of (often) intersecting and conflicting – combative – narratives. This orchestration accordingly serves as an important antidote to other approaches to the history of twentieth-century philosophy, such as one finds among cultural historians or historians of philosophy, that tend to absorb the particularity of these thinkers into an overarching narrative that would seek to arrive at a global answer to the question of the philosophical impact of the First World War.

Although *German Philosophy and the First World War* eschews an encompassing metanarrative through its kaleidoscopic configuration, many concepts and concerns do recur throughout, such as the critique of capitalism and the alienation of modern culture, the rejection of secularization, and the war as renewal or as the crisis that leads to renewal. Rather than organize the portraits in this book directly along these lines, the three recurring themes of "wartime," "philosophy in war," and "transformation" provide cardinal points of bearing for the discussion, argument, and interpretations of each chapter.

Wartime. Each portrait begins with the outbreak of the war, but does not end its discussion with a uniform date ("1918," for example). This variability regarding the reach of each chapter reflects not only the fact that for the thinkers here explored the war, in its philosophical and personal significance, did not uniformly end at a common moment or event, nor indeed with the November Armistice of 1918. This flexibility in temporal scope allows (in many chapters) for the interwar dimensionality of the war's aftermath during the 1920s and 1930s to enter into view; spiritually, the war did not end in 1918. In some chapters, death during the war provided a natural cut-off point (Simmel and Cohen, who both died in 1918 before the war's end); for others, the impact of the war is followed along a longer arc of development (Cassirer, Husserl, Heidegger, Scheler), but even here the endpoint is variable (the discussion of Heidegger, for example, does not extend beyond the middle of the Second World War); for others, the appearance of a major work immediately after the war (Bloch, Buber, Lukács, Rosenzweig) marks the terminal point of discussion. In each case, the discussion of each thinker begins in situ with the outbreak of the war in 1914. For reasons of approach and space, this book does not offer a preliminary panorama of nineteenth-century German philosophy, nor a detailed summary of a thinker's intellectual evolution before the war (nor, in most instances, after the war until their death). As examined as well, the experience of wartime varied according to location and movement during the war (service in the field, at the home front, in exile). Lastly, assessing the situation of philosophy in wartime is further complicated for several thinkers (Heidegger, Cassirer, Bloch, Buber, Lukács) by the Second World War, which arguably would have to be included in an assessment of the First World War's impact, thus bringing both wars into an overarching narrative.

Philosophy in war – philosophy at war. The twin questions "What has philosophy got to do with the war?" and "What did the war do to philosophy?" form the central axis of *German Philosophy and the First World War*. Not only does philosophical thinking find itself *in* war, but in several instances philosophical thinking finds itself *at* war, and not only with its mobilization within the broader phenomenon of *Kriegsphilosophie* (Scheler, Husserl, Cohen, Simmel). For several thinkers, the imperative of philosophical thinking was emphatically understood against the war (Bloch, Lukács) or against a certain narrative of the war's perceived significance (Cassirer, Rosenzweig). For many, war becomes a compelling figuration of philosophical thinking itself, whether in its contestation against other philosophical movements or in search of another beginning, a radically other future, or exodus from the contemporary wasteland of a world at war. For others, the war is given a philosophical voice, as it were, in grasping the war (and being grasped by the war) as an event calling for and calling upon a new philosophical thinking. For many, the seismic center of "the war" varied as well: outbreak of the war in 1914, cataclysmic defeat in 1918, the Russian Revolution of 1917, the German Revolution of 1919. To this consideration of "which" war is in play needs to be added the ways in which the war alternatively served as the foreground or background for a thinker's philosophical transformation; whether war is the stage upon which philosophical thinking was changed or whether it was philosophical thinking itself that served as the stage for a transformation of the war's perceived significance.

Transformation. A common denominator running through this gallery of portraits is transformation. As with the themes of "wartime" and "philosophy in war – philosophy at war," the transformation of philosophical thinking did not occur uniformly, with the same significance and consequence, nor to the same degree and promise among these thinkers. In some instances there is "a conversion," or "a turning," or "a change of heart," or even an irresolvable conflict or contradiction. In other cases there are multiple ruptures and moments of transformation, not all of which were clearly discernible or understood by the thinkers themselves. But in all of the portraits gathered in this book, philosophical thinking underwent a transformation, in different senses, that drew from a variety of catalysts, provocations, and influences. Across the multiple narratives presented here, what emerges is how German philosophical thinking seeks to transform itself into something other, or ends up finding itself somewhere other than imagined, or fails to become other than itself, despite its searching. In each case, transformation is animated by the desire for a "new thinking" and, in several cases, a new form of life for the philosopher as well as for the world that they felt the historical urgency to renew.

As a kaleidoscope, the portraits in this gallery can be viewed in any order. Each chapter unfolds along its own narrative and philosophical path in such a way that it moves from the historical situation and experience of a respective philosopher to an analysis of their philosophical works, where, in the spirit of a hermeneutical approach, original philosophical interpretations are developed with the intention of motivating a reader to return to these works in unsuspected ways. Throughout, there is an attempt to juggle – not balance – "life" and "thinking," "history" and "text," "internal" and "external," without simplistic reductions or empty generalizations, without, in other words, the juggling coming to a halt; it is the manifold tensions among these distinctions that are mapped in these studies. If anything, the aim of *German Philosophy and the First World War* is to render the portraits of these thinkers *more complex*, not less so, in the absence of an embracing metanarrative in which each of these figures would be neatly classified and hence tucked away – made familiar and distant – in either a "history of philosophy" or a "philosophy without a history." What has German philosophy got to do with the war – what did the war do to Germany philosophy? There are not only many different answers to these entwined questions, but different ways of formulating this ferment of questioning, and it is such differences that speak more to "What has philosophy got to do with the war?" than anything, in ways that continue to solicit our understanding today.

CHAPTER I

The Genius of War, the Genius of Peace
Max Scheler's Demons

A Sacred War

On August 25, 1914, three weeks after the invasion of Belgium (August 4) and two months after the fateful assassination of the Archduke Franz Ferdinand and his wife in Sarajevo (June 28), German troops entered the city of Leuven and destroyed its celebrated university library. Some 300,000 books and more than a thousand irreplaceable Medieval manuscripts were burnt along with the torching of 2,000 buildings and the killing of 248 civilians.[1] The devastation was so intense that Dietrich Mahnke, a student of Edmund Husserl's serving in the 75th Reserve Infantry Regiment, could still observe the city burning on August 27 as his company marched through the village of Korbeek-Lo a few kilometers northwest of Leuven. Outrage among intellectuals, politicians, and the public in Allied nations was swift. Romain Rolland penned an open letter to Gerhart Hauptmann on August 29 condemning this "assault on culture and humanity." In the words of British Prime Minister H. H. Asquith: "The burning of Louvain is the worst thing [the Germans] have yet done. It reminds one of the Thirty Years' War." As Sir Arthur Evans, the famed archaeologist who excavated the ruins of Knossos, declared in *The Times*: "Sir, may I be allowed to voice horror and profound indignation at the Prussian holocaust of Louvain."[2]

Two weeks after the sacking of Leuven, Reims Cathedral in France was severely damaged by German shelling. After an initial occupation, German troops were forced to withdraw to fortified positions on the outskirts of the city after the battle of the Marne, which effectively halted the sweeping German advance toward Paris and set the stage for the grim

---

[1] See J. Lipkes, *Rehearsals: The German Army in Belgium, August 1914* (Leuven: Leuven University Press, 2007).
[2] Quoted in A. Kramer, *Dynamic of Destruction: Culture and Mass Killing in the First World War* (Oxford: Oxford University Press, 2007), p. 14.

deadlock of trench warfare that would indelibly define the Western Front. Over the course of three days, German artillery set fire to the cathedral's roof and damaged its facades. Along with the destruction of Leuven University Library, the shelling of Reims Cathedral ruptured cultural relations between France (as well as England) and Germany. As Rolland indignantly wrote: "Whoever destroys this work murders more than a person, he murders the purest soul of a race." The London *Times* equated the shelling of the cathedral to the deeds of Attila the Hun. Decrying it as a "barbaric shame and horror," demands that "the beast must be killed" became widespread in newspapers and Allied propaganda. "German mentality," it was proclaimed, had "regressed to a state of barbarity."[3]

Reims Cathedral possessed a special significance as a place of remembrance and incarnation of the sacred union between France and Catholicism. As the historical location for the coronation of French kings and the site of an imposing statue of Joan of Arc, erected in 1896 in commemoration of her victory over the English and Charles VII's coronation (1429), the cathedral symbolized the divine authority of French kings and France's self-appointed defense of Christianity. The desecration of Reims Cathedral was not just a crime against French civilization by the might of Prussian *Kultur*. It was an attack on France's Catholic identity, thereby imbuing the war with religious overtones.[4] As Georges Bataille, 17 years old and serving in the 154th Infantry Regiment at the time, meditated on the cathedral's defacement in his first publication *Notre-Dame de Reims*: "I thought that corpses themselves did not mirror death more than did a shattered church as vastly in its magnificence as Notre-Dame de Reims."[5] According to the Dutch war correspondent Lodewijk Hermen Grondijs, who chronicled firsthand the German invasion of Belgium, the defilement of Catholic churches, and the killing of priests, the German army was undertaking nothing less than a "religious war."[6]

---

[3] T. Gaehtgens, *Reims on Fire: War and Reconciliation between France and Germany* (Los Angeles: Getty Research Institute, 2018), pp. 51, 53.
[4] As Léon Bloy bitterly wrote: "La où l'anglais offrait une Croix de bois à Jeanne d'Arc au bucher, l'hérétique Allemagne offre une Croix de fer aux assassins et incendiaires pour les récompenser de leurs crimes." [Where the English offered a Wooden Cross to Joan of Arc at the stake, heretical Germany offers an Iron Cross to assassins and arsonists to reward them for their crimes.] *Jeanne d'Arc et l'Allemagne* (Paris: Mercure de France, 1915), p. 263.
[5] Quoted in D. Hollier, *Against Architecture: The Writings of George Bataille* (Cambridge, MA: MIT Press, 1989), pp. 15–19.
[6] L. Grondijs, *Les Allemands en Belgique: Louvain et Aerschot* (Paris: Librairie Militaire – Berger-Levrault, 1915), p. 19. For documentation of anti-Catholic sentiments among the German soldiers of the mainly Protestant First, Second, and Third Armies, see J. Horne and A. Kramer, *German Atrocities, 1914* (New Haven, CT: Yale University Press, 2001), pp. 104–108.

From the pronouncements of intellectuals to mass propaganda, from the speeches of politicians and sermons of the clergy to private letters of soldiers, the rhetoric and ritualization of a sacred war suffused the mobilization of Europe.[7] This symbiosis of the political, the cultural, and the religious was arguably nowhere more virulently on display than with Kaiser Wilhelm II's address to the German nation on August 4. The Kaiser's speech had been authored by the liberal Protestant theologian Adolf Harnack, who served as his privy counselor and president of the Kaiser Wilhelm Foundation.[8] The nationalistic ambitions of science and religion, essential for the advancement of German culture, were exemplified in Harnack, whose influential version of Liberal Protestantism legitimated the synthesis of theology and politics, church and state in the newly forged Wilhelmine Empire.[9] In the rousing words of army pastor Otto Meyer to volunteers on the way to the front on September 9: "Your work is work for the Lord; your war service (*Kriegsdienst*) is a church service (*Gottesdienst*) [...] A bad and godless human being is never a good soldier and a genuine soldier is always a good Christian."[10]

"A Demoniacal Genius Who Stormed from the Heights"

Among numerous manifestations of *Kriegsphilosophie*, Max Scheler's *Der Genius des Krieges und der Deutsche Krieg* stands apart.[11] Occupying the "first place among German war philosophers" as "the highpoint of a philosophical veneration of war," Scheler was one of the most prolific wartime thinkers, and one of the "most colorful."[12] While Alois Riehl declared that Germany had embarked on a "war of culture" – a designation adopted by many prominent thinkers – Scheler's dithyramb to war proclaimed its metaphysical and religious significance.[13] Offering a vision of the world *sub specie belli*, *Der Genius* progresses from an exposition of

---

[7] P. Jenkins, *The Great and Holy War* (New York: HarperCollins, 2014), pp. 7–8.
[8] K. Hammer, *Deutsche Kriegstheologie* (Munich: Kösel-Verlag, 1971), p. 374.
[9] Jenkins, *The Great and Holy War*, p. 11. As Jenkins observes, "activists in most countries spoke the language of Christian warfare, but the German approach to the war still stands out for its widespread willingness to identify the nation's cause with God's will, and for the spiritual exaltation that swept the country in 1914." Indeed, "In two crucial cases, though – Germany and Russia – religious motivations were so inextricably bound up with state ideology and policy making that it is impossible to separate them from secular factors."
[10] Quoted in Hammer, *Deutsche Kriegstheologie*, p. 219.
[11] For a survey of German *Kriegesphilosophie*, Hoeres, *Krieg der Philosophen*.
[12] Flasch, *Die geistige Mobilmachung*, p. 117.
[13] A. Riehl, "1813 – Fichte – 1914 (Rede am 10 Oktober 1914)," in *Deutsche Reden in schwerer Zeit* (Berlin: Verlags-Archiv, 1914), p. 192.

the war's revelation of the "highest ethical values" through an elaboration of the specific German character of the war to the emancipatory promise of Germany's envisioned triumph for "the spiritual unity of Europe" and "humanity." Unlike the spiritual mobilization of preachers and theologians, *Der Genius des Krieges und der Deutsche Krieg* styles itself as an exposition of the "essence" of war by weaponizing Scheler's own philosophical thought. The war represented for Scheler an original awakening of the German nation, as well as, importantly, an exemplification of his own developing ethical thinking.[14]

On the eve of the war, Scheler's intellectual energies were guided by two overlapping concerns: the formation of an ethical theory of values embedded in a spiritual conception of life and objective values, on the one hand, and forging a philosophical critique of modern culture, on the other. Whereas Scheler's approach to ethics leveraged a phenomenological method of intuitionism, a material a priori of ethical values, and a synthesis of personalism and objectivity of values, his cultural critique took its bearings from sociological thinkers (Werner Sombart, Georg Simmel, Max Weber) on the origins of capitalism, modern bureaucracy, and bourgeois individualism. In his 1914 essay "The Future of Capitalism," Scheler railed against "the death of the system of life," "the deep perversion of all basic intellectual energies," and the "delusionary subversion of all meaningful orders of value." In a collection of essays, *Umsturz der Werte* (1915), Scheler ascribed the alienation of modern culture to unbridled capitalism, the mediocrity of the middle class, and rampant mechanization – common themes in the cultural pessimism of German cultural discourse. The "weariness of Empire" (*Reichsverdrossenheit*) plaguing wide swaths of the *Bildungsbürgertum* found a sophisticated expression in Scheler's writings. These cross-fertilizing directions of thought would further develop during the 1920s into an amalgam of philosophical anthropology, sociology of knowledge, and metaphysics of life. Despite envisioning systematic works and comprehensive studies, the restlessness of Scheler's temperament along with the volatility of historical circumstances propelled his thinking along different eccentric orbits around a central desire to understand the place of human existence in the cosmos and humankind's aspiration for the highest, eternal values. As Scheler writes in *The Human Place in the Cosmos* – published a year before his death – "ever since the awakening

---

[14] Flasch, *Die geistige Mobilmachung*, p. 91. As Staude remarks: "The war was undoubtedly one of the most important experiences of Scheler's life. His military service took place more in the realm of ideas than on the battlefield." J. R. Staude, *Max Scheler 1874–1928: An Intellectual Portrait* (New York: Free Press, 1967), p. 66.

of my philosophical thinking, the question 'what is the human being and what is his place in being?' has occupied me more fundamentally than any other question I have dealt with."[15]

Scheler cut an unusual figure among German philosophers. Born of a Jewish mother who converted to Protestantism and a Protestant father, Scheler converted to Catholicism in his youth due to his infatuation with a maid. By every account, he possessed – or, better, he was *possessed by* – a charismatic and tempestuous character. His friend Theodor Lessing described him as "a demoniacal genius who stormed from the heights to the depths of life seeking salvation through debauchery."[16] After an ignominious departure from the University of Munich in 1910 (accused of adultery) and banishment from academic employment, Scheler lectured in coffeehouses, *Weinstuben*, and hotel rooms (paid for by his friend Dietrich von Hildebrand), wandering between Göttingen and Berlin, before settling in Berlin in 1912. Perpetually lacking income, but philosophically undeterred, Scheler embarked on a career as a freelance writer and thinker, thus allowing him to engage a broader audience with his writings on the ethical plight of the modern world.

At the outbreak of war, Scheler was thus an established if itinerant intellectual figure who moved between academic institutions and artistic milieus. Refused for military service due to astigmatism in 1914, but drafted only to be discharged in 1915, Scheler was then enlisted by the department of psychological warfare in the Foreign Ministry to deliver lectures in Belgium, Austria, Switzerland, and Holland.[17] Writing during the first months of the war – his manuscript was finished in November – Scheler published "Der Genius des Krieges" in *Die Neue Rundschau*, followed by an expanded book version in 1915 with an additional section, "Der Deutsche Krieg." *Der Genius des Krieges und der Deutsche Krieg* was a bestseller going through three successive editions (1915, 1916, 1917) that further elevated his public status, especially in Catholic circles. Hermann Bahr praised Scheler's *Kriegsbuch* as a work that would remain significant long after the war: "Scheler's art of persuasion is unrivalled. He is a born educator; I know of no one who can lead us so easily but firmly to the truth." Yet, Scheler's *Kriegsbuch* also provoked dismay. Upon reading Scheler's work, an indignant Max Brod composed a rebuttal of Scheler's *Gesinnungsmilitarismus* ("spiritual militarism") in a short text, "The Genius

---

[15] M. Scheler, *The Human Place in the Cosmos*, trans. E. Kelly (Evanston, IL: Northwestern University Press, 2009), p. 3.
[16] Staude, *Max Scheler*, p. 6.
[17] Staude, *Max Scheler*, p. 68.

of Peace," which on account of its defiant stance against the war was never published.¹⁸ In his indictment of German intellectuals for their wanton legitimation of Germany's imperial ambitions, Hugo Ball sarcastically alluded to Scheler's *Kriegsbuch* in his *Critique of the German Intelligentsia*:

> The Holy Roman Empire of the German Nation and the heraldry of Gothic Kaisers stamped the people with a consciousness that believed service to God and its mission consisted in clanging weapons, judgeships, hangings, smashing things to pieces, and in brute force [...] Even today [1918] Germany still feels that it is both the "Genius of War" and the "moral heart" of the world.¹⁹

"Endlich ein Gott"

August 1914 was for many, especially for the middle class and those belonging to what the cultural historian Fritz Ringer dubbed the German Mandarin caste, welcomed for its "spiritual" significance.²⁰ Even if more apprehensive views prevailed privately, the war enthusiasm, or *Augusterlebnis*, that swept across Germany during the opening weeks of the war tapped into an apocalyptic narrative of German nationalism extending back to the nineteenth century.²¹ In Georg H. Heym's iconic poem *Der Krieg* (1911), the longing for a war that would release a restless youth from the blandness of life took the form of imagining war as a chthonic god awaking from subterranean depths:²²

> Aufgestanden ist er, welche lange schlief,
> Aufgestanden unten aus Gewölbe tief.

Heym did not live to witness the war he dramatically envisioned (he accidently drowned in 1912 at the age of 24) and the influence his poem would exert on the explosion of *Kriegslyrik* in 1914. Heym's image of a "war-god" was appropriated by Rainer Maria Rilke in his *Fünf Gesänge*,

---

¹⁸ Staude, *Max Scheler*, p. 89.
¹⁹ H. Ball, *Critique of the German Intelligentsia*, trans. B. Harris (New York: Columbia University Press, 1993), p. 76. As Ball continues, "Prussian militarism in its fundamentals is an institution of 'practical Christianity,' that is abundantly evident [...] It is religious militarism [...] This much is evident: the Prussian army gives cause to philosophize, and I am not joking when I say that Prussian militarism rests on 'philosophy of religion'" (p. 77).
²⁰ F. Ringer, *The Decline of the German Mandarins: The German Academic Community, 1890–1933* (London: Wesleyan University Press, 1969). See also J. Habermas, "Die deutschen Mandarine," in *Philosophische-Politische Profile* (Frankfurt: Suhrkamp, 1987): 458–468.
²¹ See K. Vondung, *The Apocalypse in Germany* (Columbia: University of Missouri Press, 2000).
²² See P. Bridgewater, *The German Poets of the First World War* (New York: St. Martin's Press, 1985), p. 23ff.

August 1914, hurriedly written on August 2 and 3 in the margins of his edition of Hölderlin's poems. In the first poem, the arrival of war is venerated as the emergence of a deity:

> ZUM erstenmal seh ich dich aufstehn, hörengesagter, fernster, unglaublicher Kriegs-Gott.

As Rilke ends this song of war:

> Endlich ein Gott. Da wir den friedlichen oft
> nicht mehr ergriffen, ergreift uns plötzlich der Schlacht-Gott,
> schleudert den Brand: und über dem Herzen voll Heimat
> schreit, den er donnernd bewohnt, sein röthlicher Himmel.[23]

In the flush of comparable enthusiasm, Scheler launches *Der Genius* with an evocation of the war's sublime advent: "At the beginning of the month of August, our German destiny took its stand before us like a single immense dark question and shook each individual to the core."[24] As "an incredible event in the moral world," the German nation faces itself, its values, and its future in an existential time of decision. The war was not just another episode in a chronological sequence of history, but a transformative event of revelation, or *kairos,* placing each individual under the existential "dictate of the hour." On a social and cultural level, Scheler envisions the war as an opportune moment for the transfiguration of capitalism and bourgeois individualism. As with other intellectuals, Scheler yearns for a new order of values and social solidarity, which he emphatically models on a Catholic idealization of Medieval community and spiritual union. On the level of national consciousness, the war represents an awakening of Germany to its unique historical mission. The war is said to expose the truth, or the untruth, of different national worldviews and their respective philosophical ways of thinking, thus underlining – at the focal point of Scheler's view – an irreconcilable difference between English utilitarianism and German *Geist*, the ethical supremacy of which the war validates. On a metaphysical level, the war reveals the highest ethical values for life, as realized through the vital and creative movement of "bellicose spirit" (*kriegerisches Geistes*). Scheler speaks decisively against both

---

[23] Rilke's exhilaration began to wane already within the course of his five cantos, and by the end of the war he had changed his view of the war entirely and came to regret his initial rush of poetic war fervor. As he writes on November 6, 1914 to Karl von der Heydt: "In den ersten Augusttagen ergriff mich die Erscheinung des Krieges, des Kriegs-Gottes [...], jetzt ist mir längst der Krieg unsichtbar geworden, ein Geist der Heimsuchung, nicht mehr ein Gott, sondern eines Gottes Entfesselung über den Völkern."

[24] M. Scheler, *Politisch-Pädagogische Schriften* (Bern: Francke Verlag, 1982), vol. IV, p. 11.

evolutionary theories of pacificism and the instrumental militarism of *Realpolitik* in advocating his own *Gesinnungsmilitarismus*, which he sees as based on a "spiritual drive," not bent on the acquisition of power but on the amplification of cultural values and spiritual realization of the highest values. This drive is "more original and stronger than the drive to maintain one's existence." Hence, for Scheler, there is "joy in deed and struggle" but also "in risk and sacrifice" over and above the "joy at the spoils of war or security and well-being."[25] The war is deemed to be "a miracle," as if answering the secret prayer of a culture in crisis, that "best remains unspoken and in the heart alone," and yet reveals "a wide and great path of the world" by promising an ecclesiastical unification of individuals into a community of love.[26]

Scheler throughout speaks of the "essence of war" as founded on "phenomenological evidence" and his idiosyncratic method of "intuition of essences," and thus considers the war as a historically fortuitous opportunity for the application of his foundational ethics. Scheler's thinking in this manner becomes deliberately weaponized, thus sharpening his rejection of alternative philosophical approaches and, most significantly, English utilitarianism. Rhetorically, *Der Genius* is composed in different styles of writing and modes of address: emphatic affirmation of Germany's "special mission," spiritual supremacy, and passionate nationalism; philosophical argumentation and technical vocabulary; popular simplifications and exhortation; clichés and commonplaces. Scheler's text can be read as a variegated performative speech act, appealing more to its illocutionary force and perlocutionary effects than the cogency of its locutionary pronouncements.[27] The war is not a theme of detached contemplation nor a topic of partisan geopolitical considerations; nor is the war reduced to merely subjective enthusiasm and chauvinism. Scheler ascertains the "essence of the war" from the war's own revelation, channeling its creativity and decoding its "sublime language," such that the war speaks "to us,"

---

[25] Scheler, *Politisch-Pädagogische Schriften*, p. 13.
[26] Scheler, *Politisch-Pädagogische Schriften*, p. 11.
[27] For a consideration of Scheler's work as a speech act, see D. Weidner, "Das Absolut des Krieges: Max Schelers Kriegsdenken und die Rhetorik des Äußersten," *Texturen des Krieges. Körper, Schriften und der erste Weltkrieg* (Göttingen: Wallstein Verlag, 2015): 85–114. As Weidner writes, "the decoupling of war from its political aims has the epistemological consequence: a grammar becomes absolutely displaced and becomes a language without a logic, becomes a new form of thinking, which is immediately warlike [...] when the grammar of war replaces or displaces the logic of philosophy, war becomes a category not in need of explanation but that itself explains" (pp. 99, 101). In Weidner's words, "we find in Scheler a post-metaphysical politics which does not admit any place or source for legitimation."

individually as well as collectively. As a creative and spiritual force that gives us meaning, the war suspends questions of legitimation and justice; its significance resides beyond politics and economics. As a speech act, the dominant chord of Scheler's war dithyramb thus consists in the instilling of faith. As Scheler exclaims: "We can only believe! Only as faith, but as firm and well-founded, is therefore meant all future-political [considerations] of the second part of this book."

This advocation of the war's metaphysical revelation occurred during a fertile period in Scheler's thinking that witnessed the continued elaboration of his seminal work of phenomenological ethics as well as influential essays and unpublished studies, along with additional writings on the war.[28] In the 1916 preface to *Formalism in Ethics and Non-Formal Ethics of Values*, Scheler remarks that, although "all parts of the work were written prior to the outbreak of the war," owing to "personal circumstances and the turmoil of war" it is only now that both parts (first published separately, in 1913 and 1916, in Husserl's *Jahrbuch für Philosophie und phänomenologische Forschung*) could be printed together. After referencing his "emotive-phenomenological" and "moral-critical" studies, Scheler refers to *Der Genius* and *Krieg und Aufbau* as "moral-critical applications" of his ethical thinking. The inclusion of these two wartime texts within his ethical endeavor is stated again in the 1921 preface to the second edition of *Formalism in Ethics*. And yet, as Scheler writes in the 1916 preface to *Der Genius*, the "new realities" and "tremendous events" that transpired since 1914 have impacted his thinking about the war, transforming his attitude to a more sanguine reflection on the prospects of social and spiritual reconstruction in *Krieg und Aufbau*. From the standpoint of 1916, *Der Genius* appears as a "document of the temperament (*Gesinnung*) and thoughts which animated [us] at the beginning of the war." It is a war book that already, over the course of the war, no longer entirely represents Scheler's evolving attitudes. This shift in Scheler's thinking is confirmed in the preface to the third edition of *Formalism in Ethics* (1926) – two years before his death – where Scheler makes known a change of thinking on "essential questions of metaphysics." Despite this change, "the ideas in this work [*Formalism*] not only remain unaffected by the change in my fundamental metaphysical position but *represent some of the reasons and intellectual motives which led to this change*." Conspicuously missing from this 1926 preface is mention of his wartime texts. Instead, Scheler

---

[28] *Krieg und Aufbau* (1916), *Die Ursachen des Deutschenhasses* (1917), a review of Johann Plenge's *1789 und 1914*, and a review of Pierre's Duhem's *La science allemande*.

refers to two lectures, "Moral und Politik" and "Die Idee des Friedens und der Pazifismus" (1927), which he hopes soon to publish and will "reveal the direction in which I would like to see the non-formal ethics of values develop" – a direction he did not live to see through.

Material Value Ethics

In his *magnum opus*, Scheler seeks to establish a "strictly scientific and positive foundation for philosophical ethics with respect to all its fundamental problems – but to deal only with the most elementary points of the problems involved."[29] Such a foundation would upend the dominance of rationalism and utilitarianism in ethics, as well as underpin an alternative to the rampant individualism, instrumentalism, and social fragmentation that Scheler considered endemic to modernity. Scheler envisions a transformation of modern life in the aspiration for solidarity, community, and cultivation of higher values (individually and collectively) based on an ethical socialism of love with strong Catholic overtones. Against Kant's formalist ethics, Scheler contends that ethical conduct is not defined by formal lawfulness of the will with respect to ethical imperatives, but grounded in the apprehension of values as the content of experience. Ethical obligations – what we ought to do – only gain traction through an affective uptake of values in our lives. Values are contingent upon experiencing diverse forms of affects, or feelings, neither arbitrary in their manner of givenness nor reducible to the capriciousness of subjective experience, since, as Scheler argues, values are structured according to a priori configurations, or essences. Based on the objective *and* subjective experience of values, as "feeling phenomena," Scheler displaces the rational ethical subject and Kantian goodwill as well as the biological-psychological subject ("human nature") with a conception of the person who, attuned to the ontological primacy of values and intimately responsible for oneself, bears an original coresponsibility with all other persons for the realization of goodness in and salvation of the world. Even with this broad vision, *Formalism* is an incomplete work: The ontological status of value essences (partly treated in Scheler's unfinished essay "Ordo Amoris"), the function of exemplary ethical individuals (partly treated in the essay "Vorbilder und Führer"), and the elaboration of God's significance for ethical life remained in need of clarification.

---

[29] M. Scheler, *Formalism in Ethics and Non-Formal Ethics of Values*, trans. M. Frings (Evanston, IL: Northwestern University Press, 1973), p. xvii.

Scheler utilizes a phenomenological approach that draws on as well as distances itself from Edmund Husserl's phenomenology. In contrast to the latter's analysis of the constitutive operations of transcendental subjectivity, "phenomenology," as Scheler writes, "is neither the name of a new science or a substitute for the word philosophy; it is the name of an attitude of spiritual seeing in which one can see or experience something which otherwise remains hidden, namely, a realm of facts of a particular kind."[30] Those particular facts are "value-essences" – the objective, non-arbitrary configurations of values – that are ordinarily taken for granted yet saliently implicit throughout our experience. By means of a shift in attitude, reflexive recuperation, and eidetic intuition, the a priori essential structure of values can be rendered into a thematic field of investigation; thereby revealed is an objective hierarchy of values. Scheler's inventory of values ranges, lower to higher, from "agreeable values," "vital values," and "spiritual-intellectual values" to "holy values."[31] On this account, values inhere in things or persons without themselves *being* a distinct thing or person: It is the table that we find agreeable; it is being a chess prodigy that we admire; it is the noble deeds of humanitarians that we find uplifting. Things (or persons) are experienced as valuable not in isolation, but within a nexus of values: the sense of wellbeing when drawing a warm bath, the pleasurable warmth of the water, the relaxation of our bodies, and the ultimate physical and psychological invigoration that seems to breathe new life into us. We are attuned to and oriented in the world through values, and indeed, for Scheler, things and persons in and of the world "announce" themselves, or "show up," as more valuable or less valuable. Experience is value laden across different ways of world disclosure. It is values, in their ontological purchase, that define what we care for and why what we care for remains important to us.

Values are distinct from their bearers (things or persons) as well as distinct from each other, yet they are indissociable from acts of experiencing. Importantly, values are not constituted by consciousness; they are disclosed to consciousness in two forms of intentionality: "intentional feelings" (as distinct from "feeling states," for example the feeling of pain) and "strivings." In both instances, a value is the intentional object of consciousness. Strivings are (mostly) prereflective and preconscious. The stirring of desire

---

[30] M. Scheler, "Phenomenology and the Theory of Cognition," in *Selected Philosophical Papers*, trans. D. Lachterman (Evanston, IL: Northwestern University Press, 1973): 136–201, p. 137.

[31] On occasion, Scheler considers "utility" as another type of value; his classification of values thus varies accordingly (*Formalism*, pp. 104–105, 255–261, 332–344).

for an attractive person or the impulse to reach for a delicious-looking apple are examples of how the value quality of a person or thing affects us before any deliberate decision or volitional act is set into motion. As Scheler writes: "For values are neither dependent upon purposes nor abstracted from them, but are the foundation of *goals of striving*, and are hence the foundation of purposes, which are themselves founded in goals."[32] In strivings and intentional feelings, values are revealed through preferences (*Vorziehen*) or "placing after" (*Nachsetzen*) between relatively "higher" and "lower" values. We are pulled toward or pushed away from, or attracted to or repulsed by, things or persons, not by qualitative experiences of isolated values as such, but by values in hierarchical relation to each other.

Preferring underlies our inclinations, decisions, and intentions, yet is open to reflective appropriation, correction, and calibration.[33] From this insight, Scheler mounts the argument that ethical obligations have their foundation in the experienced – "preferred" – disclosure of values. As Scheler writes: "Whenever we speak of an ought, the comprehension of a *value* must have occurred."[34] Not every value apprehension, however, has uptake as an ought. Judging what I ought to do, as determining my conduct, rests on the foundation of a value alive to, as it were, its possible being-real; something ought to be done in such and such a manner only because it expresses a value that itself should be. Scheler distinguishes in this regard between the "ideal ought" of a value as such and the "ought of duty," where in the latter case the ought refers to a possible decision, or a willing, the value content of which should be realized. A normative ought prescribes a certain possible conduct: I ought to act in such and such a manner. An ideal ought is independent from possible action; an ideal ought states "this ought to be." To value the lives of others is to recognize that lives should matter in the world. An ideal ought is not constrained by the ability to act, since from an ideal ought no direct obligation to act ensues.

Scheler identifies love and hate as the "highest level of our intentional emotive life."[35] Love and hate are not values per se, but "acts in which the value-realm accessible to the feeling of a being (the value-realm with which preferring is also connected) is either *extended* or *narrowed*."[36] Whereas

---

[32] Scheler, *Formalism*, p. 41.
[33] Scheler proposes that there are two orders: rank ordering of values with respect to their essential bearers (things, acts, and persons) and rank ordering of values with respect to value modalities (the agreeable, the vital, etc.).
[34] Scheler, *Formalism*, p. 184.
[35] Scheler, *Formalism*, p. 260.
[36] Scheler, *Formalism*, p. 261.

preferring discloses a bounded range of values within which we operate and navigate, shaping our dispositions for choosing and directions for acting, "[love] is, as it were, a movement in whose execution ever *new* and *higher* values flash out, i.e., values that were wholly unknown to the being concerned."[37] Love discloses new dimensions of values, moving upward along the hierarchy of values toward the holy (and ultimately toward God), opening new possibilities of valuing and trajectories of being a person. By contrast, hate narrows down the possibilities of valuing and being. Love is a movement of going beyond oneself, enriching oneself in the revelation of values that impel us to the ideal of what ought to be and who we ought to become. The movement of love passes through other persons, not things. When regarding another person in love, we behold more than who the person is, their moral character and value; we behold who the person *can be* (and *should be*) beyond their social standing and cultural encodings, and thus see the other person in the light of their own Idea; namely, their individual valuableness in terms of their goodness (or evilness). We speak of individuals as either "good" or "evil" in view of the values realized through their actions and lives. To be good or evil is not a matter of formal lawful conduct with respect to the moral law. It is a question of the realization, or instantiation, of higher values in one's life.

Individual and Collective Persons

This conception of the person resides at the center of Scheler's phenomenological ethics; it is a person who is deemed good (or evil), who exemplifies the highest (or the lowest) values, and who strives (or who does not strive) to realize goodness in the world. But rather than define the person with reference to a soul, an ego, goodwill, or inborn psychological traits, Scheler raises the fundamental question: *Who* – not what – is a person? Being a person is "given as one who executes intentional acts that are bound by a unity of sense" and experience of oneself in self-responsibility, responsiveness to values, and understanding of oneself as the author of one's own actions.[38] At the core of personhood, there is awareness of standing before one's own irrecusable responsibility "to be" a person. Freedom is couched in self-responsibility; volition is situated in responsiveness (or lack thereof) to values. As Scheler writes:

---

[37] M. Scheler, *The Nature of Sympathy*, trans. W. Stark (London: Routledge, 2008), p. 153.
[38] Scheler, *Formalism*, pp. 476, 487.

All true autonomy is first and foremost a predicate of the *person*, not a predicate of reason (Kant) or of the person only as an X that participates in the lawfulness of reason. But here we must distinguish two sorts of autonomy: the autonomy of personal *insight* into good and evil and the autonomy of personal *willing* of what is given as good and evil.[39]

An individual is constituted as both a public (or social) person and a private (Scheler speaks of the "intimate") person. While the social person embodies the cultural, social, and historical determinations of an individual, the private person, as "one's particular self-being," is the nonobjectifiable "mineness" of one's individuality. As Scheler writes:

> No matter how rich and diverse the memberships through which *each* person is enmeshed in the whole of the moral cosmos, and no matter how diverse the directions of the various kinds of co-responsibility by which the person is tied to this *whole* and its direction and sense, the person is never exhausted by these kinds of membership, nor is his self-responsibility reduced to various co-responsibilities, nor to his duties and rights to those duties and rights which derive from such membership (duties of family, office, vocation, citizenship, class, etc.).[40]

To be a person is characterized by an intimacy only known to oneself and a secret only discoverable by oneself. Other persons are known to us through their social determinations, and yet remain unknown to us as to their intimate personhood. Scheler's radical humanism affirms the uniqueness of personhood beyond objectifications of social forms, the universal principle of equality, and mutual recognition. Persons are unequal in relation to each other given each person's irreducible and nonobjectifiable uniqueness.[41] And yet, the individuality of a person is not only determined by intimate self-responsibility. A person's individuality, as a temporal becoming, is guided by "an individual personal value-essence," or personal destiny, not predetermined but self-prescribed, that must be claimed and consciously pursued.[42] An individual's value essence entails their "moral tenor" (*Gesinnung*), or disposition, along with their value inclinations, or what Scheler calls "personal salvation." Personal salvation is neither theologically ordained nor identical with the fulfillment of ethical obligation; instead, it is the "material a priori field for the formation of our possible

---

[39] Scheler, *Formalism*, pp. 494–495.
[40] Scheler, *Formalism*, p. 561.
[41] For the term "radical humanism," S. Schneck, *Persons and Polis: Max Scheler's Personalism as Political Theory* (Albany: State University of New York, 1987), p. 61ff.
[42] Scheler, *Formalism*, p. 489.

intentions" and "value-qualities which [we] alone can grasp."[43] It scopes out accordingly a range of possibility for what is good for me, individually, to accomplish, a sense of my own life as an unfolding and abiding whole, only accomplishable by me, that "places me in a *unique* position in the moral cosmos and obliges me with respect to action, deeds, and works, etc., which, when I represent them, all call 'I am for you and you are for me.'"[44] Goodness, as manifest through (higher) values, "whispers to me *for you*," of who I am to become. What I ought to do speaks to me individually, for it is only if I recognize *myself* as called upon to do what is good that moral imperatives can have traction and purchase *for me*, and not as a universal subject or noumenal self. This openness presupposes openness to oneself in "self-love" (in contrast to love of self); namely, that I value myself as a valuing being, and hence value from myself to effect goodness. The path to "personal salvation" – effecting goodness in the world that singularly becomes my calling – requires relations with other persons; that is, not just self-love but also love for others. When in love with another person, we behold more than who the person is in social terms: We behold their moral tenor and worth (good or evil) as well as who our beloved *can be and should be* in light of their individual value essence, or calling, beyond their social standing and cultural encodings. Rather than determine one's ethical conduct according to an impersonal categorical imperative, it is to others, as exemplifications of values and goodness, that individuals must turn, not in imitation, but through creative inspiration and critical self-development. As Scheler writes: "One can therefore say that the highest *effectiveness* of the good person in the moral cosmos lies in the pure *value of exemplariness* that he possesses exclusively by virtue of his *being* and *haecceity*, which are accessible to intuition and love, and not in his will or in any acts that he may execute, still less in his deeds and actions."[45]

In the final section of *Formalism*, Scheler observes: "An ethics which, like the one developed here, located the highest and ultimate meaning of the world in the possible being of (individual and collective) persons of the highest positive value must finally come to a question of great significance," namely, "are there *specific types* of persons that can be differentiated in an a priori fashion" (much as Scheler differentiated different types of values in

---

[43] Scheler, *Formalism*, p. 115.
[44] Scheler, *Formalism*, p. 490.
[45] Scheler, *Formalism*, p. 575. For a further, albeit incomplete, development of this cardinal idea of ethical exemplarity, see M. Scheler, "Vorbilder und Führer," *Schriften aus dem Nachlaß: Zur Ethik und Erkenntnislehre* (Bern: Francke Verlag, 1957): 255–344.

an a priori fashion)?⁴⁶ Ethical obligations have their foundation in the revelation of highest values, and if such values – that is, the highest – are exhibited in persons, not things, it follows that an ought of duty, as the basis for willing what ought to be done, cannot itself serve as the motivating norm. As Scheler proposes, "there can be *no norm of duty without a person who posits it* and no non-formal rightness of a norm of duty without the essential goodness of the person who posits it."⁴⁷ From this claim, Scheler identifies different types of exemplary ethical persons ("the *bon vivant*," "the leading spirit," "the hero," "the genius," and "the saint") and further argues that typified "value-persons," or functional ethical models of goodness, stand in a relation to the Goodness of the Divine; that is, God. The Goodness of God – the highest person – is not an aggregate or synthesis of persons. Rather, "one can call the pure types of the value-person perspectival sides (structured by ranks) of the simple and undivided Godhead, sides which are constitutive for the possible *modes of givenness* of the Godhead (as value-being) in a finite being, but not constitutive for the being of God."⁴⁸ There exists, in this regard, an "essential tragedy of all finite personal being," given their "essential moral imperfection." It is impossible for an individual person to embody in one life "the saint, the hero, and the genius." As Scheler wonders: "Only the hero fully values the hero; only the genius fully values the genius. Who should value both wills when it is impossible to be both perfect hero *and* perfect genius?"⁴⁹ How can one pursue being, and hence valuing either the hero *or* the genius, given that one cannot become both? The tragedy of the ethical is here not based on a conflict between incommensurable duties, nor between duty and inclinations. Within Scheler's personalism, the tragic arises in that "*equally justified provinces* of duty clash, each 'province' receiving its objective field from the value-being and the value-kind of the persons *themselves* who participate in the conflict."⁵⁰

It belongs to the individuality of the person to be a social being. As Scheler underlines: "All persons are, with *equal* originality, both individual persons and (essentially) members of a collective person."⁵¹ In *Formalism*, Scheler outlines a social ontology of groups, an implicit account of

---

⁴⁶ Scheler, *Formalism*, p. 572.
⁴⁷ Scheler, *Formalism*, p. 573.
⁴⁸ Scheler, *Formalism*, p. 590.
⁴⁹ Scheler, *Formalism*, p. 591.
⁵⁰ Scheler, *Formalism*, p. 593. What remains wanting from this statement of the tragic condition in *Formalism* is an account of God as a person and how God becomes himself manifest, or experienced, in his goodness, along with a sociology of ethical vocations, a theory of the exemplary person in its relation to historical worldviews. See also Scheler's essay on the phenomenon of the tragic.
⁵¹ Scheler, *Formalism*, p. 524.

"we-intentionality" and social acts. A collective person is constituted neither through a synthesis of individuals nor as a supra-individual person. As Scheler writes: "It is therefore *in* the person that the mutually related *individual person* and *collective person* become differentiated. The idea of one is not the 'foundation' of the other."[52] In this sense, a collective person attains consciousness in the social acts of individual persons. All individuals, for example, who experience themselves as Germans (i.e., a collective person), given their finitude, cannot encompass the entire "collective content which is experienced by the collective person and to which the person's peculiar awareness *also* belongs as a member-person."[53] The relation between collective person and individual person is thus a "special kind of relation between the universal and the individual [...] the collective person is as much a spiritual *individual* as the individual person, e.g., the Prussian state."[54]

As with values, Scheler identifies a hierarchy of collective forms of existence. In its rudimentary form, a group is constituted through mimetic behavior (the mass or herd). In a higher form, individuals possess an understanding of themselves as group members. Whereas in a herd no solidarity obtains among members, in this second kind of group a representable solidarity binds individuals to each other into a life-community, where individual responsibility is founded on coresponsibility for the conduct, volition, and intentions of the group. A life-community, however, is not yet a collective *person*; it is a collective form of life predicated on "thing-values" (*Sachwerte*), for example a farm sharing group. A third form of collective existence is society (*Gesellschaft*), in which relations among individuals are neither biologically determined nor mediated by "thing-values." What characterizes a society is that an individual decides to belong (or, alternatively, not to belong). Whereas life-communities are based on coresponsibility, in a society "all responsibility for others is based on unilateral *self-responsibility*, and all possible responsibility for others must be regarded as having come from a free and singular act of taking over certain obligations."[55] A society – Scheler's gloss on modern liberal society – is not a fully constituted collective person; the social is woven from relations of conventions and contracts, but not, on this account, mutual solidarity. In a life-community, the basic attitude is one of trust. In a society, by contrast, the basic attitude is one of distrust; solidarity is a product of coercion or calculated self-interest. Against these forms of collective existence (herd,

[52] Scheler, *Formalism*, p. 522.
[53] Scheler, *Formalism*, p. 523.
[54] Scheler, *Formalism*, p. 525.
[55] Scheler, *Formalism*, p. 529.

life-community, society), Scheler envisions the highest form of community as "*the unity of independent, spiritual, and individual single persons 'in' an independent, spiritual, and individual collective person.*" The self-valuing of an individual person ("self-love") binds itself to self-valuing of the collective person by means "of the idea of the salvational solidarity of all in the *corpus christianum*, which is founded on the Christian idea of love (and which is contrary to the mere ethos of 'society,' which denies moral solidarity)."[56] In the collective person, every individual is self-responsible as well as coresponsible for others in the community. Both the collective person (the community) and individual persons are, moreover, responsible "to the person of persons," God, in terms of self-responsibility and coresponsibility. This spiritual solidarity is "unrepresentable," since an individual person is coresponsible not only in their social position, office, and rank, but as an individual person above the social, as the bearer of a unique conscience: An individual does not ask themselves: "What positive moral value would have occurred in the world and what of negative moral value would have been avoided if I, as a representative of a place in a social structure, had comported myself differently?" Rather, an individual asks: "What would have occurred if I, as a spiritual individual, had grasped, willed, and realized the 'good-in-itself-for-me' in a superior manner?"[57]

In this highest form of communal life, there obtains an original coresponsibility of each individual for the ethical salvation of the world and "the whole of all realms of persons." Care for the community – for its culture and collective wellbeing – resides at the living center of the individual person, taking on an ultimate religious significance, for what is of ethical value (the highest value of self-love and love for others) is directed toward the world in love – for love of the world – standing before God "feeling united with the whole of the spiritual world and humanity."[58] The holy (*das Heilige*) is the highest value for individual persons; salvation (*das Heil*) is the highest value for a genuine collective person. Although Scheler thus binds individual salvation with collective salvation, he notes that personal salvation is "totally independent of its relation to the state." This envisioned ideal of "spiritual community" cannot have the form of the nation-state or national identity. In fact, individual members of a state exist in an "unequal realm of free spiritual persons" that places them "above the state and above law." There is no subordination of the individual person to the

---

[56] Scheler, *Formalism*, p. 533.
[57] Scheler, *Formalism*, p. 534.
[58] Scheler, *Formalism*, p. 534.

collective person; each has a common ethical subordination to the idea of the infinite person "in whom the division between individual persons and collective persons, necessary for finite persons, *ceases to be*."[59] Nevertheless, Scheler grants that "in extreme cases" the state can demand the sacrifice of an individual's life, in time of war for example; he rejects, however, that the state can demand the sacrifice of the person "in general," that is, "its salvation and its conscience," nor demand unlimited devotion, reserved only to God. In this light, Scheler takes issue with "thinkers of note" who oppose liberal and mechanical individualism in favor of the organic community of the supra-individual state, "for which a person must be prepared to make any sacrifice." This illicit "glorification of the German conception of the state," Scheler contends, has been abolished "*once and for all* by Jesus."[60] Expressed in Christian terms, an "eternal state" or "eternal nation" is contradictory and more than just empirically impossible: "The false assumption of such an eternal nation or state would also lead to a deadly conservatism that would obstruct a total explication of the inner possibilities of the spirit which forms the cultures and states. Every ethics of state or culture is therefore *eo ipso* 'reactionary.' Rather, there is a *moral* right to both cultural revolution and revolution against the state."[61]

The God of War

As Scheler states in the preface to *Der Genius des Krieges und der Deutsche Krieg*, "while the first part ['The Genius of War'] proceeds in such a way that what appears is only the shadow of the war that surrounds us, the shadow the war projects by virtue of the light from the eternal world of ideas, onto the wall of Being; the second part ['The German War'] shows the very same ideas completely immersed into concrete life, into action and dictates of the hour."[62] With this tacit wartime refashioning of Plato's allegory of the cave, Scheler expresses his ambition as penetrating beyond the shadows cast upon reality by the war to contemplate the essence of the war as "revealing of absolute realities." Through this optic, war is seen to disclose values that otherwise remained veiled amid the dogmatic slumber of peace, thus catalyzing the surpassing of modernity's aliments: capitalism, individualism, and utilitarianism. "Der Genius des Krieges" presents

---

[59] Moreover, a collective person cannot be based on blood, soil, or tradition (Scheler, *Formalism*, p. 543).
[60] Scheler, *Formalism*, p. 512.
[61] Scheler, *Formalism*, p. 560.
[62] Scheler, *Politisch-Pädagogische Schriften*, p. 9.

a wartime ascent of the soul along the contours of Scheler's prescribed hierarchy of values, toward the eternal and God. War is a vital and creative upsurge of life in pursuit of the highest ethical values, as configured in three stratifications of world-ordering (*Welteinrichtung*): vital, cultural-spiritual, and holy.[63] In "Der Deutsche Krieg," Scheler descends from this essential vision of the world in war to speak more directly to his compatriots, who are encouraged to "see with their own German eyes" the justness (*Gerechtigkeit*) of their struggle, and urged to embrace "concrete life, into action, and the demand of the hour."[64]

The values of the vital, the cultural-spiritual, and the holy structure Scheler's assessment of the war's force of transformation. Thus framed, the war is claimed to release a dynamism of life, allow for the constitution of a new world order according to the highest values, and lead to the realization of collective personhood in the revelation of God. The gap in *Formalism* between Scheler's conception of collective person and God – indeed, the function of God for his philosophical ethics – would seem to be illuminated in the glow and glory of war. This emphasis on war's vitality for life establishes a point of intersection between Scheler's concern with spiritual (and holy) values and personhood from *Formalism* (which only offers a muted assertion of vital values) with the subversion of vital values that Scheler vigorously identified with the *ressentiment* of bourgeois society, with its evisceration of trust and solidarity in the abstract name of equality.[65]

In a manner not untypical of late nineteenth-century thinkers, Scheler identifies the creative source of war with life. "The true root of all war," he writes, "consists in that from life itself, independent from its particular and changing environment and its stimulus, there is a tendency for amplification [*Steigerung*], towards growth and the unfolding of its manifold types inherent to life."[66] The paradox of war consists in creation, in myriad ways, through destruction.[67] This Schelerian affirmation of war's vitality

---

[63] Scheler, *Politisch-Pädagogische Schriften*, pp. 36, 53.
[64] Scheler, *Politisch-Pädagogische Schriften*, p. 9.
[65] See M. Scheler, *Ressentiment*, trans. W. Holdheim (Milwaukee, WI: Marquette University Press, 1994). In a collection of essays written between 1912 and 1914, *Vom Umsturz der Werte*, Scheler faulted utilitarianism – the dominant ideology of liberal capitalist society – for its subordination of vital values to values of utility, conformity, and efficiency.
[66] Scheler, *Politisch-Pädagogische Schriften*, p. 31.
[67] As Ruskin observes in his lecture on war in *The Crown of Wild Olives*, "national military conflict is not anathema to art, but its very basis." The paradox of war, for Ruskin, is that "it is impossible for me to write consistently of war, for the group of facts I have gathered about it leads me to two opposite conclusions: suffering and death," and yet "the most beautiful characteristics yet developed among men have been formed in war." Quoted in D. Pick, *War Machine: The Rationalisation of Slaughter in the Modern Age* (New Haven, CT: Yale University Press, 1996), pp. 69–70.

does not espouse a notion of "will to power" (prevalent among wartime appropriations of Nietzschean thought) that emphasizes the enhancement of life through conflict.[68] The force of life is not, for Scheler, without the aspiration of spirit to more than life. As he writes, "we must therefore distinguish two roots of all human struggle; the one that is responsible for economics and technology, springing from the struggle for existence and the other, its individualizing presupposition, as the drive towards amplification of power and achievement of the universality of life, culture, and the formation of the state."[69] Scheler distinguishes between violence (*Gewalt*) and power (*Macht*), whereby "power" is wedded to "spirit" in an inverse relation to the bond between life and violence. In placing the power of spirit, as opposed to the violence of life, at the heart of war, Scheler argues that material destruction and killing do not express the "essence" of war. On this view, war is not primarily the employment of physical force or a utilitarian instrument for the pursuit of political or economic ends. Rather than a "struggle for existence" (*Kampf ums Dasein*), a dominant slogan of *Kriegsphilosophie* and enshrined in the writings of Friedrich von Bernhardi and Heinrich von Treitschke, Scheler argues that war is a "struggle for higher existence" (*Kampf um ein Höheres als Dasein*), where power stands at the service of culture and freedom in the formation of an ethos, or form of life, incarnating higher values and a community of love, higher than the nation (Germany) and yet impossible without it.

With this spiritualized conception of life, Scheler objects to social evolutionary arguments for the progress of humankind toward peace, either of the kind in Herbert Spencer or Kant's perpetual peace. The rejection of Social Darwinism and biological accounts of human existence cuts both ways, against liberal pacificism as well as "instrumental militarism." Scheler's metaphysical conception of war – his *Gesinnungsmilitarismus* – subverts Clausewitz's influential definition of war as the pursuit of the political by other – violent – means. Rather, Scheler cites von Treitschke's statement that war is "politics κατά ἐξοχήν" – *par excellence*.[70] The bellicose realization of life in the collective form of the nation *is* the essence of politics – and not just an instrument of policy or national interest. The political is based on the existential decision of war for the sake of life's highest values. Despite this allegiance to Treitschke's idea of war as the essence of politics,

---

[68] See S. Aschheim, *The Nietzsche Legacy in Germany, 1890–1990* (Berkeley: University of California Press, 1994), chapter 5.
[69] Scheler, *Politisch-Pädagogische Schriften*, p. 35.
[70] Scheler, *Politisch-Pädagogische Schriften*, p. 41.

Scheler does not accept that war stems from an evolutionary clash of civilizations, or *Weltanschauungen*, nor the crude Social Darwinism that underlays Treitschke's *Realpolitik*. Unlike Treitschke and von Bernhardi, Scheler does not conceive of war as racial or biological survival of the fittest, or as a struggle for economic and geopolitical power.[71] Scheler speaks against the aim of war, as with the bastardized reading of Clausewitz's *On War* among nineteenth-century German military theorists, as "absolute" in the sense of tending toward the annihilation of the enemy. As Scheler states: "In cases where the goal of war is the physical annihilation of a group [...] there we have a misused application of the noble name of 'war.'"[72] Scheler, in other words, rejects the idea of *Vernichtungskrieg*, as is implied, for example, in Treitschke and stated in eugenic and racist terms by Eduard von Hartmann.[73] The essence of war is for Scheler not to be "total," but to be totally ethical, or better: all-embracing in a metaphysical-ethical sense.

Under the heading of *ordo amoris*, Scheler understands being-in-the-world (Scheler speaks of *Umwelt*, or environing world) in terms of both the objective structure of values in their historical-cultural determination and the subjective configuration of individuals as to their moral tenor and disposition.[74] The world is ontologically value laden; worlds show up already saturated and structured by values. According to Scheler, nations historically actualize different value-laden apprehensions of the world and thus inevitably enter into conflict with each other in terms of these differences of values and forms of life. Different cultures, based on the range of values available to them, stand in a hierarchical relationship to each other. Important in this respect is Scheler's fundamental claim that the world, historically and culturally, is experienced in terms of values. From this claim, it follows that, above and beyond economic and political interests, war is the pursuit of "the maximal spiritual dominance the planet" through the expansion of genuine communities of love, namely, of the highest values, and hence not as communities bound together contractually or in terms of rights or common interests.[75] Scheler's hierarchy of values leverages his argument for the justness and, indeed, cultural superiority of the German

---

[71] F. von Bernhardi, *Deutschland und der Nächste Krieg* (Berlin: J. G. Cotta, 1911).
[72] Scheler, *Politisch-Pädagogische Schriften*, p. 16.
[73] E. von Hartmann, *Die Phänomenologie des sittlichen Bewusstseins*, (Berlin: Duncker, 1879), p. 670: "die Kriege sind das Hauptmittel des Racenkampfs, d.h. der natürliche Zuchtwahl innerhalb der Menschheit." For his part, Treitschke explicitly argued for colonial expansion and racial wars of conquest.
[74] M. Scheler, "*Ordo Amori*," in *Selected Philosophical Papers*, pp. 98–135.
[75] Scheler, *Politisch-Pädagogische Schriften*, p. 15.

war effort. The world of the English, most notably, is structured by "lower values" of utility, whereas the world of Germany to come, as revealed in the war, will be structured by "the highest values" of the holy. Although cultures disclose worlds differently, Scheler nonetheless envisions a possible harmony among conflicting ways of world-disclosing, and hence valuing. Attaining what Scheler calls the "structure of a common-world culture" in its "display of the whole greatness and expanse of the human spirit" – the extension of the heart to embrace the highest values of *ordo amoris* – ultimately leads to embracing the love of God. Germany's war therefore proves critical for defending its ecumenical spiritual values – that is, its higher values – against the shallowness and degeneracy of English utilitarianism, mechanism, and materialism, among other idols. War is necessary in the ways of world-making (*Welteinrichtung*) toward realizing the unified and religious-moral task of humanity.[76] In this respect, Scheler insists that the destruction of the University of Leuven Library and shelling of the Cathedral of Reims are justified – spiritual collateral damage, as it were – given that Germany's struggle for "higher values" does not occur in the same value dimension, and hence world, as her enemies. The German war (in contrast to England's war) carries "an eminently positive meaning for cultural creation" and "the creative sources of national and personal spirit." As Scheler remarks: "Who would deny that the Athenian flowering in tragedy, sculpture, philosophy before and after the Persian wars would not be possible without the spiritual new birth of the Athenian state by virtue of victorious defense against the barbarians?"[77]

Against Allied images of "barbarian Germans" and calls that "the Hun must be killed!" Scheler affirms the supremacy of German spirit against the "barbarous Russians" and the "English cant" of utilitarianism. Scheler's argument for the justness of Germany's war elides, on the one hand, political and military reality while, on the other hand, advocating that Germany is essentially struggling against her enemies in a defensive war for the highest of values – "the holy." As Scheler declares: "This war – unlike any other – is a just war and hence a war sanctioned by divine right."[78] Whereas the English are motivated by secular interests of economic influence and power and the French are animated by revenge and *ressentiment*, the German war is spiritual in the name of love. Strange as it may be, Scheler contends that the desire for Germany's annihilation by

---

[76] Scheler, *Politisch-Pädagogische Schriften*, p. 44.
[77] Scheler, *Politisch-Pädagogische Schriften*, p. 45.
[78] Scheler, *Politisch-Pädagogische Schriften*, p. 107.

her enemies confirms a hatred that animates *their* war, not Germany's. As Scheler examines in *Die Ursachen des Deutschenhasses* (1917; first delivered as lectures in 1916), hatred against Germany represents an enmity of the periphery against the spiritual-moral center of Germany. In this political theology of war, Germany struggles in the service of higher values from love of those values and love of humankind as such. Germany's special mission, or *Sonderweg*, consists in its arrogated spiritual responsibility for the secular world – Europe – in attaining the highest values unto the love of God, while defending those values from degenerate values and idols of infatuation as exemplified by the British and modern culture more broadly.

Scheler's notion of the "genius" of the German war anachronistically represents a reversal to a modified Medieval-theological theory of war and can thus be said to be antimodern as well as antisecular. Whereas Clausewitz seminally defined a modern conception of war around the decisiveness of battles predicated on chance and friction ("the fog of war"), where war is the pursuit of (rational) political objectives by organized violent means, Scheler upholds in his idiosyncratic manner a premodern conception of war as a theological judgment of God. As Scheler writes: "Only here the idea of war as judgment of God becomes completely clear. If God is a God of love, then he will also give victory to the people, in which love is the richest, the deepest, the most high! [...] In this way therefore the divine judgment of war becomes an experience."[79] In sacrificial death, soldiers experience – indeed, "everyone" experiences ("Everybody becomes a metaphysician, because everyone can become a war hero") – eternal life in affording God's actuality in history to become effective in this testing judgment and benediction of the nation: "ein Gottesgericht über die Kultur der Völker."[80] War is God's *examen rigorosum*: the decision itself of victory, or, in other words, the pursuit of decisive victory *at all costs*, attests to God's preferential judgment. As Scheler writes: "And particularly here the genius of war becomes our leader (*Führer*) to God."[81]

---

[79] Scheler, *Politisch-Pädagogische Schriften*, pp. 98–99.
[80] 'A divine judgment on the culture of the peoples.' Scheler, *Politisch-Pädagogische Schriften*, p. 95.
[81] Scheler, *Politisch-Pädagogische Schriften*, p. 99. Against this theological backdrop, what distinguishes Scheler's "metaphysical conception of war" is its combination of elements from Protestant war theology with an appropriately revised Catholic theory of just war. In an echo of the Kaiser's declaration for German spiritual unification, Scheler offers a conceptualization of the war that would inhibit any internal division among German Christians, while identifying the privileged enemy of Germany as England rather than Catholic France. For the relation between Scheler's *Der Genius* and Protestant *Kriegstheologie*, N. de Warren, "Skepticism on Violence and Vigilance on Peace," *Graduate Faculty Philosophy Journal*, Vol. 41, No. 1 (2020): 279–317.

On the Eternal in Man

As Scheler remarks in the preface to the first edition, although parts of *Formalism* were written prior to the war (Part One was published in 1913; Part Two was published in 1916), "personal circumstances and the turmoil of war" delayed its publication in book form. As significantly, the war prevented Scheler from completing his foundational ethical project as well as "a major work planned for the near future" (announced in the Introduction to *Formalism*) on "non-formal ethics on the broadest possible basis of phenomenological experience."[82] What remained missing from the published form of *Formalism* was an elaboration of the ontological status of values as well as an examination of the relation between ethics and religion, and although Scheler intended to write a philosophy of religion, "On the Essence of Godliness and the Forms of His Experience," which would have completed the conceptual foundation of his philosophical ethics, this work never came to fruition. This unfinished condition of Scheler's ethics was compounded by a philosophical transformation – a conversion he himself likened to a "religious awakening" – that occurred during the winter of 1915–16 while residing at the Benedictine Abbey of Beuron.[83] Against the backdrop of Germany's waning fortunes and the *Ideenwende* among German intellectuals, Scheler's crisis was political, metaphysical, and personal. He emerged from this winter of discontent with a changed attitude toward the war and returned to embrace the Catholic Church.[84] As Martin Heidegger observed at the news of Scheler's death in 1928, "it is no accident that Scheler, who was raised a Catholic, in an age of collapse took his philosophical path again in the direction of what is called 'catholic' as a universal world-historical power, not in the sense of the Church."[85] "The brokenness of contemporary human existence," in Heidegger's characterization, that obsessively drove Scheler's thinking became more enlivened and despairing after Germany's defeat. As with Hugo Ball and Carl Schmitt, Scheler's newfound attraction to Catholicism, as a "world-historical power" and font of spiritual meaning, resided in the promise of the renewal of social order and establishment of ethical values. This change of heart further cemented the centrality of the question of human existence in relation to

---

[82] Scheler, *Formalism*, p. 5.
[83] Z. Davis, "The Values of War and Peace: Max Scheler's Political Transformations," *Symposium*, Vol. 16, No. 2 (2012): 128–149; p. 129.
[84] For the *Ideenwende* of 1915–16 and Scheler's wartime reconversion to Catholicism, see Flasch, *Die geistige Mobilmachung*.
[85] M. Heidegger, *The Metaphysical Foundations of Logic*, trans. M. Heim (Bloomington: Indiana University Press, 1984), p. 51.

"higher" – that is, eternal – values and God, with which he would wrestle until the end of his life.[86]

Scheler's philosophical conversion did not occur without a final salvo. In *Krieg und Aufbau* (1915), Scheler continues to express confidence in the prospects of German victory by taking aim at "the French idea" of democracy and its conception of a collective volition of individuals. Leaning on his own conception of the collective person from *Formalism*, Scheler argues against the ideals of liberalism that the nation is a "spiritual person in its own right." Despite this spirited defense of Germany's cause, Scheler nonetheless concedes that Germany's "world-historical mission" precariously hangs in the balance. By early 1916, beneath the somber horizon of the battle of Verdun and increased fragmentation of political discussions of the war's aims at home, Scheler decisively reversed his position on the war. Rather than consider the war, as in *Der Genius des Krieges*, as a historical opportunity for Germany's liberation from decadence, he came to see the war as a revelation of Europe's "moral and religious emptiness [and] the inner mendacity of this lying sham of European cultural community, long corroded with the poisons of nationalism, subjectivism, relativism, capitalism."[87] This dramatic shift in perspective pushed Scheler toward accepting the value of democracy and, as significantly, the importance of education and the humanities for the promotion and cultivation of values, for which his sociology of knowledge and worldviews was intended to play a vital role.[88] In his 1917 essay "Christian Democracy," Scheler idealizes Medieval communal solidarity in arguing that a desire for the highest spiritual freedom should supplant the centrality of individual political liberty. Catholicism, he proposes, represents an alternative for Germany against the skewed narrowness of Kantian-Prussian formalism.[89] In his 1917 essay "The Reconstruction of European Culture," Scheler extends his reflections on "the origins of hatred" against Germany, first broached in his essay "The Causes of Hatred against Germans" (1917). Setting aside his previous diagnosis that it was Germany's distinctive cultural values that provoked "hatred" among the Allies due to their due cultural *ressentiment*, Scheler seeks instead to understand "how can we build anew the moral and spiritual culture of Europe, which has been shaken in its deepest

---

[86] P. Spader, *Scheler's Personalism: Its Logic, Development, and Promise* (New York: Fordham University Press, 2002), p. 147ff. As Flasch remarks, "das Thema Krieg ließ ihn von 1914 bus zu seinem Tode nicht mehr los" (*Die geistige Mobilmachung*, p. 110).
[87] M. Scheler, *Krieg und Aufbau* (Leipzig: Verlag der Weissen Bücher, 1916), p. 347. See Staude, *Max Scheler*, p. 87.
[88] As Scheler develops in his *Die Wissensformen und die Gesellschaft* (1926).
[89] Scheler's late wartime writings on Catholicism brought him to the attention of Konrad Adenauer, who called him to the newly founded university of Cologne in 1919.

foundations and now – to change the image – flutters in the wind like a flag in tatters over the fields of dead? What spirit, what inner purpose must animate men to that end?"[90] Hatred against Germany, Scheler avers, carried a positive benefit: It united Europe in a common struggle. With Germany's defeat on the horizon, only "one great reconciliation with us Germans" could finally bring unity to Europe; but, as Scheler forewarns, any future peace treaty among European nations must avoid producing "a lacerated body of jealous nationalities." Needed is "a mighty spiritual unity which still has something important to give to the world," namely, a perpetual peace that addresses "life and spirit," not to be reduced to the formalism of legal treaties and maintaining the balance of power.

By the end of the war, it was clear for Scheler that a Christian pacifism of conviction among European nations in spiritual kinship with the highest values was urgently needed. Peace for a renewed Europe necessitated cultural reconstruction, the mitigation of *ressentiment* and desire for revenge, the decentralization of the state, the dismantling of European colonialism, and increased federalism along with cultural autonomy.[91] Most importantly, a spiritual-cultural reconstruction of Europe could only be achieved through collective guilt and moral solidarity in common expiation and repentance. As a corollary to Scheler's call for European repentance, Germany should not be singled out as responsible for the war. At fault is European modernity and, especially, secularization.[92] The renewal of German spirit that Scheler believed to have witnessed with the God of War in 1914 became transfigured into an ecumenical renewal of European spirit through a rekindled desire for a God of Peace. A future European Union must be based on respect for and solidarity with all European peoples, including, Scheler makes a point of noting, cultural minorities, in shared coresponsibility for what is distinctive and valuable in every nation. Speaking directly to his German audience, "we must break with the old German vice of traditionalism, that false sense of historical determination in its thousand and one habitual forms, not to mention the ten thousand and one academic theories it has fostered."[93] A first step in atonement for humanity's self-inflicted suffering among the peoples of Europe is called for, rather than "accusation and thirst for revenge." As Scheler writes: "There is nothing so clear as this: only the

---

[90] M. Scheler, *On the Eternal in Man*, trans. B. Noble (New Brunswick, NJ: Transaction Publishers, 2010), p. 405.
[91] Scheler, *On the Eternal in Man*, p. 410.
[92] For Scheler's understanding of repentance, M. Scheler, "Repentance and Rebirth," in *On the Eternal in Man*, pp. 33–66.
[93] Scheler, *On the Eternal in Man*, p. 417.

gradual raising of the whole of the European heart, mind and judgment to that sunlit plateau, only the clear vision of Europe's – and indeed the world's – inseparably interwoven *common guilt* for the late war, can even *begin* any edifice of religious renewal."[94]

In the aftermath of war, the advent of peace requires the renewal of religion as an antidote to the catastrophe of secularism: "this is by far the most significant new *ferment* in man's outlook on the world to have been born of the Great War." Scheler's demand that "no mere restoration, then, but *conversion* of culture; a radical change of heart and the serious will to build anew" represents the central theme of *On the Eternal in Man* (1921). It is a work that stands as a personal affidavit of repentance for his heady enthusiasm for the "genius" of Germany's war in 1914 and a preliminary installment of the philosophy of religion promised at the end of *Formalism*, as developed, however, from the changed vantage point of his wartime conversion. As Scheler writes, the war, "so unimaginably saturated with tears, suffering, [and] lifeblood," has awoken a "cry of longing" and "deepest yearning" for "the divine beyond finite things [such that] one may expect the call to a renewal of religion to resound through the world with such power and strength as has not been felt for centuries."[95] As with his earlier writings, *On the Eternal in Man* situates the question of human existence at the center of his thinking, here emphatically aligned to the aftermath condition of historical desolation – the wasteland – in search for "the eternal," or the highest values, in relation to God. Europe's renewal must take the form of a renewal of religion; postwar Europe will have to become a postsecular Europe. Scheler was not alone in this effort to think anew the indispensability of religion for the devastated modern world. Karl Barth, Rudolf Otto, and Friedrich Gogarten, among Protestant crisis theologians, and Franz Rosenzweig and Martin Buber, among Jewish thinkers, were equally concerned, in their respective and divergent ways, with thinking beyond the failed project of secularization. As Scheler remarks:

> Today this call [for the renewal of religion] takes on a singularly historic character in that what is stricken to the heart is nothing less than the *whole of humanity*, nothing less than this mysterious planetary species in its undivided state—that is, like one man, a man cast into the boundlessness of time and space, cast into a mute uncomprehending nature: he bends every member in a solidarity effort to win the fight for existence, but it is also a fight for the meaning of his life and for his worth and dignity.

[94] Scheler, *On the Eternal in Man*, p. 125.
[95] Scheler, *On the Eternal in Man*, p. 107.

In contrast to Protestant crisis theology, Scheler maintains the place of human existence at the center of his call for the return of religion in looking to a new humanism for a postsecular age. Although the history of humankind has been plagued by "countless sufferings" and "internecine conflict," throughout this "dark history" the vicissitudes inflicted by humans against each other "had at least one thing *above* it [...] something above man to which he imputed as it were a moral office of judge over himself, but something in which he could at the same time place a deep trust and hope and in whose bosom he could at least believe himself to lie in some way sheltered. This one thing was – *humanity*." In the aftermath of the war, faith in humanity is now "gone," Scheler writes, "because this war, rightly called the World War, was the first experience to be undergone by humanity as *its collective* experience." The original catastrophe of the twentieth century condemned the "quasi-religious pathos over humanity" that "the great being of humanity was inflated to something distant and holy." The war demystified the deification of the human in the apocalypse of a humanity at war with itself, thus propelling the problem of world peace to an elevated status by affecting "every member of the race – to a greater or lesser degree – in life, in body, in soul."[96] Adrift in the ruins of its own edification and deification, humanity must find again its place in the cosmos. "For the first time," Scheler writes, "humanity feels *alone* in the wide universe. It has seen that the god it made of itself was an idol – the basest of idols since time began – baser than graven images of wood, marble and gold." In this condition of anthropological desolation, the human can only regain a place in the cosmos by returning to God.

This argument that Enlightenment secular humanism has "collapsed into ruins" is tacitly directed against France and England. In turning to his assessment of the war's spiritual desolation with Germany in view, Scheler undertakes a critique of pantheism, which he identifies as the predominant worldview of German thinking in the nineteenth and early twentieth centuries. As Heinrich Heine once observed, "pantheism is the clandestine religion of Germany, as was predicted fifty years ago by those German writers who campaigned so intensively against Spinoza."[97] Given that neither "the positivism of humanism" nor "the religious pathos of humanity" played a considerable role in German culture, Germany witnessed instead

---

[96] Scheler, *On the Eternal in Man*, p. 108.
[97] H. Heine, *On the History of Religion and Philosophy in Germany*, ed. T. Pinkard (Cambridge, UK: Cambridge University Press, 2007), p. 59.

"manifold forms of pantheism," which "[have] been struck the hardest blow by the deep revelation of the *nature of things* which the experience of the Great War has brought in their wake."[98] On Scheler's construal, pantheism identifies God with the immanence of the world. The world, as rationally ordered, is created by God, yet this notion of God as the creator is arrived at from an understanding of the world as created. In this manner, "the god of pantheism is always a reflection of theistic belief," according to Scheler. There are, moreover, two forms of pantheism: "the noble form" of acosmic pantheism, where the world exists in God, and "the base form" of atheistic pantheism, where God exists in the world. Until the outbreak of "the Great War, *pantheism was tending more and more away from its noble to its base form, from acosmism to atheism,*" and this degeneration culminated with atheistic monism. Arguably with Ernst Haeckel in mind, whose writings on the war and his Monist League aggressively supported German nationalism (and who coined the expression "the First World War"), Scheler observes that "Pantheism was able – with certain allowances – to express as it were the religious formulation of the German temperament so long as the nation's intellectual life was lost in dreams of an ideal world of the spirit, representing the true homeland of man (for 'man' read 'German') – so long as the nation thought and felt itself to be first and foremost a *Kulturnation*."[99] Germany's identification with God walking in world history – the God of War in 1914 – is thus symptomatic of the devolution of theism into pantheism, including (for Scheler) Hegel's.

This twofold tendency toward, on the one hand, the cultural religion of pantheism, with its German nationalist affinities, and, on the other hand, the positivistic faith in humanity of European modernity (France and England) was definitively arrested by the catastrophe of war. Scheler implies that the competing ideological justifications for the war among the Germans, the French, and the British leveraged their own respective worldviews. These worldviews can no longer respond to the call for religious renewal. Contra Scheler's earlier view of the war's positive "genius" in 1914, the war's revelation is now assessed negatively. Its "genius" consists in disclosing the emptiness of European culture, the loss of faith in humanity and God, without thereby offering a positive revelation of how to regenerate human existence in relation to the eternal and to God. As Scheler writes,

[98] However, for the resurgence of pantheism during the interwar years in Germany, see B. Lazier, *God Interrupted* (Princeton, NJ: Princeton University Press, 2012), chapter 6.
[99] Scheler, *On the Eternal in Man*, p. 113. See D. Gasman, "Ernst Haeckel and the German Monist League," in *The Scientific Origins of National Socialism* (London: Routledge, 2017): 1–30.

"it is false to think that the Great War must of itself bring to birth a *new religion* [...] as it were a miraculous pin-bright new Word in answer to the Question of suffering humanity." Most significantly, the war has pushed the "question of suffering humanity" – and hence the problem of evil – to the forefront for an understanding of the place of humankind in the world in relation to God. A new religion and hence a new Europe must be forged in response to the problem of evil in its paradigmatic manifestation of war.

The Genius of Peace

In 1924, Scheler received an invitation to participate at a gathering of European writers and intellectuals, organized by Paul Desjardins, at the Abbey de Pontigny in France.[100] This event, known as the "Décades de Pontigny," the first meeting of which began in 1910, sought to foster intercultural exchange in a spirit of cosmopolitanism imbued with Christian overtones, yet without a common confessional doctrine among participants.[101] Scheler's lectures (on Augustine and Meister Eckhart) contributed to his introduction of phenomenological thinking to France during the 1920s.[102] By 1924, however, his philosophical thinking had changed again since the war. As Heidegger retrospectively observed, the "new possibility of thinking" that Scheler discovered during the war, and which came to expression in *On the Eternal in Man*, "broke down again," but once more the question "What is Man? moved to the center of his work." In this new optic, "he saw the idea of the weak God, one who cannot be God without man."[103]

A first indication of Scheler's second transformation in less than a decade (coinciding with yet another falling-out with the Catholic Church, this time formally abandoned) is found in the 1924 essay "Problems of a Sociology of Knowledge." This second conversion pushed Scheler further

---

[100] 1924 marked the beginning of political and cultural rapprochement between Germany and France under the stewardship of Gustav Stresemann, German Foreign Minister from 1924 to 1929. In 1924, the Weimar government agreed to the Dawes Plan, regulating indemnity payments for the war, followed in 1925 by the Treaty of Locarno, which recognized Germany's Western territorial borders. See M. Nolan, *The Invented Mirror: Mythologizing the Enemy in France and Germany, 1898–1914* (New York: Berghahn Books, 2004), p. 110–111.

[101] See F. Chaubet, *Paul Desjardins et les Décadees de Pontigny*, (Villeneuve d'Ascq: Septentrion, 2009). Scheler received a second invitation in 1926.

[102] See C. Dupont, *Phenomenology in French Philosophy: Early Encounters* (Dordrecht: Springer Verlag, 2014), chapter 2. *The Essence of Sympathy* was the first work of German phenomenology translated into French, in 1928.

[103] As Heidegger further comments: "All of this was far removed from a smug theism or a vague pantheism"; *The Metaphysical Foundations of Logic*, p. 51.

in the direction of searching for a renewal of religion, while decisively breaking with the theism that had defined his thinking from *Formalism* to *On the Eternal in Man*. The catalyst for this transformation in his conception of God was the unresolved question of how to make sense of the suffering of humanity at war with itself and the senseless manifestation of evil on a historically unprecedented scale. Scheler's theistic God proved to be inadequate for responding to the problem of evil. How could a theistic God – as the perfect embodiment of Goodness – stand reconciled with such vastness of (self-inflicted) human suffering? Scheler's own account of hatred, as emerging from *ressentiment* and the narrowing of the hierarchy of values, fell short, he realized, of taking full measure of the depth and virility of war's appetite for destruction. Although in "Problems of a Sociology of Knowledge" Scheler continued to reject pantheism, he would shortly thereafter adopt and formulate his own kind of pantheism, and yet not the "noble" or "base" kinds criticized in *On the Eternal in Man*, but a newfound pantheism that espoused the conception of a "weak God."[104]

In *The Human Place in the Cosmos* (1928), Scheler's theistic conception of God as the being from which all beings are created, who, as the highest person, embodies the perfection of Goodness, is displaced by an original agonistic difference between "Drive" (*Drang*) and "Spirit" (*Geist*). Neither can be reduced or derived from the other. The ontological ground of the cosmos is thus an original nonidentity of incessant discord between life and spirit. God is not the being who creates the cosmos nor a person – "the highest person" – who embodies perfected goodness. God becomes caught in the cosmic struggle between life and spirit, helpless and hapless before the spectacle of world suffering, which, in this speculative framework, stems from the unbridled drive of life. God is without being, not so much as the absence of being, but as the need for his own becoming "insofar as the historical process of the realization of the ideal *Deitas* (the realization of higher values) takes place."[105] From this original diremption of being, the place of the human in the cosmos is situated at the conflictual point of intersection between "drive" and "spirit." God is not an infinite person to which finite human persons aspire; on the contrary, God stands powerless to actualize his own being. God's becoming depends on the efforts of human striving to establish concord among themselves in the world. As played out within

---

[104] Spader, *Scheler's Personalism*, pp. 176ff. As Scheler notes, however, in the Preface to the third edition of *Formalism* in 1926, "the grounds and intellectual motives" for this transformation in his philosophy of religion remain anchored in his foundational ethics.

[105] Scheler, *The Human Place in the Cosmos*, pp. 70–71.

human existence, life cannot become sublimated into spirit, nor can spirit become vanquished by life. Spirit is itself "without power" yet graced with vision ("ideals"), whereas life is blind in its striving yet armed with power. Scheler disavows any final reconciliation or dialectical unity between life and spirit, stridently avoiding any form of monism, yet maintains that in the conflictual opposition between life and spirit, spirit can direct the forces of life toward higher values. There is, however, neither a cunning of reason nor a progressive teleology of history leading humanity toward a final reconciliation between life and spirit. The human condition is at war with itself, torn between life and spirit, and yet the spiritual aspiration of the human spirit toward the realization of higher values issues an "eternal protest" against unbridled life in the hope of peace and reconciliation between life and spirit, which must occur among humankind in order for God to become reconciled with himself and the world.

In 1926, a few years before *The Human Place in the Cosmos*, Scheler received an invitation to deliver two lectures, "Politics and Moral" and "The Idea of Perpetual Peace and Pacifism," to military officers at the behest of the liberal Minister of Defense Otto Gessler. The purpose of this invitation was to mediate between conflicting political factions in the German *Reichswehr*. Both lectures were delivered in Berlin in 1927. Scheler repeated his lecture on politics and morality at the University of Cologne and was due to deliver both lectures once more at the University of Frankfurt in 1928; a few days after the first lecture, he died. In his first lecture, Scheler's reflections are organized around a critical assessment of possible relationships between politics and morality in the Western tradition. The aim of this schematic survey is to arrive at a resolution of the endemic conflict between political power and moral values. On Scheler's view, there are four basic relations between politics and morality: the subsumption of morality to politics; the subsumption of politics to morality; the dualism between politics and morality; and the division between private morality and state morality. After examining these relational forms, Scheler faults each one for a common inability to properly balance the relation between political power and moral values, and proposes instead a mutual determination of power and morality – their egalization – under the ideal of the collective realization of human existence according to an objective order of higher values. The decisions of politicians must be framed by an "as much as possible diverse and profound commitment to the general world situation and the situation or position of their state therein."[106] The interests of the state

---

[106] Scheler, *Schriften aus dem Nachlaß*, p. 43.

The Genius of War, the Genius of Peace

are here constrained by the principle that nothing should adversely affect the "total salvation of humanity"; that is, the attainment of perpetual peace. In this sense, politicians are responsible for the salvation of their own state as well as for the salvation of humanity. This twofold aspiration for national and cosmopolitan salvation must be guided by the "law for the progressive diminution of the employment of violence" in history. The "drive to power" that animates politics must therefore be curbed and directed by the historical goal of realizing peace among nations, to which in turn morality, encoded in a system of laws, becomes subsumed for the purpose of allowing individual citizens to live according to higher values.

This subsumption of politics and morals to the historical realization of humanity under the watchword of peace is taken up again in Scheler's second lecture, "The Idea of Perpetual Peace and Pacifism," which, inter alia, can be read as a point-by-point (though he remains silent with respect to his wartime reflections) repudiation of his metaphysical conception of war. The idea of war as the pursuit of creative vitality, as cultural critique and awakening, as forging solidarity and ordering of the world (*Welteinrichtung*), and as *Gottesgericht* – these facets to the "genius of war" in 1914 are summarily rejected. This reversal hinges on the argument that the drive for increased vitality and self-realization is positively drawn by the idea of perpetual peace. Against his own understanding of the relation between war and peace in Der Genius, in 1927 peace is accorded a metaphysical significance for life, rather than war. As Scheler states: "War is not rooted in 'human nature.'"[107] If there was a genius of war in his wartime writings, there emerges in his thinking during the 1920s a genius of peace.[108]

Written in the aftermath of German defeat, Scheler extracts from the failure of the German war a lesson: "We must break with romantic war-philosophy and a romance that lacks any sense of reality (*wirklichkeitsermangelnder Romantik*)."[109] Unlike his view of peace as a negative idea and war as a positive value in Der Genius, Scheler turns to consider the idea of perpetual peace as the positive value in contrast to the negative value of war. In reversing his conception of war and peace in the aftermath of 1918, Scheler proposes that the problem of perpetual peace represents "for all time" and "for all human beings" a fundamental aspiration of human life for attaining autonomous rationality and consciousness. This primordial (*uralt*) drive toward peace for the self-realization of human freedom

---

[107] Scheler, *Schriften aus dem Nachlaß*, p. 88: "Auf der 'menschlichen Natur' beruht der Krieg nicht."
[108] For this dual conception, see Davis, "The Values of War and Peace."
[109] Scheler, *Schriften aus dem Nachlaß*, p. 121.

represents a drive toward freedom that critically entails rupture with pre-given meaning, received tradition, and an ordering of the world through violence.[110] The aspiration for perpetual peace, coupled with a drive toward autonomous freedom, underlies the world's "great cultures" (Scheler speaks of China, India, Ancient cultures, and Western Christianity) in a movement of "*stetiger Wiederkehr*." With each flourishing and hence promise of perpetual peace, eternity becomes temporalized in a historical "eternal recurrence," yet not in terms of the repetition of the same idea, for with each breakthrough in history, peace – the force of its idea – always emerges in the form of "new political and ethical theories."

And yet: "What is one to make of the real significance and historical efficacy of an idea of peace so ancient – and which in its own thousand years has come to virtually nothing, not even to certainly and clearly discernible beginnings of its realization?" Indeed, is perpetual peace – the *idea* of perpetual peace – even possible for human beings (*menschenmöglich*)? As Scheler writes: "Das Gute soll sein, auch wenn es niemals geschähe."[111] The Good must be, even if it has never occurred. The recurring idea of peace is the power of the powerless that, in its interruption of the conflict between "life" and "spirit," allows for the realization of the God – the God of Peace – in the world. This unfinished God is the unfinished history of humankind progressing toward the "World Age of Equilibrium" (*Weltalter des Ausgleichs*). As Scheler writes, "there is a kind of 'support' even for us. This is the support provided by the total process of realizing values in the world history in so far as this process has moved forward toward the making of a 'God.'"[112] It is this unshaken ideal, despite the "blood and revulsion" of world history, that awakens a world saturated with violence from its romanticism, complacency, or cynicism. In the aftermath of the "great furies" and "gruesomeness" of 1914–18, is there any exodus from the perpetual strife of the world toward peace? As Scheler remarks: "There is no escape from the harshness of this fact," that the apparent impossibility of peace in our world must nonetheless become the new God of the future, the possibility of which resides exclusively in what can only seem to be humankind's greatest possibility; namely, to overcome the seeming impossibility of a humanity no longer at war with itself.

---

[110] M. Scheler, *Schriften aus dem Nachlaß: Philosophie und Geschichte*, ed. M. Frings (Bonn: Bouvier, 1990), p. 79.
[111] Scheler, *Schriften aus dem Nachlaß: Philosophie und Geschichte*, p. 81.
[112] Scheler, *The Human Place in the Cosmos*, p. 95.

CHAPTER 2

Deutschtum und Judentum
Hermann Cohen in the Time of the Nations

"Great and Joyous to be a German Citizen"

On many fronts, 1916 marked a point of no return. After the collapse of optimism for swift victory following the outbreak of hostilities, the inconclusive bloodlettings at Verdun and the Somme, and mounting economic hardships on the home front, the prospects for German triumph seemed increasingly dim. Attitudes became more resigned to a war like no other, a war without end. Dampened expectations gave way to creeping pessimism matched by defiant fatalism. A number of prominent intellectuals and academics who in 1914 eagerly supported the war now came to express their doubts or else fell conspicuously silent regarding the fate of the nation. Once the most vocal of advocates for the war, Ernst Troeltsch began to see things differently and came to accept the political deficiencies of the Wilhelmine Empire with its deleterious militarism.[1] In a critique of his earlier endorsement of the ideas of 1914 and *Kulturkrieg*, Troeltsch argued in January 1917 at the first gathering of the *Volksbund für Freiheit und Vaterland* for "the primacy of politics" over military strategy, and urged that the "political philosophy of the struggle for existence [*Kampf um das Dasein*] should be abandoned." In the same vein, he called for a "demobilization of intellectuals" (*Demobilisierung der Geister*).[2] This change in the intellectual atmosphere would only become more pronounced during the final year of the war. And yet, 1916 likewise produced the opposite reaction of increased political radicalization, a tendency that would continue, and in many instances become further aggravated, after the war had ended during turbulent years of civil conflict. A public debate on the expansion

---

[1] See Flasch, *Die geistige Mobilmachung*, p. 279ff. Flasch speaks of the *Ideenwende* of 1916–17.
[2] Flasch, *Die geistige Mobilmachung*, p. 285–286. For Troeltsch's wartime writings and speeches, Ernst Troeltsch, *Schriften zur Politik (1914–1918)* (Berlin: Walter de Gruyter, 2002). Troeltsch's lecture provoked a substantial response, most visibly with the publication of Hans Volkelt's *Demobilisierung der Geister. Eine Auseinandersetzung vornehmlich mit Ernst Troeltsch* (Munich: Beck'sche Verlagsbuchhandlung, 1918).

of submarine operations without restrictions (a strategy that pushed the United States into the war in April 1917) saw a number of academics leveraging once again their "spiritual" prestige. Whereas Max Weber and the military historian Hans Delbrück expressed their reservations toward this intensification of submarine warfare, Adolf von Harnack and Ulrich von Wiliamowitz-Moellendorff, among others, energetically supported this desperate naval gambit. As yet another dramatic act of "spiritual mobilization," this ill-fated and ill-advised engagement contributed significantly to the collapse of German human sciences during the closing years of the war.[3]

In 1914, *Kampf um das Dasein* was the dominant rallying cry for the mobilization of the nation. Much of the public enthusiasm in August 1914, even if privately more cautious outlooks prevailed, seized upon the war as an epochal moment for the consolidation of the German nation. In his essay "Thoughts in Wartime," Thomas Mann evoked the cathartic effect of the war, with its promise of the spiritual rescue of Germany and Europe.[4] The war brought a heightened sense of anticipation as well as distress: anticipation of assured victory and spiritual deliverance, and yet distress at the widely perceived injustice of Allied aggression against Germany. Inscribed within a narrative of German historical self-fashioning reaching back to the 1813 War of Liberation and Fichte's iconic *Reden an die deutsche Nation*, the *Kriegsliteratur* of 1914–15 was animated by apocalyptic visions of the war's regenerative potential.[5]

On August 1, the day after Germany's declaration of war, Kaiser Wilhelm II ordered a general mobilization and addressed the German nation from the balcony of the Royal Palace in Berlin:

> Should there be battle, all political parties will cease to exist! I, too, have been attacked by one party or another. That was in times of peace. It is now forgiven with all my heart. I no longer think in terms of parties or confessions; today we are all German brothers and only German brothers. If our neighbors want it no other way, if our neighbors do not grant us peace, then I hope to God that our good German sword will emerge victorious from this hard battle.[6]

---

[3] H. Münkler, *Der Grosse Krieg. Die Welt 1914–1918* (Berlin: Rowohlt Taschenbuch 2015), p. 513. After the war, Delbrück claimed that Bethmann Hollweg had referred to this decision in 1917 as "our Sicilian expedition" (p. 514).

[4] T. Mann, *Reflections on a Nonpolitical Man*, trans. W. Morris (New York: New York Review Books, 2021), pp. 491–506.

[5] See Vondung, *The Apocalypse in Germany*.

[6] *Deutsche Quellen zur Geschichte des Ersten Weltkrieges*, ed. W. Bihl, (Darmstadt: WBG, 1991), p. 49. For this English translation: http://germanhistorydocs.ghi-dc.org/sub_document.cfm?document_id=815.

This imperial call for national reconciliation baptized the war as a struggle for existence on two fronts: unforgiving against Germany's external enemies, but, as significantly, forgiving of cultural, social, and political divisions within Germany. Even if Germany had been united after its military success in 1871, it remained a nation in search of its cultural and social – and spiritual – unity. The decades after unification witnessed rapid social and economic transformations along with fractious cultural and social divisions. Two contentious public debates were representative of the degree to which Germany remained in search of itself: the *Kulturkampf* instigated by Bismarck between Catholics and Protestants and the *Judenfrage* debate during the 1880s, commonly known as the Berlin anti-Semitism conflict.[7] Agitation was rife during these years. Political and social advancements in a growing liberal tradition, the establishment of the German Socialist Party, and educational reforms ran parallel to mounting conservative nationalism and *völkisch* ideology. As a marker of progressive tendencies, in 1912 the Socialist Party achieved a majority in the *Reichstag* – an unprecedented success among European socialist movements. Were it not for the failure of the Brussels July conference in 1914 of European socialist parties to make good on their commitments in the Basel declaration of 1912 to declare a general strike of workers in the event of a European war, critical war credits might have never been granted in August 1914 by the Socialist Party in Germany.

As expressed in a deluge of wartime speeches and publications, the war was eagerly greeted as a force of meaning, above all in forging cultural and social solidarity. The Kaiser's call for civic peace was especially welcomed by the acculturated German-Jewish *Bildungsbürgetum* that emerged during the mid to late nineteenth century. Entering into the cosmopolitan and liberal-minded *Bildungsbürgetum* offered Jews a path to assimilation, while allowing for the preservation of their religious identity.[8] At the outbreak of the war, the *Bildungsbürgetum* represented one of the "last guardians of the original idea of *Bildung*."[9] Wartime mobilization of the German spirit

---

[7] For anti-Semitic conflict, M. Stoetzler, *The State, the Nation & the Jews: Liberalism and the Antisemitism Dispute in Bismarck's Germany* (Lincoln, NE: University of Nebraska, 2008) and P. Pulzer, *Jews and the German State: The Political History of a Minority, 1848–1933* (Detroit, MI: Wayne State University Press, 2003).

[8] See P. Mendes-Flohr, *German Jews: A Dual Identity* (New Haven, CT: Yale University Press, 1999), p. 10ff. For Jewish emancipation in nineteenth-century Germany, see G. Aly, *Why the Germans? Why the Jews? Envy, Race Hatred, and the Prehistory of the Holocaust*, trans. J. Chase (New York: Picador, 2011). See also G. Mosse, "Jewish Emancipation: Between Bildung and Respectability," in *Jewish Response to German Culture*, ed. J. Reinharz and W. Schatzberg (Hannover, NH: University of New England Press, 1985).

[9] Adopting A. Assmann's characterization, *Arbeit am nationalen Gedächtnis* (Frankfurt: Campus Verlag, 1993), p. 91.

promised a resolution of the "Jewish question," namely, of how to reconcile the tensions within the "and" of being German *and* Jewish, of belonging to German culture while adhering to the Jewish religion, of being a citizen of the German state while remaining a member of the Jewish people. Jewish community leaders, rabbis in synagogues, and Jewish intellectuals joined the chorus of support for Germany's spiritual mobilization. This support embraced factions within the Jewish population in Germany and, importantly, offered a common ground for Zionists and anti-Zionists alike. Zionist organizations as well as more liberal Jewish groups were keen to focus their attention on the plight of Jewish communities in the East. In the words of the Zionist newspaper *Jüdische Rundschau*, German Jews were struggling to liberate "Russia and the world from unprecedented tyranny."[10]

To symbolize this newly proclaimed unity, on August 5 the Kaiser called for a national day of patriotic prayer. Jewish synagogues joined Protestant and Catholic churches in celebrating the spirit of war and encouraged their congregations to serve Germany's cause. As the largest Jewish organization in Germany, the *Centralverein deutscher Staatsbürger jüdischen Glaubens* declared: "In this faithful hour, the Fatherland calls its sons to join up [...] It goes without saying that every German Jew is ready to sacrifice property and blood as duty demands."[11] Restrictions on entering the military, officer promotions, and senior staff appointments became loosened, even if obstacles for Jewish soldiers and officers remained in an army controlled by the martial Junker class.[12] German Jews volunteered in significant numbers. With the first combat actions of the war, Jewish communities mourned and honored the sacrifice of their sons, brothers, and husbands. This reconciliation of religious divisions was exemplified by the military service of rabbis side by side with their Protestant and Catholic counterparts in ministering to the religious needs of German soldiers. Even in the private lives of many German Jews, the Kaiser's declared civic truce resonated deeply. As the prominent Zionist and journalist Ludwig Strauss

---

[10] German Jews were thus said to be engaged in nothing less than a "holy war" against the Russian oppression of local Jewish populations. This struggle against Russia was compared to the biblical struggle of the Maccabees against the Greeks. T. Grady, *A Deadly Legacy: German Jews and the Great War* (New Haven, CT: Yale University Press, 2017), p. 40 ff. For the impact of the war and the German Revolution on German Jews and Judaism in Germany, *Deutsches Judentum in Krieg und Revolution 1916–1923*, ed. W. Mosse (Tübingen: J. C. B. Mohr, 1971).

[11] Quoted in Grady, *A Deadly Legacy*, p. 27.

[12] See D. Hughes and R. Dinardo, *Imperial Germany and War: 1871–1918* (Kansas: University of Kansas Press, 2018), p. 30ff. See also D. Penslar, *Jews and the Military: A History* (Princeton, NJ: Princeton University Press, 2013). For a literary depiction of anti-Semitism in the German Army, Arnold Zweig's masterful novel *Outside Verdun* (Glasgow: Freight Books, 2014).

(who would marry Martin Buber's daughter) wrote in 1914: "I believe that after this war, in which I am firmly convinced we will be victorious, it will be great and joyous to be a German citizen."[13]

On Inner Peace

By 1916, however, German–Jewish reconciliation had become pulled in opposite and opposed directions. Even as German Jews continued to mobilize for the war effort, served at the front, endured the rigors of a wartime economy, and mourned their fallen ones, reconciling the tensions in the dual identity of being German *and* Jewish, in how it might be possible to be great and joyous to be a German *and* great and joyous to be a Jew, was by no means self-evident or guaranteed. In the midst of the war, Buber's launching of the journal *Der Jude* in 1916 reflected a heightened public consciousness – and acceptance – of Jewish culture.[14] With its promotion of interfaith dialogue, open debate concerning Zionism, discussion of Jewish literature and religious traditions, and concern for the predicament of Eastern European Jews, *Der Jude* established itself as a unique forum for dialogical understanding among German Jews. That same year, however, Arnold Metzger, who studied with Edmund Husserl before the war and now found himself serving at the front, confided to his mother: "I am convinced that a strong anti-Semitic movement will pass through Germany after the war."[15] His anxiety was not unfounded. Metzger had in view the notorious "Jewish count" (*Judenzahl*) of the German military in 1916, meant to assess the loyalty of Jewish soldiers.[16] Symbolically as well as psychologically, the "Jewish count" revealed a culturally ingrained suspicion against Jewish patriotism and simmering paranoia vis-à-vis "the enemy within." As the war progressed without an end, the demise of prospects for victory further fueled the radicalization of anti-Semitism and, significantly, normalized the cultural currency of racial stereotypes in public discourse.[17] Even before the war, Werner Sombart in his 1913 *Die Juden und das Wirtschaftsleben* legitimated academically the

---

[13] Quoted in Grady, *A Deadly Legacy*, p. 21.
[14] This unapologetic "self-assertion of Jewish identity" was "nothing short of revolutionary." Mendes-Flohr, *German Jews*, pp. 22, 56.
[15] *Philosophers at the Front: Phenomenology and the First World War*, eds. N. de Warren and T. Vongehr (Leuven: Leuven University Press, 2017), p. 204 (Letter of November 26, 1916).
[16] See A. Ullrich, "'Nun sind wir gezeichnet' – Jüdische Soldaten und die 'Judenzählung,'" in *Krieg! 1914–1918 Juden zwischen den Fronten*, ed. U. Sieg (Berlin: Hentrich & Hentrich, 2014): 217–238.
[17] Ulrich Sieg, *Jüdische Intellektuelle im Ersten Weltkrieg* (Berlin: Akademie Verlag, 2001), pp. 174–194.

anti-Semitic slander of disproportionate Jewish economic prosperity and influence. During the war, the circulation of anti-Semitic images and slogans intensified along with racist images of non-European troops in the service of France and England.[18] Unlike racist aggression against Allied colonial troops and their feared "contamination" of European nations (a prevalent theme in the German press), the rise of anti-Semitism drew on a longstanding anxiety in the German national psyche concerning an invisible and conspiratorial Jewish "state within a state." By 1916, the reconciliation between Germans and Jews implied in the Kaiser's call for civic truce hung precariously in the balance. Two conflicting horizons fluctuated simultaneously within the "and" of Germany *and* Judaism: a horizon of reconciliation drawn along the contours of a resolution to the question of Germany and Judaism, on the one hand, and a horizon of antagonism drawn along the contours of a new front in the war against an enemy within, on the other. As the latter began to crystallize more clearly, the former began to recede more rapidly from view.

Under the title *Vom inneren Frieden des Deutschen Volkes. Ein Buch gegenseitigen Verstehens und Vertrauens*, a collection of essays appeared in 1916 bringing together forty prominent professors, theologians, and intellectuals.[19] As with other wartime publications, *Vom inneren Frieden des Deutschen Volkes* bears a dedication to "our fallen brothers." As the editor Friedrich Thimme remarks in his preface, the war has made glaringly apparent divisions within German culture, thus rendering urgent the imperative of inner peace. For Kant, the condition of peace did not consist in a temporary cessation of hostilities, but in a state of perpetual peace. In a comparable sense, Thimme argues that "inner peace" is not equivalent to a condition of political or economic concord; it requires the "enduring glorious unity of the entire German peoples." As Thimme writes: "We have organized our military and economic forces to the amazement of the entire world, so now it is time to organize the spiritual forces, so that these forces can show the ways of inner peace for the people, which at the same time are the ways toward greatness."[20] While blood and iron provide the means for the attainment of "external peace," only mutual understanding and trust, as exemplified in this collection of essays, can offer the means for inner peace as the *conditio sine qua non* for any lasting peace.

---

[18] For racism and the war and, especially, in German prisoner of war camps, A. Becker, *Oubliés de la grand guerre* (Paris: Éditons Noêsis, 1998), pp. 317–325.
[19] *Vom inneren Frieden des Deutschen Volkes. Ein Buch gegenseitigen Verstehens und Vertrauens*, ed. F. Thimme (Leipzig: Hirzel Verlag, 1916).
[20] Thimme, *Vom inneren Frieden des Deutschen Volkes*, p. vi.

Vom inneren Frieden brings together authors from opposing positions: religious, political, and cultural. Many of the authors, Thimme underlines, penned their respective essays without knowledge of one another's intentions, and yet, despite their different perspectives, each author expresses a common love for the Fatherland. "This book seeks to serve the inner peace of the German people," and with this aim looks to mitigate the "acidic poison" of cultural conflict among different *Weltanschauungen*. This chorus of voices, moreover, is said to compose an "elevated song of spirit of mutual understanding and trust." As with the chorus in Greek theatre, this elevated song of spirit is meant to mediate between the dramatic action on the stage of war and the audience at the home front. Soldiers on the front lines, Thimme reminds his readers, suffer and die together without any conceit or concern for their respective religious confessions, political beliefs, or social class. This *Fronterlebnis* has forged solidarity among German soldiers, who "lie next to each other in heroic death in the resting place of graves as the symbol of unity and inner peace." As Thimme remarks, there can be "no more beautiful memorial placed on their graves" than an inner peace in honor of their sacrificial deaths.

"Deutschtum und Judentum"

Among the illustrious contributors to the volume, including Rudolf Eucken and Paul Natorp, one author in particular stands out given the odd placement of his essay. As the final contribution in the volume (the first essay is Eucken's "Die Einheit der deutschen Weltanschauung"), Hermann Cohen's "Deutschtum und Judentum" finds itself in the last section, "Peace among Nationalities," along with essays on the Polish question and on Alsace-Lothringen. The inclusion of Cohen in this prestigious volume is not in itself surprising. At the outbreak of the war, Cohen was the leading figure of Marburg Neo-Kantianism as well as an esteemed public spokesperson for the German-Jewish *Bildungsbürgetum*.[21] With his groundbreaking interpretations of Kant's three critiques followed by three installments of his own philosophical system, Cohen had established himself as a masterful advocate of Kant's transcendental idealism as well as an original post-Kantian philosopher, who conceived of his philosophical

---

[21] For Marburg Neo-Kantianism, K. Christian Köhnke, *The Rise of Neo-Kantianism: German Academic Philosophy between Idealism and Positivism*, trans. R. J. Hollingdale (Cambridge, UK: Cambridge University Press, 1991); S. Luft, *The Space of Culture* (Oxford: Oxford University Press, 2015); A. Philonenko, *L'École de Marbourg: Cohen, Natorp, Cassirer* (Paris: J. Vrin, 1989); H. Dussort, *L'École de Marbourg* (Paris: PUF, 1963).

mission as modernizing Kant's thinking, not through pedantic textual exegesis or a dogmatic return to Kantian orthodoxy, but in retrieving the actuality of Kant's thinking, unclouded by German speculative idealism and unfettered from psychological trappings, in order to progress beyond the limitations of Kant's own system. What is surprising, however, is the placement of "Deutschtum und Judentum," tucked away outside the sections reflecting on *Deutschtum*, as if *Judentum* represented a foreign nationality on a par with Poland and Alsace-Lothringen.

Having at first little enthusiasm for the war, Cohen became an ardent supporter after reading the telegrams between Kaiser Wilhelm II and Czar Nicholas II. In a letter of August 23, 1914, to Natorp, Cohen voices his profound indignation at Allied war propaganda and their denigration of German culture. "We [Germans]," he remarks, "stand innocent as angels before history." As Cohen further observes, "we have, to speak with Fichte, given in too much to foreign minds because we unfortunately have not grasped [our] German uniqueness and not wanted to understand it."[22] In bemoaning this failure, Cohen sees the war as a historical opportunity to realize in thought and deed the "ethical spirit of our people." As he explains to Natorp, "you thus see that I am not at all doubtful about the future. It seems to me that we stand before a great people's turning point." Cohen considers the hatred against German culture peddled by Allied propaganda to be analogous to hatred against the Jews, thus suggesting an inner affinity between the persecution of Germanness and the persecution of Judaism. As Cohen writes: "It is the same for the Germans as for the Jews, [and] therefore I perhaps understand our German fate better than you do."[23] As both a German and a Jew, Cohen claims to possess a unique perspective on the war. "German Humanity shall not perish," he writes in a letter from January 1915, but adds that only with "a profound insight into the essence of Germanness [*Deutschtum*] can genuine progress be made."[24]

Cohen's 1916 essay "Deutschtum and Judentum" represents a second iteration of his vision for the wartime spiritual reconciliation between Germany and Judaism, first advanced in a 1915 text bearing the same title. Cohen's engagement in public discussion of the war's significance reflected

---

[22] Bergson is singled out for especially harsh criticism. As Cohen remarks: "You see, how my [nose] correctly sniffed out the Polish Jew Bergson. You must have surely read how shamelessly this eclectic juggler [*Gaukler*] spoke about Germany. And now Herr Eucken must be ashamed." H. Holzhey, *Der Marburger Neukantianismus in Quellen: Zeugnisse kritischer Lektüre, Briefe der Marburger, Dokumente zur Philosophiepolitik der Schule* (Basel: Schwabe, 1986), vol. II, p. 429.
[23] Holzhey, *Der Marburger Neukantianismus in Quellen*, p. 439.
[24] Holzhey, *Der Marburger Neukantianismus in Quellen*, p. 441.

his Kantian commitment to the public exercise of reason; the war years saw numerous publications by him in support of the war effort. As with Fichte's *Reden an die Deutsche Nation*, Cohen does not consider there to be a contradiction between cosmopolitan idealism and his own Kantian form of socialism, with his unwavering affirmation of German nationalism in symbiotic relationship with the ethical-social ideal of Judaism.[25] In his 1915 essay, Cohen envisions that the effective pairing of *Deutschtum* and *Judentum* would allow, on the one hand, Germany to mature into its rightful cosmopolitan mission, thus preventing, inter alia, the collapse of *Judentum* into ethno-nationalist Zionism, while, on the other, imbuing *Judentum* with a refined ethical idealism, thus affirming the spiritual significance of *Judentum* against simmering wartime anti-Semitism. In both the 1915 and 1916 essays, Cohen argues that the "quintessence of [the war's] political task" resides with the reconciliation between *Deutschtum* and *Judentum* that would lead toward perpetual peace and the realization of the "messianic idea of Israelite Prophetism."[26] Both essays are constructed around the redemptive conjunction between *Deutschtum* and *Judentum*, (and) between philosophy (German Idealism) and religion (prophetic Judaism). The conjunction "and" functions as a philosophical term in Cohen's thinking, namely, as an irreducible and generative "correlation," a constitutive relation of reciprocity between related elements – in this instance, *Deutschtum* and *Judentum* – without which neither element can achieve self-realization. With this conjunction, or correlation, expectantly in view, as Cohen concludes his 1915 manifesto, "we can hope for the just ethical revelation from the war."

It should not be surprising, as Cohen begins his 1916 essay, that the unification of Germany lent renewed impetus to the conflict between *Deutschtum* and *Judentum*, and thus that the war, as an existential struggle of the German nation, would sharpen this opposition. National unity, however, is not to be understood as a pregiven reality but as a task animated by a drive toward the realization of an idea. Cohen acknowledges

---

[25] For this reconciliation of German nationalism and cosmopolitanism in Ficthe's *Reden*, a common theme during the war, see N. de Warren, "Rudolf Eucken: Philosophicus Teutonicus (1913–1914)," in *The Intellectual Response to the First World War*, eds. S. Posman, C. van Dijck, and M. Demoor (Eastbourne: Sussex Academic Press, 2017): 44–64.

[26] H. Cohen, *Deutschtum und Judentum* (Giessen: Alfred Töpelmann, 1915), p. 48. For an incisive analyses of Cohen's 1915 text, S. Schwarzschild, "Germanism and Judaism – Herman Cohen's Normative Paradigm of the German-Jewish Symbiosis," in *Jews and Germans from 1860 to 1933*, ed. D. Bronsen (Heidelberg: Carl Winter Verlag, 1979): 129–172; and M. Vatter, "Nationality, State and Global Constitutionalism in Hermann Cohen's Wartime Writings," in *100 Years of European Philosophy since the Grear War*, ed. M. Sharpe, R. Jeffs, and J. Reynolds (Dordrecht: Springer, 2017): 43–63.

that there are different senses (and hence ideas) in which a nation consolidates itself: as a racial unity (*Rasseneinheit*), as a political unity, and as a religious unity. Although the German nation attained political unification in 1871, it did not achieve racial or religious unity. When compared to other European nations, German unification occurred belatedly due to an entrenched theological division between Protestantism and Catholicism that, for Cohen, defined Germany's "religious distinctiveness." This religious antagonism exacerbated cultural tensions with other religions, most significantly Judaism. The achievement of religious unity would thus require a reconciliation between antagonisms produced by the Reformation in the form of the twofold reconciliation of Catholicism and Protestantism *with* Christianity and Judaism. The distinctive destiny of the German nation since the Reformation consists in the reconciliation of monotheism with itself, thus placing the question of "What is monotheism?" center stage in Cohen's reflections.

Of the two forms of national unity – racial and religious – Cohen dismisses the legitimacy of considering German unity in terms of race, thus casting off, in a defiant gesture, *völkisch* intellectuals of the likes of Paul Lagarde, Julius Langbehn, Guido von List, and Moeller van de Bruck with their Ario-Germanic ethno-mythologies. The "purity of a race" cannot be grounded as a "rigorous scientific concept," nor should "race" be conflated with "spiritual" or "moral" traits.[27] Cohen appeals to a "natural-scientific historical perspective" in arguing that Jews already contributed to the spiritual and cultural life of Germany during the Middle Ages. What threatened this "spiritual rapprochement" was the Reformation, which, in producing a rift within Christianity, allowed for anti-Semitism to serve as a politically expedient strategy of distraction from intertheological conflict. Jews became a scapegoat with which to alleviate Catholic and Protestant rivalry. In the long history of German–Jewish antagonism, the unification of the German nation in 1871 proved to be decisive. The reconciliation between Catholicism and Protestantism after Bismarck's *Kulturkampf* occurred, for Cohen, under the aegis of a Protestantism (led by Adolf von Harnack and Ernst Troeltsch) that claimed to represent an "original" or "absolute Christianity." On the one hand, this unification of Christianity under the idea of an "original Christianity"

---

[27] The anti-Semitic slander that Jews "possess an evil tribal character (*Stammescharakter*) is not even worthy of refutation and sits beyond the pale of any effort at *understanding*." As Cohen writes: "Against such a view I would not even enter into a discussion (*nicht in eine Verhandlung eintreten*)." H. Cohen, *Kleinere Schriften VI. 1916–1918*, ed. H. Holzhey (Hildesheim: Olms, 2002), p. 112.

sharpened the antagonism with Judaism. On the other hand, Protestant "pure Christianity," although based on the "fiction of the essence of Christianity," shifted the understanding of religion (as Christianity) away from a foundation in revelation to a foundation in *Sittlichkeit* (morality). As Cohen remarks, "modern religiosity, at least in Germany," does not depend on the dogma of revelation, but searches for the core of faith in "religious *Sittlichkeit*."[28] Cohen seizes on this Protestant emphasis on *Sittlichkeit* with the intention of surpassing the apparently irreconcilable conflict between Christianity and Judaism, especially as derived from appeals to the "materialism of racial emotions." In terms of religious *Sittlichkeit*, there exists no substantial opposition between Christianity and Judaism, but, on the contrary, concordance and convergence.

By stressing that both "original Christianity" and Judaism are founded on religious *Sittlichkeit*, Cohen would appear to betray his own insistence on the uniqueness of Judaism in the conjunction of *Deutschtum und Judentum*.[29] Cohen's ostensible privilege of German Protestantism seems, moreover, to be further compounded – and hence complicit – with the privilege granted to German spirit in its existential wartime struggle. German spirit would thus be granted a "double privilege," philosophical as well as religious, in Cohen's advocation of a "certain type of militant patriotism" in the cause of German–Jewish reconciliation. This twofold privilege subscribes to a "logic of exemplarism," namely, the argument (traceable back to Fichte's *Reden an die Deutsche Nation*) that the German nation exemplifies the universal.[30] On this logic, the particular claims the universal for itself in claiming to exemplify the universal as the essence of its own particularism. The claim to embody and hence realize cosmopolitanism betrays a conceited form of German spirit as the presumptuous spirit of humanity. Cohen's argumentation, however, subtly reverses the directionality of privilege in his reconciliation of Christianity (and hence Germanness) and Judaism. For if the reconciliation of Catholicism and Protestantism occurred under the idea of Protestantism (the directionality of the "and" flowed from Protestantism), the reconciliation of Christianity

---

[28] Cohen, *Kleinere Schriften VI*, p. 117.
[29] Gershom Scholem – staunchly against the war and favorable to Zionism – judged Cohen's thinking, especially in light of his German patriotism, as standing "under a dominant Protestant influence." G. Scholem, "What Is Judaism?" in *On the Possibility of Jewish Mysticism in Our Time and Other Essays*, trans. J. Chipman (Philadelphia: Jewish Publication Society, 1997): 114–133, p. 115.
[30] As Jacques Derrida argues in his reading of Cohen's 1915 *Deutschtum und Judentum* in "Interpretations at War: Kant, the Jew, the German," *New Literary History. Institutions of Interpretation*, Vol. 22, No. 1 (1991): 39–95.

and Judaism occurs by contrast under – and hence "from" – the idea of Judaism. What at first appears to be a concession to Christianity turns out in fact to imply the concession of Christianity to what Cohen calls the pure monotheism of Judaism and its messianic prophetism.[31]

But, even if Judaism and Christianity can be aligned in their mutual understanding of religion as based on *Sittlichkeit*, there would still appear to be an irreconcilable difference between Christianity and Judaism on the question of God – how could the Trinitarian conception of God stand reconciled with Judaism? Following Lessing and Mendelssohn, whose friendship exemplifies as well as foreshadows his own proposed reconciliation of *Deutschtum* and *Judentum*, Cohen "desymbolizes" the Trinitarian conception of God into an ideal of *Sittlichkeit*. The reconciliation between Christianity and Judaism turns on the idealization guiding the historical development of pure monotheism toward the historical and hence future realization of an ethical-religious morality. The Christian conception of God is the symbolic expression of messianic prophetism, whereas Judaism, in its Old Testament sources, expresses the pure idea of messianic prophetism without an ontological conception of God. The God of the prophets is not the *one* God, who represents the unity of all being, but the *unique* God, who exists in an original relation, or correlation, with humankind though his elected people, the Jews. On this basis, Cohen proposes that the epitome of monotheism does not reside within a Trinitarian God, but with the messianic future; namely, the final reconciliation of God and humanity in a world socially and ethically redeemed. As Cohen writes: "The messianic future is the epitome of Monotheism, [and] the root force of Jewish religion."[32] Only through an effective relationship with Judaism does the demytization of Protestantism – and, by extension, a reconciliation between Judaism and Christianity in the name of humanity – become possible.

Already in "The Style of the Prophets" (1901), Cohen argued that the prophets of the Old Testament did not understand themselves to be theologians. God's commandments were issued for the cultivation of ethical

---

[31] As Ned Curthoys writes: "I would describe Cohen's frequent paeans to the spirit of Lutheran Protestantism as a *concessio*, in which an interlocutor seemingly concedes to the opponent's point of view while undermining the entire edifice on which their argument and self-perception rests." *The Legacy of Liberal Judaism* (London: Berghan Books, 2013), p. 86. For Cohen's dialectical understanding of the relation between Protestantism and Judaism, see also his 1917 essay "The Jew in Christian Culture," trans. A. Mittelman, in *Modern Judaism*, Vol. 23, No. 1 (2003): 51–73. For an illuminating critique of Derrida's reading of Cohen's 1915 *Deutschtum und Judentum*, Vatter, "Nationality, State and Global Constitutionalism."

[32] Cohen, *Kleinere Schriften VI*, p. 122.

relations among human beings, attainment of salvation as a social calling, and hope for future redemption. Humanity designates the nation of all nations as a messianic horizon, achievable in history through the enactment of God's Commandments on earth. Judaism is founded on the correlation between *Gott und sein Reich*.[33] As Cohen states: "God's Reign is the Ideal of world history."[34] The messianic ideal of realizing God's kingdom can only occur through the world-historical unification of humanity. God's kingdom is, when thus understood, not in heaven, nor a city of God, but a future historical and social reality where humankind would exist in a world in which poverty would be abolished as well as the division between rich and poor. Against this messianic backdrop with its socialist inflection, Cohen conceptually distinguishes between "the nation" and "nationality." The nation is a political entity formed from a plurality of nationalities in a nation-state. Judaism, however, is an "unpolitical nationality," which, Cohen argues, should not take the form of a nation-state, since the world-historical election of the Jewish people consists in leading the nations of the world toward the messianic realization of humanity.[35] As an "unpolitical" and "stateless" people, "the Jews of world-history are the martyrs of a genuine religious Idealism." Judaism's messianic promise to the world is its proclamation of "the Unique God as the redeemer of humankind" and thereby, in the Jews' historical condition of exile, compelling the nations of the world to transform themselves and overcome their internecine struggles. Through "the inner necessity of our [Jewish] wanderings and suffering," the nations of the world are called forward – not backward – to the realization of a cosmopolitan and ethical humanity to come. Stridently pitched against Hegel's Christian sacralization of the nation-state with God's walking the earth on the stage of world history, Cohen's image of the messianic attainment of God's kingdom on earth insists on the overcoming of war and the conflictual separation of nations.[36] Humankind's perpetual condition of war stems from "historical idol worship" and abandonment of the covenant with God.[37] In Cohen's political theology of cosmopolitanism, Judaism's world-historical election should not to be conflated, however, with the exemplarism of the universal. The reciprocal conjunction and hence mutual self-realization of Judaism and Germany promises to institute a reconciliation between

---

[33] H. Cohen, *Judische Schriften III* (Berlin: C. A. Schwetschke, 1924), p. 175.
[34] Cohen, *Judische Schriften III*, p. 169.
[35] See H. Wiedenbach, *Die Bedeutung der Nationalität für Hermann Cohen* (Hildesheim: Olms, 1997).
[36] Vatter, "Nationality, State and Global Constitutionalism," p. 46.
[37] Cohen, *Judische Schriften*, p. 143.

German nationalism and (Jewish) cosmopolitanism, but not according to a logic of exemplarity, where a particular nation "exemplifies" the universal.[38] Rather than speak of the particularity of Judaism as a nation, Cohen conceives of Judaism's election as a nationality without a nation. Moreover, the logic of exemplarism hinges on a relation between the universal and the particular modeled on the relation between the one and the many, where "the many" represents a plurality of particulars within an embracing or absorbing unity. The God of pure monotheism is not One, but unique; likewise, Judaism is not one nation among many, but unique as a nationality without a nation. In this respect, the suffering of Judaism for the world is not comparable to the suffering of Christ. Rather, the suffering of Judaism displaces the figure of Christ, as the particular who suffers for the universal ("died for our sins"), and replaces this with the figure of dispersed people without a nation who give witness to the ethical force of pure monotheism against the injustice of humankind at war with itself or, as with Hegel, a premature closure of world history.[39] Cohen thus looks to avoid the logic of exemplarism (which, in fact, he sees with the "internationalism" that has betrayed Germany), while allaying the suspicion that Judaism represents a state within the state, or seeks to establish itself as a state *against* the German nation-state.

Stated in ideal terms, the reciprocal correlation between Germanism and Judaism is mediated through the shared historical and spiritual source of Greece and, in particular, Plato.[40] As a model for this threefold configuration of Jena, Athens, and Jerusalem, Cohen upholds the "genuine Classicism of the German National Spirit" of the eighteenth century, which represents a cultural project that remains unfinished. As Cohen writes in "Über das Eigentümliche des deutschen Geistes" (1914), "Germany is and

---

[38] Vatter, "Nationality, State and Global Constitutionalism," p. 46. As Vatter writes: "The construction of Germanism as a 'cosmopolitan nationality' can only become a reality if its idealist conception of the state can assume the kind of monotheism that Jews, and not just German Jews, are given to bear in and through their self-preservation and self-assertion" (p. 52).

[39] See S. H. Brody, "Reason, Revelation, and Election: Hermann Cohen and Michael Wyschogrod," *Toronto Journal for Jewish Thought*, Vol. 1, No. 4 (2010): 299–321.

[40] As Vatter writes: "For Cohen, the 'internal kinship' between Germanism and Judaism is made possible by the common reception of Hellenistic philosophy, and most particularly, Philo, the Alexandrian Jewish Platonist [...] Cohen's thesis is that German idealism is in effect a variant to Platonism which was bequeathed to it through the mediation of Philo, the first to offer a philosophical and cosmopolitical interpretation of Judaism and simultaneously the source of Paul's foundation of Christianity on the idea of logos as 'holy spirit' incarnated by Christ" ("Nationality, State and Global Constitutionalism," p. 52). For the kinship between Ancient Greece and German Idealism, see Cohen's 1915 essay "Der deutsche Idealismus und die Antike," in *Kleinere Schriften VI, 1916–1918*, Werke 17 (Hildersheim: Georg Ulms Verlag, 2002): 147–186.

remains in the continuity of the eighteenth century and its cosmopolitan humanity."[41] Among the exemplary figures of the German Enlightenment, Cohen considers Lessing's *Nathan the Wise* as expressing the "highest and final sense of Humanity." The narrative of the Three Rings is seen as defining a historical task for the German nation that hangs in the balance with the war. As Cohen writes in conclusion to his 1916 essay *Deutschtum und Judentum*, "we German Jews are in the especially felicitous situation to recognize the great contribution of the German spirit to the spiritual life of the Jews but recognize also as well the contribution of the religious spirit of the Jews and the science of *Judentum* to the German spirit."[42] Even "this horrific war" cannot steer the destiny of the German spirit away from its world-historical mission. As Cohen optimistically ends his reflections: "according to us, it is not the Flood that is coming, but rather the dawn of an ethical new birth shall break upon the world. And we cherish the national feeling of elation that the German spirit will have a great part to play in this work for what is best for the world."[43]

Ethics and Religion

With Cohen's retirement from Marburg at the venerable age of 70 in 1912, his reputation as a Jewish thinker was recognized with the endowment of a chair in the philosophy of Jewish religion at the *Lehranstalt für die Wissenschaft des Judentums* in Berlin.[44] From this position, Cohen continued his engagement in public debates, not only in support of the war, but also in response to the intensification of anti-Semitism as well as against the mounting popularity of Zionism.[45] Cohen's proposed synthesis of German Enlightenment *Bildung* and Judaic messianism provoked aggressive anti-Semitic reactions, most notably against his 1915 essay *Deutschtum*

---

[41] Cohen, *Werke*, 16, p. 243.
[42] Cohen, *Werke*, 17, p. 130.
[43] Cohen, *Werke*, 17, p. 128.
[44] In an influential reading of Cohen's development, Rosenzweig argued that his retirement and transition to Berlin represented "a tremendous life-change" (F. Rosenzweig, "Einleitung," *Jüdischen Schriften I*, p. xxxviii), whereby Cohen for the first time discovered intellectually his own Judaism; however, Cohen had already since his appointment at Marburg been engaged in numerous public debates concerning the "Jewish question"; see F. Beiser, *Hermann Cohen: An Intellectual Biography* (Oxford: Oxford University Press, 2018), pp. 272ff.
[45] Aside from teaching in support of the science of Judaism (*Wissenschaft des Judentums*) and numerous publications, Cohen lectured widely, and most significantly toured Russia in May of 1914 giving lectures in which he sought to intervene on behalf of East European Jewish populations. See Michael Meyer, "Jüdische Wissenschaft und jüdische Identität," in *Wissenschaft des Judentums*, ed. J. Carlebach (Darmstadt: Wissenschaftlich Buchgesellschaft, 1992): 320.

und Judentum by the editor of *Kantstudien*, Bruno Bauch, but it also caught the critical attention of Buber, with whom Cohen became involved in a spirited debate about Zionism, which he staunchly opposed.[46] Although Cohen had written on issues concerning Judaism before the war, it was not until the war years that Judaism became "a motor of philosophical thought" rather than a theme of cultural and political commentary.[47] Caught between anti-Semitism and Zionism, Cohen discovers Judaism philosophically along with this envisioned conjunction of *Deutschtum und Judentum*. This philosophical embrace of Judaism spurred a sweeping reevaluation of the relation between philosophy and religion in Cohen's thinking, leading to the new thinking of philosophy for the twentieth century in the posthumously published *Religion of Reason Out of the Sources of Judaism* (1919).[48] This reassessment of the relation between philosophy and religion occurred against the backdrop of the prewar completion of Cohen's system of philosophy, as presented in three accomplished works on knowledge, ethics, and aesthetics.[49] What defined Cohen's systematic recasting of Kant's critical idealism was surpassing a dualism between intuition and concept as well as a metaphysical (mis)interpretation of the notion of *Ding an sich*; namely, a "two worlds" interpretation. Cohen developed Kant's critique of knowledge into a logic of origins along the lines of the argument that it is not objects of the world that determine the validity of knowledge, but a priori forms of thinking itself. Rather than adopt Kant's

---

[46] In the newly established journal *Der Jude* in July 1916, Buber published a critical essay against Cohen's rejection of Zionism. Buber objected to Cohen's argument that "genuine Judaism" was a not a nation but a nationality, and the implication that Zionism represented a dangerous collapse of the Jewish people into the self-idolization of a nation-state. For Buber, the messianic task of Judaism required a national homeland for the Jewish people and hence the overcoming of diasporic wandering. Buber, moreover, objected to Cohen's synthesis of German humanism and prophetic messianism. In his reply to Buber's critique, Cohen stressed again that the Jewish people could only retain their distinctiveness and world-historical election by refusing to enter into the conflicts of power among the nation-states, and yet needed to guide nation-states toward the messianic future of humanity. The nationalism of Zionism reverts, for Cohen, to nineteenth-century Romanticism with its emphasis on ethnic community, in contrast to his endorsement of German humanism and the Enlightenment of Mendelssohn and Lessing. As Beiser comments, "Cohen's reaction to Zionism was virtually visceral. Zionism struck at the very core of his being, contradicting his most vital beliefs" (*Hermann Cohen*, p. 304). For a discussion of the debate between Buber and Cohen, U. Sieg, *Jüdische Intellektuelle im Ersten Weltkrieg* (Berlin: Akademie Verlag, 2001), chapter 5.

[47] S. Nordmann, *Du Singulier à l'universel. Essai sur la philosophie réligieuse de Hermann Cohen* (Paris: Vrin, 2007), p. 135.

[48] H. Cohen, *Religion of Reason Out of the Sources of Judaism*, trans. S. Kaplan (Atlanta, GA: Scholars Press, 1995).

[49] H. Cohen, *System der Philosophie, Erster Teil: Logik der reinen Erkenntnis* (Berlin: Bruno Cassirer, 1902); *System der Philosophie, Zweiter Teil: Ethik der reinen Willens* (Berlin: Bruno Cassirer, 1904); *System der Philosophie, Dritter Teil: Ästhetik der reinen Gefühls* (Berlin: Bruno Cassirer, 1912).

conception of understanding as the synthesis of intuition and concept, Cohen identifies understanding with an originating production, or "construction," based on the spontaneous production of an original and originating correlation of identity and difference, or self-differentiating logic of origins, without any residual reliance on a myth of the given.

This reformulation of Kant's discovery of the spontaneity of reason informs Cohen's recasting of Kant's conception of the pure will. As with Kant, Cohen accepts that practical reason is based on autonomy, where the pure will is not subservient to a moral law that becomes imposed externally, but, on the contrary, prescribes for itself, and hence determines itself, the moral law dictating its conduct. Kant's discovery of freedom as ethical autonomy is thus antithetical to religious subservience and binding oneself to the moral law as commanded by God. In Kant's own thinking, but reflected as well throughout German thought, Judaism represented a blind obedience to the moral law and hence a compelling illustration of the heteronomous relation between the law and ethical subjectivity. In *Religion within the Boundaries of Mere Reason*, Kant, in speaking of "Jewish theocracy," refused to acknowledge Judaism as a religion, proposing instead that, aside from heteronomous compulsion, Jewish "ritual laws" and "statutory laws" facilitated the acquisition of temporal goods, the maintenance of the state, and political, "this-worldly" gain. Judaism, thus imagined, was a particular nation with particularistic social and political laws "masquerading as religion," which would be, and should be, surpassed by the universalism of Christianity's religion of *Sittlichkeit* for "all nations," in turn then superseded by an ethics of practical reason and ethical autonomy.

In *Ethics of the Pure Will* (1904), Cohen retains a Kantian understanding of religion as situated within the bounds of reason and subsumable to an ethics of practical reason.[50] In this framework, the ethical subject is defined by the rational autonomy of self-determination with respect to moral laws. Cohen holds that categorial imperatives do not address the empirical individuality of the ethical subject, but speaks instead to their rational humanity, as a member of the Kingdom of Ends. In determining what one ought to do, an ethical subject determines their motivation with respect to the formal universality of the Law. The ethical subject acts as would all other rationally self-determining ethical subjects. The subjectivity of the ethical subject is here "the I of humanity" abiding in every individual, not the

---

[50] For this transformation of Cohen's thinking, see Nordmann, *Du Singulier à l'universel*. For a detailed treatment of Cohen's work, see S. Zac, *La Philosophie réligieuse de Hermann Cohen* (Paris: Vrin, 1984).

singular individual per se. As Cohen elaborates this Kantian position, "the correlation between the individual and the whole is to be recognized as the genuine problem of ethics. The ethical subject must [...] be the whole and individual at the same time."⁵¹ The desiderata of a philosophical ethics is accordingly twofold: to provide an account of how individual subjects are reconciled with universal laws (where the ethical subject is the "I of humanity," not the empirical person) and, thereby, to understand how humanity can become reconciled with itself through the achievement of a moral community. On Cohen's Neo-Kantian view, "humanity" is a regulative idea that designated an ethical-social horizon for the reconciliation of humanity with itself, where God stands as the ideal unity of *Sittlichkeit* with the implicitly messianic promise of achieving the "we" of humanity in the world.⁵² A notable innovation in Cohen's *Ethics of the Pure Will* consists in the argument that, much as a critical theory of knowledge takes its bearings from "scientific facts," from which to inquire into the a priori conditions of cognition, a critical ethical theory must likewise take its bearings from "facts." In this respect, Cohen argues that ethical idealism must find its bearings in jurisprudence (*Rechtswissenschaft*). Through a recursive analysis of the a priori conditions of jurisprudence, Cohen's ethics of the pure will circumvents the reduction of ethical moral laws to psychological facts, while accentuating the social bearing of ethics insofar as moral imperatives must be codified into legal doctrine.⁵³ Moreover, given that the correlation between the ethical subject and the moral law is intrinsically social, the relation between politics and ethics becomes reconfigured in turn around the centrality of a theory of rights, rule of law, and universal suffrage. When properly based on ethically sound jurisprudence, the nation-state is a *Rechtstaat*, and not a *Machtstaat*, which allows for the cultivation of a moral community of ethical subjects. Rather than a subsumption of the ethical to the political, the political is subsumed to an ethical idea of humanity as the Kingdom of Ends. It is only when a nation-state stands itself beholden to the rule of law, equality before the law, and procedural fairness that an ethical subject can be both "general" and "individual," as exemplified, for Cohen, in a citizen's right to vote.

---

[51] Cohen, *Ethik der reinen Willens*, p. 71.
[52] For Cohen's ethics, Wiedebach, *Die Bedeutung der Nationalität für Hermann Cohen*; and P. Nahma, *Hermann Cohen and the Crisis of Liberalism: The Enchantment of the Public Sphere* (Bloomington: Indiana University Press, 2019).
[53] For the relation between ethics and law, see J. Trejo-Mathys, "Neo-Kantianism and the Philosophy of Law: Its Value and Actuality," in *New Approaches to Neo-Kantianism*, ed. N. de Warren and A. Staiti (Cambridge, UK: Cambridge University Press, 2015).

Cohen's liberal conception of *Rechtstaat* carries an important consequence for the relation between the state and religion. Given that the state ensures the realization of *Sittlichkeit* and hence a reconciliation between the individual and the universal (in both senses of intersubjective community and the moral law), religion sits within the bounds of the political (and hence reason), since, on Cohen's thinking in *Ethics of the Pure Will*, religion – Judaism being no exception – represents a form of particularism, its presumed universality notwithstanding.[54] Although the state is also bound to particularity (i.e., "German"), when transformed from a *Machtstaat* into a *Rechtstaat* under what Cohen calls the "socialist imperative," the state becomes the bearer of universality; namely, humanity.[55] Politics must be based on the "ethical ideal of socialism," which Cohen understands as the realization of the biblical commandment "love thy neighbor," which, in turn, forms the "core truth of belief in God."[56] In fact, Cohen advocates that Kant is the "true originator of German socialism" with his foundational idea of the human being as an end in itself, which Cohen infuses with a socially attuned ethics of responsibility for one's neighbor from the Old Testament. The "Job of our times" is a socialist Job who decries the inequity of the world and the exploitation of modern capitalism.

Plato and Prophetic Messianism

The wartime transformation of Cohen's thinking on the relation between ethics and religion finds expression in several publications, most significantly "The Concept of Religion within the Limits of Philosophy" (1915) and "The Social Ideal in Plato and the Prophets" (1916), as well as *Religion of Reason Out of the Sources of Judaism*. In "The Social Ideal in Plato and the Prophets," Cohen identifies Plato and Old Testament prophets as the two sources of modern (European) culture. As with *Deutschtum und Judentum*, Cohen's thinking operates around the axis of two sources for Western spirit: Athens (philosophy) and Jerusalem (monotheism). Neither source – taken

---

[54] Cohen, *Ethik der reinen Willens*, p. 71.
[55] The State, as *Rechtstaat*, is not bound to race, social class, or ethnicity. This cosmopolitan dimension of the state as *Rechtstaat* is a defining aspect of Cohen's political thought. Cohen stands here under the influence of F. A. Lange, who originally brought him to Marburg and who, in addition to his academic work (*History of Materialism*), was an engaged socialist thinker. Cohen absorbs and reformulates a number of key ideas from Lange's socialism.
[56] For Cohen's Kantian socialism, see *Politische Philosophie in Deutschland* (Darmstadt: DTV Deutscher Taschenbuch, 1985), p. 105ff; D. Hollander, *Ethics Out of Law: Hermann Cohen and the 'Neighbor'* (Toronto: University of Toronto Press, 2021); and H. van der Linden, *Kantian Ethics and Socialism* (Indianapolis: Hackett Publishing, 1988), chapter 6.

in its idealized form – can be effective without the other, for each can only come to fruition in interactive correlation with the other. In the argument of *Deutschtum und Judentum*, the correlation between German Idealism and Old Testament prophets required the mediation of Greece; in "The Social Ideal in Plato and the Prophets," it is German Idealism that mediates the interaction between Plato and the prophets.[57] Plato is credited with the inauguration of the philosophical project of grounding knowledge on the basis of reason, the trajectory of which proceeds directly to German Idealism (Kant), whereas Judaism is identified as the source of monotheism; that is, (true) religion. On Cohen's reading, Plato discovers the idea of *Erkenntniskritik* and thus anticipates Kant's critical idealism, according to which forms of knowledge are investigated regarding their validity, the source of which resides in a priori forms of cognition and the spontaneity of reason. Rather than unquestioningly accept what knowledge claims to know, Plato transforms conceptual knowledge into a question by asking *how* knowledge is at all valid. Viewed through this Neo-Kantian lens, Plato's doctrine of Ideas represents a "knowledge of knowledge," namely, a knowledge of the a priori conditions under which knowledge of experience is at all possible. As Cohen elaborates, Plato's notion of the Idea draws on the term *logos* (more exactly, the locution *logon didonai* – "to give a reason" / "to provide an account" / "justification") and *hypothesis*. The latter Cohen reads in terms of the dual meanings of "seeing" (*Schauen*) and "fore-seeing," or "presentiment" (*Ahnung*); that is, a prospective view or envisioned Idea. A Platonic Idea thus becomes conceived in a dynamic sense, as aiming toward a justification in view of a priori forms of validity. Plato's discovery of Idealism carries a decisive consequence with respect to ethics, for, as Cohen underlines, Plato recognizes that the Idea of the Good stands apart from other Ideas and a priori forms of cognition. In Plato's characterization, the Good is "beyond being" – *epekeina tes ousias* (Republic, 509b). As Cohen writes: "The Good is not Being; but it therefore need not be withdrawn from the value of the idea; it is thus the idea 'beyond the being.'"[58] Forms of knowing what "is" – beings – cannot be applied to the transcendent sense of the Good, even though the Good is not without intelligibility and practical realizability. Whether in a Platonic form as the transcendence of the Good beyond Being or in the Kantian form of the moral Law and the autonomy of the rational will, Idealism is predicated on an ontological difference between the Being and the Good,

[57] Cohen, *Werke*, 17, p. 300.
[58] Cohen, *Werke*, 17, p. 304.

whereby the sense and validity of what ought (to be) cannot be reduced to the sense and validity of what it is to be.

Despite this inauguration of Idealism, Plato's thinking nonetheless remained exposed to "the danger of a dualism" between the idealism of science (knowledge of what is, or beings) and the idealism of ethics (determination of what one ought to do). This danger played itself out with the subsumption of religion to reason, along with the absorption of ethics into a form of knowledge. But, as Cohen argues, ethics must draw on two sources, namely, philosophy and religion; or, in other words, Plato *and* the Old Testament prophets. Cohen grants that the prophets remained ignorant of reason, and hence of philosophical Idealism. However, the meaning of "knowledge," often invoked by the prophets, carries the meaning of love in Hebrew. The prophets founded a "social religion" based on the conscientiousness of love, and yet remained suspicious of any mystical notions of a loving God. The transcendence of the Good translates in biblical terms into God as defined by love and, more specifically, by the divine commandment "to love" in the dual form: "I am your God you shall have no other" and "love thy neighbor." The God of the prophets is not a metaphysical God, a God "of being," who can be known as to its being or as the Being.[59] Rather, the God of the prophets is the God of *Sittlichkeit* beyond being and otherwise than beings, as manifest through the commandment of love and hospitality toward the stranger. Whereas Plato speaks of the Idea *of* the Good, the prophets write that God *is* Goodness, yet the meaning of "is" should not be interpreted ontologically, as the supreme Being, as "the One," who reigns over creation (or the manifold of beings). The "is" of God's Goodness must instead be understood in terms of the messianic Idea of humanity. Plato's doctrine of Ideas, emerging from the problem of knowledge, addressed the problem of the one and the many (the unity of multiplicity) in ontological terms, and, despite Plato's discovery of the Good "beyond beings," the legacy of Platonism determines God as substantially "the Being"; that is, as the one of the many. By contrast, the pure monotheism of Judaism does not announce that there is "one" God as a unitary being (*Einheit*), who stands above the manifold of creation as its ontological ground and unity, but that God is unique (*Einzig*), and this uniqueness of God stands in an original correlation with humankind, to wit, in a covenant with the Jewish people who are elected to bear witness

---

[59] The Babylonian God as creator of the world – as the original form for Cohen of an ontological conception of God – becomes transformed and discarded by the Judaic God as creator of humankind in an ethical-religious sense.

to God's uniqueness. The God of the Old Testament prophets is neither the God of the philosophers nor the God of the theologians.

God's commandment "to love" establishes an interactive interdependency between God and humanity, as an original "betweenness" or correlation. As an irreducible relation, this original correlation, or covenant, between God and human beings is mutually "exchanging" (*Wechsel*) and "effectuating" (*Wirkung*). Love of God, in terms of which the correlation-relation between God and humanity becomes realized, gravitates around ethical concern for the social suffering of other human beings. Moreover, as Cohen emphasizes, the biblical wisdom of the prophets recognizes other human beings as singular individuals in the form of Thou, and hence not in terms of the universal subject of reason. Through the interhuman concern for others as Thou, as socially situated, the relation between a singular human being and a unique God becomes anchored in the correlative relation of I and Thou; namely, other human beings in their singular existence. For Cohen, the ethical wisdom of the prophets is that the love of God is directed toward love for one's neighbor and is lived in responsibility for the suffering of others.

"God Is Not the Father of Heroes"

Although Plato discovered an irreducible difference between Being and the Good – indeed, the transcendence of the Good from beings – the historical legacy of Platonism failed to grasp the sense of the Good in terms of God's uniqueness, and hence that ethics must address humans in their singular existence, and not as the universal subject of reason.[60] Religion, in the sense of pure monotheism, discovers the singularity of humans' existence, in their suffering and vulnerability, in the correlation with the uniqueness of God. The philosophical-Platonic heritage placed God, as it were, into ontological captivity along with a notion of ethics predicated on the idea that the moral law stemmed from reason as addressed to a universal subject ("the I of humanity"). Cohen sees a crucial political ramification as well to this Platonic legacy. In commenting on the *Republic*, Cohen calls into question Plato's view that the polis should be governed by philosopher-kings. This proposition is of special interest given that Plato suggested (473c–d) that suffering among human beings will not come to end until kings shall be philosophers and philosophers shall be kings. While endorsing the alleviation of suffering as the

---

[60] Cohen, *Werke*, 17, p. 314.

basis for ethics and, by extension, an ethical politics, Cohen rejects the inequality between the few who are to be philosopher-kings and other classes in Plato's idealized polis, and turns instead to the Old Testament prophets who, in his view, argued that that all human beings are equal with respect to each other in common relation to God.[61] Plato's conception of the polis is based on the particularity, and hence partisanship, of city-states and their races (*Stämme*). Despite Plato's tripartite division of classes, the polis absorbs the individual into the whole under the rule of the one; namely, the philosopher-king who functions as the guardian of the polis. These philosopher-guardians, Cohen underlines, are warriors, with the implication that "the condition of war is the actual foundation of the entire state."[62] When seen in this light, the source of the "ills of the polis" resides neither with class division nor political hierarchy, but rather with the distinction between "friend" and "enemy," or friend and stranger. It is this distinction between friend and stranger that underlies the permanent condition of war among Greek city-states. Plato's political philosophy historically provided the model for the state as *Machtstaat* based on the ontological distinction between "friend" and "enemy," and thus for the notion that "war belongs in the ideal image of humanity."[63]

On this point – that the state, as *Machtstaat*, is based on the permanent footing for war – there emerges another categorical difference between Plato and the prophets. As Cohen observes, there are numerous passages in the Old Testament declaring that the peoples of the earth should no longer learn to wage war. For prophetic thinking, it is "strange and unthinkable" that the condition of war is the "source of life" as well as the basis for the nation-state. Even though Plato's thinking claims that the "root of everything human" is found in knowledge, the division of the polis into classes of the ruled and the rulers (and the later division between warriors and philosophers) would seem to contradict his proto-critical Idealism. Indeed, the notion of a permanent war footing of the polis does not follow from "the land of the Idea, but from the political reality to which Plato's ideal vision remains captive."[64] Plato's thinking remained captive to his political reality even as his Idealism gestured beyond the bounds of experience toward a critical examination of the basic conditions of validity for knowledge, ethics, and politics. Lacking a prophetic vision of ethical humanity

---

[61] Cohen, *Werke*, 17, p. 317.
[62] Cohen, *Werke*, 17, p. 317.
[63] Cohen, *Werke*, 17, p. 328.
[64] Cohen, *Werke*, 17, p. 320.

and the messianic temporality of the future, Plato not only defined the human in terms of a political ontology, but identified philosophy with the tacit acceptance of war itself, insofar as the true object of morality was not recognized to be perpetual peace among the nations of the earth. If (Plato's) "Athens" represents a political ontology wedded to the legitimacy of *Machtstaat*, (Cohen's) "Jerusalem" represents a political theology wedded to the Kingdom of God as reflected in the Idea of ethical humanity. Jerusalem, however, does not refer to a geographical location. For the prophets, "the earth and the universe is almost entirely concentrated on time."[65] In its idealized significance, Jerusalem designates a "time to come," such that the earth and Jerusalem do not exist in a condition of rest, but are related in reciprocal movement, reaching out toward a reconciliation among the nations of the earth as well as between God and humankind.

The prophets did not only speak for the eradication of war and advent of perpetual peace through the messianic realization of pure monotheism. God's holiness resides with the virtue of peace, as the God of peace and purest expression of the Ideal of *Sittlichkeit*. The radicalism of monotheism, as sourced from the Old Testament, consists in the radicality of a divinely commanded love for and hospitality toward the stranger that sets humankind upon a historical trajectory of overcoming enmity between friend and stranger. The ideal of messianic peace is that of an earthly condition where there are only strangers without enemies, where each is a stranger to the other, and hence a friend of their fellow human. Whereas Cohen faults polytheism for a cultural distinction between "friend" and "barbarian," the political ontology of Platonism is faulted for an ontological distinction between "friend" and "enemy." Cohen rejects as well secular universalism for its abstraction from the individual, and thus although an Enlightenment view of human brotherhood represents in its own way the ideal of peace, it does so at the cost of a utopia where there would only be friends without strangers. Neither secular humanism, Platonism as a moniker for a political ontology stemming from friend–enemy distinction, or polytheism as a conceptual stand-in for cultural conflicts among worldviews is able to envision the genuine conditions for peace among nations. As Cohen writes: "But as soon as the unique God loves the barbarian and declares the hostile peoples to be his own, like his own (*Eigentum*) Israel, the horizon of the human being becomes illuminated. Messianism demands and compels this development, which leads to

---

[65] Cohen, *Werke*, 17, p. 326.

cosmopolitanism."⁶⁶ In a pronouncement that surely would have caught the attention of his contemporary readers, he maintains: "God is not the father of heroes, and heroes are not designated as those favored or loved by God, rather, God 'loves the stranger' (*liebt den Fremdling*)."⁶⁷

It is unclear whether Cohen himself registered the full implications of these words – his own – in 1916. Then as now, that "God is the not Father of heroes" and "heroes are not the blessed ones of God" are impossible not to hear as an emphatic contestation of Protestant war theology and the sacralization of *Deutschtum* – indeed, any political ontology based on the existential distinction between friend and enemy – that animated the spiritual mobilization of German academics and intellectuals, including Cohen himself. To be sure, Cohen's advocation of the war's "ethical revelation" does not appeal to the passion of Christ-like sacrifice of soldiers, nor refer to a German Pentecost in its world-historical mission. And yet, if the nation of all nations – Israel – calls upon humankind to realize the commandment of God's love for strangers on earth, how can the Judaic God of strangers become reconciled with the Germanic God of heroes? How, in other words, is the symbiosis of *Deutschtum* and *Judentum* possible if God is not the Father of heroes, German or Jewish?

A Cohen at war with himself across his wartime publications – not necessarily a conflict of personal attitudes but a conflict of philosophical orientations, inscribed within the movement and countermovement of the conjunction–correlation "and" – is manifestly on display with his unapologetic defense of German militarism, issued in the same year as his advocation of messianic peace in opposition to the Platonic heritage of political ontology. In his 1916 essay "Kantian Thoughts in German Militarism," Cohen stridently responds to the accusation by French and British intellectuals of an intrinsic militarism to German philosophy (mainly Kant and Hegel).⁶⁸ Cohen is bewildered that "we Germans are presently called barbarians," given Germany's commitment to "humanism and love of peace." On the contrary, it is Germany that finds itself surrounded by "true barbarians." Expressing personal as well as national anger, Cohen takes umbrage at this "unchivalrous insult against the memory of our national heroes" and "the great military army leaders of our War of Liberation against Gallic-Corsican wantonness."⁶⁹ Rather than disabuse Allied propaganda of this perception

---

⁶⁶ Cohen, *Werke*, 17, p. 309.
⁶⁷ Cohen, *Werke*, 17, p. 309.
⁶⁸ For a review of this debate, Hoeres, *Krieg der Philosophen*.
⁶⁹ Cohen, *Werke*, 17, p. 136.

of German militarism, Cohen on the contrary seeks to illuminate and legitimate its function in the formation of what distinguishes Germany culturally, for, as he writes, "when a critique hurts, it usually contains a seed of truth."[70]

In this essay, Cohen argues that the German nation is founded on "two concentric middle-points": Luther's call for universal education and General von Scharnhorst's call for universal military conscription. While mandatory education for citizens represents – on Cohen's reckoning – a German instantiation of how the prophets envisioned a nation becoming unified as a people through education, von Scharnhorst's universal conscription enables the constitution of the nation as a nation of warriors. These Germanic institutions are claimed to be consonant with "discipline for Kant's Idealism."[71] Indeed, Cohen underlines the pervasive influence of Kant's thinking on the development of German militarism: The reform of the Prussian army during the Napoleonic Wars was fostered by Kant's students (identified as von Scharnhorst, von Gneisenau, and von Clausewitz). Given this connection between Kant's Idealism and the Prussian military, the authenticity of "our Idealism" cannot be called into question on the spurious charge that "our military forces" represent a "degenerate type of Idealism." The forging of the German nation in the War of Liberation against "a genuinely barbarian greed for conquest and against national destruction" (which, Cohen adds, "is no less shameful today") gave rise to a people's national army, not an army of mercenaries (an implicit critique of the employment of colonial troops by the British and the French). As Cohen continues, "the great fortune of our classical age," namely, eighteenth-century German Classicism, would have been impossible without an ethical striving to bring together the "profound power of thinking and the powerful force of creativity" for the sake of "one's own nation" and "the entirety of humanity." For as Cohen writes: "One does not speak about perpetual peace when the wounds are still bleeding and there is no end in sight for when the human heart shall be free from this yammering. But is it not a meaningful phenomenon that the founder of our military forces is the person who wrote the treatise on perpetual peace?"[72] *Our* philosophy, *our* common emotional life, and *our* politics – each is an "instrument" in *our* art of war (*unsere Kriegskunst*).[73] Even as Cohen was writing such inflammatory words, he was simultaneously composing a messianic vision

---

[70] Cohen, *Werke*, 17, p. 347.
[71] Cohen, *Werke*, 17, p. 137.
[72] Cohen, *Werke*, 17, p. 146.
[73] Cohen, *Werke*, 17, p. 146.

of perpetual peace in *The Religion of Reason from the Sources of Judaism*, which appeared in the aftermath of his nation's cataclysmic defeat, largely at the hands of its own venerated art of war.

God Loves the Stranger

Published after Cohen's death in 1919, *The Religion of Reason Out of the Sources of Judaism* arguably vanished from memory the moment it appeared, its immediate forgetting overlaid with the bitter remembrance of his idealist reconciliation of *Deutschtum* and *Judentum,* besieged, on the one hand, by Zionism and, on the other, by anti-Semitism, and ultimately defeated by the war itself. Despite this eclipse by the careening of war's aftermath toward another, greater catastrophe, Cohen's magistral work projected a spectral presence across twentieth-century thinking for Franz Rosenzweig, Buber, and Emmanuel Levinas. As Rosenzweig remarked, Cohen's concept of "correlation" undermined the foundation of idealism – including Cohen's own systematic philosophy – and announced a "new thinking of our times." As Ernst Cassirer recalls, aside from his relationship with Rosenzweig, "the war was the last and greatest experience for Cohen," and though he believed in the rightness of the German cause and its prospect of final victory (Cohen died in April 1918), "the first dark shadows were cast on this belief" in 1917. These dark shadows coming over Cohen's thinking were not cast only by historical circumstance; shadows emerged from within his own thinking as well. After having buttressed Kant's critical Idealism at the end of the nineteenth century and then completed his own systematic philosophy in the first decade of the twentieth, Cohen embarked, after retiring academically from philosophy, on surpassing himself by forging a new thinking in *The Religion of Reason*, centered on a sweeping reconfiguration of the relation between ethics and religion in response to Kant's enduring question: "What may I hope for?'" Internal shadows, not as the unthought-of thinking but as a thinking otherwise than thought, can come, however, in different shadings from various angles. All the while defending German militarism and professing his German "chauvinism," as Franz Rosenzweig had called him out, Cohen at the same time articulates in *The Religion of Reason* an unshakeable faithfulness to messianism in its promissory significance for perpetual peace among nations.[74] *The Religion of Reason* emerges from Cohen's thinking as

---

[74] P. Bouretz, *Witnesses for the Future*, trans. M. Smith (Baltimore: Johns Hopkins University Press, 2010), p. 21. For Rosenzweig's response to Cohen's war chauvinism, B. Galli, "Rosenzweig's Response to Hermann Cohen's 'Deutschtum und Judentum" in *Shofar*, Vol. 14, No. 4 (1996): 60–78.

the force of its own interruption and emancipation, redeeming – posthumously – Cohen at war with himself. In another sense, as Rosenzweig recognized, *The Religion of Reason* continues along the trajectory of Cohen's efforts to reconcile "two at first sight radically opposed languages: the prophetic language of the Old Testament and the Kantian language of German idealism and reason." As Rosenzweig remarks: "Cohen inverted the hierarchy between these two languages, in the course of an adventure resembling that of Christopher Columbus."[75] Another fitting image for the adventure launched in *The Religion of Reason*, rather than Columbus, would be Toni Cassirer's recollection of Cohen as a "prophet from the Old Testament," who, one may add, does not so much speak to the present from an archaic past, but instead urges the present to address and redress itself for an immemorial future.[76] Rather than Ulysses returning to his philosophical homeland, Cohen in *The Religion of Reason* is an Abraham who goes forth out of this patriotic country and from his philosophical kindred into the land which the God of the Old Testament shall shew.

In *The Religion of Reason*, Cohen argues that pure monotheism, drawn from the sources of Judaism, constitutes an ethical religion of reason based on the transcendence of God's uniqueness (*Einzigkeit*). Already formulated in "The Social Idea in Plato and the Prophets," Cohen further elaborates how, based on readings of the Old Testament, God's uniqueness is not to be understood as numerically one (*Einheit*), but as singularly abiding in a correlation of reciprocal relatedness with humanity. God's biblical pronouncement "I am your God, there is no other" reveals God as "unique," and not as "the one God" in contrast with other gods. When read in conjunction with God's response to Moses – "I Am That I Am: and he said, Thus, shalt thou say unto the children of Israel, I Am hath sent me unto you" (Exodus 3:14) – God's uniqueness stands in an essentially intersubjective dimension with humankind. As Cohen writes: "God is conditioned by the correlation with man. And man is conditioned by the correlation with God." God, therefore, cannot exist outside

---

[75] F. Rosenzweig, *Zweistromland: Kleinere Schriften zu Glauben und Denken*, in *Franz Rosenzweig Gesammelte Schriften*, Vol. III (Dordrecht: Springer Verlag, 2004), p. 230.
[76] T. Cassirer, *Mein Leben mit Ernst Cassirer* (Hamburg: Meiner Verlag, 2003), p. 74. Rosenzweig recalls in a letter: "Then I experienced an unprecedented surprise. Being accustomed to finding in philosophy chairs intelligent people, well-honed wits, acute, lofty, profound, or whatever adjective you could find to characterize that spirit when you want to praise the virtues of a thinker, I found a philosopher. Instead of the tightrope walkers who, on the wire of thought, presenting their more or less daring skillful or graceful leaps, I saw a man [...] What magic spell inhabited this man's words?" F. Rosenzweig, *Der Mensch und sein Werk. Gesammelte Schriften* (The Hague: Martinus Nijhoff, 1979), II, p. 623.

a relation to humanity, nor can humanity attain its genuine form of intersubjective existence without a living and historically realized relation to God. Importantly, this original correlation, of both separation and proximity, between God and humanity does not abrogate the ontological difference between God as creator and the creaturely condition of humanity. God and humanity, however, can only attain their respective actualization in relation to each other. Living in relation to God, according to his commandments, and hence with a form of rationality, depends on the discovery of other human beings as the neighbor or "fellowman" (*Mitmensch*), as the Thou. This revelation of other human beings as Thou makes of the neighbor not just another human being who exists numerically next to me as another man (*Nebenmensch*), but as uniquely "with" me, for whom I bear a responsibility and must welcome in hospitality. This revelation of the Thou depends on recognizing the suffering and vulnerability of others. Of special significance for Cohen is that overcoming social inequality and poverty are essential for the communal togetherness of neighbors in heed of God's commandment to love.

It is this discovery of the other person as Thou in relation to oneself as an I that distinguishes ethical religion, and, more specifically, Judaism, from philosophical (or rationalist) ethics, on the one hand, and mythical and pagan religions, on the other. In Cohen's thinking, ethics (in its paradigmatic Kantian form) and hence philosophy (paradigmatically as critical Idealism) are predicated on a notion of the ethical subject as an impersonal or universal subject. An ethical subject determines themselves in relation to a universal moral imperative, and thus acts, in prescribing for themselves what they ought to do, as a universal subject. The singularity of the "I" remains outside the frame of ethics; in its Kantian form, the materiality of the I in relation to others remains unthinkable. Ethics only considers other ethical subjects as another subject of moral law and pure will, and thus fails to recognize the materiality of their suffering and hence one's own responsibility toward the vulnerability of others. As Cohen argues, the other as Thou is not a second person among other persons, but the "fellow human" – a neighbor – who reveals to me that I, myself, am an I, who becomes aware of myself as a self in relation to the Thou. The concern for ethics originates in the spectacle of suffering that puts into question one's own orientation in the world. The paradox of ethics, in other words, is that it is unable to acknowledge and respond to the condition of human suffering even though it originates in human suffering. Religion, understood as pure monotheism, mediates between the rational and abstract subject of ethics with the concrete individual, as revealed in suffering, and in this sense religion completes ethics. Living in nearness to God requires living in nearness with others, and in this revelation of the other as the neighbor, the other stands before oneself as a Thou, in relation to the transformation of oneself as I. Suffering opens the world of intersubjectivity; this is not just the Kingdom of Ends, but the world of *Mitmenschen*, in which the other is a concrete Other, a Thou.

Whereas Kantian morality is organized around the moral law carried within the goodwill within in each ethical subject, Cohen argues that the ethical must find its source in a responsibility toward the other, as set forth in Deuteronomy with the figures of "the stranger, the orphan, and the widow" (Deuteronomy 27:19). To discover the other human being as "other," namely, as Thou, is to relate to one's "fellow human" as the stranger, much as I am the stranger, the fellow human, for the other. With the figures of the poor, the orphan, the widow, and the stranger, Cohen identifies as the essence of Judaism the mission of social justice within the messianic trajectory of humanity. Among different forms of suffering, poverty, however, is the "suffering that most properly belongs to the human species." As Cohen writes:

> The social differentiation between poor and rich poses the most difficult question for the concept of man, for the unity and equality of men. The "another man" (*Nebenmensch*) becomes unavoidably the "opposing man" (*Gegenmensch*), for the social differentiation does not appear to be organized according to rank and order of coexistence, but according to subordination and subjugation [...] Even more than the question of the stranger, the question of rich and poor is asked in one's native land and among one's own people; this human question is asked with regard to every man, with regard to every fellow man.[77]

This special status is due to the imminently social condition of poverty; unlike other forms of suffering, poverty is socially produced. As Cohen suggests, inequality between the rich and the poor represents the most challenging problem for human existence and obstacle to the unification of human beings in peace. The other person who is poor finds themselves submitted to the social order of inequality, for which all others are responsible. The face of Thou emerges along the contours of their suffering as disclosed in compassion (*Mitleid*), which provides a catalyst for action as the "motor for the pure will." With the recognition of another's suffering, I am both moved toward the other in social action and moved toward myself in responsibility: I take part or have

---

[77] Cohen, *Religion of Reason*, p. 128.

a part in the suffering of Others as social suffering. In this sense, then, suffering is the pivot for the passage from ethics (the other as a subject of moral law) to religion (the other as suffering) as the passage from *Nebenmensch* to *Mitmensch*. Suffering marks the limit of ethics and "this limit that illuminates the horizon of religion as the horizon of the human is given in suffering." Social action in response to a socially produced evil, anchored in the materiality of compassion for the suffering of others, "inaugurates through the Other the world in reciprocity." The community (*Genossenschaft*) of *Mitmensch* is based on reciprocity and the recognition and relation of each, the I and the Thou, as singular: Each is unique within a plurality.

In becoming aware of oneself as a responsible I in relation to the neighbor, there emerges an awareness of responsibility for one's own faults as a sinner; that is, as culpable before God. Through the discovery of the other in their suffering, there is a transformation of the other from "he" (or "she") to "Thou," from *Nebenmensch* to *Mitmensch*, but only through a reflection on one's own, singular moral frailty is the discovery of the Other as Thou, and hence of human existence, complete. This turn toward the Other as a turn toward oneself depends on repentance as well as trust in redemption through repentance. To repent is to come to terms with, and hence recognize, one's proper weakness and accountability. For Cohen, it is only in the consciousness of guilt and sin, as revealed through repentance and atonement, that "absolute" individuality is attained. However, it is crucial for Cohen's thinking that repentance and responsibility do not only occur horizontally among humans. The possibility of self-transformation that constitutes the self as an I (standing in relation to Thou) equally depends on return to and repentance before God. In Cohen's reading of the Old Testament, atonement represents the "cardinal point of monotheism," such that Cohen's discussion of forgiveness (Chapter 11) and the Day of Reconciliation (Chapter 12) in *Religion of Reason* can rightly be seen as the axis for the messianic promise of redemption. For Cohen, "the maturity of monotheism is reached when the correlation between man and God ceases to be based purely on the respecting of prescriptive rituals or sacrificial practices and is expressed through the concrete forms of interhuman relations."[78] Although social morality (*Sittlichkeit*) is "the main point of monotheism," with the Book of Ezekiel (and in light of Deuteronomy) social morality becomes expanded

---

[78] Bouretz, *Witnesses for the Future*, p. 54.

into the genuinely ethical.[79] Cohen writes: "The individual first should unfold himself as I only through sin," not in a merely social sense, which only "knows plurality," but in the emphatic sense of sin against God.[80] God thereby attains new significance: God's uniqueness only comes fully into view in the condition of sinning before God. With this distinction and relation between "social sin" (against other humans) and "individual sin" (against God), Cohen remarks in passing that "the World War is an acute occasion for it [social sin]. And besides, war to the prophets meant what we today more profoundly recognize as capitalistic world trade."[81] If war is a social sin, genuine peace among the nations of earth must therefore alleviate not only the sinning of humans against humans, but the sinning of humanity against God.

The narrative of suffering, repentance, and forgiveness is integral to the messianic attainment of redemption. For Cohen, Ezekiel's discovery is that to sin before God opens the way to redemption *with* God, thus formulating an understanding of repentance and atonement as "self-sanctification and the return as the creation as much of a new way as of a new heart and a new spirit," where self-sanctification "arrives at its infinite conclusion in the *forgiveness* of sin by God."[82] In turning to the Tractate Yoma, Cohen gives priority to intersubjective relation in the ritual of forgiveness; the reconciliation between humans and God is dependent on interhuman reconciliation between I and Thou.[83] The redemption of humankind, therefore, cannot be the prerogative of God alone, for God's forgiveness is dependent on the forgiveness of humans toward each other, thus inscribing God's forgiveness into the messianic horizon of history. By the same token, humankind must participate in the fulfillment of God's redemption of creation. For Cohen, "God, even in the ethical sense, is not the Good (*das Gute*) but the Good One (*der Gute*)," where "God as the Good One must therefore accomplish a kind of personal achievement in goodness." This messianic fulfillment cannot be attained through God's holiness alone, but only through a historical realization of forgiveness among humanity in the form of peace among nations. The overcoming of the condition of war, as a "social sin," thus conditions the redemptive narrative of God's creation, a narrative essentially centered on forgiveness and reconciliation/mutual understanding (*Versöhnung und Verständigung*), as Cohen, during the

---

[79] Cohen, *Religion of Reason*, p. 178.
[80] Cohen, *Religion of Reason*, p. 184.
[81] Cohen, *Religion of Reason*, p. 187.
[82] Cohen, *Religion of Reason*, p. 207.
[83] Cohen, *Religion of Reason*, p. 220.

war, had expectantly envisioned for *Deutschtum* and *Judentum*. As Cohen writes: "*The forgiveness of sins becomes the special and most appropriate function of God's goodness.*"[84] If God, as "the Unique Good (One)," transcends "beyond being," God's uniqueness in correlation with humankind's election must realize itself through an unending process of forgiveness "beyond being," unto infinity, as the messianic trajectory of human history.

In the Time of Nations

God's goodness reveals itself in the twofold commandment of love. In heeding God's commandment, the correlation between humankind and God becomes known. Revelation is thus not antithetical to reason (understood as recognition of correlation and its logic of origins) and only to the extent that religion becomes objectified into the culture of humanity, in its messianic progress toward redemption and reconciliation, does monotheism avoid collapsing into myth or scholasticism. At the basis of the ethical religion of Judaism, as the religion of reason inscribed within the correlation of love, is the injunction of Noahide hospitality toward the stranger. As stated in Leviticus (cited by Cohen): "One and the same Law is valid for you: for the stranger as well as the neighbor, for I am eternal your God."[85] In this fashion, Noahide laws, which Cohen understands as a biblical antecedent to modern natural rights, preceded the territorialization of Nomos and distinction, indeed exclusion, between "the foreigner" (or stranger) and "the native," the friend and the enemy. In stressing that the Noahide law of hospitality is more archaic, and hence immemorial, than the Ten Commandments, Cohen argues that responsibility and hospitality for others, in the figures of the widow, the orphan, and the stranger, are the foundation of ethical life for pure monotheism. As Cohen writes, "the Talmud elaborates a figure of the stranger that is not bound by the Law of Moses but must respect only the seven commandments imposed on all men in exchange for God's promise of protecting the living."

In the lineage of the sons of Noah, Judaism represents a religion of reason based on the discovery of the human as Other and election to world-historical significance. The commandment of love for all human beings

---

[84] Cohen, *Religion of Reason*, p. 209. There are three orders of time for Jewish consciousness: remembrance of the past of enslavement; the presence of the present in the consecration of the Temple by Solomon; and anticipation of the messianic future.

[85] "One law shall be to him that is home-born, and to the foreigner who resides in your country" (Exodus 12:49).

does not rest on an ontological unity or commonality among humans, for its universality is predicated on hospitality to the stranger; every person is a stranger to the other, and hence none can claim a universality based on exclusion of the other. As it is written in Exodus 22:20: "You shall not wrong a stranger or oppress him; for you were strangers in the land of Egypt." This element of alterity, or "strangeness," marks the elected condition of the Jewish people, who, paradoxically, must remain hence exiled from the time of the nations in order to bring about a reconciliation of the nations and hence humanity. The mission of Judaism is suffering for the advancement of peace. As Cohen argues: "Israel's suffering is the tragic chastisement which is to bring about peace among men."[86] Messianism brings about the universality and uniqueness of humanity in the unity of the actual condition of human life with the future of human existence. According to Cohen, Israel exists without a state, because the absence of a state represents its universal vocation. In short, the Jewish people must remain strangers among the nations. This aspiration toward universality in the testimony of God's uniqueness defines the singularity of Judaism not only vis-à-vis other nations, but in the relation to God (as distinct from paganism, pantheism, polytheism), as inscribed within a prophetic and messianic horizon of reconciliation and understanding among all nations, indeed of reconciling humanity in relation to a unique God.

Religion of Reason concludes with a discussion of the virtues of justice, courage, faithfulness, and peace. Peace is the object of *Sittlichkeit* and the principle of the messianic finality of the world, and hence the realization of God's *Reich*: "Messianism is, and remains, the fundamental power of Jewish consciousness, and the Messiah is the 'Prince of Peace.'" As Cohen adds: "what is the epitome of human life in the spirit of the Bible? It is peace."[87] With this vision of the God of pure monotheism as the God of peace, Cohen opposes monotheism to war and the conflict of political ontologies. He writes:

> one may recognize the inner opposition of monotheism to the principle of all sophistry, which lies in the Heraclitan saying that war is the father of all things. War is not the original cause of the moral universe; the end of peace becomes the cause. Peace, which is the goal of the moral world, must also be valid as its originating power. God is peace, and this is the profound expression of God's covenant.[88]

---

[86] Cohen, *Religion of Reason*, p. 284.
[87] Cohen, *Religion of Reason*, p. 460.
[88] Cohen, *Religion of Reason*, p. 448.

Peace, however, is not merely an interhuman condition; it is a virtue of the soul that necessitates the expulsion of hatred from the human heart. Although Cohen admits that the Old Testament does not explicitly formulate the commandment "love thy enemy," he argues nonetheless that the prophets advocated the prohibition of hatred for others ("Thou shalt not hate thy brother in thy heart," Lev. 19:17). As Cohen observes: "The Old Testament does not contain this commend, but it contains, in fundamental expressions, the prohibition of enmity, of hatred for men." Given that Cohen identifies hatred with vanity, he denies that it expresses a power of the soul. As he writes: "As long as hatred threatens me, my own or another man's, I cannot hope for peace and for genuine contentment. If the misery of war did not rage about us, then even the specter of war, the mere danger of war, would constitute a contradiction to the peace of the world, as well as to the peace of the soul."[89] Messianism promises the reconciliation of humanity with itself, for without the confidence that hatred among the nations of the earth could be eradicated and, indeed, "destroyed from the consciousness of mankind," there can be no peace for the individual. For one's own peace, there needs to be a fundamental faithfulness to the injunction of messianic peace. In this sense, the faithfulness of the messianic promise of peace leverages a critique of and resistance against regimes of war and empires of political ontology. The messianic future does not announce the end of history, but represents the infinite horizon of the disruptive transcendence of the contradictions and conflicts that afflict the present orders of being, understood as a condition of war, the idol, or false father, of all things.

As Cohen reflects: "what does the peace of the soul secure in order to root out the hatred from the human heart?" In the religious orientation of messianic monotheism, peace becomes secured through God's love through the interhuman love of neighbors, and this expels hatred from humankind; hence the significance of the commandment "love thy enemy." Peace manifests itself in the empathy of being moved by the suffering of others as well as the feeling of joy for the manifestation of Goodness in the world.[90] Joy in peace is "the main power of Jewish virtue," and

---

[89] Cohen, *Religion of Reason*, p. 553.
[90] "The conciliatory element in the virtue of peace forms the mediating link between this virtue and the essence of religion, which is constituted by the reconciliation between man and God, which presupposes the reconciliation of man with himself. Without the peace which I establish with my fellowman, I cannot have any hope of reconciliation with God, and as little can I hope for inner peace in myself. But the feeling of being moved, of which I become capable, disclosed to me the hope that the power of peace is not yet extinguished in my soul." Cohen, *Religion of Reason*, p. 456.

when moved on the messianic trajectory toward universal peace, reconciliation of humans with humans, and reconciliation of humankind with God, peace is the "virtue of eternity." As Cohen reminds his readers in the concluding section to *The Religion of Reason*, the Hebrew word for world, *olam*, is also the word for eternity: "He hath set the world [*olam*] in their heart" (Eccl. 3:11). As Cohen writes:

> But this eternity is only the continuation of the earthly life – the same root comprises both sides of existence; hence, peace, as it leads to eternity, is also the guide to earthly life, to the beginning of all historical survival, which lies in it. Peace is the sign of eternity and also the watchword for human life, in its individual conduct as well as in the eternity of its historical calling. In this historical eternity the mission of peace for messianic mankind is completed.[91]

---

[91] Cohen, *Religion of Reason*, p. 462.

CHAPTER 3

I and Thou
Martin Buber and Dialogical Creation

War Scoundrel

Throughout his life, Martin Buber insisted that his dialogical thinking was "not the result of reading but of personal experience." This emphasis on his own generative experience does not vitiate the fact that, as Buber likewise acknowledged, "in all ages it has undoubtedly been glimpsed that the reciprocal essential relationship between two beings signifies a primal opportunity of being, and one, in fact, that enters into the phenomenon that the human being exists."[1] Although historical antecedents pointed toward Buber's dialogical thinking, its crystallization occurred during the tumultuous years of the First World War, when he underwent a conversion, personal as well as intellectual, from the mysticism of his prewar writings to his signature postwar dialogical thinking. This transformation was not provoked by a single experience but matured through a series of wartime encounters between Buber and his friends, acquaintances, and even strangers.[2] It was a time when individuals became closed off from one another as never before, armored with nationalist ardor. It was also a time, more rarely, when individuals were called upon as never before to discover, or rediscover, the acceptance of others in a world where the lights had gone out. Buber's newfound dialogical approach continued to address established concerns from his thinking before the war: the spiritual crisis of modernity, the absence of communal existence, and the revival of Judaism's spiritual potency. Spanning Buber's prewar mysticism and his postwar dialogical endeavor was an intense quest for a response to the eclipse of religious life and obscuration of the relationship to God in the modern world – namely,

---

[1] As Buber outlines in "On the History of the Dialogical Principle," predecessors of dialogical thinking can be found in the seminal ideas of Jacobi and Feuerbach. In: *Between Man and Man*, trans. R. Gregor-Smith (London: Routledge, 2002): 249–264, p. 249.
[2] See M. Buber, *Meetings: Autobiographical Fragments* (London: Routledge, 2002).

the "death of God" – along with the erosion of human existence and intersubjective relatedness – the "death of humankind."[3] Stated in Nietzschean terms – an influential thinker for Buber – the war represented the denouement of "the Last Men" from which a new humanism and *homo religiosus* desperately needed to take dialogical form. As Buber once stated: "It was the First World War that changed my thought."[4]

Buber's transformation began under the gathering clouds of war. A few weeks before the fateful assassination of Archduke Ferdinand, a group of kindred spirits, including Buber, from different European countries gathered in Potsdam for three days of discussion in June 1914, with a shared "undefined presentiment of the catastrophe" to come.[5] This fellowship of intellectuals convened under the guidance of the Dutch social activist, poet, and writer Frederick van Eeden, who enjoyed a wide circle of contact with, among others, Tagore, Gandhi, and Upton Sinclair.[6] In addition to van Eeden, this group included Poul Bjerre, Henri Borel, Theodor Däubler, Erich Gutkind, Gustav Landauer, and Florens Christian Rang. Roman Rolland, also invited, was unable to attend. What brought these European intellectuals together was the common need for spiritual renewal and communal life that would overcome the nationalism, ethnic rivalries, and instrumental materialism that defined the modern world. After intense discussions during the three days of their gathering, this intrepid group planned to convene again in September at Forte dei Marmi, Italy, with the resolution of establishing themselves formally as a unified spiritual collective.

The arrival of war in August 1914 prevented this fellowship, since known as the Forte Kreis, from ever meeting again. The outbreak of hostilities in Europe provoked internal disputes among the group, leading precipitously to the collapse of their common aspiration that had first brought them together a few months earlier. In a circular letter to members of the group, the theologically minded Rang, who volunteered for service in the German Army, spoke of the transformation he experienced when wearing his military uniform in mystical terms. With the war, he wrote,

---

[3] M. Buber, *I and Thou*, trans. W. Kaufmann (New York: Touchstone Books, 1970), p. 171. In the 1957 Afterword to *I and Thou*, Buber recalls that "when I drafted the first sketch of this book (more than forty years ago), I felt impelled by an inner necessity." As he also writes: "A vision that had affected me repeatedly since my youth but had always been dimmed again, had now achieved a constant clarity that was so evidently supra-personal that I soon knew that I ought to bear witness to it."

[4] Quoted in M. Friedman, *Martin Buber's Life and Work* (New York: E. P. Dutton, 1981), p. 205. See also H. Kohn, *Martin Buber. Sein Werk und seine Zeit* (Wiesbaden: Fourier Verlag, 1979), p. 151ff.

[5] M. Buber, *Between Man and Man* (New York: Martino Fine Books, 2014), p. 6.

[6] For the Forte Kreis, C. Holste, *Der Forte-Kreis (1910–1915): Rekonstruktion eines utopischen Versuchs* (Stuttgart: M & P, 1992); and M. Poorthuis, "The Forte-Kreis. A Utopian Attempt to Spiritual Leadership over Europe," *Religion and Theology*, Vol. 24, Nos. 1–2: 32–53.

"something beyond contention, absolutely necessary, transcendental, is breaking through the surface. Man is once again obeying God in freedom."[7] Van Eeden, in private correspondence as well as public declarations in newspapers, sharply criticized the bellicose conceit of German intellectuals, including his fellow Forte Kreis member Rang. In a letter of rebuke to Van Eeden, Buber sided with Rang (even as privately he begrudgingly recognized Rang's Protestant nationalism) and asserted his own German patriotism. As Buber declares, "never has the concept of *Volkschaft* become such a reality to me as during these weeks."[8] Fractured along nationalist lines, the Forte Kreis, in its moment of conception, was put to a test that it did not survive, despite the arrival of a war that had been foreseen by many in this fellowship (most presciently by Landauer, who staunchly opposed the war). The break-up of the Forte Kreis reflected in its microcosm the macrocosmic rupture of European solidarity among reform-minded intellectuals and artists, united in word, if not deed, against a widely decried complicity of nationalism, capitalism, and instrumental rationality. For Buber personally, this collapse of dialogical fellowship of different religious affiliations and national cultures set in motion a conversion in his thinking, the significance of which would only become fully realized with an event in 1918 that violently terminated the life of one of his most cherished friends – a death he experienced as "his own."[9]

Over the course of the war, Buber recalls that he could only "imagine the real." On the home front the world at war had fluctuated in and out of view, but by 1918 Buber grasped that he had "been terribly influenced" by events around him. "I felt something rather strange," he reports, "that I had been strongly influenced by something that came to an end just then [1918]."[10] Violence had hitherto remained at the periphery of Buber's life, yet during the chaotic ending of the war followed by German revolution, violence pushed into the home environment and, as with Buber, affected the lives of many who had remained as civilians removed from the front. As Buber recounts, what proved decisive for the urgent realization of his new thinking was "a certain episode in May nineteen [1919] when a friend

---

[7] *The Letters of Martin Buber*, eds. N. Glatzer and P. Mendes-Flohr (Syracuse, NY: Syracuse University Press, 1996), p. 158.
[8] Glatzer and Mendes-Flohr, *The Letters of Martin Buber*, p. 160.
[9] Quoted in P. Mendes-Flohr, *Martin Buber: A Life of Faith and Dissent* (New Haven, CT: Yale University Press, 2019), p. 126. See also M. Buber, *The Holy Way: A Word to the Jew and to the Nations*, published in 1919 "in Memory of my Friend Gustav Landauer," in: *On Judaism*, ed. N. Glatzer (New York: Schocken Books, 1967): 108–148.
[10] *The Martin Buber–Carl Rogers Dialogue: A New Transcript with Commentary*, eds. R. Anderson and K. Cissna (Albany: State University of New York Press, 1997), p. 22.

of mine, a great friend, a great man, was killed by anti-revolutionary soldiers in a very barbaric way." On May 2, 1919, Landauer, who played a prominent role in the Bavarian Soviet Republic, was savagely murdered by members of the Freikorps under the approving nod of the Socialist government in Berlin. Landauer's death weighed on Buber, for it was "this great man" who earlier in the war had saved him from his initial enthusiastic support for it, from being a *Kriegsbuber* ("War Boy" or alternatively "War Scoundrel"), as Landauer had sarcastically called him then.

In the introduction to the inaugural issue of the journal *Der Jude* in 1916, Buber – drawing on terminology from his prewar mystical dialogues *Daniel* – presented a religious appraisal of the war and accentuated the role of Jewish soldiers in "Europe's fateful hour on the battlefield," who serve "not from compulsion but in fulfillment of duty." Echoing the Kaiser's call for national reconciliation, Buber embraced the war as forging "nothing but community" with the revelation of the elemental reality of "religiosity." As Buber writes in a contemporaneous letter:

> The elemental notion I am speaking of has not yet attained its pure expression, its true direction. But what is happening to the Germans proves that this emotion has at last been wakened – and I feel certain that it will not be lulled to sleep again but will grow more and more conscious of its direction and in doing so create its own world.[11]

An ardent pacificist and anarchist, who warned of an impending war after the Second Morocco Crisis in 1911, Landauer sharply rebuked Buber for his flagrant chauvinism. As he writes in a letter: "Your 'Watchword' [Buber's introduction to *Der Jude*] and these passages belong together and are very painful to me, very repugnant, and border on incomprehensibility."[12] In Landauer's unsparing critique, Buber has no right to take a stand on the war and "tuck [its] tangled events into your philosophical scheme: what results is inadequate and outrageous [...] That is the language of a man whose clarity of mind has been seriously disturbed, not of one who knows how to act nor of a man of vision." Alluding to his own utopic vision of community in *Revolution* (1907) and *Call to Socialism* (1911), Landauer pleads that "the community that we need stands fundamentally apart from all that today is called war; the origins and nature of war can be plainly recognized, need no interpretation and can bear none." More pointedly:

---

[11] Glatzer and Mendes-Flohr, *The Letters of Martin Buber*, p. 164.
[12] Glatzer and Mendes-Flohr, *The Letters of Martin Buber*, p. 189.

> Dear Buber, at some point you should have at least acknowledged that among hundreds of thousands of Jews there were, say, twenty-three or thirty-seven who did not go off to war from a sense of overwhelming duty or passionate craving [...] A pity for the Jewish blood, yes indeed; a pity for every drop of blood that is spilled in this war; a pity for every human soul; a pity, too, that you have gone astray in this war.[13]

After a face-to-face meeting at Landauer's home in July 1916 where a reconciliation between the two friends occurred, Buber became convinced of the error of his wayward *Kriegsbuber*, and converted against the war in heed of Landauer's appeal: "In the future you will not take part in the German war against the other peoples of Europe, nor in the war of Europe against itself, as you now do in your profound confusion and bewilderment."[14] Landauer had not only disabused Buber of his wartime *Kriegsbuber*. Along with the exorcism of this *Doppelgänger*, Buber abandoned his conception of mystical experience and the "godless mysticism" leveraged in support of the war. For Landauer, Buber's war enthusiasm confirmed the obfuscation of political reality facilitated by a mystical outlook bereft of socialist orientation and utopic directive.[15] Most importantly, their reconciliation cemented the restorative and redemptive power of dialogical encounter, as exemplified in the I–Thou relation of friendship, only to be cruelly interrupted by Landauer's murder in a world wasted by war where endemic violence among human beings, and hence the seeming impossibility of dialogical togetherness, appeared to have no end in sight.

In the Beginning Was the Word

Buber began drafting *I and Thou*, published in 1923, in the winter of 1915–16 during his confrontation and reconciliation with Landauer. At first, Buber envisioned *I and Thou* as the first installment of a five-volume work, but then abandoned this grand scheme given its "alienating

---

[13] Glatzer and Mendes-Flohr, *The Letters of Martin Buber*, p. 191.
[14] Glatzer and Mendes-Flohr, *The Letters of Martin Buber*, p. 192. As Mendes-Flohr argues: "Whatever transpired [at their meeting], it is evident that their time together occasioned a radical transformation in Buber's thinking – marked by a fundamental break with his *Erlebnis*-mysticism. This transformation paved the way for his philosophy of dialogue, which would be formally inaugurated by the publication of *I and Thou* in 1923"; *Martin Buber*, p. 108. See also P. Mendes-Flohr, *From Mysticism to Dialogue: Martin Buber's Transformation of German Social Thought* (Detroit, MI: Wayne State University Press, 1989).
[15] As Mendes-Flohr remarks, "Landauer's letter of May 12, 1916, was of major significance in Buber's personal and intellectual biography. Further, this letter, ex hypothesi, was a pivotal factor (among others), in Buber's turn from mysticism – his *Erlebnis*-mysticism – to the philosophy of dialogue"; *From Mysticism to Dialogue*, p. 102.

systematic character."¹⁶ By 1919, a "still awkward draft" was finished, after which Buber decided to suspend his readings in philosophy and concentrate instead on his study of Hasidic writings.¹⁷ His friendship with Franz Rosenzweig, kindled during the war, and invitation to lecture in 1922 at Rosenzweig's newly founded *Freie Jüdisches Lehrhaus* in Frankfurt provided a significant catalyst for the completion of *I and Thou*, and, most importantly, for surpassing traditional conceptions of God toward what Buber named "the Eternal Thou."¹⁸ These lectures, "Religion as Presence," brought to an end a two-year "spiritual *ascesis.*" Of equal importance for Buber's return to the writing of *I and Thou* was Ferdinand Ebner's *The Word and the Spiritual Realities* (1921), a work that "showed [him], as no other since then, here and there in an almost uncanny nearness, that in this our time men of different kinds and traditions had devoted themselves to the search for the buried treasure."¹⁹ The years 1917–21, during which Buber discovered the buried treasure of his dialogical thinking, witnessed a constellation of thinkers for whom "penetrating into the mystery of speech as the ever-new establishment of the relation between I and Thou" represented an urgent response to the crisis of "the human relation to reality" and the "horror of meaninglessness" in the modern world.²⁰ As Buber later recalled:

> During the First World War it became clear to me that a process was going on which before then I had only surmised. This was the growing difficulty of genuine dialogue, and most especially of genuine dialogue between men of different kinds and convictions [...] I began to understand at that time, more than thirty years ago, that this is the central question for the fate of mankind.²¹

---

¹⁶ According to an outline from 1916, *Ich und Du* was to be composed in three sections: "Word, History, God." In the published text, these titles would be omitted.
¹⁷ Friedman, *Martin Buber's Life and Work*, p. 297.
¹⁸ Significant parts of these lectures, copied by a stenographer along with Buber's responses to questions, made their way into the published form *I and You*. See R. Horwitz, *Buber's Way to I and Thou: The Development of Martin Buber's Thought and His Religion as Presence Lectures* (Heidelberg: Verlag Lambert Schneider, 1979).
¹⁹ Readings of other thinkers in search of the same buried treasure also proved important: Herman Cohen's *Religion of Reason from the Sources of Judaism* and Franz Rosenzweig's *Star of Redemption*; although Buber recalls having discovered these two works "too late to affect my own thought"; Friedman, *Martin Buber's Life and Work*, p. 301.
²⁰ Friedman, *Martin Buber's Life and Work*, p. 284.
²¹ Speaking these words in 1951, Buber adds: "The human world is today, as never before, split into camps, each of which understands the other as the embodiment of falsehood and itself as the embodiment of truth [...] Each side has assumed monopoly of the sunlight and has plunged its antagonist into night, and each side demands that you decided between day and night"; Anderson and Cissna, *The Martin Buber–Carl Rogers Dialogue*, p. 22.

I and Thou is artfully composed as a performance of the dialogical thinking it espouses. *I and Thou* is not a book "about" a theory or a doctrine of dialogical thinking; rather, it bespeaks dialogical thinking in a text woven from poetical images, aphoristic pronouncements, bursts of rhapsodic prose, moments of sober analysis, and sprightly neologisms. As Buber stated: "I must say it again and again: I have no teaching. I only show something. I am showing reality [...] I have no teaching, but I am leading a conversation."[22] The dialogical dimensions of *I and Thou* are, however, not immediately apparent, nor does *I and Thou* enter into conversation with a single addressee. *I and Thou* instantiates a multifaceted dialogue: with Buber himself, with its historical epoch, with its reader, and (silently) with the Eternal Thou. Only after a reader has been drawn into *I and Thou* in Section One (and they only become addressed directly as a reader at the section's end) do the multifaceted dimensions of *I and Thou* manifest themselves in Section Two, where Buber responds to the distress of the modern world and attunes his reader to the approaching reflections on the Eternal Thou encountered in Section Three.

Section One of *I and Thou* begins with the word: In the beginning was the *logos*. Not the *logos* of God, nor the *logos* of the human as a rational being, but the *logos* of the dialogical "ground-word" (*Grundwort*). Buber's recasting of the origin of the world in the word, as "ground-word," seeks to restore what he considers, under the influence of Hasidism, the bespoken word as the "in-between" of the world, human existence, and God. Originally there are two ground-words, I–Thou and I–It, each not a single word, each a relationality of the word, and each inseparable from the other. This is not a "word" in a linguistic or psychological sense, neither sign nor idea, and least of all a dialectical array of identities prefigured in a *logos* that becomes one. The ground-word is the "word," or *logos*, in the ontological sense of "the between as such," neither reducible to a psychological consciousness nor an objective phenomenon, but, in this differential or "betweenness," as structuring a fundamental sense of what it is to be. Relationality, in the ontological facticity of "betweenness," is there from the beginning in its twofold significance, inscribing within the human condition a polarity,

---

[22] M. Buber, *Schriften zu Philosophie und Religion* (Gütersloh: Gütersloher Verlagshaus, 2017), p. 471. As Buber writes: "I call my philosophy 'dialogical philosophy' not without a certain irony because basically it cannot be pursued otherwise than dialogically, but the writings dealing with it have been cast into the, for the most part, quite undialogically constituted human world of this hour – and must be cast there"; *Philosophical Interrogations: Interrogations of Martin Buber, John Wild, Jean Wahl, Brand Blanshard, Paul Weiss, Charles Hartshorne, Paul Tillich*, ed. S. Rome and B. Rome (New York: Holt, Rinehart and Winston, 1964), p. 23.

and hence a dramatic tension, that should not be confused with a dualism or a dichotomy.[23] As conflicting orientations within human existence, both ground-words – I–Thou and I–It – span the three spheres of creation: nature, the social (other human beings), and "spiritual beings" (works of art and achievements of knowledge).[24] When oriented along the I–Thou relation, each sphere of creation gives witness to the wafting of a breath silently tracing a trajectory toward the Eternal Thou. When "we gaze towards the trailing hem of the Eternal Thou," we stand at the edge of the finite onto the infinite. We feel ourselves silently addressed and answer this call through our participation in the world's dialogical realization, without being able to utter, and hence possess, the proper name of the Eternal Thou. This dialogical interrelation between human existence and the Eternal Thou contrasts with, and yet remains inseparable from, the dialogical I–Thou interrelation among human beings, when we stand directed toward one another in the reciprocity of saying I-and-Thou. The I–Thou relation in the sphere of human life contrasts with the I–Thou relation in the sphere of nature. Standing in the presence of animals, we sense the mute stirring of an address that remains incapable of reaching us. Something speaks to us without us knowing what or whom, nor to what end.

In the form of an I–It relation, an object of experience – a tree, for example – can be manifest in many ways: as an object of perceptual experience, as an object of aesthetic delight, as an object of arboreal knowledge, as represented in an image, as a propositional object ("the tree is green"), as determined by laws of nature. The I–It relation is not reducible to a psychological or epistemological relation. It shapes an ontological determination of the sense of being in connection with a typification of language organized around categorial predication based on the primacy of the verb. When speaking of a "greening tree," Buber's idiosyncratic description suggests that the traditional substance-based ontology of things and their predicate attributes is grounded in the verbal *greening* tree. It is not that the tree *is* green; *it* "trees" and "greens," as it were, in terms of which we are able to pronounce "that the tree is green."

Nature is not only experienced in the form of I–It relations. A dialogical attunement to nature is available to human life, although not in any replete sense of encountering nature as a Thou. A tree, for example, can be encountered "with an eye to its way of life" – its way of being as a tree – without thereby imbuing any personification of the tree into a Thou, empathetic

---

[23] Buber, *I and Thou*, p. 69: "In the beginning is the relation."
[24] Buber identifies Goethe as the paradigmatic thinker of the I and Thou relation with regard to nature, Socrates for the I and Thou relation among humans, and Jesus for the relation between I and the Eternal Thou.

communion, or objectification into an "It." In such instances, the tree "bodies forth against me (*er leibt mir gegenüber*) and has to do with me, as I with it – only in a different way."[25] Full-bodied dialogical interrelations are only possible with other human beings, but conversely, other human beings can be experienced in the form of "It." For another person to be an "It" is to experience their alterity to an *alter ego*, as an ego other than my own, whose presence limits the reach and realization of my own freedom; or as an ego other than my own with whom I have empathetic relations, without, however, participating dialogically in their lives, without, in other words, any investment of my own being in theirs. Under the sway of I–It relations, we "experience" others yet fail to "encounter" them as a Thou. As Buber writes: "The human being to whom I say Thou I do not experience (*erleben*). But I stand in relation to him, in the sacred ground-word."[26] This distinction between "experience" (*Erlebnis*) and "encounter" (*Begegnung*) underpins Buber's critique of the psychologizing tendencies of the modern world, including psychoanalysis, and its reduction of intersubjective relations to the constitutive sphere of immanence, or the interiority of subjectivity.[27]

In dialogical encounters, the Thou does not stand before me as an object of consciousness, as an *alter ego* set against my own self, or as subsumable to an identity. In an I–Thou relation, the I stands before the other, not in a moment of recognition or sympathetic feeling, but in the stance of response and address, responding to and addressing the being of the other, as otherness, in a grounded responsibility for and trust in the other. This is not to deny the perceptual experience of another as an embodied individual with whom I can interact and communicate. Whereas in an I–It relation, I experience others as standing before me through mediated forms of interaction as an "object" (*Gegenstand*), in a dialogical relation. I encounter others in standing before them (as a Thou) in a presence (*Gegenwart*) not of my own. The I can only achieve "actuality" or "effective realization" (*Wirklichkeit*) in directedness toward the Thou (and likewise, the Thou can only achieve actuality as an I in directedness toward me as their Thou). To participate in the lives of others, as Thou, turns on the mutual inclusion of my life in yours as well as your life in mine, without either my life or yours becoming

---

[25] Buber, *I and Thou*, p. 59.
[26] Buber, *I and Thou*, p. 60.
[27] Mendes-Flohr, *From Mysticism to Dialogue*, p. 321ff. This critique of *Erlebnis* incorporates self-critique against Buber's own prewar conception of experience with its mystical overtones of self-realization, as presented in *Daniel*. As Buber confided to Walter Kaufmann: "The psychological reduction of being, its psychologizing, had a destructive effect on me in my youth because it removed from me the foundation of human reality, the 'to-one-another.' Only much later, in the revolution of my thinking that taught me to fight and to gain ground, did I [return to] reality."

entirely absorbed into or dominated by the other. Much as the Thou is "in" me as well as "not in me," when the world becomes opened through dialogical encounters with others, the world stands "in" me as well as "not in me."

Dialogical life unfolds in the interspace of the "human in between" (*Zwischenmenschlichen*). What underpins dialogical life is neither recognition nor empathy, but trust and entrustment in the interspace of mutual participation. Recognition and empathy are enhanced and grounded in the dialogical affordance of being not just with others, but *for* others. The Thou is the singular person to whom my own existence singularly responds. That is to say, entering into a dialogical encounter does not consist in approaching the other armed with the question "What art Thou to me?" or "Who art Thou?" but to begin with, and never abandon, the self-disarming question "Who am I to be for Thou?" The "effective reality" (*Wirklichkeit*) of dialogical encounters occurs through the realization (*Verwirklichung*) of I-being for being-Thou (*Ich-wirkenden-Du*) as well as Thou-being for being-me (*Du-wirkenden-Ich*) in a performative "Thou-saying" (*Du-sagen*). An election takes place in the twofold sense of I choosing to respond directly to Thou and of Thou choosing to address me directly.[28] The I elects to become herself decentered from her drive for self-affirmation and self-satisfaction. In the reciprocity of participation, we realize ourselves as human beings; in this dialogical sense, "all real life is encounter."[29]

In terms of temporality, I–It relations are structured in the form of succession, while dialogical relations are self-temporalizing. An I–Thou relation does not just occur "in" time; it *is* temporalizing. As Buber writes, "only through the fact that the Thou becomes present, the present arises [*nur dadurch, daß das Du gegenwärtig wird, ensteht Gegenwart*]."[30] The "ground-word" of I–Thou is accorded an original temporalization, thus bringing together being and time in the bespoken word of dialogical existence. As what presently originates between us and as what is rendered as the present for us, the encounter of I and Thou gives rise to the temporal present. The present, however, must inevitably come to pass in passing away, and through this passage the presence of the Thou, neither an objective phenomenon nor a subjective consciousness, becomes an object, or "It." The I, in turn, becomes thrown back onto itself, devolving into an "ego," self-centered and self-driven, and set apart from dialogical relatedness toward the Thou. The dialogical present

---

[28] In Buber's terminology, dialogical relation involves "volition" on the side of the I and "grace" of the side of the You.

[29] Buber, *I and Thou*, p. 62. As Buber writes: The human becomes an I "on the Thou" ("Der Mensch wird am Du zum Ich").

[30] Buber, *I and Thou*, p. 16.

remains essentially oriented toward the future – namely, the not yet present – in an nonobjectified sense of the Thou. It is in this temporal sense that "whoever says Thou does not have something; he has nothing. But he stands in relation." Buber does not, however, tacitly suggest a "negative theology" or "negative determination" of the Thou.[31] To speak of the Thou as "nothing" yet "immediate" should not be understood in the ontological sense of an I–It relation. To *have* nothing of the Thou as an object (*Gegenstand*) is to *be* in the presence (*Gegenwart*) of the Thou, standing before me in the openness of a future not belonging to me to which I am elected to participate in and hence enter. This directedness toward the future passing, as it were, through the Thou contrasts with the pastness of I–It relations, where what it is "to be" becomes settled into "having been." The Thou stands before me as the present which I await (*Gegenwart*), not, however, in the passive sense of waiting for the arrival or givenness of the Thou, nor in anticipation of what will never arrive – for the Thou is already here insofar as I am always there for them in their otherness. The futural thrust of participation, the substance of dialogical realization, invites the I to walk along with – and not wait for – the Thou. In participating in the lives of others, we engage in a participatory sense-making of our lives as well as theirs, and through this realization of what it is to be as beings of this world and of this being the world.

Sublime Melancholy

Everyday concourse and commerce with others mainly occur in accordance with I–It relations. We experience others in the world, and yet regularly fall short of encountering one another as a Thou. It is not that others hide themselves; it is that we restrain ourselves from opening who we are to one another as a Thou, keeping each other at arm's length in the mutual self-interest of reliability and predictability. As Buber characterizes the familiarity of the It-world: "Be calm, everything happens as it must happen, but nothing is directed at you, you are not meant; it is just 'the world', you can experience it as you like, but whatever you make of it in yourself proceed from you alone, nothing is required of you, you are not addressed, all is quiet."[32]

However, when standing before the "mystery" of who Thou art, the "density and duration" of the It-world become interrupted and unveiled as "originally alien," but not because the "real world" or "world in itself"

---

[31] Against Michael Theunissen's argument in *The Other: Studies in the Social Ontology of Husserl, Heidegger, Sartre, and Buber*, trans. C. Macann (Cambridge, MA: MIT Press, 1986).
[32] Buber, *Between Man and Man*, p. 12.

stands hidden behind the world's apparent familiarity. In the absence of dialogical encounters with the Thou, the world does not address us; it is merely there for our experience and utility with its reliability, predictability, and familiarity. In the It-world "one has to live and also can live comfortably," and yet nothing of this world immediately speaks to us. As Buber remarks, the world does not "give itself or anything to you" nor call upon our participation for its actuality. In breaking through the comfort and complacency of being in the It-world, the encounter with the Thou emerges "as wonderful lyric-dramatic episodes" within an otherwise assuring but nonetheless unfulfilling chronicle of everyday life.[33] Without, in other words, I–Thou encounters, the world, despite its reliability and predictability, is not a home to which we sense ourselves *actually* belonging. We are not faced, however, with a choice between the It-world and I–Thou relations, for as Buber insists, without being in the world, structured according to It-relations, "you cannot remain alive; its reliability preserves you." And yet, "if you were to die into it, then you would be buried in nothingness."[34] Were life to succumb completely to the world, as entirely determined by I–It relations, the course of life would be nothing more than a useless passion, from dust to dust, ashes to ashes, without the ultimate meaningfulness of encountering others as Thou. This, then, is "the sublime melancholy of our fate," that Buber addresses directly to his reader at the end of Section One: "Hey you, and in all seriousness of the truth, without It, human beings cannot live. But whoever lives only with It is not human."[35]

This tension between I–It and I–Thou relations recasts Goethe's drama of "two souls" as the sublime melancholy to which human existence is fated.[36] An I–Thou relation, although interrupting the reification of It-relations, inevitably falls captive to the world. As Buber writes: "All response binds the Thou into the It-world."[37] An I–Thou relation endures through its own submission to an I–It relation, for it is only in binding itself

[33] Buber, *I and Thou*, p. 84.
[34] Buber, *I and Thou*, p. 83.
[35] Translation modified.
[36] Neither a duality nor a dichotomy, the *coincidentia oppositorum* of the I–It and I–Thou ground-words forms a nonsublimating polarity in Goethe's sense, as with the two souls of Faust's declaration:

> Zwei Seelen wohnen, ach! in meiner Brust,
> die eine will sich von der andern trennen:
> Die eine hält in derber Liebeslust
> sich an die Welt mit klammernden Organen;
> die andre hebt gewaltsam sich vom Dust
> zu den Gefilden hoher Ahnen.

[37] Buber, *I and Thou*, p. 89.

to the world that an I–Thou relation gains permanence; on the other hand, an I–Thou relation must endure, in the sense of survive, its own alienation in the It-world. Everyday life is never neatly demarcated between I–Thou and I–It relations. We are beholden to the It-world's stability, predictability, and symbolic ordering, without which human life could not prevail. And yet, were life to succumb entirely to the immanence of the It-world, human existence would be impoverished of restorative vitality and absolute significance; that is, of spirit. In the "frozen spirit" of the It-world, the embers of dialogical origination can "catch fire and become present, returning to the element from which it issued, to be beheld and lived by men as present."[38] In this unbinding of spirit, I–It relations become "deconvoluted" (*Entwandlung*) back into the I–Thou relatedness from which they originally sprang, not for the purpose of surpassing the world into a beyond or "third realm," but rather for the regeneration and revitalization of being in the It-world through renewed encounters with the Thou.[39]

Buber's image of a "frozen spirit catching fire" in the It-world with the return of a dialogical encounter between I and Thou, by means of which the It-world becomes repaired and restored, reveals the enduring imprint of Jewish thinking, specifically in its Hasidic form, on Buber's thought.[40] In his essay "Spirit and Body of the Hasidic Movement," Buber specifically refers to the Lurianic Kabbalistic doctrine of *tzimtzum* when speaking of God's contraction as "wanting to allow relation to emerge" from a nondual and nonrelational unity.[41] In *I and Thou*, the binding of the Thou into an I–It relation, in which the I–Thou relation becomes exiled yet from which it can potentially become unbound and hence restored through renewed dialogical encounter, is characterized as an original contraction or withdrawal. The temporality of the interaction between I–Thou and I–It relations occurs in a

---

[38] Buber, *I and Thou*, p. 90.
[39] "This essential twofoldness cannot be overcome by invoking a 'world of ideas' as a third element that might transcend this opposition"; Buber, *I and Thou*, p. 65.
[40] The war years were also for Buber a transformative period of reflection on the significance and fate of Judaism in the modern world. In addition to a contentious debate with Cohen over Zionism, Buber's intellectual and personal relationship with Rosenzweig, along with their joint translation project of the Hebrew Bible (completed after Rosenzweig's untimely death), affected his thinking about Judaism in relation to his nascent dialogical thinking. Most significantly, Rosenzweig's 1914 article "Atheistic Theology," where he silently critiques Buber's influential "Three Speeches on Judaism" for its anthropomorphic understanding of the relationship to God, incited Buber to rethink the pronounced mysticism in his vision of "realization" through "cosmic unification" – a language that Buber had mobilized in his early enthusiasm for war. Rosenzweig objected to what he judged as the abandonment of revelation and the otherness of God in modern Judaism, of which Buber's dialogues *Daniel* proved no exception.
[41] Friedman, *Martin Buber's Life and Work*, p. 120.

threefold movement of contraction, exile, and restorative return. The world is caught in an incessant flux of creation, decreation, and recreation, pulsating, as it were, between the poles of I–Thou and I–It. The primordial present of I–Thou contracts in expulsing itself into the world of I–It relations. In this self-contraction, the I–Thou becomes bound to the It-world while at the same time, in this withdrawal, leaving behind the traces of its origination as the embers of spirit awaiting restoration and return. Through this self-contraction, the I–Thou relation gives space and time for the arrangement of an ordered world of I–It relations, without which human life would be insubstantial. The Thou becomes an It when "permeated by means" in terms of the instrumentalization and functionalization of interpersonal relations through fixtures of the It-world. The cultural norms, symbolic encodings, and functional benefits of friendship, for example, represent diverse forms of friendship as an I–It relation, yet what gives spirit to a genuine friendship is participation in the life of the other as other, as afforded, in trust, in the dialogical encounter of I and Thou.

The original relation of I–Thou, as "the present," is not however an original unity that, in its self-contraction (or "becoming"), would thereby subsequentially become relational. In the beginning, there is an original ontological difference between I–Thou and I–It, between "the present" and the "pastness of the present" without which things and others of the world would have no permanence. The original present is "two in one" as an original relatedness of nonidentity in nonindifference: nonidentity with the Thou, or a present not my own; nonindifference toward the Thou, to whom I respond in my being. The creative breath of real presence between I and Thou comes to pass, and in its necessary becoming the present becomes contracted, not, however, by withdrawing into the past, but, on the contrary, by drawing forth the future. It is through this withdrawal of the present toward the future – a future held open in the Thou – that the present becomes past, thrown, as it were, into the It-world, which, in turn, stands poised and primed for future restoration through a renewal of I–Thou relatedness. The future that stands open in the present is the future of the potential return of the I–Thou relation to itself. Unbound from the binding and burden of the world, the Thou returns in a renewed present, only to find itself fated once more to thinghood, from which, in a spiraling movement, it holds out the promise of releasing itself once more, time and again. In the return of I–Thou from the future it itself holds open, in withdrawing from the It-world, there is no escape or flight from the world, but, on the contrary, an attunement to the "deeper mystery" – the mystery of creation refracted in the sublime melancholy of the human condition – irradiating this one and only world.

"Watchmen, How Much Longer of This Night?"

Section Two of *I and Thou* begins with an unexpected declaration that "the progressive increase of the It-world is clearly discernible in history." Although Buber grants that dialogical openness can be severely thwarted when human life becomes all too resigned to the It-world, the possibility for the restoration of dialogical realization can never become entirely extinguished given that I–Thou relationality, contracted into I–It relations, always leaves behind embers for its own spiritual revitalization, rekindled by the reinfused breath of Thou-saying. The historicity of human cultures in their manifest diversity is marbled by the ebb and flow of I–Thou and I–It relations, the sublime melancholy of our fate. And yet the modern era, it would seem, evinces an unprecedented disjointedness in the polarity of the human condition. On Buber's argument, modernity is not to be identified with enlightenment and emancipation, but, on the contrary, represents the unrelenting dominance of It-relations in the dual forms of "experience" (*Erfahren*) and "utility" (*Gebrauchen*) over I–Thou relatedness. As Buber writes: "the improvement of the capacity for experience and use generally involves a decrease in the human being's power to relate – that power which alone can enable the human being to live with spirit." In the modern world, experiencing and utility are endangering the potentiality of human existence to realize itself dialogically in the life of spirit, and, in this sense, to exist as authentically human. Modern life is not only without spirit; it has become a ghostly semblance of human existence dominated by the golem of bureaucratic (and instrumental) rationality in the total mobilization of a drive for power and profit.

The revealing term in Buber's critique of modernity is spirit (*Geist*). As with other thinkers of his generation, Buber joins the chorus of rejecting materialism, naturalism, and positivism. Central to this generational revolt is the distinction between *Gesellschaft* and *Gemeinschaft*. Modern society (*Gesellschaft*) is bifurcated into "two neatly defined districts" of anonymous institutions, on the one hand, and self-absorbed lived experience (*Erlebnis*), on the other. Under the capacious heading of institutions (*Einrichtungen*), Buber understands the fixtures of modern *Gesellschaft* that impose systems of classification, schemata of recognition, and norms of conduct. In the modern It-world, human life has become subservient to capitalism and the nation-state. The dominance of economic forces represents a detachment of the drive for profit from any spiritual guidance and constraint, whereas the dominance of political forces represents the detachment of the drive for power. Both drives are not only uprooted from a spiritual foundation in dialogical relatedness; each drive has become an idol for the modern world with its worship of power and profit for their own sake. Economics and the nation-state govern the sphere of "exteriority" – the public and social spheres of modern life – while the sphere of interiority stands under the sway of lived experience and the aestheticization of feeling. Modern notions of subjectivity, whether in Max Stirner's paean to egotistic self-centeredness in *Das Ego und sein Eigentum* or Wilhelm Dilthey's *Lebensphilosophie* in *Das Erlebnis und die Dichtung*, are part and parcel of the fragmentation of modern alienation. Caught in an intolerable oscillation between the pageant of individual lived experience (*Erlebnis*) and the blandness of institutionalized bureaucracy, neither sphere "knows the person or community" nor "has access to actual life."[42] Unlike other partisans of *Geist* and *Gemeinschaft*, for example Rudolf Eucken or the *völkisch* writer Paul Lagarde, Buber's critique of modern *Gesellschaft* is divorced from a Germanic revitalizing vision of *Kultur*. In a remark that discreetly rejects the reigning discourse of spirit among such nationalist thinkers, spirit for Buber is not "like the blood that circulates in you but like the air that you breathe." To live in spirit (*im Geist leben*) is to breathe in the "Thou-saying" (*Du-Sagen*) through which the breadth of the world in communal existence becomes expanded and enriched. As Buber remarks, "the relentlessly growing It-world grows over [human beings] like weeds, his own I loses its actuality, until the incubus over him and the phantom inside him exchange in whispered confession of their need for redemption."[43] Given the phantom, or zombie-like, condition of modern existence, redemption can only be achieved through the restorative breath of actual life in Thou-saying and the formation of genuine community through dialogical encounters gathered around an unique living center of Spirit.

That Buber must have been keenly aware that his call for spiritual renewal would fall upon deaf ears or meet with outright skepticism is apparent from an unidentified interlocutor who abruptly enters the scene of Buber's reflections, voicing the objection: "But isn't the communal life of modern human beings bound to be submerged in the It-world?"[44] Consider, this interlocutor continues, the "two chambers of this life," namely, the economy and the nation-state: are both "thinkable in their present dimensions and ramifications" on the basis of a "superior renunciation of all 'immediacy' [… and] resolute repudiation of any 'alien' authority that does not

---

[42] Buber, *I and Thou*, p. 93.
[43] Buber, *I and Thou*, p. 96.
[44] Buber, *I and Thou*, p. 96.

itself have its source in this area?"[45] Economic "goods and services" as well as political "opinions and aspirations" alone provide for the "firm structure of the great 'objective' fabric" of the modern world. As this interlocutor concludes: "It would be absurd to try to reverse this development; and if one could bring off this absurdity, the tremendous precision instrument of this civilization would be destroyed at the same time, although this alone makes life possible for the tremendously increased numbers of humanity."[46]

As would be discernible by his contemporary readers, Buber here ventriloquizes in this staged dialogical setting Max Weber's influential wartime lectures, "The Vocation of the Scholar" and "The Vocation of the Politician."[47] Given the circumstances in which Weber presented these lectures, one can imagine the charged expectations among his mostly youthful and war-fatigued audience as he stepped up to the lectern in 1917 and 1919.[48] In the midst of an impending defeat in 1917 and the subsequent upheaval of the German Revolution in 1919, the vocations of culture and of politics were not merely academic questions, but existentially pressing concerns, especially in light of the mobilization of German scholars in clamorous support of the war in 1914 (to which Weber himself had succumbed), which had discredited the vocation of the humanities in German universities.

As Weber remarks in his 1919 lecture against the backdrop of revolution, what lies ahead of Germany "for the time being is a polar night of icy darkness and hardness." Weber's image of "polar night" accentuates his diagnosis of the disenchanted condition of modernity, which he expressed with his characterization of the modern world as an "iron cage" – in Talcott Parsons' influential mistranslation of Weber's celebrated metaphor. In the original German "steel-hard housing" (*das stahlharte Gehäuse*), steel underlines Weber's central argument that the modern world is built upon technological artefacts and bureaucratic rationality;

---

[45] Buber, *I and Thou*, p. 96.
[46] Buber, *I and Thou*, p. 97.
[47] The occasion for Weber's two lectures was not without personal bearing for Buber. Weber had been invited to deliver a public lecture on the topic of the scholar's vocation in 1917 by the *Freie Studentenschaft* in Munich, an organization of students eager to reform the German university system and, more broadly, German culture. Weber, not without symbolic irony given his antipathy toward Marxism and socialist revolutionaries, gave his lecture on the same day as the momentous launching of the Russian Revolution (November 7). Weber was subsequently invited to lecture again, but at first hesitated given the group's political orientation, although he then accepted this invitation after hearing that Kurt Eisner, then Prime Minister of the Republic of Bavaria, whom Weber despised, would have been invited, should he have refused. His second lecture, "The Scholar of the Politician," was given on January 1919. J. Radkau, *Max Weber: A Biography*, trans. P. Camiller (Cambridge, UK: Polity Press, 2009), p. 514.
[48] As Karl Löwith remembered, Weber's "face, with a shaggy beard growing all around it, recalled the mournful glow of the Bamberg prophets"; Radkau, *Max Weber*, p. 487.

unlike iron, a natural element, steel is human made. As an encompassing metaphor for capitalism in its social, and not just economic, dimensions, the image of steel-hardened housing "implies not only a new dwelling for modern human beings, but a transformed nature: homo sapiens has become a *different* being, a degraded being."[49] This degradation of human life, in tandem with the disenchantment of the world (*die Entzauberung der Welt*), was ever more pronounced in the aftermath of the war and catastrophic German defeat. Encased within a nonnatural fabrication, the enchantment of "worldliness," anchored in the transcendent meaningfulness of it all, was supplanted by ruthless efficiency and rationalization. We moderns exist in a world that is predictable, reliable, and familiar (much as Buber describes the It-world). As Weber observes, we depend on the functioning of a tram without needing to know anything about how a tram, and the complex institutions supporting its operation (engineering, signaling, electric power), works. In a world overdetermined by instrumental rationality, we go about our lives in a "fog of incomprehensibility" concerning the world. As Weber argues, "increasing rationalization and intellectualization does not mean a greater knowledge of the conditions we live under," and hence mastery of how to exist in this world. We live in the assurance that should we need to know how things work, we could in principle find out, yet this confidence is acquired at a high price: "there are no mysterious uncalculatable forces intervening in our lives." The modern world is disenchanted, made of steel, without transcendent and, especially, religiously sanctioned meaning. As echoed by Buber's virtual interlocutor, any appeal to a spiritual center beyond the world of economics and politics must be relegated to superstition or nostalgia.

Weber's image of the disenchanted modern world as "steel-hardened housing" offers a contemporary counterpoint to Plato's allegory of the cave. As Weber remarks, the value of knowledge for Plato was inseparable from the conduct of life and how to lead a just life as a citizen of the polis. In Plato's allegory, the world was a natural cave (not a steel-hardened housing) that stood, when discovered in philosophical awakening, in relation to the transcendence of the Good and the pursuit of life in truth, individually as well as collectively, in terms of which the meaningfulness of values structuring the world could be anchored. In the modern world, by contrast, politics no longer concerns itself with the highest Good, but

---

[49] P. Baehr, "The 'Iron Cage' and the 'Shell as Hard as Steel': Parsons, Weber, and the Stahlhartes Gehäuse Metaphor in the Protestant Ethic and the Spirit of Capitalism," *History and Theory*, Vol. 40, No. 2 (May 2001): 153–169; pp. 161, 164.

has devolved into instrumental rationality and bureaucratic expertise; the value of knowledge for life has been made subservient to utilitarian purpose. Encased in a "steel-hardened housing" without transcendence, the modern world is populated by "lifeless, derivative ghosts" that have replaced the shadow figures on the walls of Plato's cave. These "derivative ghosts" are not appearances beyond which the true, the good, and the beautiful reside, giving transcendental ground to the cavernous world of appearances. The distinction between "appearance" and "reality" has been supplanted by ghosts in the shell. Within the "steel-hardened housing" of the modern world, there is neither truth nor the supreme Good beyond or behind appearances, given scientific rationality's foreclosure of transcendence. The production of knowledge, as Weber wryly remarks, is perpetually haunted by immediate obsolescence: in pursuit of the ever new, everything becomes forever old. The meaningfulness of science for life, over and above its prodigious technical efficiency and predicative power, as with the meaningfulness of cultural values (including the endeavor of academia), has become decapitated from transcendence. As Weber writes: "Even if such 'meaning' existed, how could we ever find it? If science can do anything, it is precisely to uproot and destroy the belief that the world has *any such thing* as a 'meaning'!" Scientific rationality offers a path neither to worldly fulfillment nor to other-worldly salvation. As Weber writes: "Science is meaningless, because it provides no answer for the only question that matters: 'What should we do? How should we live?'" The question "is life worth living, and under what circumstances?" has been rendered unintelligible.[50] The question of ultimate meaningfulness becomes itself ultimately meaningless, a matter of idle speculation for bewitching philosophers or seductive spiritual gurus.

We are thus left with "nothing but an eternal struggle among gods" where no system of values – the gods – for life can secure its own foundation.[51] Given this modern condition, it is senseless "to advocate one position or another," one value instead of another, since different value systems in the world are in conflict with each other.[52] As Weber writes:

> Today, though, "everyday life" is our religion. Having lost their magic, the multiple gods of the past rise up from their graves in the form of impersonal forces, fighting for power over our lives and thus beginning anew their

---

[50] M. Weber, *Charisma and Disenchantment: The Vocation Lectures*, eds. P. Reitter and Chad Wellmon (New York: New York Review Books, 2020), p. 24.
[51] Weber, *The Vocation Lectures*, p. 41.
[52] Weber, *The Vocation Lectures*, p. 30.

eternal struggle against one another [...] what is hard for us modern men and women, first and foremost the younger generation, is precisely meeting the challenge of this *everyday* life. All the hunting after "authentic experience" to be found on all sides derives from this weakness. For it is weakness to be unable to face the destiny of the age head-on.[53]

The hardness of the times – Europe's and not just Germany's polar night – must be faced nonetheless; neither resignation nor Romanticism is an option. For Weber, "the various possible attitudes toward life are in irresolvable conflict, irreconcilable, so in the end we all must *make a choice*," and this choice, as the necessary existential presupposition for the meaningfulness of life's claimed purpose, demands a new ethics and sense of calling. The meaningfulness of life, however, cannot be established by scientific rationalism or objective knowledge; it is likewise not to be found in the interiority of lived experience, nor can we rely on inherited forms of religion or appeals to divine revelation. In answer to the question "Which of the warring gods should we serve?" only a prophet or a savior can answer; but when there are no longer any such figures, or if their message is no longer credible, only we can take responsibility for ourselves. But how?

In his lecture on the vocation of politics, Weber argues that "all ethically oriented action is guided by one of *two* fundamentally different, irredeemably opposed maxims: either an 'ethics of personal conviction' (*Gesinnungsethik*) or an 'ethics of responsibility' (*Verantwortungsethik*)."[54] Whereas the former is defined by the purity of ideals and unshakeable convictions ("He who lives by an ethics of personal conviction cannot tolerate the ethical irrationality of the world"), the latter is defined in view of actions and their consequences. It proves impossible, however, to reconcile an ethics of personal conviction with an ethics of responsibility.[55] With Kurt Eisner and Gustav Landauer in his peripheral vision, Weber judges that those who pursue "the future of Socialism" or "international peace" evince an ethics of conviction; "in a war among different beliefs, [they risk] damaging and discrediting the cause for generations to come, because the true believer takes no responsibility for the *consequences* of his actions, remaining unaware of the demonic powers in play."

---

[53] Weber, *The Vocation Lectures*, p. 32.
[54] Weber, *The Vocation Lectures*, p. 103. Weber's distinction between "ethics of conviction" and "ethics of responsibility" owed much to his discussions with György Lukács, and especially their common fascination with Dostoevsky's *The Brothers Karamazov*; Z. Tarr, "A Note on Weber and Lukács," *International Journal of Politics, Culture, and Society*, Vol. 3, No. 1 (1989): 131–139.
[55] Weber, *The Vocation Lectures*, p. 106.

Aside from this critique of utopic socialists, the dangers of an ethics of conviction were made glaringly evident by the war. The spiritual mobilization of ideas and ideals was a manifestation of the mythologization of secular nationalism, where "battles" rage "among the various 'gods' of the different systems of value" and culture. As Weber remarks: "I have no idea how anyone could give a 'scholarly,' 'scientific' proof that French culture is *worth more* than German culture or vice-versa."[56] Human conflict remains intractable given the flight of the gods and the instrumentalization of reason: "the conflict rages between this god and that, and will continue until the end of time, much as it raged in the ancient world." Whereas the Greeks once offered sacrifices to the gods of their city-states in times of war, in the contemporary world the "behavior is the same, though stripped of its magic and mythical (but psychologically true) trappings." Agamemnon sacrificed his daughter Iphigenia for success at the onset of war; citizens are today sacrificed to and by the nation-state for victory as war. As Weber writes, it is "our destiny to live in an age without prophets, far from God." As echoed by Buber's virtual interlocutor in *I and Thou*, coming to terms with the disenchantment of the modern world and the hardness of humankind's polar night depends on not "obscuring this basic fact."[57] As Weber concludes his lecture: "despite all the multitudes yearning for new prophets and saviors, the situation today is much the same as the one described in the Book of Isaiah, in the beautiful song of the Edomite watchman during the time of exile: 'Watchman, how much longer of this night? Watchman, how much longer of this night? The watchman sayeth, The morning cometh.'"

Holy Insecurity

In response to Weber's spectral presence, Buber concedes that "it would be absurd to reverse this development [of modernity]." Unlike Landauer, who idealized Medieval community life and its spiritual unity in his utopic vision of revolution, Buber does not reject outright the institutions of the modern world. Nonetheless, Buber implicitly calls into question Weber's ethics of responsibility as a fitting response to the disenchantment of culture and, especially, politics. An ethics of responsibility presupposes that a deliberative and reflective command of the economy and the state remains viable. Against his virtual interlocutor, Buber claims, however, that he "speaks too late," since the state as well as the economy "are no

[56] Weber, *The Vocation Lectures*, p. 30.
[57] Weber, *The Vocation Lectures*, p. 37.

longer led" – "the leaders merely *seem* to rule the racing engines."[58] The war has revealed the extent to which the modern world, driven by capitalism and state-sponsored nationalism, has become a "golem" under the domain of which "there is nothing [...] but the despotism of the proliferating It under which the I, more and more impotent, is still dreaming that it is in command."[59] This despotism is not only to be understood in economic and political terms with the worship of power and profit as the idols of modern life. Buber moreover considers the veneration of sociobiological "laws of life" and the "struggle for existence," which animated German nationalism during the war, as further evidence of the abdication of human responsibility in dialogical relatedness.

The resignation to the modern It-world found another manifestation with the cultural pessimism of Oswald Spengler's *The Decline of the West*, a work composed during the war and an immediate bestseller on its publication in 1918 (first installment) and 1922 (second installment).[60] In implicitly responding to Oswald's influential work, Buber inter alia in the same breath takes issue with Max Stirner's *Das Ego und sein Eigentum* (which had experienced a resurgent vogue of influence during the 1890s) and its idolization of self-affirmation and "demonic" individualism.[61] With both of these authors in mind, Buber refers to the modern specter of "the demonic," of a subjectivity for whom there is no possible openness toward a Thou. A "demonic individual" elevates themselves into a "god" or "idol" in relating exclusively to themselves in the phantasy of being "self-caused," thus attempting to efface their own creaturely, and hence dialogical, condition. "The demonic" is considered by Buber to represent a distinctively modern pathology of the self; others are viewed as "machines" at the disposal and behest of an aggrandized self. All are nothing to him, even he himself, as the self-positing I, is strictly speaking not a self. He speaks on behalf of himself without any duality within him, and thus, in his atrophied state, betrays the "hopelessness of its own self-contradiction." For Buber, the deactualization of Thou-saying occurs when the demonic I seeks to unfold itself within its constricted space in rejection of dialogical relatedness. Caught in the self-contradiction of a finite being aspiring to unlimited power, the demonic I searches in themself

---

[58] Buber, *I and Thou*, p. 97.
[59] Buber, *I and Thou*, p. 97.
[60] See J. Farrenkopft, *Prophet of Decline: Spengler on World History and Politics* (Baton Rouge: Louisiana State University Press, 2001), chapter 2.
[61] M. Stirner, *The Ego and Its Own*, ed. D. Leopold (Cambridge, UK: Cambridge University Press, 2009). For a reassessment of Stirner's thought, J. Blumenfeld, *All Things Are Nothing to Me: The Unique Philosophy of Max Stirner* (London: Zero Books, 2018).

for "otherness," only to find the "horror of the Doppelgänger" – themself as defaced other – from which there is no escape. In Buber's thinking, the temptation toward "the demonic" – hypertrophic individualism – arises in reaction to the "golem" of bureaucratic and instrumental rationality. Unlike previous eras of cultural turbulence, when the dominance of the It-world nonetheless craved for redemption through the Thou-saying power of dialogical encounter, the "doom" of the modern world forecloses the return of spirit. In a striking image, the modern It-world has become an "incubus" that "lurks inside us," sucking the dialogical relatedness from the marrow of human existence. We have become ghosts in the shell – or zombies, robbed of "actuality," that is, interhuman presence.[62] What defines the modern predicament is therefore not "crisis," in the sense of a decisive moment and opportunity for "healing" by enlivening the "sparks" of spirit, but "doom," where what stands endangered is dialogical spirit itself, obscured beyond recognition and recall. As Buber writes, tacitly citing Hölderlin's poem *Patmos*, "Shall we have to follow this path all the way to the end, to the test of the final darkness? But where there is danger, what saves grows as well."[63]

In defiance of this doomed century, Buber insists that "humankind's communal life cannot dispense any more than he himself with the It-world – over which the presence of the Thou floats like the spirit over the face of the waters." How, then, to bring back into balance the polarity of I–Thou and I–It relations in a world where the temporality of dialogical actualization has been thrown out of joint? In alluding to Genesis 1:2 ("the presence of the Thou floats like the spirit over the face of the waters"), the religious thrust of Buber's response to Weber's dour realism becomes apparent: The modern It-world is a wasteland in need of redemption through a new genesis, or creation, as effectuated through the Thou-saying spirit of dialogical encounter and community. As Buber writes:

> The spirit is truly "at home with itself" when it can confront the world that is opened up to it, give itself to the world, and redeem it and, through the world, also itself. But the spirituality that represents the spirit nowadays is so scattered, weakened, degenerate, and full of contradictions that it could not possibly do this until it had first returned to the essence of the spirit: being able to say Thou.[64]

---

[62] Buber's evocation of postwar modern life as inhabited by humans robbed of actuality, as haunted by the "incubus," and "ghosts" is telling of the impact of the war on the emergence of horror films (*Cabinet of Dr. Caligari*, etc.). See W. Scott Poole, *The Great War and the Origins of Modern Horror* (Berkeley, CA: Counterpoint Press, 2020).
[63] Buber, *I and Thou*, p. 105.
[64] Buber, *I and Thou*, p. 100.

To say "Thou" requires a "decision" to step before the face (*Angesicht*) of the other, and through this revitalizing face-to-face encounter of dialogical in-betweenness, the cosmos becomes in turn a home for humankind in contrast to the steel-hard housing in which human life "must accommodate itself to a world of objects that no longer achieves any presence for it."

After this response to a ventriloquized Weber, Buber's discussion unexpectedly changes tack with a theatrical *coup de main*. A reader could be excused for thinking that Buber's argument for the reenchantment of the world through the spirit of "Thou-saying," sharpened against Weber's diagnosis of disenchantment, had now settled the matter, and yet, immediately thereafter, Buber conjures the virtual presence of another intertextual figure, who could just as much stand for Buber himself as for a still unconvinced reader, or indeed both. As he writes: "at times when a human being is overcome by the horror of the alienation between I and world, it occurs to him that something might be done."[65] In what can be labeled a theatrical vignette inserted into *I and Thou*, Buber, setting the reader into the imagination of the text itself, paints a dramatic scene of an unspecified individual – "a man" – in "the dreadful midnight hour" who is "tormented by a waking dream." It is if Buber's earlier response to Weber did not stand adequate to the task it had set for itself. In this staged vision, this virtual personage is said to experience, while lying in their bed, the collapse of the walls in their room; they plunge into an abyss, with a shattering of the "self-possession of the ego." This individual "screams," and in this anxiety, with both "object" and "subject" suspended, the question "How to live?" hovers over this welter and waste.[66] As Buber continues this imaginative portrait, an individual in such existential despair can attempt to summon confidence by means of painting for themselves "world-pictures." To the left and right of our virtual personage's bed, two irreconcilable worldviews appear, beneath each of which is written "one and all." In the first "world-picture," the I is contained in the world; there is no I. In the second "world-picture," the world is contained in the I; there is no world. Either the I cannot be harmed by the world, for there is no I that stands against and outside the world; or the world cannot harm the I, for the world is a product of one's own will and representation. Each worldview would appear at first to console and calm the anxiety of existence; yet each singularly fails, for the

---

[65] Buber, *I and Thou*, p. 120.
[66] Buber draws on Kierkegaard's conception of anxiety for the formulation of what he calls "holy insecurity" – a concept that reaches back his prewar 1913 *Daniel*.

despairing individual finds himself caught in the contradiction between both worldviews. Both flash before their eyes at once, and in this blink of an eye, blinded by two conflicting pictures:

> he looks up and sees a picture; and whichever he sees, it does not matter, either the empty I is stuffed full of world or it is submerged in the flood of the world, and he calms down. But the moment will come, and it is near, when man, overcome by horror, looks up and in a flash sees both pictures at once. And he is seized by a deeper horror.[67]

The Morning Cometh

This "deeper horror" conjured up at the end of Section Two leaves a reader suspended over an abyss without apparent hope or consolation. In quietly turning the page to begin Section Three on the Eternal Thou, something nonetheless occurs with this transition in the blink of an eye, with neither motivation nor ceremony. In the harrowing silence spanning both sections, something speaks to us in this passage, from the loss of trust in the world and inability to respond resolutely to the doom of the world at the end of Section Two to the redemptive promise of the Eternal Thou addressed in Section Three. We are meant to *hear* a question dawning upon us; it is a silent question that Buber himself heard throughout his life, time and again. As Buber remarks in his lecture "The Silent Question": "From time to time, I seem to hear a question echoing out of the depths of stillness."[68] It is not a question that we ourselves ask. Strictly speaking, it is a question asked of us in the solemnity of its own mutely bespoken address. One abides in this question, not as a self-possessed subject in a relation to an object of questioning, but in finding oneself interpolated by a question already sounded. It is this question that "the world of today" asks of religion, a question, according to Buber, pursued by all religions in the name of God or the gods: "Are you, perhaps, the power that can help me? Can you teach me to believe?"[69]

The deeper horror breached at the end of Section Two in *I and Thou* reflected as well as a personal crisis of faith. As Buber recounts, stirrings of doubt regarding his understanding of God, as presented in *Daniel: Dialogues on Realization* (1913), began to seize him before the outbreak of war. During a conversation in April 1914 with the Anglican clergyman

---

[67] Buber, *I and Thou*, p. 122.
[68] M. Buber, *On Judaism*, ed. N. Glatzer (New York: Schocken Books, 1995), p. 202.
[69] Buber, *On Judaism*, p. 202.

(and friend to Theodore Herzl) William Hechler, Buber was suddenly bewildered by his own faltering response to Hechler's question: "Tell me, do you believe in God?" Buber's vague affirmation, uttered without conviction, continued to haunt him throughout the war. It was not until 1921, with yet another unexpected illumination, this time while traveling on a train, that Buber realized: "If to believe in God means to speak *about* him in the third person, then to be sure I do not believe in God, or at least I do not know whether I am allowed to say that I believe in God."[70] God, Buber now came to understand, can be spoken of neither as an object of knowledge nor as an infinite substance, an entity or being. This unfolding revelation liberated him from his "godless mysticism" and earlier belief in a pantheistic God, manifest through "inner experience" (*Erlebnis*), as the noumenal unity of the world.[71] In rejecting these misconceptions, Buber returned to the God of the Old Testament in dialogical relation with human beings, not a God *about* which we speak, but a God *to whom* one responds, and who, in turn, addresses us.[72]

The question "Are you, perhaps, the power that can help me? Can you teach me to believe?" was not only a personal one and a dialogical stage in the trajectory of *I and Thou* toward the Eternal Thou. Not only for philosophy, the First World War was equally (and inseparably) an original catastrophe for theology. In Germany, the war ushered in the collapse of Protestant liberal theology by exposing the hollowness of its identification of religion with morality as well as its humanization and nationalization of God.[73] The aftermath of war witnessed the emergence of a soteriological "crisis theology" with an emphasis on God's radical alterity and humankind's fallen worldly condition. Rudolf Otto's *The Idea of the Holy* (1917) and Karl Barth's *The Epistle to the Romans* (first edition 1919; significantly revised for the second edition of 1922) initiated this seismic shift in theological thinking.[74] The war, as Barth remarked in a wartime sermon, was

---

[70] M. Buber, "Religion as Gegenwart," in R. Horwitz, *Buber's Way to 'I and Thou': An Historical Analysis and the First Publication of Martin Buber's Lectures 'Religion als Gegenwart'* (Heidelberg: Verlag Lambert Scheider, 1978), p. 128.

[71] See Mendes-Flohr, *From Mysticism to Dialogue*, chapter 5.

[72] His transformative understanding of God as the Eternal Thou first became articulated in his 1922 lectures "Religion als Gegenwart," delivered at *Das Freie Jüdische Lehrhaus* (founded after the war in 1920) at the invitation of his friend Franz Rosenzweig, which served as the basis for Section Three of *I and Thou*. For the importance of these lectures for *I and Thou*, see Horwitz, *Buber's Way to 'I and Thou.'*

[73] For the spiritual mobilization of theology during the war, *Urkatastophe. Die Erfahrung des Krieges 1914–1918 im Spiegel zeitgenössischer Theologie*, eds. J. Negel and K. Pinggéra (Freiburg: Verlag Herder, 2016).

[74] See Lazier, *God Interrupted*. For the fascination with Marcionism in Bloch and Carl Schmitt, R. Faber, *Political Demonology: On Modern Marcionism* (Eugene, OR: Cascade Books, 2018).

a "unique time of God" passing judgment on the failure of humanity's claim to self-mastery and rationalization of belief. "Faith," Barth proclaimed, is the "evidence of things not seen," and it is "precisely the hidden things, inaccessible to perception, that are displayed by the Spirit of God." Nonetheless, the ambiguity of our fate, "powerful in hope," is that "God cries out to us that He is coming quickly – and yet He seems deaf to every cry for human help."[75] This ambiguity of cries unto God falling on deaf ears also shapes Buber's approach to dialogical actuality – urgently in need of rediscovery – between human life and the Eternal Thou, and thus, not surprisingly, Buber situates his own response to the "deeper horror" within the broader landscape of a reawakening of theology. In the aftermath of war, not only in its Protestant manifestation but as significantly in its Jewish form with Rosenzweig's *The Star of Redemption*, as well as its Catholic expression with Max Scheler's *On the Eternal in Man*, this renewal of religious and theological thinking gravitated around the themes of revelation and redemption and, most fundamentally, the question of God.[76]

Barth's dismay at the theological support for the war – *Kriegstheologie* – among his fellow Protestant pastors and theologians, as exemplified in Adolf von Harnack and Wilhelm Herrmann's signing of the 1914 declaration "An die Kulturwelt!," provoked a sweeping revision of his conception of God, whose distance from the world and radical otherness – "unapproachably different and unutterably strange" – became affirmed without compromise. As Barth argued in his commentary on St. Paul's letters to the Romans, God is *totaliter aliter*. In Barth's dynamic eschatology, the drama of humankind's relation to God is understood as moving from the unending corruption of the cosmos and the reign of death to redemption and life in God's dialectic reconciliation of the human and the divine. The importance of St. Paul consists in his emphasis on humankind's fallen condition of being in the world, unredeemable without God's grace, and the promise of God's deliverance from inauthentic existence. St. Paul's stringent opposition between the Law and Grace becomes sharpened in Barth, who assumes an immemorial and forgotten original identity between the human and God, where

---

[75] K. Barth, *The Epistle to the Romans*, trans. E. Hoskins (London: Oxford University Press, 1965), p. 21. However, for Barth's view of the war in 1914 as "a unique time of God" drawing God nearer to humanity and hence redemption, K. Barth, *A Unique Time of God: Karl Barth's WWI Sermons*, trans. W. Klempa (Louisville, KY: Westminster John Knox Press, 2016).

[76] As Leo Strauss observes: "Most characteristic of the post-World War I world was the resurgence of theory: Karl Barth. Wholly independently of Barth, Jewish theology was resurrected from a deep slumber by Franz Rosenzweig"; *Jewish Philosophy and Crisis of Modernity* (Albany: State University of New York Press, 1997), p. 460.

God remains "totally other," eclipsing the identity of creaturely existence with the creator. It is the otherness of God that "rules the negative dialectic of all mundane and human realms."[77] Humankind's sinful condition stood irrecusably before and in need of an otherworldly God. It is not surprising, then, that Barth was impressed as well as alarmed by the perceived affinity between his theology of God's alienness to the world and the reappearance of Marcion's Gnostic doctrine of the alien God and separation between the Law and Grace in Adolf von Harnack's *Marcion: The Gospel of the Alien God* (1921). According to Barth, "religion is an abyss" and "terror," yet unlike Marcion's Gnosticism, whose alien God brings deliverance, "all we know is that the union between God and man has been changed from divine pre-supposition to human supposition, and that, consequently, every human position has suffered dislocation. On the very brink of human possibility there has, moreover, appeared a final human capacity – the capacity of knowing God to be unknowable and wholly Other."[78]

Set against acculturated liberal Protestantism (with which he was eminently associated), Harnack's retrieval of Marcion and endorsement of this "Arch-Heretic" heralded a resurgent interest in Gnosticism after the war. As von Harnack writes: "Was not Marcion right in his relationship to Christianity at large, both then and in the present time?"[79] Marcion's gospel of an alien God standing remote and against the misery of creation "was bound to deeply move readers for whom, through war and revolution, the cruelty, the counter-divine meaninglessness of fate, had become a horrific experience."[80] Yet at the same time, Marcion taught the coming of the Redeemer, "who is perfect love and nothing but love; no more punitive justice, no more legality!"[81] The God of the Old Testament, as the God of creation, is not, for Marcion, the true God, for the true God is the alien God of revelation, whose alterity stands beyond the immanence of creation, and whose manifestation in Jesus Christ heralds a redemption of the fallenness of the creation. While the God of the Old Testament is the God of the Law, the God of the New Testament is the God of grace and salvation (an opposition that implicitly sharpened the rejection of Judaism). The God of the Old Testament is unveiled to be a malign demiurge whose

---

[77] J. Taubes, "Theodicy and Theology: A Philosophical Analysis of Karl Barth's Dialectical Theology," in *From Cult to Culture* (Stanford, CA: Stanford University Press, 2010): 177–194; p. 186.
[78] Lazier, *God Interrupted*, p. 32.
[79] For a critical reappraisal of Harnack's Marcion, S. Moll, *The Arch-Heretic Marcion* (Tübingen: Mohr Siebeck, 2010).
[80] As Harnack's daughter recalls in her biography of her father. Quoted in Faber, *Political Demonology*, p. ix.
[81] Quoted in Faber, *Political Demonology*, p. ix.

creation bears the contamination of corruption. The God of the New Testament announces to the world the Gospel of salvation, love, and grace. Until the advent of Christ, human existence was alienated from itself as well as from God; only with the arrival of the alien God, incarnated in Christ, can human existence – until then a stranger to itself – become extracted from the world and "received in a new father's house." As Harnack writes: "Is it not always a failed undertaking when one strives to harmonize the essence and nature of faith, its ground and hope, with the 'world' – that is, to comprehend faith from the perspective of reason?"[82] Whereas the Gnostic slide of the Protestant Harnack hinged on accentuating God's "wholly otherness" and "infinitely alienness" to creation, thus sharing, only in this respect, an emphasis on God's other-worldly alterity in Barth, the interwar attraction to Pantheism (critically commented upon in Scheler's *On the Eternal in Man*) accentuated, by contrast, the collapse of distance between God and the world, and indeed the dissolution of a personal or theistic God. Both tendencies in postwar religious thought attested to a shattered faith in humanism, scientific rationalism, and human mastery over the world. An existential anxiety in humankind's inability to bestow sense upon the fallenness of the world and suffering fertilized the cultural and philosophical uptake of Gnosticism as well as Pantheism.

The discussion of the Eternal Thou functions on an existential level in responding to the "deeper horror" instantiated in *I and Thou*, as well as providing a response to the pervasive crisis of religious thought in Germany and, for Buber equally unacceptable, the alternatives of the radical otherness of God and the radical identification of God with the world. There is yet another dimension in which Buber's discussion operates; namely, with regard to the dialogical ambiguity of the human condition itself. As established in *I and Thou*, the "in-betweenness" of human existence is defined by the polarity of two souls: "a force of disorder without purpose" (I–It relations) and "movement of the Good 'in the direction of home'" (I–Thou relations).[83] I–Thou relations suffer from a discontinuity that can only be alleviated – paradoxically – by becoming frozen, and hence arrested, into the permanence and continuity of I–It relations. This discontinuity of I–Thou relations (contracted and withdrawn, and yet latent) represents "the fundamental question from which," as Buber writes, "alone we may grasp what may be rightly called religion. It is the question of the continuity

---

[82] A. von Harnack, *Marcion: The Gospel of the Alien God*, trans. J. Steely and L. Bierma (Eugene, OR: Wipf & Stock, 2007), p. 30.

[83] P. Bouretz, *Witnesses for the Future: Philosophy and Messianism*, trans. M. Smit (Baltimore, MD: Johns Hopkins University Press, 2010), p. 400.

of the Thou, of the unconditionality of the Thou."[84] It is this fragility of the I–Thou relation that is experienced in the "deeper horror" from which there issues a cry in the desert to the Eternal Thou as the silent question of the redemptive imperative.

Rather than speak *of* God, Buber's dialogical relation to the Eternal Thou effects an ontological rupture with conceptions of God as "infinite substance," "perfected being," and "self-created being." The locution "the Eternal Thou" expresses in dialogical speech the unspoken appellation of God that wafts across the diversity of human religions. As Buber writes: "all names of God remain hallowed – because they have been used not only to speak *of* God but also to speak *to* him."[85] God is not an "object" determinable in terms of an I–It relation, nor encapsulated in a subjective, however intense, lived experience. "Eternal" is not an attribute of something; the Thou "is" the Eternal (*der Ewige*). With this adjectival substantive, Buber displaces a substance nominative–based ontology of God with the living dialogical word "to God."[86] Buber's "deontologization" of God opens an alternative to God either remaining in the world or God being found outside, or beyond, the world. As with Otto and Barth, Buber advocates a renewal of religion, but places the source of religious life not with the noumenal "Holy" (as with Otto) or the utterly alien (as with Barth). In an I–Thou relation, the I stands before the Thou not as object of recognition or feeling, but in the mode of response, responding to the *being* of the other, as otherness. Every I–Thou relation among human beings carries within itself an "extended line" that reaches forth and offers a glimpse of the Eternal Thou. God is both "the ground" and "the way." God's dialogical presence speaks to us not only through us, but through things as well, and hence through nature and the world, summoning human beings to a responsibility for creation. Indeed, Buber contends that a silent dialogue with God is refracted and thus glimpsed in dialogical relation with others. We stand, in this sense, "in" God's presence, and yet God, as Eternal Thou, stands beyond the world. What inhibits losing ourselves in the noumenal unity of God's presence, as with Buber's prewar *Erlebnis* mysticism, is this anchoring and relatedness to others; and yet, what prevents us from losing ourselves entirely into the world of It-relations, to which I–Thou relations inevitably succumb, is the transcendence of God's presence.

---

[84] M. Buber, "Religion als Gegenwart," Band 12, *Schriften zu Philosophie und Religion*, ed. A. Noor and K. Schreck (Gütersloh: Gütersloher Verlagshaus, 2018): 87–160, p. 108.
[85] Buber, *I and Thou*, p. 123.
[86] S. Bergman, *Dialogical Philosophy from Kierkegaard to Buber*, trans. A. Gersten (Albany: State University of New York, 1991), pp. 154–155.

This approach entails that the human is likewise no longer understood as a created being from a God who stands either remote from creation or immanent to it. "Of course," Buber writes, "God is 'the wholly other'" – in tacit reference to Otto – but "he is also wholly the same: the wholly present."[87] This proximity of distance is, however, not to be characterized as a feeling of dependence (as with Schleiermacher) or creature feeling (Otto, for his part, distinguishes between "creature" and "creaturehood"). The feeling of creaturehood is not, as with Otto, "nothingness before God," but by the same token, the otherness of God is not, as with Barth, beyond the actualization of human dialogical relations in the world. God is neither immanent to the world nor transcendent from the world. As Buber writes: "One does not find God if one remains in the world; one does not find God if one leaves the world." God is "wholly other" *and* "wholly the same," and in this sense, God is both "the *mysterium tremendum*" and the "mystery of the obvious that is closer to me than my own I," namely, as abiding in I–Thou relations.[88] In this regard, Buber speaks of the Eternal Thou as "the becoming of the existing God" (*ein Werden des seienden Gottes*); in God's becoming, we ourselves participate in creation, and hence encounter "the creator," not as the ontological cause of being or a supreme being, but in a living commemoration of and confidence in God's dialogical creation. In the relation to the Eternal Thou, unconditional exclusiveness and unconditional inclusiveness are one in the sense that nothing retains importance outside of it and everything outside of it only gains importance within it. The Eternal Thou is encountered in the face of every person encountered as a Thou, and yet cannot be identified with any Thou in particular nor fall into the form of an It. Dialogical relatedness to the Eternal Thou is singularly lived, and hence not universal, through the particularity of other human beings, not a "person" in whom one "believes," but a presence in which one stands in living with others in community and communion. As Buber writes: "it is the reality of the between in its unconditional, that is, absolute."

Dialogical relatedness to the Eternal Thou must be embedded in relations to others, and hence in a social community of living together in trust and confidence. This triadic dialogical relation (I and Thou, I and Eternal Thou, Eternal Thou and community of "Thous") instills trust or, more accurately stated, faith as trust and confidence, and this trust is lived in a

---

[87] Buber, *I and Thou*, p. 127. For the theological and wartime contexts for Otto's *Das Heilige*, P. Almond, *Rudolf Otto: An Introduction to His Philosophical Theology* (Chapel Hill: University of North Carolina Press, 1984).
[88] Buber, *I and Thou*, p. 127.

twofold relation: to God and to other humans. This trust is categorically different to a sense of security and safety vis-à-vis the risks of the It-world; it is also not a postulate of reason or a prudential principle, but the manner of being in the world – existing – and orientation toward the world. Robustly, trust is not a feeling but an "entrance into reality"; indeed, an "existential reality," through which, or in which, God becomes lived as a person along with others as well.[89] As Buber writes: "[trust] is essentially the act of holding fast to God. And that does not mean holding fast to the faith in God one has conceived. It means holding fast to the existing God."[90] Love is a personal relation in trust of God and others, but also standing elected to be oneself entrusted with responsibility for others, and the world, in God. God is thus the between as the Absolute: transcendent and immanent, of the world and beyond it, presence and absence, hidden and yet always silently addressing us from behind our backs, and this "and," in the multiple declinations, is not static but a movement, in fact a tension inscribed within an incessant excitation of polarity. The presence of the Eternal Thou is the eccentric center for the interhuman in terms of which the earth becomes a place of dwelling, a "house and home."[91] On earth, we walk together with others in communion with the unfinished narrative of creation itself. In a letter to Franz Werfel in 1917, Buber writes:

> God reveals himself in your wanting to become, not in your waiting for grace [...] It is not I who wait, God waits that he can say to me, to you, to *every single person* what, according to the report of the Hebrew Gospel the spirit spoke to Jesus when he raised him in baptism to sonship: My son, I have awaited you in all the prophets, that you shall come and I should find peace in you. You are indeed my peace.[92]

We do not wait for "God" – the Eternal Thou – but walk toward the Eternal Thou in participating, in trust and entrustment, in the dialogical creation of the world, human community, and the Eternal Thou's abiding presence to the world. As Buber writes: "Creation happens to us, burns itself into us, recasts us in burning – we tremble and are faint, we submit, we partake in creation, meet the Creator, reach out to Him, helpers and companions."[93]

---

[89] Buber, *I and Thou*, p. 80.
[90] Buber, *I and Thou*, p. 170.
[91] Quoted in Friedman, *Martin Buber's Life and Work*, p. 347.
[92] Quoted in Friedman, *Martin Buber's Life and Work*, p. 364.
[93] Buber, *I and Thou*, p. 83.

CHAPTER 4

More than Life
Georg Simmel's Philosophical Testament

"Life Has Not Vanquished Me"

On March 21, 1918, the German Army launched "Operation Michael" against British positions around Arras as the first stage of an offensive along the Western Front. Bolstered by reinforcements from the Eastern Front after the October 1917 Revolution and cessation of hostilities with Russia, the *Kaiserschlacht*, as it was called, represented a final gambit to win the war. A few days after the start of this titanic onslaught, Georg Simmel confided in a letter of March 25 to his friend Hermann Graf von Keyserling:

> Now I am in the midst of very difficult ethical and metaphysical investigations […] If I can still finish them, they shall represent my testament […] I am at an age [60] when the harvest must be brought in, and no further delay is allowed […] How difficult these years have been, and still remain, need not to be said, for these years have aged me at least two or three times the normal effect of time.[1]

It was not only premature aging that conspired against reaping his philosophical harvest: Simmel had been diagnosed with terminal liver cancer. As he writes to his friend, he finds himself in "very bad health" and severely reduced in "intellectual energy." In a subsequent letter of May 18, against the backdrop of a failed offensive that had run its course by the end of April (but continued in fits and starts until July), Simmel sympathizes with the Graf's existential despair that "the fate of the world has shattered the ground beneath one's feet" and wonders as well "whether the broken pieces that have been irreparably torn asunder can ever be put back together again – this suffering I understand well, since I, too, feel it to a high degree."[2] Throughout his life, he considered himself to be

---

[1] G. Simmel, *Briefe 1912–1918. Jugendbriefe*, eds. O. and A. Rammstedt (Frankfurt: Suhrkamp, 2008), p. 928.
[2] Simmel, *Briefe 1912–1918*, p. 952.

"a good German" and yet without contradiction also "a good European." That Europe is now lost, and Germany as well, "at least for my lifetime, is a sorrow that I shall never be able to overcome."[3] Already before the war, he notes, he had diagnosed Europe's collapse due to "exclusive capitalist valuation" and the "appalling age of the machine," and although he could not foresee then how the tragedy of modern culture would come to an end, he nonetheless believed "to have perceived certain indications of a new spirituality, true, as yet weak and without orientation, but in my eyes entirely unambiguous [...] But that's all over now." In 1918, on the brink of Germany's downfall, the broken pieces of modernity could never be made whole. Life had become groundless.

As the war labored its way to an end, Simmel lay dying. On September 11, Simmel writes to the painter Sabine Lepsius – a member of the Stefan Georg circle, whose son, Stefan, died at the front in 1917 – that he has put the finishing touches on a book. Knowing that his cancer has progressed beyond remission, Simmel takes leave of his friend: "I depart in profound gratitude and with the conviction that it is the right moment, and that life has not vanquished me."[4] In a letter of September 15 to Max and Marianne Weber, Simmel writes that "my life stands before me with unexpected completeness. I have just brought into safe harbor my final book, *Lebensanschauung*, and it will appear soon." As to other friends, Simmel closes his letter by bidding farewell: "And please accept my heartfelt gratitude for all the friendship and love that you have graced me with. So long as I can still breathe, I will feel this as a great gain of my life."[5] On September 26, Simmel passed away.[6] His "very difficult ethical and metaphysical investigations," *The View of Life: Four Metaphysics Chapters*, as his wife Gertrud (herself an author of philosophical works under the pseudonym Marie Luise Enckendorff) informs Graf von Keyserling on October 7, is set to appear in print. As she remarks: "He called it the final conclusion of his wisdom – I think it offers a cornucopia for all who understand how to receive that wisdom."

Published in December, Simmel considered *The View of Life* "his most mature work." Completed during the waning of Simmel's extraordinarily curious, prolific, and influential life, during the last gasps of a war he

---

[3] Simmel, *Briefe 1912–1918*, p. 953.
[4] Simmel, *Briefe 1912–1918*, p. 1015.
[5] Simmel, *Briefe 1912–1918*, p. 1024.
[6] As Marianne Weber recalls, Simmel's wife had written to her: "Let us count as a great fortune that he did not experience the last weeks" of Germany's collapse; *Buch des Dankes an Georg Simmel*, eds. K. Gassen and M. Landmann (Berlin: Duncker & Humblot, 1958), p. 218.

intimately understood to have spelled the end for an already tragic world, *The View of Life* bears testimony to a philosophical life nearing its end, amid a world in ruins, in pursuit of a thinking beyond itself.[7] Composed under the duress not merely of accelerated aging but of cancerous death, along with Germany's and Europe's demise, Simmel's testament – part finale, part overture – reaches forth into an unknown future. As Simmel writes in a letter to Margarete Susman, "the war placed a punctuation mark where I had expected a semi-colon. I am convinced that a new epoch of the world begins and that I have grown old. Of course, I do not believe as with others to be able to affect the future, but the world has taken a turn [...] My doing and thinking stretches into the future, what will now become a present, and that I have to spread the seed where there is no farmland."[8]

Border Fortress

The twilight of Simmel's life occurred in a condition of internal displacement, both geographically and intellectually. With French forces advancing in 1917, Simmel and his wife were forced to evacuate Strasbourg and relocate to Kassel. But then again, exile was not an unfamiliar condition for Simmel, as his career had been marked by academic marginality, despite the cultural reach of his thinking, as well as his dislocation from fashionable trends and entrenched forms of thought. Repeatedly thwarted on account of anti-Semitism from obtaining a chair in philosophy or promotion at the University of Berlin, where Simmel had taught since 1885, he finally obtained in 1914 a professorship at the University of Strasbourg. Although a recent territorial acquisition after the Franco-Prussian War, Alsace-Lorraine effectively remained outside the sphere of prestigious inland German universities. This borderland status became further exacerbated with the outbreak of war. On August 1, Strasbourg was placed under the command of the military governor of the fortress

---

[7] Simmel began work on this book in 1914 when he arrived in Strasbourg. Frisby rightly notes an increasing sense of disillusionment in Simmel's letters after his move to Strasbourg; see D. Frisby, *Georg Simmel* (London: Routledge, 2002), p. 33. As Goodstein writes: "In his final four years, working not just under the globally terrible conditions of wartime, but in the acute circumstances of the garrison town, Simmel produced a series of essays and talks in which he strove publicly to convey that vision – a striving that culminates in the beautiful and profound work that he would call his 'last word of wisdom'"; E. Goodstein, *Georg Simmel and the Disciplinary Imaginary* (Stanford, CA: Stanford University Press, 2017), p. 340.

[8] Simmel, *Briefe 1912–1918*, p. 534. As Simmel writes in his Journal Aphorisms: "I know that I shall die without spiritual heirs (and that is as it should be). Mine is like a cash legacy divided among many heirs, and each converts his share into whatever business suits *his* nature, in which the provenance from that legacy cannot be seen."

in a state of emergency. On August 2, Simmel writes on a postcard to Hugo Liepmann: "I am experiencing the most tumultuous days of my life. Yet, one cannot imagine what it means to be in a border-fortress."[9] Public gatherings and political organizations were banned; newspapers were monitored; letters had to be mailed in unsealed envelopes; telephone lines and railway connections to Switzerland and Germany were severed. In a letter to the Jastrows (August 16), Simmel speaks of "the great fortune we three [Simmel, his wife, and their son] are living on an island." The city is "as if it had died out," quotidian life was suspended, and only military activity could be seen on the streets. As he observes: "I have the impression that the proximity to the events here produces an entirely different atmosphere. There is no trace of victory-enthusiasm in this serious, still, and nearly abandoned city."[10] During outings in the surrounding forests, he occasionally hears the thunder of artillery fire – "knowing that it is tearing apart human bodies into pieces" – from the Vosges mountains, and this proximity to the front lines produced a palpable tension on a "quiet Sunday afternoon in a happy corner of the earth." This borderland existence between the front lines in France and the home front in Germany was mirrored in his experience of temporal liminality. As Simmel writes (August 22) to Susman, his "lived experience" is profoundly disjointed, for a "thick line has been drawn" separating the past from the future:

> Life stands on an entirely new basis, the breadth and depth of which I did not anticipate. It is unimaginable that as long as we live we could return impartially to old assumptions. An unprecedented experience, the destiny of an entire world of culture that becomes immediately felt as entirely personal, not as a part, but as the whole, and each individual carries the whole; the peculiar feeling to embrace the whole and at the same time with this expansion, which nearly explodes, the thought of destruction. I am not truly a chauvinist but I shall be proud about Germany until the end and Germany can rise to the hour of its fate. But what is most heavy still lies before us.[11]

Simmel's borderland existence manifested itself as well in an internalized conflict, attested to throughout his letters, between an urgency to contribute directly to the war effort and regret at his inability to do so; indeed, guilt at having been unable to enlist: "It is as if one made an egotistical exception for oneself when one cannot sacrifice anything while the most noble blood of Germany is spilled."[12] His wife and son were enlisted

---

[9] Simmel, *Briefe 1912–1918*, p. 359.
[10] Simmel, *Briefe 1912–1918*, p. 386.
[11] Simmel, *Briefe 1912–1918*, p. 372.
[12] Simmel, *Briefe 1912–1918*, p. 461.

in tending to wounded soldiers, however, and Simmel himself served as a military telephone operator and censor in the communications bureau. As he writes in a letter:

> what impresses me every hour but which gives me nightmares is the madness of this world-destiny and European destruction. If I were a warrior, I would declare: No, I do not fight for a general humanist value, I fight for Germany, because I love Germany and want that it lives and breathes and is not trampled to death by Cossacks and Turks. No one in Germany wants to destroy the enemy but the enemy wants to destroy Germany, and this is the chaos of our world today, that our enemies want to destroy us radically. The super-personal is however today the most personal affair.[13]

This fusion of *Das Überpersönliches* and *Das persönlichste* found expression in Simmel's prolific contributions to the spiritual mobilization of the nation.[14] In addition to giving public lectures in Germany, often for the purpose of raising charity funds for wounded soldiers and widows, Simmel took it upon himself to shape public perception of the war in neutral countries and respond to Allied anti-German vitriol, most notably against Bergson, despite the latter's significant influence on Simmel's thinking. As Simmel argues to the Danish philosopher Harald Høffding in a letter of October 2, 1914, it is incontrovertible that Germany was forced into the war. Germany has everything to lose and nothing to gain. "Who are the real barbarians," Simmel asks, "given that Germany represents a bulwark against Russian hordes? If Cossacks were to defile the Brandenburg Gate, that would be something never to forget nor to forgive."[15] By 1916, however, Simmel had decided to curtail his efforts at influencing public opinion abroad since, as he writes, too much has happened, and to no avail, in this respect.[16] Nevertheless, Simmel continued to exercise his rhetorical prowess at home by offering lectures for soldiers on the front lines in courses at the "flying university," organized by the German military for the spiritual welfare of wounded and resting troops. As he reports on one occasion to Susman:

> I have spent a strange week giving a course at the front [...] it was a marvelous experience to lecture on Plato's theory of ideas with cannons at Verdun thundering above! [...] Our one and only task should be nothing else than,

---

[13] Simmel, *Briefe 1912–1918*, p. 371.
[14] For a discussion of Simmel's war writings, P. Watier, "Georg Simmel et la guerre," in *Kultur und Krieg. Die Rolle der Intellektuellen, Künstler und Schriftsteller im Ersten Weltkrieg*, ed. W. Mommsen (Berlin: Walter de Gruyter, 1995): 31–47.
[15] Simmel, *Briefe 1912–1918*, p. 400.
[16] Simmel, *Briefe 1912–1918*, p. 461.

from morning until evening, to spin the threads leading to the spirit of the future; even the thinnest of threads can be of service.[17]

Spiritual Decisions

Bereft of assurances that he would live to witness the end of the war and knowing that not much time remained for him to "spin threads of service," however thin, Simmel was keen to impart "a little wisdom" to posterity.[18] Simmel's final philosophical testament, *The View of Life*, cannot be disassociated, however, from another testament bequeathed to posterity in 1917.[19] Announced by his publisher as Simmel's *Kriegsbuch*, *Der Krieg und die geistigen Entscheidungen* brings together four texts: "Deutschlands innere Wandlung" (1914); "Die Dialektik des deutschen Geistes" (1916); "Die Krisis der Kultur" (1916); and "Die Idee Europa" (1916). Simmel's decision to publish this selection is not without intrigue, since it contravened an official government order from 1915 that he refrain from publishing his views on the war due to essays that had caught the disapproving eye and ire of military censors in Strasbourg.[20] Faced with a disciplinary hearing, Simmel was compelled to defend himself against charges of "un-German conduct" and "anti-German sentiments" by the Imperial Governor.[21] Avoiding dismissal from his university position, Simmel was cleared of these charges, but not without a stern reprimand that such conduct was unbecoming of a German university professor. Public pronouncements concerning the war were "unconditionally to cease." In 1917, Simmel must have nonetheless felt compelled by the deterioration of Germany's situation (as well as his own health) to defy this prohibition. In the preface to his *Kriegsbuch*, written in April 1917 with a dedication "To my friends in Straßburg im Elsaß," Simmel writes of wanting to give a "permanent literary form" to his interpretation of the "inner side of world destiny" in

---

[17] Simmel, *Briefe 1912–1918*, p. 834.
[18] According to Helle: "When he felt himself to be incurably ill, he asked his doctor: How long do I still have to live? He needed to know because his most important book still had to be finished. The doctor told him the truth and Simmel withdrew and completed: *Lebensanschauung*"; H. J. Helle, *Messages from Georg Simmel* (Leiden: Brill, 2012), p. 87.
[19] As Hans Joas and Wolfgang Knöbl observe, Simmel's lectures and writings in support of the war "certainly do not represent a break in his thinking"; *Kriegsverdrängung. Ein Problem in der Geschichte der Sozialtheorie* (Frankfurt: Suhrkamp, 2008), p. 186. See also S. Moebius, "Georg Simmel's Political Thought: Socialism and Nietzschean Aristocratism," *Journal of Classical Sociology* (2021): 1–43, https://doi.org/10.1177/1468795X211053993.
[20] The first essay was published in Sweden: "Kulturarbetet efter Kriget" in *Svenska Dagbladet*, May 17, 1915. The second essay, "Europa und Amerika," in *Berliner Tageblatt*, July 4, 1915.
[21] G. Simmel, *Gesamelte Ausgabe* 16 (Frankfurt: Suhrkamp, 1999), p. 429. Hereafter GA.

view of what is to come. Of course, he remarks, previsions and predictions for the future can either be refuted or confirmed by what has not yet happened; nonetheless, "these contemporary documents" sketch the "decisive contour" of the future to come, or what he likewise calls a "co-decisive contour of the future," as if his essays were circumscribing figurations of a possible, indeed desired, future after the war, toward which his reflections were meant to lead.[22] As is evident in his correspondence, wartime lectures, and publications, Simmel's attitude toward the war fluctuated considerably until his death, although he never wavered in supporting his Fatherland.[23] In 1914, Simmel, as with other academic thinkers and intellectuals, sees the war as an opportunity to transform modern culture and galvanize the unity of the German nation. During the *Ideenwende* of 1915–16, Simmel becomes increasingly concerned with the Americanization of Europe – a theme of reflection already sounded in his 1896 essay "Money and Modern Culture," where he warned of the potential Americanization of the twentieth century – given America's material support of the Allies and, eventually, entrance into the war in April 1917.

Delivered in November 1914 as a public lecture in Strasbourg, "Deutschlands innere Wandlung" opens with the evocation of "the absolute situation" in which Simmel and his compatriots find themselves. The shock affecting "every soul" in Germany is deemed comparable to moments of "epochal transformation," for example the millennial year 1000, when the end of the world was thought nigh "without people knowing whether they were damned or saved." We live, Simmel continues, under circumstances of fundamental uncertainty regarding the future, yet existential decisions – individually as well as collectively – still need to be made. In this war, Germany must become radically other, and even if no positive image can yet be formed for the Germany to come, Simmel assures his audience that it shall not be a restoration of "old Germany," but the fulfillment of 1871 on an "entirely new basis." Although the war shattered the "pregiven conditions of life," one can glimpse in this absolute situation the horizon for an "othering of life into more than life as it was and is." As Simmel states, "the greatest gain of these great times is the decisiveness with which each individual must stand before an existential decision about what matters most." Practical and utilitarian interests must therefore cede to the imperative that individuals need to bind themselves to the nation

---

[22] Simmel, GA 16, p. 9.
[23] Leck identifies three stages in Simmel's assessment of the war, but fails to recognize *Lebensanschauung* as essential for Simmel's "search for a postwar world"; R. Leck, *Georg Simmel and Avant-Garde Sociology* (Lexington, KY: Humanity Books, 2000).

based on an intimate decision, and hence, in personal freedom and responsibility, to participate in the realization of the nation. This "new kind of relation," binding "the most personal" with "the supra-personal," proves difficult to articulate, but Simmel nonetheless sees it exemplified by "the warrior on the battlefield," who subsumes his individual existence to the supra-personal value of the nation. As Simmel writes: "That is the most wonderful thing about these times that the day reaches above the day, that everything practical, everything of the moment, is significant for the shaping of Germany in an unforeseeable future." The absolute situation in which each individual has been thrown by the war represents the advent of salvation from the fragmentation and alienation of modern life. "Actual history," Simmel proposes, requires the birth of the (as yet) nonexistent that ruptures the complacency of everyday life. Prior to 1914, everyday life was determined by the "oscillation of hunger and love" and cyclical rhythms of transitoriness, not by a striving for an existence beyond the transitory toward the timeless, which, in this historicizing time of war, becomes a responsibility for each of us. There is, however, no "profound historical necessity" for the war – indeed, Simmel is convinced that without "the blindness and criminal frivolity of a few individuals this war would never have happened" – yet the war nonetheless demands sacrifice. A higher dimension of purposiveness becomes revealed as an objective *ethos* for everyone, with every individual encouraged to "reach beyond the day" for more than life. Each of us, Simmel argues, is responsible "as never before," thus imparting "gravity to our decisions and actions, but also their supreme value."[24] In this characterization of the war as an absolute situation, the term "absolute" serves as an "appellative metaphor," meant to persuade his audience to view the war as a decisive moment for the surpassing of the relativism and indecisiveness of modernity to which they had become all too accustomed or resigned.[25]

And yet, Simmel still wonders: "who can tell if future generations, our great-grand-children, will look back at this catastrophe to curse it or bless it for the loss of so many precious human beings?" Regardless of how the future will retrospectively assess the war, Simmel reiterates his confidence that from this absolute situation of "not-knowing knowledge," a "new form of human existence" and "new axial age" will emerge: "life shall be a different one." This anticipated "metamorphosis of life," moreover, will be

---

[24] As Simmel parenthetically remarks, "that our victory requires the sacrifice of a wonderful old cathedral is a symbol for what stands before us"; GA 16, p. 21.

[25] M. Riedel, *Metaphysik des Irgendwie. Georg Simmel als Philosoph* (Freiburg: Alber Verlag, 2021), p. 175.

indissociable from a "metamorphosis of culture," one that promises to surmount "the tragedy of modern culture."[26] Given the economic deprivation befalling Germany (due to Allied blockades) but nonetheless the solidarity emerging from the shattering of everyday existence, Simmel anticipates the dissolution of a cultural malaise that, in his view, progressively gained dominance over the modern world; what he terms Mammonism. Under this heading, Simmel does not understand what the Bible speaks of as greed ("Ye cannot serve God and Mammon," Matthew 6:24). The modern manifestation of Mammonism, for Simmel, cannot be associated with a psychological affliction of inordinate and insatiable desires, but refers instead to the transformation of money into an all-encompassing form of objectivity and saturating of the valuing of life with metaphysical pretension.[27] As Simmel argues in *The Philosophy of Money*, "money has become the God of our time [...] Just as with the truly pious believer, he prays to his God not because he wants something or needs something from God, but because God is the absolute."[28]

What characterizes modern life is a pervasive relativism and interminable conflict of values. In *The Philosophy of Money*, Simmel looks to the phenomenon of money to develop a "philosophy of relativism." In the modern world, money expresses and encapsulates the relativism of modern life, but, by the same token, money, in its historically unprecedented autonomy, allows for the mediation and stabilization of conflicts. Money has been anointed a "new God," for "the most profound essence of the concept of God is reached in its ability to unify the multiplicity and contradictions of the world." In this regard, money girds the plasticity of social relations and individual differentiation in granting individuals extensive social mobility along with an intensification of self-differentiation (as exemplified in fashion). The power of consumer purchase lies in acquiring ever novel social associations and identities; the acceleration of reciprocal relationships (*Wechselwirkungen*) and dissolution of fixed social hierarchies is likewise enabled by the modern economy. As Simmel writes, "the more the life of society becomes determined by money economy, the more effectively and distinctly conscious life becomes of its relative character of existence." The circulation of money symbolizes the dissolution of substantial forms and fixed social orders through an incessant movement of *Wechselwirkungen*,

---

[26] Simmel, GA 16, p. 16.
[27] As Leck observes: "it is very important that Simmel found it necessary to express his critique of monetary culture from within a tradition, Christianity, which his Nietzschean philosophy had so consistently and thoroughly rejected"; *Georg Simmel and Avant-Garde Sociology*, p. 185.
[28] G. Simmel, *The Philosophy of Money*, trans. T. Bottomore and D. Frisby (London: Routledge, 2011).

but what remains constant throughout is the spectral autonomy of money itself, this new God. As a universal medium of exchange for value that itself lacks intrinsic value, "money has increasingly become an absolutely self-sufficient expression and equivalent of all values."[29] The value of value becomes transmogrified into value without substance or subjectivity, and thus, on the one hand, conditions the intensification of individualism (consumer buying power, individual differentiation) and, on the other, the intensification of social fragmentation and indifference toward culture as a whole. A modern individual is paradoxically determined by the value objectification of money *while* considering themselves emancipated from social conformity through the power of purchase and consumer self-affirmation. The circulation of money and its paramount social symbolism sustain a unity without a dialectical resolution between individual differentiation (individuals as affirmed in their difference from each other) and the absence of a collective ethical life (indifference toward others and social wellbeing in general). The ruse of money is to give a unified dynamic to modern life while obscuring its contradictions and conflicts. As significantly, money's ubiquitous function of mediation reveals the presence of "the somehow" – that *somehow* everything is bound and connected with everything else, that *somehow* the complexity of modern social relations belongs to a whole – that defines modernity, but also Simmel's own style of thinking and writing about modern life. Hence the fragmentary, essayistic, and open style of his writing, as with *The Philosophy of Money*, that refuses systematicity and fixity.[30]

The war, however, promises to strip the facade away from acculturated money to reveal what matters most existentially. Simmel sounds an optimistic note that sacrifice at the front and economic hardship at home will prove decisive in overcoming Mammonism. Monetary and instrumental rationality, he proposes, will give way to an experience of genuine meaningfulness for life and culture. This prognosis, predicated on German victory in a spiritually transformative and material (on the battlefield) sense, became tenuous in Simmel's mind with America's creeping entrance into the war. In the essays "Europa und America" (1915) and "Die Idee Europa" (1915), Simmel speaks of "the suicide of Europe," which, he fears, is paving the way for the global ascension of America.[31] Even without the war,

---

[29] Simmel, GA 16, p. 63.
[30] As Riedel insightfully argues, "dieses *Irgendwie* ist ein geradzu methodisches Element des Simmel'schen Philosophierens"; *Metaphysik des Irgendwie*, p. 16.
[31] The essay was published in the newspaper *Berliner Tageblatt* (a prominent liberal newspaper) in July 1915 (Spring 1915 saw the Shell Crisis in England).

Simmel acknowledges that the future of Europe will be American, which, as with Max Weber, represented the epitome of the modern disenchantment of the world.[32] Europe, and not just Germany, would ultimately be the loser of the war. As Simmel writes to Graf von Keyserling on March 25, 1918, not just "the reality, but the *Idea* of Europe has disappeared, since it is finally not an eternal idea as with humanity or beauty, but an historical Idea." As he continues, one "could be resigned to the hope that in many decades and perhaps in another form this idea would once again emerge – if America would not exist."

In "Krisis der Kultur" (a lecture delivered in Vienna in 1916), Simmel sharpens his focus on the tragedy of modern culture through the lens of the war.[33] Understood broadly, culture is the patterned assemblage of forms of meaning (aesthetic, social, ethical values, institutions, etc.) that are indispensable for the manifestation of (human) life. The soul, in Simmel's language, cannot achieve "actuality" without the mediation of cultural forms that give purposiveness to life through configured relations of means and ends. Historically variable and culturally diverse forms of purposiveness are held together in a unified whole under the aegis of an encompassing transcendent idea – God, for example, in Medieval Christianity. What distinguishes modern culture is not only its fragmentation, but the absence of any standpoint or transcendental signifier (God, for example) under which to integrate the multiplicity of forms into a whole. This pervasive relativism is accentuated with the estrangement of modern life from its own cultural forms, experienced as external and autonomous, and armed with a purposiveness no longer in concert with life itself. The "tremendous and extensive growth of technology" enmeshes life in a complex network of means and ends without an overarching goal; that is, meaningfulness. With the quickening pace of technological advancements, modern life perpetually feels itself to be too late, falling behind the next innovation, while also sensing itself to be too early, waiting in vain for technological miracles to resolve life's fundamental conflicts.[34] Parsed in subjective terms, modern life is adrift in a self-perpetuating movement of "more" – more consumption, more technological progress, more money – without

---

[32] J.-L. Evard, "La philosophie de la vie part en guerre," in *Georg Simmel face à la guerre* (Paris: Éditions Rue d'Ulm, 2015), p. 97ff.

[33] For an unsurpassed discussion of Simmel's sociology of modern culture and its resonance among his contemporaries, Leck, *Georg Simmel and Avant-Garde Sociology*.

[34] For the broader turn-of-the-century context for the acceleration of cultural experience and the First World War, S. Kern, *The Culture of Time and Space, 1880–1918* (Cambridge, MA: Harvard University Press, 2003).

fundamental significance; in objective terms, cultural forms reign over life as an autonomous and lifeless empire ruled and running according to their own obscure norms and opaque directives. The tragedy of modern culture thus consists in a qualitative alienation of subjective and objective, along with a quantitative formless infinity. The drive for infinite consumption and the manic imperative to differentiate one's individuality ad infinitum are exemplary of "formless infinity." The hyperindividualism of fetishized freedom contributes to and becomes reinforced by social fragmentation and indifference. The oppressiveness of modern life makes itself felt in being overwhelmed by countless unassimilable elements of culture. The culture of things (as with gadgets and consumer products) proliferates without end in both senses: without limit and without ultimate purpose. The capacity for living becomes more restrictive and narrow, less able to find itself, or recognize itself, in a world of increasing complexity, mediation, and indifference.[35]

In his essay "Konflikt der modernen Kultur" (published in July and August of 1918 and first delivered as a lecture in Berlin in January 1918), Simmel reformulates his view of the tragedy of modern culture. There is an inevitable conflict between spirit ("life beyond animality") and culture. This Heraclitan flux of cultural-historical existence expresses the "infinite fruitfulness of life," but equally the "profound contradiction between eternal becoming and self-transformation against objective norms" – "*Es bewegt sich zwischen Stirb und Werde – Werde und Stirb.*"[36] In the twilight of 1918, Simmel argues that a new phase in this "ancient struggle" has set upon Europe, with the epoch-defining qualification that it is no longer a question of a conflict between vital emergent forms and deadened forms of the past, such that life renews its spiritual vitality through the overcoming of the old and the creation of the new. What distinguishes the plight of the modern world, grotesquely manifest in a war seemingly without end, is that life has turned against form as such, thus rendering life groundless and astray in a world of forms through which it can no longer find orientation and significance. Every cultural epoch is structured through oppositions, transformations, and conflicts, and yet every cultural epoch has historically been united under a transcendental, or highest, value: for Classical Greeks, in the Idea of Being; for the Medieval world, God. Developments leading up to 1914 witnessed a deviation from ingrained patterns of cultural transformation, where new forms replaced established forms. Rather than a desire

---

[35] Simmel, GA 16, p. 39.
[36] Simmel, GA 16, p. 186.

for new forms of wholeness, modernity has devolved into the fetishism of fragments in opposition to the principle of form as such.[37] What characterizes the exceptionality of the modern age is the rejection of a metanarrative or an axial center. Modernity is a postaxial age. As Simmel writes, "of a cultural idea that would reign over the whole man and his activities we no longer hear about anymore." In fact, when asked "under what idea do you exist?," we can only offer specific answers since we have lost the meaningfulness of posing the question of the sense of being as such. As Simmel writes: "We gaze into an abyss of unformed life beneath our feet. But perhaps this formlessness is the appropriate form for contemporary life."

We Hollow Beings

As Susman, one of Simmel's most astute readers (and students), writes: "Simmel's death at the end of the First World War marks the boundary from which a new form of thinking becomes deployed."[38] This new form of thinking winding across the meditative pages of *The View of Life* arose from Simmel's experience of the war as a time out of joint, profoundly scarred by the devastation of human existence. As Susman remarks: "Western philosophy as a whole had truly arrived at its end. Needed was a new thinking as well as a new language to express the problems of a new age," indeed, "an Exodus from previous philosophy," from Parmenides to Hegel, that stood speechless before the question of human existence. At the center of Simmel's philosophical testament, human existence is confronted against the backdrop of the disappearance and disenchantment of transcendence. The eclipsing of transcendence, once giving fundamental significance and orientation in the world to human life, was for Simmel both subversive and emancipatory. According Susman, "no Western thinker has thus far gone so far in the dissolution of all transcendence, and from this dissolution sought to win a new faith, and a new faith in the integral religiosity of the human," not, however, religion as faith in the supersensible nor faith

---

[37] Simmel, GA 16, p. 190.
[38] M. Susman, *Die Geistige Gestalt Georg Simmels* (Tübingen: J. C. B. Mohr, 1959), p. 35. As Goodstein likewise argues, Simmel responds to a "crisis of meaning in European life," a faltering of "transcendent truth," and "destruction of the cultural world that had given meaning to his life." "His meditations on life's transcendence disclose the possibility of meaning in mortality; his conception of the 'individual law' locates ethical action within the very fragmentation and disenchantment of post-theological existence; his vision of cultural life as self-overcoming creation of forms affirms human being in a world devoid of enduring standards of truth or value, where nihilism of instrumental reason and the vacuity of the forms of objectivity fostered by the money economy were becoming apparent"; *Georg Simmel and the Disciplinary Imaginary*, p. 339.

in any traditional form, but as a "pure transcendence without a concept of the beyond," a transcendence immanent to yet more than life. In a world without gods afflicted with the worship of golden calves, how is authentic existence, given its contingency and singularity, possible?

What Simmel felt to be the truth, but also the question of his life, was reflected in the truth, but also the question, of life itself. As he writes in an aphorism appended to *The View of Life*: "By my existence I am nothing more than an empty place, an outline, that is reserved within being in general. Given with it, though, is the duty to fill this empty place. That is my life."[39] We, hollow beings, are bound to fill and thereby fulfill – actualize – ourselves through culture, values, knowledge, art, and so on. This empty place of our existence stands as a placeholder for meaning – meanings that live and die, emerge and pass away. Throughout this ebb and flow, the direction, and hence the endurance, of spiritual life remains assured. All of this has changed with modernity, only to have been further accelerated by the war to a breaking point of no return. As Simmel writes in a letter to Susman, "before 1914 it was not paradise, but at least there was the perfume of nostalgia; and now with the war, we are looking to the future for a new form of life." In a world abandoned by the gods and in the refusal of transcendental forms, how can the formlessness of life become itself the source of its own meaningfulness? How can human existence orient itself toward transcendence in a world defined by the foreclosure of transcendence? How can we hollow beings achieve something more than life, finding it nowhere else than with the formless depth of life itself?[40] And so, by his own allowance, Simmel's final philosophical testament, deepening a constellation of questions that had preoccupied his thinking since the end of the nineteenth century, confronted what he discerned as the "new basic motif" of the twentieth century still to come: the formlessness, or groundlessness, of existence. As he writes: "What life is, because we ourselves are part of life, cannot be said. It must and will be left consciously ungrounded and unconceptual. The ultimate certainty that supported classical metaphysical positions becomes replaced by the final uncertainty."[41]

This final uncertainty animates the searching style of *The View of Life* and Simmel's pursuit of an "absolute" that could remain truthful to the "perhaps," or "somehow," of life. A book unlike any other, it is composed

---

[39] G. Simmel, *The View of Life*, trans. J. Andrews and D. Levine (Chicago: University of Chicago Press, 2010), p. 170.
[40] Simmel, GA, 12, p. 160.
[41] Quoted in Riedel, *Metaphysik des Irgendwie*, p. 149.

of four intermeshed essays.[42] In the first essay, "Transcendence of Life," Simmel reflects on human existence as characterized by self-transcendence in a twofold sense: as more life and as more than life. From this assessment, Simmel's thinking winds its way across three chapters: "The Turn Towards the Idea," "Death and Immortality," and "The Law of the Individual," weaving together the interconnected themes of "life," "world," "death," and "responsibility."[43]

In "Transcendence of Life," Simmel defines the facticity of life, or existence, as necessarily standing within boundaries that provide place, orientation, and meaning in the world. We are bounded beings, existing within limits, structures, and forms in the incessant ebb and flow of their settlement, transgression, and transformation. Boundaries delimit a range between higher and lower, more or less – a space of variable meaning. To be so determined is to exist between two poles, pulled and pushed in conflicting directions at once. This, then, characterizes the finitude of human existence: to exist in a situated manner within a tensile field of conflictual meanings. If life is thus always bound to a situation, it is also the case that every boundary, and hence situated form of existence, can be surpassed, as with the shifting borders of knowledge and ignorance regarding, for example, the consequences of our actions. This malleable relationality of boundaries is further exemplified by technology: telescopes and microscopes have broadened our perceptual experience, in so doing surpassing and reconfiguring the bounds of sense. With the spectacular technological transformations of the modern world, "we have thus transcended the compass of our natural being in certain directions; that is, the adaptation between our total organization and our world of perception."[44] The technological reconfiguration of perceptual boundaries corresponds to a transformation of social categories and ways of world disclosure. As Simmel observes, modernity has produced an outward displacement of boundaries into "the realm of the measureless," with the rebounding effect that we are "pressed back into our consciousness to the magnitude boundary of an infinitesimal point."[45]

---

[42] As Lizardo remarks, *The View of Life* is "a book like no other written by a classical theorist"; O. Lizardo, "The Resilience of Life: On Simmel's Last Testament," *Contemporary Sociology*, Vol. 41, No. 3 (2012): 302–304; p. 303.

[43] The second essay draws from the 1916 essay "Proto-forms of Ideas"; the third essay draws from the 1913 essay "Towards a Metaphysics of Death"; and the fourth essay draws from the 1913 essay "The Law of the Individual: An Essay toward the Principle of Ethics."

[44] Simmel, *The View of Life*, p. 4.

[45] Simmel, *The View of Life*, p. 4.

Insofar as we *are* boundaries, they no longer necessarily bind us, since in knowing ourselves to be the boundaries that we are, we have already stepped beyond them. As Simmel writes: "We deny the boundary the moment we know its one-sidedness, without thereby ceasing to stand within it. This is the only thing that allows us to be released from our despair about it, about our finiteness and mortality: that we do not simply stand *within* these boundaries."[46] To exist is "to be" and "not to be" in the situation in which we find ourselves. This does not represent a logical contradiction or dialectical opposition awaiting sublimation into a higher unity. We are beholden to the world in defined ways – historical, cultural, social – as well as projecting ourselves beyond our boundedness. Expressed in Simmel's Goethean language, life is animated by the polarity between becoming who we are and unbecoming who we have been, between bounded immanence and unbounded transcendence.[47] All forms and boundaries are hence intrinsically relative; that is, to be transgressed as well as transformed. The import of this metaphysical facticity is that the human is the limited being who possesses no limit: "we are bounded in every direction, and we are bounded by no direction."[48] Or, as Simmel eloquently states: "the human soul is the greatest cosmic endeavor with unsuitable means."[49] How are we able to fill the hollow of our being with something absolute, not just giving ourselves more life and hence, paradoxically, more hollowness, but something cosmically more than life, despite, it would seem, our unsuitableness to be anything other – more – than our hollow selves?

With these reflections in play, Simmel turns to the relation between temporality and existence. Time, he argues, can be understood in two ways: in chronological terms as the linear sequence of now-moments or in nonlinear terms as *durée* (here inspired by Bergson). With the former, we consider human existence to be "in time." With the latter, we consider human existence to be temporal through and through. In chronological time, each now-moment marks a boundary for "the collision of past and future." When we measure time – strictly speaking, events in time – what is measured is not the moment per se (since it lacks, on this account, extension, i.e., duration), but the span of time between two moments.

---

[46] Simmel, *The View of Life*, p. 5.
[47] Simmel, *The View of Life*, p. 9: "Life is at once flux without pause and yet something enclosed in its bearers and contents, formed about individualized midpoints, and contrarily it is therefore always a bounded form that continually oversteps its bounds; that is, its essence."
[48] Simmel, *The View of Life*, p. 2.
[49] Simmel, *The View of Life*, p. 166.

Echoing Aristotle's seminal definition, time is the number of motion (or change) with regard to the before and the after. Simmel repeats an established objection that with this notion of time, the now-moment is defined as instantaneous, and hence without temporal duration; time is composed of now-moments that are themselves nontemporal. Since the past and the future do not exist, reality would only occur in a nontemporal now-moment. As Simmel formulates this paradox: "time is not in reality, and reality is not in time."[50]

Unlike chronological time, the reality of life possesses an intrinsic temporality in which past, present, and future are not external to each other. With the temporality of human existence, the past is carried in the present: I *am* my past. The pastness of one's life, moreover, is not monolithic but composed of sedimented layers and "countless *individual* elements" that have not vanished in significance, but that protrude – "live for the day" (*Hineinleben*) – into the present. Many are the ways in which the past shapes and informs the present: as remembrance, habit, and so on. We exist beyond the present of our lives from the standpoint of the past inhering within it. The present always comes to pass; the past never ceases to be present. As significantly, Simmel argues that the future is not adequately understood when conceived merely in terms of anticipation. What it is to have a future – that is, living into a future – cannot be reduced to a conception of life as a "goal-setting being" whereby the future is modeled on the projection of a *telos* at a fixed point ahead of us, as if positioned on a line yet to be traversed. Although Simmel does not discount the relationality of means and ends, and hence a correlative temporalization of life, a goal (the future as goal directed) can only be projected based on an original protrusion (*Hineinleben*) of the future into the present. The projection of a goal or possibility into the future presupposes an original openness of the future. The future, as an indeterminate openness, must already have arrived, as it were, in the present in order for the present to stand directed in determined ways toward the future. The openness of life toward its own future resides in a facticity without a pregiven or prescribed *telos*. Human existence is without purpose in this temporal sense, in other words without a defined end, other than existing for the future as such.

Every lived moment is transcended in a twofold sense: through the protrusion of the past as well as the protrusion of the future. As Simmel writes: "We live perpetually in a border region that belongs as much to the past as to the future as to the present [and] insofar as life's essence

---

[50] Simmel, *The View of Life*, p. 6.

goes, transcendence is immanent to it (it is not something that might be added to its being, but instead is constitutive of its being)."[51] The temporality of existence sets life into an interactive relation of unity and difference, which, inspired by Goethe, Simmel conceives not in the manner of Hegelian dialectics or Kantian synthesis, but as a dialectical polarity. In this twofold condition of polarity, human existence is temporalized as "more life" and "more than life," as transience and transcendence. Along the vector of "more life," life is transient in traversing through itself, as it were, as its own temporal becoming: Each moment of my life is both more than the past of who I was, yet still am, and less than who I am yet to become, and still to be. Along the vector of "more than life," life seeks to transcend itself from within its own immanent transience. Cultural forms of meaning, relations of purposiveness, and other "spiritual forms" are expressions of life's movement of "more than life," without which life cannot meaningfully exist; that is, endure its own transience. Simmel in this regard speaks of the "turn towards Ideas" as encompassing the whole of cultural forms, as offering a transcendent horizon of significance.

Worlds upon Worlds

With these reflections in motion, Simmel repositions his view of the tragedy of culture within this encompassing view of life. In his prewar writings, two salient features characterized the predicament of modernity: the estrangement of life from its cultural forms and the loss of an embracing meaningfulness of being in the world. What, however, does it mean to be in a world? In the broadest sense, a world refers to the totality of what is real, whether known or unknown. Such a conception, however, fails to recognize that even if the totality of objects in the world are accessible to us, we would still not have an adequate conception of a world. A world is composed of a nexus of relations that allow disparate and different objects – fragments of the world – to interact with each other and, in this integrated sense, find a place in the world. "Reciprocal interaction" (*Wechselwirkung*) among its elements is thus essential for the composition of a world. Significantly, this conception of a world as composed through reciprocal interactions implies that the unknown can be related to the known; there cannot be a world that does not include the unknown, and hence openness toward the future.

---

[51] Simmel, *The View of Life*, p. 9.

Such a conception of "world" is still abstract, for what remains to be specified is the "differentiated idea of a pervading sense of being," weaving together different regions and domains of reality into a whole.[52] The constitution of a world depends on an overarching idea under which objects are encountered as belonging to *this* world, thus establishing the fundamental *sense* of what it is for something to *be* in the world (for example, the fundamental sense of being as "created being" for the Medieval world). Historically, philosophers interpreted the world with different transcendental distinctions: the distinction between being and becoming, the distinction between matter and spirit, the distinction between created being and uncreated (or self-created) being. Such transcendental distinctions determine a world ontologically, the gearing of categories of meaning into the world, and different ways of world disclosure. For Simmel, a world is intrinsically plural, historical, and cultural; that is, ontologically variable.[53]

There is, however, another complementary conception of "world" according to which objects are situated in a world with reference to an activity of spirit, as with the world of art, the world of religion, or the world of knowledge. Such worlds can be self-enclosed and exclude other worlds, or intersect with and fertilize other worlds. Worlds in this sense are liable to attain independence (*Eigengesetzlichkeit*) from the world-bestowing activity of spirit and operate with an internal coherence that stands opposed to "the activity of generative spirit." With this conception, variability and relativity are inescapable. As Simmel argues, apprehending "the stuff of the world" – what *is* in the world; that is, some determinate content or object – always takes place within a scheme of categories, or, in other words, an order of things. Blue, for instance, can be experienced as a sensation in the practical world (a blue cup), in a painting (Matisse's blue), on the color spectrum (blue as understood scientifically), and so on. For Simmel, a world is the form "through which we assemble the whole of the given – actual or potential – into a unity. Depending upon the ultimate concept directing this unification, multiple worlds arise out of the same material: the world of knowledge, the artistic, the religious."[54] These reflections on being in the world accentuate the relativity, contingency, and multiplicity of worlds; it is by virtue of historical circumstance and the contingency of our cognitive apparatus that these categories, and not different ones, exist to form worlds.[55] Lived experience always finds

---

[52] Simmel, *The View of Life*, p. 20.
[53] Simmel, *The View of Life*, p. 20.
[54] Simmel, *The View of Life*, p. 55.
[55] Simmel, *The View of Life*, p. 23.

itself situated in a world, whether imaginary (the world of Madame Bovary), ideal (the world of mathematics), or actual (the perceptual world). This multiplicity of worlds can be understood as different dimensions of meaning and acting through which an individual life navigates, all the while adopting, rejecting, or interpolating fragments from various dimensions of the world. As Simmel notes, "if we view this from the point of view of life, this fragmentariness is united in the life process like waves of a stream; it is in each case *one* life that produces them as it pulse-beats."[56]

The radicalism of Simmel's relativism – Ernst Troeltsch claimed that Simmel's philosophy represented "the bleakest relativism and historicism" – becomes apparent with his argument that the content of any truth depends upon the form of life in question, for whom such a truth has purchase and traction in the world; namely, purposiveness. To take Simmel's example, the truths of an Indian yogi are incomprehensibly distant for a Berlin stockbroker. A truth cannot be divorced from a form of life and hence a determinate way of being in the world. Our knowledge of what counts as true (what carries the value of truth) does not only mean, or refer to, something that one can express with concepts; we *live* our truths as the "real pulse-beats of life" that provide life with an ideal *telos*, or purposiveness. Truth gives a sense of purposiveness to being in the world. The value of truth stands inseparable from the value of truth for life. As Simmel remarks, "it is a half-baked idea to think that there is an absolute truth valid for all beings and gradually conquered by human intelligence." Given that there are as many "truths" (where truth is wedded to purposiveness) as there are forms of life, a human being is "too many-sided a creature to be able to exist in the world in so linearly teleological a manner as a plant," since a human life is never fully determined, or determinable, by one form of life. A human life exists in a multiplicity of worlds; a life, it can be said, struggles to find itself across a multiplicity of lives, its own.[57] In this regard, means–ends categories possess a much narrower significance for human existence than one thinks, and insofar as Simmel argues that freedom defines the fundamental sense, or animation, of life, freedom becomes disassociated, in its primary significance, from either a Kantian notion of autonomy (pure will) or a notion of freedom hemmed in by coercion and external impediments. The freedom that distinguishes human life stands beyond purpose; indeed, life's "distinctive value" resides in "acting without purpose." As Simmel writes: "If we understand

---

[56] Simmel, *The View of Life*, p. 25.
[57] Simmel, *The View of Life*, p. 36.

'goal-setting' as the consciously rational form of purpose, then the human being is a goal-setting creature; yet this is only a part of life; all constructs pass through the stage of purposiveness before ascending to a stage of pure being for themselves: freedom." Viewed overall, "the human being is the least teleological creature."[58]

The Gift of Death

"Death and Immortality" represents a pivotal moment in *The View of Life*. Simmel's sinuous reflections on human existence, temporality, and the relativity of worlds arrives at the suggestion that it is the unity of a life that brings together fragments of worlds into a way of being in the world, but that, by the same token, the unity of an individual life cannot be reduced to a purpose or goal. With these considerations in mind, Simmel turns, as he writes, to his real task: "For all their transcendence, worlds are intimately entwined with life; what is their genesis and how do they fit into life?"[59] In pursuit of this question, Simmel reflects on death in its ethical-ontological significance for how we hollow beings, "the least teleological creature," are able to achieve authenticity and responsibility in a world defined by conflictual orders of meaning where there are no longer any gods. Death's significance turns on the tension, tracked throughout Simmel's meditations, between the transience of life – more life – and the transcendence of life – more than life. Though the contours of Simmel's confrontation with mortality were outlined before the war, his preoccupation with a metaphysics of death became intensified as well as sharpened during the war.[60] Many of the insights on death in *The View of Life* found expression in a 1915 lecture given in Berlin, "On Death in Art," and in his monograph on Rembrandt (1916).[61] As Simmel reported to Heinrich Rickert after his Berlin lecture: "Amazing and sublime is this interest in philosophy during these times (the lectures were overflowing in attendance), when Germany is struggling for its bare existence. Otherwise, life is afflicted by a heaviness that is hardly bearable – whereby I don't have to tell you anything new."[62]

---

[58] Simmel, *The View of Life*, p. 29.
[59] Simmel, *The View of Life*, p. 25.
[60] G. Simmel, "Metaphysic of Death," *LOGOS*, Vol. 1 (1910): 57–70.
[61] G. Simmel, *Rembrandt: An Essay in the Philosophy of Art*, trans. A. Scott and H. Staubmann (London: Routledge, 2005). "On Death in Art" was delivered as two lectures to the Kant-Gesellschaft in Berlin on January 4 and 5, 1915; G. Simmel, *Aufsätze und Abhandlungen 1909–1918*, GA 13.
[62] Simmel, *Briefe 1912–1918*, p. 482.

As Simmel observes in the opening remarks to his Berlin lecture, during these past months of witnessing the departure of youth for war, when the gleam of their lives seemed inextinguishable and full of inexhaustible richness, our desolation at receiving the news that they have fallen at the front does not only consist in the acute sense of loss with regard to their existence, but grief that they have been "robbed" of their future, that their lives have been "stolen" from them. This "metaphysical horror" at the death of others rests on an image of death as "a foreign and unwelcomed element."[63] That we must now think of them as dead, those whom we knew in the flush of life, appears to be unthinkable, given how we ordinarily take death for granted; namely, as impossible. And yet, each of us somehow knows that even the young must die, as everyone must. Why, Simmel asks, are we distressed at the inevitable? The thought of death stands infinitely removed from living, and when death does break into life we commonly imagine death as a "fatal doom hanging over us," as befalling life rather than as belonging to life. Even as we sense that life and death are inextricably woven together – are we not mortal creatures? – the death of youth accentuates what we ordinarily take to be an irreconcilable opposition between life and death.

In contrast to such a commonplace, Simmel argues that it is "entirely certain" that death "*inhabits* life from the outset." It is not that we live then die; we live in death much as death lives in us. Death informs life from the beginning, only to gain a poignant visibility in the hour of death. Death is, therefore, not a discrete event or actuality interrupting life from the outside, as an alien intrusion; nor is death a possibility, one of many, on a par with other possibilities that life has on offer for itself, as hovering over life and awaiting felicitous circumstances for its actualization. This is not to deny that, from the standpoint of the living present, we shall die at a particular moment of time in the future. Simmel proposes, however, that the distinction between "actuality" and "possibility" falls short of grasping the sense in which life stands bound to death – its own – from within.[64] Death is likewise not to be conceived as an "end" or "goal" toward which life incessantly and necessarily moves, as a kind of moribund *telos*. If the human is "the least teleological being," it is because death does not stand outside of our existence; rather, death inhabits life itself: To be is to be mortal.

In Rembrandt's portraits, Simmel sees an awareness of death as the sacramental seal of life, its mark of baptism, and *character indelebilis*. A person's individuality in Rembrandt's paintings is rendered manifest as

---

[63] Simmel, GA 16, p. 123.
[64] Simmel, GA 16, p. 124.

the coursing of life's fragments within an embracing stream of temporality. The whole of an individual life cannot be held or arrested within a single moment, for in each moment the whole of life flows in exceedance of itself, "dissolving, as it were, into an uninterrupted life in which the paintings rarely denote a pause. It never *is*, it is always *becoming*."[65] What Simmel calls "the secret of life" consists in "that the whole of life is in each moment, and yet each moment is unmistakably different from any other."[66] This secret of life is the gift of death:

> Thus, if one grasps death not as a violent creature waiting outside – as a fate coming upon us at a certain moment – if one moreover comprehends its insoluble, deep immanence in life itself, then the death secretly casting its shadow out of so many Rembrandt portraits is only a symptom of how unconditionally, in his art, precisely the principle of life connects itself to that of individuality.[67]

Death, as traced across Rembrandt's faces, is "the always-effective actuality of every present" and "the formal moment of life that colours all its contents: the boundedness of the whole of life by death influences each of its contents and instants beforehand."[68] Rather than death as *what* happens to life or raising the question as to *why* we are mortal beings, death is "the simple concrete being-so of our life, the fundamental *how* of a life as it passes through changing forms." Death does not befall us (*wir sind nicht "dem Tod verfallen"*), for death traverses every breath of life as the transience without which we would not be breathing. As Simmel writes, "our life becomes formed as that which we know it to be, when we grow old or wither away […] insofar as *we can die*. Life only becomes what it is, formed into itself, insofar as life shall die."

Death runs through life in imprinting its baptismal seal on the transience of every lived moment. Death's molding and coloration of human existence also impel the reach of life for more than life. The polarity between more life and more than life – transience and transcendence – expresses the twofold sense in which death inhabits, indeed animates, life. The finitude of human life is Janus faced. Simmel speaks in this respect of the "mystery of the boundary," revealed to be the mystery of death itself, that life cannot face death, bespoken in every breath we take, without elevating itself toward more than death. We are death-bound to life and yet unbounded from life

---

[65] Simmel, *Rembrandt*, p. 11. For Simmel's analysis of Rembrandt, S. Symons, *More Than Life: Georg Simmel and Walter Benjamin on Art* (Evanston, IL: Northwestern University Press, 2017), chapter 2.
[66] Simmel, *Rembrandt*, p. 12.
[67] Simmel, *Rembrandt*, p. 79.
[68] Simmel, *The View of Life*, p. 65.

through death. As Simmel formulates this thought in an aphorism: "I feel in myself a life that is impelled toward death – that in every instant and every content, it will die. And I feel another life that is not headed for death. I do not know which one carries its true properties, its process and its fate."[69]

Simmel's aphorism bespeaks how death, intrinsic to the form of life, carries a bivalent meaning.[70] As with Simmel's final testament, *The View of Life* represents the "suprapersonal" of a thinking reaching beyond death that speaks immanently from death, as he lay dying of cancer while witnessing the twilight of Germany's destiny and the "suicide of Europe." It is in this respect a work of *Untergang* as well as *Übergang*, a passage to the grave as well as a speaking from, and hence passage beyond, the grave. Life does not just reach out beyond itself to leave something behind; life is already ahead of itself in projecting more than life, an "afterlife," before itself. The drive for more than life, the "life pulse" traversing the incessant movement of "more life," is distinct from a "feeling of eternity" attesting to the unconditioned and "nonteleological" character of human striving for more than life. Simmel writes:

> No single content that has risen to the level of being formulated in consciousness absorbs the psychic process entirely in itself; each one leaves a residue of life behind it that knocks on the door it has shut, as it were. From this reaching out of the life process beyond each one of its identifiable contents, arises the general feeling of eternity of the soul.[71]

In one sense, cultural forms are expressions of the drive for more than life; in another sense, there always remains an indivisible remainder of life – more than life – that can neither become fully alienated from nor fully encased in its own generated forms of meaning.

Simmel in this manner distinguishes between two senses of "more than life," namely, the drive to create enduring forms of meaning – "culture" broadly speaking – and the drive for immortality ("feeling of eternity"). Throughout the transient experience of our lives, we possess a "feeling of eternity," a sense for our singular existence as a unique whole that exceeds the manifold determinations of who we are. This self-transcendence of life finds symbolic expression in myths of the afterlife, the yearning for the eternal, and religious conceptions of immortality. But it likewise finds prosaic

---

[69] Simmel, *The View of Life*, 163.
[70] As David Frisby remarks: "the recognition of the present as transitory is countered by the search for the eternal forms that are present in the transitory itself"; D. Frisby, *Fragments of Modernity: Theories of Modernity in the Work of Simmel, Kracauer and Benjamin* (Cambridge, MA: MIT Press, 1986), p. 106.
[71] Simmel, *The View of Life*, p. 76.

expression in the poignancy of regret for the numerous unfulfilled and unclaimed possibilities that continue to haunt our lives, those residues of ourselves that litter our life as a whole. Life exists in openness to its own "nothingness," or "nonbeing," in the sense that it can be affected by its own unfulfilled possibilities as well as possibilities that never fell into the reachable orbit of actual life. Human finitude is double: internally, vis-à-vis possibilities left unanswered, and externally, vis-à-vis possibilities beyond its horizon, namely, those that never entered into the realm of possibility and hence, in this sense, remained for us impossible. As Simmel writes: "Man's possibilities are unlimited, but so too, in seeming contradiction, are his impossibilities. Between these two – the infinity of what he can do and the infinity of what he cannot do – lies his homeland."[72]

From this insight, Simmel proposes that the responsibility we nonetheless feel for those residual and unclaimed possibilities in our lives as well as for those impossibilities that remain within us, carried along in the wake of regret, inscribes an existential sense of responsibility for our lives as a whole (unbounded by the actuality of life), and thus the possibilities that life has claimed for itself. This "meta-ethical significance" of responsibility exceeds and envelops the identity of the self.[73] What defines us authentically is this unbounded yet not unmoored responsibility for ourselves, extending beyond the possible and the actual, to embrace what could never have been for us; namely, those impossibilities that still haunt us. We are shadowed, and hence shaped, by death – our own – not only as the "always-reality of every present" but equally as the "never possibility" of every present. This sense of "the impossible," for which we stand responsible before ourselves, impels imaginatively and symbolically the envisioning of immortality (as distinct from the envisioning of generational afterlife as culture). As Simmel writes: "Our narrow reality is perhaps shot through with the feeling of these unbounded tensions and potential directions and equipped with the intimation of an intensive endlessness that is projected in the time-dimension as immortality."[74]

When demythologized and read back from its existential ground in the gift of death – death as the drive for more life and more than life – Simmel considers that the desire for immortality, understood as the desire for the endurance of life beyond substantial existence or an existence unmoored

---

[72] Simmel, *The View of Life*, p. 165.
[73] R. Coyne, "Bearers of Transcendence. Simmel and Heidegger on Death and Immortality," *Human Studies*, Vol. 41, No. 1 (2018): 59–78; p. 71.
[74] As Coyne insightfully states: "the ego is haunted by the residues of life, suggesting that its sense of responsibility is not at all congruent with its sense as a self-identical entity."

from actuality and possibility, expresses an existential desire for the impossible – to live beyond death – as if life sought to reclaim what proved impossible *in* life with the impossibility of life outside or beyond life. As Simmel remarks: "Perhaps, the whole idea of the immortality of man simply signifies the accumulated feeling, heightened into a uniquely immense symbol, for the transcendence of life beyond itself." In developing this thought, Simmel argues that "the metaethical core of Christianity" consists in a conception of individual human existence as standing in a relation of absolute self-responsibility before God. This responsibility for the singularity of one's own contingency proves, however, to be unbearable. As Simmel writes: "This utterly undiluted self-responsibility achieved nowhere else in such intensity and coincident personality, is nonetheless not bearable for the majority of souls."[75] And yet, in shouldering an absolute responsibility for ourselves – the singular burden that defines what is authentically mine – "death is overcome." It is not that death becomes effaced or vanquished, thus leading to substantial immortal existence. Rather, "the individual entirely on his own balances [himself] as though on a needlepoint; in the deep sense of threat that is conjoined with his life situation, he cannot do without his grip on the thought that ultimately death can have no hold on him."[76]

The Individuality of Life

The contingency of human existence, underlined by the transience of experience, is inseparable from an impulse for transcendence. In the passage from more life to more than life, there is an exceedance of life all the while bearing the seal of death's benediction. An individual life feels viscerally that one is continuously becoming different, not just in terms of aging, but more substantially, in terms of choices made and unmade, of who one has been or could have been, or failed to be. And yet, throughout the unfolding of possibilities claimed and unclaimed, one *somehow* feels oneself to be same, even, paradoxically, the oneself that was not to be or could never have been. There is an inconstruable sense of *being* oneself that "runs through all this [the reality of life] without being at all influenced by anything in particular coming from its nature as a soul."[77] An individual life feels itself to be more than what one is, as determined by one's history,

---

[75] Simmel, *The View of Life*, p. 87.
[76] Simmel, *The View of Life*, p. 87.
[77] Simmel, *The View of Life*, p. 94.

social environment, and cultural milieu. In thus drawing an implicit distinction between *who* one is and *what* I am, Simmel does not have in mind a definition of "the who I am" as a substantial soul or transcendent ego that would persists across, or above, the temporal unfolding of life's becoming. Although Simmel grants that speaking of "constancy of presence" and "an enduring self" is fraught with possible misunderstanding, incontrovertible is the meaningful claim that *something* (or "some-who," as it were) persists – or, better, insists – in us (namely, oneself), "while we are wise men and then fools, beasts and then saints, happy and then despairing." What defines this "something" and "somehow" – the who that becomes me – cannot admittedly be spelled out directly or articulated conceptually, and yet it can still be characterized. Rather than an ontological determination of the constancy of *being* an individual, Simmel proposes an ethical-existential characterization of oneself as an abiding and absolute – that is, uniquely one's own – responsibility for oneself.

These reflections on the metaphysics of concrete life, gravitating around an irrecusable responsibility for one's own existence, deepen Simmel's treatment of the problem of the individual. Throughout his writings, Simmel deliberately avoids speaking abstractly of "the subject" and "subjectivity," but refers instead to "the individual," "the concrete human," and "the actuality of life." In his essay "Freedom and the Individual," Simmel argued that the nineteenth century witnessed a profound transformation in the conceptualization of human life.[78] Traditional conceptions of the indestructible soul, a subject organized into faculties possessing universal cognitive capacities, or the noumenal self and the rational will, were displaced by a concept of life as developed by Schopenhauer and Nietzsche (and in the early twentieth century, Bergson). This metaphysical discovery of life represents the defining novelty of modern thought.[79] In his prewar writings, Simmel's analysis of the problem of the individual (albeit without an emphasis on individual *life*) was shaped around the examination of a constitutive tension between social conditions and individual differentiation. As Simmel states, "the human being is never merely a collective entity, much as they are never merely an individual entity."[80] To

---

[78] G. Simmel, "Freedom and the Individual," in *On Individuality and Social Forms*, ed. D. Levine (Chicago: University of Chicago Press, 1971): 217–226. See also G. Simmel, *Schopenhauer and Nietzsche* (Urbana: University of Illinois Press, 1991).
[79] G. Simmel, "Henri Bergson," in *Aufsätze und Abhandlungen 1909–1918*, Band II, Gesamtausgabe 13 (Frankfurt: Suhrkamp, 2000): 53–69. Hereafter GA 13.
[80] G. Simmel, *Aufsätze 1887–1890*, Gesamtausgabe 2 (Frankfurt: Suhrkamp, 1989), p. 175. Hereafter GSG 2.

be an individual is constituted dynamically through the intersection of the "external" (the social) and the "internal" (the psychological), where no firm separation between these two relational poles, between which a field of tension becomes established, can be stabilized. Against the rational idealism of a universal subject and the Romanticism of interiority, an individual is per se neither "objective" nor "subjective," since an individual is determined by a host of relational forces and social-cultural interactions. There is no absolute substantial self or irreducible core self, but only a process of individuating self-differentiations in reciprocal interaction with other self-differentiating individuals and social-cultural conditions (institutions, values, etc.). As Simmel writes: "Only the combination and fusion of several traits in one focal point forms a personality which then in its turn imparts to each individual trait a personal-subjective character. It is not that it is this or that trait that makes a unique personality of man, but that he is this and that trait."[81]

More generally, every element (individuals, institutions, etc.) in a society is related to other elements through a variety of "reciprocal relational interactions" (*Wechselwirkungen*) – conflict, domination, exchange, and so on.[82] These interactive forms of what Simmel terms "sociation" (*Vergesellschaftung*) are ontologically primitive; social reality becomes realized, in situ and in re, through sociative forms of relational interaction. From these "delicate threads of the minimal relations between humans," the fabric of society becomes woven, torn, and mended.[83] An individual is situated in and must navigate a complexity of relational interactions and forms of differentiation. Fashion, for example, functions as a process of individual differentiation and social marking; it allows an individual to display their uniqueness while subjecting themselves to group conformity and belonging. By contrast, smug indifference, which Simmel detected to be a distinctly metropolitan phenomenon, expresses a defense against the hyperstimulation, overcomplexity, and acceleration of modern life.[84] What defines an individual is a coefficient of combinatorial belonging (or not belonging) to different social circles. An individual becomes more themselves the more they are inscribed within their social nexus; the more, in other words, reciprocal relational interaction occurs between themselves

---

[81] Simmel, *The Philosophy of Money*, p. 296.
[82] For Simmel's analysis of different forms of social interaction, G. Simmel, *Soziologie* (Frankfurt: Suhrkamp Verlag 2018), GA 11.
[83] Simmel, *Soziologie*, p. 20.
[84] G. Simmel, "Fashion" and "The Metropolis and Modern Life," in *On Individuality and Social Forms*, pp. 294–323 and 324–339.

and others.⁸⁵ A society is thus constituted from the totality of relational interactions among individuals, which, changing in configuration and forms, admits of no overall regulative principle other than the principle of *Wechselwirkung* itself.⁸⁶ Within any social nexus, individual freedom involves degrees of available latitude and leeway for actions in negotiating conflicts among values and navigating relational interactions with others.⁸⁷

The View of Life continues to address the constitution of the individual from the transformed perspective of a metaphysics of life. An individual life, as an unfolding whole, is not constituted as an aggregate or synthesis of discrete experiences and social determinations. Who one is is always "more" than what one has been, and not just in the sense of "more life" but, and in the same breath, as "more than life." This individual self-transcendence within one's own transience gravitates around the axis of life's death-bound responsibility for oneself.⁸⁸ The twofold transcendence of life – more life and more than life – means that "concrete life" is strung and stretched between two mutually interacting and yet mutually irreducible poles: "on the one hand, we are thrown into and adapted to cosmic movement, yet on the other hand we feel and conduct our individual existence from our own centre, as self-responsible and, as it were, in self-enclosed form."⁸⁹ Importantly, Simmel does not consider this interactive polarity (and hence tension) in terms of a difference between "actuality" and "possibility" or, indeed, between "being" and "becoming." As gleaned from his reflections on death, the irrecusable responsibility for oneself exceeds responsibility for our actual self, since it embraces those possibilities that were not claimed, or could not be claimed, or failed to be successfully actualized. An individual life stands before itself as more than its own actuality *and* possibility, and this "more than life," the impossibilities of life that are nonetheless one's own, is not beyond oneself, but, on the contrary, defines the oneself that stands beyond myself to which I remain intimately bound, as with those manifold regrets and guilts, for example, that haunt who I am with shadows of who I could have been, yet am no longer becoming. These shadows of who I could have been as well as who I could not have been gather, as it were, around a profound sense of not only of who I could have been, but of who I *should* have been.

---

⁸⁵ GSG 2, p. 244 ff.
⁸⁶ As Simmel himself underlines, *Wechselwirkung* is the metaphysical principle of this thinking; Gassen and Landmann, *Buch des Dankes*, p. 9.
⁸⁷ Riedel, *Metaphysik des Irgendwie*, p. 48 ff.
⁸⁸ See O. Pyyhtinen, "Life, Death and Individuation: Simmel on the Problem of Life Itself," *Theory, Culture & Society*, Vol. 29, Nos. 7–8 (2012): 78–100.
⁸⁹ Simmel, GA 16, p. 319.

What proves crucial for understanding the existential difference between "actuality" and "the ought" is that "actuality" is always determined by contingent and changing – culturally and historically – forms. "Actuality" itself is a form of experience – in fact, *one* among many forms – in terms of which we shape and apprehend experience and thus "has no more intimate or privileged relation to that content than do the categories of science, art, wish, and value."[90] As with any form of experience, "actuality" stands in interactive relations with other forms, yet nonetheless enjoys a "monopoly" among forms, given that all objects of experience are determined by actuality; namely, as "something existing or something that is." This monopoly of actuality, or stated more exactly "actuality-possibility," does not fully extend, however, across an individual's life, since Simmel identifies "the ought" as a "second category according to which we continually experience our life, one which is somewhat parallel to actuality, but in no way reducible to it."[91] As existential determinations of life, "actuality" and "the ought" are in a productive tension with each other. Life cannot exclusively and exhaustively be determined *ontologically* in terms of actuality, for in striving for "more than life," an individual confronts their life in light who they *ought* to be. An individual life stands before oneself as incessantly "challenged to better oneself," and this demand does not issue from a moral law or authority exterior to life (God, for example), but from life itself. The "ought" can thus be said to be something like an "Individual Law" that prescribes an existential "mode of living one's whole life." However, as Simmel cautions, one can "never extract, from the fact of the Ought, *what* we ought, content-wise, to do," since the content of this existential Ought is "utterly variegated, accidental, determined in each case historically and psychologically, and in no way form[s] a systematic order."[92]

Become Who You Ought to Be

This discovery of an existential Ought, or the Law of the Individual, motivated the reformulation of an ambiguity that repeatedly confronted Simmel's thinking: how to reconcile the relativity of the world with the possibility of individual authenticity.[93] How can an individual be singularly –

---

[90] Simmel, *The View of Life*, p. 99.
[91] Simmel, *The View of Life*, p. 100.
[92] Simmel, *The View of Life*, p. 102.
[93] As K. Christian Köhnke argues, the "law of individual" emerged in Simmel's writings as early as 1900 to form the "normative center" of Simmel's thinking; *Der junge Simmel in Theoriebeziehungen und sozialen Bewegungen* (Frankfurt: Suhrkamp, 1996). For Hans-Peter Müller, Simmel's law of

that is, absolutely – responsible for themselves in a world of changing values and interminable conflicts? Where is absolute meaningfulness to be found for a death-bound life? Where can one find the absolute in a world without gods? As Simmel observes, "we are determined by a thousand influences that affect others similarly, we are graded by social institutions and stratifications, and colored by general historical conditions; precisely as empirical beings we are governed by natural law with its deindividualizing general validity, just as we also submit, as empirical beings, to the universal laws of justice." Bound to and defined by the world, the struggle of becoming oneself involves, as Simmel discussed in his prewar writings, navigating a constitutive tension between external determinations and internal dispositions; these continually pass into each other in the process of shaping one's life as a whole from a multitude of fragments, influences, and conditions. If the world and history can no longer provide an overarching meaningfulness to it all, can life find a wholeness of meaningfulness for its own individual existence? Rather than a restatement of the problem of the one and the many (projected onto the question of what it is to have life) in the vernacular of "being" and "becoming," "substance" and "attribute," "transcendental" and "empirical," Simmel recasts the question of life in the mold of his existential distinction between "actuality" and "ought." It is important to stress that Simmel does not understand this reformulation as the problem of freedom in terms of determinism and indeterminism. In the same vein, Simmel's question of concrete life stands removed from the ontological primacy of an ontological difference between "being" and "becoming" (or beings), on the basis of Simmel's claim that the "ought" must be recognized in its facticity; that is, as "an absolutely primary category." By the same token, the Kantian difference between "actuality" (empirical determinations and the empirical self) and "ought" (noumenal freedom and the noumenal self) becomes supplanted with an existential difference, inscribed within life itself, between "actuality" and "Ought." As Simmel writes: "Only when we understand the Ought, beyond all of its particular contents, as a primary mode in which the individual consciousness experiences a whole life does it become understandable why one can never extract, from the fact of the Ought, *what* we ought, content-wise, to do."

---

the individual represents a Nietzschean "aristocratic individualism." As he argues: "Thanks to spiritual education and aesthetic experience, aristocratic individualism is able to shape its own path in life and create its own distinctive personal lifestyle. This aristocratic individuality, Simmel has no illusions about that, is reserved only for a minority and probably only for a small elite"; *Krise und Kritik. Klassiker der soziologischen Zeitdiagnose* (Berlin: Suhrkamp, 2021), p. 284. For Simmel's Nietzscheanism and its influence, Leck, *Georg Simmel and Avant-Garde Sociology.*

With this original distinction in mind, Simmel rejects two possible misconceptions of the relation between the actuality of life and the ought to life. On the one hand, the existential ought should not be associated with "wish-images" and "ideals" that would stem from subjective phantasy (i.e., who I would wish to be) or imposed upon life from an external source and authority (God or nature, for example). On the other hand, the Law of the Individual should not be conflated with a fact of reason and autonomy of the moral will. The existential ought "in" me does not command a universal form of conduct or prescribe a content to my maxim in formal accordance with the moral law. On Simmel's understanding, Kant's moral law represents a universal Law "that issues from a different order than that from which life springs," namely, from rationality and the noumenal realm of freedom. Simmel thus effects a double displacement of the concept of life from "reason" and "the will." The ought to life is not synonymous with Kantian autonomy nor with Schopenhauer's blind and nonindividuated will in itself. The Law of the Individual speaks to actual life as an insistence on one's own responsibility to be oneself, where the freedom here in play – to become, and hence decide, who one ought to be – is not identified with freedom of choice among possibilities (as with Simmel's earlier conception), nor with Kantian autonomy and rational self-determination. Whereas freedom of choice refers to a set of possible actions, and not the whole of life as such, Kant's moral law addresses the rational and universal subject, and thus, in this sense, the subject as a whole, and yet not the facticity of life as an *individual* whole. What Kant failed to recognize is that "actuality" embraces the whole of a life and not just the empirical content and maxim of the ethical subject. Kant's "superindividual reason" and "noumenal self" obscured the discovery of the existential "ought" for life. As Simmel writes: "What I have endeavored to show is that life, proceeding in its totality as Ought, means law for the very same life that proceeds in its totality as actuality; Kant, however, transfers the dualism into the totality of life itself, by splitting this totality between the real or rational ego and the sensuousness that is only peripheral or opposed to it."[94] The existential Ought represents a deformalization of the moral law and deontification of what is symbolically expressed with the idea of God's will. For Simmel, "none of these substantiations of the Ought has proven to be sufficiently and durably sound. Being-as-Ought is just as irreducible as being-as-actual."[95]

[94] Simmel, *The View of Life*, p. 107.
[95] Simmel, *The View of Life*, p. 101.

Embedded in every choice of action and conduct, whether implicitly or explicitly, is a self-embracing decision to become the person one "ought" to be. Bound to oneself, this decision does not occur in the noumenal realm of freedom, and hence outside or before time, nor does it emerge as the consequence or aggregate of an individual's particular choices. In every act, the entirety of one's life is at stake. Yet the Law of the Individual does not prescribe a content of action, nor can the Law of (each) Individual become universalized, since it bears on *me* specifically and absolutely. Indeed, one cannot, strictly speaking, speak of a "choice" in terms of a decision among different possibilities, since the individual life that one bears, or has, is not one possibility among many, much as (my) death is not one among many possibilities of life. As with the singularity of death, to which one is bound, inhabiting the form of life, the Law of the Individual inhabits one's way of life. The choice to prescribe for oneself what one ought to do, and act upon this self-prescription, implies a prescription regarding who one ought to be, such that, on this account, decisions for a particular action and conduct in the world tacitly imply and invoke an existential decision regarding oneself. Beneath every choice to act in a determinate manner, there is an existential decision concerning oneself; each action becomes effectuated on the ground of this self-choosing from which it arises, but likewise, the resoluteness to be oneself rebounds back upon itself from the choices one makes to act. As Simmel writes: "Thus the whole of life is responsible for every act, and every act for the whole of life."[96] This back and forth, or polarity, between "actuality" and "ought," between what I choose to do (under given contingent circumstances) and who I ought to be, paves the grounded path for an individual life from within the groundlessness of life itself. Stated in these terms, Simmel proposes that "the ultimate metaphysical problematic of life" consists in the interactive polarity between "actuality" and "the ought." An individual life is animated by an internal tension between "consciousness of life as it actually is" and "consciousness of life as it ought to be." "The ought" is "precisely a mode by which life becomes aware of itself," and although "we thereby appear to lead two lives," namely, between actuality and the ought, "what we sense as the unity of life is in no way destroyed."[97] We are both near and far from ourselves: far from who we ought to be as measured by the nearness of who we have actually become.

---

[96] Simmel, *The View of Life*, p. 153.
[97] Simmel, *The View of Life*, p. 101.

In developing this account of an "existential Ought," Simmel draws significantly, albeit silently, on Goethe in speaking of the Ought as "a categorical *Ur-phenomenon*." As a "primary phenomenon," the impulsion to become who one ought to be, as prescribed to oneself in situ through the actuality of decisions and actions taken or not, an individual life becomes set upon the adventure of its own self-discovery and self-determination without following or adhering to an overarching purpose beyond the death-bound project of living itself. Life is a purposiveness without a purpose, animated by its own creative play at forming itself. As with death that binds life to itself in absolute self-responsibility, the Ought is "purposeless" – there is no prescribed *telos* or goal to life other than life's own becoming more than life. As Simmel writes:

> We are obliged, not from such a purpose, but from ourselves; the Ought as such is no teleological process. This naturally does not apply to the *content* of the Ought, which in fact continually presents itself under the category of purpose [...] But *that* we should do this, that it claims us under the category of duty – this again is not itself dependent on the purpose we serve with the actuality [*Tatsächlichkeit*] of such action.[98]

Historically, the ethical demand upon the self was defined either as "a decision based on personal conscience, or it comes from the objective, from a superindividual precept drawing its validity from its material-conceptual consequences." Simmel proposes a third way: "the objective Ought of this very individual, the demand imposed from *his* life onto *his* life and in principle independent of whether he really recognizes it or not." As a function of the whole life, the Law of the Individual bespeaks a secret destiny into the heart of life, only to be known and discovered, or missed and forgotten, by individual life itself. There is, thus, a "double incompatibility" of life with itself. The Ought is as unprovable to others as it is incontrovertible for oneself; it can neither be imparted to others nor substituted for another's. In facing oneself as a yet unknown adventure, an individual lives within an intimate dimension of solitude – not to be confused with loneliness or alienation. Whether achieved or failed, an individual stands before itself in absolute responsibility for a life that calls to be achieved and accomplished, come what may.

The "purposiveness without purpose" of becoming who we ought to be circumscribes an open horizon, or unbounded finitude, within which determined purposes can be claimed for oneself, but equally discarded and

---

[98] Simmel, *The View of Life*, p. 141.

transformed. Much as death animates life with the impulsion of more life (transience) as well as more than life (transcendence), the latter stands under the lodestar of an "ought" discoverable only to me. The Ought, when conceived as the Law of the Individual, is not a prescriptive command per se, but a compelling manner of becoming aware of oneself in terms of the demand for and hence pursuit of authenticity, to become, and hence decide to become, who one should be within given contingent circumstances. Awareness of one's life under the call of this demand "to become who one ought to be" entails a striving to become "other" than who one has been, in the pursuit of more than life rather than merely more life. Straddling who one is and who one ought to be, an individual leads their life simultaneously on two nonsynchronous planes: the life one has been (actually) living and could continue to lead, and the life one ought to pursue. In this existential-ethical sense, an individual life is both "subject" and "object," both "I and Thou" for oneself, as, for example, when one addresses oneself with the question: Who shall I be? The tension between "actuality" and "ought" within oneself suggests for Simmel that an individual cannot merely posit or affirm themselves, and hence constitute themselves absolutely, for what is demanded of a life is to negotiate the interplay, on the one hand within themselves (between actuality and ought) and on the other hand with their world. This interplay between "self-positing" and "alien-positing" (*Fremdsetzung*) reflects the condition that one's own-most – namely, one's Individual Law – confronts one, in one's actual existence, as *alien*, or other; namely, as the demand to become other than who one has been in order to accomplish who one should be.[99] The impulsion to become who one ought to be thus involves becoming other than oneself in order to be oneself. This otherness of oneself is experienced in the obscurity of the Ought itself, which, speaking from the depth of a life, calls upon life to not just more life, but to more than life. As Simmel writes:

> This vitalizing and individualizing of ethicality is so foreign to all egoism and subjectivism [...] many of our acts, pardonable sins examined in isolation, only attain their full weight when we make clear to ourselves that our entire existence has pushed toward them, and that they will define our existence perhaps for the entire future—a criterion, however, that can only be valid for this individual life, and would be utterly senseless if generalized to any others who are not absolutely identical to me.

[99] For the Goethean sources of this conception of the passage through one's own otherness in order to become oneself, G. Simmel, "Einheit und Zwiespalt. Zeitgemäßes in Goethes Weltanschauung," *Aufsätze und Abhandlungen*, II, GA 13: 165–173.

Simmel's existential thinking ascribes to an ethical life an infinitely more difficult responsibility. It is not only that an individual is responsible for choosing their particular actions and conduct in relation to the moral Law. An individual must choose themselves to be the kind of person who would decide at all to be moral, and thus to establish the conditions within their own existence for the traction and uptake of duties and norms. In this sense, there is a "creative element to the ethical realm, with its dangers and responsibilities," that, for Simmel, Kant's categorical imperative obscures as well as alleviates, since it spares life from being self-creating and thus fails to grasp the authentic autonomy of life itself (as opposed to autonomy of the rational will as a source of action) in its death-bound singularity.

In his closing reflections on the Law of the Individual, Simmel proposes that "because the flowing formation of life proceeds as Ought, because the absolute of the demand becomes in this sense a historical one – but this historical demand is an absolute one – the normative strictness goes deep below the level on which alone ethics previously sought the responsibility of man, namely, whether he actually acts according to the existing Ought." So deep, in fact, as to inhabit Simmel's thinking to the point of a certain betrayal. In thinking about the relation between the historical situatedness of life and its responsibility toward its individualized existential Ought, Simmel offers "a simple example" of how the "firmly individualized life exists as an objective fact in the full sense," where life's ideal Ought (not just what I ought to do, but more primarily who I ought to be) makes of an individual life a "historical" and "objectively valid thing, in such a fashion that true and false notions about it can be formed, both by its subject and by other subjects." Let us imagine, he writes, "an anti-militarist who is convinced that the war and the military are utterly condemnable and evil, and who avoids patriotic duty, not only in peaceful conscience, but also with the sacred conviction of thereby doing the ethically right and unconditionally required thing." Simmel considers that a pacifist's refusal to do his duty should be judged negatively, since it is an ethical duty to fulfill one's patriotic duty, regardless of how one thinks about it subjectively. The Ought of military duty, however, cannot be conflated with the coercive power of the state, and even if God or some other authority demanded of the pacificist to serve, his can only be considered an ethical ought in an existential sense if the claim made on him comes from an Ought "located in *his* being."[100] Although the nation demands service, it is the individual who must, in her conscience, first demand it of herself. How, then, to

---

[100] Simmel, *The View of Life*, p. 143.

reconcile that neither God nor the Fatherland can function as the ethical Ought with a subjective refusal to serve, which must nonetheless be overcome by an Ought stemming from the individual herself? How can the pacifist become who he "ought" to be, from himself, against his own (subjective) conscience? For Simmel, the resolution of these issues seems evident: "I certainly believe […] that the anti-militarist really is ethically obligated to armed service, although his subjective moral consciousness condemns it." For although "subjectively" the pacifist opposes military service, given that he lives in the form of an "ought to be" that can never be "ahistorical" and "nonmaterial," and, moreover, that his citizenship shapes an ineluctable aspect of his individuality, the fulfillment of this demand to serve stems, it is here argued, from the "indissoluble interweaving of nation-state powers and values into his individual existence." Although it is a historically contingent fact that the pacifist is German (and not French, for example), he must nonetheless fulfill the demand to serve as necessary – what he ought to be – to his being German. As Simmel proposes: "The decisive element […] is that the individual life is not anything subjective, but rather – without somehow losing its limitation to this individual – is thoroughly objective as an ethical Ought."

One might think Simmel's reasoning to be inconsistent, even within his own framework, but clearly this reconciliation between the personal and the "suprapersonal" in an "absolute situation," which he had championed as the demand of Germany's greatest hour of historical destiny, proved essential to Simmel's twofold final testament, not just his view of life, but his view of life in wartime.[101] In his 1915 lecture on death and art, Simmel concludes his reflections with a reference to Rilke's insight from *das Stunden-Buch* that "jeder seinen *eigenen* Tod stirbt."[102] As Simmel comments: "Whoever is unique, whose form disappears with him, he alone dies so to speak definitively: in the depths of individuality as such is the fate of death anchored […] the individual being dies *am gründlichsten*, because he lived *am gründlichsten*."[103] In sacrifice for the Fatherland, the soldier gives himself freely from the intimate "ought" of his own existence, and in this absolute of self-sacrifice "there lives in this depth another individual: the great individuality of the people; a generality not opposed to individuality," as Simmel sees in "the singing soldiers of Langemarck,

---

[101] As argued by M.-S. Lotter, "Das individuelle Gesetz. Zu Simmels Kritik an der Lebensfremdheit der kantischen Moralphilosophie," *Kant-Studien*, Vol. 91, No. 2 (2000): 178–203; p. 200.
[102] Simmel, GA 16, p. 131.
[103] Simmel, GA 16, p. 130.

as the rapture and intoxication of life are the small meaning of life and small meaning of death become sublated [*aufheben*] in the great sense of life."[104] From death out of one's own, unique freedom (*der Tod aus seiner eigenen Freiheit heraus*) there arises the authenticity of life in absolute responsibility for oneself, as the gift of death that, one can only surmise, the exposed propaganda myth of *der Kindermord bei Ypern* (alternatively called *Kindermord bei Langemarck*) could not falsify for Simmel (even if he were to be disabused of this wartime fabrication) the truth of his final testament for life.[105] It is not that a soldier's sacrifice would reflect a decision to die for the Fatherland for eternity; it is that his sacrifice would define his life here and now entirely, absolutely, for nothing and from nothing other than one's own mortal life. As Simmel reflects on his view of life:

> Instead of the truly bleak Nietzschean thought – 'Can you desire that this action of yours recur infinitely often?' – I propose: 'Can you desire that this action of yours should define your entire life?'[106]

---

[104] Simmel, GA 16, p. 132.
[105] For the fabrication of the myth, K. Unruh, *Langemarck, Legende und Wirklichkeit* (Koblenz: Bernhard & Graefe, 1986). See also *Der Langemarck-Mythos in Dichtung und Unterricht*, ed. R. Ditmar (Luchterhand: Neuwied, 1992).
[106] Simmel, *The View of Life*, p. 151.

CHAPTER 5

The Apocalypse of Hope
Ernst Bloch's Phenomenology of Utopic Spirit

What Now?

"What now? Enough is enough. Now we have to begin. Into our hands, life has been given."[1] With these exasperated words, Ernst Bloch's *The Spirit of Utopia* begins like no other work of philosophy. In anger and aspiration, it does not begin with a pedantic preface or scholarly introduction. It begins in situ with a catastrophe that has thrown human existence back upon itself, from which no deliverance seems to be at hand. What is to be done? How can one survive? Caught in the condition of pitching "senselessly back and forth," *something* nonetheless endures, we know not what, we know not how, but with nothing in our hands save our own obscurity, life still darkly speaks, for which, in this end of days, we want to be its initiative as well as its end.

Written between 1915 and 1917, significantly revised into a second edition (1923) in the aftermath of Germany's defeat, the October Russian Revolution, the failed Munich Revolution, and the death of his wife, Else von Stritzky, historical and personal tumult intersect in the syncopated cadences of *The Spirit of Utopia*'s two editions, to which, as an extensive coda, *Thomas Münzer als Theologe der Revolution* (1921) can be appended. The question haunting *The Spirit of Utopia* is not "What actually happened?" but "Has anything actually occurred?" To be sure, a war has been endured, the after-effects of which, during Bloch's rewriting of the second edition, continued to be dramatically experienced. And yet, despite the bellicose clamor of salvation shouted to the heavens in the *Augusterlebnis* of 1914 and for all the countless sacrifices for the Fatherland, the war essentially transformed nothing. Mass destruction and untold suffering have failed to incite an awakening. Contrary to expectations, whether those of socialist revolution for postwar Germany or those of conservative postwar regeneration for *das Vaterland*, the dreamed-for apocalypse did not occur.

---

[1] E. Bloch, *The Spirit of Utopia*, trans. A. Nassar (Stanford, CA: Stanford University Press, 2000), p. 1.

In a series of opening reflections entitled "Objective," Bloch situates his work amid the wasteland of its hopeful composition. Capitalism, materialism, and militarism, along with the perversion of culture into entertainment – the mass decoration of modernity's disenchantment – are submitted to unsparing critique, the broad contours of which Bloch shares with other voices of early twentieth-century cultural discontent. What distinguishes Bloch's critique is its emphasis on the foreclosure of the future as the consequence of war's aftermath. Despite a frightful cost in lives, collective stupidity, and the hypocrisy of European values, the war did not provoke a fundamental transformation of human existence *for the better*. It is not, for Bloch, that the trauma of the war has been repressed or ideologically muted. The trauma is not what has happened but what has *not* happened – the "not yet" that is "no longer." The Great War was not the war to end all wars; it was the war to end all futures, understood in Bloch's utopic sense as the possibility of otherness, of becoming other than who we have been, both collectively and individually. Hope is the placeholder of time allowing us to hold ourselves in place in the present *and* the place held open for a future beyond the grip of the past to which we are held captive.

In the ruins of aftermath, we are left empty-handed with the bitter question: "Who was defended?" As Bloch writes, "what was young had to fall, was forced to die for ends so alien and inimical to the spirit, but the despicable ones were saved, and now they sit there in their comfortable drawing rooms."[2] The war served the interests of capitalism, but likewise, the war's ferocity exceeded the rationality of capitalist realism – the war was not just the pursuit of capitalism by other means. Under the aegis of Prussian militarism, the war certified the *Apriori der Machineware* and that ours was to be the age of remoteness from God. What survived the war was the military state apparatus and godless capitalism, but most of all, the spiritless mediocrity and rank stupidity that afflicted German society before the war. For Bloch, "there has never been a more dismal military objective than Imperial Germany's: a suffocating coercion imposed by mediocrities and tolerated by mediocrities; a triumph of stupidity, guarded by the gendarme, acclaimed by the intellectuals who did not have enough brains to provide slogans."

These scathing words of indictment and introduction for a book the title of which surely touched on something profound among its contemporary readers (and continues to profoundly affect readers who find themselves in a world in which they can no longer breathe), even as it would have sounded dreamy and anachronistic – one thinks of Max Weber's

---

[2] Bloch, *The Spirit of Utopia*, p. 1.

sobering vocation lectures or Oswald Spengler's *The Downfall of the West* – are scarred by the fatigue of war and the calamity of defeat. Even if nothing changed on account of the war, the hoped-for transformation – a new future – did not become extinguished with the defeated apocalypse of 1918.[3] The star of a new beginning burst forth with the October Revolution in Russia, then briefly flashed upon the scene in Germany with the Bavarian Revolution and Munich's *Räterepublik*. And so a new dawn for Germany, as well as for Europe, seemed possible after all. The call for revolution at the end of Ernst Toller's wartime play *Transformation* could now, or so it seemed, finally come to pass.[4] Was it not Toller, the anarchist poet war veteran, and president for six fleeting days of the Bavarian Soviet Republic, who found himself, with Gustav Landauer and others, at the helm of a new society toward a new humanity? But pass it did. With Kurt Eisner's assassination on the day of his resignation and the suppression of the dreamland of the Munich *Räterepublik* (Landauer's brutal murder, Toller's imprisonment, extrajuridical executions on the streets of Munich) under the approving nod of the governing Social Democrats in Berlin in complicity with the self-serving reactionary *Freikorps*, the despair of the war's aftermath became compounded. As Bloch remarks: "The War ended, the Revolution began, and along with the Revolution, doors opened. But of course, they soon shut." The mediocrity of the bourgeoisie, Prussian militarism, pathological nationalism, and voracious capitalism continued apace. In Bloch's prescient assessment, "those who apparently have been restored completely reenact what the reaction of a century ago auditioned: the slogans about native soil, the traditionalism of *Vaterland*, and that oblivious Romanticism that forgot the Peasant's War and saw only knight's castles rising into enchanted, moonlit nights."[5]

In Munich, the city of *Der Blaue Reiter* and the fugitive seat of power for revolutionary poet-anarchists, the profiteering farmer, the *grand bourgeois*, and the panicked *petit bourgeois* have closed ranks, thus propelling Bavaria politically, along with Germany in its swell, toward another cataclysm against which fewer than fifteen years later Bloch would have to engage,

---

[3] As Walter Benjamin observed: "It may confidently be asserted that the revolution of 1918, which was defeated by the petty-bourgeois, parvenu spirit of German Social Democracy, did more to radicalize this generation than did the war itself." W. Benjamin, *Selected Writings*, Vol. 2, Part 1, 1927–1930 (Harvard, MA: Belknap Press, 2005), p. 20.
[4] "Brothers, raise on high your tortured hand, / Sound a joyous end to persecution! / Let revolution stride through our free land, / Revolution! Revolution!"; E. Toller, *Plays One*, trans. A. R. Pearlman (London: Oberon Books, 2001), p. 118.
[5] Bloch, *The Spirit of Utopia*, p. 3.

once again, "in hand-to-hand combat" in *Heritage of the Times*. In the aftermath of war time became unhinged, thus setting the stage for the triumph of Nazism, sprouted from the seed of the Thule Society in postwar Munich. "Authentic reality," Bloch argues in *Heritage of the Times*, is discontinuous with itself: "not all people exist in the same Now."[6] What defines modern society is the "simultaneity of the non-simultaneous." The historical present is not contemporaneous with itself, given its cacophony of premodern mentalities, prejudices, and *ressentiment* along with spectacular advances in technology, scientific achievements, and industrialization. As diagnosed by Bloch during the 1930s, signs of which were readily apparent to him after the failed revolutions of 1918–19, the temporal disjointedness of modern life was ripe for exploitation and manipulation by yet another, more aggressive fantasy of national salvation. Mythology, occultism, and *völkisch* religion spoke as never before to a collapsed modernity's longing for epic salvation. Marxism, by contrast, with its reductive form of dialectical materialism, failed to understand this resurgent desire for myth, fantasy, and dreams – the "warm stream of culture" – and, in its own waywardness, succumbed to ineffectiveness. The thwarted hopes of 1918–19 continued to haunt Germany and precipitated the country's unrestrained embrace of a profligate barbarism in the 1930s. As Bloch remarks in his reflection "Objective," "what just was will probably soon be forgotten. Only an empty, awful memory hangs in the air." It might all have been just an awful dream.

Socialism or Barbarism

In 1914, artists, intellectuals, and academics were complicit in a collective flag-waving that doomed an entire generation. For Bloch, if there is one institution that did not survive the war, it was the university. Along with his friend György Lukács, Bloch vigorously opposed the war from the beginning and objected to the spiritual mobilization of German thinking, or rather, the vampiric possession of a spirit long since eviscerated. As Bloch decries, "the universities have truly become the spirit's burial mound, filled with the stink of corruption and immovable gloom." Even before 1914, philosophy had long since perished, ever since the eclipse of German Idealism and Marx. The parroting of war slogans by German thinkers in 1914 reflected an intellectual lassitude and moral collapse seeking to resuscitate itself through the pursuit of philosophy by illicit means. Even the "great" thinkers of our times – "Lask, Simmel, Rickert, yes, even

---

[6] E. Bloch, *Heritage of Our Times* (London: Polity Press, 1991), p. 97.

Husserl" – have abandoned the genuine vocation of philosophy. Each in their own way blithely asks: "'What is metaphysics to me?'"[7] In response to the bankruptcy of philosophy, flagrantly on display with the weaponization of German thought, Bloch resuscitates a speculative thinking of the Absolute beyond the separation of theory and praxis, appearance and thing in itself, spirit and materiality, as the future of philosophy, as the philosophy of the future – a "new German metaphysics," as Margarete Susman astutely assessed *The Spirit of Utopia* to be.

Bloch's dismay was both philosophical and personal. After obtaining a PhD in Würzburg, he arrived in Berlin in 1908 and fell under the spell of Georg Simmel's idiosyncratic brilliance, entering into the circle of gifted students attending Simmel's private home seminars. For Bloch, Simmel "was the only living philosopher who really interested me," and this intellectual appeal reflected the boldness of his thinking and avant-garde sociological-philosophical approach to modernity.[8] In 1914, however, Simmel's lectures on the situation of Germany's existential hour of decision proved insufferable for Bloch. How could Simmel's anti-establishment thinking and trenchant critique of modern life, which inspired progressive thinkers such as Kurt Hiller and Helene Stöcker, mobilize his own left-wing Nietzschean life philosophy in support of the war?[9] Above all, Bloch was baffled at how his teacher, "Bergson's friend, the lover and admirer of French culture, of French cuisine and wines," who, as a Jew, never received a position in Berlin, and whose seminars were overfilled with students, yet who was shunned by the mediocrities of academia, and who once confided in him that "a future history will establish that the two great times of unhappiness for Germany were, first, the Thirty-Years War and, second, Wilhelm II" – how could such a sophisticated mind capitulate to the crass rhetoric of the war? As Bloch writes in a letter to Simmel: "You never sought a definitive answer to anything, never. The Absolute was always suspicious and closed

---

[7] Quoted in P. Zudeick, *Hintern des Teufels: Ernst Bloch – Leben und Werk* (Zurich: Elster Verlag, 1987), p. 246.
[8] From an interview in 1976: "Was German university philosophy of importance for the development of your philosophy? Bloch: No; since this no longer existed"; E. Bloch, *Tagträume vom aufrechten Gang* (Frankfurt: Edition Suhrkamp, 1977), p. 101. As Lukács wrote in his obituary: "Georg Simmel was unquestionably the most important and the most interesting transitional figure in all of modern philosophy. Therefore, he was – for all the truly philosophical talents of the young generation of thinkers (who were more than purely intelligent or fluid scholars in individual philosophical disciplines) – so exceedingly alluring that there are hardly any among them who for a short or long period of time were not slain by the magic of his thought." G. Lukács, *Buch des Dankes an Georg Simmel*, eds. K. Gassen and M. Landmann (Berlin: Duncker & Humboldt, 1958): 171–175; p. 172.
[9] For the significance of Simmel's thinking for progressive avant-garde figures and social reformers, see Leck, *Georg Simmel and Avant-Garde Sociology*.

off to you, even the striving for an Absolute was closed off. Hail to You! Now you have finally found it. The metaphysical Absolute is for you now in the German trenches!"[10]

Bloch's friendship with Lukács, whom he met at Simmel's seminar in Berlin, also suffered from the war, though philosophical differences between the men were already apparent before that. As Bloch recalls: "With the war, distinct political phenomena became visible, which more or less necessarily lead to Marxism, which we knew in theory, but not in connection with any type of praxis."[11] Despite a common rejection of the war, whereas Bloch considered that the intellectual was now called upon – as he himself would call upon intellectuals with his numerous newspaper articles and editorials for an antiwar newspaper in Switzerland – to become engaged politically, Lukács, as with his role in the Hungarian Revolution, thought that the detached position of the intellectual, however engaged with their pen, needed to be abandoned. This parting of ways between Bloch and Lukács, centering as well as on their dispute regarding aesthetics and Expressionism that would reignite in the 1930s, occurred with the collapse of Max Weber's intellectual circle in Heidelberg (both had moved to Heidelberg from Berlin before the war). Bloch and Lukács made for an unusual, if brilliant, odd couple – "two figures from opposite poles," in Marianne Weber's recollection – in Weber's orbit. Bloch would later fondly recall these years in Heidelberg as a "bachelor's life with Lukács, led like princes of erudition."[12] Weber, for his part, was less than impressed, indeed annoyed by Bloch's mystical and prophetic demeanor. "Whenever I have spoken with Lukács," Weber once remarked, "I have to think about it for days. When, on the other hand, I see Bloch again, I must begin by working myself back into our last conversation; this man is full of his God, and I am a scientist."[13] When he was appointed director of a military hospital in Heidelberg, Bloch took umbrage at Weber's parading in his reserve officer uniform, and despised the pathological nationalism of the Stefan Georg circle around the literary scholar Friedrich Gundolf.

Among Weber's circle, Karl Jaspers, Gustav Radbruch, and Emil Lederer were, as with Bloch, resolutely against the war. With Jaspers' assistance, Bloch

---

[10] Bloch, *Tagträume vom aufrechten Gang*, p 5.
[11] This divergence on the role of the intellectual was mirrored in their dispute surrounding Expressionism and their respective conceptions of aesthetics and metaphysics of tragedy. By 1916, regular exchange of letters ceased between them. In a letter to a friend, Bloch speaks of the *decrescendo* in his relationship with Lukács during the war (Zudeick, *Hintern des Teufels*, pp. 50–51).
[12] Cited in Bouretz, *Witnesses for the Future*, p. 426.
[13] P. Honigsheim, *The Unknown Max Weber*, trans. J. A. Beegle (New Brunswick, NJ: Transaction Publishers, 2003), p. 151.

obtained a medical release from military duty. Weber and Radbruch followed suit by facilitating a stipend for Bloch to research antiwar movements in Switzerland. After completing the manuscript of *The Spirit of Utopia*, Bloch left for Bern in May 1917, and entered into the vibrant community of exiled German artists and intellectuals. During his two years of exile, he wrote more than 100 newspaper articles for the journal *Freie Zeitung*, often under pseudonyms. Bloch befriended Hugo Ball, Walter Benjamin, Hermann Hesse, Annette Kolb, and René Schickele. The exposure to Dadaism, Kurt Hiller's *Aktivismus*, and the anarchist socialism of the avant-garde provided fertile ground for his radicalization in the direction of Marxism; these formative years of exile were also infused, through the influence of Ball and, especially, Bloch's wife, with a religious and messianic temperament. His articles in Switzerland caught the attention of German military censors, however, as did the first edition of *The Spirit of Utopia*.[14] In the words of the censor's report: "There is nothing new to state about Bloch's conduct [in Switzerland]: the theoretical ideology of his radical standpoint lacks any practical application and thus demonstrates itself, at least in this present essay [*The Spirit of Utopia*], as fairly undangerous for the interests of leading the war."[15]

At the end of "Objective" in *The Spirit of Utopia*, Bloch wonders whether any possibilities remain for life other than subservience to authority and distraction in frivolity. In the aftermath of war, we have become resigned to "dancing around the golden calf" and no longer possess meaningful answers to "Why is there culture?" For Bloch, the future has been cancelled, and in this condition of disenchanted realism – the steel-hardened housing of modern life – we have "become the poorest of vertebrates" in "worshipping" either "our bellies" or the state, or both: "everything else has sunk to the level of a joke, of entertainment." We find ourselves where "we have no idea of socialism" and are thus faced with the stark reality of having to decide for either socialism *or* barbarism, which, for Bloch, in echo of Rosa Luxemburg, stands as *the* question of the twentieth century.[16] Here, then, in the midst of the impossible, a "new beginning" must nonetheless be set

---

[14] For the influence of Ball's Catholic anarchism, interest in the mysticism of von Baader, and the Chiliastic revolutionary figure Thomas Münzer, as well as the resonances between *Critique of the German Intelligentsia* and *The Spirit of Utopia*, and Bloch's reaction against Ball's anti-Semitism, see A. Rabinbach, *In the Shadow of Catastrophe: German Intellectuals between Apocalypse and Enlightenment* (Berkeley: University of California Press, 1997), chapter 2.
[15] Cited in Zudeick, *Hintern des Teufels*, p. 76.
[16] Luxemburg formulated the statement "Socialism or Barbarism," as a choice between the triumph of socialism or the definitive collapse of culture into barbarism, in her antiwar pamphlet, written in prison in 1915 and clandestinely distributed: "The Crisis in German Social Democracy," also known as "The Junius Pamphlet" (www.marxists.org/archive/luxemburg/1915/junius).

into motion by which "an unlost heritage takes possession of itself," with the hope that "what rises above all the masquerades and the expired civilization is the one, the eternal goal, the one presentiment, the one conscience, the one salvation." What remains unbroken is "the realest part of our waking dreams: that is, from the last thing remaining to us, the only thing worthy to remain." In these pages, we are invited to embark on a "fantastic journey" in the interpretation of "our waking dream" and the "implementation of the central concept of utopia," a metaphysical exodus seeking "the true, the real, where the merely factual disappears – *incipit vita nova*."[17]

Ye Olde Pitcher

Amid the wasteland evoked in Bloch's opening reflections, *The Spirit of Utopia* begins with a meditation from a first-person point of view on an old water pitcher (*ein alter Krug*), standing strangely as a relic from a shipwrecked culture, equally "real" and "unreal," we know not why or how. Abruptly, a voice begins to speak. By adopting a first-person stance, Bloch begins with the singularity of existence, not with a universal subject or humanity at large. Yet the "I" of Bloch's fable-like beginning does not just index Bloch himself; it speaks to and of every reader who would embark upon *The Spirit of Utopia* through this lyrical incantation. Bloch's staging of a meditation on an old pitcher depends for its internal coherence on the indexicality of Bloch himself as the I who speaks; it depends for its external coherence on the indexicality of the I of the reader, who here becomes bespoken. Neither the internal ("Bloch as I") nor the external ("the reader as I") is subordinated to each other. The I finds its place *before* the pitcher in the allure of its singsong presence; the standpoint of the I (Bloch, the reader) stands *after* the old pitcher in pursuit of its secret. It begins with the object as giving forth a first-person standpoint, as situating the first person with regard and respect to itself, through which the first person can discover, or encounter, herself. Against Edmund Husserl, Bloch's phenomenology of spirit, as exemplified in his meditations on an old pitcher, is not a descriptive science of how consciousness constitutes objects. Against Hegel, it is an adventure of self-encounter that surpasses the reconciled identity of subject and object.

In moving and speaking about the world, I am not entirely with myself. I am "at myself," or "on myself" (*Ich bin an mir*), yet I do not possess myself completely. When, to use Bloch's example, I take a glass in my

[17] Bloch, *The Spirit of Utopia*, p. 3.

hand from which to drink, the glass is there for me as something useful. It stands before me with functional purpose and design. I am myself in a relation to its affordances: to drink from it, to pick it up, to wash it, and so on. In handling the glass, I do not, however, apprehend myself entirely even as I do experience myself as myself, even as I am "at myself." The purpose and design of who I am "to be" elude me. I am myself, but I do not have myself. Sitting amid the comfort and docility of everyday objects, we rarely realize how close, and yet how far, we are from ourselves, always sitting on the precipice of self-discovery.

And now there sits before me an old pitcher, not a mass-produced object, but an "expensive bearded pitcher, beautifully preserved and deliberately sculpted and elaborately fluted."[18] The design of this old pitcher embodies its usefulness, and yet manifests something else (and not just something more). Something otherwise speaks to me that exceeds the pitcher's utility, but that cannot be divorced from its objective form nor reduced to subjective caprice. Something about its aura escapes the intentionality of subject and object as well as the correlation of mind and world. The old pitcher is an arche-fossil, not of an immemorial past, but of an immemorial future pitched from the past. The pitcher's "enigmatic wildman's bearded face" and "significant, snail-shaped solar emblem on the curvature" are ornamental in a way that cannot be identified with mere decorative flourishes; it is imbued with a fairytale that "speaks to us from a time when they say the long-eared hare could still be seen dancing with the fiery man on Hessian fields." The "once upon a time" of the pitcher's bespoken fairytale moves in its own time: The primeval forests of Germany are "very near to us." A faint aroma of long-forgotten drink wafts forth. This old pitcher before us is, we are told by Bloch, a Bartmann Krug from the Rhine-Franconian region of Germany. The image of the bearded man originated from the archaic myth of a wild man "from Nordic lands," which originally served as a talisman for magical pitchers containing vital water and harboring "the secret of life against death."

This old pitcher does not motivate a question, nor does it confound us in a specifiable way. It is neither an aesthetic object of disinterested contemplation nor (merely) an object of practical use. Our transfixed amazement at this old pitcher remains inconstruable. We stand beholden in the suspense of an "endless, curious children's question," wondering without yet knowing why, what for, or where to. Objectively speaking, the old pitcher is insignificant and aesthetically outmoded – even ugly.

---

[18] Bloch, *The Spirit of Utopia*, p. 8.

Subjectively speaking, the enchantment cast upon us does not resonate with any definable interest within us. In fact, this old pitcher seems to be a discarded object, a knick-knack of colportage, a trace of one knows not what, a thing ostracized from the present, something anachronistic from a remote past. The old pitcher's expressive surplus, its sung transcendence, pulls us toward a yet undisclosed future.

Considering the pitcher further, Bloch remarks that if he beholds long enough the presence of this old pitcher, "I could probably be formed like the pitcher, see myself as something brown, something peculiarly organic [...] and not just mimetically or simply empathetically, but so that I thus become for my part richer, more present, cultivated further toward myself by this artefact that participates in me."[19] It is not that I see myself in this pitcher, nor that I see myself as this pitcher. There is neither identification nor unification with the pitcher. There is an impulse toward oneself, or self-encounter, into a great outdoors beyond, for this old pitcher leads toward a "strange, new territory, and returns with us formed as we could not be in life, adorned with a certain, however weak sign, the self of our self."[20] When I peer into the dark interior of the pitcher, I gaze into the darkness of my own life, of who am I "to be," unknown to myself, at myself in the double entendre of always "toward myself" and already "with myself." The self, for Bloch, is the genuine *Ding an sich*, where the miniscule term *an* indicates a temporalizing crack, or gap, within the self. The self is always on the verge of being itself, held open as both the promise and the secret of the future. Gazing into the pitcher's warm darkness, "one feels oneself looking down a long, sunlit corridor with a door at the far end."[21] As we ourselves begin to peer into *The Spirit of Utopia* through this opening meditation on an old pitcher, we feel ourselves pulled – not pushed – down a long sunlit corridor with a door at the far end of its beyond. What lies behind this door we know not yet. *Nous sommes embarqués.*

Philosophical Expressionism

Characterized by Bloch as *ein Sturm und Drang Buch*, *The Spirit of Utopia* reads like an apocalyptic phenomenology of utopic spirit with a decisively anti-Hegelian and anti-systematic thrust. Unlike Hegel's phenomenology, spirit does not arrive at itself in its own absolute that would provide the

---

[19] Bloch, *The Spirit of Utopia*, p. 9.
[20] Bloch, *The Spirit of Utopia*, p. 9.
[21] As Bloch notes in a 1974 interview: "Every sentence about the pitcher possesses a hidden relation to that which comes after"; Bloch, *Tagträume vom aufrechten Gang*, p. 163.

premise for a science of logic and speculative thinking of God as he is in his eternal essence before creation. Bloch's thinking is not configured in dialectical terms, nor is there a discernible method to the composition of scenes through which *The Spirit of Utopia* traces its journey. There is, instead, an incessant deformalization of dialectical thinking that breaks with the lynchpin of identity and closure of the rationality of the real. With the sonorous quality of its inimitable prose, leitmotifs that become reconfigured, and an uncanny double vision of the (unseemly) actual present and (seemingly) impossible future, *The Spirit of Utopia* presents a philosophical narrative in a montage of expressionist prose. With its paratactic composition and "formal unheard-of-ness" (*formale Urerhörtheit*), Bloch's magisterial work represents an avant-garde philosophy in search of the futurity of spirit's homecoming, the Absolute.[22] It does not progress toward an ultimate revelation where every element of the past would find itself reconciled with the consummate whole; nor does it progress through an eidetic variation that looks for the invariant, essential morphology of objectivity and the structure of reason. As Bloch remarks, "truth is not a scientific or phenomenological category, it is a utopic category. Reality is not suspended or put out of action, it is discarded: utopic *Wesenschau*."[23]

This journey begins with a childlike amazement for a discarded object – the old pitcher – that offers a point of entry for "self-encounter" (*Selbstbegegnung*). Divided into two unequal parts, "The Self-Encounter" and "Karl Marx, Death, and the Apocalypse," Bloch's thinking moves from the interiority of subjectivity, or "self-encounter," to the transcendence of the We, the Idea of socialism, and the Absolute of spirit coming home to itself as the utopic future. In "Self-Encounter," Bloch tackles the philosophical dichotomies of "subject–object," "appearance–thing in itself," and "theory–praxis" – the legacy of German Idealism – through a reflection on art. His aim is not to offer a theoretical solution to this cluster of outstanding problems, but an intimation of the Absolute in the inwardness of subjectivity beyond a logic of identity and dialectic of self-reconciliation. What becomes revealed through the prism of art is "the I-problem" and that "the *unknown*, or *incognito*, first glimpsed with the meditations on the old pitcher, is the subject itself," centered on the "darkness of the lived moment."[24] From this self-encounter, the interiority of the subject discovers itself to be haunted

---

[22] Adapting here Carlo Mierendorff's characterization of Expressionist prose: C. Mierendorff, "Wortkunst / Von der Novelle zum Roman" (1920), in *Prosa des Expressionismus*, ed. F. Martini (Stuttgart: Reclam, 1970): 194–197.
[23] Zudeick, *Hintern des Teufels*, p. 62.
[24] Bloch, *Tagträume vom aufrechten Gang*, p. 163.

by its own "not yet consciousness," and thus fractured from within by the transcendence of its own nonidentity. In "Karl Marx, Death, and the Apocalypse," Bloch passes from the I-problem (inwardness as discovered in and expressed through artworks) to the "We-problem," exteriority in the world and the beyond of the utopic future, progressing from the standpoint of aesthetic contemplation to social-political praxis.

Bloch's conception of art, as developed in the section "Self-Encounter" (divided into two parts, "The Production of the Ornament" and "The Philosophy of Music"), draws inspiration from Expressionism and, more specifically, *Der Blaue Reiter*. As Bloch observes, "my book *Spirit of Utopia* is through and through stamped by the sensibility of Expressionism. Because the goal of creation is the human, Expressionism wanted a new world, a new human being, a new sensibility to create."[25] Significantly, "the concluding part of *Spirit of Utopia* [...] corresponds completely to the Stimmung of 1914/1915, the *Blaue Reiter*, and expressionist painting and poetry: *Karl Marx, Death, and the Apocalypse*."[26] On offer, however, is neither a philosophy of Expressionism nor, strictly speaking, a theory of aesthetics, nor indeed a philosophy of art. In keeping with the avant-garde spirit of cross-fertilization, Bloch effects a philosophical "refunctioning" of Expressionism, capitalizing on its utopic impulse and pursuit of the creative transcendence of aesthetic novelty.[27] Under the designation of "ornament," Bloch seeks to grasp the significance of art in terms of both its surplus of meaning – reaching toward the not yet possible – and its deepening of subjective inwardness. The artwork as ornament is not to be considered as incidental or frivolous, nor as bound to a conventional aesthetic notion of form. It is the dynamic expression of spirit that molds itself along the contours of the ornament (as, for example, with Kandinsky's painted compositions) in such a manner that it breaks with representational or mimetic aesthetics without falling into decorative abstraction. The artwork as ornament is characterized – as with the old pitcher – as a "masked communication" (*vermummte Auskunft*) of self-encounter: the external form of ornament allows for the disclosure of *Innerlichkeit*.

Bloch's aesthetics of the expressionism of spirit aims at surpassing the philosophical aesthetics of Kant (and the influence of Kant's formalism

---

[25] As Bloch recalls, "I was in complete amazement for *Der Blaue Reiter*, which I came to know in Munich"; Bloch, *Tagträume vom aufrechten Gang*, p. 108.
[26] Bloch, *Tagträume vom aufrechten Gang*, p. 169.
[27] In "The Production of the Ornament" (*The Spirit of Utopia*, pp. 10–33), Bloch responds inter alia to Lukács' aesthetics, as developed in his unfinished *Heidelberg Philosophy of Art* and *Heidelberg Aesthetics*.

on nineteenth-century art theory) and Hegel. Bloch rejects the dualism between "appearance" and "thing in itself" as well as the identity of appearance with the thing-in-itself. Developed through the exposition of the ornament and music, the thing-in-itself is not, as with Kant, an epistemological figure of thought, nor, as with Hegel, reconciled in self-identity, but an "objective real incognito," neither "agnostic or transcendent or as finished-stable."[28] As Bloch writes: "The thing-in-itself [...] is what lies in the closest distance, in the actuality of the blue of objects agitates and dreams [*treibt und träumt*]; *it is this, what not yet is, that which is lost, anticipated*, ours in darkness, in the latency of every lived-through moment of hidden self-encounter."[29] The thing-in-itself is not an indeterminate "nothing" but the "not-yet-becoming" of a thing. It is importantly for Bloch a material concept, exemplified in the creative transcendence of artworks, understood as "the at-itself [*das Ansich*] of a still ongoing root-darkness of the material nucleus itself [*noch währendes Wurzel-Dunkel des materiellen Kern selbst*], along with the tremendous cosmic correlation to the darkness of the lived moment."[30] The materiality of an artwork brings about a new and futurally directed openness of possibility of meaning and, in this sense, a "not-yet-becoming" of itself. This incognito on the side of the art object leads to an incognito on the side of the subject, and hence transcendence of the identity of subject and object, indeed, its rupture, in a negative dialectics of surplus and utopic difference. The X of the actual blue, or the driving core in objects (*der treibende Kern in den Objekten*), is indeterminate, and does not have the content of its own ground; the intelligibility of its own being lies in the future, pulling it along in the material world of process. Against a Hegelian reconciliation of objective and subjective identity in the spirit's symbolic manifestation in artworks, the fracture of ontological identity, conceived under the heading of "ornament," releases the possibility of "to be" as the essence of the ornament itself. Artworks open onto a beyond that returns us to ourselves, in self-encounter, in order to transcend who we have been, revealing the inconstruable depth of our own existence in the potentiality of our own "to be." As Bloch writes:

> Things thus become like the inhabitants of one's own interior, and if the visible world seems to be crumbling anyway, to be increasingly emptying itself of its own soul, becoming uncategorical, then in it and through it the sounds of the invisible world correspondingly want to become pictoriality [...] here

---

[28] E. Bloch, *Philosophische Aufsätze zur objektiven Phantasie* (Frankfurt: Suhrkamp, 1985), p. 157.
[29] Bloch, *Philosophische Aufsätze zur objektiven Phantasie*, p. 157.
[30] Bloch, *Philosophische Aufsätze zur objektiven Phantasie*, p. 158.

the pictures, strangely familiar, can appear like magical mirrors where we glimpse our future, like the masked ornaments of our inmost shape, [...] of our glory vibrating within mystery, of our secret divine existence.[31]

The actuality of an artwork, as "ornament," is an event of ontological "decategorization," whereby established categories of meaning and symbolic orders of signification become confronted with an "unknown," not beyond time, but as an unknown future made possible where we might encounter ourselves and our world anew, as otherwise than how we have known ourselves to be in the world.

Bloch's anti-Hegelian aesthetics deformalizes the dialectical through a conception of appearance, in the form of artworks as ornaments, that destabilizes the distinction between exteriority and interiority, phenomenal and noumenal, immanence and transcendence. Artworks bear the traces of a messianic beyond, "cutting the dialectical at its central point," in Adorno's trenchant remark.[32] As cultural artefacts, artworks exemplify the "daydream" or "waking dream" of anticipation, "sufficiently diversified and open to avoid being an absolute knowledge, but sufficiently mediated to delineate a habitable world" – "a non-mortal home for mortal beings."[33] In this sense, artworks avoid the flimsiness of a bad infinity or wishful thinking, while expressing a diversified territory of the imagination that, once created materially in works of art, *could* (*and should*) become populated by new subjectivities, who would, so to speak, need to become the capacity of perceiving or hearing what they cannot as yet. As with the aspirations of *Der Blaue Reiter* movement, works of art are prefigurations, and hence salvations, of subjectivity rescued from the facticity and obscurity of the present to which it seemingly stands beholden. In Bloch's memorable words, an artwork is a "moment of being that escapes the damnation of the unfinished." To draw on a later Blochian expression, artworks are not "appearances" or "illusions" but "pre-appearances" (*Vorschein*) of a "better life" that upturns the forms of the world and their ideological entrapments, allowing for an exodus of life, and, indeed human potential, from the dominion of what is.[34]

It is with music that Bloch's philosophical aesthetics arrives at the utopian transcendence of art in its purest manifestation. If Bloch's discussion

---

[31] Bloch, *The Spirit of Utopia*, p. 32.
[32] Bouretz, *Witnesses for the Future*, p. 436.
[33] Bouretz, *Witnesses for the Future*, p. 447. For the notion of a "non-mortal home for human beings," H. Arendt, *The Human Condition* (Chicago: University of Chicago Press, 2018), p. 168.
[34] E. Bloch, *The Principle of Hope*, trans. N. Plaice and S. Plaice (Cambridge, MA: MIT Press, 1995), p. 215.

of the ornament attended to how interiority becomes disclosed through the plastic arts and hence objects of visual perception, with musical sonority the depths of the self, or "self-encounter," becomes sounded more profoundly and decisively. At this stage in Bloch's phenomenology of utopic spirit, with this passage to music we witness a subtle transition in its narrative voice. When speaking of music, Bloch switches from "I" to "We." Rather than how "I am at myself" (*Ich bin an mir*), Bloch begins "The Philosophy of Music" with the declaration: "We hear only ourselves." This invocation of "we" becomes sustained throughout Bloch's treatment of music. In the lengthiest part of *The Spirit of Utopia*, Bloch undertakes, in rough and rapid strokes, a philosophical genealogy of Western musical forms, beginning with the originating experience of singing to oneself and dancing.[35] From this creative font, musical sonority and the performing musical self remain "nameless." In the primal experience of singing to oneself and dancing, musicality is intimately bound up with movements of the body, giving expression to the materiality of human embodiment. With structured melodic singing and arrangements, musical experience fosters "self-encounter." It is only with melodic form, the origins of which remain historically obscure, that sonorous expressivity becomes "amply and securely equipped" as musical composition. Unlike the plastic arts, music is not a visible object. The musical organization of tones expresses the intrinsic "mystery of sensibility" in terms that language and symbols cannot. Music does not only speak to us in ways unknown to language; it lets us see in ways unseeable by vision, outstripping the world's visible texture. As Bloch writes:

> The clairvoyance [of the world] is long extinguished, but should not however a clairaudience, a new kind of seeing from within, be imminent, which, now that the visible world has become too weak to hold the spirit, will call forth the audible world, the refuge of the light, the primacy of inner flame instead of the former primacy of seeing, if ever the hour to speak in music comes?[36]

With breathtaking staccato, Bloch plays out the history of modern music in terms of a phenomenology of the spirit's self-discovery of interiority, ranging from the "small sacred self" of Bach to the "small secular self" of Mozart, and beyond to the great symphonic and operatic compositions of the nineteenth century. The symphony, the sonata form, and opera in their evolution from Beethoven to Wagner incarnate "the *great*

---

[35] Bloch, *The Spirit of Utopia*, p. 34.
[36] Bloch, *The Spirit of Utopia*, p. 163.

Luciferian self, questing, rebellious, not to be satisfied by anything given, full of militant presentiments of a higher life." In contrast to an interpretation of music as the expression of emotions or the will, music for Bloch is itself expression; it expresses itself as music, and in this self-expression opens beyond itself, not however to an ideal harmony or system of values, but to the future of what is not yet. In its utopian potential, music is the shaping of material sounds; the sounds are entirely temporal and transient and yet, in the medium of their transience, there is an immediacy of affectivity that transcends without suppressing or abandoning the transience of materiality, thus confounding the stability of a distinction between objective time and subjective temporality. Music is the sensuous manifestation in sound of the primal utopic impulse for the realization of what is lacking in the presentiment of what should be. In the rapturous absorption of listening, musical experience is paradigmatic of "the daydream" in hearing of a possibility for a future horizon of sensibility and selfhood that breaks into the present from afar. In the nonverbal expressivity of music, the not-yet-consciousness becomes manifest, not, however, in terms of an "unconscious" (as with Schopenhauer) nor in terms of a "beyond conscious." In the "not-yet-conscious" of musical experience "there is exposed a new self, the self [that is] experienced during listening, for whom hearing is hope."[37] Works of art, whether as ornament or as music, speak to us from a time that is not yet and prefigures in the present a possibility and significance that have not been understood or established before. In this sense, works of art initiate a movement toward the future as well as a movement of self-transformation. Music, however, given its resonance within our own material embodiment and the mystery of its affective unconditionality, speaks to us more profoundly, calling us toward something more and, indeed, transforming us into someone else. "Music," as Bloch states, "is the sole subjective magic."[38]

As the purest aesthetic manifestation, music is the "anamnesis of the modern age, ever more closely circling the Unconditional" through which what can be rescued is "what is most authentic, most genuine from all of the world's unknowing and error."[39] The breakthrough of utopian potency that transcends cultural and social context opens toward "the Infinite."

---

[37] Bloch, *The Spirit of Utopia*, p. 139.
[38] Bloch, *The Spirit of Utopia*, p. 59. For an extensive analysis of Bloch's philosophy of music, B. Korstvedt, *Listening for Utopia in Ernst Bloch's Musical Philosophy* (Cambridge, UK: Cambridge University Press, 2010).
[39] Bloch, *The Spirit of Utopia*, p. 172.

The other truth of which music speaks, to which it calls, is the "indirect correlation to the unseen Man, of the Servants, the eschatological ground of the soul, the restoration of Cosmic man, of *the secret, absolute figure of humanity, from the labyrinth of the world.*"[40] In Beethoven's "Ode to Joy," we hear "the cry of the Beethovenian subject whom nothing in this illusionary life satisfies, a passion for leaving behind the merely inner life, the self-enclosed stillness of interiority, one that transforms the self into a true cosmic structure so high and so deep that suns, moons, and stars could rise and set without colliding, that the entire circuit of humanity has a place." We are transformed from "self-encounter" to the dawn of the We in a new community to come, as with the call that "all people become brothers." Transformed into a discovery of the We, self-encounter, through music, becomes a homecoming, a reconciliation of nature and humanity, human to human: coming to be ourselves as coming together with ourselves, our genuine home. Homecoming is not a movement of return or recuperation. Homecoming is the messianic movement of the utopic future. As Bloch writes, "the We and the Absolute finally meet in the spirit of music" where "the We hears itself, where the fraternally shared ground of the world echoes."[41] We hear "our utopia calling out to itself through goodness, music, metaphysics, but unrealizable in mundane terms."[42] Or, in a contemporary idiom: "The Universe is in My Voice / The Universe Speaks through the Dawn / To Those of Earth and Other Worlds / Listen While You Have the Chance."[43]

Bloch's utopic enthusiasm for Beethoven – his son Jan reports that *Fidelio* was an especially meaningful composition for Bloch – is not without resonance to the historical situation to which and from which he speaks. In September 1914, Herman Hesse published an essay, "O Freunde, nicht diese Töne," in which he took to task his compatriot writers and artists for their cacophonous support of the war. Hesse is incensed by those whose stoking of hatred against France and other nations has carried "the war into the realm of the spirit."[44] Hesse was not wrong with this concern for the spiritual mobilization of Beethoven: Whether for German soldiers who were accompanied to the front by Beethoven's marches or the wartime dominance of Beethoven's compositions in the concert halls,

---

[40] Bloch, *The Spirit of Utopia*, p. 159.
[41] Bloch, *The Spirit of Utopia*, pp. 65–66.
[42] Bloch, *The Spirit of Utopia*, p. 159.
[43] In the words of the incomparable Sun Ra.
[44] H. Hesse, *If this War Goes On … Reflections on War and Politics*, trans. R. Manheim (Edinburgh: Canongate Press, 2018).

"Beethoven's music was synchronized with the German war effort."⁴⁵ In an open letter of 1917 "To a Cabinet Minister," Hesse sought to reclaim Beethoven from this wartime appropriation and perversion. He writes in this letter how listening to a Beethoven sonata after a day's work had proved redemptive: "With its angelic voices the music recalled me from the bustle and worry of the real world, to the one reality in which and for which we live." Later that evening, Hesse read from the Sermon on the Mount and was immediately struck by the commandment "Thou Shall Not Kill." As he writes: "Beethoven's music and the words of the Bible told me exactly the same thing; they were water from the same spring, the only spring from which man derives good." Hesse goes on to admonish the minister and challenges him to listen to Beethoven's "sublime music": "Oh, if this hour of music, this return to true reality, could somehow come your way! You would hear the voice of mankind, you would shut yourself up in your room and weep. And the next day you would go out and do your duty toward mankind." As with Bloch – Bloch befriended Hesse in Switzerland – Hesse hears in Beethoven's music the cosmopolitan utopia of peace and humanity, which, once emancipated from the cries of war – *O Freunde, nicht diese Töne!* – releases a force of interruption in bespeaking the absolute commandment Thou Shall Not Kill. When Kurt Eisner, who studied with Hermann Cohen, ascended to becoming prime minister of Bavaria in 1919, he organized a revolutionary festival to herald the dawn of a new world at the establishment of the Bavarian Republic with a public performance of Beethoven's *Leonore*.⁴⁶ As Eisner conveyed to the audience before the performance:

> My friends, the tones which penetrated your souls portray the enormity of a tyrannical absurdity; the world appears sunken and shattered in the abyss. Suddenly, out of the darkness and despair there is heard a trumpet fanfare which announces a new world, a new mankind, a new freedom […] At the moment when the senselessness of the world had appeared to reach the peak of horror, new hope, new confidence is announced by the distant fanfare of trumpets. Friends, what we have experienced in these days is a fairy tale becoming reality.⁴⁷

---

⁴⁵ D. Dennis, *Beethoven in German Politics, 1870–1989* (New Haven, CT: Yale University Press, 1996), p. 66.
⁴⁶ As Eisner once remarked: "Intellectual influence on my innermost was something only one person ever gained: Hermann Cohen." See M. Benner, "Between Hermann Cohen and Karl Marx: The Jewish Dimension of Kurt Eisner's Revolution in Bavaria, 1918–19," *Modern Judaism – A Journal of Jewish Ideas and Experience*, Vol. 40, No. 1 (2020): 17–36.
⁴⁷ Dennis, *Beethoven in German Politics*, p. 87.

The Inconstruable Question

Running athwart the settled world of mechanism, money, and machines, artworks, in the plastic form of the ornament or the ensouled expressivity of music, rupture the identity of subject and object. Standing before us, an artwork, with its singular materiality and form, effects a decategorization of experience. In art, rather than alienating life from itself, spirit discovers itself anew in its creative potential for imagining a future beyond what has been. Without artworks, we would lack an organ for self-encounter and the discovery of an inward self-transcendence, where our inner gaze becomes captivated in the amazement of "I know not what," as when peering into the obscure hollow of Bloch's old pitcher. Our routine self-forgetting in the mundane and manufactured world becomes arrested; we are brought back to ourselves: "The inward human being stands half still, motivated and attracted cognitively, but what remains or is even reinforced is the presentiment of our hidden power, our latent ascent, our genuine possession, finally unhusked, finally drawn perfectly near."[48] It is not, however, a question of self-knowledge or spirit's self-identification as subject and object, and hence reconciliation with itself, for what becomes disclosed in this "presentiment of our hidden power" is the creative potency of nonidentity with oneself. Creativity is the power of transcending what is (thus far) possible, where the imaginary reaches beyond itself to become utopic. The I is awoken from within to "a transcendence without transcendence," where neither otherworldly transcendence nor immanent certitude of self-presence is discovered. On the contrary, what is discovered as the beating heart of existence is "the darkness of the lived moment" and "the not yet consciousness," braced in "the inconstruable question" that I have become for myself. "I am at myself" (*Ich bin an mir*), always on the edge of a self-questioning, the sense of which both eludes and interpolates me. As Bloch writes, "what is *most inward* in us itself simply lies in deep shadow even past the insubstantial fog, incognito to itself, *in a moral-metaphysical incognito*."[49]

Thrust into the obscurity of our own inwardness, as Bloch writes, "all we can do for the moment is prepare, provide words and concepts, until an identification takes them up and grants equivalence." Self-encounter destructures existence from the mediated forms of essences and symbolic encodings by operating an ontological decategorization of subjectivity

---

[48] Bloch, *The Spirit of Utopia*, p. 168.
[49] Bloch, *The Spirit of Utopia*, p. 172.

itself. We are, indeed, unknown to ourselves, always standing before ourselves as a question only dimly construed according to established ways of knowing. In the hollowness of inwardness, subjectivity awaits the revelation and realization of a final truth as to its own self-identity. Human existence, in this sense, remains an ontologically unfinished adventure, and finds within itself, as creative potential, the "not yet consciousness" of itself. To be an inconstruable question for oneself is not to lack an answer; it is to lack a proper sense of the question itself, the question that becomes me. This question that the self becomes for itself haunts every moment of existence, unknowingly while we are lost to ourselves in our attentiveness to the manufactured world. Once broached, the darkness of the lived moment, in its mysterious allure and accent, eludes any congruence with concepts: "the soul," "the ego," even "humanity," are at best placeholders and "sites of prayer" for an identity, and hence an actuality – indeed, a life – to come. Once we arrive at the incognito of ourselves – the animating incognito of the subject; that is, the subjectivity of the subject – we have arrived in Bloch's phenomenology of spirit at the point of absolute unknowing, and hence a point of departure for *vita nova*.

The depth of this inwardness (namely, the subjectivity of the subject) was explored by Kant and Hegel with their respective conceptions of subjectivity in its primary ethical-metaphysical unconditionality. What attracts Bloch to both thinkers is how subjectivity becomes defined principally in ethical – not ontological – terms, but also how this ethical conception of subjectivity becomes inscribed in the movement of history. Kant is the thinker of subjectivity as autonomy; he is not the thinker of the finite subject within the bounds of sense and understanding, but rather the thinker of finitude bound to the unconditional. The ethical subject becomes itself in determining for itself what it ought to do with respect to the moral law. Most significantly, with Kant, "we first, finally become free, and the outer encirclement breaks; the genuine self steps forward [...] *in hope*."[50] Whereas theoretical knowledge, and hence the knowing subject, finds itself restricted and conditioned, the ethical self opens "another rationalism [other] than the thinking, theoretical Cartesian subject." Absence of self-knowledge does not preclude determining what one ought to do; it is, in fact, the condition for autonomy insofar as self-knowledge is not a condition for acting unconditionally. The ethical subject is affected by the unconditional, the absolute of the moral law, from within, out of respect.

---

[50] Bloch, *The Spirit of Utopia*, p. 178.

Bloch in this regard speaks of the "melancholic honor" of the ought-to-be: practical reason can never fully close the circle between itself and itself, insofar as the perfection of the will to the moral law remains unattainable, and yet, in this infinite movement, the law does not stand outside, or external to, subjectivity. What is and what ought to be, in the domain of practical reason, can never coincide or stand identical with each other. This polarity inscribes an adventure into the movement of subjectivity, which, for Bloch, reflects the principle of hope that is integral to Kantian autonomy. The purchase of freedom for human life is measured by a sense of hope that cannot be bound to the objectivity of the world or the finitude of the subject. As Bloch states, Kant discovers "the great and honest metaphysics of the ethical subject, contemporary with the remoteness of God."[51] Hegel expands on Kant's discovery of autonomy with his inscription of individual freedom into a community of *Sittlichkeit* and the march of "world-historical spirit." The dualism inherent to Kant's "bad infinity" between what is and what ought to be – the moral will and the moral law – becomes surpassed with Hegel's argument that the inwardness of the I must breathe the air of a historically unfolding world toward "the We-problem." What ought to be becomes realizable in history and the nation-state, at the price, however, of falling into a "panlogism" of the *Encyclopedia* and finality of world history. Kant's "bad infinity" has been exchanged for Hegel's "false absolute." The self has been lost to the Absolute, closed off into it, rather than the self-encountering of itself in the Absolute, opened onto it. More significantly, as Bloch writes, "Hegel's theory that everything rational is already real concludes a premature and total truce with the world." The ruse of reason is unmasked as a sleight of hand in the cheat of reason: "heavenly cards are shuffled into the earthly deck, as if they belonged there and had always been part of it."[52] Hegel's dialectical philosophy of the absolute, in its world-historical contemplation, represents nothing less than the effacement of suffering and evil, with which, however, no peace or reconciliation should so easily be found. The aim of dialectical thinking, in Bloch's deformalization, is *never* to make peace with the world as it has been, or is; nor to impose a form of consolation in the face of evil and suffering so as to "relieve consciousness of its speculative torments" – as with the catastrophe of the First World War.[53] As Bloch writes:

---

[51] Bloch, *The Spirit of Utopia*, p. 176.
[52] Bloch, *The Spirit of Utopia*, pp. 181, 182.
[53] For this formulation, Bouretz, *Witnesses for the Future*, p. 442.

> In Hegel, philosophy becomes a headmaster, or an impassive lawyer for the Being that hired him, and the night of the world withdraws into the uneducated subject. Thus, the good warm atmosphere of the study spreads out, in order that everything painful, unbearable and unjust in life […] can be set forth as something anodyne, something that always happens, that never happens, the strict analysis of which either is found only on the blackboard, or is but a simple ceremony.[54]

Against a false peace and reconciliation with the world, Bloch proposes that we must "let Kant burn through Hegel" and return to the darkness of the self in its lived moment of existence, yet we must also, in turn, allow the darkness of the lived moment to burn through Kant's autonomous subjectivity. As Bloch asks: "When does one really live, when is one consciously present oneself in the vicinity of one's moments?"[55] With this question, Bloch suspends established conceptions of subjectivity and, in particular, subjectivity as spontaneity and self-presence, and returns to the temporality of lived experience. The temporality of subjectivity subtends the ontological determination of the subject as "soul," "consciousness," and so on. How the self exists is inseparable from a temporality – its own – that never lets oneself *just* be. The lived moment incessantly slips away and yet remains shadowed by its own obscuration; within each lived moment there abides a dark ground of absence, thus undercutting self-presence as well as self-identity. I am always *at* myself, on the edge of myself, caught at the border of knowing and not knowing what for and where to I am, much as I am, in every lived moment, "at the now," caught at the border of the not yet and the no longer. In Bloch's phrasing, "we live (*leben*) ourselves, but we do not experience (*er-leben*) ourselves." In this constitutive fracture between "living" and "experiencing," the unfurling of temporality does not refer to the reverse side of consciousness as its unconscious, but refers instead to oneself as *not yet conscious*, and not as no longer conscious or as consciousness of the not yet. The darkness of the lived moment, as "not yet conscious," is, moreover, not to be conflated with a repressed consciousness, or unconscious. The darkness of the lived moment cannot be associated with a notion of the lived moment – "the now" – as slipping away into the past. On the contrary, the darkness of the lived moment consists in the future as "not yet," as having already slipped into the present, thus dislocating the present from itself (and rupturing self-presence). The lived moment slips, or passes, away into the "no longer now" only

---

[54] Bloch, *The Spirit of Utopia*, p. 185.
[55] Bloch, *The Spirit of Utopia*, p. 188.

because the "not yet now" has already ejected the present from itself. Lived temporality, our own, does not so much flow away, murmuring within its silent breath the incessant passage of being into nonbeing; that is, death. Rather, lived temporality comes to pass in the sense of coming into passage from the surplus of the future – our own not yet being. Bloch inverts the traditional relation between time and being in refusing to understand temporality as first and foremost a passage from being toward nonbeing. Lived temporality becomes flipped on its head: no longer the experience of nonbeing, of life passing away, but as an interpolation of being by a transcendence – the future – beyond the essence of what has been, or what is. This is not to deny that lived temporality is experienced as passage; it is, however, to indicate within temporality an original fissure, or fault line, between the present and the past, through which the present can become emancipated from the hold of what has been toward what is yet to be. Time passes away because we already stand before the not yet of our own future. At the core of subjectivity in its temporalized existence is a hole in its own being toward which subjectivity is pulled, pushed away from itself *and* pulled toward itself. In casting for a characterization of this consciousness of hope at the heart of temporality, Bloch speaks of the "waking dream" and "higher-order unconscious, the *fundus intimus, the latency of the primordial secret in itself moving within the Now,* in short the creative unconscious of our spiritual *coronation*."[56]

In life, Bloch reflects, we go shopping and feel that something is missing, without knowing exactly what is missing. We peruse things on offer in a shopping mall, and end up purchasing things we never really need, having forgotten the wonderment of the child. The unconditional wonder at the world, without inclination for its possession or impulse for domination, moves us to discover *that* something is missing. Once we have disencumbered ourselves of prefabricated concepts, social norms, and cultural forms that obscure this wonder at ourselves, we stand before ourselves as a child in amazement – we are not bewildered, but captivated: we are at once, as with a child, "constantly impatient" and dumbstruck that we *are* unfinished and that, as such, what it means to be is that we are still "to be." In this amazement, "the surplus of the *moral-metaphysical existence-meaning in itself*" becomes lived as the question we are for ourselves. This amazement is childlike: We know not what we are asking or searching for, we are held by the innocence of a question without motivation or interest,

---

[56] Bloch, *The Spirit of Utopia*, p. 192.

we are disinterested yet entirely captivated.⁵⁷ The inconstruable question we become for ourselves is a remembrance, or *anamnesis*, not of lost time or the authentic self we once were; it is a remembrance of the future, as the origin of the future, that disrupts the settled answers to a question we can no longer take for granted or assume to be – construe as – known: to be oneself. To be is to be in question, yet not to be construed as a project that I knowingly pursue, but as an adventure to which I am unknowingly called. The "final goal" is "the question directed towards us, not as indication to an answer; but the inconstruable question as itself the answer to the question." Nothing becomes revealed in the present for everything becomes revealed as not yet. In this sense, the being who I am, who is "here" and "now," is a being not toward death, but toward life *in* hope. As Bloch remarks: "We were not only born to accept or write down what was and how it was, when we were not there, but everything waits for us, things seek their poets and want to be related to us."

The amazement (i.e., the inconstruable question) that illuminates the darkness of the lived moment discloses the world as not yet accomplished along with an impulse to realize its completion. Pulsating through every lived moment is the pull of the future; we are pulled toward the future, not just dragged away into the past; and, indeed, it is the pull of the future that, as it were, is the Real, as the force of interruption and differentiation that incessantly haunts the continuity of time, the stability of ontological categories, and historical conceits. The origin is withdrawn from the present, yet not behind us in the past. The origin *is* the future, as the not yet of being who we are to become and should be. This utopic-ontological difference eludes the logic of identity as well as the mythology of origins. As Bloch writes, "the origin in the strict sense has itself not yet arisen."⁵⁸ Rather than an ontological movement of "difference" in the sense of deferral, there is

---

⁵⁷ Bloch's darkness of the lived moment, as Jürgen Habermas argues, draws significantly from Schelling and Böhme; J. Habermas, "Ernst Bloch – A Marxist Romantic," *Salmagundi*, Vol. 10/11 (1969–70): 311–325. But as Przemyslaw Tacik has convincingly argued, Bloch finds direct inspiration for this conception in the writings of Isaac Luria and the Kabbalist's notion of *tsimtsum*. As Tacik writes: "In Chaim Vidal's portrayal of the *tsimtsum*, God's initial contraction has two concurrent consequences: first, it empties the space for the creation of the world and second, it expulses the powers of judgement out of God [...] whereas in the Lurianic *tsimtsum* contracts the fullness of the Ein-Sof in order to open the space for creation, the Blochian lived moment crushes and contracts the stiff amassment of the past in order to pave the way for the radically new. The past is contracted and thrust open, with its content forcefully pushed into the future [...] as if ultimately the origin of the world was not at the beginning but at the end of the world"; P. Tacik, "Ernst Bloch as a Non-Simultaneous Jewish Marxist," *Religions*, Vol. 9, No. 11 (2018): 346.

⁵⁸ As Bloch writes in *The Principle of Hope* (p. 307): "The origin remains the incognito of the core which moves throughout all times, but which has not yet moved out of itself," and in this sense, every moment is the "year zero of the beginning of the world."

an ontological movement of difference in the sense of proffering. In the immediacy of the darkness of the lived experience as haunted by "not yet consciousness," a utopic impulse arrests and confounds the settlement of ontologies. This utopic impulse haunts the lived moment from the future, toward the future. In every lived moment, not only is the world still to be ontologically accomplished, but subjectivity itself – humanity – remains not just unknown to itself, but unidentifiable and unaccomplished. The dark ground of the lived moment is a contraction: withdrawal and expulsion. As Bloch states in *The Principle of Hope*, looking back to *The Spirit of Utopia*, with this conception of a "cracked ontology," the future inhabits being under the guise of possibility; "it is not a terrifying dimension into which we are thrust from our cozy home, but our real homeland to which we travel from the unhospitable world of the past."[59]

Marx, Death, and Apocalypse

"Now we have to begin. Into our hands, life has been given. To itself it became empty already long ago."[60] With these words, Bloch begins the final section of *The Spirit of Utopia*, "Karl Marx, Death, and the Apocalypse," in echo of the anger and aspiration with which he began: "So we repeat: What just was will probably soon be forgotten […] We repeat again: And of course, as though one had not been burned badly enough, this is how it remains even today. The War ended, the Revolution began and with it, seemingly, the open doors. But correct, these soon closed again." With this (near) verbatim version of pronouncements from "Objective," we appear to have come full circle, finding ourselves no farther than the beginning, as if Bloch's phenomenology of utopic spirit – from the ornament to music to the inward wonder of the inconstruable question – were but a waking dream, a promised adventure having yet to begin. Has all of this effort been in vain? Is this return to the beginning not a confirmation that the future remains foreclosed? In this return to the beginning, spirit, however, does not turn back to where it began, for in this movement of Kierkegaardian repetition, spirit finds itself beyond itself along the contours of a hairline fracture between the hopelessness of "the just then" and the hopefulness of "the just now." Bloch's artfully constructed *The Spirit of Utopia* is itself a philosophical ornament that, in its narrative arc, does not come full circle upon itself nor stand fully enclosed within its own historical situation.

---

[59] Bloch, *The Principle of Hope*, II, p. 312.
[60] Bloch, *The Spirit of Utopia*, p. 233.

With this repetition of the beginning, the historical present – the aftermath of the war – is brought once more into the foreground, now illuminated by the brilliant star of socialism that has since broken into history on the horizon of the East: "Meanwhile the West with its millions of proletarians has not yet spoken; meanwhile there stands, unbowed, a Marxist Republic in Russia; and the eternal questions of our longing, of our religious conscience still burn, undiminished, unbent, unredeemed in their absolute claim."[61] Here, then, we find the inaugural gesture of Bloch's daring ambition to superimpose a religious quest for redemption on Marxism's pursuit of world revolution. This passage from the unfinished legacy of Kant and Hegel to the unfulfilled dream of Marx is, among other claims, predicated on an attitude of rejecting any complacency or compromise – indeed, consolation – with the world. As Bloch writes:

> This book – which will never make peace with the world – led the reader all the way through, first to our still unused nature, to our secret Head, our figure and awakening convocation, to the center of our artistic principle; precisely this already rang out by our interpretation of a simple pitcher, interpreted as the *a priori* latent theme of all the "visual" arts, and then as central to all the magic of music, illustrated finally by the ultimate possible self-encounter, by the comprehended darkness of the lived moment, which leaps up and hears itself in the essence of the inconstruable, the absolute question, in the very problem of the We.

Only in moving upward to the We-problem can we "break through the error of this world."[62] Across this threshold, outward into the world and upward to the We-problem from the inwardness of the I-problem, Bloch's phenomenology of utopic spirit transitions from the ethical to the political, from contemplation to praxis, from the immanence of subjectivity and its unfinished yearning "not yet" to the transcendence of intersubjectivity and its unfinished yearning "not yet." The darkness of the lived present opens a fissure through which one becomes moved from the "inner sanctum onto a broader domain" of the question of who *we* are to become. In this passage from the "lonely waking dream of inner self-encounter to the dream that goes out to shape the world," there reverberates the cosmic "salvific intention" and "desperate rebelliousness" against the state along with the utopic imperative for revolution.[63] For we can only genuinely live after what is false has fallen away, and what is false in the world is

---

[61] Bloch, *The Spirit of Utopia*, p. 236.
[62] Bloch, *The Spirit of Utopia*, p. 247.
[63] Bloch, *The Spirit of Utopia*, p. 238.

enforced through coercion: the falsity of the world stands inseparable from the political realism of a world structured by violence, social oppression, economic exploitation, and worship of false idols.

Bloch adopts Weber's seminal definition of the modern nation-state as organized around the monopolization of violence and the instrumentalization of the law by means of which, here following Marx instead, "the ruling class protects its interests." The law and the nation-state promote social degradation and injustice. Revolution, envisioned by Bloch as the eschatological goal of world history, must strive, however, for more than a material-social transformation of relations of power and abolition of class structure. Rather than accept a positivist conception of Marxism wedded to laws of history and economic reductionism, Bloch argues against the occlusion of subjectivity, in its inwardness, as the unfinished "not yet" consciousness; it is from the inwardness of subjectivity that the radicalism of utopian orientation breaks through in its anticipatory and productive function. In the *incognito* of the soul ("inwardness") there agitates the *incognito* of who we – humanity – should become. In this manner, Bloch rehabilitates utopia as both a fundamental ontological and political category in its diverse productive functions: cognitive, anticipatory, educative, and causal.[64] Against the charge that utopianism represents a wishful Romantic form of subjectivism, Bloch contends that although the "utopic impulse is absolutely eccentrically to time as the inventory of Oughts," as presentiments of the goal, or *eschaton*, of world history, it nonetheless takes its bearings from a series of "super-historical" Oughts, each of which testifies to the unfinished character of historical reality. In Bloch's survey of modern thought, he identifies three kinds of Oughts: Kant's Kingdom of Ends and Idea of Perpetual Peace; Hegel's Absolute Spirit of World History; and Marx's Proletarian Revolution. Rather than understand the problem of utopia, as framed by what reality ought to become, in terms of how to extrapolate an ideal arrangement for the future from the present, Bloch reverses the utopic equation into the question of how to relate to the present from a future that is not yet. As that which is not yet but should be, the dream image of utopia reveals and hence awakens the unfinished, that is, the inadequate and unacceptable character of what has hitherto been taken to be.

What distinguishes Bloch's renewal of utopic thinking in "Karl Marx, Death, and the Apocalypse" is the superlative accent on redemption for the fallenness and corruption of the world, not only in terms of economic

---

[64] W. Hudson, *The Marxist Philosophy of Ernst Bloch* (London: Wayne Hudson, 1992), pp. 50–51.

and political structures, as championed by Marx, but as a triumph over death. There can be no "peace with the world," which, in the final messianic pages of *The Spirit of Utopia*, Bloch characterizes in overtly religious terms: "the mere physical world is still an impediment in itself; it is the collapsed house in which no one lived, is a rubbish heap of cheated, deceased, degraded, misled and ruined life, is the kingdom of Edom."[65] The question of "Socialism or Barbarism," raised in the opening remarks of *The Spirit of Utopia*, has been transformed, over the course of its development, into the question of Jacob and Esau; the Edomites were said to be the descendants of Esau, and were claimed in the Old Testament to be responsible for the destruction of Jerusalem (Ezekiel 35:1–5; Psalms 137:7). At the center of Bloch's call for salvation stands human suffering, not only in its socioeconomic dimensions but, metaphysically weighted, for human suffering *as such*. In this respect, Marxism falls short of heeding the revolutionary imperative of salvation for human suffering, which only humans can achieve for themselves. Marx's insistence on social revolution – the abolition of class conflict and oppression – must be supplemented by the Judeo-Christian insistence on salvation of human suffering and triumph over the sovereignty of death.

Viewed in these terms, what utopia must essentially struggle against is death, or "anti-utopia." Death poses a crucial problem for utopian thinking, for death opposes hope in both a social and a political sense: how can I be committed to a utopic, that is, revolutionary, transformation of the world, for a future "we" beyond our own mortality, namely, for a future form of human existence other than and exceeding our own, a future that I shall never witness? Responding to the anti-utopic challenge of death entails the possibility of interrupting the dominance of *lex talionis* – the cycle of retaliation and revenge – as well as subjection to the materiality of being; namely, the power of what *is*. As Bloch writes: "death is nothing other than the power of that which merely is." This identification of death with ontology – the power of being – contests the bond between meaning and attachment to the world, such that, on the contrary, the question of being and nonbeing is not the be-all and end-all of humanity. The temporality of human possibility, as revealed in the "not yet consciousness," is not anchored in "being-towards-death" but, on the contrary, in hope beyond being and hence death.[66] In this manner, the question of

---

[65] Bloch, *The Spirit of Utopia*, p. 271.
[66] See E. Levinas, *God, Death, and Time*, trans. B. Bergo (Stanford, CA: Stanford University Press, 1992), pp. 92ff.

meaning for human existence becomes disassociated from the primacy of the question "To be or not to be?" To this end, Bloch reflects upon the universality of myths and beliefs in immortality and the afterlife among human cultures. These "fairytales" are expressions of what distinguishes human life: We are material organisms that can dream beyond the alternative of being and nonbeing. We exist as a dreaming materiality. Images of the afterlife and the religious quest for redemption in the afterlife symbolize an ethical-metaphysical hope and aspiration for otherness, understood in terms of a world other than the world as we have known it, and, indeed, another world of goodness, justice, and freedom that, from the point of view of the present, encumbered with the substance of the past, appears to be impossible. Higher than actuality is not the possibility of death, or nonbeing, for higher than the possibility of death is the impossibility of life after death, an impossibility that nonetheless affects and hence moves us more powerfully than the conditionality of our finitude. False in one sense, myths of the afterlife are nonetheless true as to their utopic aspiration. As with the ornament, religious narratives give expression to a "not yet consciousness" and the force of the imaginary against what would seem to be ontologically impermeable. Dreams of the afterlife and mythological narratives of the quest for immortality do not shield or protect us from the anxiety of death, however. In the materiality of death, there is also the materiality of the dream to surpass death. Myths of the afterlife are not deceptive wish-fulfillments or expressions of subjective caprice. We do not escape into fantasy. On the contrary, the Real penetrates into the world, disruptively and originally, through "fairytales" and the utopic imaginary, which moves in its own time as otherwise than being and beyond essence.[67] For Bloch, images of the transmigration of souls attest to "an indiscernible something" that agitates within us toward the realization of "the still undiscovered world-idea" and the We of humanity: "Everything could pass away, but the house of humanity must remain preserved and stand illuminated at full strength, so that one day, when destruction rages outside, what we have gained can live there, and help us—which leads us directly from the transmigration of souls to the meaning of the true social, historical and cultural ideology."[68] In dreaming of the afterlife, we dream of homecoming, not as transcendence beyond the world and history, but, on the contrary, as a transcendence of the impossible – the present state of

---

[67] A. Bielik-Robson, "Dreams of Matter. Ernst Bloch on Religion as Organized Matter," *Revue internationale de philosophie*, Vol. 3 (2019): 333–360.
[68] Bloch, *The Spirit of Utopia*, p. 266.

the world, apparently unchangeable – toward the possibility for the realization of a humanity at one with itself in peace. Stated thus, the utopic impulse aspires toward a future, not according to a pregiven plan or model for human collective existence, nor as a place, or *topos*, whether on earth or elsewhere, that does not exist but should. The utopic aspiration opens a messianic temporality of salvation for humanity in broaching an ontological interspace between the present and the future. Through this fissure in being, the identity of who we are yet to be, and need to become, becomes graspable in the present for a time yet to come, and which ought to be. The rift between what has been and what should be reveals hope *now* for homecoming. It is, however, not God who remains hidden in our awaiting of messianic fulfillment but us, our future humanity, as *homo absconditus*.[69] Humanity remains unknown and unfinished for itself until the apocalyptic end of days when humanity shall finally be able to walk hand in hand toward a common table of concord and goodness.

There is a further significant aspect to Bloch's argument that utopia, in this Messianic-Marxist configuration, must confront death, or anti-utopia, where death is understood as "the power of that which merely is." There is nothing more unimaginable than emancipation from the materiality of being, and yet there is nothing more materially significant for human existence than overcoming the realism of being. On this conception, death is the power of being and nonbeing, or, in other words, the power of ontology itself. When situated in the context of the war and its aftermath, the utopic struggle against anti-utopia represents a struggle against the ontopolitical mobilization of death. As Bloch decries at both the beginning and the end of *The Spirit of Utopia*, the war has been "forgotten." What has survived is capitalist exploitation, social oppression, consumer culture, and Prussian militarism. It is not only that the deaths of millions have been in vain, leading neither to an awakening nor a transformation of humanity. It is that the deaths of millions proved to be politically and economically expedient for the maintenance of the status quo. The total mobilization of European nations revealed the extent to which modernity is determined by necro-politics. Millions have been sacrificed for the Fatherland, called upon to die for the sake of society and culture. Death, in other words, is not merely an ontological category; it is inextricably a political category as well, understood in terms of the production of social death. When translated into Bloch's Marxist-Messianic

---

[69] J. Siebers, "Noch Nicht," in *Bloch-Wörterbuch. Leitbegriffe der Philosophie Ernst* Blochs, eds. B. Dietschy, D. Zeilinger, and R. Zimmermann (Berlin: De Gruyter, 2012): 403–408.

framework, modern capitalism sustains itself through the social production of death in various forms: social alienation, cultural oppression, economic exploitation, and racial colonialism. The elimination of death, as the aim of utopic salvation, entails the elimination of the production of social death. In this sense, a biophilic revolution is integral to Bloch's phenomenology of utopic spirit in its struggle against the "absolute anti-utopia that sanctifies and makes death absolute."[70] Although Bloch rejects the revolutionary transformation of one particular domain (class, gender, etc.) or idea (happiness, freedom, etc.) as holding the key to the transformation of the world, the totality of transformation falling under the universality of the "we-problem" hinges on the surpassing of economic exploitation and the degradation of human life, and the triumph over social death. Socialism, in this messianic sense, refers to the utopian promise of alleviating the suffering of inhumanly produced society in its modern configuration; otherwise, we are left with the barbarism of necropolitics, as became patently apparent with the war. Hence the existential threat posed to barbarism by the hope of socialism, given the social production of death and the economic predation without which modern capitalism and its biopolitics could not sustain itself.

The imperative for utopic transformation can only be genuinely grasped in religious terms, hence the syncretic blending of Marxism and Christian-Judeo messianism in Bloch's thinking. What the Judeo-Christian heritage emphasized as the cosmic struggle against evil and death, against which Jesus declared war, provides the original transcendental-historical schema for revolution. As Bloch retrospectively remarked in an Afterword from 1963, *The Spirit of Utopia* is a

> *Sturm und Drang* book entrenched and carried out by night, against the War, as well as about a first work – built around the *nos ipse* – of a new, utopian kind of philosophy. Its revolutionary Romanticism (as in my monograph on Thomas Münzer) attains measure and definition in *The Principle of Hope* and the books that followed. There, what was specific to *The Spirit of Utopia* became especially definite, something entrusted peculiarly to evil, as to its remedy: revolutionary gnosis.

The appeal of Gnosticism, with strong accents of Marcionism, consists in the promise of an emancipation from death as the power of being. For Bloch, the figure of Christ represents an apocalyptic triumph over the final enemy of death (1 Corinthians 15:26). As Bloch writes: "Precisely that too

---

[70] M. Ott, "Something's Missing. A Study of the Dialectic of Utopia in the Theories of Adorno and Bloch," *Heathwood Journal of Critical Theory*, Vol. 1, No. 1 (2015): 133–173; p. 136.

was messianically meant by the Second Coming, and in an explosion, it flies at the outside, the put-in-the-way, Satan the Demon of Death, the encrusted *ritardando* of the world, everything that is not of us or even obstructs us, of the plural Singular who hopes for himself, of our heavenly glory."[71] The coming of Christ, in this Blochian figuration, stands for the revelation of the "secret Human Being, something always meant, always utopianly present," that would become realized as the homecoming of humanity to itself. And yet, the secret of religion consists in the notion that "atheism with concrete utopia is at one and same time the annihilation of religion and the realization of its heretical hope, now set on human feet."

This, then, is the messianic depth of human existence, the purest expression of the utopic imaginary: God must become human, and hence empty himself, while humankind must empty itself, and hence become "godly." The attraction of Marcionism resides (inverted, however, from a gospel of the alien God to the gospel of alien humanity) with this proposal that we are still waiting for the alien human to become revealed in an apocalypse of hope that would redeem creation; that is, the realm of being. As Bloch writes: "The ultimate fulfillment of the messianic principle will thus be the utopian transformation of the real." But this transformation of the real occurs through the intrusion of the Real, or Absolute, that would save us from creation – the realm of ontology – in the form of an "enabling traumatism."[72] The figure of Christ stands for the Son of Man, not the Son of God, as the future of a humankind reconciled with itself. As the figure of Hope, Christ initiates the "entire new" as the anti-demiurgic principle that rebels against mystifications of state power and, most crucially, the ontological power of death. For this transformation of the Real is not as a cosmic escape to another world that leaves the material cosmos untransformed, but as a radical "humanization of nature," or what Bloch calls "naturalization of man and humanization of nature."[73] With Bloch's Marxian inspiration, this would entail a social and ecological dimension – namely, the reconciliation between humanity and nature – within the messianic arc of a final inversion by which "the inward can become the outward and the outward like the inward."[74] Bloch's own work, written in the midst of war and its aftermath, is issued as a waking dream in which

---

[71] Bloch, *The Spirit of Utopia*, p. 277.
[72] A. Bielik-Robson, *Jewish Cryptotheologies of Late Modernity: Philosophical Marranos* (London: Routledge, 2014).
[73] E. Bloch, *Atheism of Christianity*, trans. J. T. Swann (London: Verso, 2009), pp. 212–213, 232.
[74] Bloch, *The Spirit of Utopia*, p. 231.

the Real disturbs us, which Bloch considers exemplified in an image from stories of Baal Shem: "The messiah can only come when all the guests have sat down at the table," where "we can wipe each other's tears."[75] When we finally become reconciled with each other, only then shall there "arise in the world something which appears to us all in childhood, and in which none of us yet was – home."[76]

---

[75] Bloch, *The Spirit of Utopia*, p. 246.
[76] Bloch, *The Philosophy of Hope*.

CHAPTER 6

The Road to Damascus in the Age of Capitalism
György Lukács and History and Class Consciousness

"The Second International Is Dead"

In July 1914, Vladimir Lenin and his comrade Gregory Zinoviev found themselves as political émigrés "in a god-forsaken little mountain village in Galicia."¹ Under gathering clouds of war, Zinoviev recalls making a bet with Lenin that the German Social Democratic Party would never support financing a war. Lenin gladly took up this wager in full confidence that European socialist parties, as declared by the Second International, would call for a general strike of the proletariat in the event of war. As Zinoviev recalls, Lenin observed that "no, they [German Socialist Party or SPD] are not such scoundrels as all that. They will not, of course, fight the war, but they will, to ease their conscience, vote against the credits lest the working class revolts against them."² When the SPD newspaper *Vorwärts* arrived announcing that war credits had been approved, Lenin refused to accept this confounding news. "It cannot be," he exclaimed, "it must be a forged number." Reality quickly disabused Lenin of his incredulousness. In Zinoviev's words: "Neither of us had taken the full measure of the flunkeyism of the social patriots. The European Social Democrats proved completely bankrupt." As Lenin remarked: "The Second International is dead!"³

More than a hundred years later, one can wonder whether Europe ever recovered from this fateful decision in 1914.⁴ In his assessment of Germany in

---

¹ V. Sebestyen, *Lenin: The Man, the Dictator, and the Master of Terror* (New York: Vintage Books, 2017), p. 231.
² "Lenin: Speech to the Petrograd Soviet by Gregory Zinoviev Celebrating Lenin's Recovery from Wounds Received in the Attempt Made on his Life on August 30, 1918," www.marxists.org/archive/zinoviev/works/1918/lenin/index.htm.
³ Sebestyen, *Lenin*, p. 232.
⁴ As the historian Ferdinand Braudel observes: "L'Occident, en 1914, *autant qu'au bord de la guerre, se trouve au bord du socialism*. Celui-ci est sur le point de se saisir au pouvoir, de fabriquer une Europe aussi modern, et plus peut-être qu'elle ne l'est actuellement. En quelques jours, en quelques heures, la guerre aura ruiné ces espoirs"; F. Braudel, *Grammaire des civilisations* (Paris: Flammarion, 2008), p. 526. See also L. Canfora, *1914* (Palermo: Sellerio Editore, 2006), chapter 1. As Nicola

Die Bilanz der Moderne (1904), Samuel Lublinski identified 1890 as the pivotal year for the emergence of socialism.[5] The revocation of Bismarck's anti-Socialist law in 1890, which had banned the socialist party since 1878, allowed for opposition against the Prussian Junkers and entrenched conservatives. This ascent of socialism in Germany mirrored a broader European tendency. Toward the end of the nineteenth century and the beginning of the twentieth, socialist parties in France and Italy, as well as the labor movement in England, gained in political viability and electoral support. In 1889, delegates of socialist and labor parties from twenty countries established the Second International Socialist Bureau in Paris, with the ambition of forming a united front against the expansion of capitalism and the imperialism of European nation-states – more radical elements advocated the overthrow of both – as well as to promote women's rights, the empowerment of the working class, and social reforms. Central to the platform of the Second International was the abolition of war, as well as antimilitarism and pacificism.[6]

The Second Morocco Crisis in 1911 further emboldened the Second International's antiwar stance, despite Gustav Landauer's prescient caution against premature optimism that the threat of war on the Continent had subsided with the resolution of this colonial dispute between France, England, and Germany. Europe had never been – and remained – so close to war. In response to this crisis, European socialist parties convened in Basel in July 1912 to reaffirm their antiwar solidarity. The Basel conference represented the height of the Second International's standing as a movement that had become, for many of its members, almost "religious in feeling."[7] Antiwar demonstrations throughout Europe in October and

---

Chiaromonte likewise observes: "In 1952, when I lived in Paris, I was puzzling over the question of why socialism, the strongest and more intellectually fertile endeavour to further the cause of justice and freedom in Europe, had been destroyed by the outbreak of the First World War. How could an idea be defeated by an event? Yet socialism had, indeed, been defeated by the war it failed to resist successfully. The victory of Bolshevism was the flagrant confirmation of this defeat, for, as Rosa Luxemburg saw at once, it was precisely by rejecting democratic socialism that the Bolsheviks came to power"; *The Paradox of History* (Philadelphia: University of Pennsylvania Press, 1985), p. 1.

[5] As he writes: "The fall of Bismarck marked the end of the major achievement that defined his statecraft during his final years in office: the emergency law against Social Democracy of 1878. This law signified a complete turning point in Germany's political life; it was without a doubt the most significant event since the founding of the Reich"; S. Lublinski, *Die Bilanz der Moderne* (Tübingen: Niemeyer, 1974), p. 409.

[6] As a historian of socialism comments: "in the confused and restless years preceding World War I the socialist international was considered the most important anti-militarist political force in the world: the international did not merely declare 'war on war' but believed itself capable of mobilizing an army of five million organized workers in the active struggle for peace"; G. Haupt, *Socialism and the Great War: The Collapse of the Second International* (Oxford: Clarendon Press, 1972), p. 85.

[7] J. Joll, *The Second International 1889–1914* (London: Weidenfeld and Nicolson, 1955), p. 157.

November 1912 added to the Second International's optimism that a future war could be avoided. The diffusion of the Balkan crisis in 1913 cemented this optimism, and was bolstered by Jean Jaures and Karl Kautsky, who argued that the interests of modern capitalism would surely inhibit conflict among European nations. Modern finance capitalism – the imperial extension of financial markets and monopolies – would mitigate against war; a view that actually undermined the socialist position that war among capitalist countries could only be avoided through a general strike of the working class and revolution.[8] Even Lenin, who had wagered on a military conflagration in Europe as early as 1900, "waged for the division of colonies, a struggle for markets, and for the freedom to loot foreign territories" – wrote to his mother and sister in November 1912: "There is much talk about war here as you can see from the papers [...] but I do not believe there will be a war."[9] Increasingly, socialist intellectuals and party leaders were convinced that war ran counter to the benefit of capitalism and national self-interest, thus galvanizing their sanguine attitude that military conflict in Europe was unthinkable. In 1913, the Second International was nominated for the Nobel Peace Prize.

The assassination of Archduke Franz Ferdinand and his wife in Sarajevo plunged Europe into yet another crisis, in response to which socialist parties once again gathered, this time in Brussels on July 29 and 30.[10] The Brussels conference occurred, however, within a transfigured landscape of resurgent national allegiances among socialist parties. Despite the declaration of the 1912 Basel conference for a general strike in the event of war, the SPD voiced fears about Russia and the "barbarous Slavs." Should Russia side with Serbia, "we will not have our women and children sacrificed to the brutality of the Cossacks."[11] On August 4, the SPD voted for the approval of war loans in the *Reichstag* in alignment with the Kaiser's call for national unity. The war could now finally begin.

Lenin immediately grasped how this fateful decision encapsulated the historical significance of a war "in which an entire world disappeared: not only the idyllic bourgeois faith in progress, but *also* the socialist movement that accompanied it."[12] In opposition to this socialist benediction of war, Karl Liebknecht (elected to the Reichstag in 1912), Clara Zetkin,

---

[8] R. Hilferding, *Das Finanzkapital. Eine Studie über die jüngste Entwicklung des Kapitalismus* (Vienna: Wiener Volksbuchhandlung, 1910).
[9] Quoted in Sebestyen, *Lenin*, p. 231.
[10] The 21st Universal Peace Congress was scheduled to convene in Vienna later in September.
[11] Quoted in Joll, *The Second International 1889–1914*, p. 169.
[12] S. Žižek, *Lenin: The Day after the Revolution* (London: Verso, 2017), p. xv.

and Rosa Luxemburg broke away from the SPD to continue the cause of proletarian class struggle with the creation of the Spartacus League.[13] More dramatically, the visionary architect Paul Scheerbart went on a hunger strike at news of the war's outbreak and died as a result in 1915. In his *Gedächtniskranz auf Paul Scheerbarts Grab* (1919), Anselm Reust observed:

> He was hit by no bullet, by no grenade nor bomb from the airships he so feared – and yet the titanic destructive power of this war had already sapped and undermined him far earlier than was visible to others. Indeed, Scheerbart had a last dream for humanity, a dream of the future like Victor Hugo's.[14]

Hugo's vision of a United States of Europe, universal peace, and socialist humanism had been betrayed by European socialists themselves. This "flunkeyism of the social patriots" impressed on Lenin the urgent need for a theoretical reevaluation of Marxism's fundamental principles along with the aggressive pursuit of Proletarian revolution; indeed, a conjunction of theory *and* praxis that would once and for all rescue humanity from imperialism and capitalism, while also rejecting Neo-Romantic visions of utopic salvation.[15] With the collapse of European socialism in 1914, the question was not only "What is to be done?" but as significantly "What is one to think?" In *State and Revolution* (1917), Lenin sought answers to these entwined questions in seeking to "articulate the Truth of the catastrophe [and] discern the unique chance for revolution."[16]

Permanent Mood of Despair

As György Lukács observes in his 1962 preface to *The Theory of the Novel*, it was the outbreak of war and "the effect which its acclamation by the social-democratic parties had upon the European left" that was the "triggering moment" for the publication of his work in 1916.[17] When conceived in 1914, *The Theory of the Novel* was to take the form of a dialogue among "a group of young people withdrawn from the war psychosis of their environment, just as the story-tellers of the *Decameron* had withdrawn from the

---

[13] In 1915, Liebknecht was arrested for his revolutionary antiwar publications and sent to the eastern front for punitive military service.
[14] *Glass! Love!! Perpetual Motion!!! A Paul Scheerbart Reader*, eds. J. McElheny and C. Burgin (Chicago: University of Chicago Press, 2014), p. 268.
[15] Theoretically as well as practically, the war, as Rosa Luxemburg stated after the November Armistice, confronted Europe with the stark alternative of "socialism or barbarism"; either "salvation for humanity" and "abolition of capitalism" or "continuation of capitalism, new wars, and imminent decline into chaos and anarchy." www.marxists.org/archive/luxemburg/1918/12/14.htm.
[16] Žižek, *The Day After the Revolution*, p. xv.
[17] G. Lukács, *The Theory of the Novel*, trans. A. Bostock (Cambridge, MA: MIT Press, 1971), p. 11.

plague."[18] In contemplation of the world enflamed, these "young people" would have been led toward a vision of hope and salvation. As Lukács remarks, however, a "permanent mood of despair over the state of the world" made this dialogical form, as well as any theoretical refuge from the world gone under, impossible, while also rendering an attitude of intellectual indifference untenable.

Lukács' decision to abandon a dialogical form for *The Theory of the Novel* reflected as well the collapse of his own vibrant intellectual milieu in Heidelberg. The war provoked sharp antagonisms within Max Weber's circle, not helped by Weber's enthusiasm for his appointment as a reserve officer in charge of organizing local hospitals.[19] When Marianne Weber remarked to Lukács that the war ushered in "an hour of the greatest solemnity of depersonalization," "ardent love of community," and "noble acts of individual heroism," Lukács brusquely retorted: "The better, the worse." As Lukács recalls: "All the social forces I had hated since my youth, and which I aimed in spirit to annihilate, now came together to unleash the first global war; at the same time, they [intellectuals] were globally without any ideas, the very enemies of ideas. Right from the beginning, I was among those who said no."[20] Of the numerous disputes with friends and colleagues, especially distressing was his rift with Georg Simmel, but also with his Hungarian friend Béla Balázs and the playwright Paul Ernst, on whose plays he had written the concluding essay to *Soul and Form* (1911).[21] In a letter to Ernst in letter of April 14, 1915, Lukács writes that

> the power of structures seems to be increasing unabatedly, and for most people it represents the existing reality more accurately then does the really existent [itself]. But – and for me this is *the* ultimate lesson coming out of the war experience – we cannot permit that. We have to stress again that after all, we and our souls, are the only essentiality; and even all the eternal a priori

---

[18] Lukács would figuratively appear in discussions withdrawn from the war psychosis of their environment in the character of Leo Naphta, a Jewish-Jesuit Communist, in Thomas Mann's *The Magic Mountain* in 1924. For the relation between Mann and Lukács, J. Markus, *Georg Lukács and Thomas Mann: A Study in the Sociology of Literature* (Amherst: University of Massachusetts Press, 1988).
[19] Weber had become critical of the war by 1915–16, however.
[20] G. Lukács, *Gelebtes Denken* (Frankfurt: Suhrkamp, 1981), p. 24.
[21] The original Hungarian edition of *Soul and Form* was published in 1908 followed by an expanded German version in 1911. Balázs' essay "The Aesthetics of Death" (1906) was influential for Lukács. Although, to Lukács' dismay, Balázs volunteered for service, he became disillusioned with the war and embraced pacifism. In 1916, he published a collection of antiwar stories in *Soul in War*. He was the librettist for Béla Bartók's "Bluebeard's Castle."

objectifications of the soul are (to recall the beautiful metaphor of Ernst Bloch) nothing but paper money, of value only when redeemable in gold.[22]

Lukács rails against the "cardinal sin against Spirit" propagated by German thinkers since Hegel, who administered "a metaphysical sanctification of all power." The state wields power over the real, yet does it stand, he asks, that the identification of state power over the world should therefore be recognized in "the utopian sense of philosophy in the sense of true ethics acting at the level of the essentiality of the soul?" – that is, the salvation of humanity, as professed by the wartime mobilization of German Spirit. Lukács hopes to develop a "vehement protest against" modern state power in a work on Dostoevsky, he informs his friend, which he is currently writing. In a letter of April 28, 1915, Ernst responds that the state "fills a part of our being" and does not require "metaphysical sanctification" since it is "a part of myself, my being." As Ernst writes: "But I am not just I, but I live with others, and in this war we have a contraction of the I into the nation, and here we have a harmony, and that is why I think that the state is something Holy."[23] In a reply to Ernst on August 2, 1915, Lukács frankly admits that he possesses "no understanding" of Ernst's essay "National Character and the State," and in fact recognizes "a great danger in his views" regarding his sacralization of the state.[24] As Lukács formulates their dispute, "one can speak of an eventual understanding but not of being convinced," and refers in this regard to an essay he intends to write for Weber's journal *Archiv für Sozialwissenschaft und Sozialpolitik*, "The German Intellectuals and the War."[25] A few months after mentioning his work on Dostoevsky – his "vehement protest" against the war – Lukács writes that he has decided to abandon his book – it has become too large a project – but plans nonetheless to publish from this project "a large-scale essay, 'The Aesthetics of the Novel'"; to wit, *The Theory of the Novel*. In addition to this and other intellectual disputes about the war, Lukács grieved the battlefield deaths in 1915 of two friends, Emil Lask and Béla Zalai, who both influenced his thinking, all of which interrupted his literary philosophical ambitions.[26]

---

[22] G. Lukács, *Selected Correspondence 1902–1920*, trans. J. Marcus and Z. Tar (New York: Columbia University Press, 1986), p. 246.
[23] G. Lukács, *Briefwechsel 1902–1917* (Stuttgart: J. B. Metzler, 1982), p. 350.
[24] *Vossische Zeitung* (May 27, 1915).
[25] Lukács, *Selected Correspondence 1902–1920*, p. 252.
[26] For the importance of Zalai, B. Smith, "Bela Zalai und die Metaphysik des reinen Seins," Brentano Studien. Internationales Jahrbuch der Franz Brentano Forschung, Vol. 5 (1994): 59–68. For the importance of Lask, R. Hartmutt, *Emil Lask als Lehrer von Georg Lukács. Zur Form ihres Gegenstandsbegriffs* (Bonn: Bouvier, 1975).

In "The German Intellectuals and the War," Lukács critiques the wartime seduction of German intellectuals, for whom the war arrived like a "gust of fresh air" and escape from "the intolerable situation" of modern life.[27] Thomas Mann and Simmel are singled out as exemplary of those who welcomed the advent of war in the hope of fostering the realization of "another Germany."[28] In the discourse of *Kriegsphilosophie*, the war was championed as bringing about *Gemeinschaft* through collective solidarity in the face of existential danger – an experience that, Lukács wryly notes, was understood to be specifically German and would thus necessarily fail to be comprehended by Allied intellectuals. That the war is deemed "spiritual" does not represent, Lukács reasons, a "patriotic experience per se," for it is more akin to an "inexpressible religious experience," thus revealing not only the profound spiritual plight of the modern world but, as significantly, the conflation of war with an ethics of salvation. As an echo of his dispute with Marianne Weber, Lukács rejects the view that the war calls forth a uniquely German type of hero. What defines the "emergence of a new heroism" is that the hero has become anonymous in mechanically fulfilling his duty without a critical assessment of the war's objective. As Lukács writes: "Just as the present economy has replaced the independent worker with the machine and the workers who serve it, thereby causing the personal value of work to disappear, so does the present war pit against one another no longer men but machines and servants of machines."[29] The soldier is a "thing" whose "personality has become subsumed entirely to *Sachlichkeit und Schlichtheit.*"

This view of the war as revealing the commodification of social relations in capitalist society mirrored the argument of Emil Lederer (also a member

---

[27] G. Lukács, "Die deutschen Intellektuellen und der Krieg," *Text + Kritik*, Vol. 39/40 (1973): 65–69. In *The Destruction of Reason*, Lukács underlines the role played by *Lebensphilosophie* and its vitalism in the mobilization of *Kriegsphilosophie*. As he writes: "Despite the superficiality of these wartime products, despite their total worthlessness and insignificance from a philosophical point of view, they were nevertheless of import as the beginnings of a new phase in German vitalism. The old basic antithesis of 'life' versus 'rigidity' and the 'moribund' was naturally preserved, but it acquired a new and seasonal content. The 'German character' [*das deutsche Wesen*] which was 'to restore the world's health' now constituted the 'life' of conception, and the national character of other peoples (chiefly the Western democracies and especially England) was what was moribund and rigid"; *The Destruction of Reason*, trans. P. Palmer (London: Verso, 2021), p. 460.

[28] For the wartime relation between Lukács and Mann, Markus, *Georg Lukács and Thomas Mann*.

[29] In his 1917 article "On the Philosophy of the Present War," Gustav Radbruch speaks of the war as a golem that "thanks to a cabalistic parchment in its mouth has mysteriously succeeded in acquiring a soul of its own, and which subsequently unfurls a life that is blind, stupid, and terrifying, yet quite omnipotent"; in J. Marcus, G. Lukács, and T. Mann, *A Study in the Sociology of Literature* (Amherst: University of Massachusetts Press, 1982). In a letter to Radbruch, Lukács writes: "I agree completely with your analysis"; G. Radbruch, "Zur Philosophie des Krieges. Eine methodologische Abhandlung," *Archiv für Sozialwissenschaft und Sozialpolitik*, Vol. 44 (1917/18): 139–160.

of Weber's circle in Heidelberg) in "Zur Soziologie des Weltkriegs" (1915), published in *Archiv für Sozialwissenschaft und Sozialpolitik*.[30] In this seminal essay, Lederer argues that the modern nation-state is defined by the power of total mobilization of cultural and intellectual life, in addition to economic and social forces. The modern state harnesses and channels cultural values, civil law, personal affiliations, and social institutions for the purpose of forging a "fabricated unity of people under one state." Lederer sees in universal conscription the exemplification of the interaction between modern industrialization, the logic of increased productivity, and social production of skilled workers, through which a nation-state becomes coeval with society as whole; conscripted subjects feel themselves to be individual even though they are abstract, indeed expendable, objects of the nation-state at war. In the universal medium of the army, society achieves consciousness of itself as an united "subject" (i.e., the *Volksgemeinschaft* praised by partisans of *Kriegsphilosophie*) without recognizing, however, that this universal consciousness is in fact fabricated state ideology.[31] War effects a total mobilization that imposes a homogeneity of time, and hence a form of experience, through coordination of individual activities into a public standardized temporality.[32]

Lukács contrasts in his essay (which should have been published with Lederer's but never was) the "extermination of decorative heroism" – namely, the commodification of the soldier – with the "terrorist hero of the great Russian Revolution," having in mind the revolutionary protagonist in Boris Savinkov's novel *Pale Horse* (1909) (which his Russian wife Jelena Grabenko, herself a revolutionary, had read to him from Russian into German). Lukács' admiration of this novel proved contentious, however, as it spurred a heated exchange with Ernst, who, for his part, viewed Savinkov's hero as "an image of the sickness of an individual without a state, of an isolated I, who then turns to crime." Lukács counters in a letter that *Pale Horse* must not be read as "a symptom of a disease but rather [as] a new manifestation of an old conflict between the first ethic (duties towards social structures) and the second [ethics] (imperatives of the soul)."[33] What

---

[30] E. Lederer, *Kapitalismus, Klassenstruktur und Probleme der Demokratie in Deutschland 1910–1940* (Göttingen: Vandenhoeck & Ruprecht, 1979): 119–144. For a discussion of Lederer's essay, H. Joas, "Kriegsideologien. Der Erste Weltkrieg im Spiegel der zeitgenössischen Sozialwissenschaften," *Leviathan*, Vol. 23, No. 3 (1995): 336–350.
[31] M. Královcová, "Emil Lederer: On the Sociology of World War," *Central European Papers*, Vol. 2, No. 2 (2014): 51–57; p. 56.
[32] Kern, *The Culture of Time and Space*, p. 33–34.
[33] Lukács, *Selected Correspondence 1902–1920*, p. 248. Letter of May 4, 1915.

fascinates Lukács in *Pale Horse* is Savinkov's Dostoyevskian molding of the ethical dilemma of political violence. "We know that the world lives by untruths. Where is there truth, tell me?" the mystically inclined revolutionary Vanya asks in the novel as he struggles to justify his decision to assassinate Grand Duke Sergei Aleksandrovich (Savinkov's narrative is a fictional retelling of the Grand Duke's assassination in 1905, in which he himself actually participated). Vanya's devotion to the destruction of "evil social order" for the sake of creating a new world, where humans would exist according to (what Lukács calls) the "second ethics" of brotherly love, sets him on a path toward redemptive political violence. As he states: "Yes, I say, kill so that no one else kills later. Kill, so that people will live according to God's will, so that love sanctifies the world."[34] As Lukács explains to Ernst: "One must become a cruel *Realpolitiker* out of a mystical ethic and has to violate the absolute commandment: 'Thou shalt not kill', which is clearly *not* an obligation toward the structures."[35] In essence, Lukács continues, this represents "a very ancient problem expressed most pointedly perhaps by Hebbel's Judith: 'and if God had placed sin between me and the act of ordered for me to so, who am I to be able to escape it?'"

In contrast to Karl Jaspers and Gustav Radbruch, who also opposed the war among Weber's Heidelberg circle, Lukács' opposition did not reflect a commitment to pacifism. As Lukács recalls: "My emphatic repudiation [and] condemnation of the war was neither pacifist nor Western and democratic in its inspiration but motivated instead by Fichte's idea that ours was the age of absolute sinfulness." The war laid bare the failure of pacificism, the compromise of socialist parties, and the fallenness of the modern world, but also, in this predicament, an existential imperative for another ethics – "a second ethics" – over and above established ethical forms, that were centered either on adherence to social and political norms, or on abstract and anonymous obligations, all of which too easily succumbed to a war psychosis from which there seemed, despairingly, no escape. There was, nevertheless, one glimmer of hope: Karl Liebknecht's courageous stance in the *Reichstag* suggested to Lukács that, in this age of absolute sinfulness, a "concrete political viewpoint was possible."[36] In December 1914,

---

[34] B. Savinkov, *Pale Horse*, trans. M. Katz (Pittsburgh, PA: University of Pittsburgh Press, 2019), p. 51. For *Pale Horse* and literary fascination with the abolition of death and its impact on socialism and communism in Russia, I. Masing-Deling, *Abolishing Death: A Salvation Myth of Russian Twentieth-Century Literature* (Stanford, CA: Stanford University Press, 1992), pp. 48–49.
[35] Lukács, *Selected Correspondence 1902–1920*, p. 248.
[36] G. Lukács, *Record of a Life: An Autobiographical Sketch* (London: Verso Books, 1985), p. 47.

Liebknecht voted against another installment of war loans and published a passionate statement against the war. As Liebknecht writes:

> This war, which none of the peoples involved desired, was not started for the benefit of the German or of any other people. It is an Imperialist war, a war for capitalist domination of the world markets and for the political domination of the important countries in the interest of industrial and financial capitalism. Arising out of the armament race, it is a preventative war provoked by the German and Austrian war parties in the obscurity of semi-absolutism and of secret diplomacy.[37]

For Lukács, the war revealed the "absolute sinfulness" of this age, from which no escape or consolation was possible, but within this ethical condemnation of his times, the hint of political action dimly and defiantly made itself apparent. What was needed was not simply peace, in the sense of an orderly and pacified rearrangement of the status quo, let alone understanding, in the sense of a historical explanation of the world's "sinfulness." More radically, what was needed was a politics of redemption as the redemption of politics itself by means of world transfiguration in a collective awakening of consciousness to a novel ethical possibility.

"I Cannot Bear an Inessential Life"

The war did not only produce fractures among friends as well as force Lukács' displacement from Germany back to Hungary, effectively – indeed, permanently – interrupting his pursuit of an academic career.[38] It also transformed his attitude toward "the age of absolute sinfulness" in shifting, as he recalled, "the center of [my] interests from aesthetics to ethics." The aesthetic and the ethical were in fact conjoined in his quest for existential significance. During his Heidelberg years, Lukács was intensely preoccupied with developing a philosophy of art that would extend and enrich his diagnosis of the tragedy of modern culture explored in *Soul*

---

[37] www.marxists.org/archive/liebknecht-k/works/1914/12/17.htm. As he writes: "our brothers on the field of battle, and those wounded and sick, for whom I have the warmest compassion [...] But my protest is against the war, against those responsible for it, against those who are directing it; against the capitalistic ends for which it is being pursued, against the violation of the neutrality of Belgium and Luxemburg, against military dictation, and against the complete neglect of social and political duties of which the Government and the dominant class are guilty to-day."

[38] Lukács is called up for military service in Hungary in 1915, but is declared unfit for duty and is assigned to work in the postal censor bureau. In 1916, he returns briefly to Heidelberg, but then returns to Budapest in 1917, which allows him to reconnect into the intellectually vibrant Sunday Circle. See M. Gluck, *Georg Lukács and His Generation, 1900–1918* (Cambridge, MA: Harvard University Press, 1991).

and Form – a work considered by Lucien Goldmann as a precursor of existentialism.[39] In the final essay of *Soul and Form*, "The Metaphysics of Tragedy" on the theatrical works of Ernst, Lukács trenchantly expressed his view of the irresolvable alienation of life from objective forms of meaning – the central theme of his essays. The essay form adopted by Lukács' thinking embodied the problematic situation of modern life: Without a robust backdrop of life "which gave Plato and mystics their strength," but equally without naive faith in the value of books as their own robust reality, the essay, in its reflective self-searching, provides the medium in which the thinker attains conscious of himself in relation to that of which he speaks, so as to "build something of his own out of himself."[40] If "salvation can only come from accentuating the problems to the maximum degree," Lukács, the essayist thinker, is "a Schopenhauer" who writes while waiting for the arrival of his own book to come, like a literary John the Baptist, who "goes out to preach in the wilderness about another who is still to come." Unlike the literary works discussed in *Soul and Form*, Lukács' essays neither proclaim the advent of salvation nor offer a solution to the tragedy of modern life. Each of his essays is an experiment in waiting without heralding any redemptive announcement, which would risk the possibility of becoming superfluous or represent an ill-afforded luxury for that which does not arrive. Strictly speaking, the essayist does not claim anything; he whispers through the writings of others but cannot "awaken others to life and action." And yet, "the one who whispers […] is the great value-definer of aesthetics, the one who is always about to arrive, the one who is never quite yet there, the only one who has been called to judge."[41]

An objective form is "the highest judgment of life," and as a form giving to life, every form is an "ethic"; that is, a value judgment that opens a possibility for life. Objective forms, however, impose limitations on life; indeed, life loses its individuality, when determined by cultural and aesthetic forms of meaning without which, at the same time, an individual life could not exist. These objective forms of mediation are relative and not absolute. Moreover, as with Simmel's "tragedy of culture," forms of meaning turn against, and hence alienate, life from itself. Life, Lukács writes, is "an anarchy of light and dark: nothing is ever completely fulfilled in life […] everything flows" and becomes mixed, destroyed; nothing ever

---

[39] L. Goldmann, *Lukács and Heidegger: Towards a New Philosophy*, trans. W. Boelhower (London: Routledge & Kegan Paul, 1977).
[40] G. Lukács, *Soul and Form*, trans. A. Bostock (Cambridge, MA: MIT Press, 1978), p. 15.
[41] Lukács, *Soul and Form*, p. 16.

flows into "real life."⁴² Drawing on Wilhelm Dilthey's notion of *Erlebnis*, "to live," Lukács states, "is to live something through the end: but *life* means that nothing is ever fully and completely lived through the end."⁴³ Life, therefore, cannot not be fully lived, and thus can only be described negatively without the realization of revelation of genuine – complete and whole – life as such. In this respect, "real life is always unreal, always impossible, in the midst of empirical life."⁴⁴ And yet, within the anarchy of light and dark, there nonetheless can occur "suddenly a gleam, a lightening that illumines the banal paths of empirical life [...] the miracle"; these glimmers of the soul's essentiality notwithstanding, "one has to fall back into numbness," namely, into the relativity of objective forms. Tragically, empirical life must be renounced to live essentially, without thereby *being* able to abide essentially within life. As Lukács writes: "The deepest longing of human existence is the metaphysical root of tragedy: the longing of man for selfhood, the longing to transform the narrow peak of his existence into a wide plain with the path of his life winding across it, and his meaning into a daily reality."⁴⁵ A soul awakened to what is truly real of its individuality would be carried to its "uttermost limit" and thus live "adequate to its idea" (an implicit nod in the direction of Simmel's conception of the "Law of the Individual"). Tragedy's verdict, as with the inscription over the gate of Hell in Dante, is, however, to for all who enter to abandon hope – life.

As illustrated in the play *Ninon de l'Enclos* (based on a celebrated courtesan during the reign of Louis XIV), Ernst's heroine struggles for freedom against social norms and anonymous conventions. She becomes "strong enough to be able to breathe the air of tragedy, to live within the periphery of tragedy," for she has emancipated herself from objective forms and limitations, but still failed to achieve a consecration of life; namely, "freedom born out of her innermost self, identical with the highest necessity – not the completion of her life." For Lukács, "her freedom is the freedom of harlots."⁴⁶ This harlot's tragic heroism is in principle no different from the Knight of Faith's given that Kierkegaard sought to fashion an "absolute

---

⁴² See G. Márkus, "Life and the Soul: The Young Lukács and the Problem of Culture," in *Lukács Revalued*, ed. A. Heller (Oxford: Basil Blackwell, 1983): 177–190.
⁴³ In 1962 preface to *The Theory of the Novel*, Lukács speaks of his "youthful enthusiasm for the work of Dilthey" and "the fascination exercised by Dilthey's *Das Erlebnis und die Dichtung*" (pp. 12–13). Despite his unsparing critique of Dilthey's "irrationalism" in *The Destruction of Reason*, Lukács nonetheless admits that Dilthey was "all in all a man of exceptional knowledge and genuine learning"; p. 420.
⁴⁴ Lukács, *Soul and Form*, p. 153.
⁴⁵ Lukács, *Soul and Form*, p. 162.
⁴⁶ Lukács, *Soul and Form*, p. 173.

life" oriented toward God with this renunciation of Regine Olsen, and yet nonetheless failed to reconcile "ordinary life" with "absolute life." Kierkegaard's honesty resided with his wanting to live his own tragedy ordinarily, as it were, that, in turning to divine love against love on earth, he wanted to live what cannot be lived.[47] The tragedy is that a poet's life – one might add, a philosopher's life as well – "is null and worthless because it is never absolute, never a thing in itself and for itself, because it is always there only *in relation to something*, and this relation is meaningless and yet it completely absorbs the life – for a moment at least; but then life is made up of nothing but such moments."

As with Bloch, Lukács' interest in aesthetics was animated by a will to transcendence against the disenchantment of modern life and life's alienation from existing cultural forms of meaning. Plans for a philosophy of art already took shape prior to his arrival in Heidelberg in 1912 with Bloch, whom he had befriended in Simmel's private home seminars in Berlin.[48] The war interrupted the completion of his project, despite having drafted a substantial manuscript "Heidelberg Philosophy of Art," abandoned at the outbreak of the war, followed by an unsuccessful attempt at a Habilitation thesis, "Heidelberg Aesthetics," in turn abandoned in 1918.[49] The centerpiece of Lukács' aesthetic thinking is the artwork as an integrated totality through which transcendence from empirical (and fragmentary) reality could be experienced as well as the fulfillment of a "more profound longing for community and unity with one another." As Lukács writes: "Art takes over the function of a this-worldly salvation, no matter how this may be interpreted. It provides a *salvation* from the routines of everyday life, and especially from the increasing pressures of theoretical and practical rationalism."[50] Adopting a Neo-Kantian framework, Lukács attempts to understand how the artwork is constituted as an object independently of an experiencing subject and judgment of taste, albeit without adopting a Hegelian symbolic identification of subject and object. In his effort to

[47] Lukács, *Soul and Form*, p. 40.
[48] As Lukács recalled: "The experience of meeting Bloch (1910) convinced me that philosophy in the classical sense was nevertheless possible. I spent the winter of 1911–12 in Florence under the influence of this experience [...] In the spring of 1912 Bloch came to Florence and persuaded me to go to Heidelberg with him where the environment was favourable to our work." Quoted in F. Tőkei, "Lukacs and Hungarian Culture," *New Hungarian Quarterly*, Vol. XII, No. 47 (1972): 108–122, p. 114.
[49] Both manuscripts – "Heidelberg Philosophy of Art" (1912–14) and "Heidelberg Aesthetics" (1916–18) – were placed by Lukács in a Heidelberg bank deposit box upon his departure for Hungary in 1917 and only discovered in 1973.
[50] Quoted in R. Westerman, *Lukács's Phenomenology of Capitalism* (London: Palgrave Macmillan, 2019), p. 87. As Westerman argues, "the method that Lukács used to explain the meaning of works of art [...] was the basis for the method he later used to interpret social relations in HCC"; p. 36.

develop an ontology of the art, an artwork is a "totality," as a unity of meaning, that cannot be reduced to its composing elements and composed content. The artist as well as the viewing subject occupy their own respective stance of intentionality toward the artwork that transcends both. Unlike empirical reality, an artwork enjoys an ideal unity of form and content, and in this sense possesses "concrete totality." In his unfinished Habilitation writings, Lukács argues that artworks are constituted in aesthetic experience as autonomous unities of form and content, such that, as an "immanent utopia," aesthetic form prescribes the standpoint of the subject in relation to itself as an artwork, thus reconciling objectivity and subjectivity in itself. Unlike Bloch's conception of artworks as "ornaments" – that is, as messianic figurations of future reconciliation between subject and object, and hence totality, to come – Lukács seeks to fashion a philosophy of art that would resolve the antinomy between cultural forms and life in the present, thus fulfilling the immanent utopic longing of the soul.[51]

Lukács' interest in the ontology of the artwork cannot be divorced from his ongoing struggle with ethics, gravitating around, as he writes in a diary entry from 1911, his "nervous feeling for the purity of the soul" and "the demand for relationships." As he writes: "above all, are they [this nervous feeling and demand] not the proof of my inability to religion, to existence? Or – though the question will be more complicated, but more understandable – are they not the proof of my boundlessness (e.g., I do not have any bound in myself)."[52] This existential despair was rendered acute by his unrequited love for Irma Seidler, and her suicide in May 1911, from which Lukács struggled to extricate, indeed resurrect, himself, philosophically as well as personally. Throughout his grief-stricken self-questioning, his readings in German Idealism, Husserl, Neo-Kantianism, and art theory folded into his own intimate pursuit of existential significance. As he remarks: "And everything goes back to the old question: how can I be a philosopher? I.e. as human I cannot leave the ethical sphere – how can I form the

---

[51] Bloch and Lukács worked intensely on aesthetics from 1912 to 1914, with however diverging reactions to German Expressionism, at the center of which stood the fundamental disagreement on the relation between art, reality, and politics. The debate between the men on Expressionism would ignite on the eve of the Second World War in 1938, by which time Lukács had moved far afield from his Heidelberg philosophy of art and *History and Class Consciousness*, but was still insisting on, and indeed sharpening, his basic objection to Expressionism for its "pseudo-revolutionary" subjective pretense and its neglect of form, i.e., failure to grasp the totality of social conditions in modern capitalism; it is, in this sense, another symptom of "bourgeois decadence," in his highly rhetorical language of the 1930s. For this debate, T. Adorno, W. Benjamin, E. Bloch, B. Brecht, and G. Lukács, *Aesthetics and Politics* (London: Verso Press, 2007).

[52] *The Lukács Reader*, ed. A. Kadarkay (London: Blackwell, 1995), p. 32.

meaningful?"⁵³ In his 1910–11 diary, Lukács, on the precipice of suicide himself, wonders when the miracle of salvation will happen, and whether he will ever find his "road to Damascus."⁵⁴

Mounting despair after Seidler's suicide reached a pitch of intensity, blending the philosophical and the personal, in the 1912 essay "On Poverty of Spirit"⁵⁵ Resonant with the essay "Metaphysics of Tragedy," the conflict between soul and form becomes recast into the alienation of life from formal ethics, or what he generally subsumes under the heading "first ethics," namely, an ethics of norms and universal imperatives.⁵⁶ "To be sure," Lukács writes, "most people live without life, without ever being aware of it. Their existence is merely social and interpersonal." In accordance with moral duties and social norms, such existence lacks "real life"; that is, authentic existence: "The real life is beyond forms, whereas everyday life lies on this side of forms." In contrast to the "first ethics" of "impure and sterile forms," Lukács evokes a transcending and transformative openness to goodness. The metaphysical longing of "real life" is identified with a longing for goodness as "the gift of grace to break through the forms for the sake of works."⁵⁷ Goodness is "useless" and without foundation; indeed, it is "divine" and "metaphysical" in contrast to the world of mechanical forces, thus allowing for an overcoming of the alienation of forms through the advent of a "genuine community" where individuals could enter into immediate relation with each other, and where "subject and object collapse into each other." Characters from Dostoevsky's novels – Sonya, Prince Myshkin, and Alexei Karamazov – are exalted as incarnations of goodness; "fruitless, chaotic and futile." Myshkin's world "was beyond tragedy, for it was purely ethical, or, if you wish, purely cosmic." As with Kierkegaard's Abraham, Myshkin has "left the world of tragic conflict and heroes, the world of Agamemnon, and his sacrifice."⁵⁸ What Lukács identifies as "the poverty of spirit" is

---

⁵³ Quoted in B. Szabados, "Georg Lukács in Heidelberg: A Crossroad between the Academic and Political Career," *Filozofia*, Vol. 75, No. 1 (2020): 51–64; p. 53.
⁵⁴ M. Löwy, *Georg Lukács – From Romanticism to Bolshevism*, trans. P. Camiller (London: NLB, 1979), p. 107. For the "social-revolutionary intentions" of "On Poverty of Spirit" and Lukács' intransient rejection of the bourgeois world before the war, A. Arato and P. Breines, *The Young Lukacs and the Origins of Western Marxism* (London: Pluto Press, 1979).
⁵⁵ For the connection of this essay to Irma Seidler's suicide, A. Heller, "Georg Lukács and Irma Seidler," *New German Critique*, Vol. 18 (1979): 74–106.
⁵⁶ G. Lukács, "On Poverty of Spirit: A Conversation and a Letter," in Kadarkay, *The Lukács Reader*, pp. 42–56. For an analysis of this text and his 1911 journal, Löwy, *From Romanticism to Bolshevism*, pp. 102–109.
⁵⁷ Kadarkay, *The Lukács Reader*, p. 44.
⁵⁸ Kadarkay, *The Lukács Reader*, p. 45.

the condition of "searching for the meaning of life – the redemption." As he notes in his 1911 diary: "I cannot bear an inessential life."[59]

Transcendental Homelessness

The outbreak of the war precipitated Lukács' abandonment of his philosophy of art and begin instead a study of Dostoevsky (under the influence of an intense reading of Kierkegaard) that sought to elaborate "a second ethics" of salvation and goodness (already adumbrated in "On the Poverty of Spirit" and his letters).[60] This project was abandoned, however, in 1915 given its "too large scope" (as he informs Ernst), but arguably as well given his despondency over the war. In 1911, Lukács could not bear an inessential life; in 1915, this despair became coupled with the impossibility of bearing an inessential and self-destructive history. This aborted project nonetheless bore fruit, namely, *The Theory of the Novel*, as an extended prolegomena to his unfinished book on Dostoevsky. Published in 1916 "in opposition to the barbarity of capitalism" and the "wretchedness of German conservatism," *The Theory of the Novel*, as Lukács retrospectively remarked, is "not conservative but subversive in nature," even if based on "a highly naïve and totally unfounded utopianism – the hope that a natural life worthy of man can spring from the disintegration of capitalism and the destruction, seen as identical with that disintegration, of the lifeless and life-denying social and economic categories."[61]

The originality of *The Theory of the Novel* with its search for an ethical utopia from the ruins of the modern novel was lost to many of Lukács' friends, and it remains a complicated work, despite its significant influence.[62] As Jaspers politely wrote to Lukács: "I am unable to follow easily your line of thought with real comprehension because I am not familiar with your presuppositions – indeed, I don't even know what they are. Even the words I am familiar with, and with whose conceptual meaning I am at home […] I don't seem to recognize readily in the context of your work."[63] As Weber, who facilitated its publication, candidly remarked to Lukács: "As I told you before, it is also my opinion that the first part is almost unintelligible to anyone but those who *know you* intimately."[64]

---

[59] Kadarkay, *The Lukács Reader*, p. 37.
[60] L. Congdon, *The Young Lukács* (Charlottesville: University of North Carolina Press, 1983), p. 98 ff.
[61] Lukács, *The Theory of the Novel*, p. 20.
[62] See *Hundert Jahre "transzendentale Obdachlosigkeit." Georg Lukács', Theorie des Romans' neu gelesen*, eds. R. Dannemann and M. Meyzaud (Bielefeld: Aisthesis Verlag, 2018).
[63] Lukács, *Selected Correspondence 1902–1920*, p. 267. Letter of 20 October 1916.
[64] Lukács, *Selected Correspondence 1902–1920*, p. 255. Letter of 23 December 1915.

The Theory of the Novel can be read as an original – and intimately motivated – assessment of the disenchantment of the modern world from the perspective of an historical ontology of literary forms. On Lukács' argument, literary genres – the epic and the novel – are expressions of the world from which they emerge, where the totality of a world, in its social configuration and understanding of what it is to be, attains self-consciousness. A literary artwork is thus an objectivization of "spirit" – not just a form – that possesses an autonomy of signification from subjective experience (the author as well as reader) that, in turn, cannot be absorbed or reduced to philosophy. The literary forms of the epic and the novel reveal the makeup of the world to which they respectively attest, in their ontological and social constitution, and yet because the conditions of different historical ages vary, different literary forms express different configurations of being in the world. What distinguishes the modern world, as expressed in the genre of the novel, is the condition of "transcendental homelessness," not as the loss of "home" in the sense of *Heimat*, but in the sense of *Obdachlosigkeit* – without a sheltering sky. Taking his cue from Hegel's observation in his *Aesthetics* that "a novel in the modern sense of the word presupposes a world already prosaically ordered […] For the whole state of the world today has assumed a form diametrically opposed in its prosaic organization to the requirements […] for the genuine epic," Lukács argues that the modern novel gives expression to the loss of as well as the search for a transcendental abode, understood in terms of an encompassing meaningfulness, or totality, in which objective culture forms and subjective life could be reconciled. In the modern world, relations between individuals are mediated by objective social institutions that in fact alienate individuals from each other and the world. The consequent fragmentation of social existence, implicating a loss of wholeness for life, finds expression in the novel in its attempts to reconstitute a totality in literary form that in fact remains impossible in actual life.

In Lukács' sweeping narrative, *Don Quixote* inaugurates the modern novel, for it is in Cervantes' masterpiece that "the abandonment of the world by God manifests itself in the incommensurability of soul and work, of interiority and adventure – in the absence of a transcendental 'place' allotted to human endeavour."[65] From this inaugural work, the

---

[65] In the words of the novelist Milan Kundera, who would echo Lukács' thinking in his essay "The Depreciated Legacy of Cervantes": "As God slowly departed from the seat whence he had directed the universe and its order of values, distinguished good from evil, and endowed each thing with meaning, Don Quixote set forth from his house into a world he could no longer recognize. In the absence of the Supreme Judge, the world suddenly appeared in its fearsome ambiguity; the single divine Truth decomposed into myriad relative truths parceled out by men. Thus was born the world

development of the novel form repeatedly gives expression to the modern challenge of how an individual life can find a place in a world determined by an increased complexity of social relations, fragmentation of totality, and estrangement from cultural norms. The world has "become infinitely large and each of its corners [...] richer in gifts and dangers than the world of the Greeks," yet this openness "cancels out the positive meaning – totality – upon which their life was based."[66] In the modern novel, life becomes conscious of itself in the separation between the interiority of the self and the conventionality of the objective world; an "unbridgeable chasm separates 'cognition and action' and soul and created structure and self and world, and essence and substance."[67] By contrast, the epic form of Antiquity expressed the ontological condition of the Classical world, where life existed immanently within an encompassing world in which there is no separation between world and life, oneself and others. As Lukács writes: "The epic gives form to a totality of life that is rounded from within; the novel seeks, by giving form, to uncover and construct the concealed totality of life."[68] In the premodern closed universe, the "soul goes out to seek adventure" in the world, and yet the soul never risks encountering "real danger," since although wide and unpredictable, the world always remained an abode of integrated meaningfulness for life. The Greeks, in this regard, "knew only answers but no questions, only solutions (even if enigmatic ones) but no riddles, only forms but no chaos." Life always returned to itself in its adventures in the world, given that the world was experienced as a totality of belonging.[69]

Although mystery and incomprehension were nonetheless experienced, the perfect circular motion of the cosmos could never become unsettled. Within such a rounded world, life could be threatened and destroyed, but never the meaningfulness of it all, the sense of being as such.[70] It is clear for

---

of the Modern Era, and with it the novel, the image and model of that world"; M. Kundera, *The Art of the* Novel, trans. L. Asher (New York: Harper Perennial, 1986), p. 6.

[66] Lukács, *The Theory of the Novel*, p. 34.
[67] Lukács, *The Theory of the Novel*, p. 34.
[68] Lukács, *The Theory of the Novel*, p. 60.
[69] Lukács, *The Theory of the Novel*, p. 30.
[70] The Greek age moved through three stages of "the great and timeless paradigmatic forms of world literature: epic, tragedy, philosophy," where the transition from epic to philosophy represents a transition from an anchored existence of answers without question to an unmoored existence of questions without answers of "how can life become essential." The transformation from epic to tragedy to philosophy (echoing Nietzsche) represents the progressive ejection of meaning from the immanence of life in the world, and hence a progressive fracture and alienation between life and the world, life and artistic form. The tragic hero takes over from Homer's living man, and Plato's new man, the wise man, "unmasks the tragic hero and illuminates the dark peril the hero has vanquished."

Lukács that there is no possibility of return to the rounded and anchored sense of being in the world enjoyed in Antiquity. Adrift in the modern condition of transcendental homelessness, the only possibility of salvation lies with a future that would seem impossible because unimaginable.

In Lukács' anti-Hegelian narrative of modernity, transcendental homeliness stems from the awakening of spirit to itself as form-giving activity, with the consequence that spirit cannot find a home in a world of its own shaping, and hence cannot become reconciled with itself – at home with itself. In discovering the "true substance" of spirit in the creation of forms, spirit becomes alienated from the world. The loss of the rounded totality of being in the world corresponds to ontological separation between the interiority of subjective life and the exteriority of the world as anonymous. With this tragic form of Kantianism, although spirit constitutes the world, it does so at the expense of no longer finding itself at home in the world. In the same vein, this time expressed in Hegelian terms, substance and subjectivity become ruptured from within, giving rise to a rupture between self and world and, more profoundly, a chasm within the self, a "menacing abyss between us and our own selves." Given this transcendental predicament, the soul either becomes narrower than the world or broader than the world.[71] In the first case, the narrowing of the soul leads to "abstract idealism." In the second case, the expansiveness of the soul leads to "romanticism of disillusionment." With abstract idealism, the soul sets upon an adventure in the world toward the realization of an ideal while remaining oblivious to the unbridgeable distance and inevitable friction between the real and the ideal. When reality fails the demand for the ideal, the soul becomes "demonic" in its relentless pursuit of the ideal at all costs. For heroic idealism, the struggle to attain the ideal in the world perpetually falters and yet, myopically fixated upon the ideal, the hero is unaffected by the real, since "the soul is at rest in the transcendent existence it has achieved on the far side of all problems; no doubts, no search, no despair can arise within it so as to take it out of itself and set it into motion."[72] Paradoxically, the "complete absence of any inwardly experienced problematic transforms such a soul into pure activity," and yet this pure activity effects nothing in the world. In this typology of the novel into two subgenres, the demonically narrowed soul of abstract idealism is confronted with the dilemma that "either it must give up all relationship to life or it must lose its immediate roots in the true world of ideas." In contrast

---

[71] Lukács, *The Theory of the Novel*, p. 97.
[72] Lukács, *The Theory of the Novel*, p. 99.

to abstract idealism, Romanticism is characterized by a widening of the soul beyond the bounds the world has on offer. As with abstract idealism, this expansive movement of the soul, where it is the world that proves too narrow, collapses into a fetishism of feeling that inwardly becomes resigned to the world onto itself. Disillusionment feeds from the elevation of interiority to the status of a completely independent world, and yet the soul's imagined self-sufficiency reveals itself to be a desperate self-defense against reality: "it is the abandonment of any struggle to realize the soul in the outside world, a struggle which is seen *a priori* as hopeless and merely humiliating."[73]

The novel attempts to reimagine, and hence reconstitute, the immediate relation between life and the world; indeed, a closed totality of immanence. The novel is animated by a search for utopia, understood as the concrete and immanent totality closed upon itself.[74] The interminable opposition between abstract idealism and Romantic disillusionment reaches a transformative threshold with Tolstoy and Dostoevsky.[75] Tolstoy "aspires to a life based on a community of feeling among simple human beings closely bound to nature, a life which is intimately adapted to the great rhythm of nature," and though abstract idealism and Romantic disillusionment would appear surpassed, there nonetheless remains an "insoluble problematic [...] since the totality of men and events are only possible on basis of culture." Tolstoy in his own way succumbs to the insoluble aporia that, on an individual level, characterized Kierkegaard's renunciation of his love for Regine Olsen for the sake of God: Tolstoy's grand gesture to find an absolute form of life devoted to God fails since it could not become lived as a culture; that is, as ordinary reality.[76] This ontological diagnosis of the disenchantment of the modern world turns on an unfulfilled – literally and figuratively – gesture toward a utopia on the order of an "second ethics" to come, which Lukács glimpses in the pages of Dostoevsky, who, in fulfilling the desire of the modern novel to attain totality, dissolves its aesthetic form into a new form of writing. Dostoevsky succeeds in portraying "pure soul-reality, where man exists as man, neither as a social being nor

---

[73] Lukács, *The Theory of the Novel*, p. 114.
[74] See F. Jameson, *Marxism and Form* (Princeton, NJ: Princeton University Press, 1971), chapter 3.
[75] Goethe's *Wilhelm Meister* stands between these two types as its attempted synthesis, but even here, Lukács judges this reconciliation to have failed. Lukács examines Goethe's literary works in greater depth in *Goethe and His Age*. As he argues, *Faust* is "an Iliad of modern life" (quoting Pushkin), where what defines "modern" is that "intellectual depth, the totality of social and human categories, and artistic perfection are no longer joined in a naïve and self-evident unity; rather they are sharply at odds with one another"; *Goethe and His Age*, trans. R. Anchor (London: Merlin Press, 1968), p. 157.
[76] Lukács, *The Theory of the Novel*, p. 147.

as an isolated, unique, pure and therefore abstract interiority."[77] In this regard, Dostoevsky did "not write novels," nor revert to the form of the epic, since "he belongs to the new world – we will have to decide whether we are really about to leave the age of absolute sinfulness or whether the new has no other herald but our hopes."[78]

October 1917

In notes for his study of Dostoevsky, Lukács outlined a distinction (already introduced in "On the Poverty of Spirit" as well as in his wartime letters) between "a first ethics" and "a second ethics." Under the heading of a first ethics, Lukács subsumes Kant's ethics of individual autonomy and formal lawfulness of the rational will as well as Hegel's collective *Sittlichkeit* and its embodiment in the modern nation-state. Under the heading of a second ethics, Lukács envisions a "mystical ethics," or "metaphysical ethics," meant to displace a "first ethics" and, significantly, surpass the antinomy of soul and form, namely, the modern condition of "transcendental homelessness" – in short, the age of sinfulness. In Dostoevsky, Lukács discovered a utopic image of relations among individuals that was not conditioned by alienating and anonymous social forms. With the foundation of a new community with Alyosha's Speech at Stone in *The Brothers Karamazov*, we are provided with a glimpse of a world organized around "active love" – symbolically expressed in the community of children gathered around Alyosha – that would dissolve the intolerable oscillation between abstract idealism and Romantic disillusionment without, however, recurring to an organic notion of the community as with Tolstoy. This salvation presented by "the Idea of Russia" – a theme often discussed with Weber – promised a reconciliation of "subject" and "object," yet not through an aesthetic form (Dostoevsky "did not write novels"), but through the literary inauguration of a communitarian and personalist ethics of goodness and quasi-mystical redemption. Lukács' vision of a second ethics was equally informed by the Russian revolutionary in *Pale Horse* and its advocacy of political violence as "the highest

---

[77] Lukács, *The Theory of the Novel*, p. 152. As Lukács writes in his study of Béla Balázs in 1918: "Positing soul-reality as the only reality means a radical shift in man's sociological stance: on the level of soul-reality all these bonds through which soul was normally bound to its social position, class, origin, etc., are separated from it and in their place new, concrete relations between soul and soul are put. The discovery of this world was Dostoevsky's great achievement." For reference to the Béla Balázs essay and this quotation, K. Kavoulakos, *Georg Lukács's Philosophy of Praxis* (London: Bloomsbury, 2018), p. 154.

[78] Lukács, *The Theory of the Novel*, p. 153.

expression of mystical atheism."[79] This atheism of the heroic militant, tied to individual praxis, contrasted with the mass mobilization of commodified soldiers sacrificed for the Fatherland (as Lukács discussed in "The German Intellectuals and the War"). Political terrorism for revolutionary aims, involving an individual leap of faith, offered a way to merge revolutionary praxis and redemptive utopia, thus supplementing the absence of political agency in Dostoevsky. And yet, the appeal of revolutionary violence for the sake of a higher justice thrust Lukács' thinking into a Faustian dilemma of choosing between revolutionary Marxism in the age of Western capitalism and Dostoevskyian salvation in an age of sinfulness.[80] Caught within this predicament of "either/or," Lukács' interest in Kierkegaard (he began but never completed an essay on the Danish thinker's critique of Hegel during the war) both sharpened this internal conflict and intensified the imperative for a decision.[81]

It was neither a theoretical insight nor a personal revelation that emancipated Lukács from his Faustian dilemma, but a historical event – the Russian Revolution of 1917 – that, as he writes, "really opened a window to the future [...] at last! at last! a way for humankind to escape from war and capitalism."[82] If the solution to Faust's ethical dilemma was only possible in the "wide world" of Part Two of Goethe's play, something comparable could be said of Lukács: The solution to his own Faustian dilemma could only be found in the "wide world" of Part Two, albeit a second Lukács, as it were, which, in contrast to Goethe's *Faust*, would not complete a Part One, but initiate instead the unfolding of another drama; indeed, another tragedy. On the road to Damascus, the October Revolution of 1917 did not only reveal an answer to the question posed by the war – "Who will save us from Western civilization?" As Lukács remarked decades later:

> The grim years of the First World War, which were full of abrupt changes of fortune, and the ensuing period brought a marked change of mood. The subjectivist tendency remained, but its basic tenor, its atmosphere was completely altered. No longer was the world a great, multi-purpose stage upon which the I, in ever-changing costumes and continually transforming the scenery at will, could play out its own inner tragedies and comedies. It had now become a devasted area.[83]

---

[79] Kavoulakos, *Georg Lukács's Philosophy of Praxis*, p. 156.
[80] For this Faustian dialectic, Löwy, *From Romanticism to Bolshevism*, p. 128.
[81] For the importance of Kierkegaard, R. Westerman, "The Irrational Act: Traces of Kierkegaard in Lukács's Revolutionary Subject," *Studies in East European Thought*, Vol. 67, No. 3/4 (2015): 229–247.
[82] G. Lukács, *History and Class Consciousness*, trans. R. Livingstone (Cambridge, MA: MIT Press, 1971), p. xi.
[83] Lukács, *The Destruction of Reason*, p. 490.

On this collapsed stage of world history, where the individual could no longer aspire to heroism – saintly or militant – Lukács discovered the world-historical praxis of the proletariat, thereby becoming himself, philosophically and personally, transformed – to the surprise of many – into an engaged participant in the cause of revolution in Hungary as a member of the newly founded Hungarian Communist Party (which he joined in November 1918).[84] His friend Anna Lesznai likened it to a conversion "from Saul to Paul."[85] Bolshevism, in the wake of the failed Second International and the ravages of a war without end, appeared to be the only way to overcome and purge the age of sinfulness. It was not an irrational decision, however, but an existential commitment in word and deed, neither to a rigid idea (as with abstract idealism) nor an expansiveness of self (as with Romantic disillusionment), but to an engaged praxis of political redemption. Caught between Alyosha and Vanya (from *Pale Horse*), Lukács rediscovers through Marx in the light of Hegel the effective dimension of history in relation to objective spirit and the proletariat, thus allowing him to recognize that his critique of the age of sinfulness and aspiration for utopic transformation needed to be reconceptualized for the sake of the transformation of social conditions of existence and the empowerment of collective – and not individual – agency. "Soul," "inwardness," and "form purified to the ethical" – these notions of Lukács' struggle to envision an ethical utopia and second ethics were exposed to an internal demystification and, through this self-demystification of himself in thought and deed, Lukács became armed with the means to expose – indeed, transform – the ideological structure of capitalism, which he unwittingly had himself embodied and expressed. As he writes in *History*

---

[84] In an autobiographical text from 1933, "My Road to Marx," Lukács laid down the narrative of his conversion to Marxism, or, as he writes, his "apprenticeship in Marxism," in view of the subsequent repudiation of *History and Class Consciousness*. G. Lukacs, *Utam Marxhoz* [My Road to Marx] (Budapest, 1971), pp. 30–31.

[85] Gluck, *Georg Lukács and His Generation*, p. 176 and chapter 6 for Lukács' conversion and the break-up of the Sunday Circle in Budapest. Lukács joined the Hungarian Communist Party in November 1918 and served briefly as Commissar for Public Education in the Hungarian Soviet Republic (March–August 1919). In 1919, after the collapse of the short-lived Hungarian Soviet Republic, he fled to Vienna, was arrested, and would have faced execution but was not extradited back to Hungary due to the public intervention of Thomas Mann, Ernst Bloch, and others. This launched him on intense political activism and writing until 1929 and this text on the Blum theses. See L. Congdon, *Exile and Social Thought: Hungarian Intellectuals in Germany and Austria, 1919–1933* (Princeton, NJ: Princeton University Press, 2014), pp. 45–46. As he states in "My Road to Marx," although he had read Marx in high school, it was only during the war that he read Marx intently as well as discovered Hegel, but also read and interacted with Rosa Luxemburg and was influenced by Sorel's syndicalism and voluntarism ("general strike") through his friend Ervin Szabó. As he writes in the 1967 preface to *History and Class Consciousness*, his thinking "hovered between the acquisition of Marxism and political activism" and the "constant intensification of my purely idealistic ethical preoccupations."

and Class Consciousness (looking back inter alia to his earlier writings): "the union of *inwardness*, purified to the point of *total abstraction* and stripped of all traces of *flesh and blood*, with a *transcendental philosophy of history* does indeed correspond to the *basic ideological structure of capitalism*."[86]

This transformative break with himself is encapsulated in his critique of Bloch's *The Spirit of Utopia*. The wartime divergence between these thinkers, despite shared points of theoretical orientation and friendship before the war, could not be more pronounced, and in this respect represents more broadly a parting of the ways of twentieth-century philosophy, given their respective influence on subsequent thinkers and veins of critical thought. Lukács rejected Bloch's premise that an awakening of inwardness offered a point of leverage for genuine revolutionary change of social and political arrangements in the world. As Lukács writes in *History and Class Consciousness*, "when he [Bloch] conceives of economics as a concern with objective things to which *soul and inwardness* are to be opposed, he overlooks the fact that the real social revolution can only mean the restructuring of the *real and concrete* life of man."[87] *Thomas Münzer as Theologian of the Revolution* (1921) further confirmed Bloch's voluntarism and failure to understand Marx's dialectical materialism. Economic forms that defined "real life" and, correspondingly, forms of thought, as Marx taught Lukács to appreciate, are forms of existence, or being, that must be grasped in their historical-social dialectic unfolding. As Lukács states, "the revolutionary sects [before 1917] were forced to evade this problem because in their historical situation such a restructuring of life and even of the definition of the problem was objectively impossible." The Russian Revolution revealed how the impossible could and needed to be true; it is the event that renders possible, and hence thinkable, what hitherto had remained impossible as well as unthinkable, namely, that the material conditions of reality *can* be transformed, and that this social revolution of the real, world history itself, can be made through usurpation and transformation of objective forms and relations through the collective agency of the working class.[88]

---

[86] Lukács, *History and Class Consciousness*, p. 192. In his 1962 preface to *The Theory of the Novel*, Lukács speaks of his earlier attempted fusion of a "left ethics" and "right" epistemology, i.e., a fusion of the ethics of inwardness and transcendence with a conventional epistemology-ontology of reality; p. 12.

[87] Lukács, *History and Class Consciousness*, p. 193.

[88] In Bloch's review of *History and Class Consciousness*, although he gestures in the direction of Lukács' Hegelian "subject-object" identification of proletarian class consciousness, he objects to Lukács' "closed totality" and "one-dimensional linearity" of world-history; "Aktualität und Utopie zu Lukács' *Geschichte und Klassenbewusstsein*" (1923) in E. Bloch, *Philosophische Aufsätze zur Objektiven Phantasie* (Frankfurt: Suhrkamp, 1969), GA 10, p. 619 ff. Lukács would, however, subsequently judge *History and Class Consciousness* as still utopian in outlook; Lukács, *History and Class Consciousness*, p. xviii.

In his first publication after joining the Hungarian Party, "Bolshevism as an Ethical Problem" (1918), Lukács looks beyond the practical aspects of Bolshevism's seizure of power to the ethical question posed by Bolshevism; namely, whether historical and socioeconomic conditions can be ripe for revolution to such a degree as to abrogate the ethical ramifications of revolutionary violence. Whether social conditions occasion or cause revolution is, in fact, as insoluble problem, for as Lukács argues, "there never is a situation where one can actually know and foresee things with an absolute certainty."[89] A distinction therefore needs to be drawn between the utopian postulate of Marxist thought and Marxist sociological analysis, given that there exists a gap between historical actuality and what historically ought to be. As Lukács writes, "the proletarian class struggle, whose appointed task is to create a new world order, *qua* class struggle, does not yet contain this world order." In opposition to a mechanistic or deterministic reduction of Marxism (which Lukács identified with the Second International), the realm of freedom "transcends sociological postulates and laws," since it depends on a "will to a world order; a democratic order" that cannot merely be derived from social conditions. This new will for a future order, fulfilling the ethical vision of utopia earlier considered under the heading of a "second ethics," is here identified with the world-historical mission of the proletariat. As Lukács remarks: "The will to new order designates the proletariat as the socialist redeemers of humanity, the messianic class of world history."[90]

Whereas the ethical idealism of Kant and Hegel ("the first ethics") sought to bring about a revolution "to lift the old world off its hinges – metaphysically," Marx's understanding of the proletariat as the genuine subject of world history transforms Kant's theoretical Copernican revolution into a political Copernican revolution based on revolutionary praxis. The self-transforming awakening of the proletariat bridges "soulless empirical reality" and "human, utopian ethical will." At the center of this transformation is an ethical-political decision: Either Communism must be realized along with the dictatorship of the proletariat, and thus necessarily involve "terror and class oppression," or a new world order by means of democracy is to be created and "thereby run the risk that most of humanity is disinterested in the new world" – disinterested because lacking the mobilization of the proletariat in its revolutionary potential in view of social totality. Each horn of this dilemma carries "potentially terrifying

---

[89] Kadarkay, *The Lukács Reader*, p. 216.
[90] Kadarkay, *The Lukács Reader*, p. 216.

sins and countless errors." Bolshevism's "fascinating power" consists in that "it frees us from compromise" given its absolute demand for democracy based on a classless society; however, in this first blush of Lukács' attraction to Bolshevism, the dictatorship of the proletariat could not rule out a future world in which conflict would be abolished. Nonetheless, the messianic class of the proletariat must attain dominance ("dictatorship of the proletariat") at any cost. "Can the good be achieved by evil means?," here inscribed in political-revolutionary terms, demands the acceptance of faith that, while accepting evil and the necessary tragedy of revolution, the required oppression of proletarian power will not in turn offer an opportunity for a new form of tyranny, but lead instead to a new "democratic" world. As Lukács remarks: "Bolshevism rests on the metaphysical assumption that good can issue from evil, that it is possible, as Razumikhin says in *Crime and Punishment*, to lie our way through to the truth. This writer cannot share this faith and therefore sees at the root of Bolshevism an insoluble ethical dilemma."[91]

This "insoluble dilemma" is addressed once again in "Tactics and Ethics" (1919), where Lukács further delineated his vision of proletarian class consciousness in Hegelian-Marxist terms as the self-consciousness of the total historical process in which the "subject" (the proletariat) and the "object" (social reality) are identical. The utopic messianism of a "second ethics" that defined Lukács' orientation becomes recast during his political conversion into a dialectical interaction between individual responsibility and collective action, as embedded within a concrete historical situation, namely, revolutionary praxis. Faced with the tactical question "What is to be done?" the ethical responsibility of an individual enters into conflict with societal obligations and moral norms, and yet, given the objective imperative of (proletarian) revolution, the individual "must raise himself above the level of its merely real facticity and reflect on its world-historical mission and the consciousness of its responsibility." The objective class consciousness of the proletariat, where the proletariat grasps itself as the genuine subject of history, mediates and hence resolves the tragedy between individual ethical decision and historical conditionality. Through the praxis of revolutionary struggle, the engaged individual "confronts an authentically tragic dilemma which [she] is compelled to answer through the sacrifice of [her] moral conscience for the sake of realizing the objectively possible, collective goal," namely, what she ought to do for the sake of revolution. As Lukács writes: "For every socialist, then, morally correct

---

[91] Kadarkay, *The Lukács Reader*, p. 220.

action is related fundamentally to the correct perception of the given historical-philosophical situation which in turn is only feasible through the efforts of every individual to make this self-consciousness consciousness for himself."[92] With such statements, it is clear that the apocalyptic shadow of Savinkov's *Pale Horse* still looms large over Lukács' thinking: "murder is not allowed, it is an absolute and unpardonable sin; it 'may' not, but yet it 'must' be committed." And yet, as Lukács writes: "To express this sense of the most profound human tragedy in the incomparably beautiful words of Hebbel's *Judith*: 'Even if God had placed sin between me and the deed enjoined upon me – who am I to be able to escape it?'"[93]

Orthodox Marxism

Gathering a series of essays written during years of civil strife and exile in Vienna between 1919 and 1922, *History and Class Consciousness*, as Lukács remarks, "was born in the midst of the crises of this transitional period." The war's turbulent aftermath in Central Europe left an indelible mark on the searching character of Lukács' thinking so as to make of these essays a text "yet to be written."[94] Unlike the essays of *Soul and Form*, composed by a literary John the Baptist who "goes out to preach in the wilderness about another who is still to come" and for whom "salvation can only come from accentuating the problems to the maximum degree," the multifaceted essays in *History and Class Consciousness* were composed in tandem with the rapidly changing and, indeed, deteriorating situation of revolution. The Kapp Putsch, the Spartacus Uprising, Polish–Soviet conflict, and social unrest in Italy and other countries, as Lukács observes, "strengthened our belief in the imminence of world revolution and the total transformation of the civilized world." And yet, with the failed revolutions of 1919 in Hungary and Germany followed by the emergence of what he would in hindsight recognize as "a prelude of fascist philosophy" in the form of a transfigured vitalism mobilized by *Kriegsphilosophie*, Lukács felt the urgent need in situ to "clarify the theoretical problems of the revolutionary movement" and thus redeem, and thereby reinvigorate, the

---

[92] G. Lukács, *Tactics and Ethics 1919–1929* (London: Verso Press, 2014), p. 9.
[93] Lukács, *Tactics and Ethics 1919–1929*, p. 11.
[94] F. Jameson, *Valences of the Dialectic* (London: Verso, 2009), p. 222. As Merleau-Ponty states in his celebrated essay "Western Marxism": "We must, however, recall this lively and vigorous work which revives the youth of the revolution and that of Marxism in order to take stock of today's communism and to realize what it has renounced and to what it has resigned itself"; M. Merleau-Ponty, *Adventures of the Dialectic*, trans. J. Bien (Evanston, IL: Northwest University Press, 1973), p. 161.

possibility of Marxist revolution to which he had existentially converted.[95] Weber's warning in 1920 looms large over the run of these essays: "Most esteemed friend, *of course* we are separated by our political views! (I am absolutely convinced that these experiments [1919 Revolutions] *can* and will only have the consequences of discrediting socialism for the coming 100 years)." The Second International had discredited socialism in 1914; would the failed revolutions of 1919, in which Lukács himself participated in Hungary, prove equally calamitous? Against Weber's conviction, *History and Class Consciousness* – for Maurice Merleau-Ponty the groundbreaking work of "Western Marxism" – proposes a theoretical reaccreditation of Marxism for the twentieth century for the purpose of reinforcing an absolute conviction in the world-historical promise of proletarian revolution.[96]

To this end, Lukács combined an unsparing critique of the positivist and historical evolutionary doctrines of Marxism that underpinned the failed Second International with a genial philosophical foundation for Lenin's vision of revolutionary praxis. Before undertaking a "thorough study of Lenin's theory" during his exile in Vienna, Lukács knew little of Lenin's writings, but his discovery of Lenin's adaptive reformulations of Marxist tenets in the aftermath of the collapse of the Second International, the war, and a successful – if still savagely embattled – Russian Revolution convinced Lukács that his own thinking remained plagued by an "unresolvable dualism" and the naive belief that the "correct solution went in the direction of an abstract utopianism in the realm of cultural politics" (i.e., a second ethics). Lenin's "effectiveness rests on the fact that he has developed the practical essence of Marxism to a pitch of clarity and concreteness never before achieved," while his theoretical achievement "placed in our hands the key to [the correct] understanding of Marxist method." This indebtedness to Lenin notwithstanding, Lukács, in returning to the question "What is Orthodox Marxism?," rejected Lenin's adoption of Engel's notion of dialectical materialism as well as Lenin's theory of reflection. Central to Lukács' twofold rejection of the Marxism of the Second International and critical recalibration of Lenin's "effectiveness" is a proper understanding of Marx's thinking as defined by a dialectical

---

[95] At the antipode of *History and Class Consciousness* stood Oswald Spengler's *The Decline of the West* (1919; 1922), which, for Lukács, "had such a powerful and lasting effect" because it gave a "most radical expression" to this change in postwar vitalism as a pathological bourgeois manifestation of the fetishism of soul and inwardness; Lukács, *The Destruction of Reason*, pp. 460–461.

[96] Lukács, *Selected Correspondence 1902–1920*, p. 281. As Lukács remarked after the Second World War: "as a result of this failure in 1918 [German Revolution], the masses were increasingly ensnared under the imperialist reactionary leadership in their national aspirations," thus leading to "a revival of aggressive German imperialism"; Lukács, *The Destruction of Reason*, p. 720.

method of thinking and praxis for the purpose of overthrowing capitalism in its totality. Orthodox Marxism, Lukács argues, is neither a set of convictions, a profession of faith, nor an exegesis of sacred texts; it is a method that opens onto an understanding of the whole of reality, or "totality," not "abstractly" – that is, speculatively – but concretely – that is, historically and socioeconomically. Rather than an intellectual method of analysis detached from or awaiting praxis, dialectical thinking cannot unfold outside actual revolutionary praxis, as with Lukács' own engagement during the writing of *History and Class Consciousness* (or Lenin during the war and Russian Revolution). As with Marx's *Das Kapital*, *History and Class Consciousness* offers a "critique of political economy" – it aims to understand, through its interlocking essays, the totality of capitalist society by uncovering its categorical presuppositions and conditions of possibility; it is, in this sense, both a critical "exposé" and transformative "critique."[97] As Lukács indicates, the sequence of essays represents a progression of thinking, with each essay "arising from actual work for the party to clarify theoretical problems of the revolutionary moment," from a critique of commodification and reification, to a critique of German Idealism as the epitome of the reification of bourgeois thinking, to an argument for the political organization of the party and the historical perspective of the proletariat.

The concept of "totality," as the dialectically mediated relations of social and historical reality, presents an alternative to "illusionary evolutionism" and "undialectical separation of means and ends" that characterized "vulgar Marxism," but also presciently forewarns against the increased bureaucratization of the Communist movement (as would occur with the Stalinization of the Third International).[98] As Lukács writes: "Only in this context [dialectical] which sees the isolated facts of social life as aspects of the historical process and integrates them in a *totality*, can knowledge of the facts hope to become knowledge of *reality*."[99] The methodological standpoint of totality allows for the demystification of the unmediated and independent elements of capitalist society, to reveal instead constitutive forces, albeit veiled and obscured by the ideological structures of (bourgeois) consciousness, that mold empirical facts within a concrete whole. Only the entire historical movement, in its dynamic unfolding toward an

---

[97] See Marx's letter of February 22, 1858, to Ferdinand Lasalle, https://marxists.architexturez.net/archive/marx/works/1858/letters/58_02_22.htm.

[98] I. Mészáros, *Beyond Capital: Toward a Theory of Transition* (New York: Monthly Review Press, 2010), p. 310.

[99] Lukács, *History and Class Consciousness*, p. 8.

end, namely, the abolition of capitalism, sets particular social relations into an intelligible reality. Importantly, as Lukács writes: "the category of totality does not reduce its various elements to an undifferentiated uniformity, to identity. The apparent independence and autonomy which they possess in the capitalist system of production is an illusion only in so far as they are involved in a dynamic dialectical relationship." When analyzed in terms of interactive social relations, and not as a process between unchanging or inert objects, but, on the contrary, as a process wherein "objective forms of all social phenomena change constantly in the course of their ceaseless dialectical interactions," dialectical thinking reveals how objective categories are constituted – materialized – through social relations. In Lukács' thinking, the dialectic mediation of social relations is inseparable from a concrete and dynamic totality. Following Marx, economic relations must be understood as social processes; these forms of objectivity are primarily not categories of thinking, but forms of (social) existence.

The failure to grasp social conditions within an overarching unfolding of history, tending toward the overcoming of capitalism through revolutionary praxis, accounted for the reformist conservatism of the Second International and its uncritical assumption that economic conditions alone would catalyze social transformation. Social existence encompasses the totality of all structures, including economic relations, and hence only through a transformation of social existence as such can economic relations become transformed. By the same token, any transformation in forms of thinking must be predicated on a transformation in the material conditions of thinking, namely, social forms of existence, and yet, it is only through the theoretical discovery of dialectical thinking that the constitutive social processes of reality can be discerned at all. This reciprocal relationship, or "zigzag," as it were, between theory and praxis is, in turn, mediated by an understanding of praxis as the collective agency of the proletariat in its coming to self-awareness and empowerment as the subject of history, rather than, more limitedly, as the transformation of material nature through labor. Praxis is a consciousness in action, or enactive collective consciousness, imbued with a constative and constitutive statement of human freedom and social salvation.[100] As Lukács states: "The individual can never become the measure of all things. For when the individual confronts objective reality he is faced by a complex of ready-made and unalterable objects which allow him only the subjective responses of

---

[100] For the originality of Lukács' conception of praxis, A. Feenberg, *The Philosophy of Praxis: Marx, Lukács, and the Frankfurt School* (London: Verso, 2014).

recognition or rejection. Only the class can relate to the whole of reality in a practical revolutionary way."[101] Expressed in Lukács' Hegelian terminology, the proletarian class in its revolutionary self-discovery is both the "subject" and "object" of world history, for it is only the proletariat who can arrive at a consciousness of totality in order to transform it completely; that is, abolish a capitalist society based on class division and conflict.

In the essay widely considered to be the centerpiece of *History and Class Consciousness*, "Reification and the Consciousness of the Proletariat," Lukács applies his dialectical method of thinking to the commodity. As Lukács observes, it is no accident that Marx began *Das Kapital* with an analysis of the commodity, for "at this stage of humankind" – that is, in modern capitalism – "there is no problem that does not ultimately lead back to that question and there is no solution that could not be found in the solution to the riddle of commodity-*structure*."[102] With this emphasis on structure, the commodity is not one form of objectivity among others, but, on the contrary, the dominant form of objectivity in a capitalist society. In this encompassing sense, commodification, as the form of objectivity as such (*Gegenständlichkeitsform*), determines not only the form of objects as value objectivities, but inseparably the relationship between objects and subjective consciousness.[103] As Lukács writes, the commodity form is the "original schema of all forms of objectivity and all forms of subjectivity that correspond to them."[104] Much as Lukács argued in his writings on aesthetics that the artwork, as an independent totality of form and content, prescribes the orientation from which a viewer experiences the artwork, such that the viewer does not stand outside the artwork but is prescribed a place from within the artwork itself, the commodity form, as structuring objectivity as such, prescribes, and in this sense subjectifies, the conduct, attitudes, and consciousness of subjects within a capitalist society. In the objective dimension, the commodity structure determines the form of an object's value in terms of a formal equality between qualitatively different objects. Qualitative and individual differences of an object's use value are exclusively measured, and hence reduced, to its quantitative exchange value, thus allowing for the circulation of objects (commodities) within a system of economic relations (the market). Moreover,

---

[101] Lukács, *History and Class Consciousness*, p. 193.
[102] Lukács, *History and Class Consciousness*, p. 83.
[103] For the Neo-Kantian sources and emphasis on the commodity as *Gegenständlichkeitsform*, see R. Westerman, *Lukács's Phenomenology of Capitalism* (Dordrecht: Springer Verlag, 2019) and Kavoulakos, *Georg Lukács's Philosophy of Praxis*.
[104] Lukács, *History and Class Consciousness*, p. 94.

the value of a commodified object is neither "objective" (intrinsic to the object) nor merely "subjective" (based on use value for an individual). The commodity structure displaces the notion of intentionality; the relation between "object" and "subject" is determined a priori by the original schema of the commodity. A commodity, as illustrated for example by advertisement, prescribes and hence predisposes an individual's desire and perception. It is not only that commodities speak to each other, as Marx famously stated; it is that commodities speak to us, indeed bespeak us, such that we are already spoken for. Commodities, as it were, magically appear to us, there for the satisfaction of desires that they in fact prescribe. As Lukács writes:

> The transformation of the commodity relation into a thing of "ghostly objectivity" cannot therefore content itself with the reduction of all objects for the gratification of human needs to commodities. It stamps its imprint upon the whole consciousness of man; his qualities and abilities are no longer an organic part of his personality, they are things which he can "own" or "dispose of" like the various objects of the external world.[105]

If, following Marx, we can speak of the "spectrality" or "ghostly" character of the commodity, we can likewise speak of the "spectrality" or "ghostly" – alienated – character of subjectivity. In the subjective dimension, the leveling effect of commodification imposes the mechanization and specialization of labor through industrial production. As Lukács writes: "The universality of the commodity form determines [...] an abstraction of the human labour objectified in commodities"[106] – "abstraction" through the dominance of calculative and instrumental rationality along with the bureaucratization of social relations. The ontological-social bifurcation between subject and object is connected as well to the objectification (i.e., commodification) of labor power (i.e., wage labor), with its destructive effect on social relations that bind individuals into a community.[107] The transformation of human activities "into a commodity reveals in all its starkness the dehumanized and dehumanizing function of the commodity relation" and "the specialization of skills leads to the destruction of every image of the whole."[108] The commodified objectification of things thus correlates with a fragmentation of the subjective life, which no longer experiences the social world of its own production as a home.

---

[105] Lukács, *History and Class Consciousness*, p. 100.
[106] Lukács, *History and Class Consciousness*, p. 95.
[107] Lukács, *History and Class Consciousness*, p. 101.
[108] Lukács, *History and Class Consciousness*, p. 102.

The commodity structure reconfigures the totality of modern society, and, indeed, renders society a totality, structured by a pervasive form of objectivity in relation to subjectivity. As Lukács writes: "The commodity can only be understood in its undistorted essence when it becomes the universal category of the overall social being. Only in this context does the reification that results from the commodity relation assume decisive importance for both the objective evolution of society and for the behaviour of men towards it."[109] Reification (*Verdinglichung*) arises from the objectification of commodification – and should not be conflated with commodification per se – as the "mystification" of objectification through its "naturalization" in conjunction with an ideology, or "false consciousness," embedded in social institutions that veil the commodification process itself. Reification is thus neither an "anthropological constant" (as argued by Axel Honneth) nor based on a "metaphysical philosophy of history" (as argued by Jürgen Habermas).[110] For Lukács, "reification is [...] the necessary, immediate reality of every person living in capitalist society," as exemplified by a consciousness of the world as governed by autonomous and mechanistic laws and the bureaucratization of social relations; that is, the anonymity of social processes.[111] This condition of alienation (affecting the bourgeois class as well as the proletariat) manifests itself in a contemplative stance toward the world: The world of commodities appear to us as "alien" and "other" in the sense of possessing an independent (and hence apparently unmediated) existence. Reification pertains to being and thinking; dereification requires the transformation of both, in thought and deed.[112]

Historically conditioned reification is exemplified by the antinomies of bourgeois thought that defined German Idealism, which can only be resolved through a transformation of social reality itself. Lukács argues that the theoretical question of how to understand the relation between "form" and "content," and more generally reconcile the dualism between "object" (world) and "subject" (mind), where different positions appealed either to a

---

[109] Lukács, *History and Class Consciousness*, p. 97. Marx in *Das Kapital* (Book III, chapter 48) describes reification as "mystification of the capitalist mode of production," "the reification of social relations," and "the immediate coalescence of the material relations with their historical and social specificity."

[110] The conflation or confusion between "objectification" and "reification" pervades a number of influential interpreters: Adorno, Habermas, and Honneth. For a critique of these misunderstandings and argument for the distinction between objectification and reification, see Kavoulakos, *Georg Lukács's Philosophy of Praxis*, pp. 141–149.

[111] Lukács, *History and Class Consciousness*, p. 267.

[112] Dannemann stresses these dual aspects of reification: as ideology and as real reification, i.e., distortion of relations of production. R. Dannemann, *Das Prinzip Verdinglichung: Studie zur Philosophie Georg Lukács'* (Frankfurt: Sendler, 1987).

myth of the given (the irrational content, or the *alogon*), a rational holism, or an a priori correlation (intentionality, synthesis of pure concepts and forms of intuition), stems from an underlying (and veiled) reality of social reification. Whether Kant's epistemological dualism between "appearance" and "thing in itself" or Fichte's ethical hiatus between actuality and the ought, the struggle to reconcile subject and object, or being and the ought, cannot find a possible theoretical solution, for these antinomies reflect the naturalization of reification, whereby commodities are encountered as alien and other than the social relations of their production. In this regard, *History and Class Consciousness* inaugurates a postphilosophical thinking that insists on the social – that is, material – conditions of theoretical ("philosophical") problems that, intrinsically, theory (and hence philosophy) does not have the means to solve, lacking as it does, as embodied in the essays of *History of Class Consciousness*, the method of dialectical thinking enacted in thought and deed. Although Fichte and Hegel abandoned a contemplative subject standing against the world, the active self-positing of Fichte's ego (as the identical subject-object), who posits an objective world as other than in itself, remains beholden to an individual subject in relation to an alien reality.[113] Schiller's aesthetic, where art is predicated on the creation of a self-enclosed totality – the ideal unity of form and content – is also deemed an example of reification. In Lukács' view, Hegel points toward an adequate solution to the structural antinomy of German Idealism with an understanding of history as a self-reconciling whole, as the manifestation of Spirit, as the "we" of *Sittlichkeit* and the state, that resolves the opposition between "form and content."[114] Following Marx, Lukács considers that "the demiurgic role of Spirit" in Hegel's thinking reverts to conceptual mythology with its sacralization of modern state power (a theme of contention in his wartime correspondence with Ernst). The absolute cannot have a speculative or theoretical solution; it dissolves into the reconciliation of social existence with itself, and thus we pass from theory to praxis, from thinking to revolution. Modern thought – German Idealism – found itself in the historically paradoxical situation that it looked for a theoretical solution to its problem that only a solution in praxis could resolve, while obscuring this for itself. The solution to the antinomies of modern reason can only be found with "the end of bourgeois society" and the "resurrection in thought of a humanity destroyed in that society and by it." Bourgeois modes of thinking, including philosophy, cannot overcome reification and the antinomies of modern thought,

---

[113] Lukács, *History and Class Consciousness*, p. 124 ff.
[114] Lukács, *History and Class Consciousness*, p. 146.

for only the proletariat, in becoming aware of itself as a "reified consciousness," can transform itself, and hence emancipate itself and the social world, from reification and the dominance of commodification.

Revolutionary Class Consciousness

The theoretical clarification of this antinomy of modern thought through dialectical thinking stands within the political engagement of revolutionary praxis. Knowledge does not duplicate or double social reality through reflection, however critical it aspires to be; thinking can only claim to be dialectical as an integral moment of contributing to the transformation of its object; namely, social reality as a whole (as exemplified by *History and Class Consciousness*). This represents what Lukács calls the "we of genesis when the proletariat discovers within itself as basis of its life experience the identical subject-object."[115] The process of the subjectification of the proletariat – the genesis of the collective We – must involve the "dereification" of the proletarian consciousness through a struggle to transform actual relations, the economic organization of production, and social institutions. The proletarian class is therefore privileged in dual respects: It is called upon to transform the totality of social reality under capitalism and thus overcome economic exploitation and the social alienation of humanity (in its contemporary historical condition), as well as establish the epistemological vantage point for a complete understanding of social reality, as articulated by a Communist engaged thinker like Lukács himself. History becomes aware of itself in word and deed in the self-awakening of the proletarian class to its own self-actualized truth. In the same vein, the theory of orthodox Marxism, as espoused in *History and Class Consciousness*, is the self-awareness of the Communist movement in its revolutionary actuality. In the unity of the object and the subject of history, proletarian self-awareness entails ethical-normative and epistemological aspects.[116]

The function of theory, in its dialectical efficacy, consists in galvanizing a revolutionary leap into praxis, and this can only occur when a historical situation arises in which proletarian class consciousness comes to understand itself in relation to social reality as such. The awakening of the proletariat hinges on discovering itself as "the subject-object" of world history – that is, as the subject that produces itself as well its social reality – thus

---

[115] Lukács, *History and Class Consciousness*, p. 184.
[116] L. Kolakowski, *Main Currents of Marxism*, trans. P. S. Falla (Oxford: Oxford University Press, 1981), III, p. 272.

rupturing with its own reified consciousness in its passive and contemplative attitude toward a world to which it falsely understands itself to be beholden and historically fated. In its alienated condition, the proletariat is prescribed a contemplative stance toward the world by the dominant structure of commodification; in revolutionary class consciousness, the relation to the world becomes inverted. Lukács alternates between two characterizations of the passage, or subversive inversion, from the alienation and contemplative attitude of the proletariat (where reflective thinking beholds the world) to revolutionary praxis (where revolutionary thinking, embedded in praxis, seizes the world as the product of proletarian agency). On one account, Lukács argues that the proletariat awaken to their collective interest and agency by exploiting their own dialectical contradiction. In becoming aware of their existence (commodification of labor, economic exploitation, and so on) in view of the totality of social reality, where "external reality" becomes seized as their own "internal production," the proletarian emancipates itself from reification through its transformative praxis of rendering itself the subject-object of the totality of social reality. On another account, Lukács distinguishes between "empirical" (or actual) class consciousness and "imputed" or "prescribed" (*zugerechnet*) class consciousness, by which the (actual) reified class consciousness imputes to itself its own "objective possibility" to come; that is, what it ought to become.[117] Such "imputed consciousness" is an ideal type of consciousness in its enacted aspiration to transform the conditions of its own existence in pursuit of fulfilling its world-historical mission.[118] Consciousness imputes, or prescribes, to itself an objective consciousness of its own enactive possibility. In this self-objectified class consciousness, proletarian consciousness prescribes for itself the objective subjectivity that it must become in the future, as an objective possibility it gives to itself and as the subject that prescribes this historical possibility to itself, and hence as the identity of subject and object as forged through revolutionary praxis. Imputed objective consciousness, as prefiguring an objective reality in revolutionary making (i.e., through praxis), is neither a merely heuristic device, a utopic model, nor an abstract possibility. It is also not a program that is imposed unilaterally on proletarian consciousness by a party or group of intellectuals. As Maurice Merleau-Ponty suggests, imputed

---

[117] Lukács, *History and Class Consciousness*, p. 62.
[118] Lukács, *History and Class Consciousness*, p. 51: "Now class consciousness consists in the fact of the appropriate and rational reactions 'imputed' to a particular typical position in the process of production. This consciousness is, therefore, neither the sum nor the average of what is thought or felt by the single individuals who make up the class."

objective consciousness passes beyond the dilemma of subjectivist intention or objective model or idea.[119] Revolutionary praxis does not follow or realize a pregiven plan or idea; it crystallizes in situ practical possibilities through actions within definite historical conditions in pursuit of the complete transformation of social reality.[120]

In this fashion, the dialectical process of proletarian self-awareness and practical self-empowerment is neither mechanical nor causal, for it realizes collective freedom, which Lukács characterizes with Simmel's term of "interactive reciprocity" (*Wechselwirkung*).[121] The interactive reciprocity between actual consciousness in the historical situation of the proletariat and its future-directed imputed objective possibility reflects Marx's insistence that one should not speak of human existence in general or abstractly. For Lukács, the originality of Marx's humanism consists in its "refusal to see in the categories of reflection a 'permanent' of human knowledge," and thus, through the discovery of the dialectic, the historicity of social being and categories of thought are discovered to be immanent to the unfolding of history. Praxis cannot be divorced from knowledge, and it is through praxis, as the refusal and abolition of "actual forms of social life" along with the "disruption of the reified structure of existence," that the contradictions of capitalism become transformed and surpassed.[122] What this means, as Lukács writes, is that "in addition to the mere contradiction – the automatic product of capitalism – a *new* element is required: the consciousness of the proletariat must become deed."[123] This emergence of the "new" entails that "the problem of the constitution of the ascribed consciousness is precisely the problem of the emergence of a *radically new form of consciousness*, beyond the one that corresponds to the economic position of the proletariat and its subsequent demand for its improvement within the given social content."[124] The conversion from actuality to possibility, from what is to what ought to be, hinges on making, as it were, the impossible true. As Lukács writes:

---

[119] Merleau-Ponty, *Adventures of the Dialectic*, p. 46 ff. As Löwy argues, "it is not as a rigid metaphysical duality but as a historical *process* through which the class, assisted by its vanguard, rises to its own imputed consciousness through its own experience of struggle"; *From Romanticism to Bolshevism*, p. 169.

[120] Lukács, *History and Class Consciousness*, p. 225.

[121] As Merleau-Ponty states: "since the revolutionary politics is to be invented, not being already there, implicit in the existing proletariat, it cannot bypass this moment when it dares to step into the unknown"; *Adventures of the Dialectic*, p. 52.

[122] Lukács, *History and Class Consciousness*, pp. 177, 197.

[123] Lukács, *History and Class Consciousness*, p. 178.

[124] Lukács, *History and Class Consciousness*, p. 184.

The leap is rather a lengthy, arduous process. Its character as a leap is expressed in the fact that on every occasion it denotes *a turning in the direction of something qualitatively new*; that it expresses the conscious action directed towards the comprehended totality of society; and therefore in the fact that it belongs—in its intention and fundament—to the realm of freedom.[125]

Lukács stresses that "the *conscious* desire for the realm of freedom can only mean taking the steps that will really lead to it," and that this does not transpire in one sudden miraculous leap, but by leaps and bounds, the "first arduous, uncertain and groping steps" he identified with the "collective will of the Communist Party."[126] The role of the party in the organization of class consciousness is to bridge the gap, and hence facilitate the leap, between actual class consciousness and the true class consciousness of the proletariat; here following Lenin, placed in alignment with Marx's humanism and emphasis on freedom, the party provides the mediating link between the agency of the proletariat and the totality of history, thus allowing for the unity of theory and practice. However, this Leninist stress on the will of the party in world-historical perspective carries over, in a transformed manner, the centrality of the ethical, which had always been the guiding point of reference for Lukács' quest to overcome the age of absolute sinfulness. As Lukács writes, "class consciousness is the 'ethics' of the proletariat, the unity of its theory and its practice, the point at which the economic necessity of its struggle for liberation changes dialectically into freedom" and this connects to the notion that "the true strength of the party is *moral*."[127]

1924

In his book on Lenin published the year of Lenin's death in 1924, Lukács argues that Lenin's grounding and guiding thought was the "actuality of the revolution."[128] In turning back to Lenin, Lukacs rejects the establishment

---

[125] Lukács, *History and Class Consciousness*, p. 315. Lukács breaks here with his friend Bloch: "Real actions then appear—precisely in their objective, revolutionary sense—wholly independent of the religious utopia: the latter can neither lead them in any real sense, nor can it offer concrete objectives or concrete proposals for their realization"; pp. 192–193.

[126] Lukács, *History and Class Consciousness*, p. 315. Merleau-Ponty, *Adventures of the Dialectic*, p. 47 ff. Merleau-Ponty argues that freedom is central to Lukács' notion of the proletariat. As Merleau-Ponty argues, class consciousness is not a "state of mind" or knowledge, and thus not "top down" positing or changing of society according to a plan or fixed idea – abstract idealism – nor expansiveness of a purely subjective world (Romantic anti-capitalism), but a transformation of forms of objectivity and social relations, and thus a denaturalization of fixed social structures and positions, and openness to intervention and configuration.

[127] Lukács, *History and Class Consciousness*, p. 42.

[128] G. Lukács, *Lenin: A Study on the Unity of His Thought*, trans. N. Jacobs (London: Verso Books, 2009), p. 23.

of the soviets and syndicalism as permanent forms of organization and endorses instead the party and worker unions. Historical materialism, as the theory of the proletarian revolution that reaches its highest point as theory in becoming praxis, as personified in Lenin himself, could only be theoretically formulated in a historical moment as well as set in motion and formulated in its practical actuality as the order of the day, or demand of the hour, of history. For, as he writes, there can be no ideological and organizational maturity that contributes to the proletariat being decisive and resolute for struggle when this is not a consequence of the objective economic and social situation of the world. Lenin expressed his position most clearly at the Stuttgart congress of the Second International and warned of the imminent threat of an "imperial world war" and what in reaction was to be done against this war. This position of Lenin and Luxemburg was adopted and later ratified in Copenhagen and Basel. And yet, in August 1914, Lenin stood alone in his position and, as Lukács remarks, his standing alone was not accidental, not just a psychological or moral circumstance but a theoretical one: "the attitude or position of the individual socialist tendencies in August 1914 were direct, thematic consequences of their preceding theoretical, tactical, etc., comportment." Lenin recognized that the final stage in the evolution of capitalism is the "decisive struggle" between the bourgeoisie and the proletariat. What hung in the balance with this apocalyptic hour of decision/resolution was nothing less than the salvation of humanity.

However, there is a difference between Lenin and Lukács, which reveals how far Lukács has moved beyond the framework of the Second International to which Lenin remains beholden.[129] Imputed class consciousness must be brought "from without" and "from within," by which Lukács understands a dialectical process between a political process and a socioeconomic process. The question of the historical situation of the proletariat is not the choice between peace and freedom, which was the dominant view of the Second International and led to compromise, but the choice between imperialistic war and civil war.[130] The necessity of civil war as the defense of the proletariat against imperialism arises from the conditions of struggle that are demanded by the development of capitalist production. Lenin already recognized as early as 1905 that the weapon

---

[129] For this argument, A. Feenberg, "Post-Utopian Marxism: Lukács and the Dilemmas of Organization," in *Confronting Mass Democracy and Industrial Technology*, ed. J. McCormick (Durham, NC: Duke University Press, 2002), p. 56 ff. Lenin remains beholden to the framework of Plekhanov and Kautsky.

[130] See also Lukács' remark on the Second International in *History and Class Consciousness*, p. 301.

of general strike was insufficient, thus he had already established theoretically the necessary tactic of the proletariat in world war. This results in the transformation of the very concept of war. As Lukács remarks: "The revolutionary essence of an age expresses itself most clearly when the struggle of classes and parties no longer has the character of internal struggle against a state order but begins to explode its borders; the state becomes itself a weapon in the struggle of class." In answer to the question posed by the war – How shall we be saved from this age of sinfulness? – the 1917 October "world revolution" was the answer. The theory of historical materialism has as its presupposition the "world-historical actuality of the proletarian revolution." In this regard, according to Lukács, the objective foundation of an entire epoch – the present – as well as the perspective of understanding, object and subject in other words, forms the center of Marxist doctrine.[131] But, as Lukács still wonders in 1924: "But have we entered the period of decisive revolutionary struggles? Has the moment already come when the proletariat, on pain of its own destruction, is forced to take up its task of changing the world?"[132]

In his opening address in June 1924 to the Fifth Comintern Congress in Moscow of the Third International, general secretary Zinoviev condemned *History and Class Consciousness* as an idealist and revisionist work on account of Lukács' critique of "vulgar Marxism" and the socioeconomic determinism of the Second International. This public denunciation coincided with Lenin's death and the transformation of the aspirations of the Russian Revolution that marked a parting of the ways in the development of Marxism in thought and deed. Although Lukács defended his position against other attacks, his existential commitment to his conversion to Communism in the interest of world history compelled him to conform to the imposition of Stalinism and finally renounce *History and Class Consciousness* in 1929.[133]

---

[131] Lukács, *Lenin*, p. 57.
[132] Lukács, *Lenin*, p. 62.
[133] For Lukács' defense of *History and Class Consciousness* in a text only recently discovered and most likely written in 1926 or 1926, *Tailism and the Dialectic*, trans. E. Leslie (London: Verso, 2000).

CHAPTER 7

From Death into Life
Franz Rosenzweig's Redemptions

"Then I Came to Know 'Everything'"

For countless soldiers, revelation as to the significance of their lives entwined with the fate of God, the Nation, or whatever Absolute claimed to give meaning to it all could occur in the most fearful of situations, but also in the most inauspicious of moments. For many, the war was experienced as a rite of passage and self-discovery. Many emerged from the war transfigured, set upon a new course of life. There were those, as with Ernst Jünger, who entered the war with an adventurous heart in search of something more than what domestic life had on offer; there were those, as with Karl Löwith, who did not go to war adventuring but in need of an ill-defined alternative, returning from the war scarred for life; there were those, as with Dietrich Mahnke, who through the war found confirmation of what had already been known but as yet existentially evidenced; there were those whose philosophical promise was extinguished on the battlefield, as with the deaths of Emil Lask and Adolf Reinach; and there were those who, philosophically active before 1914, disappeared from the stage of history after 1918, whose postwar quietude, as with Johannes Daubert, poignantly bespoke the extinguishing of thinking. But if philosophy – and not just philosophers – could thus become a casualty of war, it could just as well find rebirth, for there were those for whom the war became a crucible for the origination of a new thinking, indeed a new way of *living*, the brilliance of which continued to shine long after the war had receded from memory.

In a far-flung corner of Macedonia, removed from the titanic struggles of the western and eastern Fronts, Franz Rosenzweig had a revelation in October 1917 as he stumbled along a path during a nighttime march in the vicinity of Prilep. As Rosenzweig writes to Martin Buber after the war, he experienced that night a redemptive insight into the relation between creation and revelation while stepping on "a nasty prickly plant."[1] In a theatre of conflict – "the most controversial of all the so-called sideshows," in the words of a military historian – situated between Europe and Asia Minor, Rosenzweig "came to know everything." In a surge of inspiration six weeks later, Rosenzweig wrote a letter (November 18, 1917), known as the *Urzelle*, to his cousin Rudolf Ehrenberg, where this illumination began to take shape and direction. "Already a month ago now," Rosenzweig wrote, "I achieved something important, so at least it seemed to me at first [...] Here it is: my philosophical Archimedean point, long sought after."[2] What dawned on him was "the perspicuous interconnections of thoughts" for a comprehensive understanding of "the whole" – of God, the world, and human beings – where previously in his mind there had been "mere aperçus pushed one in front of the other." At the center of this revelation stood the singularity of human existence, Rosenzweig's own, as "a completely common private-subject, I fore- and surname, I dust and ashes," within a constellation of the whole – the All of what is. Rosenzweig came to see how human life exists in "a twofold relation to the Absolute, one where it has him, but still a second where he has *it*."[3]

What was set in motion during that fateful night march did not spring Minerva-like fully formed into existence. From the embryonic *Urzelle*, Rosenzweig composed over the course of the next two years *The Star of Redemption*. As Rosenzweig informed Ehrenberg in September 1918, his book "is really nothing but the development of my letter to you of last November. It contains really everything that is in me, consequently all the influences I have undergone."[4] It would be wrong to think that Rosenzweig's revelation graced him in one stroke with a lucid vision of the systematic argument and existential purchase of his eventual book.[5] Much of the thinking in *The Star of Redemption* was set down on postcards to his mother and missives sent back from the front. Rosenzweig's thinking materialized in dialogue with a handful of friends and, most importantly, Margrit Rosenstock (his friend Eugen Rosenstock's wife), with whom he became amorously involved toward the end of 1917. In his letters to Gritli, as he affectionately called her, *The Star of Redemption* crystallized along with

---

[1] Rosenzweig, *Gesammelte Schriften*, I/2, p. 816.
[2] Rosenzweig, *Gesammelte Schriften*, I/2, p. 816.
[3] F. Rosenzweig, *Philosophical and Theological Writings*, trans. P. Franks and M. Morgan (Indianapolis: Hackett Publishing, 2000), p. 51.
[4] Rosenzweig, *Gesammelte Schriften*, I/2, p. 604.
[5] He writes most of the *Star* in late 1918 and, after being demobilized at the end of 1918, finishes the manuscript in Kassel and Berlin on February 16, 1919.

an attachment to his immortal beloved. "Hermann Cohen and Gritli," Rosenzweig writes to Ehrenberg, are the two "great names" from which the "the *Star of Redemption* issues, and not gratuitously, as a book that insists on the heaven of the *future*, of what one 'hopes.'"[6] As a prolific letter writer on account of the war, the epistolary discourse of Rosenzweig's "speech-thinking," as he called it, cut across a distinction between written and oral expressions. In the ebb and flow of address and response, thinking was indissociable from the agency of time itself in dialogical enactment of the word: the sending of and waiting for letters, pauses for thought between letters, and the conception of ideas in the lap of writing. Wartime isolation at the front became transcended by a dialogical interspace, spanning different war fronts as well as the home front, that allowed Rosenzweig to cultivate solitude without being alone. As Rosenzweig writes to Hans Ehrenberg in October 1916:

> I have been on Dub mountain now for almost exactly three months as an anti-aircraft observer, and I hardly ever get down; I still feel no desire to be relieved [...] up here I lead a hermit's existence [...] I've been reading a lot in Tertullian and studying Aramaic assiduously [...] I've also developed a great taste for writing and write endless letters.[7]

A year after his revelation – six weeks into the writing of *The Star of Redemption* – Rosenzweig reports to Margrit Rosenstock on a vision he experienced while working on his manuscript:

> I was still finishing the Transition chapter last night [from the first part to the second part]; it became quite crazy, and all the spirits were so let-loose that I couldn't sleep anymore after midnight [...] these are the moments in which one sees oneself as doubled because one is no longer glued right firmly in one's body. So, it all happened that I was between two parts and as a consequence the Star [...] suddenly shone as strongly as in the first days when it began. I saw it again with eyes and everything individual in it [...] Thus I saw the Star and strangely enough it rotated around itself and therein everything that I still have to write was to be seen [...] I really needed this night "between the pieces" again in the immediate sight of the whole.[8]

---

[6] Rosenzweig, *Gesammelte Schriften*, I/2, p. 643. As Pierre Bouretz insightfully remarks: "That a polarity should thus be established between a Judaism embodied in a father figure always venerated but often the object of revolt and a Christianity represented by a woman who is herself a symbol of love – this can tell us much about Rosenzweig's split personality, and about the speculative tension formerly opened up by his temptation to convert, and reflected at the heart of his great work"; Bouretz, *Witnesses for the Future*, p. 99.

[7] Rosenzweig, *Gesammelte Schriften*, I/2, p. 243.

[8] F. Rosenzweig, *Die "Gritli"-Briefe. Briefe an Margrit Rosenstock-Huessy*, eds. I. Rühle and R. Mayer (Tübingen: Bilam Verlag, 2002), pp. 159–160.

The configuration of *The Star of Redemption* descended on Rosenzweig in a visionary self-shaping of the book itself, while he, in this intellectual intuition of its articulated whole, experiences himself as doubled, inside and outside of his thinking, as "strongly as in the first days when it began." It is not merely Rosenzweig who thinks *The Star*; it is just as much *The Star*'s thinking that lays claim to him, transcribing for him a path that his own life was to follow. In a de facto preface to his magnum opus, Rosenzweig observes in his essay "The New Thinking" (1925) that for a philosophical book to be worth reading, a reader cannot already know "what one is driving at from the beginning," since a book is only worth reading if one does not understand its beginning or understands it wrongly. As Rosenzweig comments with respect to his own work, "where the whole becomes surveyable at a glance cannot be predicted; in general, already well before the last page, but scarcely before the middle of the book; and certainly hardly at exactly the same point for two readers."[9] Each reader will find themselves somewhere else with this new thinking, and yet find themselves nowhere else than within a systematic thinking of the meaningfulness of it all. A reader should thus enjoin a twofold relation to *The Star of Redemption* – where it has them, where they have it. Although books generally "can be written and read without any concern for the time passing," *The Star of Redemption* moves in its own temporal register, challenging not only what it is to read a work of philosophy, but what it is *to be* a work in philosophy; that is, what significance philosophy, in this new configuration of promise, enjoys and enjoins for life itself.

As Rosenzweig advises, *The Star of Redemption* is neither "a Jewish book," nor a "philosophy of religion," nor a philosophical work in any conventional sense. It develops a systematic philosophy – a constellation in motion – where the meaning of philosophy becomes recast into a metaphysical thinking of the interactive relations between God, the world, and human existence, without the reduction of each to the other, nor the isolation of one from the other. This threefold declination of irreducible yet inseparable senses of what there is – that there is God, that there is the world (cosmos), that there is human existence – is articulated in word and deed, as language and time, in terms of an ecstatic threefold temporality of creation, revelation, and redemption. The question of the sense of what it is "to be" cannot be understood otherwise than through the reciprocal interaction between God, the world, and human existence. There is not *one* fundamental sense of what it means to be, but *three*. This threefold

---

[9] Rosenzweig, *Philosophical and Theological Writings*, p. 114.

declination of what is cannot become subsumed into a seamless totality closed upon an identity with itself nor reduced to one of the three elemental senses of being (God, human existence, the world). As a further enrichment of the bold intricacy of *The Star of Redemption*'s configuration, the relationality and, hence, openness of each to the other, of God, the world, and human existence, becomes set into place and motion, into time and narrative, through an effective relationality between creation, revelation, and redemption. In short, we behold not a traditional metaphysical thinking turning in circles around the axis of "is-questions," but a thinking otherwise than being, breaking with the principle of identity and reduction of the many to the one. Rather than an obsessive concern with the ontological thinking of the "is," Rosenzweig's new thinking conjugates multiple senses of "the little word 'and' [as] the basic word of all experience, to which its [philosophy] tongue is unaccustomed. God and the world and man. This 'and' was the first of experience; so it must also recur in the ultimate of truth."[10]

Written in a manner to which the historical languages of philosophy, from Ionia to Jena, are unaccustomed, *The Star of Redemption* speaks in tongues. And yet, *The Star of Redemption*'s vision of the whole promises more than just another revolution in the history of philosophy. As Rosenzweig states, his is a "philosophy which does not want to bring about a mere 'Copernican Revolution' of thinking, after which he who has performed it sees all things upside down, although they are still the same things he had seen before, rather [it is] a philosophy which wants to bring about the total renewal of thinking." From this renewal of thinking there issues a renewal of life. Rosenzweig's vision of the whole and its articulation in speech-thinking cannot be identified as a theory dragging along a praxis. We arrive at philosophical knowledge – or better, wisdom – when we arrive at ourselves, in the world, with others, and in relation to God. In what Rosenzweig calls his "messianic theory of knowledge," *The Star* culls the "elements" of existence prior to thinking, and configures them into a course of thinking leading toward a gate exiting from the book into life, passing from thinking through being to living, to existence after thinking, to life lived under the lodestar of redemption. It is this configured vision of the whole, beginning from the mute facticity of existence, leading through thinking, as philosophical narrative, to life organized around the power of redemptive speech, with others in community, in prayer and ritual. If life is said to be not worth living without

[10] Rosenzweig, *Philosophical and Theological Writings*, p. 135.

philosophy, philosophy should in turn be said to be not worth thinking without living, and that which makes life worth living (and hence thinking) is abiding in hope for the redemption of creaturely existence. We have never genuinely entered life, knowing and living it as we think we do every day, if we have not, once in our lifetime, traversed "the day of the life of the All" from creation through revelation to redemption. As with Abraham's vision in Genesis 15:1, to which Rosenzweig's beholding of a rotating star in his letter to Gritli alludes: "After these things, the word of God came to Abraham in a vision saying, 'Don't be afraid, Abraham, I am your shield. Your reward is great.'"[11] Such, then, can be said of *The Star of Redemption*: It was only worth writing because Rosenzweig himself could not understand its beginning, much as life would not be worth living if its fate were already known from the beginning. Time still had to run its course in a world where the course of history, the future of thinking, the concert of nations, and, most significantly, an orientation toward God were thrown out of joint.

"I Therefore Remain a Jew"

The Archimedean point revealed to Rosenzweig in 1917 opened a way to exodus from a personal and intellectual crisis that had engulfed his life since before the war. As Rosenzweig writes in his *Urzelle* letter, his nighttime illumination resonated with a spiritual crisis that had inhibited him from finding his way in the world after his university studies. As he recalls to a friend, on a tour of the Harz mountains in 1914 "we had just stepped out of a fir forest [...] and spoke about whether and how one could delimit – purely philosophically or even only in general – revelation from all properly human knowledge by any demonstrable criteria whatsoever."[12] The question of revelation, of a witnessed unimpeachable truth regarding the sense of what it is to be, according to which one could live, haunted Rosenzweig across intersecting registers: in relation to the confrontation between Christianity and Judaism; with regard to the conflict between faith and reason; with respect to the meaning of history and the Absolute. While working on his doctoral dissertation on the development of Hegel's political thinking (*Hegel and the State*, completed in 1912

---

[11] For the connection between Rosenzweig's vision in October 1918 and Abraham, see B. Pollock, *Franz Rosenzweig and the Systematic Task of Philosophy* (Cambridge, UK: Cambridge University Press, 2009), pp. 265–266.
[12] Rosenzweig, *Philosophical and Theological Writings*, p. 48.

but only published in 1920) under the supervision of Friedrich Meinecke, Rosenzweig befriended Eugen Rosenstock at a conference of Hegelian-inspired students in Baden-Baden in 1910. Both men had strong misgivings about Hegel's historical theodicy of absolute spirit as well as Neo-Hegelian schools of historicism. Even while writing his Hegel thesis, as he observes in a letter to Rudolf Hallo after the war, "I considered the Hegelian philosophy to be harmful."[13] As early as 1910, Rosenzweig recognized that "the struggle against history in the nineteenth-century," and hence, inter alia, against Hegel, "is for us identical with the struggle for religion in the twentieth-century sense."[14] *For us*, namely, for us Jews, "religion is the 'only authentic theodicy,'" whereas "for Hegel, history was a divine theodicy."[15] Caught between an equally unacceptable sacralized thinking of the Hegelian absolute and the profane relativism of *Weltanschauung* theories, his friend Rosenstock had found refuge by converting from Judaism to Protestantism. Faith in revelation, for Rosenstock, was anchored in the historical manifestation of God in his openness toward human existence with the advent of Christ. A vibrant debate ensued between these two friends, drawing in Ehrenberg as well, which reached a point of crisis on the night of July 7, 1913.

As Rosenstock recounts, he, Ehrenberg, and Rosenzweig found themselves that evening in Leipzig engaged in a "heated discussion of science and religion" stemming from their disagreement over the final sentence in Selma Lagerlöf's novel *The Miracles of the Antichrist*: "Nobody can redeem men from their suffering, but much shall be forgiven him who re-encourages them to bear these sufferings."[16] Eugen read this statement as a profession of Christian faith, whereas Franz understood it as suggesting skepticism against Christianity. Debating long into the night, Rosenzweig finally became convinced under the sway of Rosenstock's staunch Christian faith that he, too, should convert. As he writes in a letter: "You were the witness to how from this knowledge for me the building of a world could begin anew. In this world – and related to this inside an unrelated outside I no longer allowed to obtain or be valid [...] – in this world therefore it

---

[13] Rosenzweig, *Gesammelte Schriften*, I/2, p. 889.
[14] Rosenzweig, *Gesammelte Schriften*, I/1, p. 113.
[15] Rosenzweig, *Gesammelte Schriften*, I/2, p. 112.
[16] For this account of the *Leipzigernachtgesprach*, see E. Rosenstock-Huessy, *Judaism despite Christianity: The 1916 Wartime Correspondence between Eugen Rosenstock-Huessy and Franz Rosenzweig* (Chicago: University of Chicago Press, 2011), pp. 72–74. For Rosenzweig's sketchy account in his letters, see his letter to Rudolf Ehrenberg of October 31, 1913, Rosenzweig, *Briefe und Tagebücher: 1900–1918*, Band I, p. 137, *Gesammelte Schriften* I.

seemed that there was no place for Judaism." Convinced that there was no longer a place for Judaism in history nor for himself as a Jew in the world, conversion to Christianity, based on the primacy of revelation, seemed to be the only viable course for avoiding historical and cultural relativism. Rosenzweig's decision to convert likewise disabused him of a flirtation with Marcionism. As he writes to Ehrenberg:

> In that night's conversation Rosenstock shoved me step by step out of the last relativistic position that I still occupied and forced me to take an absolute standpoint [...] Had I back then against him supported my dualism between revelation and world with my dualism between God and the Devil, I would have been unassailable. But the first line of Genesis prevented me from this. This common piece allowed me to withstand him [...] Any form of relativism is now impossible for me.[17]

Rather than accept the revelation of the Absolute in history as its culmination or succumb to the relativism of history, Rosenzweig had entertained a Marcionite rejection of creation, and with it the God of creation from the Old Testament, in the Gnostic hope of salvation through the revelation of hidden and alien God. But as Rosenzweig remarks in a note from 1916: "What it means that God created the world and [is] not just the God of revelation – this I know precisely from the Leipzig night-conversation of 7.7.13. At that time, I was on the best road to Marcionism."[18] Both temptations – historicism and Marcionism – could be avoided with the embrace of Christianity. He decided, however, to convert under one condition: to convert as a Jew.

Set upon conversion as a "conscious Jew such as Saul of Taurus," a few months after his Leipzig decision Rosenzweig attended services for the Day of Atonement at an orthodox Synagogue in Berlin on October 23, 1913. Profoundly affected by the observed ritual of fasting, prayer, and repentance, he suddenly decided to break with his announced conversion.[19] As he writes to Ehrenberg: "I have reversed my decision. It no longer seems necessary to me, and therefore, being what I am, no longer possible. I will remain a Jew."[20] Given the assimilated background of his

---

[17] Rosenzweig, *Gesammelte Schriften*, I/1, 133.
[18] Rosenzweig, *Gesammelte Schriften*, I/1, p. 133. For the importance of the temptation to Marcionism and Lagerlöf's novel for Rosenzweig's conversion, B. Pollack, *Franz Rosenzweig's Conversions: World Denial and World Redemption* (Bloomington: Indiana University Press, 2014).
[19] The details of what Rosenzweig witnessed at this decisive Day of Atonement service remain unknown; neither in his letters nor in the testimony of his friends do we find a direct account of his revelation that day.
[20] Rosenzweig, *Gesammelte Schriften*, I/1, p. 132.

family's Jewish identity, Rosenzweig returns with this countermanding of his own decision to convert to a Judaism that had never truly been his own, but now needed to become his own, as the focal point of intellectual engagement and personal devotion, on terms yet to be discovered. As Rosenzweig announces to Ehrenberg: "I am about to interpret for myself the entire system of Jewish doctrine on its own Jewish basis."[21] This return to his native Jewishness and "dissimilation" from Christianity and Hegelianism coincided with the fateful befriending of Hermann Cohen at the *Hochschule für die Wissenschaft des Judentums* in Berlin. As Rosenzweig recalls his encounter with Cohen:

> Then I experienced an unprecedented surprise. Being accustomed to finding in philosophy chairs intelligent people, well-honed wits, acute, lofty, profound, or whatever adjective you could find to characterize that spirit when you want to praise the virtues of a thinker, I found a philosopher. Instead of the tightrope walkers who, on the wire of thought, presenting their more or less daring skillful or graceful leaps, I saw a man [...] What magic spell inhabited this man's words?[22]

Beginning in 1914 until the venerable philosopher's death in April 1918, Cohen lectured on what would become *Religion of Reason Out of the Sources of Judaism* (which Rosenzweig read in manuscript). Cohen's newfound understanding of Judaism, as Rosenzweig suggested in his introduction to Cohen's posthumously published *Jüdische Schriften*, was Cohen's "great *teshuvah*."[23] After his own "great *teshuvah*" in Berlin, Rosenzweig lost contact with Rosenstock (who apparently had not realized that Rosenzweig had decided "to remain a Jew") without any resolution as to their dispute. The onset of war provided the fortuitous occasion for the resumption of their unsettled debate. In an exchange of letters between May and June 1916, Rosenzweig combatted Rosenstock (serving at Verdun) in seeking "to wrench Judaism from the alienation" imposed on it by Christianity and the denial of its otherness and originality. Rosenstock, for his part, continued in his besieging of Rosenzweig with the universal world-historical mission of Christianity and sought to disabuse him of a "Jewish stubbornness" in resisting assimilation and reconciliation on the terms set

---

[21] Rosenzweig, *Gesammelte Schriften*, I/1, p. 137.
[22] Rosenzweig, *Gesammelte Schriften*, II, p. 623.
[23] As Rosenzweig writes to his parents, he has experienced many "famous philosophy professors, Lipps, Rickert, Windelband, Jonas Cohn, Riehl, Dessoir, Cassirer, Stumpf, Simmel, Lask, Eucken, Wundt, Spranger," but with none of them did he have at all the feeling of standing in the presence of "a philosopher"; Rosenzweig, *Gesammelte Schriften*, I/1, p. 442.

forth by Christianity.[24] Rosenzweig staunchly rejected the dialectical sublation of Judaism into Christianity as well as Christian tolerance or the enlightened humanism of Lessing's *Nathan the Wise*. As Rosenzweig writes to his friend, whereas "Christianity identifies with the Empire (the *world* of today)," "Judaism identifies with its own *self*," and this insistence on its "own self" demands a "decision" for grasping the "metaphysical election of Judaism" – not "stubbornness" – at the price that "we have to remain strangers to Western culture."[25]

Rosenzweig's decision in 1913 "to remain a Jew" by returning to Judaism marked an existential and intellectual caesura. As he writes in a letter to Hans Ehrenberg from October 1916, since the summer of 1910 and the Baden-Baden conference he was – without knowing and wanting to believe it – "seeking to begin life on a location and with a new staff." In 1913, "my new vitality emerged."[26] As Rosenzweig also explains in a 1920 letter to Meinecke: "In 1913 something happened to me for which *collapse* is the only fitting name. I suddenly found myself on a heap of wreckage, or rather I realized that the road I was then pursuing was flanked by unrealities."[27] These unrealities were the "forms of history," that is, inherited schemas of meaning, as well as his academic "talents" for historical research: "I began to sense how meaningless such a subjection to the rule of one's talent was and what abject servitude of the self it involved [...] I remember how sinister [was] my insatiable hunger for 'forms' – a hunger without goal or meaning [...] History was to me a purveyor of forms, no more." Rosenzweig's "collapsed" life was set upon a course of rebirth and yet simultaneously held in suspended animation, given that a direction for his life's meaning and thinking continued to elude him: How can one remain a stranger in the world and yet live fully, in word and deed, for – and not against – the world? How can the God of the Old Testament remain alien and strange to the history of the world, and hence resist assimilation into world-spirit, while nonetheless offering a path toward the redemption of creation? An academic trajectory, upon which Rosenzweig could have embarked as a career (and offered to him by Meinecke after the war), no longer spoke to

---

[24] Rosenstock was serving at the front in Verdun, Rosenzweig in the Balkans. As Stéphane Mosès remarks: "The correspondence between Franz Rosenzweig and Eugen Rosenstock represents one of the most deeply moving episodes in the Jewish-Christian dialogue of the twentieth-century"; *The Angel of History: Rosenzweig, Benjamin, Scholem*, trans. B. Harshav (Stanford, CA: Stanford University Press, 2008), p. 20.
[25] Rosenzweig, *Gesammelte Schriften*, I/1, p. 305.
[26] Rosenzweig, *Gesammelte Schriften*, I/1, p. 242.
[27] Rosenzweig, *Gesammelte Schriften*, I/2, p. 679.

him. Christianity and Christian culture as well as Hegel's totalizing philosophy of dialectical reconciliation, and hence philosophy tout court in the conceit of its Western completion, could not provide an answer either. In this condition, Rosenzweig felt compelled to "descend into the vaults of my being, to a place whither talents could not follow me; that I approached the ancient treasure chest whose existence I had never wholly forgotten," and, emerging from this descent, retrieving his ancient treasure, ascended from a historian to a philosopher – his collapsed life was driven toward self-discovery "under the rule of a 'dark drive' which I'm aware that I merely *name* by calling 'my Judaism.'"[28] This ascent toward philosophy, catalyzed by the revelation of 1917, coincided with the discovery of his dark drive, casting a haunting shadow across philosophy and Christianity, as yet only named but not thought, and hence yet to be fully lived.

With his life in suspended animation, Rosenzweig experienced the arrival of war, unlike tens of thousands of others, as neither a moment of rapture nor a transformative event. The war found Rosenzweig's life already in tatters. History as a source of meaning was already, with his rejection of Hegel and Christianity, demolished and in this void of "forms of history," the war, it would seem, could only be distantly heard as an echo of the cacophony within. As Rosenzweig remarks in a letter (October 1916) to Hans Ehrenberg: "The war itself does not represent a major break of any sort to me; I had already experienced so many things in 1913 that nothing could have occurred in 1914 that impressed me at all, short of the world's total collapse." As he continues:

> I haven't experienced the war and know nothing about it […] I neither expect nor hope anything from it, but carry my life through it, as Cervantes did his poem (not even in the left but in the right hand; with the left I master as much of the war as I can). Whether this vacation from life's responsibility, which I have feared and still do, will or will not benefit me, I do not know; in a sense I enjoy it, as I will not have another such chance. To enjoy it *entirely* would be equivalent to experiencing the war, which I am prevented from doing by my future life, whose servant I am even now, in every leisure moment.

That he experienced military service as a "vacation from life's responsibilities" is amply attested to in Rosenzweig's letters.[29] His decision to

---

[28] Rosenzweig, *Gesammelte Schriften*, I/1, p. 243.
[29] November 24, 1916 to his parents: "Unfortunately, I am a poor soldier, since I am so unpractical and awkward […] nevertheless, I get some fun out of it. My solitary tour of duty as an aircraft observer has made a romantic childhood dream come true: to be 'alone' on a high mountain with a magnificent view." Rosenzweig, *Gesammelte Schriften*, I/1, p. 293.

enlist was not motivated by intense nationalism. In fact, the opposite was the case. As Rosenzweig writes in a letter to his parents on September 9, 1914: "I had never before realized to what extent I do not feel myself to be a German since the outbreak of the war [...] hopefully it is soon over. Of course, peace after German victory will probably be so disgusting that one will perhaps wish to return to the condition of these war months."[30] Rosenzweig's letters are characterized by the conspicuous absence of reporting on the miseries of a soldier's life at the front or fear of death and injury. There is noticeably a "touristic" quality to many of his letters: requesting an edition of Tertullian be sent to him, sharing his latest reflections on literature, asking for swimwear and strings for his violin, and communicating his cultural observations of Jewish communities in Poland and other visited territories. Whether a repression or sublimation of his war experiences can be discerned in these letters, or just guarded awareness of military censorship, remains unclear. His letters, however, reveal a novel dimension of this modern war with its massive logistical apparatus and rear echelons, where thousands of troops operated in supporting and administrative roles, which, given an efficient postal system, rotation of home leave and (as was the case with Rosenzweig) sick leave, created a veritable theatre of war between the fighting front lines and the domestic home front.

Although Rosenzweig had entered the war, the war had barely entered him. The war, it seemed, was placed on the stage of Rosenzweig's inner struggle rather than his life having been placed on the historical stage of the war. As Rosenzweig reports in a letter:

> I received your letter just as I was assigned to an observation post on Dub mountain. I am still here, as I declined to be relieved. I live more primitively here, but on the other hand am removed from the whole enervating mechanism of commanding and obeying [...] On the mountain we have a concrete shelter, so that we are quite safe, though not while actually on duty.

In the opening years of world conflict, Rosenzweig was engaged in a *gigantomachia peri tes ousias* on his own spiritual front. In a revealing letter, Rosenzweig takes leave by remarking "so much for 'Franz R.' That it

---

[30] Rosenzweig, *Gesammelte Schriften*, I/1, p. 174. In a letter to Eugen Rosenstock of November 7, 1916, Rosenzweig explains that the extent to which a Jew can participate in the life of the people cannot be prescribed by himself. It is prescribed for him. He remarks that he personally placed himself at the service of the state in purely legal terms, namely, from a sense of duty, and for that reason did *not* – he stresses – enter as a volunteer, but rather offered his services to the International Red Cross. When his draft year was finally called, he then decided to report as a "volunteer" to an artillery regiment in Kassel; Rosenzweig, *Gesammelte Schriften*, I/1, p. 287.

is premature and therefore pointless to speak about him (exempli gratia), I have written already before." His life, he muses, is

> a ship that can never get lost, whose crew cannot suffer shipwreck, and there is only one of these kinds of ships, that sails on all the seas and its crew only comes above deck at night [...] it is the spectral ship, and until today, 1914, 1915, 1916, Senta has not been found. But the flying Dutchmen will always want, again and again, to go ashore, and one day will find it; lasciava ogni cos, except one thing: der *Speranza*. From God's throne the Jew, it is said, is asked *only this one* question: Have you hoped for salvation?[31]

"Now Everything Is Gone"

In July 1917, a few months before his October revelation near Prilep, Rosenzweig confided to his parents: "I am inconsolable." It must have been a surprising admission to his parents, for since the outbreak of war Rosenzweig had frequently expressed in his letters that the war meant nothing to him. He had enlisted in 1914 seeking neither salvation nor glory, and, in fact, objected strongly to German nationalism, Cohen's as well as his mother's. As he wrote to her: "Cohen's spiritual *Deutschtum* is as precarious as your social *Deutschtum*, and neither can be maintained without true acrobatics."[32] And yet, a shift in attitude toward the war becomes registered in his letters beginning in 1917. In this July letter to his parents, Rosenzweig bemoans the resignation of Chancellor Bethmann-Hollweg under the pressure of the German High Command and makes known his growing consternation at Germany's faltering situation in the war. Signs of political turmoil were already apparent to Rosenzweig earlier in the year. "Were he [Bethmann-Hollweg] not to exist (and what he represents)," he writes to his parents in February, "so it would not be a shame if Germany goes under. But, therefore, [resignation was at the time not imminent] it is certain that there is still a future for the people of Goethe."[33] With the arrival of summer, Bethmann-Hollweg's resignation represented nothing less than, as Rosenzweig observes, "a renunciation of Germany, of its future for the epoch until the next war." As he confides: "I had been carried away by this man and interested in something that didn't concern me at all; that is now over with; I am no

---

[31] Rosenzweig, *Gesammelte Schriften*, I/1, pp. 288–289. In Wagner's opera *The Flying Dutchman*, Senta is the daughter of Daland, the ghostly ship's captain.
[32] Rosenzweig, *Gesammelte Schriften*, I/1, p. 445.
[33] Rosenzweig, *Gesammelte Schriften*, I/1, p. 350.

longer interested in 'strong men.'"³⁴ In contrast to his muted reaction toward the war in 1914, Rosenzweig increasingly becomes personally and intellectually affected by Germany's waning fortunes as the war nears its catastrophic end. In the twilight years of 1917–18, the war finally came home to Rosenzweig. As he writes to Rudolf Ehrenberg on March 5, 1918:

> Strangely I have, for the first time, "forebodings," temporally related to March, and as I arrived here [in Macedonia] I noticed that an offensive is in the air. Wouldn't do any harm. I am very down [*Ich bin sehr down*], truly really "shattered" and *yet* in high spirits. A real devouring for death should he come to grab me – I feel that I am presently also closed off to you. Excuse me.³⁵

This transformation in his geopolitical assessment of the war reflected to a considerable degree an enthusiasm for the project of *Mittel-Europa*, as proposed by Friedrich Naumann in his influential *Mitteleuropa* (1915).³⁶ After the lifting of an official prohibition on public debate of Germany's war aims, Naumann argued that the war should be seized as an opportunity to establish an Central European sphere of political cooperation, economic free trade, and cultural exchange, thus setting the conditions for a postwar multiethnic peace undergirded by a Central European economic nation [*mitteleuropäische Wirtschaftsvolk*].³⁷ Against a militarist and expansionist agenda for Germany's war aims, Naumann's vision of a Germanic postwar Central Europe exercised considerable influence on, among others, Bethmann-Hollweg and continued to resonate during the turbulent Weimar Republic on, among others, Martin Heidegger.³⁸ Along with his friend Ehrenberg, Rosenzweig subscribed to his own vision of *Mittel-Europa* and published a series of articles, written at the front, in support of Naumann's overall conception. In

---

³⁴ Rosenzweig, *Gesammelte Schriften*, I/1, p. 422. To his parents, October 13, 1916: "everything against Bethmann is proof for the kind of human beings who are the average Germans. It goes without saying that the entire thing is a piece of war-psychosis." With Bethmann-Hollweg's dismissal, Rosenzweig rightly fears – a candid expression of critique in letters that were routinely censored – the usurpation of political power by Hindenburg and Ludendorff.
³⁵ Rosenzweig, *Gesammelte Schriften*, I/1, p, 515. In March 1918 it is no longer possible, as Regine Munz suggests, for Rosenzweig to uncouple the events of war from his "inner experience"; R. Munz, "Ob's nach dem Krieg schön zu leben sein wird?" in *Franz Rosenzweig und Ludwig Wittgensteins Schreiben im 1. Weltkrieg, Freiburger Zeitschrift für Philosophie und Theologie*, Vol. 45, No. 3 (2012): 480–505; p. 489.
³⁶ F. Naumann, *Central Europe*, trans. C. Meredith (New York: A. A. Knopf, 1917).
³⁷ M. Zimmermann, "A Road Not Taken – Friedrich Naumann's Attempt at a Modern German Nationalism," *Journal of Contemporary History*, Vol. 17, No. 4 (1982): 689–708.
³⁸ For Heidegger's reception of Naumann, D. Losurdo, *Heidegger and the Ideology of War: Community, Death, and the West*, trans. M. and J. Morris (Amherst, MA: Humanities Books, 2001).

his essay "Die neue Levante," Rosenzweig advocates for the creation of a United States of Europe, formed through a unification of Germany, the Austro-Hungarian Empire, and the Balkan territories, as the guarantee for world peace. Adjusting Naumann's idea of *Mittel-Europa* to his own newly discovered fascination for the Balkans and the Middle East, Rosenzweig conceives of this cosmopolitan "New Levante" as a necessary bulwark against European nationalism and future conflicts on the European continent.[39]

Bethmann-Hollweg's resignation in July 1917 signaled, however, the collapse of this geopolitical ambition for Germany. With the de facto military dictatorship of Hindenburg and Ludendorff, the prospects of guiding the German war effort toward the foundation of a "New Levante" became starkly impossible; there could now never be genuine peace. A month before the Armistice, while recovering from malaria in a military hospital in Belgrade, Rosenzweig writes to his mother: "peace is now absolutely certain. And thereby is also my up-to-now most durable unpublished war-opera [...] no longer relevant [...] since *Mittel-Europa* is toast."[40] In speaking of his "war-opera," Rosenzweig has in mind an ambitious geophilosophical narrative of Western Europe and study of "the grounds of war" that he began writing in 1917. In fact, during the years of 1915–17, when Germany's fate hung in the balance, the war's significance from a world-historical perspective became something of an obsession for Rosenzweig. Publishing under the pseudonyms "Adam Bund" and "Macedonicus," he authored several texts on the war, including a short appraisal of military strategy ("Cannä und Gorlice"), an essay on the aims of the war ("Das Kriegsziel"), and reflections on politics ("Vox Dei?," "Die Reichsverfassung in Krieg und Frieden").[41] At the front, Rosenzweig gave lectures on his ideas to his comrades. In a letter, he speaks with pride of having delivered, and with much success, his first baptismal lecture to his fellow soldiers in the field.[42]

Whatever hopes Rosenzweig still entertained for the redemption of Germany's war effort, despite the collapse of the idea of *Mittel-Europa*

---

[39] Rosenzweig, *Gesammelte Schriften*, III, pp. 309–312. See J. Kreienbock, "Franz Rosenzweig's Mitteleuropa as a New Levante," in *Personal Narratives, Peripheral Theatres: Essays on the Great War (1914–18)*, eds. A. Barker, M. E. Pereira, M. T. Cortez, P. A. Pereira, and O. Martins (Dordrecht: Springer, 2018): 185–200; and, for an extensive treatment, W. Herzfeld, *Rosenzweig, "Mitteleuropa" und der Erste Weltkrieg: Rosenzweigs Politische Ideen im Zeitgeschichtlichen Kontext* (Freiburg: Karl Albert Verlag, 2013).
[40] Rosenzweig, *Gesammelte Schriften*, I/1, pp. 611–612.
[41] For these and other writings, Rosenzweig, *Gesammelte Schriften*, III.
[42] Rosenzweig, *Gesammelte Schriften*, I/1, p. 478.

in 1917, definitively fell apart with Germany's defeat in 1918. In a letter to Margrit Rosenstock on the day of the Armistice, Rosenzweig writes:

> I learned only afterwards to feel myself not only as a German but also – *completely* new – to feel myself a Prussian. I believe that after this experience, I will *never* again be a "democrat." It is as impossible as pacificism. For all time there shall be domination and war. Freedom and peace only lie beyond. Between all that has happened I also had the feeling of being able to breathe again ("that it will become again our world"). But since the revolution no longer. And even now interiority is narrowed down in suffocation.[43]

Redemption, in the form of peace and freedom, no longer proved possible on the shattered stage of world history, nor could refuge or consolation be found within oneself, in retreat from the world. As Rosenzweig continues: "Do you know what is the truly terrible feature of our defeat (how easy the 'we' now flows for me from my lips in relation to Germany! For five years I have spoken of Germany in the third person, and only now do I feel again belonging to Germany)? All of our fallen-ones are fallen for nothing [*alle unsre Gefallenen sind fehlgefallen*]." In a letter to his mother shortly after the Armistice, while awaiting transport back to Germany, he writes:

> I don't feel myself settled or well at all. I had indeed kept my cool at the beginning of the war, but now it pulls at my heart. I never imagined a defeat in 1914, at most a Hubertusburg, in other words, a non-victory, but a retaining of the results of Bismarck. And I believed this until this year. Now everything is gone, and the world as I imagined it is no longer there.[44]

While his mother frets about a shortage of paper for the publication of his Hegel thesis, Rosenzweig fears instead a lack of readership: "Who would then read this book about this bloody Germany [sic: *diesen bloody Germany*], who would still believe in this unholy Alliance [...] I have only now noticed how much I am a monarchist; I feel so bad for Wilhelm [...] I want a *king* [...] The end is terrible; Wilhelm has fallen, without anyone giving him a hand."[45]

"A Field of Ruins"

Rosenzweig completed his PhD thesis *Hegel and State* before the war, but did not publish it until 1920; by then, however, the demise of world-historical spirit along with the forlorn hope for geopolitical salvation had

---

[43] Rosenzweig, *Die "Gritli"-Briefe*, p. 184.
[44] Rosenzweig, *Gesammelte Schriften*, I/1 p. 614. Rosenzweig's reference here is to the 1763 Treaty of Hubertusburg ending the Third Silesian War between Prussia, Austria, and Saxony.
[45] Rosenzweig, *Gesammelte Schriften*, I/1, p. 614.

summarily condemned this work to be nothing more than a funeral stone for an age and an aspiration that were no longer. As Rosenzweig remarks to Gertrud Oppenheim: "The book stands entirely behind me."[46] In his original thesis, Rosenzweig had chosen not to include a preface, but with its postwar publication this could no longer be avoided since, as he writes in his 1920 Preface, a reader "has a right to know, immediately at the threshold, that the book could only still be completed in the year 1919; I could not have started it anymore." As Rosenzweig adds, "I do not know how today one could muster the courage to write a German history. Back then, as this book took shape, there was hope that the Bismarckian state, its breathing restricted both internally and externally, would expand itself into a free empire breathing the air of the world."[47] With this tacit invocation of Naumann's *Mittel-Europa*, Rosenzweig's Hegel study was intended to be a "small contribution" toward the realization of this ecumenical vision by means of an analysis, influenced by Meinecke's *Weltbürgertum und Nationalstaat*, of the development of Hegel's political thinking. *Hegel and the State*, however, is not only a meticulous study of the concept of the state in Hegel's writings; it at the same time argues that Hegel's conception of the modern state plays a constitutive function for the realization of Spirit in its world-historical manifestation. In Rosenzweig's account, Hegel's political thinking was animated by the need to reconcile individual subjective freedom with the objective historical unfolding of the world. Only in the form of the state, where the freedom of subjective spirit becomes worldly through its subjection to the command of law and the realm of *Sittlichkeit*, does Spirit become fully embodied in the world. "The march of God in the world," Hegel once professed, "that is what the state is."[48] As Rosenzweig comments, "on the basis of a completely fundamental knowledge of Christianity's value of eternity, Hegel arrives at a kind of community that is beyond the state and lacking state-like forms of organization – at a Church, in a sense, the invisible head of which is, in his view, the law of world-history, the 'World Spirit.'"[49] This world-historical march of

---

[46] Rosenzweig, *Gesammelte Schriften*, I/2, p. 628.
[47] Rosenzweig, *Gesammelte Schriften*, III, p. 50. "'Forward' and 'Concluding Remark' to *Hegel and the State*, Rosenzweig, *Philosophical and Theological Writings*, pp. 73–83.
[48] G. W. F. Hegel, *Elements of the Philosophy of Right*, trans. H. B. Nisbet (Cambridge, UK: Cambridge University Press, 1991), § 258. And Hegel continues: "The basis of the state is the power of reason actualising itself as will. In considering the Idea of the state, we must not have our eyes on particular states or on particular institutions. Instead we must consider the Idea, this actual God, by itself."
[49] F. Rosenzweig, *Hegel und der Staat* (Frankfurt: Suhrkamp Verlag, 2010), p. 375.

Spirit, achieving its apotheosis with the modern state under the benediction of "what is rational is real," is dialectically woven from the Christian doctrine of the word made flesh in time.⁵⁰ Hegel's thinking effects the synthesis of Christianity (Rome) and philosophy (Athens) with its immanentization of the eschaton of the world in history, as its fulfillment, and hence the immanentization of eternity in time. Rosenzweig acknowledges that Hegel's conception of the modern state is not imbued with the nationalist conceit of later nineteenth-century political thinkers such as Friedrich Dahlmann and Heinrich von Treitschke. Nevertheless, for Hegel (as well as these ethnonationalist thinkers), the "state is the goal," but whereas Hegel guides the individual toward their fulfillment in the state, Treitschke and others guided the individual toward their fulfillment in the German nation. In the aftermath of the war, however, the tribunal of world history had decisively spoken against Hegel's march of God in the world. As Rosenzweig writes in concluding remarks appended to his book: "We are at the end. We feel the extent to which we are at the end today, when the century of Bismarck, at whose gate the Hegelian life stands like the thought before the deed, has collapsed." He continues, "things have turned out differently. A field of ruins marks the spot where the empire previously stood."⁵¹ The empire – of philosophy as culminating in Hegel, of the modern state as culminating in the German nation, and of Christianity as culminating in the dominant Protestantism to which Rosenzweig had nearly converted – stood no more.

In this field of ruins more than one of Rosenzweig's own literary remains were buried. In addition to rendering *Hegel and State* anachronistic, the collapse of any prospect for *Mittel-Europa* and the "New Levante" (with Bethmann-Hollweg's resignation and the military usurpation of power by Hindenburg and Ludendorff) spelled the abandonment, or "abortion" as he writes in a letter, of a sprawling manuscript that Rosenzweig worked on during 1917 – his "war-opera" – entitled *Globus: Studien zur weltgeschichtlichen Raumlehre*. Dividing the work into two parts, "Ökumene. Zur Geschichte der geschichtlichen Welt" and "Thalatta. Seeherrschaft und Meeresfreiheit," Rosenzweig set his sights on understanding "the grounds of war" in the sweeping context of the geopolitical development of Europe since the Holy Roman Empire.⁵² Influenced in part by Rudolf

---

⁵⁰ For this reading of Rosenzweig's interpretation of Hegel, G. Petitdemange, "Hegel et Rosenzweig, la différance se faisant," *Cahiers de la Nuit surveillée. Franz Rosenzweig*, Vol. 1 (1982): 157–170; see also Bouretz, *Witnesses for the Future*, p. 115.
⁵¹ Rosenzweig, *Philosophical and Theological Writings*, p. 82.
⁵² Rosenzweig, *Gesammelte Schriften*, III: 313–368.

Kjellén's conception of geopolitics, Rosenzweig's analyses moved beyond the historical framework and methodological approach of *Hegel and the State* to a planetary perspective of the West. To this end, Rosenzweig employs the idea of "Oecumene" (οἰκουμένη) – central to the formation of the Holy Roman Empire – for his world-historical narrative centered on the geopolitical transformation of the indeterminate earth into a plurality of worlds, rooted in defined territories, in conflict with each other. This grand philosophical world history allowed Rosenzweig to situate the – at the time of his writing still undecided – significance of the war. As he writes in the introductory remarks to "Ökumene": "I don't know if the present war will still be called by our grandchildren with the same term with which we immediately called it: as a world-war." Viewed from a world-historical perspective, the war augurs the transition from a European epoch of internecine conflict to a coming planetary age that, optimistically in early 1917 (the manuscript for "Ökumene" was drafted in January), would lead to the emergence of a "New Levante" and cosmopolitan world peace. Rosenzweig's elaborate tapestry of European geopolitics since the fall of the Roman Empire is organized around an appropriation of Schelling's three epochs of Western history (the Petrine, the Pauline, and the Johannine) and the unfolding plot of world history – "the globe" – toward redemption.[53] In 1914, the Imperial powers of Germany, England, and Russia represented three different ideas of the nation-state vying for supremacy on the stage of world history in the Johannine age. Among these three powers, Germany, guided by the idea of *Mittel-Europa*, would usher in a reconstitution of the ideal of the Holy Roman Empire and bring about planetary ecumenical peace.[54]

Setting aside the details of Rosenzweig's narrative, *Globus* stages the development of the West as a metaphysical-historical drama between two conflicting drives – "the Land" and "the Sea" – within an overarching eschatological trajectory toward an ecumenical unity of the planet and humankind. Whereas "the Land" designates the outward-pushing drive of territorial possession and self-affirmation of subjectivities (communities, nations, individuals), "the Sea" represents an obscure pulling toward an overcoming of territorial boundaries and exclusionary identities in view of the "glimmer of the boundless ocean." The drive of "the Land" pushes outward from a center of identity to claim and conquer space; the

---

[53] F. W. J. Schelling, *Philosophy of Revelation* (1841–42), trans. K. Ottmann (Thompson: Spring Publications, 2020), p. 322ff.

[54] See Rosenzweig's letter of January 27, 1917, Rosenzweig, *Gesammelte Schriften*, I/1, p. 340.

drive of "the Sea" pulls away from self-attachment and spatial totalization-territorialization toward a cosmopolitanism without borders in perpetual peace. In this frame of thinking, world history begins with the demarcation and division of the earth into exclusive territorial possessions, rooted places of habitation, and territorialized identities. As Rosenzweig writes: "What we call world-history is nothing other than the becoming of the earth into a closed historical space, a 'world.'" Carved into a plurality of worlds, the establishment of an "ego," or subjectivity, centered on its own identity, claims a determinate place as its own, its home, against its rival neighbors.

For Rosenzweig, the logic of identity and totality, as ontological determinations, is inseparable from the historical geopolitics of territory and the antagonistic opposition between "us and them." As he writes, "with the mine [the first human] created what is yours and what is ours." The indeterminate earth becomes historical through human territorialization involving boundaries and borders in a spatial-ontological sense, thus producing conflict among worlds and their (self)-attached subjectivities. Borders englobe space, and progressively expand toward englobing the earth into a globe under the totalizing identity of one people's self-affirmation. As Rosenzweig writes: "all world-history is now the further movement of this first border, is now the ever again renewed telescoping [*Ineinanderschieben*] of the mine, yours, and theirs, in always more expanding-grasping accentuations of I and Thou relations from the undifferentiated chaos of It." Attachment to place and identity allows for the differentiation of a primordial "there is" of undifferentiated earth; namely, "the chaos of the It." The positing of identity and territorial possession represents a constitutive ontological violence that transforms the anonymity of the earth into a familiar world, at the price, however, of conflict with the territorial possession and self-positing identities of others. In desiring to claim a home and an identity for oneself, struggle inevitably arises as the engine of world history among different "we-communities" striving to realize "the unlimited final we" and thereby perpetual peace, on terms, however, set forth by the drive for power and totality, and hence on the condition of the world-historical supremacy of one empire; namely, one's own.

Within an original undifferentiated chaos of the It, from which the drive for self-attachment and territorial possession emerges, there agitates as well the drive of "the Sea." In opposition to the drive of "the Land," which represents the arche-chthonic grounding of being in the world, "the Sea" represents the yearning for boundless existence beyond borders, divisions, and conflict. "Globus opposes the Sea," and yet "Globus" is haunted by the future – "the boundless sea" – as "the most archaic memory of humankind." This *telos* of the earth becoming the sea remains suppressed by the drive of "the Land," and yet nonetheless impels human existence towards peace on earth. The image of the infinite – the Sea! the Sea! – is the remembrance of the future as the prefiguration of cosmopolitan unity to come. As Rosenzweig writes:

> to the extent that a fragment of this image shines [the boundlessness of the sea], it is impossible for man to devote himself, with satisfaction, to a land with rigid boundaries, and to confine himself to his own people [...] eternally reawakened and pushed from here to beyond, among the things he possesses, he continues to keep the memory of what is not possessed [...] the unity of the earth is the driving force behind historical becoming.[55]

In effect, Rosenzweig's *Globus* outlines a historical ontology of war. The geopolitical history of warfare is obscurely drawn toward oceanic peace, which does not stand at the beginning of history, but, on the contrary, as the eschatological end of history. Rosenzweig inserts his historical ontology of war into a tripartite division of Western history in its progress through the Petrine Age of Roman Catholicism, the Pauline Age of Protestantism, and the Johannine Age of secularized modern nation-states. Throughout, the eschaton of world history – "the Sea" – becomes incessantly misrecognized by political configurations (nation, church, empire) engaged in mimetic rivalry. Rather than the realization of "the boundless Sea," the (contemporary) Johannine Age is the Age of Empire, and hence a failure of Christianity to realize universal peace and planetary unity. As revealed by the war, nation-states are parochial delimitations of "us" against "them" armed with national identities as secularized religions. Modern nation-states are pitched in a struggle of mimetic secularization – nation-states proclaim their own identity and people as elected to realize the universal and yet remain caught in a mimetic rivalry of misrecognition: Each nation misrecognizes the end of history in considering itself elected to establish an empire (and hence peace under the aegis of empire) on earth.[56] Structured by a logic of exemplarity, a modern nation-state claims to exemplify the universal, and yet misrecognizes its genuine ecumenical meaning, with the result being endemic mimetic violence among nations of the world. Nationalism represents, on this view, a secularized-eschatological claim to represent humanity in the conflictual stage of

---

[55] Rosenzweig, *Gesammelte Schriften*, III, p. 313.
[56] G. Bensussan, "Rosenzweig and War. A Question of 'Point of View': Between Creation, Revelation, and Redemption," *New Centennial Review*, Vol. 13, No. 1 (2013): 115–136; p. 132.

world-historical significance. Along with this mimetic rivalry of modern secular religions (i.e., nationalism), citizens are elected – called upon – to sacrifice themselves for their own nation. In Rosenzweig's outlook, the war is the historical-ontological condition of conflicting powers and identities, each misrecognizing the "glimmer image of boundless sea" and hence forsaking the prophetic image of a cosmopolitan world in ecumenical peace.[57] "The Land" and "the Sea" represent two contrasting images of the world, or *Okumeme:* the Homeric and the biblical. In the Homeric image, the Sea is bordered by Land as the expanse traversed to conquer land (as with Ulysses); or, as with the model of the Roman Empire encircling the Sea, thus making of the Sea "land" (*mare nostrum*). By contrast, the biblical image (Rosenzweig draws from Deutero-Isaiah) situates Land at the center of the Sea. As with the sending forth of Abraham, the land is "open to the unknown" and "the immense indeterminate [...] the islands of Deutero-Isaiah spread across the infinite sea, faraway in the middle of nowhere, beyond land [...] the gaping abyss where sailors and ships are in danger of sinking."

The collapse of any prospect for the establishment of *Mittel-Europa* followed by German defeat in 1918 spelt the demise of the eschatological promise of the Johannine Age of ecumenical peace. As Rosenzweig writes to Gertrud Oppenheim, his work *Ökumeme*, which, as he informs her, he began planning around 1910–11, was meant to offer "a history of the reason for war from 1494 until the English-German war of 19."[58] When he first envisioned this work before the war, as he remarks, he had deliberately left the year of his narrative vacant ("19") – although in expectation of an imminent Anglo-German conflict. Only later, after the outbreak of war, did he fill in the year "1914." But now, he writes in 1917, he has been forced to abandon his project altogether and "no longer believes in it anymore."[59] The end of war did not announce for Rosenzweig the advent of peace; rather, the war's bitter end heralded an age of war without end. As he writes to his mother the day after the Armistice: "Yes, sadness and shame, and additionally personal dread for the future. How I had earlier rejoiced at the moment when I would take off my uniform;

---

[57] The dynamic of the land, as an elemental force of war, separation, exclusion, and englobing, is opposed to the oceanic force, or pull, of "perpetual peace," but not a peace in terms of pacifism, which Rosenzweig rejects. For his distinction between peace before the war (heavenly peace) and peace after the war (messianic peace), see the letter of September 1, 1916, Rosenzweig, *Gesammelte Schriften*, III, p. 314.

[58] Rosenzweig, *Gesammelte Schriften*, I, p. 398.

[59] Rosenzweig, *Gesammelte Schriften*, II, p. 617.

now the feeling is completely different."⁶⁰ November 1918 was a historical revelation, uneasily juxtaposed with his October revelation of 1917, where the significances of these two revelations are not sequentially aligned but paratactically set next to each other. Straddled across the paratactic "and" of these two revelations, 1917 and 1918, while the prewar PhD thesis on Hegel appears anachronistic and the incomplete geopolitical *Globus* lay in ruins, the emerging *The Star of Redemption* aspired toward a new future.

Who Hears Me When I Cry Out?

The Star of Redemption is a work unlike any another. It begins in neither word nor deed, not even in silence, but with a cry of despair unto the heavens regarding the meaningfulness of it all. "From death" – the first utterance of *The Star of Redemption* – Rosenzweig's adventurous thinking sets sail under the lodestar of redemption in a twofold sense as "exodus from" and "emergence to." In coursing its way from the polarity of being and nothingness that defines the order of creation to the revelation of divine love in Thou who art God and an unconditional responsibility toward other human beings to the possibility of life abiding in the trust of eternal redemption, Rosenzweig's thinking traces a path of exodus *in philosophos! in theologos! in tyrannos!*⁶¹ "Against" in this threefold sense, *The Star of Redemption* operates a demobilization, not only in the personal sense that Rosenzweig composed his masterpiece during his demobilization from military service, but, inseparably, as a demobilization of Western thought in its threefold configuration of philosophy, theology, and political theory. In charting a course of redemption "from death," *The Star of Redemption* facilitates a return as well to a "new thinking" (as a system of philosophy, and hence as the redemption of philosophical thinking), to a spiritually reinvigorated Judaism (and hence as a redemption of Judaism as a faith to live by, although Rosenzweig cautions against reading his work as merely a "Jewish book"), and, above all, to a regeneration of life beyond the book itself in the world at large in the aftermath of its wartime devastation.⁶²

After his demobilization, Rosenzweig decided to abandon the pursuit of an academic career and committed himself instead to his newly founded *Freies Jüdisches Lehrhaus*, a center for adult education dedicated to the

---

⁶⁰ Rosenzweig, *Gesammelte Schriften*, I/2, p. 34.
⁶¹ *In philosophos! in theologos! in tyrannos!* – appended respectively to the introductions of each of the three sections in *The Star of Redemption*.
⁶² Rosenzweig, *Philosophical and Theological Writings*, p. 110.

instruction and promotion of Jewish culture. Along with this pedagogical mission, Rosenzweig undertook the monumental task, with Martin Buber, of translating the Hebrew Bible – "one of the great controversial texts in the history of Western translation" – the completion of which he did not live to see.[63] Rosenzweig understood there to be a direct connection between *The Star of Redemption* and his translation of the Hebrew Bible: both texts sought to revitalize the centrality of revelation for modern life and renew the significance of religious life in the form of a Judaism breaking with Enlightenment and historicist traditions.[64] In an encompassing spiritual sense, *The Star of Redemption* rides forth in its splendor on behalf of truth in the world, a humility of human existence, and hope for God's justice. More than a book, it is a rite of passage and self-transformative work, for an individual, for a community, indeed for a century to come. Issuing "from death," as the factual situation of thinking and anterior moment of the "Not-Yet-Book," the Abrahamic journey of Rosenzweig's thinking across the All of what is arrives at "the Gate," opened at the end of the book, through which Rosenzweig (but also his readers) steps through into the "No-Longer-Book" of the living. What calls upon thinking is the celebration "to life" in traversing "the day of the life of the All."[65] What therefore renders *The Star of Redemption* unique is its point of departure "before the book" and point of exit "after the book," as if the book, once traversed, would no longer be needed, having facilitated the passage to not just a new thinking, but a new life.[66]

Yet we are ahead of ourselves, for all things move in their own time, a time birthmarked by death. In the grasp of death, *The Star of Redemption* begins with an elemental cry at the threshold of speech. As Rosenzweig writes:

> That man may crawl like a worm into the folds of the naked earth before the whizzing projectiles of blind, pitiless death, or that there he may feel as violently inevitable that which he never feels otherwise: his I would only be an It if it were to die; and he may cry out his I with every cry still in his throat against the Pitiless One by whom he is threatened with such an unimaginable annihilation […].[67]

---

[63] L. Rosenwald, "On the Reception of Buber and Rosenzweig's Bible," *Prooftexts*, Vol. 15, No. 2 (1994): 141–165; p. 141.

[64] See M. Benjamin, *Rosenzweig's Bible: Reinventing Scripture for Jewish Modernity* (Cambridge, UK: Cambridge University Press, 2009).

[65] Rosenzweig, *Philosophical and Theological Writings*, p. 137.

[66] Rosenzweig did not, however, abandon philosophical reflection or writing. Aside from the essay "New Thinking" and other essays, he restated his philosophical outlook in *Understanding the Sick and the Healthy: A View of World, Man, and God*, trans. N. Galtzer (Cambridge, MA: Harvard University Press, 1999).

[67] Rosenzweig, *The Star of Redemption*, in *Understanding the Sick and the Healthy*, p. 11.

In reading these words, we are meant to feel the fear and trembling of our own mortal condition, whether crawling under a hail of projectiles or sensing during idle hours the slow creep of our inevitable demise. From the facticity of death, "all thinking of the All begins." This incontrovertible fact, that each of us dies, that, in other words, nothingness intimately belongs to our existence, is neither produced nor posited by thinking. This elemental fact should not be conflated with an indeterminate negation or a determinate negation in the dialectical self-unfolding of thinking. On the contrary, death, as much as life, haunts thinking as its unreachable "before," as that before which we stand as well as that which sits before thinking itself. The nothingness of one's own being – *my* death – is the nonconstituted condition for thinking *that* I am mortal, which always remains prior to thinking; to wit, as unthinkable. Although to each their own mortality, death cannot therefore be claimed, on Rosenzweig's view, as one's "ownmost," nor be invested with the self-rallying power of authenticity.[68] When confronted by their own "inconceivable annihilation," an individual experiences "terrifying poverty, loneliness, and tornness from the whole world," in sensing "that his I would only be an It if it died." Death returns me to the dark folds of creation – the ebb and flow of being and nonbeing – from which I issued. Being toward death imbues one's existence with forlornness from the world, and yet, in the fear of death, there resonates as well "the angst of the earthly." In the anxiety over our own death, there murmurs an anxiety of creation itself, in which we human creatures participate, standing not only in its midst but in the middle, insofar as it is we who know ourselves to be creaturely. As Rosenzweig writes: "Everything mortal [*das Sterbliche*] lives in this angst of death, every new birth increases the angst for a new reason [*Grund*], since it increases those entities that die [*das Sterbliche*]." We mortal creatures exist in the acute awareness, albeit mute and obscure, that with every birth – most poignantly one's own – there issues another, and hence more death to the world: "The womb of the inexhaustible earth ceaselessly gives birth to what is new, and each one is subject to death." In the endless recurrence of life and death and ceaseless proliferation of being and nothingness, what distinguishes human existence is fearing,

---

[68] For the contrast between Rosenzweig's understanding of death and Martin Heidegger's "being towards death," K. Löwith, "M. Heidegger and F. Rosenzweig or Temporality and Eternity," *Philosophy and Phenomenological Research*, Vol. 3, No. 1 (1942): 53–77. For a comparison of the two thinkers, P. Gordon, *Rosenzweig and Heidegger: Between Judaism and German Philosophy* (Berkeley: University of California Press, 2003).

and hence in this sense knowing, ourselves *to be* created beings; a being that knows itself to die is a being that knows not to have created itself. With this breathless accentuation of our creaturely condition, we participate in a creation seemingly without purpose or end, for what sense to it all is there, other than to be and not to be? Is that all that there is? Is that all that I am, dust to dust, ashes to ashes? It is not the infinite silence of it all that we fear but the incessant murmur of it all – that all that there is is that there is, and nothing more, always and ever more. And yet, within the cry of despair from death, from which the thinking of the All begins, a defiant protest and accusation against "the Pitiless One" is dimly sounded, that I shall not be abandoned and forsaken to die as an It, in the quiet hope that there must be something stronger and other than death, that death be not proud nor encompass the sense of it All.

The Flight of Philosophy from Ionia to Jena

From death, then, the thinking of it All called philosopher emerges. This elemental impulse should not be conflated with a desire for knowledge, wonderment that there is, or an interest of pure reason. Philosophical thinking, in its aspiration to systematically understand the meaning of it All, responds to the unsettling of existence in the questionability of the meaningfulness of it All exposed by death. In the fear of death, it is not only one's own existence that becomes questionable, but the sense of it All, given that one's own death partakes in the cosmic drama of creation in the ebb and flow of being and nothingness. Our "annihilation" remains "inconceivable," and hence unthinkable, and yet thinking cannot *not* think about death, insofar as death haunts thinking as the dark ground of its own issue, over which it lacks mastery and self-possession. From this double bind of thinking and death, Western philosophy has perpetually sought to take flight. As Rosenzweig writes:

> upon all this misery philosophy smiles its empty smile and, with its outstretched index finger, shows the creature, whose limbs are trembling in fear for its life in this world, a world beyond, of which it wants to know nothing at all [...] when around the earthly it weaves the thick blue haze of its idea of the All.

Ever since its Eleatic inception, according to Rosenzweig, Western philosophy rests on two reinforcing conceits: that the All – the unified manifold totality of being – is knowable ("thinkable"), where thinking means the determination of what is in terms of what is "essential," or an essence; and that, as pronounced by Parmenides, the same thing is for thinking and for being, namely: "That which is there to be spoken and thought of must be. For it is possible for it to be, but not possible for nothing to be." If the determination of what is in terms of an essence adheres to an ontological distinction between "being" and "becoming" – being cannot be thought otherwise than essence – the identity of being and thinking establishes the centerpiece of Idealism: that every being that is identical with itself. This principle of identity, underwriting Western philosophy, further ingrains the thought, in terms of which the unity of the All becomes thinkable, that all things that have being partake in this common trait of identity, and hence that among the manifold, or plurality, of beings there is one Being – God, Nature, and so on – that fundamentally defines the beingness of beings. The unity of a being with itself, its self-same identity, is also its unity with Being, however "Being" is to be understood. These two premises (the distinction between being and becoming in terms of essence and existence; the principle of identity) underpin the totalizing and reductive effort of Western thought to ascribe one fundamental sense of Being that would encompass and unify the many senses of what it is to be.

Given the Eleatic identity of being and thinking, traditional thinking of the All bases itself on the presupposition that "nothing" cannot be thought. This ejection of nothing from the purview of thinking rests, however, on a repression and falsification of death; the elemental facticity of death, in its singularity as belonging to an individual (human) existence, is rendered "unthinkable" while, by the same token, the "nothingness" of death becomes falsified into a notion of either "indeterminate negation" or "determination negation" through the transposition of nothingness into negation. Philosophy presupposes "nothing" in the twofold sense that it wants to know nothing of nothing (i.e., death) and can know nothing of nothing, insofar as nothingness becomes mischaracterized, and hence obscured, as "negation," in terms of which it becomes absorbed and given a place within the idealism of thinking. This ejection of the elemental nothingness of death from the remit of philosophical thinking is reflected in the philosophical claim that thinking is presuppositionless or, in other words, grounds itself in the thinkability of the principle of identity. In this fashion, the principle of identity (as the thinkability of being) excises the dark ground, or "prethinking," of its own possibility; that is, the nothingness of death.

Stated differently, philosophical thought from Ionia to Jena has been dominated by a totalizing effort to reduce the "outside" of thinking – death as the elemental trace of nothingness – and the multiplicity of what is to *one* sense of being as identified in thinking. As Rosenzweig argues, however, "in the 'what-is' question directed at everything, lies the entire error of the answers."⁶⁹ This error in answers to the question of being is exemplified by the subsumption of human existence to an essence, whereby the nothingness that inherently belongs to human life becomes relegated as either unthinkable or accidental to the essence of the human. A human being, nonetheless, does not exist in abstraction nor as a universal subject, for a human being is a mortal individual; death does not obtain generally, but singularly, as the birthmark of one's own existence (where mortality is not synonymous for Rosenzweig with finitude). The flight of philosophy to an enduring realm of essences and ideas betrays its denial of death for the purpose of duping life. Philosophy, in this sense, is the Grand Lie. As Rosenzweig writes: "For clearly: an All would not die, and in the All, nothing would die. Only that which is singular can die, and everything that is mortal is solitary. This, the fact that philosophy must exclude from the world that which is singular, this exclusion of the something is also the reason why it has to be idealistic."⁷⁰ This reductive drive of Western thought in its quest for a presuppositionless thinking of it All plays itself out as well in the conflict between revelation and reason, where revelation names a source of meaning beyond or before thinking, to which thinking itself remains beholden or becomes surpassed. Rosenzweig considers that Hegel has brought the history of philosophy to its end, the catastrophic political meaning of which becomes revealed with the war. For Hegel has achieved a systematic thinking of the All based on the reconciliation of revelation (faith) and reason, or, in other words, a reconciliation between Christianity (Rome) and the Greeks (Athens). Moreover, this Hegelian achievement reconciles thinking and history, where the intelligibility of world history is understood as the self-realization of Absolute Spirit in the world.

Philosophical thought arises from the fear and trembling of death, but seeks, in its systematic attempt to think the All, to suppress this earthly fear, and hence the creatureliness of being. The suppression of death represents the "cancelation" (*Abschaffung*) of creation; namely, the "decreating" or "unmaking" of the human as a created being. And yet, as Rosenzweig experienced on the night of his revelation in October 1917 while stepping on a prickly bush, "the reality of death cannot be banished from the world." In the angst of one's earthly – that is, creaturely – existence, the facticity of one's own irreducible existence, forlorn and torn, becomes

---

⁶⁹ Rosenzweig, *Philosophical and Theological Writings*, p. 116.
⁷⁰ Rosenzweig, *The Star of Redemption*, p 11.

experienced. This singularity of mortality cannot, in turn, be captured by a logic of identity and difference, as it escapes the conceptual distinction between "essence" and "existence." Nowhere is the sublation of an individual's irreducible facticity more apparent than with Hegel's reflections on war, where sacrifice sublates the singularity of death into the historical realization of the state and Spirit. As Hegel argues: "Sacrifice on behalf of the 'individuality' of the state is the substantial tie between the state and its members—and so is a universal duty."[71] It is this obliteration of the individuality of death for the sake of the universal – the state – that the war has revealed in its absurdity, thus undermining the Hegelian conceit that "the rational is real, and the real is rational." But, as Rosenzweig argues, "the All [as thinkable] can no longer pretend to be all: it has lost its unique character" in the face of the irreducible elementality of an individual's creatureliness. "From death" – philosophy remains deaf to this cry, or, rather, remains haunted by this cry of the earthly. From this cry of despair, and the questionability of existence called death – is that All there is, to be and not to be? – the flight of philosophy must be rejected, but equally the evasion of suicide, for, as Rosenzweig insists, the human being knows that it wants to live with its mortality, not against or beyond it. How, then, to live with neither the "compassionate lie" of philosophy nor the vanity of suicide? As Rosenzweig writes: "Man should not cast aside from him the fear of the earthly; in his fear of death he should – stay."[72] This requires that "the fear of the earthly should be removed from him only with the earthly itself."

"In Nothingness I Hope to Find Everything"

Much as Rosenzweig, as he recounted in a letter to Gritli, was entranced by a vision of the self-shaping of his book while writing it, *The Star of Redemption* virtually configures itself for a reader, whose own thinking, in following the course of this unique book's unfolding, takes on the gestalt of the Star of David that progressively emerges from the conjoining of two triangles constructed out of its three main sections ("The Elements," "The Path," and "The Figure"). Beginning with primitive "elements," shaped into the constellation of the All in its threefold relationality between God, human existence, and the world, leading toward the figure (*Gestalt*) of redemption, *The Star of Redemption* moves in the medium of

---

[71] Hegel, *Elements of the Philosophy of Right*, p. 308.
[72] Rosenzweig, *The Star of Redemption*, p. 10.

its own time and speech.⁷³ There is no thinking without time, not in the trivial sense of a time in which thinking happens, but as the happening of time itself in thinking. And if there is no thinking without an intrinsic self-temporalization, it is because there is no thinking without language, or what Rosenzweig calls the "time-word."⁷⁴ Rather than presuppose language for thinking, Rosenzweig argues that language is the organon of thinking. In this regard, *The Star of Redemption* provides for the reader its own configuration of language for its new thinking. In fact, the completed configuration of *The Star of Redemption* is said by Rosenzweig to form not only a "mouth" but indeed "a face" (with "ears," "eyes," "nose," and "mouth") that becomes projected onto the two superimposed triangles of the Star. *The Star of Redemption* figuratively constitutes itself as a face that speaks to us, but likewise as the countenance bestowed upon us. Rather than a philosophical language traditionally composed from substance words (mirroring a thinking of essences in answer to the what-is question) and established categories ("being and becoming," "identify and difference," "substance and accident"), Rosenzweig's "speaking-thinking" is organized around the primacy of the verb and enactment of meaning in thinking. Each of the three sections in *The Star of Redemption* speaks through its own organon of language: the mathematical organon, the grammatical organon, and the liturgical organon. This constitutive significance accorded to language, in its varied ways of speaking and hence thinking, serves as the vehicle for a tacit translation of scripture into Rosenzweig's new thinking, which, on the one hand, facilitates a passage beyond the self-enclosed totality of Western thought, while, on the other hand, renewing, in a complex act of repetition, the wisdom of the Hebrew Bible in modern form. Rosenzweig's literary masterpiece speaks in tongues, sounding at once archaic and prophetic, premodern as well as postmodern, through its multilingual textured prose.⁷⁵

---

⁷³ The composition of Rosenzweig's book involves the formation and intersection of two triangles into the Star of Jacob. The first triangle is formed from three points – God (top), human existence, and the world (bottom corners). This figure exhibits the irreducibility *and* relation of God–the human/God–world/the human–world. A second triangle is formed from the three points of creation, revelation, and redemption. These two triangles represent the triadic interplay of God, human existence, and the world as well as the triadic interplay of creation, revelation, and redemption. Both triangles come together in the final configuration of the Star. For analysis of this figure, P. Ricoeur, "La 'figure' dans *L'étoile de la Rédemption* de Franz Rosenzweig," *Lectures 3* (Paris: Seuil, 1994): 63–81.
⁷⁴ Rosenzweig, *Philosophical and Theological Writings*, p. 122.
⁷⁵ In a letter to Richard Koch (2 September 1928) shortly before his death, Rosenzweig makes known that after having "suddenly become a philosopher in 1913," the idea of writing his "life's work" occurred to him at the end of 1916 in the form of a commentary on the Bible, which he abandoned to write instead *The Star of Redemption*; *Gesammelte Schriften*, 1.2, p. 1179. For a comparison between

In Section One, "The Elements," Rosenzweig deformalizes established philosophical categories (the one and the many, substance and accident, being and becoming, identity and difference, essence and existence) in beginning with the ruins of totality as "thinkable." The cry of death, from which *The Star of Redemption* issues, embodied a visceral experience of the facticity of human existence, the facticity of the world (as when crawling in the folds of the earth), and the facticity of God (as with the accusation against the Pitiless One). Rather than accept the presumption that philosophical thinking is geared to answering the "what-is" question in terms of essence, Rosenzweig returns, in the aftermath of the war amid its field of ruins (philosophical, theological, and historical), to a primitive, prephilosophical experience of facticity (*Tatsächlichkeit*), shorn of sedimented conceptualizations and essentializations. In what Rosenzweig refers to as "common experience" – that is, deformalized experience – we intuitively grasp the facticity of three separate elements: God, human existence, and the world. In each instance, we obscurely sense *that* (somehow) there is God (without yet being able to name "God"), *that* I am mortal (without yet being able to grasp what for or where to), and *that* there is a world (without yet being able to understand the meaningfulness of it All). This intuitive knowledge *that* there is, in a threefold elementary sense, does not grant or garner knowledge as to *what* there is. This gap between knowing that there is and not knowing what there is constitutes the specificity of the elementals, grasped in absolute separation; that is, without any implication or relation to each other. Each element stands irreducible to the other; likewise, in their respective irreducibility, each element cannot be reduced to itself, since, strictly speaking, the facticity of each element lacks self-identity given our ignorance as to what the world is, who God is, and who the human is. The intuitive experience of these elements does not instantiate a positive knowledge *of* something nor, on the other hand, a self-voiding ignorance. In their elemental primordiality, each element is wanting of actuality (*Wirklichkeit*) and, hence, bereft of a determined temporal tense. None of these elements is identical with itself, nor are these elements an alterity, and hence utterly unfamiliar. Neither "past," "present," nor

> the (implicit) task of biblical translation in the modern thinking of *The Star of Redemption* and translating the Torah into modern German, B. Casper, "Franz Rosenzweig. Die Herausforderung zu einer neuen Zukunft," in *Rosenzweig als Leser: Kontextuelle Kommentare zum "Stern der Erlosung,"* ed. M. Brasser (Tübingen: Max Niemeyer Verlag, 2004): 209–222; and H.-C. Askani, "Schöpfung der Welt und Grammatik der Sprache. Zum Verhältnis von philosophischem Gedanken und biblischem Text im Stern der Erlösung," in *Rosenzweig als Leser*, 411–428.

"future," the elements can only be thought in the fashion of "once upon a time" in the immemorial everlastingness of their facticity. In this sense, the elements are not themselves a ground or a beginning, but akin to an original and obscure potency, as elements for a beginning yet to come. In the nothingness, or dark ground, of we know not what, there is neither an implicit negation (of something) nor an indeterminate negation. For "something" makes itself known in the "nonknowing" of the elements, prior to thought and being, as less than being yet more than nothing. Neither immanent nor transcendent, neither a substantial being nor a fleeting becoming, there abides in these elements an uncanny familiarity in the obscurity of knowing "that there is" without knowing what there is as to this something. These elements are "shadows" or "phantoms," hovering on the other side of being and nothingness, as otherwise than being or nothingness. The elemental experience of facticity cannot be equated with a night in which all cows are black. As Rosenzweig writes:

> It is highly significant that our thinking, which a short while ago was understood as proposing the All as its one and universal object, is not understood now as being thrown back into a one and universal *ignoramus*. The nothing of our knowledge is not a singular nothing, but a threefold one. And that is why we may hope, as did Faust, to find again in this nothing, in this threefold nothing of knowledge, the All that we had to cut into pieces. "Disappear then into the abyss! I could also say: arise!"

With this threefold facticity of elemental nothingness, Rosenzweig decisively parts ways with the Eleatic principle of identity and its underlying assumption of an ontological distinction between (one) being and (one) nothingness. When cast as elemental facticity, "nothingness" (dislodged from its conflation with negation) is experienced in the disjointedness of plurality, where numerical identity cannot be said of each element, given that an elemental facticity is neither an "identity" nor a "difference" (i.e., an identity other than another identity). In the mute certainty that there is God, that there is human existence, and that there is a world, nothing can be thought or spoken of – these elements have yet to come into actuality and manifestation. Given the experienced muteness of the elements, the logos of their facticity cannot be articulated by language as such. According to Rosenzweig, the organon for thinking the logos of the elements is provided by mathematics, and more specifically differential calculus, in its philosophical elaboration, which is "nothing other than the constant deviation of a something – and never more than one something, one some-thing – out of Nothing, and never out of the empty universal Nothing, rather always out of 'its' nothing, out of the nothing of just this something."[76] Rosenzweig here creatively adapts Cohen's logic of origins for this differential logos of the elements. In arriving at the transcendental operation of pure thinking from differential calculus, Cohen argued that thinking cannot discover or derive something from something prior to it (for example, the conceptual cannot be anchored in intuition, as with the myth of the given), nor does Cohen accept Hegel's dialectical reconciliation of identity and difference in the self-actualization of Spirit. In the former instance, the pure thinking of the concept would lead to an infinite regress; thinking could not be the origin of its own conceptualization. In the latter instance, dialectical self-differentiation presupposes the principle of identity. In what Cohen called the logic of origins, "something" emerges from "primal nothing" (not to be conflated with the mathematical idea of zero or logical negation) through an original differential between "nothing" and "something." Neither "being as such" nor "nothingness as such" is the first moment in the unfolding of pure thinking. The differential itself, between "nothingness" and "something," occurs through itself. Cohen's transcendental conceptualization of differential calculus (as the logic of pure thinking) leads to a new thinking of the problem of the one and the many as well as the interaction of identity and difference.[77] Unlike Cohen, however, Rosenzweig's differential logic of the elements does not discover a logic of origins in pure thinking. On the contrary, Rosenzweig discovers the metalogic of "pre-thinking" and "pre-being" insofar as the elements are not posited or constructed *in* thinking. Each element rests within its own dark ground before thinking and being (as actuality); each is an element of the All resting in itself wanting and waiting for itself.[78]

The elements of God, human existence, and the world (what Rosenzweig calls "metaphysics, "metaethics," "metalogic," where "meta" means "beyond" as immemorial) correspond to the three traditional themes of philosophy: theology, psychology-anthropology, and cosmology. Against the totalizing imperative of Western thought, Rosenzweig argues that "none of the three great concepts of philosophical thinking can be reduced to another."[79] The determination of the sense of being in terms of essence led to a reduction of the manifold senses of elemental being to one Being

---

[76] Rosenzweig, *The Star of Redemption*, p. 150.
[77] P. Gordon, "Rosenzweig Redux: The Reception of German-Jewish Thought," *Jewish Social Studies*, Vol. 8, No. 1 (2001): 1–57.
[78] Rosenzweig, *The Star of Redemption*, p. 20.
[79] Rosenzweig, *Philosophical and Theological Writings*, p. 117.

in answer to the presumed fundamental "what-is" question. Historically, the development of philosophy from Ionia to Jena passed through three epochs of thinking. As Rosenzweig writes: "As ever, the possibilities of the 'reduction' of each to one to the other are untiringly permutated, [possibilities] that seen in large, seem to characterize the three epochs of European philosophy – cosmological antiquity, the theological Middle Ages, [and] anthropological modernity. In particular, of course, the darling idea of the modern era, the reduction to the 'I.'"[80] Ancient thought elevated the world to totality: Everything that exists, gods and humans included, is encompassed within the immanence of the world. For Medieval thought, God is elevated to the principle of totality: God is the creator of all beings. With modern thought, the human is elevated to the fundamental being as the measure of all things.

In addition to this critique of Western thought and its three historical epochs, Rosenzweig's treatment of the elements formulates a distinction between paganism and religion (i.e., Abrahamic monotheism). For the pagan Greeks, the world is understood to be a self-enclosed totality without transcendence. The plasticity of the world, in its ever-changing forms, remains stable, caught in the eternal recurrence of the same, as manifest with the perfect motion of the starry heavens above with neither beginning nor end. Within this rounded cosmos, the elemental God remains hidden, veiled by the pantheon of divinities who exist immanently in the world. Likewise, human existence is only dimly aware of "something above itself" that, in the Greek world, is conceived as anonymous fate. For Rosenzweig, the tragic hero embodies a mute solitude that defines human existence in the Ancient world. The tragic hero participates in the world and relates to others, but in their defiance against fate "in the glacial solitude of the self," there is a mute cry for exteriority. The tragic hero cannot grasp the significance of the fate that befalls them; they can neither speak to it nor speak for it. Within the self-enclosed immanence of the pagan world, there is an intimation of exteriority, but it remains "blind and mute" until the biblical advent of God's revelation in dialogical address to human existence. Only in relation to a revealed God, who thus becomes manifest to the world as well as for itself, does human existence become open to transcendence in terms of which human life accedes to the veritable standing as "a soul." The pagan world, despite an obscure sentiment of transcendence, not only does not "know anything of this outside, but wants to know nothing of it."

---

[80] Rosenzweig, *Philosophical and Theological Writings*, p. 115.

Miracles of Revelation

Rather than begin with philosophy's "favorite word 'reality,'" Rosenzweig, with his treatment of the elements, begins with the word "and" as "the basic word of all experience."[81] God *and* human existence *and* the world are introduced in their mutual disjunction of potencies as cast members for the drama of reality and meaningfulness of it All that commences in Section Two, "The Path." With this transition to the configuration of elements into the coursing of reality, the organon of thinking correspondingly changes from the mathematical organon (differential calculus) to the grammatical organon of language structured by the verbal tenses of time (past, present, future) and the declension of personal pronouns (I, Thou, We). Whereas "all concepts that attempt to embrace reality [in the history of Western thought] universally try to adopt the form of the past," that is, "cause, origin, presupposition, a priori," Rosenzweig argues that "to know God, world, and the human means to know what in these tenses of actuality they do or what happens to them, what they do to each other and what occurs by one another."[82] The "doing" (in echo of Goethe's celebrated line *Im Anfang war die Tat*) of effective reality (or actuality – *Wirklichkeit*) entails the "self-opening of something closed," namely, the elements, as revelation (*Offenbarung*), taken to mean the effecting of actuality as well as rendering manifest. The effective reality of an element must emerge, however, from the element itself. As Rosenzweig proposes:

> How should the elements come into the course of actuality? May we lead them to the current from the outside! Never! [...] No, the course of the flowing movement must take its origins out of the elements themselves, and out of the elements alone [...] The elements themselves must hide within themselves the force out of which movement rises, and within themselves the ground of their order, in which they enter the stream.[83]

Drawing from Schelling's notion of "dark ground," each element – God, human existence, the world – harbors an inner restlessness on account of its want of identity. Each element "knows itself to have an outside" and yet "knows nothing of this outside and – worse – wants nothing from it." Marked by its own nonidentity, as lack of itself, the everlasting "thereness" of an element is characterized by anonymity as an "It." There is no "what" or "who" to speak of, only the mute facticity that there is.

---

[81] Rosenzweig, *Philosophical and Theological Writings*, p. 135.
[82] Rosenzweig, *The Star of Redemption*, p. 124.
[83] Rosenzweig, *The Star of Redemption*, p. 170.

An element becomes transformed, opened from itself, in reaching out toward another in a dialogical act of speech through which relationality between God, human existence, and the world arises in their "triple birth from out of the dark ground." This passage from muteness to speech occurs "miraculously," according to Rosenzweig, given that what defines a dialogue, as an ontological occurrence, is not only the unexpectedness of what comes next, but an interactive self-transformation with otherness. In coming to "speak," as it were, *with* each other, each element enters into the course of manifest actuality, where each in turn becomes transformed through its self-transcendence, or reach, toward an exteriority.[84] What is "miraculous" is not only the transfiguration of each element into an effective (and relational) actuality, but that, in opening itself to otherness (another element that is irreducible to it), actuality (whether of God, human existence, the world) preserves its own elementary otherness. In becoming other than itself, each element actually becomes itself; that is, attains its own proper interactive and articulated (relational) actuality. The actuality of God, human existence, and the world respectively enters into a reciprocal and constitutive correlation ("and") in terms of which each remains irreducible, and yet dependent on, another. God, human existence, and the world, entering into effective actuality in relation to each other, "cannot be spoken of in the third person," as with the anonymity of the "there is" of the elements. With the genesis of effective reality from a primordial separation of the elements, the All (the whole of what is) becomes articulated grammatically according to the temporality of past, present, and future, as well as the personal pronouns I, Thou, and We. Dialogical relationality does not dialectically sublate God, human existence, and the world into a seamless unity. On the contrary, dialogical relationality allows for the unified constellation of it All to emerge through the fuguing of "and." The threefold conjunction of "and" (as opposed to one fundamental meaning of "is") is furthermore expressed in the three relations (joined with a form of temporality and dialogical address) of creation, revelation, and redemption. Creation is the miraculous self-transcendence of God from itself toward the world; revelation is the miraculous self-transcendence of God from itself toward human existence; redemption is the miraculous self-transcendence of human existence toward the world. As Rosenzweig writes, "the genuine

---

[84] Rosenzweig credits Ludwig Feuerbach with discovering dialogue as method for a new thinking and acknowledges the importance of Eugen Rosenstock for his conception of the "time-word"; Rosenzweig, *Philosophical and Theological Writings*, p. 127.

notion of revelation is going-out-of-self, belonging-to-each-other, and coming-to-each-other of the three 'factual' elements of the All."[85]

Divine creation is an act of speech in which God externalizes itself to the world as creator of the world. God speaking is the miracle of creation as the fulfillment of the mute beginning of everlasting facticity. God as God the Creator becomes revealed – no longer hidden – not only to the world, but just as much to itself. In a dialogical speech act, the element of the world and the element of God become mutually transformed. Rosenzweig in this respect calls attention to the phrasing of Genesis, "in the beginning, *when* God created heaven and earth," to propose that, although the world's facticity "was already there" in its immobile everlastingness, it is only through God's creative act that the world becomes recreated into a singular, unique whole. There obtains "a real process" between the world as "already-there" and God's power of creation.[86] The world becomes transfigured into a whole by virtue of God's act of creation, and set into temporal actuality, whereby the "already-thereness" of the world becomes reconfigured into "to be is to have been created." The actuality of the world becomes created in the sense of "renewed every morning." In a subtle argument, Rosenzweig maintains that God's creation is neither instantaneous "in the past" nor continuous across the unfolding of creation. Nor does God withdraw, in contraction, from creation to remain hidden from the world. Breaking with the anonymity of the "there is," the created world "gathers all the singular in itself." It is this singularity of the world – its uniqueness – that becomes renewed every morning, not continuously as the "same" world, but as the world born ever anew (in contrast to being everlasting). The miraculous opening of God toward the world is surprising, moreover, for God itself. In this self-transcendence, God comes to know itself and exist in actuality.[87] God, in other words, becomes emancipated from its own remote solitude and obscurity through the relational act of creation.[88] God, in this sense, becomes an "I" in relating to the "I" of the world. God is thereby, however, through creation, not yet a "Thou." God's creation of the world does not allow God to stand completely as an I, since this requires that God becomes revealed as Thou for another I, who in turns stands addressed

---

[85] Rosenzweig, *The Star of Redemption*, p. 185.
[86] Rosenzweig, *The Star of Redemption*, p. 143.
[87] For the notion of miracle, R. Wiehl, "Experience in Rosenzweig's New Thinking," in *The Philosophy of Franz Rosenzweig*, ed. P. Mendes-Flohr (Hanover, NH: University Press of New Hampshire, 1988): 42–68.
[88] Rosenzweig, *The Star of Redemption*, p. 124.

as Thou. Only through God's revelation to human existence does God become an I in (dialogical) relation with the Thou of human existence.[89] God's relation to the human is singular (not humanity as such, but each human uniquely), much as God is not a "universal" but unique. In Rosenzweig's formulation, God and human existence respectively attain a proper name in relation to each other.

The creation of the human in the narrative of Genesis, when God declares "Let us make man," does not yet afford God the witnessing of another in terms of which God becomes a Thou (and hence fully an I). And yet, when God "saw everything that He had made, and behold, it was very good" (Genesis 1:31), God's benediction of it All imparted the seal of death upon creation. Death enters the world through God's act of creation; but it is only with the creation of the human that death becomes a salient feature of creation in the dual form of an awareness of discontinuity from creation ("torn from the world") and in the revelation of an intimate relation to God. Only because the human is the creature who fears for their own mortality is revelation open to them. As Rosenzweig writes: "As keystone of Creation, death imprints everything created with the indelible stamp of its condition as creature, with words 'has been,'" but with the advent of the human and the revelation of God to the human in the revelation of love, God becomes entrusted to the human in the sense that God's creation becomes entrusted to human existence.[90] God's revelation to human existence is the miraculous self-transcendence of love, and through this revelation of love God entrusts itself to human existence, but by the same token the world – God's creation – becomes entrusted to human existence. The drama of creation, with this passage to God's relation to human existence in revelation, becomes slowly discernable across the pages of *The Star of Redemption* as hanging on the plotline from the Song of Solomon (8:6): "love is strong as death," indeed, so strong as to lead to life itself. The three sections of *The Star of Redemption*, mirroring the three ages of the world (creation, revelation, redemption), trace an arc from death through love to life.

Only when God addresses Adam with "Where art Thou?" can human existence open itself to stand before God in response as an I, and thereby God as a Thou for humans. It is the openness of the question addressed to

---

[89] More specifically expressed in Rosenzweig's terms, the "elementary" human discovers itself as "Self" and "individual." The individual stands as a Self in dialogical relation to the Thou.

[90] Rosenzweig, *The Star of Redemption*, p. 169.

Adam that characterizes the dialogical revelation of God to human existence. By hiding himself in shame, Adam leaves the question addressed to him open. For Rosenzweig, the human creature thereby remains mute, and hence not fully actual as a Thou. In God's address to the human, there is the advent of language itself as "the wedding gift of the Creator to humanity." As Rosenzweig writes, "the question-and-answer play of thinking" surges forth through "the whole actual becoming-spoken of language," thus making of language intrinsically dialogical.[91] God's I "discovers itself in the moment when it claims the existence of the Thou through the question after the where of the Thou." The human achieves the I, a place to stand in the world, when addressed by God by the proper name: "Here I am."[92] The call of God is responded to in opening the self in hearing: The call is heard as the commandment – "You shall love eternally your God with all your heart, with all your soul and with all your power." According to Rosenzweig, this "is not only the greatest of commandments, but in truth the only commandment, the sense and essence of all the commandments that were ever spoken from the mouth of God."

Whereas in creation God's freedom reverses itself into the ground of creation (God as an element is not the ground for itself, but its own "dark ground"), with revelation God the creator (as ground and unconditional being) reverses itself in the act of love to become a conditioned being. In the revelation of love for human existence, God becomes other than itself qua necessary ground and unconditional being. God's love springs miraculously upon God itself from its own dark ground as an enabling trauma. God becomes ruptured from its own unconditionality in transcending itself toward the human in a dialogical relation of I and Thou. In this sense, the traumatic transcendence of God from itself to the human enables dialogical attainment of God's own actuality as a Thou. On Rosenzweig's understanding, God's commandment of love – "I am You God, there is no Other" – must be heeded through the human's love for God, which bears witness to, and thus validates, God's love, thus affording God an enduring existence, indeed an ever-renewed existence. As Rosenzweig states: "God's eternal essence awakens anew to each moment as ever young, ever first – love."[93] The commandment of love bespeaks:

---

[91] Rosenzweig, *The Star of Redemption*, pp. 120, 174.
[92] When Abraham responds "here I am" (Genesis 22:1), this is understood by Rosenzweig as responding to Adam's silence when God asked "where art Thou?" (Genesis 3:9).
[93] Rosenzweig, *The Star of Redemption*, p. 182.

"If you bear witness to me, then I am God, and otherwise not." It is thus through the testimony of "the living soul" – the ensouled love of God in the human – that "God achieves his tasteable and visible actuality this side of His hiddenness [...] in that the soul confesses before God's face and therewith confesses God's being and bears witness, God too, the revealed being, first achieves being."[94]

For the human, God's absolute and unconditional commandment to love is experienced as traumatic – "shocking, seizing, tearing" – since it ruptures the self-attachment to oneself. The defiant pride that defines the self becomes unsettled in hearing the commandment of love, which is heard as the double commandment "love thy God," "love thy neighbor." In Rosenzweig's reading of scripture, the mutism of Adam's shame before God's address becomes transformed into the human's avowal of weakness and "fault," not as an original sin of the past, but in an avowal of humankind's continuous fallibility and weakness. Repentance for one's fallibility to endure the absolute commandment of love as well as atonement for the faultiness of one's shouldering this responsibility – toward God and toward others – are integral to the avowal of love for God as well as others. The commandment "Thou shall love your God" is experienced as an enabling trauma; the human becomes ruptured from itself in an openness to the otherness of God, and in response the human is impelled to turn toward other human beings, as the neighbor, standing as a Thou, under the commandment of love.[95] The enabling trauma of God's commandment is endured and endures in the love of the neighbor: "the love of God should express itself in the love of the neighbor, and thus the I passes to the Thou and into the We: into life and toward redemption of the All, that is, realization of the All."[96] The soul becomes open toward the neighbor under the commandment of love, but in turning toward the other as other, the human gains eyes for the world in the transcendence of redemption. Redemption is not a relation between human existence and God, but between human existence and the world through intersubjective relations to others, as a community of "Thous" forming into a "We," in the name of God. Redemption is both "other-worldly" and "this-worldly," of the eternal future and in the now.

---

[94] Rosenzweig, *The Star of Redemption*, p. 182.
[95] This represents for Rosenzweig the "conversion" of the soul into an I: In responding to God's commandment by addressing other human beings, the human turns toward God, standing before God as an I.
[96] For the notion of enabling trauma, Bielik-Robson, *Jewish Cryptotheologies of Late Modernity*, pp. 227–231.

The Star and the Cross

The passage from Section Two, "The Path," to Section Three, "The Figure," projects historically on the transition from Ancient paganism to the religion of revelation in the dual (and conflicting) manifestations of Judaism and Christianity, the latter passing through the three epochs of the Church (taken up in Rosenzweig's unfinished *Globus*) until the aftermath of the war. Much of Rosenzweig's struggle with the relation between revelation and redemption, stemming from his 1913 crisis and wartime debates with his friend Rosenstock, is mirrored in his effort to understand the essence of Christianity and Judaism in their respective distinctiveness and ultimate relationship. With this transition to the theme of redemption in Section Three, the organon of thinking becomes displaced from "grammar" to "prayer," in conjunction with progressing from the temporality of past–present–future to the cyclical temporality of eternity in relation to time. Rosenzweig maintains that what God, what human existence, and what the world "is" cannot be known other than "what they do, or what is done to them."[97] Christianity and Judaism represent two different yet juxtaposed forms that mirror "the ever-renewed actuality" of creation in their different orientation toward eternity. This relationship to eternity is connected to the sociological composition of Christianity and Judaism as "we-communities" as shaped by their respective orientations toward redemption. Both religions of the Book (but also Islam, sporadically discussed by Rosenzweig) relate to the world in its uniqueness under the promise of redemption.

The contrast between Christianity and Judaism proves central to Rosenzweig's thinking. In many respects, the conflict and distinction outlined in his unfinished manuscript *Globus* between "the Land" and "the Sea," and hence the drama between "the Homeric" and "the biblical," become reconfigured into the relation between Christianity and Judaism in Section Three of *The Star of Redemption*. For Rosenzweig, what defines Christian eschatology is not only anticipation of redemption in eternity, but the fulfillment of the historically immanent solicitation of Christ for salvation. Christianity, as Rosenzweig writes, "pushes its roots into the night of the earth, which, although dead, furnish nonetheless life [...] In the ground, with its domination and territory, here is firmly anchored their will for eternity." Christianity seeks to master time and the world through the immanentization of eternity, with the consequence of inducing either the divinization of the world or the "worldification" of God. Moreover, given this impulse for mastery over time

---

[97] Rosenzweig, *Philosophical and Theological Writings*, p. 132.

and the earth, with its inevitable will to totality; war, on Rosenzweig's thinking, occupies the center of Christian historical existence. In contrast to the wars of Antiquity, which for Rosenzweig were waged for territorial defense, Christian wars of faith are waged in the name of sacrifice and culture.

By contrast, what defines Judaic messianism is the anticipation of redemption "outside" and "beyond" history. Jews are neither a people "of the earth" nor of history; the Jewish people exist "in themselves" through a community of blood, where blood is the symbolic medium for continuity and transmission of identity, orientation, and heritage.[98] Above all, blood is the signet of hope. As the people of blood, Jews embody a cyclical transmission of an anticipation of eternity from one generation to the next. The temporal continuity of Jewish communal life on earth is not anchored in territory or language. Blood likewise symbolizes mortality and the hope for redemption, around which the rituals of the Jewish religion and practices of Jewish life are formed. On this view, the Jewish people are not a national people and have no "visible place in the world." Jews, in this sense, do not participate in history, which, echoing his geopolitical thinking in *Globus*, Rosenzweig understands as a history of territorial domination and incessant conflict. The Jewish people exist "trans-historically," given their orientation toward a redemption of creation in eternity, lived from the standpoint of the present. This "trans-historical" existence and refusal to participate in the world-historical plot of domination over creation lend Judaism an interruptive force against the closure of world history, or, in other words, the march of God in a Hegelian sense. Rather than time as the moving image of eternity, for Judaism, eternity is the moving image of time. In the cyclical temporality of the Jewish people, they live in anticipation of eternity and hence in redemption, where the future is the "motive power" such that the cyclical movement of temporality is neither pushed forward by the past nor fleeing away from the present. It is the future that pulls cyclical time forward, and with each liturgical cycle moves closer to a future redemption. As Rosenzweig writes: "For eternity is precisely this, that between the present moment and the completion time may no longer claim a place, but as early as in the today every future is graspable."[99]

What distinguishes the Jewish people is that they do not attach themselves to the earth in taking possession of territory; they are anchored in the ritual

---

[98] On the complexities of Rosenzweig's nonracial understanding of blood and consanguinity of community, H. Dagan, "The Motif of Blood and Procreation in Franz Rosenzweig," *AJS Review*, Vol. 26, No. 2 (2002): 241–249.
[99] Rosenzweig, *The Star of Redemption*, p. 348.

and cyclical life of community oriented beyond time to eternity. This is the sense in which Jews are both elected and in exile, "homeless" in the sense of without the possession of territory. Rosenzweig argues that Christianity is characterized by "constant life in the war of faith," whereas for Judaism all wars can only be political: "the Jew is really the only man in the Christian world who cannot take war seriously, and therefore is the only genuine 'pacifist.'" Living in cyclical temporality in the mutual participation of community with God, "he no longer needs to win in the long march of a world history." This, then, is the sense in which Judaism stands outside of history, history as history of war, and hence stands outside the world: "by living in eternal peace, it stands outside of a warlike temporality; by resting at the goal that it anticipates in hope, it is separated from the march of those who draw near to it in the toil of centuries."[100] Judaism resides in itself, is at home in itself – in fact, the Jewish "home" resides in a communal existence oriented towards eternity – but from the point of view of the earth and history, Jews are in exile: "The Creation itself as a whole, however, is held together with Redemption in all time, as long as Redemption is still in its coming, only through the Eternal People placed outside all World History."[101] As Rosenzweig argues: "Jewish people do not have a national life or visible place in the world [...] nor in a territory properly belong to [it], firmly grounded and delimited on earth." Whereas Christianity is based on the Law, Judaism is organized around the cyclical temporality of liturgy, and the three main festivals in the Jewish calendar as sacred time: Shabbat (creation), Passover, Shavuot, and Sukkot (revelation), and Rosh Hashanah (New Year) and Yom Kippur (redemption). Prayer is a speech act of redemption; narrative is the language of creation; and dialogue the speech of revelation. As Rosenzweig writes: "here is the ultimate result arrived at in Revelation: prayer." Prayer is a mode of speech that cannot be measured by its "satisfaction," and revelation arrives at "the cry of an open question," which is prayer, and this cry moves the human beyond dialogue to God, and he becomes open to the world. The human opens their eyes to the world: The commandment of God's love becomes the commandment to love the neighbor, and this is the passage from revelation to redemption. As Rosenzweig writes: "the neighbor is not loved for themselves, he is not loved for his beautiful eyes, but uniquely because he exists, precisely because he is my neighbor."

The Jewish people exist "beyond the opposition" that shapes "the actual moving power in the life of the peoples," namely, the opposition between

---

[100] Rosenzweig, *The Star of Redemption*, p. 351.
[101] Rosenzweig, *The Star of Redemption*, p. 355.

particularity and universal (as world history), heaven and earth, homeland and faith, and thus, the Jewish people "does not know war." As Rosenzweig elaborates: "For a people, war means staking life for the sake of life," such that a people risks its own death in war, and this is only possible if a people understands itself as elected, or chosen, and hence not as mortal; and thus claims for itself the embodiment of eternity.[102] "To keep the image of the true mutual participation intact it must not be allowed the satisfaction that the peoples of the world have continuously in the State," he writes.[103] The state is "the ever-changing form under which time moves to eternity step by step," and this means that the state is "the attempt, inevitably always to be renewed, to give to the peoples eternity in time."[104] On Rosenzweig's thinking, the nation-state is the political manifestation of conquest not just of territory, but of eternity in time. But Judaism anticipates eternity without state and possession. As Rosenzweig writes, the state represents the "attempt to confer to peoples an eternity in time," and thus to attain possession of and mastery over history; this means that violence and the state belong together intrinsically, and this plays itself out in the law. This sets up opposition between life and the state and the law that it maintains through violence; the "false eternity" of the state depends on its perpetuation of violence. The law of the state, for the preservation of life (in contrast to the renewal of life), requires violence to reconcile the contradiction between preservation of life and life's renewal: "Therefore war and revolution are the only reality that the State knows, and in every moment where neither one nor the other would take place – and be it only in shape of a thought of war or revolution – it would no longer be State. At no moment can it lay down the sword from its hand […]." Where there is no state, there is no world history: "And that is why the true eternity of the eternal people must remain always foreign and annoying to the State and world history."[105]

According to Rosenzweig, then, "before God therefore, both Jew and Christian, are workers on the same task. He cannot dispense with either. Between the two, he set an enmity for all time, and yet he binds them together

---

[102] Rosenzweig, *The Star of Redemption*, p. 348.
[103] Rosenzweig, *The Star of Redemption*, p. 352.
[104] See Hegel, *Elements of the Philosophy of Right*, § 270: "The state is the divine will, in the sense that it is mind present on earth, unfolding itself to be the actual shape and organisation of a world. Those who insist on stopping at the form of *religion,* as opposed to the state, are acting like those logicians who think they are right if they continually stop at the essence and refuse to advance beyond that abstraction to existence, or like those moralists (see Remark to § 140) who will only good in the abstract and leave it to caprice to decide what is good."
[105] Rosenzweig, *The Star of Redemption*, p. 354.

in the narrowest reciprocity."[106] Christianity is the anticipation of redemption in history and thus represents the immanentization of historical *eschaton*. Judaism stands "outside history" and, as a consequence, does not enjoin visibility in the history of nation-states and the mimetic rivalry for power. Judaism, as a communal form of living, lives in its own parallel temporality. Judaism haunts history and the foundation of nation-states – politics – in violence, for it is precisely the "people of eternity" who have opted out of mimetic rivalry *and* interrupted the logic of sacrifice that cannot be accepted by peoples devoted to the realization of redemption immanently within historical time. The force of Judaism consists in the incessant disruption and interruption of false messianism in historical time; namely, redemption within history through the violent immanentization of the eschaton. However, without Christianity, Judaism would in turn not have a historical stage where its cyclical temporality could play itself out in its messianic sway. Judaism remains, in this regard, the stranger to history, yet finds a place in the world in which it can live as a community oriented toward a messianic redemption as the people of eternity through time (and not "from" or "above" time).

The Gate toward Life

If *The Star of Redemption* opened upon the broad panorama of creation with the question of the meaningfulness of it All as initiated from the fear and trembling of death, with the unmistakable war-torn "whizzing of projectiles" and "pestilential breath of Hades," it closes with an opening beyond, set before our eyes with the triangular typesetting of Rosenzweig's text, as if to puncture a hole in the penultimate page of the book itself, through which, with shielded courage, we are asked to "walk humbly with God," leading nowhere else than *into life*. *The Star of Redemption* ends as a book by opening a gate through which one can enter the "No-longer-Book" of life. As Rosenzweig writes:

> No-longer-book is the enraptured-startled knowledge that in this beholding the "world-likeness in the countenance of God" in this seizing of all being in the immediacy of a moment and blink of an eye, the limit of humanity is entered. No-longer-book is also becoming aware that this step of the book toward the limit can only be atoned for by – ending the book. An ending which is also a beginning and a midpoint: stepping into the midst of everyday life.[107]

---

[106] Rosenzweig, *The Star of Redemption*, p. 438.
[107] Rosenzweig, *Philosophical and Theological Writings*, p. 136. As Rosenzweig writes in a letter to Buber in 1919: ""I see my future only in life, no longer in writing," F. Rosenzweig, *Ninety-Two*

In stepping into life, the meaningfulness of it All flashes brilliantly forth in its configuration, "the world-likeness in the countenance of God," but in this stepping forth into a new life, the book must be shouldered as a responsibility in everyday life. From the Elements to the Path to the Figure through the Gate, *The Star of Redemption* enacts in narration "the day of the life of the All," which, once traversed, allows a reader to live for the future in trust and confidence, or what Rosenzweig calls the "verification truth of his messianic theory of knowledge," that the truth of the Book must be lived, and hence verified, through a lived trust and entrustment recreated daily. As Rosenzweig writes: "Such trust in experience might well constitute what is teachable and transmissible with respect to the new thinking." The arc from death through love to life configurates the Star as a "countenance that looks upon me and from out of which I look"; not God but God's truth becomes the mirror opening the doors of sanctuary; this vision of beyond life is already at the center of life. The Star is the inner sanctuary that is a gate through which we can walk into life, toward redemption hand in hand, as it were, with God along with others: "To walk humbly with your God – nothing more is asked for here than a wholly present trust."[108] We want to remain holding on to our creatureliness, death notwithstanding. The reader is left, in passing through the gate "to life" of the closing page in *The Star of Redemption*, not with a solution or answer to the meaningfulness of it All, but with trust in the meaningfulness of it All under the lodestar of redemption; in this way Rosenzweig sees a convergence between "the greatest poet of the Jews" and "the greatest poet of the Germans." "My words are too difficult for you, for which reason they seem too simple to you" – thus spoke Judah Halevi. "Many a riddle must be solved there," states Faust, to which Mephistopheles replies: "yet many a riddle is also propounded."[109]

Poems and Hymns of Yehuda Halevi, trans. T. Kovach, E. Jospe, and G. G. Schmidt (Albany: State University of New York Press, 2000). Rosenzweig continued nonetheless to write, including his translation work on the Bible and the poems of Yehudah Halevi, but also his gem *Understanding the Sick and the Healthy*.

[108] Rosenzweig, *The Star of Redemption*, p. 447.

[109] In 1922, Rosenzweig was diagnosed with amyotrophic lateral sclerosis, or Lou Gehrig's disease, which progressively left him paralyzed to the point that a special apparatus had to be constructed for him to communicate based on the blinking of his eyes and modified typewriter. Rosenzweig's final words, tapped out on this apparatus, were the unfinished statement: "And now it comes, the point of all points, which the Lord has truly revealed to me in my sleep, the point of all points for which there …"

CHAPTER 8

"A Journey around the World"
Ernst Cassirer, Freedom in Ways of Worldmaking

"But the Day Is Really So Absurd and Confused"

At the outbreak of the war, Ernst Cassirer enjoyed an international reputation as a leading figure in the Marburg School of Neo-Kantianism.[1] Still a *Privatdozent* after years at the University of Berlin and repeatedly thwarted from obtaining a chair of philosophy in Germany due to entrenched anti-Semitism, Cassirer's erudite publications had garnered widespread recognition. Rudolf Eucken, recipient of the Nobel Prize and "a famous man," as Cassirer writes to this wife, Toni, in 1911 even asked him out to lunch when invited to speak at the University of Jena. Numerous professors and "a huge crowd of other people" were in attendance. His works were on display in bookshop windows along with the announcement of his lecture in the spiritual capital of Weimar Classicism. A year before the war, Cassirer was offered an appointment to teach at Harvard University as a visiting professor for the academic year 1913–14. This prestigious invitation – "normally received only by famous scholars" – took him by surprise. Ignorant as to the whereabouts of Harvard, Cassirer pleasantly discovered that it was in Boston – "the most beautiful city in America known for its resemblance to a European city."[2] Undertaking a trip to "this unknown world, of which we knew next to nothing, where things could get really wild and strawberries purchased in winter" seemed too daunting, however. With two young sons and a lack of proficiency in English, Cassirer felt unsuited to world travel, let alone prolonged separation from his family.[3] Years later, Toni

---

[1] For the movement of Neo-Kantianism, see F. Beiser, *The Genesis of Neo-Kantianism, 1796–1880* (Oxford: Oxford University Press, 2017); and Köhnke, *The Rise of Neo-Kantianism*. For Marburg Neo-Kantianism, see Luft, *The Space of Culture*; and Philonenko, *L'École de Marbourg*.
[2] Cassirer, *Mein Leben mit Ernst Cassirer*, p. 109.
[3] Cassirer's letter of July 15, 1913, to Harvard President Abbott Lawrence Lowell, in E. Cassirer, *Nachgelassene Manuscripte und Texte* (Hamburg: Felix Meiner Verlag, 2009), 18, p. 21. Cassirer received a second invitation for 1914–15.

often imagined what might have been, had they accepted this invitation to discover an unknown world where strawberries were in abundance in wintertime. What would have become of "Ernst's entire [philosophical] development," she wondered, had they left for America in 1913 and then been unable to return to Germany because of the war?[4]

When enemy airplanes were sighted over Nuremberg on July 30, 1914, Toni and the children were away on holiday at the Baltic Coast. As with other middle-class Germans, war had interrupted their summer vacation. At Germany's declaration of war against Russia on August 1, she rushed home with the children. Arriving in Berlin, she discovered the city "completely changed," and was unable to comprehend what was happening around her. Ernst, despite his "understanding of history and historical developments," remained as baffled as she: "even he found himself all of a sudden perplexed for the first time in finding himself in a completely changed world." The world of yesterday was no more. The Cassirers had until then enjoyed an assimilated life among artists and scholars insulated from politics. Suddenly, "everything French was suspicious." French art, once venerated, was now "undesirable." "Foreign languages, which one struggled to learn with steely resolve," were now frowned upon. Good friends, citizens of "enemy powers," had to be avoided. And why? "Because encircled Germany – assaulted by its neighbors – found itself in a war of life and death."[5] Overnight, European art and literature become weaponized. Strangers in an unrecognizable land, Cassirer and his wife were appalled by the lack of critical judgment among their educated peers. As Toni writes: "All around us – from the spiritual-moral leaders of Germany down to the youngest child – flowered the blindest form of nationalism. Any trace of objectivity had disappeared." This was especially pronounced among the German-Jewish *Bildungsbürgertum*. As Toni dryly observes: "There was nothing more 'German' than the German Jews at that time – no one who surpassed them in patriotic short-sightedness."[6]

By happenstance, Cassirer was exempt from military service: A mild skin irritation was diagnosed by military doctors as an illness that would prevent him from wearing a uniform. By 1916, the war nonetheless caught up with Cassirer; he was enlisted as a civil servant in the French language department of the *Kriegspresseamt* (War Press Office), newly formed in 1915 after the loosening of an official prohibition against public debate of the

---

[4] Cassirer, *Mein Leben mit Ernst Cassirer*, p. 110.
[5] Cassirer, *Mein Leben mit Ernst Cassirer*, p. 117.
[6] Cassirer, *Mein Leben mit Ernst Cassirer*, p. 118.

war's aims.[7] In addition to censoring publications and surveillance of political attitudes, the *Kriegspresseamt* vetted newspaper reporting about the war so as to leave no doubts about the surety of victory.[8] Cassirer was responsible for monitoring French news announcements and altering their battlefield reports to conform with the communications of the *Kriegspresseamt*. His talents did not go unnoticed; he attained the rank of "surrogate officer" and was promoted to lead his section. Diligent in his duties, Cassirer nonetheless "felt like a cog" and, "as with every soldier, robbed of personal responsibility." As he complains to Paul Natorp, "because of my work in the War Press Office, which normally also occupies my Sundays, I have had only one free morning at my disposal in the past two months."[9]

From his vantage point, it became clear that the war was lost for Germany. This realization spurred Cassirer to redress Germany's spiritual blindness "in his characteristic manner," namely, by writing a book.[10] "What can *philosophy* do in this struggle against political myths?" Cassirer asked decades later in 1945.[11] Arguably, it is a question that he had already wondered about in 1916, without then being able to imagine how this question would shadow the development of his thinking, leading him gingerly to admit "that we [philosophers] have greatly underrated the strength of political myths" in the closing months of another world war whose end he would not live to see. In hindsight, Cassirer could have realized that he had been given a glimpse into the resurgence of mythical power, in the distinctive modern form he would decades later critically examine in *The Myth of the State*, with his service in the *Kriegspresseamt* and its promotion of war propaganda, as "one of the greatest triumphs of modern political warfare." As he writes: "From now [on] myth was no longer an incalculable and uncontrollable thing. It could be made at pleasure; it became an artificial compound manufactured in the great laboratory of politics."[12]

---

[7] For the *Kriegspresseamt*, see D. Welch, *Germany and Propaganda in World War I* (London: I. B. Taurus, 2014), pp. 39–42.
[8] Welch, *Germany and Propaganda in World War I*, p. 60.
[9] Cassirer, *Nachgelassene Manuscripte und Texte*, p. 31. Letter of January 1, 1917.
[10] Cassirer, *Mein Leben mit Ernst Cassirer*, p. 119. As Toni recalls: "At first, the work in this office was very interesting for him; but it inevitably led to the destruction of any illusion about the war and especially about 'the German cause.'"
[11] E. Cassirer, "The Technique of Our Modern Political Myths," in *Symbol, Myth, and Culture*, ed. D. P. Verene (New Haven, CT: Yale University Press, 1981): 242–267; p. 266.
[12] E. Cassirer, "Judaism and the Modern Political Myth," in *Nachgelassene Manuskripte und Texte*, p. 269. In *Myth of the State*, Cassirer argues that Nazism "invented a new technique of myth [… that] can be manufactured in the same sense and according to the same methods as any other modern weapon […] That is a new thing – and a thing of crucial importance. It has changed the whole form of our social life"; E. Cassirer, *Myth of the State* (New Haven, CT: Yale University Press, 1961), p. 235.

Even without this acuteness of vision from the 1940s, the corrosive effects of national myths and political propaganda on Germany's spiritual legacy must have already been evident in 1916. To save Germany from its self-destructive parochial complexes, Cassirer discreetly undertook at his office, all the while falsifying French reports of the war for homeland consumption ("this condemnable society game which he nonetheless executed in an exemplary manner"), an alternative narrative of the German spirit.[13] Published in June 1916 while the German Army persisted (and perished) at Verdun and British-French armies were amassing on the Somme, *Freiheit und Form: Studien zur Deutschen Geistesgeschichte* is an isolated wartime affirmation of the bond among the German spirit, political liberalism, and creative cultural freedom. With an endorsement of Classical Weimar humanism, the aesthetic and ethical ideals of eighteenth-century German Enlightenment, and cosmopolitan *Bildung*, Cassirer issues his own call to the German nation in the hope of safeguarding "the image of an indestructible and eternal Germany, which was in the clutches of becoming entirely and definitively unrecognizable from the slag-heaps on which it had thrown itself."[14]

While writing *Freedom and Form*, Cassirer might have recalled Goethe's despair toward the end of his life amid a world falling apart. As Goethe writes to Wilhelm von Humboldt in 1829: "No one knows himself anymore, no one understands the element in which he lives and moves, no one understands the material which he shapes. There can be no talk of pure simplicity, but of simple nonsense there is plenty." Five days before his death in 1832, and haunted by disturbing recollections of the July 1830 Revolution, Goethe confides to Humboldt:

> But the day is really so absurd and confused that I am convinced that the honest efforts with which I have labored so long on this strange edifice [*Faust*, Part II] would be ill repaid; they would be driven upon the shore, lie there like a shattered hulk, only to be covered over by the drifting sands of time. Confused theories for confused actions hold sway over the earth; I have nothing better to do than, where possible, to augment what is my own and has been left to me, to distill and redistill my own individuality, just as you, also, my esteemed friend, are doing in your castle.[15]

---

[13] Cassirer, *Mein Leben mit Ernst Cassirer*, p. 120.
[14] Cassirer, *Mein Leben mit Ernst Cassirer*, p. 120.
[15] Cited in K. Löwith, *From Hegel to Nietzsche*, trans. D. Green (New York: Columbia University Press, 1964), p. 28.

A Counter-History of Spirit

Although the initiative for *Freedom and Form* predated the war, it was Cassirer's growing dismay at the fate of German spiritual life that motivated the plan of his work to become clearly defined and pressingly in need of completion.[16] Had it not been for the past two years, Cassirer observes in his Preface, he would never have mustered the "resolution and courage" to publish *Freedom and Form*. In a public lecture given in Berlin at the *Lehranstalt für die Wissenschaft des Judentums* in March 1916, "Der Deutsche Idealismus and das Staatsproblem" (mirrored in the final chapter of *Freedom and Form*), Cassirer declares that "one of the unique manifestations of this war" is that a "conflict of thoughts and theories" has emerged alongside "the conflict of weapons."[17] Cassirer rejects the view advocated by Allied intellectuals, most notably Henri Bergson, that the war pitted German thought against French and British thought, and he does not accept a distinction between German Idealism and Prussian militarism, with the fault of war befalling the latter. These attacks against the "German essence" (*Wesen*) brought into sharper relief what was at stake in this conflict, but, in contrast to the shrill chorus of *Kriegsphilosophie*, Cassirer grasped that what hung in the balance was whether the German spirit would collapse into pathological nationalism or elevate itself to cosmopolitan significance.

The war represents, in this sense, "a great turning point" for the German nation. What before the war seemed an "abstract problem" – namely, a critical reflection on historical configurations of the idea of freedom in modern thought – became transformed by the war into an "immediate and living interest of our present times." Although historical in scope, *Freedom and Form* speaks to the present times through a critical self-reflection on the essence of the German nation, or *Deutschtum*.

---

[16] E. Cassirer, *Freiheit und Form. Studien zur Deutschen Geistesgeschichte*, (Darmstadt: Wissenschaftliche Buchgesellschaft, 1975), p. xi. At the end of the second volume of *Das Erkenntnisproblem* (1907), Cassirer noted that the question of *das Ding an Sich* could not be resolved within a purely theoretical standpoint, but required instead the progression to an ethical standpoint, within which the opposition between freedom and causality could be reconciled. With this transition to practical philosophy, Cassirer suggested that that critical philosophy "finds its true nature as philosophy of freedom, in which knowledge and morality cannot be reduced to external conditionality but find their own conditionality in their own autonomous law"; E. Cassirer, *Das Erkenntnisproblem in der Philosophie und Wissenschaft der neueren Zeit* (Berlin: Bruno Cassirer, 1906–1907), II. See M. Ferrari, *Ernst Cassirer. Stationen einer philosophischen Biographie* (Hamburg: Felix Meiner Verlag, 2003), p. 53.

[17] E. Cassirer, *Zur Philosophie und Politik* (Nachgelassene Manuskripte und Texte Band 9), eds. J. M. Krois and C. Möckel (Hamburg: Felix Meiner Verlag, 2008), p. 3.

Cassirer presents a counter-history of spirit in defiance of the spiritual mobilization of *Kriegsphilosophie*. The clamor of *Kriegsphilosophie* evinces a dismaying provincialization of spirit against which *Freedom and Form* strives to reclaim German spirit's universalism and "world-historical" – that is, cosmopolitan – mission by means of a recovery of "the active and productive forces on which the future configuration of our existence essentially depends."

The wartime provincialization of spirit afflicted Cassirer's Neo-Kantian colleagues. Hermann Cohen and Natorp both leveraged the cultural prestige and philosophical import of German Idealism in their support of the war. Cohen (whom Cassirer held in high esteem) argued for a wartime alliance of *Deutschtum* – centered on eighteenth-century German humanism and Kantian Idealism – with the prophetic messianism of *Judentum*.[18] Natorp advocated Germany's "world-historical mission" and "spiritual conquest of Europe." In *Deutscher Weltberuf. Geschichtsphilosophische Richtlinien*, Natorp outlined the development of Europe that stressed the distinctiveness of German faith, Eckhart's mysticism, and the Germanic ideal of freedom in its struggle against positivism, rationalism, and the "British Faustian drive for fabrication."[19] Rudolf Eucken, in his 1916 popularization of German Idealism, issued to soldiers at the front, celebrated Fichte as the *Kriegsphilosophe* par excellence.[20] The venerable Wilhelm Windelband, in his final publication before his death in 1915, *Geschichtsphilosophie. Eine Kriegsvorlesung*, warned of the "annihilation of Europe" should Germany fail to prevail. Wilhelm Wundt, in *Die Nationen und ihre Philosophie: ein Kapitel zum Weltkrieg*, interpreted Nietzsche's *Übermensch* as incarnating the obligatory duty of sacrifice under the imperative "you should sacrifice yourself for the task given to you by the world!" – *der Idealismus der Tat und Hingabe*.[21]

Amid this mobilization of Neo-Kantianism, Cassirer conspicuously avoids a direct confrontation with his war-enthused contemporaries and colleagues. This reticence might reflect the specter of censorship, of which

---

[18] See T. R. Keck, *Kant and Socialism* (Ann Arbor: University of Michigan Press, 1975), pp. 364–412. For contrast with Cohen and Natorp, Ferrari, *Stationen einer philosophischen Biographie*, pp. 35–38.
[19] For Natorp's war writings, N. Brun, *Vom Kulturkritiker zum "Kulturkrieger." Paul Natorps Weg in den "Krieg der Geister"* (Würzburg: Köningshausen & Neumann, 2007).
[20] For Eucken's war writings, de Warren, "Rudolf Eucken."
[21] W. Wundt, *Die Nationen und ihre Philosophie: ein Kapitel zum Weltkrieg*, 2 (Leipzig: Kröner, 1915), p. 114. As Ferrari writes, "the fracture of the war profoundly transformed the entire context of debates in Neo-Kantianism" just as "the last generation of Neo-Kantians arrived at maturity when belle epoque began decline"; *Stationen einer philosophischen Biographie*, p. 140. For an extensive treatment of *Kriegsphilosophie*, Hoeres, *Krieg der Philosophen*.

Cassirer would have been clearly informed, or patrician discretion (as with his confrontation with Martin Heidegger in Davos, Switzerland, in 1929). And yet, *Freedom and Form* is neither anti-German nor explicitly against the war, and was, in fact, favorably reviewed for its "vital history" of German spirit.[22] Cassirer's reserved attitude can also be seen as anticipating a statement made decades later in *The Myth of the State* that "myth cannot be overcome by logical and rational argument." In 1916, Cassirer responds to the political and cultural myths of his time not by argument, but with a demythologizing counter-narrative of spirit. His strategy consists in challenging the widely proclaimed irreconcilable conflict between German *Kultur* and European civilization by examining the fertile cross-cultural exchange between Germany and European nations since the Renaissance *and* the Reformation. The distinctiveness of German spirit remains affirmed throughout, yet becomes situated within the cosmopolitan horizon of European modernity beyond national parochialism.[23] By appealing to the openness of German spirit, Cassirer seeks to surpass the opposition between "particular" and "universal," and hence a logic of exemplarity, intrinsic to the historical vision of *Kriegsphilosophie*, whereby the particular (German) nation claims to exemplify, and hence possess, the universal at the exclusion of other nations; whereby the universal is claimed (as with the Allied powers) in cancelation of the cultural values of a particular nation (namely, Germany). For Cassirer, the universality of freedom emerged from the spiritual development of the German nation in dialectical relation with the heritage of Renaissance humanism, and thus embodied a transnational significance that neither abolished nor absorbed the particularity of individual nations, nor illegitimately universalized a particular nation above others.

Methodologically, Cassirer rejects a narrative of spirit based on the "implementation of abstract historical-philosophical principles that are belatedly demonstrated on particular facts." His counter-history of German spirit is woven instead from "concrete intuitions of the things themselves and their

---

[22] For contemporary reviews of Cassirer's work, H. Bahr, "Über Ernst Cassirer," *Die neue Rundschau*, Vol. XXVIII (1917): 1483–1499; H. Lindau, "*Rezension*," *Kant-Studien*, XXII (1918): 125–134; E. Troeltsch, "Ernst Cassirer: Freiheit und Form (1916)," *Theologischen Literatur-Zeitung*, XVII/XIX (1917): 368–371. As Georg Simmel writes to Gottfried Salomon on December 28, 1916: "Have you seen Cassirer's new book *Form and Freedom*? [sic] It appears to be entirely excellent"; Simmel, *Briefe 1912–1918*, p. 720.

[23] D. Gawronksy, "Ernst Cassirer: His Life and His Work," in *The Philosophy of Ernst Cassirer*, ed. P. A. Schilpp (La Salle: Open Court, 1945): 1–38; p. 23. See also Ferrari, *Stationen einer philosophischen Biographie*, p. 33 ff.

spiritual connections."²⁴ The style of thinking in *Freedom and Form*, blending historical narrative and philosophical argument, possesses an epistemological function.²⁵ Cassirer implicitly effects a synthesis of Goethe's morphological genealogy with Kant's transcendental critique. Rather than determine the meaning of historical-cultural phenomena from a "fixed and firmly put together logical definition," Cassirer's historical-phenomenological narrative transposes Kant's reflective judgment onto the field of culture by investigating the "spiritual connections" of religion, philosophy, art, politics, and poetry.²⁶ These "mobile and imaginative thought-symbols" reveal their respective meaning when related to a "highest universal" – the idea of freedom – and yet the "entire sense of this universal" can only be understood through the relations and connections among different thought symbols. In guiding the unity of modern cultural development, the idea of freedom becomes progressively realized through its multiple forms, across the full range of human experience, thus bringing together the universal and the particular as well as the potential and the actual into an embracing movement of spirit's self-discovery and self-realization.

Addressed to the historical present, *Freedom and Form* does not sacrifice "the rigor of conceptual development and the difficulty of the problems" for the sake of achieving a "popularity of presentation." This disengagement from the stage of popular appeal does not reflect a depolitical thinker, but, on the contrary, affirms the political significance of the autonomy of thinking and historical critique *against* the wartime mobilization of spirit. In a later essay, "Albert Schweitzer as Critic of Nineteenth-Century Ethics," Cassirer endorses Schweitzer's characterization of the philosopher as "the watchman." Against Hegel's iconic image of philosophy taking flight at dusk, and hence belatedly arriving on the scene of history in benediction of its closure, Cassirer argues that the courage for truth resides in a Socratic manner, with a responsibility to speak the truth against falsity in striving for self-knowledge and understanding

---

[24] Cassirer would repeat this methodological device of counter-history, as a means to reactualize the unfinished trajectory of the Enlightenment as philosophical modernity based on freedom and reason, during the 1930s with *The Philosophy of Enlightenment* (1932). Along with *The Individual and the Cosmos in Renaissance Philosophy* (1927), these critical historical works can be seen as further elaborations and extensions of *Freedom and Form*. For Cassirer's studies of the Enlightenment as counter-history, P. Gordon, *Continental Divide* (Cambridge, MA: Harvard University Press, 2010), p. 292 ff; and Curthoys, *The Legacy of Liberal Judaism*, chapter 5.
[25] B. Naumann, "Styles of Change: Ernst Cassirer's Philosophical Writing," in *Symbolic Forms and Cultural Studies: Ernst Cassirer's Theory of Culture*, eds. C. Hamlin and J.-M. Krois (Berlin: Walter de Gruyter, 2008): 78–98.
[26] Cassirer, *Freiheit und Form*, p. xiii.

of the whole. With this ethical imperative of self-reflection, philosophy is neither "too late," a retrospective reconciliation in thought of the whole with itself, nor "too early," a prescriptive thinking for the whole of its necessary end. The "principal duty" of *Selbstbesinnung* is not to "yield to the pressure of external forces" and, in this unyielding remembrance of its own responsibility, reflection exemplifies the autonomy of spirit as *Selbstbefreiung*.[27]

The Spirit of 1914

Cassirer was not wrong to think that posterity would consider as "one the strangest aspects of the total image of these times how during the hardest struggles for the political-material existence of the German people the question concerning its spiritual kind of being and its world-historical determination became energetically and with ever more generality posed."[28] Although the meaning of what was perceived as a titanic struggle remained shrouded, the sublime advent of war – *Groß und wunderbar* in the words of Max Weber to his wife Marianne – was widely experienced as the "acme of existence (*Dasein*)."[29] Within the first months of conflict, the war gave rise to a storm of speeches, pamphlets, and books concerning German *Eigentumlichkeit*, or *Deutschtum*.[30] As Thomas Mann remarked in his popular essay "Thoughts in War" for *Die Neue Rundschau* in November 1914, German poets "sang as if in competition with each other the praises of war, with deep passion, as if they and the people, whose voice they are, saw nothing better, nothing more beautiful than to fight many enemies." What inspired the poets, however, was not "economic domination" or "empire" but "the war itself, as a visitation and moral necessity."[31] In

---

[27] As Ursula Renz remarks: "Cassirer's writings were not entirely unpolitical, but they display a specific understanding of the political and societal task of philosophy that is marked by the notion of the functional autonomy of philosophical insight in modernity"; "Cassirer's Enlightenment: On philosophy and the 'Denkform' of Reason," *British Journal for the History of Philosophy*, Vol. 28, No. 3 (2020): 636–652; p. 638. As Cassirer writes in *The Philosophy of Enlightenment* (Princeton, NJ: Princeton University Press, 2009): "No account of the history of philosophy can be oriented to history alone" (p. xi). For Cassirer's view of the "duty of philosophy" in Schweitzer, *Symbol, Myth, and Culture*, pp. 230–232.

[28] Cassirer, *Freiheit und Form*, p. xiii.

[29] M. Weber, *Max Weber: A Biography*, trans. H. Zohn (London: Wiley, 1975), p. 521.

[30] For "the Spirit of 1914" and "the Idea of 1914," see J. Verhey, *The Spirit of 1914: Militarism, Myth and Mobilization in Germany* (Cambridge, UK: Cambridge University Press, 2000); Flasch, *Die geistige Mobilmachung*, pp. 15–62; W. Mommsen, *Bürgerliche Kultur und künstlerische Avantgarde. Kultur und Politik im deutschen Kaiserreich 1870–1919* (Frankfurt: Propyläen, 1994); and Lübbe, *Politische Philosophie in Deutschland*.

[31] T. Mann, "Thoughts in War," in *Reflections of a Nonpolitical Man*, p. 497.

Hermann Bahr's words, "we know for the first time who we really are" – "being German has manifested itself to us."[32] As Siegfried Kracauer argued in "Vom Erleben des Krieges" (1915), "Love of the Fatherland" appealed to a broad psychological and social spectrum.[33] Nationalism was not only a political passion; it was imbued with a metaphysical significance centering on an experience of freedom, "German Freedom," and embrace of an ideal for existence.[34]

Under the dual banners of "the Idea of 1914" and "the Spirit of 1914," this intellectualization of the war propagated an aggressive cultural typification of Germany's enemies: the English as "merchants," the French as "frivolous," and the Russians as "barbarians." This hardening of stereotypes accompanied an apocalyptic narrative whereby the war of 1914 was imagined as the repetition, and indeed fulfillment, of the *Befreiungskrieg* of 1813, spooling back even farther into the depths of Germany's resistant origins with Arminius' legendary victory over the Roman legions of Varus at the battle of Teutoburg Forest. For many, the war promised a "liberation of existence through an Ideal [at] the profound center of the soul." What prewar Germany lacked was wholeness, due to social fragmentation, professionalization, and everyday life with its chaotic "accidental impressions." Without an edifying and unifying Ideal, existence (*Dasein*) remained adrift in "zusammenhangsloser Lebensregungen."[35]

In his influential *Die Idee von 1914*, Rudolf Kjellén spoke of the war as the "battlefield of spirit" and as a "struggle between 1789 and 1914."[36] Following the popularized ideas of Johann Plenge, the war is depicted as not just involving a revolution of ideas, but, more significantly, as the opportunity for a national-social revolution leading to the establishment of a novel "German organization" of society. Kjellén praises Germany's "incomparable national social organization," namely, the total mobilization of society and economics, and "concentration of the life of the state" as a bulwark against the "anarchy lurking on the ground of the individualism

---

[32] H. Bahr, *Kriegssegen* (Munich: Delphin Verlag, 1915), p. 5ff.
[33] S. Kracauer, "Vom Erleben des Krieges," *Preussisches Jahrbuch*, Vol. 158, No. 3 (July–September 1915): 410–422. For Kracauer's disillusionment with the war after this 1915 essay, see J. Später, *Kracauer: A Biography*, trans. D. Steuer (London: Polity Press, 2020), pp. 33–34.
[34] For the metaphysical experience of the war's outbreak in a broader cultural and artistic context, M. Eksteins, *Rites of Spring: The Great War and the Birth of the Modern Age* (Boston, MA: Houghton Mifflin, 1989), chapter 6.
[35] S. Kracauer, *Schriften. Aufsätze*, 5–1 (Frankfurt: Suhrkamp, 1990), p. 17.
[36] R. Kjellén, *Die Idee von 1914* (Leipzig: G. Hirzel, 1915), p. 5; J. Plenge, *1789 und 1914. Die symbolischen Jahre in der Geschichte des politischen Geistes* (Berlin: J. Springer, 1916); M. Krahmann, *Krieg und Volkswirtschaft* (Berlin: Leonhard Simion, 1915).

of 1789." In this struggle for a new society, symbols possess an incomparable value. Indeed, Kjellén viewed history as centrally a struggle about "words and between words," as with the conflict between the Idea of 1789 and the Idea of 1914. "Every epoch," he writes, "has its word that holds its spiritual riddle, its secret word that has power over an epoch, against which any form of critique bounces off, and which permeates the air, sits on the walls, and penetrates everything on earth and in every corner." The symbols that gave expression to the French Revolution in 1789 – "individual freedom," "equality," and "fraternity" – have become eclipsed by "keywords for a new epoch of Ideas of 1914." Among these, "greater than all others," is *Ordnung*. As Kjellén writes: "Order is therefore the great word, the first word of 1914, which should destroy the random degenerate freedom of 1789. We have hungered for order."[37]

German Greatness

In seeking to rescue Germany from the "spiritually narrow chauvinism of these times," Cassirer does not reject Germany's *geistigen Wesensart*, nor its world-historical significance. And yet, how can German spirit be affirmed without succumbing to a jargon of authenticity or myth-making propaganda? In *Freedom and Form*, Cassirer charts a course through scenes of a forgotten Enlightenment, namely, the *German* eighteenth-century Enlightenment that had been prematurely eclipsed by reactionary Romanticism and ethnonationalism in the mid to late nineteenth century.[38] The parting of the ways that defines for Cassirer the unfinished adventure of German spirit turns on the opposition between Hegel and Goethe.[39] While a direct vein leads from Hegel to the "spiritually narrow chauvinism of these times," another trajectory of German development, and hence another future for Germany in the twentieth century – the road not yet taken – resides with Goethe; more specifically, with the axis of Kant and Goethe, which Cassirer defines neither as doctrine nor dogma, but as "an inexhaustible problem."[40]

---

[37] Kjellén, *Die Idee von 1914*, p. 24; Verhey, *The Spirit of 1914*, p. 138.
[38] For a significant recovery of the German Enlightenment, T. J. Reed, *Light in Germany: Scenes from an Unknown Enlightenment* (Chicago: University of Chicago Press, 2013). The expression "scenes from an unknown enlightenment" I have freely adopted here.
[39] For this opposition, D. Wellbery, "The Imagination of Freedom: Goethe and Hegel as Contemporaries," in *Goethe's Ghosts: Reading and the Persistence of Literature,* ed. S. Richter (London: Camden House, 2013): 271–239.
[40] E. Cassirer, *Gesammelte Werke. Aufsätze und kleine Schriften 1922–1926* (Hamburg: Felix Meiner Verlag, 2003), p. 471.

In Cassirer's counter-history of spirit, Luther's Reformation is credited with initiating the development of the modern conception of individual freedom. Rather than consider Luther as seeding an idea of freedom based on *Obrigkeit* and *Pflicht*, as championed by Protestant *Kriegstheologie* and advocates of the Idea of 1914, Cassirer offers a humanist recasting of Luther's conceptions of individual conscience and volition along with his rejection of Medieval hierarchical social structures. With this emphasis on the individual in the cosmos, Luther's Reformation does not run against the cosmopolitan orientation of the Renaissance.[41] From these two sources of modernity, Cassirer surveys decisive moments in the phenomenology of (mainly German) spirit: Leibniz, "the aesthetic form-world" of eighteenth-century German thinking, the discovery of autonomy, and the a priori that defines German Idealism, the indominable Goethe, the idea of freedom and aesthetic education in Schiller, and the cultured state in Fichte and Humboldt. The progressive realization of the idea of freedom attains its genuine form with the conjunction of Kantian self-prescribing autonomy with Goethe's conception of creative self-formation.[42] Notably, *Freedom and Form* culminates with the chapter "Freiheitsidee und Staatsidee" on Fichte and Hegel, thus foreshadowing the relation between morality and politics that would become central to *The Myth of the State*.

Beginning with Luther, Cassirer maintains that the relation between the individual, the people (*das Volk*), and the state developed on a distinct conceptual trajectory in seventeenth- and eighteenth-century German thinking. What distinguishes the German tradition of political thought in its attempts to determine the idea, or "form," of the state, in contrast to those of the French, Italian, and English, is that the state attains the status of a "metaphysical question" in relation to the cultivation of individual creative autonomy. In other European nations, the concept of the state was defined primarily along the lines of *raison d'état* and monarchial

---

[41] D. Lipton, *Ernst Cassirer: The Dilemma of a Liberal Intellectual in Germany, 1914–1933* (Buffalo: University of Toronto Press, 1974), p. 56. In *The Philosophy of the Enlightenment*, Cassirer echoes the call issued in *Freedom and Form*, but in the context of the 1930s it is addressed not to Germany alone but to Europe: "More than ever before, it seems to me, the time is again ripe for applying self-criticism to the present age, for holding up to it that bright clear mirror fashioned by the Enlightenment: *sapere aude*. [...] We must find a way not only to see that age in its own shape but to release again those original forces which brought forth and molded this shape"; *The Philosophy of the Enlightenment*, p. xi.

[42] As Gregory Moyhan observes, "it would be difficult to overstate the importance of Cassirer's reading of Goethe in *Freedom and Form*"; *Ernst Cassirer and the Critical Science of Germany: 1889–1919* (London: Anthem Press, 2013), p. 173.

sovereignty, with its centralized authority and monopolization of violence. Monarchial statehood is wedded to an epistemological relation between the universal and the particular, as well as a metaphysics of substance; the state is the universal substance encompassing particulars; namely, individual members. Moreover, the state is constituted in terms of power – a *Machtstaat* – as an anonymous and sovereign will to which individual interests and volitions must be subsumed. An alternative conception of the state, and hence of the relation between individuals and the state, took form with German thinkers. The lack of national unity and political fragmentation among German lands proved fortuitous, according to Cassirer, for cultivating "a disposition for reflective thinking." In the absence of a unified nation-state, German thinkers conceived of the state as a *Machtstaat* that needed to be transformed into a *Rechtstaat*.[43] Because Germany possessed no political reality, on Goethe's epigram, Germans should expend their efforts in becoming human.[44]

Central to this German liberal tradition is the development of natural rights theory, the rule of law, the inalienability of individual rights, and the values of *Bildung*. Although in other European nations monarchial sovereignty was a criterion of social hierarchy and hence inequality, in German aristocratic domains sovereignty became blunted and gradated along with social divisions. As one of the foundational ideas of the eighteenth-century German Enlightenment, the individual was imbued with intrinsic rights, stemming from rational moral duty, that could not be derived or abrogated by social contract, political power, or historical tradition.[45] Based on the principle of sufficient reason, Leibniz established a framework for both natural law and positive law, each adhering to the triumph of legality as a metaphysical idea, which allowed for the subordination of the law to its justification and reasoning; law lost an independent or divine basis of authority and became bound to reason and the science of jurisprudence.[46] For Leibniz, individual natural rights are not derived from a principle of equality, given that equality remains an abstract notion. Individual rights are situated within the overarching principle of harmony, or concordance, where individuals preserve their differences among themselves yet strive to cultivate themselves within an all-encompassing political community. From this Leibnizian footing, Cassirer traces the development of

---

[43] Cassirer, *Freiheit und Form*, p. 309.
[44] J. Adler, *Johann Wolfgang Goethe* (London: Reaktion Books, 2020), p. 118.
[45] Cassirer, *Freiheit und Form*, p. 315.
[46] R. Berkowitz, *The Gift of Science: Leibniz and the Modern Legal Tradition* (New York: Fordham University Press, 2010), chapter 1.

individual rights through Christian Wolff to Kant's essay on perpetual peace, where the rationality of individual self-governance, or autonomy, is brought together with the republican constitution of nation-states. As Cassirer writes: "The new position and dignity which is attained for the moral law through Kant's categorical imperative demands nothing less than a complete 'revolution in the manner of thinking,' as well as a completely new transformation of a world-view."[47] With Kant, "genuine sovereignty, which the state must establish and represent is the sovereignty of rational wills, and only in terms of the self-legislation of rational agents in legislation for each other." The idea of natural right thus receives a new form, such that the state and individual freedom are placed in a reciprocal relation under the historical *telos* of striving toward perpetual peace through the cultivation of individuals and society as a whole.

A little more than a decade later, in his defense of the Weimar Republic in 1929 in his public lecture "The Idea of the Republican Constitution," Cassirer would once again, as Rector of the University of Hamburg, and this time with greater urgency, call attention to the cornerstone of individual rights and rule of law for the legitimacy of the modern nation-state. As Cassirer remarks in this lecture in troubled times, Leibniz was the "first great European thinker who placed the principle of the inalienable basic rights of the individual at the foundation of his ethics and his philosophy of right and the state."[48] The European "world of ideas" adheres to the sanctity of individual rights and the subsumption of *Machtstaat* to a cosmopolitan-oriented *Rechtstaat*. Kant's *Critique of Practical Reason* (1788) and the French Revolution (1789) represent "a great historical turning point" – philosophical and political – that, as Cassirer emphasizes in 1929 as well as in 1916, emerged from the native ground of German spirit. Human rights, rule of law, and individual autonomy are not strangers nor intruders to Germany.[49]

Within this genealogy of Weimar liberalism presented in 1916, Cassirer's contemporary readers would surely have grasped the significance of his portrait of Frederick the Great as embodying "the unity between thinker and sovereign," and hence between theory and practice, but equally as the

---

[47] Cassirer, *Zu Philosophie und Politik*, p. 16.
[48] E. Cassirer, "Die Idee der republikanischer Verfassung," in *Gesammelte Werke. Aufsätze und kleine Schriften 1927–1931* (Hamburg: Felix Meiner Verlag, 2004): 291–307; p. 296.
[49] During the 1930s, Cassirer would intensify and expand his counter-history of spirit with his studies of the Renaissance and the Enlightenment, and argue especially for a rapprochement between Germany and France by means of a conceptual axis of Kant–Rousseau and their respective arguments for the value of the individual.

founder of a "new form of the state." There exists for Cassirer an inner affinity between Kant and Frederick the Great: "Frederick the Great thoroughly belongs as a philosopher as well as a political leader in the development leading from Leibniz to Kant."[50] In *Briefe über die Vaterlandsliebe* (1779), Frederick the Great reflected on the question: "Can one actually love one's Fatherland? Can one love one's people [*Volk*]?"[51] On Cassirer's construal, the unity of the state is neither abstract (a formal universal entity) nor an aggregate of individuals. As defined by Frederick the Great, the unity of the state is forged through "doing and effecting [*im Tun und Wirken*]." Nationalism, therefore, is neither a "mystical" nor an "intellectual" love for the Fatherland, but must be anchored in individual "doing and effecting," and thus not reduced to a "blind or sensual passion." The unity of the state is not based on historical tradition, "the mystical political body," or Machiavellian power of the princes, nor is the organization of the state solely composed from the "truss of rules and regulations" – an implicit rejection of the veneration of "order," "duty," and "authority" surrounding the Idea of 1914. Instead, the state is constituted on the basis of the "ethical idea" of freedom and the unity of individual wills.

With Schiller's *Briefe über die ästhetische Beziehung* and Wilhelm von Humboldt, Cassirer identifies a further stage in the phenomenology of German spirit. For these thinkers of *Bildung*, freedom was the indispensable and integral essence in humanity's historical self-realization. Freedom is thus understood neither as liberty from external constraints nor as freedom of choice among a range of pregiven possibilities nor as Kantian moral autonomy, but in terms of the formation, or cultivation, of the self, its capacities for creative meaning formation. With an eminently political significance, aesthetic education, for Schiller, entailed a harmonization of receptivity to complex particularities of the world and active shaping of complexity into unified, rational understanding.[52] Aesthetic *Bildung*, as freedom of self-cultivation, promotes the unity of real and ideal, *Sinnlichkeit* and *Geistigkeit*. The imperative to cultivate/educate oneself – *bilde Dich selbst!* – must be guaranteed and promoted by the state, whereby, for Humboldt, the state is reduced to a minimal and "mechanistic function" so as to allow for the flowering of the "culture of its citizens." This Humboldtian vision of *Bildung* and a minimalist state

---

[50] Cassirer, *Zu Philosophie und Politik*, p. 13.
[51] It stands to reason that Cassirer's discussion of Frederick the Great tacitly responds to Thomas Mann's 1915 book *Frederick and the Great Coalition*.
[52] J. Herdt, *Forming Humanity: Redeeming the German Bildung Tradition* (Chicago: University of Chicago Press, 2019), p. 127. For a discussion of Humboldt and Schiller, chapter 4.

apparatus emphasizes the variety and uniqueness of individuality within a holistic development of the individual as a person. Politically, as Cassirer stresses, the collective development of individuals into a society depends on diversifying and intensifying "linkages" and "connections" within a culture. Cultural pluralism entails a twofold task: to become oneself a diversified whole, as well as to become oneself a part of the diversified whole of society.

From this conception of *Bildung*, Cassirer suggests that "the true genuine completion of the concept of the state in German Idealism could not emerge from the pathos of aesthetic perspective, but only from the moral deed with Fichte," who envisioned Germany as a project, not only in historical terms but, more significantly, in metaphysical terms, as the project to realize an Idea of Freedom, in its primary ethical meaning, for "humanity." In *Rede an die Deutsche Nation*, Fichte surpassed the apparent opposition between nationalism and cosmopolitanism with his appeal for a humanization of culture and a culture of humanity. As Fichte argued, individual freedom becomes actual in relation to the "not-ego" – that is, "foreign subjects" (*fremder Subjekte*) – whereby the "not-ego," or other person, is regarded not as a "physical-material object," but as an autonomous individual other than oneself who makes claim on oneself. As Fichte writes: "I must in all cases recognize the free being outside of me as a free being, i.e., I must limit my freedom through the concept of the possibility of his freedom." The activity of self-positing and striving to be an individual ethical person must at the same time and in the same measure posit outside of itself other ethical subjects as a "Thou" (*Du*). As Cassirer explains: "The finite rational agent cannot, in other words, ascribe to itself any free *Wirksamkeit* in the sensible world without ascribing free *Wirksamkeit* to others."[53] For Fichte, right does not derive from the plurality of rational subjects; on the contrary, the recognition of the validity of rights provides the condition for the recognition of other ethical persons. Rights define how rational agents relate to each other, and it is this relation between individuals that is crucial, since individual relations are mediated through rights. In this respect, Fichte's *Foundations of Natural Right* develops a transcendental conception of intersubjectivity based on the constitutive function of reciprocal recognition for self-consciousness.

Rather than accept an irresolvable conflict between "the Idea of 1789" and "the Idea of 1914," Cassirer argues that the Idea of 1789 and the French Revolution stemmed from the French Enlightenment thinkers *and*

---

[53] Cassirer, *Freiheit und Form*, p. 341.

eighteenth-century German humanism. In the constellation of German Idealism – Kant, Schiller, Fichte, Humboldt – Cassirer sees an alternative to a narrowing of the Idea of 1789 and its degeneration into the anarchy of revolutionary France, followed by the reactionary impulse to empire. This appeal to German humanism likewise provides a counterpoint to the chauvinism of the Idea of 1914. In this light, Cassirer contests the image of Fichte as the "war philosopher" as celebrated in the discourse of *Kriegsphilosophie*. A Republican Fichte represents instead a "transcendental translation" of the idea of the French Revolution.[54] Cassirer upholds in the midst of the First World War the foundation of modern culture on individual freedom, the Republican constitution of nation-states, and the "continual self-renewing work of spirit on the way to the future." This opening of the future critically depends on sustaining an ontological difference between "actuality" and "ought," theoretically as well as historically. In Fichte's *Grundzüge des gegenwärtigen Zeitalters*, Cassirer recognizes the paramount significance of the separation between "ought" (*Sollen*) and "being" (*Sein*) for political thought. As Cassirer writes, "genuine reality" becomes constituted through the "infinite task of the Ought," thus sustaining a space of critique for the present and openness of creativity toward the future.[55]

Against Hegel's unification of "the ought," or the "Idea," and "being," or "actuality," with his identification of the state, in its historical conditionality, with the culmination of world-historical spirit – epitomized in Hegel's statement that the state is "the march of God in the world, the foundation of which is violence of reason realizing itself as will" – Cassirer insists on the openness of cosmopolitan spirit. As Cassirer writes:

> If for [Hegel] reason is not a mere ideal of the Ought, but signifies an "infinite power," which reveals itself in the world of events, and manifests itself as itself in history – this determination, however sublime it appears, obscures the simple insight, that the medium, through which the realization occurs, merely in moral work, which the individual has performed. The force which resides in this work, would be blunted if it is predicated on an "absolute consequence of world-spirit in history."[56]

Hegel fails in his reconciliation of freedom and form not only on account of his collapse of the difference and hence distance between "Sein" and "Sollen." Reason, for Cassirer, cannot be realized historically through

---

[54] Ferrari, *Stationen einer philosophischen Biographie*, p. 43.
[55] Cassirer, *Freiheit und Form*, p. 349.
[56] Cassirer, *Freiheit und Form*, p. 366.

the "infinite power" of state-sponsored and incarnated spirit.⁵⁷ Indeed, it is the responsibility of freedom "to be suspicious of reality and to criticize the existing form of the state."⁵⁸ Bound to ethical self-responsibility, the duty of philosophy demands a "heroism of renunciation."⁵⁹ In his essay "Hölderlin und der deutscher Idealismus," Cassirer further opposes Hölderlin and Hegel. Whereas Hegel subsumes the individual as well as the "Ought" to the historical actualization of the modern state as the abode of *Sittlichkeit*, Hölderlin "does not pretend to solve this primordial conflict, but strives only to show it and poetically realize its depth."⁶⁰ Hölderlin's nation is just as much Goethe's – a nation of individuals who strive to attain their ownmost through participation in a culture of ethical and aesthetic values, as well as critical reflection.

In *Freedom and Form* as well as his Berlin lecture on the state, Cassirer breaks off his discussion with a parting of ways between a republican Fichte and a conservative Hegel.⁶¹ Cassirer's silence on German political thinking in the mid to late nineteenth century is telling of a silent condemnation of the nationalism and *Realpolitik* of Leopold von Ranke and Heinrich von Treitschke. Implicit here is that the rise and decline of German political liberalism are bookended by calls for national liberation in 1813–15 and the Prussian unification of Germany in 1871.⁶² This abrupt ending of Cassirer's narrative suggests that the development of German spirit, centered on the relation between freedom and cultural forms, remains in suspended animation. In his Berlin lecture, Cassirer takes a further step in proposing that the liberal cosmopolitanism of German Idealism culminates with Hermann Cohen's cosmopolitan humanism, drawn from the sources of the Old Testament prophets in correlation to his restatement of Kantian ethics and political thought. In Cassirer's own reconciliation of *Deutschtum* and *Judentum* in his 1929 essay "Die Idee der Religion bei Lessing und Mendelssohn," the legacy of German eighteenth-century humanism resides with a dynamic conception of reason, a cosmopolitan vision of culture, and a religiously inflected humanism.⁶³

---

⁵⁷ Cassirer, *Freiheit und Form*, p. 366.
⁵⁸ Cassirer, *Freiheit und Form*, p. 366.
⁵⁹ E. Cassirer, *Descartes: Lehre-Persönlichkeit-Wirkung* (Hamburg: Felix Meiner Verlag, 1995), p. 275.
⁶⁰ E. Cassirer, *Idee und Gestalt. Goethe/Schiller/Hölderlin/Kleist. Fünf Aufsätze* (Berlin: Bruno Cassirer, 1921), p. 155.
⁶¹ Cassirer grants that Hegel's political conservatism was more a matter of the Right Hegelians than intrinsic to Hegel's thinking.
⁶² See L. Krieger, *The German Idea of Freedom: A History of a Political Tradition* (Boston, MA: Beacon Press, 1957).
⁶³ For Cassirer and the Liberal Jewish tradition of Cohen, Curthoys, *The Legacy of Liberal Judaism*.

In both texts from 1916, Cassirer insists that "the conception of the German state is one which must still be won" in turning to Schiller's unfinished poem "German Greatness" (*Deutsche Grösse*).[64] In commenting on Schiller's fragment, Cassirer calls attention to the unfinished trajectory of German humanism – a trajectory that has been abducted by the "spiritually narrow chauvinism" of post-Hegelian thinking. The power of the German state must draw from the power of German culture, not the other way around. The world-historical mission of German spirit – "elected by the world-spirit" – consists in struggling for the sake of *Menschenbildung* against empire and "the command of princes." In Friedrich Schlegel's words: "the genuine national gods are not Hermann and Wotan, but art and science." As Cassirer closes his appeal to the German nation: "We feel it more and more that the thought of the German state, as it was understood by thinkers of the eighteenth and nineteenth centuries, stands before its genuinely hardest and most profound historical test."[65] The future must decide, at this "decisive turning point, [whether] German Spirit has not become extinguished."[66]

World Philosophy

By the summer of 1917, the economic situation in Germany had become dire. During the *Kohlrübenwinter* of 1916–17, the home front experienced chronic shortages of potatoes, meat, and other essential products, thus compelling the Cassirers to relocate to West Berlin, closer to a plot of land on which they could grow their own cabbage and potatoes. Cassirer needed to travel one-and-half hours by tram to reach his *Kriegspresseamt* office, often without a seat in overcrowded and dirty carriages, and tried to make the most of his daily commutes, standing at the end of the carriage while reading, book in one hand, his other hand firmly on the railing.[67] On June 13, 1917, while riding home from his office, Cassirer experienced a sudden realization: The idea of symbolic forms "flashed upon him; a few minutes later, when he reached his home, the whole plan of this new

---

[64] Drafted in 1801 shortly after the peace accord of Lunéville.
[65] Cassirer, *Freiheit und Form*, p. 367.
[66] Cassirer, *Freiheit und Form*, p. 358. As David Lipton writes: "The war marked a philosophical turning point in his thinking and forced him to reconceive not only the idea of philosophy but the historical development of German thinking and with that European thinking it was during the war that he finally broke from his earlier philosophical thinking. It was during the war that he first proposed a cosmopolitan view of German history and understood the development of Germany as inseparable from the development of Europe"; *The Dilemma of a Liberal Intellectual in Germany*, p. 50.
[67] Cassirer, *Mein Leben mit Ernst Cassirer*, p. 120.

voluminous work was already in his mind, in essentially the form in which it was carried out in the course of the subsequent ten years."[68] Cassirer hurriedly sketched a project entitled "Philosophy of the Symbolic." This revelation launched him on a multidisciplinary exploration of the myriad forms of human cultural life, while retaining, indeed refashioning, his commitment to the transcendental orientation of Kant's enterprise:

> Suddenly the one-sidedness of the Kant-Cohen theory of knowledge became quite clear [...] It is not true that only human reason opens the door which leads to the understanding of reality, it is rather the whole of the human spirit, with all its functions and impulses, all its potencies of imagination, emotion, volition, and logical thinking [...] which determines and molds our conception of reality.[69]

In his thirty-two-page outline, Cassirer divided his project into different sections.[70] In the first section, "Psychology of the Symbolic," Cassirer sought to overcome the "false dualism" between "the internal" and "the external" through an analysis of the phenomenon of expression, which would reveal the necessary correlation between embodiment and "the soul." From this basis, Cassirer formulated the idea that consciousness (*das Psychische*) transcends itself and "means," or "signifies," something other than itself (the influence of Franz Brentano and Edmund Husserl and their respective theories of intentionality is here evident). What Cassirer calls the original function of presentation (*Vorstellung*) consists in the exhibition (*Darstellung*) – and not representation – of the "not-now in the now." The transcendent character of consciousness possesses an intrinsic temporal form that, Cassirer aimed to argue, undercut a strict distinction between "theoretical" and "practical." With this examination of expression in hand, Cassirer moved to consider the idea of "symbolic function," thus establishing a framework for his subsequent sections: "Logic of the Symbolic" would offer an analysis of logic and conceptual knowledge in terms of symbolic functions; "General Theory of Knowledge" would broaden this approach to include a theory of knowledge as such; "The Basic Problems of Aesthetics" would apply symbolic functions to aesthetics (a theme that remains missing from *The Philosophy of Symbolic Forms*). "Philosophy of the Symbolic" was meant to culminate in a final section,

---

[68] As told to Dmitry Gawronsky, "Ernst Cassirer: His Life and His Work," p. 24.
[69] Gawronsky, "Ernst Cassirer: His Life and His Work," p. 25.
[70] Cassirer's manuscript is held at the Beinecke Library at Yale University and has been published in A. Schubbach, *Die Genese des Symbolischen: Zu den Anfängen von Ernst Cassirers Kulturphilosophie* (Hamburg: Felix Meiner Verlag, 2016), pp. 367–435.

"Metaphysics of the Symbolic," on the "fundamental problem of metaphysics: the relation between truth and reality."

A first step in this newfound direction of thinking appeared in *Idee und Gestalt* (1921), a collection of essays on Schiller, Kleist, Hölderlin, and Goethe, which Cassirer conceived as an extension of *Freedom and Form*, thus splicing his discovered idea of symbolic forms into his counter-history of German spirit. In both works, the dominant figure emerging from Cassirer's counter-history is Goethe – "liberator of the Germans" (*Befreier der Deutschen*), as Goethe once called himself.[71] In two essays on Goethe, Cassirer establishes the pairing of Kant and Goethe as the axis of German humanism. From *Freedom and Form* and *Idee und Gestalt* until his final writings, this pairing, tilting toward Goethe, provides the mouthpiece as well as the source for Cassirer's philosophical thinking.[72] For Cassirer, Goethe fashioned a new form of life and a new form of art – indeed, a new form of thinking – with his discovery of the function of "the imagination for the truth of the real" that departed from the static dualism of "one-sided subjectivity" and a mimetic conception of art. As Cassirer writes: "The imagination [*Phantasie*] is for him [Goethe] the organ with which he not only builds new and beyond worlds 'over' reality but rather with which he interprets and comprehends this reality itself – be it 'inner' or 'outer' – in its whole configuration." In his poetry, philosophy of nature, scientific research, and literary writings, Goethe arrived at a "new form of objective life of spirit." In the figure of Prometheus, Goethe recognized the autonomy of creativity, centered on the production of forms, which liberated human life from "external and conventional life-forces." The human is the symbol-producing creature, who fashions objective mediations and hence meaningful ways of being in the world that animate and bind life to itself as well as allow for life to transcend itself. The mediation between "the subjective" and "the objective" is understood dynamically in terms of a correlation between the "becoming of objective forms" and "the concrete symbol" that life itself becomes. Where Cassirer would have once spoken of "function," he now, following Goethe, speaks of "dynamic form"; where once he would have looked to rational cognition, he now turns to the creativity of self-objectification, where life, in transmuting itself into spirit, becomes open to the world in the "living-momentary revelation of the not

[71] Cassirer, *Freiheit und Form*, p. 171.
[72] For the reception of Goethe in Neo-Kantianism and *Lebensphilosophie* (Dilthey, Gundolf, Simmel, George, Vorländer), see H. Kindermann, *Das Goethebild des 20. Jahrhunderts* (Darmstadt: WBG, 1966); and M. Saman, "Constructions of Goethe versus Constructions of Kant in German Intellectual Culture, 1900–1925," *Goethe Yearbook*, Vol. 21 (2014): 157–189.

yet explored [*lebendig-augenblickliche Offenbarung des Unerforschlichen*]."[73] The reciprocal interaction between finite, objective forms of meaning, stemming from the creative, or "spiritual," form-bestowal activity of life, and "the infinite" expanse of the world beyond, as the "not yet explored," reflects a nurturing polarity between self-knowledge and knowledge of the world. Life comes to increasingly know, and hence cultivate itself, the more life comes to know the world, and hence participate in a culture of vibrant forms of meaning; and it is only by means of bounded forms of meaning that the world becomes an unbounded horizon to be discovered and explored anew, as other than how we have known it, and hence as other than have we have come to know ourselves. Throughout the maturation of Cassirer's philosophy of symbolic forms, there is a creative employment of Goethe's quotations and figures of thinking (the morphology of forms, correlation as structured by polarity, not dialectical resolution, the rhythm of life in systolic and diastolic movements of spirit) in a reciprocal interplay with Cassirer's refashioning of a Kantian direction of questioning — to the point that there is a doubling of Goethe *in* Cassirer, much as there is a doubling of Cassirer *in* Goethe, passing through the mediating conjunction of Kant.[74]

As Cassirer argues, Kant's three critiques exhibit a movement of "expansion and enrichment," proceeding from logic to ethics to aesthetics, that establishes the unity of reason as well as the intelligible unity of nature and spirit. In this progression, the transcendental becomes decoupled from an exclusive orientation toward theoretical knowledge and mathematical (Newtonian) physics. Kant's discovery of the synthetic unity of knowledge, as structured by a priori forms of understanding and sensibility under the power of judgment, needs, however, to be extended into all "forms of spiritual *Gesetzlichkeit*," in which objectivity within all domains of human experience emerges. As Cassirer emphasizes, echoed as well in *Kants Leben und Lehre* (1919), Kant's Copernican revolution transformed how to problematize the relation between knowledge and its objects. Knowledge is the synthetic accomplishment of judgment, but here Cassirer is drawn to reflective judgment in the *Critique of Power of Judgment* (in contrast to determinate judgment in the *Critique of Pure Reason*). As he writes: "Nowhere else than on the particular is the function of the 'general' representable, as now becomes apparent. In this respect, the thought toward which the doctrine

---

[73] Cassirer, *Freiheit und Form*, p. 258.
[74] Cassirer, *Freiheit und Form*, p. 242. For Cassirer's "doubling" of Goethe, B. Naumann, *Philosophie und Poetik des Symbols. Cassirer und Goethe* (Munich: W. Fink Verlag, 1998).

of schematism aims has found its decisive completion and fulfillment only in *The Critique of the Power of Judgment*."[75] Rather than the application of concepts to the manifold of sensible givens, a symbolic form allows Cassirer to understand how objective forms of meaning are manifest in the particular "from below," as it were, within the warp and weft of experience itself. This reformulation of reflective judgment into symbolic forms opens the differentiated expanse of cultural configuration of meaning to transcendental reflection that attends to the "process" of constitution. Wherever there is a "determinate formation of being," one can inquire into the "how" of its meaning bestowal by uncovering the "creative activity of spirit [...] as what is authentically that which is original," that is, the source, from which forms of experience and hence meaning emerge.[76] The expression "creative activity of spirit" marks a cross-fertilization of Goethe and Kant, for although Kant critically investigated the three basic forms in which "the spontaneity of the spiritual" manifests itself, this threefold distinction of reason (mapped in Kant's three critiques) "does not exhaust the total concept of spiritual energies." Kant and Goethe, as two poles within an idealized reciprocal correlation, opened a "new way of understanding" and "new 'sense' of the world" that, on the one hand, remain "inexhaustible," but of which, on the other, Cassirer understands his "philosophy of the symbolic" to be its twentieth-century realization.[77] As Cassirer states in *Einstein's Theory of Relativity* (1921): "It is the task of systematic philosophy, which extends far beyond epistemology, to free the world from this one-sidedness. It has to grasp the whole system of symbolic forms [...] such as the general forms of theoretical, ethical, aesthetic, and religious understandings of the world."[78]

This transformation of an epistemologically oriented Kantian critical philosophy into a philosophy of the symbolic passes through the problem of language, as formulated by Humboldt and Goethe, each of whom discovers the presupposition of language for transcendental critique. In Kant, as Cassirer observes, the "cosmos of 'reason' is developed and laid out for us without its most important tool, without the *logos* that is alive and effective in language and belongs to it."[79] Following Humboldt,

---

[75] Cassirer, *Zur Philosophie und Politik*, p. 211.
[76] Cassirer, *Idee und Gestalt*, p. 68.
[77] E. Cassirer, "Kant und Goethe," in *Aufsätze und kleine Schriften (1922–1926)*, Ed. B von Recki, Ernst Cassirer Werke Hamburger Ausgabe 16 (Hamburg: Felix Meiner, 2003), p. 475.
[78] E. Cassirer, "Einstein's Theory of Relativity Considered from the Epistemological Standpoint," *The Monist*, Vol. 32, No. 3 (1922): 89–134.
[79] E. Cassirer, *The Warburg Years (1919–1933)*, trans. S. G. Lofts (New Haven, CT: Yale University Press, 2013), p. 104.

language is not merely an instrument of communication, a medium of representation, or a system of signs. Language is the "organ of thinking" through which the world receives "a spiritual imprint" of meaning. Language underpins and shapes, indeed animates, as the expression of "the soul's vital energy," the mediation between "consciousness" and "world." This transcendental embrace of language allows Cassirer to avoid a psychologization of transcendental concepts, insofar as concepts of the understanding are displaced by symbolic forms of meaning, while also opening the breadth of culture, and hence objective forms of experience, to transcendental analysis.[80] This symbolic recasting of transcendental critique becomes phenomenological in Cassirer's sense (again, under the sway of Goethe): The conditions of possibility cannot be specified without reference to the historical development of symbolic forms of objectification and their morphological variations.

The transformation of Cassirer's thinking from a (prewar) critical philosophy of reason to a (postwar) critical philosophy of culture received further impetus for broadening his horizon with his discovery of the Warburg Library, when he arrived in Hamburg to take up the chair of philosophy at the newly established University of Hamburg in 1919.[81] Cassirer recalls how his first visit to Warburg's library revealed in embodied literary form what had preoccupied with "for a long time": "for here, the history of art, the history of myth and religion, the history of language and culture were not only juxtaposed but also related to each other and to a common ideal center."[82] This "ideal center" is that "the

---

[80] See E. Cassirer, "The Concept of Symbolic Form in the Construction of the Human Sciences" and "The Kantian Elements in Wilhelm von Humboldt's Philosophy of Language" in *The Warburg Years*, pp. 72–100, 101–129.

[81] For Cassirer in Hamburg during the 1920s, E. Levine, *Dreamland of Humanists: Warburg, Cassirer, Panofsky, and the Hamburg School* (Chicago: University of Chicago Press, 2013). In 1920, the director of the Warburg Library, Fritz Saxl, recalled that Cassirer "listened attentively as I explained to him Warburg's intentions in placing books on philosophy next to books on astrology, magic, and folklore, and in linking the sections on art with those on literature, religion, and philosophy." As Saxl remarks: "Cassirer understood at once," and when he left, he declared: "This library is dangerous. I shall either have to avoid it altogether or imprison myself here for years. The philosophical problems involved are close to my own, but the concrete historical material which Warburg has collected is overwhelming." As Saxl further noted: "In one hour, this man had understood more of the essential ideas embodied in that library than anybody I had met before." Warburg at the time was a patient under Binswanger's care at the Bellevue asylum in Kreuzlingen, Switzerland, after having succumbed to a mental breakdown in October 1918. See K. Lang, *Chaos and Cosmos: On the Image in Aesthetics and History* (Ithaca, NY: Cornell University Press, 2006), chapter 3. For significant differences between Cassirer's symbolic form and Warburg's *Pathosformel*, G. Didi-Huberman, *Atlas, or the Anxious Gay Science*, trans. S. Lillis (Chicago: University of Chicago Press, 2018); and C. Johnson, *Memory, Metaphor, and Aby Warburg's Atlas of Images* (Ithaca, NY: Cornell University Press, 2012), chapter 4.

[82] Cassirer, *The Warburg Years*, pp. 72–73.

spiritual," in its manifold symbolic forms of realization, "can fulfill itself in no other way than in its history, but it does not remain in this *one* dimension of the historical." What the Warburg Library fertilized for Cassirer was his basic contention that the senses of being are multiple, as historically and culturally configured, and that spirit itself achieves its own being ("raised to the form of being") in no other manner than through these manifold forms of symbolic becoming. A shared fascination with Goethe's theory of symbols prompted a cross-fertilization between Cassirer's and Warburg's conceptions of the symbolic form, the movement of "near" and "distant" within symbolic meaning constitution, and the dynamic of polarity. The intellectual and cultural environment of Hamburg, gathered around the university and the Warburg Library, as well as the optimism of embarking on the establishment of a new culture in the aftermath of war, channeling the ideals of Weimar Classicism and *Bildung*, served as both a confirmation and a catalyst for the crystallization of Cassirer's thinking. Hamburg – "the dreamland of Humanists" – provided a counterpoint to the pervasive malaise and outlook of crisis increasingly brewing in the aftermath of Germany's defeat. This interwar gloom represented, as Cassirer remarked years later, "an imminent threat to the whole extent of our ethical and cultural life."[83] This broadening of Cassirer's intellectual vision, fostered by his revelatory discovery of the Warburg Library as a "set of problems" – his second, compounding revelation after the tram-ride revelation in 1917 – effectively transformed his philosophy program into a "world philosophy," as much a philosophy of the world in its historical and cultural diversity as a philosophy *for* the world with its cosmopolitan vision of diverse ways of world manifestation.

Journey around the World

The Philosophy of Symbolic Forms appeared in three volumes: on language (1923); on mythical thinking (1925); and a phenomenology of knowledge (1929). A fourth and culminating volume, begun in 1928, was never completed on account of Cassirer's time-consuming duties as Rector of the University of Hamburg and his exile from Germany in 1933. At the center of Cassirer's reformulated transcendental critique is neither the problem

---

[83] E. Cassirer, *An Essay on Man: An Introduction to a Philosophy of Human Culture* (New Haven, CT: Yale University Press, 1946), p. 18.

of knowledge in the sense of scientific cognition nor the threefold dimensions of reason (knowledge, ethics, aesthetics), but the fundamental forms of "world understanding" (*Weltverstehen*).[84] As Cassirer explains, "the 'philosophy of symbolic forms' grows from the critical transcendental question and builds upon it. It is 'pure contemplation,' not of a single form, but of all – the cosmos of pure forms – and it seeks to trace this cosmos back to the 'conditions of possibility.'"[85] With this enlargement and enrichment of critical idealism's mandate to reflect upon the a priori conditions of possibility of experience, Cassirer transforms the traditional faculties of reason into ways of world understanding, as structured by symbolic forms. "Reason," he writes, "is a very inadequate term with which to comprehend the forms of man's cultural life in all their richness and variety."[86] Indeed, there occurs a radicalization of Kant's "revolution in the manner of thinking" and novel direction of questioning. Rather than inquire as to "what there is," Kant advanced the fundamental question of *how* "what there is" can be experienced at all, thus placing the question of sense (*Sinn*) at the focal point of transcendental thought rather than the question of being *or* knowledge; ontology as well as epistemology must be recast within the framework of the problem of sense. As Cassirer writes in his 1927 essay "Erkenntnistheorie nebst den Grenzfragen der Logik und Denkpsychologie":

> More and more we have been forced to recognize that that sphere of theoretical meaning that we designate with the names "knowledge" and "truth" represents only *one*, however, significant and fundamental, layer of meaning. [...] We must, in other words, grasp the problem of knowledge and the problem of truth as particular cases of the more general problem of meaning [*Sinn*].

This "general problem of meaning" (or "sense" [*Sinn*]) is reflected in the configuration of the three volumes of *The Philosophy of Symbolic Forms*. Beginning with an analysis of language as a symbolic form (Volume One), Cassirer progresses to an analysis of mythical thinking as symbolic of form (Volume Two), before addressing the problem of knowledge and truth in

---

[84] As Cassirer remarks: "the philosophy of symbolic forms directs its regard not exclusively and not in the first place to pure scientific, exact apprehensions of the world [*Weltbegreifen*], but to all directions of understanding the world [*Weltverstehens*]"; E. Cassirer, *The Philosophy of Symbolic Forms*, I, trans. R. Manheim (New Haven, CT: Yale University Press, 1965), p. 16.
[85] E. Cassirer, *The Philosophy of Symbolic Forms*, IV, trans. J. M. Krois (New Haven, CT: Yale University Press, 1996), p. 189.
[86] Cassirer, *An Essay on Man*, p. 26.

Volume Three.[87] The domain covered by the analyses of language, mythical thinking, and perceptual experience – falling under the symbolic forms of expression and presentation – represents "the natural world concept" and "naive" relationship between "intuition" and "concept" (reconfigured into symbolic forms). The passage to a critical reflection and theory of the concept – namely, a theory of scientific cognition and "pure signification" – requires a phenomenology of knowledge, the subtitle of Volume Three. As Cassirer writes:

> The philosophy of symbolic forms does not want to be a metaphysics of knowledge, but a phenomenology of knowledge. It takes the word "knowledge" in the broadest and most comprehensive sense. It understands by it not only the act of scientific comprehension and theoretical explanation, but every mental activity, in which we build up a "world" in its characteristic design, in its order and in its "being-so."[88]

In speaking of a phenomenology of knowledge, Cassirer specifies that "I am using the word 'phenomenology' not in its modern sense but with its fundamental meaning as established and systematically grounded by Hegel." Cassirer understands "modern phenomenology" as "starting much less from Kant than from Brentano's concept of consciousness" as intentionality, and further developed in Husserl's transcendental phenomenology.[89] By distinguishing his phenomenology from Husserl's, Cassirer offers an alternative reconfiguration of transcendental thinking, not along the contours of a rigorous science based on the constitutive accomplishments of transcendental subjectivity, but, aligned with Hegel, a phenomenology of symbolic forms as ways of world understanding and self-realizations of spirit. As Cassirer remarks, "we start with the concept of the whole: the whole is the true (Hegel). But the truth of the whole [*die Wahrheit ist das Ganze*] can always only be grasped in a particular 'aspect.' This is 'knowledge' in the *broadest* sense – 'seeing' the whole 'in' an aspect, through the

---

[87] Cassirer's analysis of symbolic forms in his three volumes does not in principle exclude investigations of other symbolic forms. In the Preface to the second volume, he mentions other symbolic forms – economics, technology, morality, and law – not included in his own studies. For Cassirer's analysis of technology as a symbolic form, N. de Warren, "Spirit in the Age of Technical Production," in *Interpreting Cassirer*, ed. S. Truwant (Cambridge, UK: Cambridge University Press, 2020): 109–129.
[88] E. Cassirer, "Zur Logik des Symbolbegriffs," in *Wesen und Wirkung des Symbolbegriffs* (Darmstadt: Wissenschaftliche Buchgesellschaft, 1956): 201–230; p. 208.
[89] E. Cassirer, *The Philosophy of Symbolic Forms*, III, trans. R. Manheim (New Haven, CT: Yale University Press, 1965), p. 196. For the relation between Cassirer and Husserl, N. de Warren, "*Eine Reise um die Welt*: Cassirer's Cosmological Phenomenology," in *New Approaches to Neo-Kantianism*, pp. 82–108.

medium of this aspect."⁹⁰ The "concrete whole" of spirit must be rendered intelligible in terms of the totality of its diverse manifestations, as related to each other and gravitating around a common center; namely, *freedom*. Spirit becomes manifest through symbolic forms of objectification in "the rhythm [of spirit] in the self-movement of concepts." The term "rhythm" reveals once again Goethe's spectral doubling; it is not the dialectical movement of concepts but a systolic–diastolic polarity that is the "proper and unique substantial element of spirit itself." Rather than the movement of the Hegelian concept coming to itself in the self-realization of spirit, there is the movement of symbolic forms opening onto self-knowledge of the concrete whole of spirit.

This crucial difference, marking the doubling of Goethe, is evinced by Cassirer's (most likely) deliberate misquotation of Hegel's celebrated statement *das Wahre ist das Ganze*.⁹¹ This discrepancy between Hegel's statement and Cassirer's *die Wahrheit ist das Ganze* is telling of a difference between the closed totality of Hegel's *Logic of Science* and *Encyclopedia of the Philosophical Sciences* (from which Hegel's statement is drawn) and Cassirer's open whole of *The Philosophy of Symbolic Forms*.⁹² Rather than an encyclopedia of knowledge (Hegel) or an archive of phenomenological archeological finds (Husserl), Cassirer's is the philosophy of the world library – the accumulated ways of world understanding open to transcendental reflection on the dynamic conditions of possibility. As Cassirer writes: "Reason has another function than deriving the manifold of forms of culture, but the unity of reason manifests itself in revealing directions in which culture progresses unendingly."⁹³ Not a suspension of the world in search of constitutive acts of consciousness but research into cultural and historical forms, Cassirer proposes a "journey around the world," exploring within a transcendental framework the different forms of meaning formation ("symbolic functions") and ways of world understanding in a cosmological (and cosmopolitan) vision of the whole in the making.

---

⁹⁰ Cassirer, *The Philosophy of Symbolic Forms*, III, p. 193.
⁹¹ G. W. Hegel, *The Phenomenology of Spirit*, trans. A. V. Miller (Oxford: Oxford University Press, 1977), p. 11.
⁹² D. Verene, *The Origins of the Philosophy of Symbolic Forms* (Evanston, IL: Northwestern University Press, 2011), p. 45. As Verene remarks: "Given Cassirer's great power of learning and memory, it seems unlikely that he misremembers how Hegel phrases this famous assertion." For differences between Hegel and Cassirer, pp. 45–48, 78 ff. See also Philonenko, *L'école de Marbourg*, p. 150 ff. As Philonenko observes: "En 1907 Cassirer conçoit encore la phénoménologie dans le sens de Hegel et Lambert"; p. 128.
⁹³ Cassirer, *Freiheit und Form*, p. 372.

It should not be surprising that Cassirer begins this three-volume project with an investigation of language as a symbolic form for his transformation of a critique of reason into a critique of culture, for it is the discovery of language as an "organ of thinking" and "vital energy of spirit" in Humboldt and Goethe that enabled Kant's transcendental directive to embrace the full range of meaning formations, insofar as language sets up a world between consciousness and its objects, a world of meaning in which humanity achieves self-expression. Through this engagement with the problem of language, Cassirer formulates three kinds of symbolic forms that populate *The Philosophy of Symbolic Forms*: expression, or expressive meaning (*Ausdruck*); presentative meanings (*Darstellung*); and pure signification (*reine Bedeutung*). Each of these symbolic forms is keyed to a different conception of language: as mimetic reproduction (where the sign enacts and absorbs the signified); as analogical presentation (where the sign and the signified are distinguished and set in a relation of correspondence); and as symbolic expression (where invariant, pure relational forms, and the function of signification itself, are grasped in their self-sufficiency, that is, the self-regulated bestowal of signification).[94]

Symbolic forms are "ways by which spirit proceeds in its objectivation," yet each symbolic form must be described in both its "subjective" and "objective" aspects. Expression, presentation, and pure signification correspond to the objective forms of myth, language, and scientific cognition and mathematics. These are the different objective manifestations of spirit, and although Cassirer only examines myth, language, and scientific cognition in *The Philosophy of Symbolic Forms*, he recognizes that religion, technology, and art (as initially envisioned in his 1917 outline) would require their own analysis as symbolic forms. These objective functions cannot be separated from subjective functions, understood as different modes of consciousness. As exemplified by "mythical thinking," in the symbolic form of expression, consciousness does not experience the world at a distance from itself; that is, there is no separation between "consciousness" and "world" or "appearance" and "reality." Rather than an objectified world posited "as independent being," the world is understood as saturated with magical forces and mythic significance; affectivity predominates for "mythical

---

[94] This threefold structure draws significantly from Goethe's "Simple Imitation of Nature, Manner, Style" (1789), where style is defined as "the highest expression of objectivity, but not the simple objectivity of existence, but rather the objectivity of artistic spirit [...] that is, the both free and regulated nature of form-giving"; Cassirer, "Der Begriff der Symbolischen Form im Aufbau der Geisteswissenschaften," in *Schriften zur Philosophie der symbolischen Formen*, ed. M. Lauschte (Hamburg: Felix Meiner Verlag, 2009), p. 183.

consciousness." With "exhibition function" (*Darstellungsfunktion*), by contrast, the world becomes experienced in terms of consciousness and objectified presentations (*Darstellungen*).

A central aim of Cassirer's phenomenology of knowledge is to show how the "construction of the world of perception" entails "ever-richer and more-diverse sense-functions." Symbolic functions gain traction on the basis of what Cassirer calls "symbolic pregnance," by which he understands "how a lived-perceptive-experience, as a 'sensible' lived-experience, contains in itself at the same time a certain non-intuitive 'sense' and brings it to immediate concrete perception."[95] In this manner, Cassirer rejects a dualism between "content" and "form," "intuition" and "concept," as well as, significantly, a conception of consciousness either as passive receptivity or as actively constructing objects of sense experience (in both senses: sensible and imbued with sense or meaning). With "symbolic pregnance," Cassirer's insight is not just the claim that "matter," or perceptual content, is always "saturated" by a determinate (symbolic) form of sense, but that the content of perceptual experience is never fixed to one determinate form. Since the relation between "matter" and "form" is relative, not absolute, the synthesis of perceptual content and its possible forms of meaning is itself variable. As Cassirer writes: "Here we are not dealing with bare perceptive data, one to which some sort of apperceptive acts are later grafted, through which they are interpreted, judged, transformed."[96] Each particular perception of the world is both a "differential" – a distinct aspect of the world rendered salient – as well as an "integral of experience," by which Cassirer understands a concentrated apprehension of a totality of experience, as reflected and refracted along further horizons, or "lines," of symbolic relations. More trenchantly expressed, each perceptual experience of the world is a "vector" of ever diversified (and self-diversifying) experiences.

By way of illustration, Cassirer takes the perception of "a simple line." Depending on the symbolic function in play, a line (drawn on a chalkboard, etched in wood, etc.) can "mean" differently: a mood is expressed in a line drawn by Matisse; a geometrical object is cognitively apprehended on a line drawn in a geometry textbook; a boundary between spaces is marked by a line drawn in the sand. In each instance, the visibility of the line, its materiality, is meshed with its legibility of meaning, with the "sense" of meaning in each instance varying: an expression of mood, a visualization

---

[95] Cassirer, *The Philosophy of Symbolic Forms*, III, p. 239.
[96] Cassirer, *The Philosophy of Symbolic Forms*, III, p. 202.

of geometrical form, and so on. Perceptual experience is imbued with an "articulation" of a determinate *Sinnfügung*. The line appears differently since it means differently (i.e., it incarnates different senses). In each of these cases, for example with the prosaic line expressing a mood, "we do not merely read our own inner states subjectively and arbitrarily into the spatial form [of the line]; rather, the form gives itself to us as an animated totality, an independent manifestation of life."[97] Meaning inheres *in* perceptual sensation; the mood is expressed *in the animation of the line itself*. The "same" physical inscription can thus take on different forms of visibility *and* legibility: "its [the line's] pure visibility is never conceivable outside and independently of a determinate form of vision." There is, in other words, no underlying inscription ("primary sensation") of a line onto which is (then) grafted a particular sense as "mood," "geometrical object," and so on. The concept of "symbolic pregnance" entwines "visibility" and "legibility" (or "speakability," as it were) into the manifestation of the world.

Although a symbolic form "saturates" the content of experience, meaning is thereby not *in* consciousness but in the world. As Cassirer writes: "content is not simply *in* consciousness, filling it by its mere existence—rather, it speaks to consciousness and tells it something."[98] Symbolic ways of world making are not the singular achievements of a pure consciousness; the world as constituted transcendentally is not "carried" *in* consciousness, but instead "flows through" consciousness "like a single stream of life."[99] In this way, symbolic forms do not "bridge" a finished inner world and a finished outer world, since on the contrary symbolic forms originally constitute the "separation and sorting out of the I and the world."[100] Symbolic forms are transcendental forms of tension, the original "in-between" or "spacing" of mind and world, giving sense and direction to both. As Cassirer writes, a philosophy of symbolic forms is "concerned with the dynamics of the giving of meaning in and through which the growth and delimitation of specific spheres of being and meaning occur in the first place."[101] In this respect, the transcendental dynamic of symbolic forms is neither "active" nor "passive." Consciousness is not a necromancer that would enliven what is merely given and "dead." The original phenomenon of "symbolic pregnance," "without which neither

---

[97] Cassirer, *The Philosophy of Symbolic Forms*, III, p. 200.
[98] Cassirer, *The Philosophy of Symbolic Forms*, III, p. 191.
[99] Cassirer, *The Philosophy of Symbolic Forms*, III, p. 202.
[100] Cassirer, *The Philosophy of Symbolic Forms*, IV, p. 60.
[101] Cassirer, *The Philosophy of Symbolic Forms*, IV, p. 4.

an object nor a subject, neither a unity of the thing nor a unity of the self would be given to us," can be said to be *medial* in character. The discovery of "symbolic pregnance," as anchoring a "true phenomenology of perception," reveals "a new angle on how the analysis of consciousness *can never lead back to absolute elements*: it is precisely the pure relation which governs the constitution of consciousness and which stands out in it as a genuine a priori, an essentially first factor."[102]

With the "function of signification" (*Bedeutungsfunktion*) as operative in scientific cognition (the natural sciences and mathematics), objects of experience are not understood as substantial entities existing independently of consciousness, nor as inseparable from the affective and expressive manifestation of consciousness. "Pure thinking" attains "genuine objectivity" defined by relationality, invariance of structure, and lawfulness.[103] Scientific thinking discovers a functional understanding of "what there is" based on an invariance of experience open to a "new synthesis"; that is, new discoveries and formations of significance. From the vantage point of "pure thinking," the "truth of the whole" becomes disclosed; namely, that "the one reality can only be indicated and defined as the ideal boundary of the many changing theories; however, the positing of this boundary itself is not arbitrary, but indispensable, insofar as it is only through it that the *continuity of experience* is established."[104] This "continuity of experience" is not fixed or absolute, however, for as Cassirer writes: "We do not need the objectivity of absolute things, but rather the objective determinateness of the *paths of experience itself*." These "paths of experience" are opened through bounded symbolic forms, leading spirit further on its journey around the world into the "unexplored." Importantly, with the attainment of mathematics and scientific cognition, "spirit for the first time truly discovers itself as that which contains within itself the principle, the beginning of movement."[105] Spirit becomes conscious of itself in attaining scientific knowledge of objective reality – not that it recognizes itself in objective being, but it discovers objective being as "created by thought itself [...] in full freedom, in pure self-activity of spirit."[106]

---

[102] Cassirer, *The Philosophy of Symbolic Forms*, III, p. 203.
[103] As he writes: "It is characteristic of philosophical knowledge as the 'self-knowledge of reason' that it does not create a principally new symbolic form, it does not found in this sense a new creative modality—but grasps the entire modalities as that which are: as characteristic symbolic forms"; Cassirer, *The Philosophy of Symbolic Forms*, III, p. 232.
[104] Cassirer, *The Philosophy of Symbolic Forms*, III, p. 550.
[105] Cassirer, *The Philosophy of Symbolic Forms*, III, p. 341.
[106] Cassirer, *The Philosophy of Symbolic Forms*, III, p. 335.

Although Cassirer stresses that symbolic forms are irreducible to each other, he nonetheless places them in a progressive movement from expression to presentation to pure signification. The progression from myth to language to scientific knowledge does not involve dialectical sublation of a "lower" form into a "higher" form. There is no universal *telos* to the development of humanity, but an incessant development of novel forms of meaning, as structured by the dynamic of symbolic forms, and each a distinct view of the world according to its own lawfulness or norms.[107] The symbolic forms of myth, language, and pure concept correspond respectively to three forms of world understanding: expression, representation, and scientific cognition. Each of these symbolic forms structures in an a priori manner a way of having the world in view, as well as an orientation of subjectivity within the world. All symbolic forms, on this view, are related to the determination of "truth as such," which can only be grasped as knowledge of the whole, where the whole is refracted in each symbolic form. With the progression from expression to representation to thinking, the world becomes progressively (historically as well as systematically) expanded and diversified through a multiplication of "bands of meaning."

In this sense, Cassirer's symbolic morphology of culture emphasizes the value of interaction among cultural forms and their mutual irreducibility as well as, implicitly, a critique of the reduction of humanity's cultural diversity to one form of understanding. This intrinsic valuation of complexity and relationality suggests that the culture of humanity is an irreducible complexity of *possible* ways of world understanding, the conditions of which are examined in *The Philosophy of Symbolic Forms* as realizations of human freedom.[108] Ultimately, the cultivation of diversity, converging toward the truth of the world, will "point to a source of truth emanating from beyond the sphere of the human representation and of human will, a transcendental source of the Good that, over and again, Cassirer qualified in Platonic terms as a 'truth beyond being' (*epekeina tes ousias*)."[109]

---

[107] See J.-M. Krois, "Urworte: Cassirer als Goethe-Interpret," in *Kulturkritik nach Ernst Cassirer*, eds. E. Rudolph and B-O. Küpers (Hamburg: Felix Meiner Verlag, 1995): 297–324.

[108] See E. Rudolph, "From Culture to Politics: The 'Aufhebung' of Ethics in Ernst Cassirer's Political Philosophy in Comparison with the 'Political Theology' of Ernst Kantorowicz," in *Symbolic Forms and Cultural Studies: Ernst Cassirer's Theory of Culture*, eds. Cyrus Hamlin and John Michael Krois (New Haven, CT: Yale University Press, 2004): 117–126; p. 120. As Rudolph argues: "In *Myth of the State* Cassirer complements his implicit ethos of cultural complexity with the outline of a philosophy of politics […] In my opinion, the value of this text […] lies in the fact that it takes the political message *implicit* in his 1920s philosophy of culture and renders it *explicit*"; p. 119. In *Myth of the State* "the destruction of freedom as an act of freedom may well lead to cultural suicide."

[109] J. Barash, "Der Ort der Religion bei Ernst Cassirer," in *Die Gegenwärtigkeit deutsch-jüdischen Denkens*, eds. A. Noor and J. Matveev (Munich: Fink Verlag, 2011): 383–394.

"Eins und Alles"

In May 1933, a few months after Hitler's consolidation of dictatorial power in March, Cassirer resigned his professorship in Hamburg and went into exile with his family, first at All Souls College in Oxford, then at the University of Göteborg in Sweden, and finally in 1941 at Yale University. This forced displacement permanently interrupted the completion of *The Philosophy of Symbolic Forms*, thus condemning Cassirer's magnum opus to philosophical exile in its unfinished state as well as into historical exile, insofar as European humanity and culture, already under threat in 1914–18, now seemed to have been definitively destroyed, at least for Cassirer, who died before the end of the Second World War. This catastrophic intrusion, once again, of history and, more specifically, the "spiritually narrow chauvinism of these times" into Cassirer's life and thought did not, however, spell an end to his indefatigable writing. Although history had eclipsed his cosmopolitan thinking, it could not extinguish the source of its creative freedom and, in fact, arguably sent Cassirer back to where it all began in *Freedom and Form*, retold and reconceived in his final (and posthumously published) work, *The Myth of the State*.

In the preface to the third volume of *The Philosophy of Symbolic Forms*, Cassirer indicates that a "final chapter defining and justifying the basic attitude of the Philosophy of Symbolic Forms toward present-day philosophy as a whole" – indeed, "the crucial part that should have concluded this volume" – should have been included, but owing to the already sizable dimensions of this phenomenology of knowledge, he judged it prudent to reserve this text for a future publication, "'Life' and 'Spirit' – Toward a Critique of Contemporary Philosophy." In this de facto conclusion to the third volume, where his phenomenology of knowledge arrives at the metaphysical interaction between life and spirit, Cassirer critically engages with representatives of *Lebensphilosophie* (Nietzsche, Bergson, Scheler, and Simmel) as well as, crucially given his legendary confrontation at Davos, Heidegger. These reflections on "life and spirit" are meant as well to motivate and situate the never completed final (and fourth) volume, *The Metaphysics of Symbolic Forms*, which would have brought his project to completion from its initial revelation in 1917, and for which only a fragmentary draft exists, entitled *Basisphänomene* (written in 1940).

In taking stock of "the long path of investigations" in the three volumes of *The Philosophy of Symbolic Forms*, Cassirer remarks in "'Life' and 'Spirit'" that a philosophy of symbolic forms "cannot stop here," namely, with the treatment of "pure signification" and the foundations of natural-scientific thinking.[110] What has been learned, however, from this phenomenology of knowledge is that symbolic forms cannot be understood as spanning "a *finished* 'inner world' and a *finished* 'outer world'" or "an 'I' and 'non-I' as given and fixed starting points." As Cassirer writes, "the world of spirit is no more 'immanent' within the world of 'life' than it is 'transcendent' of it," and this enfolding of inside and outside (as developed in the three volumes of his work) is differently configured according to various symbolic forms. And yet, what remains to be understood is how this plurality of symbolic ways of world understanding itself is grounded, and indeed arises from life itself. The threefold symbolic dimensions of expression, representation, and signification contribute to a "living web of relations" – worlds upon worlds. These different ways of "worlding," as it were, in conjunction with different forms of life, constitute the "actual concrete reality of Spirit," which "consists in the fact that all its different basic aspects mesh with one another and coalesce, that, in the true sense of the word, they are 'concrescent.'"[111] Although different ways of world understanding are unified into a whole, they are not reducible to a single origin or principle. Cassirer thus rejects any form of monism, where the plurality of ways of world-making would be expressions of a common substance ("Being") or substantialized spirit. Having rejected an ontological foundation to ways of worlding, a promising alternative would seem to reside with Kant's transcendental approach, which looks for the ground of objectivity ("objective spirit") in the constitutive activity of subjectivity or, as with Heidegger, in a fundamental ontology of Dasein's ways of being-in-the-world. It would seem, in other words, that "all these different forms and directions of culture meet and come together again and again in creative subjectivity itself," hence pointing to an understanding of the subjectivity of the subject as the foundation for the meaning-bestowal function of symbolic forms.

This turn to the problem of subjectivity as the basis for a phenomenology of symbolic forms should not be taken as an answer to a question, however, but rather as the starting point for recasting the problem that had traditionally been understood as the problem of subjectivity. With this contention, Cassirer seeks to develop a "new conception of the problem [of subjectivity]," beyond the framework of Kant's cognitive subjectivity (reason as a system of faculties) or Hegel's absolute spirit. In so doing, Cassirer turns to

---

[110] Cassirer, *The Philosophy of Symbolic Forms*, IV, p. 4.
[111] Cassirer, *The Philosophy of Symbolic Forms*, IV, p. 5.

the concept of life as an alternative to traditional notions of the soul and consciousness. Under the influence of Georg Simmel's *The View of Life*, Cassirer argues that the metaphysical discovery of life represents a uniquely modern form of conceptualization, which displaced the substance ontology of classical metaphysics as well as the spontaneity metaphysics of German Idealism. Moreover, the problem of life, in its metaphysical significance, displaces the classical metaphysical problems of nature and freedom, being and becoming, the one and the many.[112] As Cassirer writes: "The opposites of 'Being' and 'Becoming,' of 'One' and 'Many,' 'Matter' and 'Form,' 'Soul' and 'Body' all appear now to have been dissolved into this one completely fundamental antithesis" between life and spirit. Neither life nor spirit is to be taken, nevertheless, as a modern surrogate for the classical idea of God or Being. Against "the older metaphysics" of substance as well as the transcendental faculties of reason (and its distinction between sensibility, thinking, and volition), the concept of life "recognizes no substantiality other than that which consists of pure actuality alone"; yet the "pure actuality of life" cannot by the same token be determined as the spontaneity of the understanding (Kant), the self-positing of the ego (Fichte), or the dialectical reconciliation, and hence self-identity, with itself as spirit (Hegel). Cassirer looks beyond this triumvirate of German Idealism to Goethe, for whom the "actual movement" of life consists in "an oscillation between two extreme phases," namely, form-making and form-transcending, self-binding and self-unbinding. As Cassirer writes: "Becoming is in essence neither mere life nor mere form; rather, it is the becoming of form – *genesis eis ousian* or genesis into being."[113] Or, phrased in another lexicon meant to stave off the temptation of reading into Cassirer's a Goethean morphogenetic pantheism: "The *forma formans* that becomes *forma formata*, which it must become for the sake of its own self-preservation without ever becoming reduced to it, retains the power to regain itself from it, to be born again as *forma formans* – this is what is distinctive of Spirit and culture."

From this primordial difference between life and spirit, Cassirer contours a philosophical anthropology that he planned to develop further as the basis for the human sciences along two parallel directions: the human as "the subject-object of culture" and as "the subject-object of nature." In this manner, centered on an understanding of *homo symbolicus*

---

[112] "Of all the thinkers who are part of this movement [*Lebensphilosophie*], perhaps no one has so strongly felt its origin and brought it so clearly to consciousness as Simmel has done"; Cassirer, *The Philosophy of Symbolic Forms*, IV, p. 8.
[113] Cassirer, *The Philosophy of Symbolic Forms*, IV, p. 15. Cassirer here quotes Plato's *Philebus* (26d8).

(or, alternatively, the *animal symbolicum*) as *homo interrogans,* Cassirer's philosophical anthropology recasts the question of the human:

> In fact, we can now predict that the fundamental answer to the question of the "essential concept" of humankind which it seeks can come only from a philosophy of "symbolic forms" [...] In the medium of language and art, in myth and theoretical knowledge, that turnabout or intellectual revolution takes place which permits humankind to set the world aside in order to draw it closer. By virtue of these "forms" humankind attains proximity to the world and a distance from it which no other creature possesses.[114]

In a complex weave of arguments, for which Cassirer in his 1940 manuscript *Basisphänomene* provided the barest of outlines, the foundation for his phenomenology of symbolic forms is placed within what Goethe called the "basis phenomenon" (or "primordial phenomenon"). As with other aspects of Cassirer's *Doppelgänger* relationship with Goethe's thinking, Cassirer creatively tailors this fecund conception to his own ends, even as he looks to mirror, indeed amplify, Goethe's original discovery. Cassirer's own reflections on the "primordial phenomenon" are clustered around three statements from Goethe's *Maxims and Reflections* (from the morphological reflections of 1822); each of these statements expresses a different "primordial phenomenon," and yet each of these expressions mirrors the concept of primordial phenomena as such, which can only be grasped through a myriad of crystalline reflections. For Goethe, "primordial phenomena" are characterized by a constitutive obscurity and creative play of visibility and invisibility that catalyze symbolic formation. For his part, Cassirer identifies three primordial phenomena of *Ich-phenomenon, Wirkens-phenomenon,* and *Werk-phenomenon*. In keeping with Goethe's understanding of the enactive relation between primordial phenomenon and symbolic expression, each of these primordial phenomena underpins "symbolic pregnance." In adopting Goethe's "primordial phenomenon" for the nonfoundational foundation of his own philosophy of the symbolic, Cassirer recognizes a basic tension within his thinking, one that risks fracturing, if not exploding, the methodological and systematic presuppositions of his (form of) transcendental idealism. As he wonders: "How can we do justice to the Goethean demand for the recognition of 'primordial phenomena' and to the Cartesian-Kantian demand for 'reflection' in knowledge and philosophy?"[115] For, indeed, primordial phenomena are

---

[114] Cassirer, *The Philosophy of Symbolic Forms*, IV, p. 38.
[115] For a discussion of the changes in Cassirer's conceptions of life and spirit, and relation to three basis phenomena, see T. Bayer, *Cassirer's Metaphysics of Symbolic Forms* (New Haven, CT: Yale University Press, 2001), pp. 149–152.

more original than a priori conditions of cognition and transcendental operations of consciousness, and, in this sense, can be characterized as movements of manifestation at the core of which an essential nonmanifestation abides, "before-thinking" and "before posited being"; hence, in his 1940 manuscript, Cassirer's interest in theories of common sense, immediate experience, and belief. And yet, primordial phenomena are animated by a polarity between *arche* and *telos*; namely, an origin as well as a finality. As Goethe observes: "Natural system: a contradictory expression. Nature has no system; she has – she is – life and development from an unknown centre toward an unknowable periphery. Thus, observation of nature is limitless."[116]

Goethe's Maxim 391: "Life is the rotating movement about itself [and] impulse to nurture this life." From this image of life as an incessant transition from one state to another, which, for Cassirer, underpins "the biological, the psychological, and the transcendental," the rotating movement of the "monad" of life manifests itself through a metamorphosis of symbolic forms. Across this plurality of symbol forms, the uniqueness and unity of life become expressed in a self-mirroring perspectivism, or what Goethe called *"wiederholten Spiegelungen,"* where each symbolic formation is a manifest radiation of primordial life.[117] Life in this original movement is "a streaming being-moved" without rest, incessantly binding and unbinding itself to its transitory states. This monadic manifestation of life shows itself as a "stream of consciousness" that Cassirer associates with the primordial temporality of life's Heraclitean flux. The temporality of life is neither "active" nor "passive." It is not a temporality produced by consciousness nor registered by consciousness; the living stream of "self-movement" and "self-temporalization [...] encompasses the totality of all aspects of life, the present, past, and future." This first primordial phenomenon of monadic life is characterized as the "I-phenomenon" or the "phenomenon of the self," as materialized in the feeling of life.[118]

Goethe's Maxim 392: the living monad intervenes in its surrounding world and thus becomes aware of its internal lack of limits as well as its external limitation. The monadic rotation of life, as radiating from itself in turning about itself, becomes expressive through the second primordial phenomenon of what Cassirer broadly calls "effects" or "actions" (*Wirken*), covering "volition" and "the ethical" as well as the experiencing of oneself

---

[116] Goethe, *Scientific Studies*, trans. D. Miller (Princeton, NJ: Princeton University Press, 1995), Collected Works 12, p. 43.
[117] Cassirer, *The Philosophy of Symbolic Forms*, IV, p. 139.
[118] Cassirer, *The Philosophy of Symbolic Forms*, IV, p. 149.

as a willing "expression of action or influence on others." The unbounded volition of life becomes defined and limited in a shared space of action in relation to others in terms of praxis – action on the world directed toward an effect, whether on the world or on others – and interaction with others, who are defined as "Thou." The I emerges in relation to the Thou. As Cassirer writes: "The ethical primordial phenomenon: the 'I' recognizes others 'next' to it, 'outside' itself, not *extra* but *praeter nos* and enters into an active relationship toward them."[119] With this transition to the "phenomenon of action and effects," Cassirer distinguishes between life and spirit. Life and spirit are set in a rotating relation of polarity. Life is a "primordial fact of dispersion in a multitude of different directions" and yet it obtains a "deep unshakable unity in this divergency."[120] Spirit is a movement of diversity and unity, and it is only in relation to life that spirit becomes manifest in different ways and that different symbolic forms are held together in spirit.[121] The movement of spirit proceeds in a "double-direction," and this doubling of direction is constitutive of symbolic meaning formation. Life has a drive to produce meaning through symbolic forms; this is the sense in which human beings are symbolic animals. The movement of life "consists in the creation of ever new forms and in their destruction."[122]

Goethe's Maxim 393: in directing itself toward the outer world, spirited life creates something more enduring than its own activity: cultural productions, knowledge, and history. This is what Cassirer broadly calls "works" or the poetic (*poiesis*), in contrast to the praxis and actions of the second primordial phenomenon. If purpose and utility define praxis, "nondetermination" defines work: "the poetic 'arises' and 'endures' outside every 'intention' […] It is 'without interest.' It dwells within itself and is 'blessed in itself.'"[123] With this third primordial phenomenon, we arrive at the fundamental experience of freedom. As Cassirer writes:

> In this act of becoming conscious and of making himself conscious we do not find the power of fate which governs organic processes. Here we attain the realm of freedom. The true and highest achievement of every "symbolic form" consists in its contribution toward this goal; by means of its resources and its own unique way, every symbolic form works toward the transition from the realm of "nature" to that of "freedom."[124]

---

[119] Cassirer, *The Philosophy of Symbolic Forms*, IV, p. 133.
[120] Cassirer, *The Philosophy of Symbolic Forms*, IV, p. 225.
[121] Cassirer, *The Philosophy of Symbolic Forms*, IV, p. 230.
[122] Cassirer, *The Philosophy of Symbolic Forms*, IV, p. 226.
[123] Cassirer, *The Philosophy of Symbolic Forms*, IV, p. 183.
[124] Cassirer, *The Philosophy of Symbolic Forms*, IV, p. 111.

Spirit realizes itself more fully and knows itself as creative. It is in terms of the third primordial phenomenon that the world of objective reality becomes produced and sustained. In contrast to the transience of life and life's action in view of the future, the phenomenon of works allows for the temporal endurance of values and meaning formations. This endurance of cultural-symbolic works (artworks, literature, etc.) opens within temporal becoming a dimension of transtemporal eternity: "This is its eternity which enables it to have continuing effects that the creative individual, the *monas*, could never foresee."[125] These three primordial phenomena, interacting with and through each other, as contoured in Cassirer's fragmentary reflections, are arguably condensely expressed in Goethe's poem "Eins und Alles":

> To take what's made and then re-make it,
> To fight rigidity and break it,
> Eternal living action quest.
> What never was grows real and fuller,
> As pure clean suns, as worlds with colour,
> And in becoming never rest.
> It all must move, make new creations,
> First take form, then transformations;
> For moments it just seems held fast.
> In all things life's perpetuated,
> And all must be annihilated
> That existence strives to last.

---

[125] Cassirer, *The Philosophy of Symbolic Forms*, IV, p. 141.

CHAPTER 9

Martin Heidegger and the Titanic Struggle over Being

Life during Wartime

On September 13, 1918, as autumn settled upon the Western Front after the costly failure of Ludendorff's Spring Offensive and ensuing loss of strategic initiative against strengthening Allied Armies, Martin Heidegger, serving in a weather unit in the vicinity of Verdun, sat down in the early morning at his observation post to write a letter to his recently betrothed Elfriede, at home in Freiburg with their newborn son. He is sitting "at the telephone and passing huge quantities of numbers on to the artillery, airship men, [and] gas officers" against the backdrop of "heavy artillery" and the "thunder of bombs, making everything in the hut shake."[1] He reassures Elfriede that she has nothing to fear; "we already have the truck for retreat as well" – but doesn't think that it will be needed, "as there are good people stationed here." All in all, he adds, "I'm very well – taking pleasure in the new things I see." Heidegger is fascinated ("getting his money's worth now") by the sight of convoys passing through a village while "assault battalions march through, young rather pale faces – resolute in their eyes – no laughing, no singing, even less diffidence or despondency – but quite unflagging strength." Looking toward the front lines, an assault battalion comes into view "in the glow of a sunset behind some woods [...] marching along the road at a pretty brisk pace – with steel helmets & all loaded up, the men bent forward somewhat – the muzzles of their rifles pointing sharp into the air." There are "wonderful horses with taunted muscles," shouted commands, and "cars [tearing] along the road, motorcycles in the other direction." Amid this cacophony, Heidegger sits transfixed by the solemn procession of destiny: "the men are all silent, lost in thought, a few kilometers and they're in Hell."[2]

---

[1] M. Heidegger, *Letters to His Wife 1915–1970*, trans. R. Glasgow (London: Polity Press, 2010), p. 51.
[2] Heidegger, *Letters to His Wife 1915–1970*, p. 52.

Throughout Heidegger's sporadic wartime service, he was never among those resolutely silent men descending into Hell, and this proximity, as fascinated observer but not as participant, to those who are going to have died brought home a difference between him and them that made of the war a no less defining experience. As Heidegger writes in a letter, while teaching as a lecturer at the University of Freiburg in 1916, to his then fiancée (he met Elfriede in his seminar in the winter of 1915), a "young field surgeon," who attended his seminar on Kant's *Prolegomena*, "came up to me afterwards & thanked me." Heidegger continues: "I immediately invited him to return for the next few classes; I could see in his eyes how he longed for these ultimate things – & then [he] said to me, this time next week I'll probably be 'out' again. My heart stood still as the contrast came home to me in this single moment and all I could do was squeeze the young man's hand."[3] The contrast that pulled at Heidegger's conscience was arguably twofold: between Heidegger in the seminar room and the young surgeon in the trenches; between a philosopher's pondering "ultimate things" and a soldier's eyes longing for "ultimate things." Whereas the first contrast separated the thinker from the soldier, the second contrast brought them together in common need of "these ultimate things," which, implied in Heidegger's letter, it would be his responsibility to discover and deliver.

In a subsequent letter to Elfriede after the end of term, Heidegger confides that "today I know that there *can* be a philosophy of vibrant life – that I *can* declare war on rationalism right through to the bitter end – without falling victim to the anathema of unscientific thought."[4] Heidegger declares that philosophical thinking must be "produced as living truth & as a creation of the personality valuably & powerfully." The Kantian question of how knowledge is possible is not only "*wrongly* put," but fails "to capture the problem; this is much richer & deeper." His war against rationalism, by which Heidegger primarily understands Neo-Kantianism, was not just a personal crusade, and certainly not merely an academic affair, for it urgently spoke to the dire predicament of the historical present and its lost generation with which he identifies. As Heidegger writes: "We must not give our young heroes stones instead of bread when they come back hungry from the battlefield, not unreal & dead categories, not shadowy forms and bloodless compartments in which to keep a life ground down by rationalism neat and tidy and let it moulder away."[5] Heidegger's biblical

---

[3] Heidegger, *Letters to His Wife 1915–1970*, p. 15.
[4] Heidegger, *Letters to His Wife 1915–1970*, p. 17.
[5] Heidegger, *Letters to His Wife 1915–1970*, p. 17.

allusion ("bread for stones") is telling of the spiritual, indeed religious, significance he ascribes to his innermost calling "to produce living truth" against "rationalism" and "dead categories," in answer to a generational longing for the sense of what it fundamentally means to be.

Setting aside the discrepancies in Heidegger's various accounts of his military record, it is only in 1918 that he is called up for extended service.[6] Until then, Heidegger spent the war in and out of service, repeatedly declared unfit for combat duty. With the outbreak of war in 1914, he claims to have volunteered for duty, only to be released due to a heart condition.[7] Heidegger's attitude to the war found expression in a short essay in his regional newspaper *Heuberger Volksblatt* in 1915. The occasion for these reflections was three days of prayer and contemplation organized by German Catholic bishops for the Feast of the Three Kings. In "Das Kriegstridiuum in Messkirch," Heidegger considers the war within the "inner tumult and absolute aimlessness of the age." Evoking Nietzsche's view that "for some time now, our entire European culture has been moving us toward a catastrophe," Heidegger ascribes this historical waywardness to a "fear of thinking" and "thoughtlessness" afflicting German culture. Soldiers on the way to the front, he observes, are handed copies of the New Testament, Goethe's *Faust*, and Nietzsche's *Zarathustra*. Of these "worldviews," Christianity and Weimar Classicism are spiritually exhausted, while Nietzsche's call for a New Human to overcome the age of the Last Humans remains to be fulfilled. Heidegger rails against "the nonsense of futurism and cubism," "the worst French novel of illicit love," and "the almost insuperable confusion, insecurity, and aimlessness of someone who is moved by momentary moods and drawn by the whim of the moment." Adrift in such cultural fashions and fancies, the war calls upon the seriousness of thinking: "What then is contemplative reflection actually, and properly speaking?" In echoing the episcopate's "great call to reflection" – "like a voice of one crying in the wasteland, in the desolation and shallowness of our present culture" – Heidegger proffers his own definition of reflection as "the fathoming of sense down to its sources

---

[6] Between 1915 and 1938, Heidegger offered five different accounts of his military record. For a discussion of their discrepancies, W. Altman, *Martin Heidegger and the First World War:* Being and Time as Funeral Oration (Lexington, KY: Lexington Books, 2012), p. 83–92; and T. Sheehan, "Heidegger's Lehrjahre," in *The Collegium Phaenomenologicum: The First Ten Years*, ed. J. Sallis (Dordrecht: Kluwer, 1988): 77–137.

[7] M. Heidegger, *Reden und andere Zeugnisses eines Lebensweges* (Frankfurt: Vittorio Klostermann, 2000), p. 42–43. A question remains whether he in fact volunteered or was called up for service. Ott reports that he was "called up" on October 10, 1914; H. Ott, *Martin Heidegger: A Political Life*, trans. A. Blunden (New York: Basic Books, 1993).

It was during his off-duty days that Heidegger rediscovered Hölderlin, whose poetry "is currently turning into a new experience for me – as though I were approaching him wholly primordially for the first time." Norbert von Hellingrath's edition *Hölderlins Samtliche Werke*, along with his essays "Hölderlin und die Deutschen" and "Hölderlins Wahnsinn," proved decisive for Heidegger's poetical awakening. Hellingrath's aristocratic and military prestige added to his embodiment of Stefan Georg's ideal of the poet as a prophetic leader who would guide the German nation. In "Hölderlin und die Deutschen," Hellingrath spoke of the "ambiguity of our peoples" as caught between "the people of Goethe" and "the people of Hölderlin." As Hellingrath declared: "I call us 'Hölderlin's people' because it resides profoundly in the German essence that only in its inner embers under the slag-crust, which is Germany's surface, a secret Germany infinitely comes to light."[17] With this opposition between two poetical visions of Germany, Hellingrath's paean to Hölderlin's "secret Germany," distinct German religiosity, and symbiosis of Germany and Greece, aligned his poetry with wartime nationalism.[18] Hölderlin's fascination for the redemptive promise of human suffering in contrast to the self-sufficiency and immortality of the gods resonated strongly in Hellingrath's vision of the prophetic force of his poetry. Nonetheless, as Hölderlin reflects upon in his poem "The Rhine," the gods, as "dwellers of heaven," "require one thing, / It is heroes and humans / And other mortals." Heroic suffering allows the gods to feel their own blessedness through this sacrificial participation among humans "on their behalf."

For Heidegger, Hellingrath's battlefield death placed a sacramental seal on his anointment of Hölderlin's people and its secret destiny. As Heidegger recalled decades later:

> In 1910 Norbert v. Hellingrath, who was killed in action at Verdun in 1916, published Hölderlin's Pindar transcriptions from the manuscripts for the first time. This was followed in 1914 by the first printing of Hölderlin's late hymns. Both had an earthquake effect on us students at that time.[19]

This awakening to Hölderlin's poetry – "in the midst of the destruction, primitiveness, harshness and impoverished meaning of one's surroundings" – significantly contributed to Heidegger's philosophical calling. As

---

[17] N. von Hellingrath, *Hölderlin. Zwei Vorträge* (Munich: Hugo Bruckmann, 1922), p. 17.
[18] C. Bambach, *Heidegger's Roots: Nietzsche, National Socialism, and the Greeks* (Ithaca, NY: Cornell University Press, 2003), p. 242 ff.
[19] M. Heidegger, *Unterwegs zur Sprache* (Pfullingen: Verlag Günther Neske, 1959), p. 182.

he remarks, "this whole configuration of moods and emphases will specifically influence my own work – I hope, as soon as things are running properly, to make real progress."²⁰

At the time, however, things were far from running properly. With Germany's looming defeat on the horizon, Heidegger observes in October 1918 that "in many cases today people – even among 'intellectuals' – have become insensitive to the inner powers and deeds of spiritual struggle and experience." In a letter written during the spread of influenza in Freiburg (Husserl and his wife have taken ill, Heidegger's friend Theophil Rees has recently lost his pregnant wife to the virus), he declares to Elfriede that "only the young will save us now – and creatively allow a New Spirit to be made flesh in the world." In a letter written "in the field" on October 27, Heidegger expresses his "clear conviction that these weeks will have an effect on our entire future & this will be all the purer & more lasting, indeed, more deeply rooted, emerging from the situations imposed upon us, the more intensely, the more confidently we live."²¹ Heidegger envisions that "our rich future" already inhabits the "creative present, so that it forms part of our life's innermost center as it were – & every present is only the ever precious aliveness of past & future life – i.e., truly historical."²² For these seedling insights to germinate, "language and concepts first have to be discovered and created in silent contemplation" – a task he sets for himself, the condition of which must be a "radical self-emancipation from previous patterns of thought specific to the theory of being & nature." In addition, the problem of the sacred must be brought into the ambit of these problems. All of these efforts, however, are for an uncertain future; on the eve of capitulation, Heidegger writes:

> There was no post again today and they say the postal service as a whole has come to a halt – the wildest rumors are going round – dates for an armistice deal are mentioned, but one after another they prove to be false – the gunfire goes on the same as ever – pointless sacrifice of human lives – what our wretched politics has on its conscience – though disaster now seems to be well on its way – only through this quite radical purification will there

---

²⁰ Heidegger, *Letters to His Wife 1915–1970*, p. 49.
²¹ Heidegger, *Letters to His Wife 1915–1970*, p. 56.
²² Altman sees in this letter "a breakthrough to Heidegger's central insight about *being and time*: what he calls a 'truly historical' existence based on a schöpferische Gegenwart that unites past, present, and future – none of them regarded any longer as existing in the Zeitferne – in a Lebenszentrum infused with a wertvolle Lebendigkeit. In short: Heidegger has discovered in the field a new way of being that depends on a new way of uniting past, present, and future 'in a creative present'"; *Martin Heidegger and the First World War*, p. 111.

be anything to hope for – and only through radicalism – complete commitment of the human being as a whole – will we ourselves advance as real revolutionaries of the spirit.[23]

The Hidden King

Exempt from front-line duty due to a congenital heart condition yet eventually mustered for rear echelon service during the war's twilight in 1918, Heidegger was throughout the war embroiled in struggles on personal and intellectual fronts: work on his Habilitation on Dun Scotus (1915) and faltering efforts to advance his academic career; abandonment of his Catholic faith and thwarted ambition to obtain the Catholic chair in philosophy in Freiburg; controversial marriage to Elfriede, a Protestant, to the dismay of his conservative Catholic parents; and discovery of Edmund Husserl's phenomenology, which offered a groundbreaking way for his sought-after philosophical thinking and dismantling of "the dead categories" of his contemporaries, Husserl's included.[24] All of these factors contributed to Heidegger's audacious thinking. It would be amiss to extricate one factor from this volatile crucible – "front-line experience" or "religious crisis" or "academic opportunism" – as the decisive factor that would set Heidegger upon his pursuit of the question of Being, which, as he repeatedly asserted, remained the one and only question to which his thinking stood devoted. If a philosopher genuinely thinks of but one question, it does not follow that his lifelong calling must have emerged from one point of departure or single catalyzing event. As evident from his wartime letters, it was not so much one experience ("the front line" or "crisis of faith," for example) that propelled Heidegger on his philosophical way, but wartime as such, understood along the lines of Heideggerian own's conception of *kairos* in conjunction with an eschatological expectation of *parousia*. This twofold characterization of the war in terms of *kairos* and *parousia* – rupturing event and eschatological arrival – Heidegger shared with other contemporaries (most notably Max Scheler), partaking, as it does, in the apocalyptic imagination that infused German wartime historical self-understanding in its "struggle for existence." More specifically, Heidegger aligns this perception of wartime as a time out of joint with his own conception of "situation."

---

[23] Heidegger, *Letters to His Wife 1915–1970*, p. 58. Letter of November 10, 1918.
[24] Ott, *Martin Heidegger*, p. 116. As Kiesel remarks: "The tumult of the war years is matched in tempo by the young Heidegger's religious tumult in 1917"; T. Kiesel, *The Genesis of Heidegger's* Being and Time (Berkeley: University of California Press, 1995), p. 18.

As he argues in his "Emergency War Seminar" (1919), "factical life" occurs as the "living togetherness of tendencies" and "motivational possibilities," which, for the most part, are experienced "unreflectively" and "untheoretically."[25] Existing in an environing world, "factical life" always finds itself standing before an array of possibilities that defines its historical situation. How life stands in a situation, however, is not akin to how an object is located in a room, for "the event of the situation happens *to me*" and "radiates into my own being."[26] In this sense of "happening," a situation unfolds along conflicting vectors of possibilities that befall life, thus confronting life with a set of challenges and problems, in relation to which life is called to decide how to act and, hence, exist in the world. As Heidegger writes: "Each state of affairs is inherently a problem, literally something 'thrown before' as a provocation [... that] prefigures the direction of the process of theoretical comportment." The intrinsically future directedness of "factical life" in its historical situation is marked by an openness of questioning, where life finds itself in question as to the sense of its being in the world. As a life event calling for decisiveness, Heidegger's wartime situation became a crucible in which different possibilities – personal, philosophical, religious, and academic – were forged into a new configuration and way of thinking that, developing over the course of the 1920s, would lead to the publication of *Being and Time* (1927), and, indeed, reverberate beyond, on future wayward paths, but always resonant with the sounding of wartime's urgency for another, and not just renewed, beginning.

With Heidegger's return to the University of Freiburg as Husserl's assistant in 1919, his search for another way of thinking, armed with his brilliantly transfigured phenomenological method of inquiry, determinately set itself against the "dry rationalism" and "dead concepts" of his contemporaries, mainly Neo-Kantianism and Protestant liberal theology. As Heidegger recalls in "My Way into Phenomenology," the initial impulse for his concern with the question of Being was provided by Franz Brentano's *On the Several Senses of Being in Aristotle*, followed by his discovery of intentionality, the a priori, and categorical intuition in *The Logical Investigations* – Husserl's breakthrough work that motivated Heidegger's own breakthrough to the question of Being. Phenomenological thinking, when ontologically geared toward a recovery of "factical life," offered an alternative to psychologism, Neo-Kantian theories of cognition and value,

---

[25] M. Heidegger, *Grundprobleme der Phänomenologie (1919/20)* (Frankfurt: Vittorio Klosermann, 1993), p. 208.
[26] Heidegger, *Grundprobleme der Phänomenologie*, p. 206.

as well as historicism and doctrines of "worldviews."²⁷ In Heidegger's recasting, phenomenology migrates toward a hermeneutical understanding of "factical life" (bearing the imprint of Wilhelm Dilthey's thinking), where the sense of what it means to exist, as presupposed by established notions of "the soul" and "transcendental consciousness," is inseparable from the self-understanding of how "factical life" exists in the world. As Heidegger defines in his "Emergency War Seminar," "phenomenology is the investigation of life in itself," and yet, "despite the appearance of a philosophy of life, it is really the opposite of a worldview," which, for its part, represents an "objectification and immobilization" of life. In his Freiburg courses during and immediately after the war, Heidegger develops an analysis of factical life through a phenomenology of religious life along with a phenomenological ontology keyed to different comportments toward "being" in relation to how existence, or *Dasein*, relates to itself. As he writes: "If one takes 'life' as a manner of 'being,' then 'factical life' means: our own existence (*Dasein*) as 'here.'"²⁸ Life understands its own manner of being in the world through a hermeneutic unfolding of sense that cannot be equated with theoretical or objective cognition, but neither can it be equated with psychological nor subjective experience.

In the wartime context of Heidegger's break with his native Catholicism and turn to Protestantism, a phenomenological method of analysis allows for a retrieval of the original source of religious experience in the facticity of human life. His reading of Luther (in particular) along with St. Paul, Augustine, and Kierkegaard set into place a series of reference points – "being toward death," "fallenness," "affliction and care," and "eschatological temporality" – that would guide his thinking until *Being and Time*. As Heidegger writes to his wife: "Since I have read Luther's Commentary on the Romans, much that was previously painful and dark to me has become luminous and liberating."²⁹ Influenced as well by Georg Simmel's *The View*

---

[27] As Heidegger writes to Elisabeth Blochmann in a letter of May 1, 1919: "My own work is quite concentrated, fundamental, and concrete: basic problems of phenomenological methodology, disengagement from the leftover residue of acquired standpoints, ever new forays into the true origins, preliminary work on the phenomenology of religious consciousness, disciplined preparation in order to attain an intensive and qualitatively high academic effectiveness, constantly learning in my association with Husserl"; M. Heidegger and E. Blochmann, *Briefwechsel 1918–1969* (Marbach: Deutsche Schillergesellschaft, 1989), p. 16.

[28] M. Heidegger, *Phenomenology of Religious Life*, trans. M. Fritsch and J. A. Gosetti-Ferencei (Bloomington: Indiana University Press, 2004), p. 19.

[29] Heidegger, *Letters to His Wife 1915–1970*, p. 100 (September 1919). For the formative significance of Heidegger's phenomenology of the religious life, with its emphasis on temporality, suffering, and eschatology, J. Wolfe, *Heidegger's Eschatology* (Oxford: Oxford University Press, 2013); and J. van Buren, *The Young Heidegger: Rumor of the Hidden King* (Indiana: Indiana University Press, 1994).

of Life, Heidegger considers human existence as intractably caught between its own finitude and an original impulse for "more than life," or transcendence, toward the sense of "ultimate things," God or Being. In addition to this concern with Dasein's being-in-the-world, Heidegger mints a series of ontologically suggestive expressions such as "worlding," thus transposing his philosophical lexicon away from a substantive ontology to a verbial ontology of event and existence.[30] These efforts centered around a retrieval of "the primal something" (*Ur-etwas*) – the primal sense of what it is to be in relation to Dasein's manifold ways of existing in the world.

A recurring operation in Heidegger's confrontation with the history of philosophy (and theology) is "destruction." Life must be emancipated from "dry rationalism" and "dead concepts." By the same token, philosophical thinking must be liberated from the captivity of its heritage. Throughout the development of his thinking in Freiburg (1919–22) and Marburg (1923–7), Heidegger undertakes a "destruction" of the history of metaphysics in both its philosophical and theological aspects. Methodologically, "destruction" refers to an interpretive engagement with canonical figures – St. Paul, Augustine, Aristotle, Leibniz, Descartes, Kant – that seeks to uncover the inherited "unthought" dimensions of thinking that barred a genuine beginning anew with the question of Being and (human) existence, or Dasein; "destruction" clears a space for alternative ways of conceptualization that would not merely replace "dead concepts" but extract their unthought and forgotten potential into an alternative array of meanings, and hence possibilities of understanding and being. As Heidegger writes to Karl Löwith in 1921, "the meaning and sense of philosophizing is itself historical and what matters is to find one's own – and to leave aside all the yardsticks of earlier philosophers. This has been utterly neglected."[31] Heidegger's insistence on not just a suspension of historical assumptions but "leaving aside all the yardsticks" – namely, a destruction of the inherited *logos* of philosophy – implies that the war itself did not and could not productively "destroy" Western metaphysics. Burdened by "dead concepts" that no longer spoke to the contemporary situation in which life found itself in wartime (and its aftermath), the task

---

[30] As Kiesel argues: "The importance of this groundbreaking course, in all its vital rawness and freshness pointing the way to all of Heidegger, in my view cannot be overestimated. For here he first clearly identifies and names his subject matter, his lifelong topic which, even in those early years, rapidly assumed a series of names: the primal something, life in and for itself, factic life, the historical I, the situated I, factic life experience, facticity, Dasein, being"; T. Kiesel, *The Genesis of Heidegger's* Being and Time (Berkeley: University of California Press, 1993), pp. 16–17.

[31] M. Heidegger and K. Löwith, *Correspondence: 1919–1973*, trans. J. Assaiante and S. Ewegen (London: Rowman and Littlefield, 2021), p. 20.

of thinking consisted in accomplishing what the war could not accomplish for or in lieu of thinking. Only thinking can yield another beginning for thinking, through an interpretive violence directed at and beyond itself, its historical unthought. Despite having published little during the 1920s, from his years in Freiburg to his appointment in Marburg to his return to Freiburg as Husserl's successor in 1928, Heidegger, as Hannah Arendt observed, "was hardly more than a name, but the name traveled all over Germany like the rumor of the hidden king" – a hidden king engaged in a titanic struggle over the sense of being against the burdensome history of metaphysics and the complacency of his contemporaries.

Gigantomachia peri tes ousias

To those students fascinated and inspired by this hidden king during the 1920s, it seemed self-evident that Heidegger's revolutionary retrieval of the question of Being in tandem with a concentrated destruction of Western metaphysics directly addressed the urgent need for thinking in a time left devastated and wanting by war.[32] As Löwith observes:

> One may ask how many or how few have understood the extent to which Heidegger's question of "Being" has to do not simply with "time" generally but also with the specific time in which he posed the universal question of Being; that time was the 1920s, after the First World War, when "eternal values" of the philosophy of value and culture, and the traditional content of our so-called cultural generally, had become threadbare and fragile, and Dilthey's historiological critique of reason and of traditional metaphysics became generally accepted.[33]

Despite the calamitous aftermath of war in which Heidegger's thinking matures during the 1920s, the war remains conspicuously absent from the remit of his thinking. Unlike a slew of contemporary "revolutionaries of spirit," Heidegger does not, in his seminars and lectures, nor indeed in *Being and Time,* integrate the war's significance or a reflection on the crisis of culture – two sides of the same discourse – into his self-styled revolutionary retrieval of the "forgotten" question of what it means to be.

---

[32] For these brilliant students who were anything but "children," see nonetheless R. Wolin, *Heidegger's Children* (Princeton, NJ: Princeton University Press, 2015).

[33] K. Löwith, *Martin Heidegger and European Nihilism,* trans. G. Steiner (New York: Columbia University Press, 1995), p. 130. In the same vein, Hans-Georg Gadamer remarks that "[*Being and Time*] effectively communicated to a wide public something of the new spirit that had engulfed philosophy as a result of the convulsions of World War I"; H.-G. Gadamer, *Philosophical Hermeneutics,* trans. D. Linge (Berkeley: University of California Press, 1976), p. 214.

As Heidegger remarks to Löwith in a letter of 1920: "My will, fundamentally, aspires to something else, and that is not much: living in an actual revolutionary situation, I pursue what I feel to be 'necessary' without caring to know whether a new 'culture' will emerge from it or an acceleration of decline."[34] As he explains: "I do what I must and what I consider to be necessary and do it as well as I can – I do not adapt my philosophical work to cultural needs of an unspecified today [...] I work out of my own I am." Indeed, Heidegger consistently rejects the concept of "culture" as well as its associated doctrine of worldviews. It is not, however, that Heidegger's thinking did not operate in the milieu of crisis; yet it is a distinctive feature of this thinking that he distances himself from the dominant rhetoric of cultural crisis and adopts instead a more ominous language of "danger" and "desertification," the significance of which escapes the – on his view – ontologically and historical superficial talk of crisis. What is required in this time of peril is neither "critique" nor "renewal" but *destruction*. As Heidegger remarks in notes for his winter-semester course of 1919–20:

> A pervasive helplessness lies over all contemporary life, because it has separated itself from its genuine primal sources and merely skirts the issue. Typical: scribbling about the meaning of culture and the problems of culture – on the basis of what one imagines to be a fresh perspective – as one must if one gets crazy ideas about the problem of culture, instead of actively and productively *creating* a new culture.[35]

Heidegger's response to what he routinely invoked as "the today" is not shaped around the contours of a cultural discourse of crisis; on the contrary, his polemic against the idea of a worldview distinguishes his philosophical attitude to the historical present in the aftermath of the war. In framing this thinking around the question of the sense of Being and its metaphysical obscuration, Heidegger searches for a more fundamental perspective, extending back to the origins of Western thought, in terms of a profounder (and untapped) vein of questioning the sense of what it means to be, where rather than claim to have found an answer to the question of being, Heidegger insists instead on the imperative to plumb, and indeed inhabit, the question itself, without promise of an answer or solution. Answers, as it were, including those proffered under the name of culture, must be abandoned, in fact sacrificed, for the sake of a more

---

[34] K. Löwith, *My Life in Germany Before and After 1933*, trans. E. King (Evanston, IL: University of Illinois Press, 1994), p. 29.

[35] M. Heidegger, *Grundprobleme der Phänomenologie (1919/1920)*. Gesamtausgabe Band 58 (Frankfurt: Vittorio Klostermann, 1993), p. 20.

original confrontation with the questionability of today. As Heidegger writes to Löwith in 1921: "We must *sacrifice* ourselves and find our way back into *existential* limitation and facticity, instead of deflecting these by programmes and universal problems."[36]

The vehemence of Heidegger's rejection of the concept of culture is nowhere better on display than with his acidic reaction to Husserl's *Kaizo* articles on the theme of "renewal." As Heidegger writes to Löwith on November 22, 1922:

> The old man [Husserl] is writing contributions to a Japanese newspaper. Rickert arranged it over the summer. The title of these contributions is "Renewal"! According to him, it is completely "humanities-oriented and socially ethical." [...] You would not be able to imagine in your wildest dreams how disastrous it is. In order to prevent the worst, I told his wife that something like this could never be published in Germany – it is too elementary.[37]

What appeared "too elementary" was that Husserl failed to frame his diagnosis of crisis in terms of the forgotten question of Being and the metaphysical tradition stemming from the Greek experience of Being. The obsession with culture and worldviews, which Husserl shared with Neo-Kantian thinkers as well as *Lebensphilosophen*, betrayed a thinking of modernity based on inherited metaphysical distinctions that prevented such a palaver of self-diagnosis from grasping the veritable depth and extent of the wasteland defining "the today."[38]

Heidegger's antagonistic attitude toward the cultural crisis-discourse of his contemporaries is revealing of how the war's genuine significance remained "unthought," but likewise of how the war in turn remained the "unthought" shadow of Heidegger's own thinking. In the aftermath of the war, the war is not an event that stands inert behind Heidegger's thinking in the immediate past, nor an event that, as for many of his contemporaries during the interwar years, becomes thematically present for his thinking. On the contrary, neither in the past nor in the present, the war affects, indeed silently afflicts, Heidegger's thinking as still "to be thought" from

---

[36] Heidegger and Löwith, *Correspondence: 1919–1973*, p. 31.
[37] Heidegger and Löwith, *Correspondence: 1919–1973*, p. 57. As Heidegger then observes: "And now you have a letter full of gossip. But this is the only way one can write about one's 'situation.'" Even more excoriating in 1923: "If I now look back on the *Logical Investigations* from this vantage point, I come to the following conclusion: never in his life, not even for a second, was Husserl a philosopher. He is becoming increasingly ridiculous;" Heidegger and Löwith, *Correspondence: 1919–1973*, p. 63.
[38] For Heidegger's view of Neo-Kantianism as the philosophical expression of modern culture, B. Crowe, *Heidegger's Phenomenology of Religion* (Bloomington: Indiana University Press, 2008), p. 44.

within the unfolding question of Being and the destruction of the history of metaphysics.[39] Neither thought through nor repressed, the unthought dimension of the war haunting Heidegger's thinking during the 1920s nevertheless left slim traces across his lectures and seminars.[40] In his 1924 lecture "Dasein und Wahrsein nach Aristoteles," for example, Heidegger, in engaging the question "does truth really find its ground in judgment, or has it been uprooted and displaced from a more native, or indigenous, soil [*Bodenständigkeit*]," off-handedly remarks: "The *Ruhrkampf* must become the *Titanenkampf* (*gigantomachia*) over being once fought by the great Greek philosophers, which we Germans are destined to make into our *Kampf!*"[41]

Against this backdrop, Heidegger's magnum opus opens with an invocation of "the today" in which his thinking struggles to overcome the forgetting of the question of the sense of Being. Although, as Heidegger writes, "our times" consider themselves progressive in reaffirming "metaphysics," the effort for engaging anew in a *gigantomachia peri tes ousias* remains wanting. The question that "took the breath away of Plato and Aristotle" and since then fell into silence and oblivion as a "thematic question of actual investigation" has been historically forgotten; indeed, this forgetting has itself been forgotten throughout the history of metaphysics. It is clear from Heidegger's leading statements on the historical forgetting of the question of Being – a forgetting in which metaphysics unknowingly deployed itself – that this question of questions befalls us "today" in its urgency. Much of Heidegger's effort, however, is not to pursue an answer to this here remembered and retrieved question; on the contrary, the thrust of Heidegger's thinking moves toward breaching the question of the sense of Being – a question that seems to be either impossible or meaningless, empty, in its directionless generality. The aim of *Being and Time* is not to answer the question of the sense of Being, but rather to discover and launch this question regarding "ultimate things," as the future for philosophical thinking, yet without delivering an answer or solution.

In this manner, Heidegger's ambition consists in retrieving the question of the sense of Being from its historical oblivion through a retrieval

---

[39] For this contrast between Scheler, Spengler, and others with Heidegger's silence – no public statements on the cultural crisis – and hence his "apolitical and anarchic attitude," H. Sluga, *Heidegger's Crisis: Philosophy and Politics in Nazi Germany* (Cambridge, MA: Harvard University Press, 1993), p. 136ff.

[40] In his 1925 Marburg lecture, "History of the Concept of Time," Heidegger makes this offhand remark: "Take for example a grenade suddenly striking or piercing the ground nearby and with it the sudden appresentation of the imminent approach of the explosion, which can occur at any moment"; *History of Concept of Time*, p. 288.

[41] Quoted in T. Kiesel, "Situating Rhetoric/Politics in Heidegger's Practical Ontology (1923–1925: The French Occupation of the Rhine)," *Existentia* Vol. 9 (1999): 11–30.

of a more fundamental understanding of human existence as Dasein. According to Heidegger, ontologies within the Western metaphysical tradition are based on a distribution of different senses of being across different senses of time, with an unquestioned primacy accorded to being-present, or presence: beings that have beginnings and endings, beings that have neither a beginning nor an ending, beings that are created, and so on. Ever since Greek thinking, the fundamental sense of being remains understood in terms of "to be present." Yet it is precisely this unquestioned compact between "to be" (being) and "being present" (time) that Heidegger seeks to question anew through a fundamental ontology based on Dasein's understanding of its own temporal being. In Heidegger's thinking, different ontic senses of "to be" are keyed to different senses of time, and thus, on his thinking, presuppose a horizon of temporality identified with Dasein's basic manner of existence. Dasein is from the beginning, or in its basic existence, already an openness, or "transcendence," toward beings ("what-is" or entities) as well as Being as such, and thus not only toward regions or kinds of being. Moreover, Dasein's primordial understanding of its own being in its finite existence is "more original" than any conception of *human* being. As Heidegger writes in his *Kantbuch*: "More original than man is the finitude of the *Dasein* in him."[42] To retrieve the question of being through a retrieval of a more original sense of existence as the temporality *who Dasein is* invokes a more primordial sense of temporality than is traditionally understood through the established distinctions between time and eternity, becoming and being. As Heidegger states: "time needs to be explicated primordially as the horizon for the understanding of Being, and in terms of temporality as the Being of *Dasein*, which understands Being."

Already in the 1924 lecture "The Concept of Time," rather than begin with the question "*What* is time?," Heidegger proposes instead to address the question "*Who* is time?," where the meaning of "who," as developed in *Being and Time*, refers to Dasein, whose basic structure of existence, as what Heidegger calls "care" (*Sorge*), is grounded in its temporality. Dasein is time, or, to speak more exactly, what it is for Dasein to be is to be a primordial temporality in terms of which an understanding of being is possible. In his 1930 lecture course *Hegel und das Problem der Metaphysik*, Heidegger distinguishes between a *Grundfrage* and a *Leitfrage*. The fundamental question (*Grundfrage*) of philosophy is the question of Being

---

[42] M. Heidegger, *Kant and the Problem of Metaphysics* (Bloomington: Indiana University Press, 1990), p. 156.

(*Seinsfrage*). Expressed in the very questionability of being, this possibility of understanding being defines the essence of human existence, not, however, as either *homo sapiens* or *ens creatum*, but as *Dasein*, as that being for whom the sense of being is at all an issue, and who is herself in question in questioning being. The question "Who is Dasein?" serves as the guiding question (*Leitfrage*) for the question of being; it is the question that underpins the "and" in the question of being *and* time. This intrinsic connection between the question of the sense of Being and the question of the sense of that being for whom what it means to be at all is a question – that being for whom beings are questionable; namely, Dasein – is the pivotal point of leverage for Heidegger's basic insight that authenticity for Dasein consists in accepting the impossibility of finding an answer or solution to its own problematic existence along with the impossibility of not searching for it.

Throughout Heidegger's thinking in *Being and Time*, its brilliance consists in part in the historical urgency of struggling to rethink the question of "ultimate things" and thus deliver "bread for stones" to "the today" in the aftermath of war. That the titanic struggle over being once fought by Greek philosophers, echoing throughout the pages of *Being and Time*, must also be destined for Germany to make into its own struggle remained nonetheless unspoken, indeed unthought. A few years later, however, in Heidegger's 1929–30 lecture course "The Fundamental Concepts of Metaphysics," in the context of reflecting on "*das Kommende*" in response to the predicament of an existence (Dasein) without community and authenticity, the First World War thematically enters onto the scene of Heidegger's thinking – namely, his "metaphysics of Dasein" – in the wake of *Being and Time*. As with *Being and Time*, Heidegger's guiding interest in these lectures resides with retrieving the question of Being through an existential analysis of Dasein. This existential awakening turns on abiding within a fundamental attunement in which the guiding question "Who is Dasein?" can spring forth along with the fundamental question of Being.[43] As Heidegger observes: "Our fundamental task now consists in awakening a fundamental attunement in our philosophizing. I deliberately say: in *our* philosophizing, not in some arbitrary philosophizing nor even in philosophy in itself, for there is no such thing."[44] This emphasis on the historical present reflects

---

[43] Heidegger's analysis of Dasein's temporality is performative in a double sense: it is meant to awaken human existence to its own essence, as temporality, and through this awakening of Dasein *to itself*, it is meant to awaken human existence to its own historical present. Time itself, as both temporality and "historicity" (*Geschichtlichkeit*), enters into visibility.

[44] M. Heidegger, *The Fundamental Concepts of Metaphysics*, trans. W. McNeill and N. Walker (Bloomington: Indiana University Press, 1995), p. 59.

Heidegger's election of boredom as the fundamental attunement meant to provide the guiding thread for an analysis of Dasein's temporality. The historical present is shaped by an acute consciousness of crisis, interpretations of which remain indebted to a philosophy of culture and notions of *Weltanschauung*. As Heidegger challenges, "these world-historical diagnoses and prognoses of culture do not involve us, they *do not attack us*. On the contrast, they release us from ourselves and present us to ourselves in a world-historical situation and role."[45] As Heidegger further ponders:

> We must first call for someone capable of instilling terror into our Dasein again. For how do things stand with our Dasein when an event like the Great War can to all extents and purposes pass us by without leaving a trace? Is this not perhaps a sign that no event, however momentous it may be, can assume this task if man has not prepared himself for awakening in the first place?[46]

The widespread appeal of cultural interpretations of crisis suggests for Heidegger that contemporary Dasein (human existence in its present historical condition) is affected by a profound boredom. This fundamental attunement is both transparent and veiled. In Heidegger's suggestive metaphor, "profound boredom draws back and forth like a silent fog in the abysses of Dasein."[47] This image of boredom as ebbing back and forth like a silent fog reconfigures the classical metaphor of time as a stream into a distinctive image of time's silent inquietude, while in the same gesture telegraphing Heidegger's own basic insight into Dasein's existential temporalization as both self-obscuring and self-revealing. The fundamental attunement of boredom indicates both an absence of oppressiveness and the opportunity for a "moment of vision," and this vision is afforded by a profounder form of boredom, with oneself as well as with the world. A transformative revelation of three questions becomes pressing: What is world? What is finitude? What is individuation? Within the organization of Heidegger's lecture course, the fundamental attunement of boredom solidifies in phenomenological terms the connection between the three fundamental questions of world, finitude, and individuation with the question of temporality. As Heidegger writes: "If time is tied up with boredom, and on the other hand is somehow the basis for our three questions, then the fundamental attunement of boredom constitutes an exceptional relation to time in human Dasein, and thereby offers an exceptional

---

[45] Heidegger, *The Fundamental Concepts of Metaphysics*, p. 75.
[46] Heidegger, *The Fundamental Concepts of Metaphysics*, p. 172.
[47] Heidegger, *The Fundamental Concepts of Metaphysics*, p. 77.

possibility of answering the three questions."⁴⁸ Where in 1915 Heidegger once spoke of the avoidance of "the fear of contemplation," in 1929 he now speaks of the need to "instill terror in our Dasein" – as if the horror of war were not, ontologically speaking, enough – and thus, still outstanding, against the "satiated comfort in the absence of dangerousness."

"Guests in Our House"

In March 1929, Heidegger met Ernst Cassirer in Davos, Switzerland, for a philosophical debate on Kant's philosophy. It is an event that has since passed into legend as representing a decisive "parting of ways" and "Continental divide" in twentieth-century European thought. For Hans Blumenberg, Heidegger emerged from this confrontation triumphant into the twentieth century, while Cassirer slipped from philosophical relevance – an outcome that four years later, Blumenberg observed, would be sealed "for a long time, almost up until the present."⁴⁹ For Jürgen Habermas, Cassirer embodied "the cultivated world of European Humanism against a decisionism that appealed to the originality of thinking."⁵⁰ At the time, this debate attracted international newspaper coverage. For the *Frankfurter Zeitung*, the encounter represented nothing less than a collision between "two different epochs." And yet, rather than "seeing two worlds collide, one enjoyed at most a theatre performance," according to the *Neue Züricher Zeitung*, "in which a very nice person and a very ardent one, who tried his best to be nice, spoke to one another in monologues." As that reporter wryly remarked: "everyone in the audience acted as though this was very gripping and afterwards congratulated one another for having been there."⁵¹

Despite significant philosophical differences, notwithstanding some degree of common interests, both Cassirer and Heidegger were reticent, even unwilling, to confront each other directly.⁵² Each thinker spoke at

---

⁴⁸ Heidegger, *The Fundamental Concepts of Metaphysics*, p. 81.
⁴⁹ H. Blumenberg, "Der Parteibeitrag," in *Die Verführbarkeit des Philosophen* (Frankfurt: Suhrkamp, 2000), p. 78.
⁵⁰ J. Habermas, *Philosophisch-Politische Profile* (Frankfurt: Suhrkamp, 1981), p. 52. This characterization of the confrontation at Davos has been in the main adopted by subsequent studies. For the historical and cultural context, as well as the particulars of their respective lectures, see Gordon, *Continental Divide*. See also M. Friedman, *A Parting of the Ways: Carnap, Cassirer, and Heidegger* (Chicago: Open Court Books 2000).
⁵¹ As quoted in J.-M. Krois, "Why Did Cassirer and Heidegger Not Debate in Davos?" in *Symbolic Forms and Cultural Studies*: 242–262.
⁵² See the Ritter-Bollnow protocol. As J.-M. Krois observes: "Each made statements, but there was no real debate; their remarks give the impression of two ships passing one another in the night. Cassirer in particular seemed evasive"; "Why Did Cassirer and Heidegger Not Debate in Davos?," p. 245.

the other rather than with one another. From Cassirer's vantage point, Heidegger's existential analysis of Dasein in *Being and Time* along with his "destructive" interpretation of Kant did not pose a fundamental challenge to his own *The Philosophy of Symbolic Forms* (or his reading of Kant), but, on the contrary, confirmed the importance of *Lebensphilosophie*, under which Cassirer placed Heidegger, as the contrasting point of departure for his own metaphysics of life.[53] Cassirer's thinking was at the time already firmly committed to a shift away from the centrality of the question of Being to the centrality of question of meaning, in its plural symbolic manifestations as different ways of world disclosure and understanding. Indeed, Cassirer seems to have subsequently "not thought much about" his (non) debate with Heidegger.[54] For his part, Heidegger apparently sought out a confrontation with the institutionally more established Cassirer. *Kant and the Problem of Metaphysics* as well as his discussion of Kant in *The Question Concerning the Thing* can be seen as written inter alia against Cassirer.[55] Heidegger's strident critique of the narrow epistemological optic of Cassirer's imputed Neo-Kantianism arguably missed its target, however, for Cassirer had himself abandoned (as well as criticized) this restrictive framing of the problem of knowledge. The Cassirer rejected by Heidegger in 1929 represented a "Cassirer" that Cassirer had himself rejected during the war.[56] In turn, Cassirer's critique of Heidegger's presumed *Lebensphilosophie* (sketched in his unpublished drafts for the fourth volume of *The Philosophy of Symbolic Forms* but not put forth at Davos), which Cassirer situated in an existential-religious lineage stemming from Luther, arguably missed its target as well, given the transformation of Heidegger's religiously inflected phenomenology of factical life of the early 1920s into the existential analytic of Dasein in *Being and Time*.[57] Moreover, Heidegger's thinking in 1929 had evolved from the analytic of Dasein in *Being and Time* to a "metaphysics of Dasein," on the verge of the dramatic turn in his thinking with its abandonment of the (unfinished) project of

---

[53] See Cassirer, *The Philosophy of Symbolic Forms*, 4.
[54] R. Klibansky, "Erinnerungen an Ernst Cassirer," *Internationale Zeitschrift für Philosophie*, Vol. 2 (1999): 275–288; p. 279.
[55] For Gadamer's recollection and this plausibility, D. Kaegi, "Davos und davor," in *Cassirer – Heidegger. 70 Jahre Davoser Disputation*, eds. D. Kaegi and E. Rudolph (Hamburg: Meiner Verlag, 2002): 67–105; p. 72.
[56] See Chapter 8 in this book on Cassirer.
[57] See, for example, Heidegger's rejection of the identification of his thinking in *Being and Time* with a Christian existential reflection of the human condition in the 1941 lecture course "The Metaphysics of German Idealism"; M. Heidegger, *The Metaphysics of German Idealism*, trans. I. Moore and R. Therezo (London: Polity Press, 2021).

Being and Time.⁵⁸ Rather than an encounter between two philosophical Titans, their missed encounter resembled a Titanic shadow boxing, or "two ships passing in the night" (in John Michael Krois' expression), each belaboring the other's shadow.

And yet, beneath this shadow boxing there agitated unsettled ghosts. Between the lines of this confrontational nonconfrontation, something else seemed afoot, as marked by Cassirer's prudential silence and Heidegger's elliptical aggression. As Toni Cassirer recounts, Heidegger's "enmity and pugnacity were immediately visible."⁵⁹ In particular, she recalls an effort at small talk with Heidegger, politely inquiring whether he had known Hermann Cohen while expressing her dismay at the "scandalous handling" of Cohen's funeral in 1918, when no faculty member in Berlin accompanied the coffin of this "outstanding Jewish scholar." When Heidegger showed neither sympathy nor understanding for her evident distress, she persisted in evoking her husband's admiration for Cohen, until finally receiving the "the pleasure of seeing that this hard dough [i.e., Heidegger], like a bread roll in warm milk, softened." This momentary softening did not inhibit Heidegger from parading at Davos as "the victor" while Cassirer's respectful temperament restrained him from a "frontal attack." Given such palpable tensions between the men, why did Cassirer not respond forcefully or call out Heidegger's spurious charge against his alleged Neo-Kantianism? What did Heidegger signal in targeting the shadow of Cassirer's former philosophical self? On what other scene, behind the performance of "a very nice person and a very ardent one, who tried his best to be nice," did a confrontation between two thinkers – indeed, between two epochs – *not* take place, thus haunting this shadow boxing of Titans from within?

Two months before Davos, on February 23, 1929, the Austrian philosopher and social economist Othmar Spann delivered a lecture in Munich organized by the *Kampfbund für deutscher Kultur* on "the contemporary cultural crisis."⁶⁰ As noted by the *Frankfurter Zeitung*, "his [Spann's] characterization of Neo-Kantianism should be mentioned, in which he said that

---

⁵⁸ For a trenchant critique of framing the Davos confrontation in terms of a confrontation of "the spontaneity of Spirit" in Cassirer and Heidegger's "thrownness of Dasein," see J. Barash, "Ernst Cassirer, Martin Heidegger, and the Legacy of Davos," *History and Theory*, Vol. 51, No. 3 (2012): 436–450.

⁵⁹ Cassirer, *Mein Leben mit Ernst Cassirer*, p. 188. Hans Jonas recalls: "I was later told that Cassirer was deeply repulsed [at Davos] and naturally had also felt that the hearts, the feelings of the audience were definitely with Heidegger."

⁶⁰ J. Haag, "Othmar Spann and the Quest for a 'True State'," *Austrian History Yearbook*, Vol. 12, No. 1 (2009): 227–250. As Lukács writes: "Long before Hitler's seizure of power, Spann shared most of the social views of fascism. He saw his main enemies partly in the liberal ideas of 1789, but above all in the Marxist ideas of 1917"; Lukács, *The Destruction of Reason*, p. 641.

it was sad to think of how the German people were being reminded of their own Kantian philosophy by strangers; among these 'strangers' he understood philosophers of such rank as Hermann Cohen and Ernst Cassirer."[61] Leaving no ambiguity as to Spann's diagnosis of Germany's cultural crisis, the pro-Zionist *Neue Welt* reported that "the Anti-Semite [Spann] gave a lecture on the 'Jewification' of philosophy." Spann's polemic against the plight of German culture a decade after German defeat revived an anti-Semitic attack against the "intellectualism" and "foreignness" of Marburg Neo-Kantianism. It found immediate favor with his audience. As reported by the *Neue Zeitung*: "Adolf Hitler appeared personally, whereby his numerous supporters, decorated in swastikas, gave him a loud ovation by stamping their feet and applauding, for which he thanked them."[62]

Spann's slanderous ad hominem aggression must surely have rattled Cassirer in the months leading up to Davos, not least of all because it replayed an anti-Semitic outburst directed against Cohen's *Deutschtum und Judentum* during the war.[63] At the time, Cohen's proposed reconciliation between *Deutschtum* and *Judentum* provoked an acidic response among a number of German thinkers. Most notoriously, in "Vom Begriff der Nation" (1916; published in *Kant-Studien*), Bruno Bauch (at the time editor of the journal) vigorously rejected any philosophical convergence between *Deutschtum* and *Judentum*, which, on the contrary, could only lead to a "mutual obliteration" threatening the purity of the German people. As Bauch writes: "To mix Kantian spirit and Jewish spirit fully in the fields of ethics and philosophy of religion is so grotesque that I hardly need to say anything about it [...]."[64] For this severing of the ways between *Deutschtum* and *Judentum*, Bauch appealed to an idea of the nation as forged in a community of blood among "those born into it" – a precursor to the ideology of *Blut und Boden* promoted by the Nazi regime.[65] Drawing on the discourse of *Kriegsphilosophie*, Bauch defines

---

[61] Cited in Krois, "Why Did Cassirer and Heidegger Not Debate in Davos?," p. 247.

[62] "Othmar Spann und Hitler," *Die neue Welt* (Vienna), March 8, 1929, p. 6. https://sammlungen.ub.uni-frankfurt.de/cm/periodical/titleinfo/2711694.

[63] See Chapter 2 in this book on Cohen. As Krois remarks: "Slander on this scale, aimed at Cassirer and Cohen, could neither have escaped Cassirer's notice nor left him unaffected at the Davos Hochschulkurse"; "Why Did Cassirer and Heidegger Not Debate in Davos?," p. 248.

[64] T. Meyer, *Kulturphilosophie in gefährlicher Zeit: Zum Werk Ernst Cassirers* (Hamburg: Meiner Verlag, 2007), p. 131.

[65] B. Bauch, "Vom Begriff der Nation," *Kant-Studien*, Vol. 21 (1916): 139–162. Bauch would later reference his writings from the war when promoting the removal of "Jewish influence" from German science in the 1930s. See also B. Bauch, "Erbanlage, Erziehung und Geschichte," *Blätter für deutsche Philosophie*, Vol. 10 (1936/37): 45–68; and B. Bauch, "Erbanlage, Erziehung und Geschichte," *Blätter für deutsche Philosophie*, Vol. 15 (1941): 45–68.

the (German) nation as the "divine determination of eternity," requiring "total devotion and sacrifice to the whole of the nation," with the imputation that German Jews were unwilling to sacrifice themselves for the Fatherland, thus leveraging a historically entrenched prejudice (reaching back to Hegel) that Judaism was essentially incapable of accepting (revelatory) sacrifice.[66] Bauch denied, however, any anti-Semitism on his part, although he argued that despite the assimilation of Jews into German culture and their command of the German language, "the stranger may live among us through generations and no longer be able to speak another language [...] nevertheless, his language is not ours." Jews are deemed to be "guests in our house," who could never truly be at home in the *Heimat*.[67] As Bauch stated in the populist journal *Der Panther*, "the Jewish thinker Cohen" could never genuinely understand "the German thinker Kant."[68] There shall always remain "*ein Fremdes zwischen ihm und uns.*"[69]

Bauch's polemic against Cohen opened a philosophical war front against Judaism within academic German philosophy that mirrored as well as legitimated mounting anti-Semitism during the war. This anti-Semitic *Kriegsphilosophie* against the "enemy within" traded on the stereotypical image of "the Jew" and "Judaism" as pitched in existential struggle against Germanness.[70] Already before the war, Werner Sombart in *The Jews and Economic Life* (1913) cast the opposition between Germans

---

[66] Hoeres, *Krieg der Philosophen*, p. 233 ff.
[67] B. Bauch, "Leserbrief," *Der Panther. Deutsche Monatsschrift für Politik und Volkstum*, Vol. 4, No. 6 (1916): 148–154.
[68] Bauch's article was provoked in 1916 by Lenore Ripke-Kühn's "Ein Briefwechsel," where she responds to an anonymously published article by Max Hildebert Böhm in the *Preussische Jahrbuch* entitled "Vom jüdisch-deutschen Geist" (1915). Böhm's article presented sustained anti-Semitic polemic against Cohen's German–Jewish synthesis and the "rationalism" of "Jewish Neo-Kantians." In her letter, Ripke-Kühn speaks of the "danger posed by Jewish Neo-Kantian intellectualism" and singles out as well Cohen, who is "unquestionably of the most honorable figures of Judentum and one of the most significant philosophical figures within Germany." The Neo-Kantian Bauch did not take kindly to any association with Cohen and "Jewish rationalism and intellectualism," and thus responded with his own *Der Panther* to Ripke-Kühn. M. Böhm, "Vom jüdisch-deutschen Geist," *Preussische Jahrbücher*, Vol. 162 (1915): 404–420; B. Bauch, "Brief an Frau Dr. Ripke-Kühn," *Der Panther*, Vol. 4 (1916): 742–746. See C. Streubel, *Lenore Kühn (1878–1955): neue Nationalistin und verspätete Bildungsbürgerin* (Berlin: Trafo Verlag, 2007).
[69] For the controversy provoked by Bauch's article, see Hoeres, *Krieg der Philosophen*, pp. 232–237; Sieg, *Jüdisches Intellektuelle im Ersten Weltkrieg*, pp. 231–256; Meyer, *Kulturphilosophie in gefährlicher Zeit*, p. 129 ff. Bauch's article produced a rift among the Kantian academic community. Cohen and Cassirer both left the *Kantgesellschaft*, while Rudolf Eucken tried to mediate between the parties along with Hans Vaihinger. Bauch was forced to resign, and yet continued to endorse his article. In 1918, Bauch established the "German Philosophical Society" with a nationalistic and *völkisch* orientation.
[70] D. Rupnow, *Judenforschung im Dritten Reich. Wissenschaft zwischen Politik, Propaganda und Ideologie* (Baden-Baden: Nomos, 2011), p. 288 ff.

and Jews in sociological terms as a conflict between "heroic peoples" (*Helden*) and "commercial peoples" (*Händler*), between "community" (*Gemeinschaft*) and "society" (*Gesellschaft*). "Rationalism," "individualism," and "cosmopolitanism" were said to be "the fundamental characteristics of both Judaism and capitalism." Jews were thus unable to enter into "an organic whole of culture and community." Indeed, for Sombart, Jewish civilization – *Bildungsbürgertum* – stood antithetical to German *Kultur*. With Germany's defeat in 1918 followed by civil war, economic deprivation, and national humiliation, Henrich von Treitschke's lament that "the Jews are our misfortune," as Golo Mann observed, strongly reverberated throughout German society.[71] Among conservative and *völkische* outlooks, the view that "the Jews have obstructed our course to victory and betrayed the fruits of our victory," as declared in *Ostdeutsche Rundschau* in 1919, became widely accepted, along with the convenient myth of a Jewish "stab in the back" (*Dolchstoß in den Rücken*) that allegedly precipitated Germany's downfall.[72] As Hans Blüher, a leading figure in the *Wandervogel* movement, wrote in *Secessio Judaica* (1922): "The Germans will soon know that at the core of all political questions is the Jewish question." Blüher sounded the alarm of "Jewish machinations [*Machenschaften*] against Germany" and, as exemplified with Bauch's polemic against Cohen, entrenched a cultural and philosophical paranoia against Jews as the spectral enemy, who operated "inside" and "outside," and whose "machinations" would inhibit – "obliterate" – the realization of the German spirit. The German translation of the *Protocols of the Elders of Zion* (1920) expanded Jewish "machinations" to the level of a "world conspiracy."[73] Firmly established within the political and cultural landscape of Weimar Germany, the abstract image of the Jew became an encompassing symbol for the ailments of modernity with its destruction of German indigenous roots, communal existence, and traditional values.[74] The internal enemy – "the guest in our house" – who allegedly "betrayed" Germany remained all the more threatening in the aftermath of catastrophe, an even greater, and yet unseen, danger lurking within.

---

[71] Cited in S. Friedländer, "Die politischen Veränderung der Kriegszeit," in *Deutsches Judentum in Krieg und Revolution 1916–1923*, ed. W. Mosse (Tübingen: J. C. B. Mohr, 1971): 27–67; p. 49.
[72] Cited in Friedlander, "Die politischen Veränderung der Kriegszeit," p. 53.
[73] See N. Cohn, *Warrant for Genocide: The Myth of the Jewish World Conspiracy and the Protocols of the Elders of Zion* (New York: Harper and Row, 1967).
[74] As Enzo Traverso writes: "As the personification of the abstraction that dominated the social relations of capitalism, urban, and industrial world, the Jew was stripped of his real features and became simply a metaphor for modernity"; E. Traverso, *The Origins of Nazi Violence*, trans. J. Lloyd (New York: New Press, 2003), p. 130.

In 1916, although Cassirer had urged the aging Cohen (who died in April 1918) not to dignify Bauch's anti-Semitic writing with a reply, he nonetheless took it upon himself to draft a critical essay, although he never completed it.[75] In this unpublished essay, Cassirer challenged Bauch's "abstraction of the Jew" and a priori refusal to admit any possible understanding between Germans and Jews. Moreover, Cassirer rejected the ethnonationalist talk of "the German Spirit" as a "purely dogmatic naturalism."[76] Echoing *Freedom and Form* (1916), Cassirer argued that although the idea of freedom represented the highest achievement of German Idealism, it is not "a specifically German concept." Bauch's vitriolic nationalism and dogmatic naturalization of spirit rested on a decisionism that placed his thinking beyond the reach and responsibility of genuine philosophical confrontation and debate. As Cassirer writes: "Where do we end up when in the dispute about the validity of a proposition its pure content is no longer decisive, when a decision is no longer to be taken from its logical presuppositions and reasons, but from the personality of its author?"[77] Revealingly, Cassirer decided to abruptly "break off" his discussion of Bauch, as if he realized in actu the implication of his own astute analysis, and consequently adopted an attitude of taciturn silence. As Cassirer remarks:

> Basically, of course, there is no difficulty and no serious problem for Bauch here: for the relationship between Germans and Jews is determined for him very simply according to a general schema. The Jew is a "guest in the German house": and thus his position is prescribed for him once and for all by the relationship that is to be assumed in general between "guest peoples" and "host peoples." Here there is an external coexistence [*ein äusseres Nebeneinanderleben*], which, however, can never lead to a truly inner spiritual-national relationship. For everything that could establish such a relationship is denied to the Jew.[78]

When placed within the shadow of Cassirer's unpublished – and hence silent – response to Bauch's attack against his venerated teacher during the war, it is telling that Cassirer only once referred in print to his encounter with Heidegger in Davos: at the end of his review of Heidegger's *Kantbuch*. In "my discussion with Heidegger in Davos," he did not hope to "convert"

---

[75] As Cohen writes to Paul Natorp: "Doesn't it seem as if that in the highest dangers of politics the Germans always think of the Jews"; in *Der Marburger Neukantianismus in Quellen: Zeugnisse kritischer Lektüre, Briefe der Marburger, Dokumente zur Philosophiepolitik der Schule*, ed. H. Holzhey (Basel: Schwabe, 1986), Band II, p. 456.
[76] E. Cassirer, "Zum Begriff der Nation. Eine Erwiderung auf den Aufsatz von Bruno Bauch," in *Nachgelassene Manuskripte und Texte*, IX, 29–60; p. 42.
[77] Cassirer, "Zum Begriff der Nation," p. 35.
[78] Cassirer, "Zum Begriff der Nation," p. 47.

Heidegger to his own standpoint, and yet, as he writes: "But what should be striven for in all philosophical discussion and what must be achieved in some sense is this, that even did opposites learn to see themselves correctly and that they try to understand themselves in this dichotomy." Arguably, Cassirer's silence in response to Heidegger's spectral attack against the "rationalism" and "intellectualism" of Marburg Neo-Kantianism repeated his attitude in the face of Bauch's polemic against Cohen. The malignant ghosts of a wartime philosophical anti-Semitism had returned with unsuspected vehemence, and destructive consequences that at the time no one could possibly imagine. Finding himself in the place once occupied by Cohen, in the discerning awareness that Heidegger's decisionism precluded any possibility of *Verständigung*, one could only remain dignified in silence so as not to fall victim to specters leading to the grave.[79]

Advance Outposts and Rearguard Positions

Around 1930, Heidegger began recording whispered reflections in a set of private notebooks, his *Black Notebooks*, where, over the span of forty years until his death, he set down, in an impressionistic yet single-minded manner, "the basic attunements of questioning and the directives into the extreme horizons of attempts at thinking."[80] These ensconced lines of thinking began during the transformative turn in Heidegger's thinking from 1929 to 1932, away from the unfinished project of *Being and Time* toward his searching meditations for "another beginning," with the question of Being gathered around the question of truth in its primordial (and historically obscured) Greek experience as *aletheia*. As Heidegger notes:

---

[79] In his last publication before his death, Franz Rosenzweig in his brief essay "Exchanged Fronts" identified an elective affinity between Heidegger and himself. Rosenzweig considers Cohen's posthumously published *Religion of Reason* and the Davos conference as marking a transformation from an "old" to "new thinking. Curiously, Rosenzweig argues that the "fronts have been exchanged" between Cassirer – a student of Cohen in Marburg – and Heidegger (who had been appointed in Marburg). As Daniel Herskowitz comments: "In a somewhat puzzling analysis, Rosenzweig portrays the late Cohen, Heidegger, and himself as promulgators of a shared vein of thought"; *Heidegger and His Jewish Reception* (Cambridge, UK: Cambridge University Press, 2021), p. 75. Setting aside Rosenzweig's idiosyncratic perception, what Rosenzweig failed to see is that this was not an "exchanged front" but the spectral return of the war front between Germany and Judaism. For a discussion of this piece and comparison between Rosenzweig and Heidegger that draws out contrasts and divergences, K. Löwith, "M. Heidegger and F. Rosenzweig: A Postscript to *Being and Time*," in *Nature, History, and Existentialism*, trans. Arnold Levison (Evanston, IL: Northwestern, 1966): 51–78.

[80] The first Black Notebook from 1930 remains missing. The second Notebook begins with the date October 1931.

Today (March, 1932) I am in all clarity at a place from which my entire previous literary output (*Being and Time*, "What is Metaphysics?, *Kantbuch*, and "On the Essence of Ground" I and II) has become alien to me. Alien like a path brought to an impasse, a path overgrown with grass and vegetation – a path which yet retains the fact that it leads into Da-sein as temporality.[81]

After a foray into a "metaphysics of Dasein" in the wake of *Being and Time*, Heidegger definitively abandoned the path of thinking toward the question of Being through an existential analysis of Dasein, and turned instead to what he called *Seynsgeschichtliches Denken* (adopting the idiosyncratic orthography of *Seyn* rather than *Sein*). As Heidegger writes: "the history of Being is not the history of man and humanity, nor the history of the relation of man to beings and being. The history of being is being itself and only itself."[82] With this view that the "destiny of Being determines the essence of all history," historical events are to be seen within an encompassing trajectory at the center of which no longer stands the relation of human existence (Dasein) to Being, but the unfolding of the destiny of Being in relation to the truth of Being within which the fate of human beings becomes itself situated. Historical events are "geschichtlich" (Heidegger plays on the term *Geschick/Geschichte*) – issued, or sent, and destined – within a historicity otherwise than the chronological time of punctual beginnings and endings rooted in Dasein's ecstatic temporality. It is during this turning of Heidegger's thinking that the First World War returns, emerging from the shadows of his previous thinking into the staging area for another beginning. The unthought resonances of the war beneath the surface of Heidegger's unfolding thinking during the 1920s become transfigured into an attempt to think philosophically, within his revised ontological frame of reference, the war's unthought significance for Germany as well as the West. This passage of the war from "unthought" to "thought" was first signaled in the 1929–30 lecture course "The Fundamental Concepts of Metaphysics," where Heidegger declared:

> We must first call for someone capable of instilling terror into our Dasein again. For how do things stand with our Dasein when an event like the Great War can to all extents and purposes pass us by without leaving a trace? Is this not perhaps a sign that no event, however momentous it may be, can assume this task if man has not prepared himself for awakening in the first place?[83]

---

[81] M. Heidegger, *Ponderings II–IV. Black Notebooks 1931–1938*, trans. R. Rojcewicz (Bloomington: Indiana University Press, 2016), p. 16.
[82] *Nietzsche II (1939–1946)*, ed. B. Schillbach (Frankfurt: Vittorio Klostermann, 1997), p. 447.
[83] Heidegger, *The Fundamental Concepts of Metaphysics*, p. 173.

Contemporary existence (Dasein), Heidegger there argued, remained asleep to the dangerousness of its own historical situation. Adrift and distracted in the boredom and bustle of modern culture, Heidegger's cry in the wilderness becomes an emphatic call for his contemporaries to awaken to the First World War's unfinished – that is, eschatological – eventuality from their dogmatic slumber. The war returns as philosophically unfinished, still in search of victory in the name of ultimate things.

This searching turn toward "another beginning" and *Seynsgeschichtliches Denken* coincided with the Great Depression and political-economic collapse of the Weimar Republic. The 1930s, as Heidegger writes to Karl Jaspers in 1931, promised to be "an age of revolutionary possibility," to which his own philosophical thinking would contribute, if not initiate. Containing neither sketches of projected works nor "notes for a planned system," the *Black Notebooks* are an intimate echo chamber for the amplification of Heidegger's thinking in this time of revolutionary possibilities. As Heidegger notes:

> These "ponderings" and all the previous ones are not "aphorisms" in the sense of "adages"; instead, they are inconspicuous advance outposts – and rearguard positions – within the whole of an attempt at a still ineffable meditation toward the conquest of a way for the newly inceptual questioning, which is called, in distinction from metaphysical thinking, the thinking of the history of beyng.[84]

With such a characterization of his "ponderings," or "reflective considerations" (*Überlegungen*), as "advance outposts" and "rearguard positions," Heidegger betrays an underlying ambiguity in the self-fashioning of this thinking as emboldened and embattled in a titanic struggle during the end of days for "the Last Humans."[85] The old world was becoming more and more devasted – "the flight of the gods," as Heidegger was fond of saying – while the new – "ineffable" – world struggled to emerge; today was the time of monsters. As Heidegger writes: "What is happening? The destruction of the earth [...] in the guise of what is *gigantically* unprecedented from day to day and always new and in the guise of the running down of all resistance has disappeared – and with it any capacity for awe in the face of that which is self-concealing."[86] The planetary age of "machination, the anthropomorphizing of the human being into the exploitation

---

[84] M. Heidegger, *Ponderings VII–XI. Black Notebooks 1938–1939*, trans. R. Rojcewicz (Bloomington: Indiana University Press, 2014), p. 214.
[85] As Bambach remarks: "In Nietzschean moment of visionary resolve," Heidegger's adoption of a martial language of hardness and appropriation of militant-heroic rhetoric "aimed at battling contemporary urban man and rootlessness"; *Heidegger's Roots*, p. 35.
[86] Heidegger, *Ponderings II–IV*, p. 230.

of the earth, and the calculation of the world" has achieved "unrestricted supremacy," against which "no measures can be taken to impede."[87] What exacerbates this plight of Being is the profound loss of orientation toward the historical present itself. The "today" is not in a crisis, for it stands exposed to a danger of which it remains oblivious: "we cannot *know* what is basically happening with us; such knowledge was never granted a historical age. What the age believes it knows is always different from what is happening." Caught in this double bind – without a clear path of exodus to the future, without a secure standing in the present – Heidegger defiantly maintains: "But we must grasp two things, specifically in their correlation. On the one hand, the setting of a defense against the uprooting of the West and at the same time, on the other hand, the preparation of the highest decisions of historical Da-sein."[88]

Heidegger's thinking straddles the line between "rearguard positions" and "advance postings," where struggle, in an ontological sense, rages as the cipher of Being in the "no man's land," as it were, of the present condition of indecisiveness, "de-divinization," and desertification. This front line of titanic struggle over the meaning of it all does not demarcate a clear boundary or limit.[89] It designates instead a breach into which thinking is challenged and called to adventure, where the thinker appoints himself as an ontological *Frontkämpfer* on the eschatological stage of Being. As Heidegger writes:

> We still reflect too little on the fate of those solitary ones who had to fall at their advanced outposts, seemingly without exploits and works, without illumination and transfiguration. And how great is their number, how much forgotten their individual names and sacrifices. What has the god of our history here required of the people? And yet – over and against these fallen ones of the Great War, how rare those who in solitude fall on the path of meditation and of the projection of the projections in the *polemos* of truth.[90]

In seeking to dispense bread for stones, Heidegger undertakes a communion and commemoration with "the solitary ones" – those he once witnessed resolutely going to Hell – in the fold of his own intimate struggle for a decision about the truth of Being along the onward path of his own thinking.

---

[87] M. Heidegger, *Ponderings XII–XV. Black Notebooks 1939–1941*, trans. R. Rojcewicz (Bloomington: Indiana University Press, 2017), p. 41.
[88] Heidegger, *Ponderings II–IV*, p. 214.
[89] As with Ernst Jünger in his essay "Across the Line": *Über die Linie* (Frankfurt: Vittorio Klostermann, 1950).
[90] Heidegger, *Ponderings II–IV*, p. 219.

This path "underway" to thinking, as Heidegger explains in *Contributions to Philosophy*, effects a "crossing from metaphysics to being historical thinking [*seynsgeschichtliches Denken*]," across six "joinings" (*Fugen*) – "echo, playing-forth, the leap, grounding, the one who are to come, and the last god" – meant to facilitate another beginning and repair the disjointedness of Being, that time is out of joint.[91] In this "sojourning" of thinking, ways of Being manifests themselves as self-appropriating "events" (*Ereignis*), which philosophical reflection neither masters nor directs.

Given the historical double bind in which Heidegger situates himself, "philosophy least of all is capable of eliminating the already all too severe plight (the external one) or even of pointing out the ways to that end. On the contrary, philosophy must remain hard against the plight and keep itself hard to the wind of *its own* storm." In standing fast against the desertification of the world and abandonment of Being, Heidegger cultivates a fretful consternation over the wanting indigeneity of "Germanness" from his own rooted embrace of the earth. As he writes:

> Once more: the world is in reconstruction toward itself. We are again approaching the truth and its essentiality – we are becoming mindful of everything the truth requires to take it up and to take a stand within it – to become ones who are indigenous, who stand on native soil. The one who can be indigenous is the one who derives from native soil, is nourished by it, stands on it – this is the original – that is what often vibrates in me through the body and disposition – as if I went over fields guiding a plow, or over lonely field-paths amid ripening grain, through winds and fog, sunshine and snow, paths which kept mother's blood, and that of her ancestors, circulating and pulsing [...].[92]

This yoking together of the political, the ontological, and the historical places the question of Germanness at the forefront of Heidegger's pitched battle against the disjointedness of modernity. As a rearguard action and preparation for "a secret Germany to come," Heidegger affirms the indigenous autochthony of Germanness as prophetically expressed in Hölderlin's poetry. As Heidegger states: "Only someone who is German can in an originarily new way poetize being and say being – he alone will conquer anew the essence of *theoria* and finally create a *logic*."[93] This situating of Germanness within the history of Being aligns itself with the

---

[91] M. Heidegger, *Contributions to Philosophy*, trans. P. Emad (Bloomington: Indiana University Press, 2000), p. 3ff.
[92] Heidegger, *Ponderings II–IV*, p. 29.
[93] Heidegger, *Ponderings II–IV*, p. 21. For Heidegger's adherence to Germanness in relation to the Greeks, see Bambach, *Heidegger's Roots* and Sluga, *Heidegger's Crisis*.

Machtergreifung of the Nazi Party and Adolf Hitler's appointment as *Reichskanzler* in January 1933. The Nazi ascension to power, touted as a "German Revolution," signaled for Heidegger the redemptive uptake for Germany in the aftermath of the war, thus setting the stage for his own arrival on the scene of Germany's political destiny. As Heidegger writes to Karl Jaspers in April 1933, "as dark and as questionable as so many things are, still I sense more that we are entering into a new reality and that an epoch has become old."[94]

Seeing in the eschatological orientation of National Socialism an intersection with his own aspirations for reform of German universities and, more broadly, German Spirit, Heidegger was elected Rector of the University of Freiburg in April 1933 and joined the Nazi Party in May, with the expectation of contributing to Germany's regeneration. As Heidegger writes to Elizabeth Blochmann after his appointment, mindful of the danger that current political transformations might still "adhere to the superficial," "we are preparing ourselves for a second and deeper one," namely, a transformative awakening that "we, as a historical-spiritual people, still and once again will be ourselves."[95] On May 27, Heidegger delivered his infamous Rectoral Address, "Self-Assertion of the German University," endorsing the Nazi regime.[96] Quickly thereafter, however, when Heidegger recognized his inability to push through his programmatic reform of university life and education, sidelined as he was by party bureaucrats, he resigned his Rectorship in 1934. As Löwith recalled, Heidegger's students were surprised by this decision to engage himself politically, given his (mostly) silence on political issues during the 1920s.[97]

---

[94] *Martin Heidegger – Karl Jaspers: Briefwechsel 1920–1963*, ed. W. Biemel (Frankfurt: Vittorio Klostermann, 1990), p. 152.
[95] Heidegger and Blochmann, *Briefwechsel 1918–1969*, p. 60 (March 30, 1933).
[96] Heidegger resigned his position as Rector in April 1934. The literature on his involvement with Nazism and his Rectoral Address is vast. For documentary materials: G. Neske and E. Kettering, *Martin Heidegger and National Socialism: Questions and Answers*, trans. L. Harries (New York: Paragon Press, 1990); and *The Heidegger Controversy: A Critical Reader*, ed. R. Wolin (Cambridge, MA: MIT Press, 1992). For the biographical details of Heidegger's affiliation with the Nazi Party and Rectorship, R. Safranski, *Martin Heidegger: Between Good and Evil*, trans. E. Osers (Cambridge, MA: Harvard University Press, 1999); V. Farias, *Heidegger and Nazism* (Philadelphia, PA: Temple University, 1989); and Ott, *Martin Heidegger*. For Heidegger's political thinking, G. Fried, *Heidegger's Polemos: From Being to Politics* (New Haven, CT: Yale University Press, 2000). For the *völkische* underpinnings of Heidegger's thinking and language in relation to Nazi ideology, A. Knowles, *Heidegger's Fascist Affinities: A Politics of Silence* (Stanford, CA: Stanford University Press, 2019). For the details of Heidegger's relationship with National Socialism based on archival materials and scrupulous research, H. Zaborowski, *Eine Frage von Irre und Schuld? Martin Heidegger und der Nationalsozialismus* (Frankfurt: Fischer Verlag, 2010).
[97] Löwith, *My Life in Germany*, p. 34.

Yet it must have been of equal surprise for the decorated veteran Löwith to witness the entrance of the war into Heidegger's thinking from the shadows of its suspended spiritual animation. Or maybe not so, for as Löwith astutely assessed: "The German revolution of 1933 began with the outbreak of the [First] World War. The events in Germany since 1933 have been an attempt to win the war which was lost."[98]

"The Great War Is Only Now Coming over Us"

It was a gathering of students at his former Gymnasium in Konstanz in May 1934 in commemoration of the war twenty years after its outbreak that offered Heidegger an opportunity for the thematic appearance of the war in the ambit of his thinking. In this memorial address, rather than view the war as an event "already distant from us" in the past, Heidegger invites his youthful audience to "please rise and think of them [our fallen comrades] in a different light." Commemoration (*Gedenken*) of our "fallen comrades" must not be conflated with relating to the past as an object of memory (*Erinnering*). Remembrance (*Gedenken*) does not look back upon an obscure past, but, on the contrary, looks toward the future in gathering in, and hence returning to, the present what has yet to come to pass, what, in other words, remains unsurpassed and unfulfilled of the past for the future. To whom and for what purpose, Heidegger asks, is a commemoration addressed? The dead cannot hear the speeches of the living, nor can the dead be addressed by the living. The dead, Heidegger observes, only hear silence and stillness. And yet, their silence nonetheless speaks to the present in calling upon those who remember to forge a new community – a *Volksgemeinschaft* – in communion with the dead.[99] Their deaths were "the greatest" as the "highest sacrifice for the destiny of our people," but only on the condition that their sacrifice becomes honored and mourned does the actuality of the past dawn on the present. In remembrance, the

---

[98] Löwith, *My Life in Germany*, p. 1.
[99] In this transition from memory (*Erinnerung*) of a past removed from the present to remembrance of the dead, Heidegger, presenting himself as a veteran, evokes the dead not as dead but as undefeated, and, in this sense, as the spectral guardians and conscience of the present. For this rhetorical trope and substitution of memory with "myth of the war experience," G. Mosse, *Fallen Soldiers: Reshaping the Memory of the World Wars* (Oxford: Oxford University Press, 1990), chapter 1. This shift from "memory" to "commemoration" (*Gedenken*) echoes a rewriting of the war set into place during its final stages from "defeat" to "undefeated." In November 1918, as the battered German army was making its way home after the Armistice, the Prussian War Ministry issued the explicit instructions that a "festive welcome" must be given to "our field-grey heroes [who] return to the *Heimat* undefeated, having protected the native soil from the horrors of war for four years"; R. Bessel, *Nazism and War* (New York: Modern Library, 2004), p. 8.

war dead return to the present in the form of an opened future – for us as well as for them – that their heroic deaths enabled. As Heidegger states, "the Great War is *only now* coming over us [...] for us Germans [as] a *historical* reality of our existence." As he explains: "history is not that which has been nor even what presents itself but rather what is to come and our task with respect to it."[100]

In *Being and Time*, Heidegger argued that the relation between the living and the dead "must not be grasped as a being together with something at hand which takes care of it." Given that "the deceased *himself* is no longer factically 'there,'" and thus no longer present in the world, the dead cannot partake in the community of being-with, given that "being-with always means being-with-one-another in the same world." In his 1934 Gymnasium address, Heidegger, on this score, revises his previous thinking in imparting to his audience how commemoration allows for the war dead to return *home*; namely, to a *Heimat* consecrated through their sacrifice. This newfound emphasis on sacrifice allows Heidegger to think the singularity of death together with the possibility of a genuine *Miteinandersein* (which in *Being and Time* depended on the substitution of one Dasein for another) through a community of mourning.[101] As Heidegger observes, "every human being dies their own death." The singularity of death ("always my own") consists in that it can neither be exchanged (others cannot die in my place) nor avoided (I am fated to die my own death). Death – "the deepest secret of life" – should not be imagined, however, as a discrete event that befalls Dasein nor a possibility, one among many, that awaits felicitous circumstances for its actualization. Drawing on his seminal discussion of "being-toward-death" from *Being and Time*, Heidegger teaches his youthful audience that death is "the possibility of the impossibility of any existence at all" as one's ownmost "to be." Death is thus the "not yet" that is already immanent, or present, as that before which Dasein immanently and imminently stands.

Moreover, death is not a possibility that can be "fulfilled" or "realized," for the possibility of death is not a "possibility-of-what." Death, in this existential sense, can never be "overtaken," thus fating Dasein to an existence without completion or roundedness; indeed, without a *telos*. And yet, Dasein must bear its own possibility of death. Dasein can only authentically accomplish itself – be itself – when it assumes its own death-bound

---

[100] Heidegger, *Reden*, p. 280. For a discussion of Heidegger's conception of *Geschichlichkeit* in this speech, Altman, *Martin Heidegger and the First World War*, p. 170 ff.
[101] M. Heidegger, *Being and Time*, trans. J. Staumbaugh (Albany: State University of New York Press, 2010), § 47.

existence; when, in other words, Dasein freely owns up to its mortality. As neither a possibility nor an actuality, this being unto death who I am is characterized by Heidegger as a "running on ahead into death" (*Vorlaufen zum Tode*) that discloses Dasein's possibility "to be."[102] Only because Dasein is already death bound, running headlong unto its own death, can Dasein die or perish. This death-bound trajectory renders Dasein "free to be" such that "becoming free for one's own death," or what Heidegger calls "freedom unto death" (*Freiheit zum Tode*), stands as Dasein's utmost and extreme possibility. As Heidegger writes in *Being and Time*, in the "resolute (self)-determination (*Entschlossenheit*) of self-sacrifice," Dasein defies as well as embraces the contingency of its finitude.[103] "Resoluteness," of those who are going to have died, "constitutes the loyalty of existence towards its own self." Although muted in Heidegger's meditations on death in *Being and Time*, self-sacrifice exemplifies Dasein's freedom unto death; "as fate, resoluteness is the freedom to sacrifice [*Aufgeben*] a definite resolution as demanded in a possible situation."[104] Importantly, "sacrifice" does not signify here "substitution" or "dying for." As Heidegger states: "*No one can take the other's dying away from them.* Someone can go 'to his death for another.' To sacrifice oneself for another '*in a definite manner*,'" "dying for ..." cannot imply that one's own death is taken away or given up.[105] In sacrifice, to each their own death, for in freely forsaking one's own life, one wholly assumes it, as if giving life to oneself in giving it up for oneself. In this sense, self-sacrifice, not for anything or a "what" but of oneself for oneself, breaks with the "stiff focus on existence already achieved," so as to liberate Dasein from itself for the sake of its ownmost possibilities as defined by one's own finitude. Sacrifice does not open a transcendence of finitude, nor does sacrifice adhere to or endorse an existence already achieved; sacrifice, instead, in this Heideggerian regard, reveals the truth of Dasein's existence as the impossibility of transcending its own finitude, which it nonetheless transcends in rendering it one's ownmost.

In his 1934 memorial address, this existential significance of sacrifice, touched upon in *Being and Time*, becomes freighted with amplified

---

[102] Heidegger's expression *Vorlaufen zum Tode* has less to do with a presumptive experience of the front line or combat – as proposed by Johannes Fritsche, *Historical Destiny and National Socialism in Heidegger's* Being and Time (Berkeley: University of California Press, 1999) – and more to do with Heidegger's transplantation of Luther's expression *cursus ad mortem* (see van Buren, *The Young Heidegger*).
[103] Heidegger, *Being and Time*, § 53; § 74.
[104] Heidegger, *Being and Time*, § 75 (translation modified).
[105] Heidegger, *Being and Time*, § 47, p. 223.

ontological, political, and historical heft.¹⁰⁶ Sacrifice constitutes Dasein's authentic "mineness" graced with the "power of Being." As Heidegger remarks in a welcoming address to a pre-Christmas afternoon tea at the University of Freiburg in 1933: "the hidden law of all Being – that all genuine actuality is preserved only in and through the human being's power of sacrifice."¹⁰⁷ Throughout the 1930s, this paean to the ontological power of sacrifice runs across Heidegger's thinking. Not by coincidence, beginning in 1934–5 after his resignation from the Rectorship, Heidegger launches into an intense engagement with Hölderlin, as the poet of the "secret Germany" to come, whose eschatological envisioning of German destiny promises a regeneration of the West. In part, this return to Hölderlin, first discovered during the war, allows Heidegger to work through as well as work out his disappointment with the ideology of National Socialism, which venerated Hölderlin as the poetical prophet of the Fatherland as the Kingdom to Come; namely, the Third Reich.¹⁰⁸ Heidegger's embrace of Hölderlin, extending into the 1940s, functioned as well as a conduit for his reflection on the First World War's unfinished – that is, eschatological – significance for Germany. As Heidegger remarks in "The Origin of the World of Art," "During the campaign [of the war], Hölderlin's hymns were stuffed into one's backpack right along with the cleaning gear." It could equally be said that Heidegger continued to carry on the campaign of the war in his carrying forth on the meaning of Hölderlin's hymns. As Heidegger states in the 1934–5 lecture course on the hymns "Germania" and "The Rhine," "One reads Hölderlin 'historically' and mistakes the one essential thing, that his still time-space-less work has already overcome our historical posturing and founded the beginning of a different history – that history which begins with the struggle for a decision about the arrival or flight of the god." This prophetic thrust of Hölderlin's poetry is elaborated in terms of the power of sacrifice in its political-ontological dimensions. For the people of Hölderlin, "death" and "readiness for its sacrifice first of all creates in advance the space of the community out of which comradeship emerges."¹⁰⁹ As Heidegger writes:

---

¹⁰⁶ As Löwith remarks: "In 1927, the year in which Heidegger's Sein und Zeit first appeared, I doubt that any of us would have imagined the 'one's ownmost death', radically individualized, which Heidegger exemplified by referring to Tolstoy's Death of Ivan Illich, would be travestied six years later in a celebration of NS 'hero'"; *My Life in Germany*, p. 38.

¹⁰⁷ Heidegger, *Reden*, p. 221.

¹⁰⁸ For the Nazi appropriation of Hölderlin, *Deutscher Klassiker im Nationalsozialismus: Schiller, Kleist, Hölderlin*, ed. C. Albert (Stuttgart: J. B. Metzler, 1994).

¹⁰⁹ M. Heidegger, *Hölderlin's Hymns "Germania" and "The Rhine,"* trans. W. McNeill and J. Ireland (Bloomington: Indiana University Press, 2014), p. 67.

The comradeship of soldiers on the front is based neither on the fact that people had to join together because other human beings, from whom one was removed, were absent; nor did it have its basis in people first agreeing to a shared enthusiasm. Rather, its most profound and sole basis lies in the fact that the nearness of death as a sacrifice placed everyone in advance into the same nothingness, so that the latter became the source of an unconditional belonging to one another.[110]

The death that each one dies as their own is not "given up" in sacrifice. In sacrificing oneself, one does not abandon death, nor abandon oneself in resignation to death. On the contrary, one resolutely claims death as one's ownmost. But unlike his analysis in *Being and Time*, rather than an emphasis on the singular death-bound destiny of Dasein, Heidegger steers his thinking toward a reflection on the communal destiny of the people. In the disclosure of one's own "to be," sacrifice broaches the "space for community" such that "community *is* through *each individual's* being bound in advance to something that binds and determines every individual in exceeding them."[111] What exceeds the death of an individual is the "same nothingness" opened in "free sacrifice," namely, "an exposure to Being" in the elementary and earthly clearing of the homeland. The power of the earth, as the hollow of Being, is emphatically joined to the power of sacrifice. "Homeland [*Heimat*]," Heidegger stipulates, "is not as a mere birthplace, nor as a mere landscape familiar to us, but *as the power of the Earth* upon which the human being 'dwells poetically'." This sacrificial consecration of the homeland must, however, be taken up in what Heidegger calls "holy mourning." As he states: "Mourning is neither an isolated pining over some loss or other; yet nor is it that floating, hazy, and yet burdensome sadness about everything and nothing – what we call melancholy – which can in turn be shallow or profound depending on its fundamental differences in depth and extent." In a silent dialogue with sacrifice, holy morning is "what belongs to the homeland" where "the human being first experiences himself as belonging to the Earth," and from this rootedness to Earth, for the human it "first becomes possible to experience the nothingness of his individuated I-ness." Mourning "stands within itself" in standing open

---

[110] Heidegger, *Hölderlin's Hymns*, p. 66.
[111] In the 1933–5 lecture course "Nature, History, State," Heidegger develops this relation between the state and space. The state is based on home (*Heimat*), which "finds its expression in the nativity of autochthony and the sense of being bound to the place." The home, however, becomes "a mode of the being of a people [*Volk*] only when it enters into the wider interaction of trade and traffic, commerce and communication," in other words, when it becomes a state. M. Heidegger, *Nature, History, State 1933–1935*, trans. G. Fried and R. Polt (London: Bloomsbury, 2015).

"with you" – the dead.[112] Holy mourning, in this Heideggerian sense, allows for a co-memoration in which the war dead are brought home to the resting place of thinking/remembrance giving thanks to sacrifice. In this sense, the war dead "break free" from their graves abroad in returning to the homeland, as if the ghosts of the war dead arrived from the future to the present to lead the present beyond the deadened past. As Heidegger writes: "The outbreak of our two million dead from the endless graves is only now beginning, forming a secret crown around the borders of the Reich and German-Austria."[113] The graves of the war dead in fields bordering Germany consecrate – in defending – the homeland, the contours of which Heidegger draws around the imaginary borders of *Mittel-Europa*.[114]

Heidegger concludes his 1934 Gymnasium address with a veritable call to arms: the "Great War stands before us for the first time," not only in its spiritual promise for Germany, but, more expansively, for "the entire planet." As Heidegger declares, "our *Geschlecht* – we in the most secret companionship with the dead comrades – is the bridge to the spiritual conquest of the Great War."[115] Only Germany, Heidegger stresses, among "all the nations" possesses "the inner mightiness that could rise to the test of this great trial." This "great trial of the war" will usher "the new German reality" in "the deepest and widest care for the freedom of the people."[116] In terms that amplify the war rhetoric of the Idea of 1914, Heidegger refers to *German* freedom as "binding to the innermost Law and order of our being or essence" and "awakening and enforcement of the will of the people for its unique mission."[117] This "revolutionary German socialism" requires overcoming cultural superficiality, "empty patriotism," and "indecisive Christianity," as well as the "destruction of inauthentic humanism." In

---

[112] Heidegger, *Hölderlin's Hymns*, p. 80–81.
[113] Heidegger's term *Aufbruch* ("outbreak") channels the great awakening of 1914 (*Deutscher Aufbruch von 1914*) continued and fulfilled with the "German Revolution" of 1933. We have here Heidegger channeling the three stages or movements of the aftermath of war: the period of hope for Revolution in November–December 1918, the period of decision in early 1919, and the period of disappointment in the spring of 1919; D. Peukert, *The Weimar Republic*, trans. R. Deveson (New York: Hill and Wang, 1987), p. 22 ff.
[114] As Heidegger expressly states in "Introduction to Metaphysics" and other writings during the 1930s, Germany finds itself besieged between Russia and the West. For the influence of Friedrich Naumann's idea of *Mittel-Europa* on Heidegger, Losurdo, *Heidegger and the Ideology of War*, pp. 208–213.
[115] For the intractable and untranslatable complications in Heidegger's notion of *Geschlecht*, see Jacques Derrida's essays: *Psyche: Inventions of the Other*, II, eds. P. Kamuf and E. Rottenberg (Stanford, CA: Stanford University Press, 2008) and *Geschlecht III: Sex, Race, Nation, Humanity*, ed. G. Bennington (Chicago: University of Chicago Press, 2020).
[116] Heidegger, *Reden*, p. 281.
[117] As Losurdo remarks: "The influence of *Kriegsideologie* continues to be felt, though reshaped and transformed and, in a certain sense, even radicalized" in Heidegger's thinking during the 1930s; *Heidegger and the Ideology of War*, p. 55.

this sense, "what is demanded of us [is that] the Great War must be *spiritually* conquered by us, that is, *struggle* must become the *innermost Law* of our existence [*unseres Daseins*]."[118] As a final pronouncement, Heidegger evokes Heraclitus' saying, "struggle is the father of all things," yet cautions that this "profound wisdom" must not be understood in a "philistine" manner as a conflict between two parties. Struggle is here not war in Clausewitz's sense as the pursuit of the political by other, violent means. "Struggle" means above all the "great test of all being."

Heidegger repeated this call for "the spiritual conquest of the Great War" to foreign students at the University of Freiburg in 1934. Once again, Germany's *Sonderweg* is claimed to center on "a new Freedom," that is, "German Freedom" – "binding to the law of the people's spirit [and] responsibility for the destiny of the people."[119] As Heidegger explains, "what we call 'the world war' lies beyond the question of guilt and innocence, beyond the question of imperialism or pacifism," since the question posed by the war is whether "they [nations] will become rejuvenated or become older by this event." For Germany, "the awakening of the spirit of the front in war and its solidification after the war is nothing other than the creative transformation of this event into a shaping power of future existence."[120] This evocation of the "spirit of the front" (*Frontgeist*), however, has nothing to do with militarism or "working towards a new war." For it designates "*the spiritual conquest* and creative transformation of this war," as embodied by "the national socialist revolution [that] will transform entirely German reality" and the "entire historical-spiritual existence of the people." As Heidegger communicates to his foreign audience, as an acknowledgment of his own adherence to the redemptive promise of National Socialism, Germany's historical mission lies in saving the world from spiritual devastation. As Heidegger states: "The essence of the national socialist revolution consists in that Adolf Hitler has elevated and pushed through this new spirit of community into a shaping force of a new order of the people-nation."

Götterdämmerung

In 1931, Heidegger noted to himself: "Objection to the book [*Being and Time*]: I have even today still not enough enemies – it has not brought me a Great enemy."[121] This wanting and waiting for "a Great enemy" reflected

---

[118] Heidegger, *Reden*, p. 283.
[119] Heidegger, *Reden*, p. 291.
[120] Heidegger, *Reden*, p. 299.
[121] Heidegger, *Ponderings II–VI*, p. 8.

an alienation from his earlier thinking, magnified by his disappointment at his magnum opus's mundane misinterpretation. Waywardness from the project of retrieving the question of the sense of Being, as developed during the 1920s, further accentuated an urgency regarding the "desertification of the planet" and historical "abandonment of Being." As Heidegger remarks: "The world is now out of joint; the earth is a field of destruction. What Being [*Seyn*] 'means' no one knows." Above all, this conglomeration of attunements in need of "a Great enemy" reveals how Heidegger increasingly (and impatiently) understood his thinking as embattled in a titanic struggle over Being, not only against individual thinkers and philosophical movements, but as projected onto an epic stage of ontological conflict against an enemy unlike any other. "Two decades after the world war," Heidegger writes in 1938, "despite all the upheavals, the same blind frenzy, only apparently checked but not mastered," continued to define the plight of his times, without any fundamental decision, and hence transition, having been achieved toward "another beginning." Caught amid interminable wartime, the struggle of philosophy for "ultimate things" – Heidegger's *Seynsgeschichtliches Denken* – cannot merely be an issue of "argument" or "quarrelsome wrangling," for the epic task of philosophical thinking challenged by the "desertification of the world" – the wasteland – can only measure itself against an enduring "great test" in search of a "great decision" regarding the truth of Being. Such a titanic endeavor, on Heidegger's apocalyptic reckoning, can only be achieved in confrontation with a Great enemy, as opposed to the mundane enemies populating the argumentative spaces of "quarrelsome wrangling." As Heidegger writes:

> Whoever does not know the decisions can also never know what war is, even if he has "partaken" in a war. He knows only the horrors and bitter shocks of what occurs therein, and he knows the impetuses for sacrifice and self-control within the unfolding encounters, but he never knows the ground of the truth, and the distorted ground of the fact that war and peace always live on the *one* side (the side of beings) and never harbor the power of the essential occurrence of a truth of Being [*Seyn*].[122]

This obsession with "the enemy," indeed, "the Great enemy," shaped Heidegger's thinking during the 1930s. Unlike Carl Schmitt, however, the ontological distinction between "friend" and "enemy" is not situated for Heidegger at the origin of the political, which he situates instead with the inaugural power of sacrifice and communal devotion of holy mourning.

---

[122] Heidegger, *Ponderings VII–XI*, p. 147.

The enemy does not stand at the beginning, but at the end, in these ends of days, as inhibiting "another beginning." Moreover, given that the "secret Germany" to come represents the vanguard of exodus from the "desertification of the world," the "Great enemy" must be struggled against from the autochthony of Germany's homeland and its *Volksgemeinschaft*; indeed, in defense of this (self-anointed) ontological *Heimat*. The political, as Heidegger proposes, resides with "*care of the people*," in its "becoming oneself historically against the other," such that the friend–enemy relation, aligned with the relation between the truth of Being and its falsification, presupposes "*polemos* and its metaphysical grounding."[123] The enemy, therefore, must be discovered, thus attesting to their spectrality and hence their incipient dangerousness. As Heidegger remarks in his 1933–5 lectures "Being and Truth":

> An enemy is each and every person who poses an essential threat to the Dasein of the people and its individual members. The enemy does not have to be external, and the external enemy is not even always the more dangerous one. And it can seem as if there were no enemy. Then it is a fundamental requirement to find the enemy, to expose the enemy to the light, or even first to make the enemy, so that this standing against the enemy may happen and so that Dasein may not lose its edge.[124]

This image of the hidden and secretive enemy, more threatening to the historical existence of the people – Germany – than external enemies, and to the extent that "there is no enemy," marks first and foremost a void, or emptiness, from which the enemy is said to emerge, as if conjured from nothing, and yet lurking within the existence of the people itself. The most dangerous enemy, on this construal, is not the external, but the internal who is external, the agent provocateur who is at once "internal" and "external." This Great enemy is a Great specter, against which Heidegger's thinking appoints and anoints itself as its principal adversary. As Heidegger elaborates:

> The enemy can have attached itself to the innermost roots of the Dasein of a people and can set itself against this people's own essence and act against it. The struggle is all the fiercer and harder and tougher, for the least of it consists in coming to blows with one another; it is often far more difficult and wearisome to catch sight of the enemy as such, to bring the enemy into the open, to harbor no illusions about the enemy, to keep oneself ready for

---

[123] M. Heidegger, *On Hegel's Philosophy of Right*, trans. A. Mitchell (London: Bloomsbury, 2014), p. 189.
[124] M. Heidegger, *Being and Truth*, trans. G. Fried and R. Polt (Bloomington: Indiana University Press, 2010), p. 73.

attack, to cultivate and intensify a constant readiness and to prepare the attack looking far ahead with the goal of total annihilation.[125]

This fundamental requirement to find the enemy, spilling over into an ontological paranoia in the echo chamber of Heidegger's *Black Notebooks*, is inseparable from prospectively safeguarding the secret Germany to come. Holding the line against "the Great enemy," who has "attached itself to the innermost roots of the existence of the people," demands standing fast to the essence of Germanness in its struggle against "unrootedness" and "groundlessness." With this ontological inscription of *polemos*, Heidegger is quick to caution that *polemos* – that "one word [that] stands great and simple at the beginning of [Heraclitus'] saying" – does not signify "the outward occurrence of war and celebration of what is 'military,' but rather what is decisive: standing against the enemy" in a titanic struggle over the sense of Being.[126]

Heidegger's recasting of the question of Germanness in the mold of an existential struggle against "the enemy," as set on the stage of his conception of the "fated-history of Being," became leveraged to distance himself from his affiliation with National Socialism, while at the same time co-opting and transforming its "revolutionary" and, indeed, apocalyptic potential into an envisioning of his own. As Heidegger reflects in 1939: "Thinking purely 'metaphysically' (i.e., heeding the history of Being [*Seyn*]) during the years 1930–1934 I saw in National Socialism the possibility of a transition to another beginning and interpreted it that way. Thereby I mistook and undervalued this 'movement' in its genuine powers and inner necessities as also in the extent and kind of its greatness."[127] Heidegger thus recognizes that what initially attracted him to National Socialism was a shared apocalyptic and eschatological vision, which, intensified by the First World War, reached back to the 1813 War of Liberation and Fichte's iconoclastic *Reden an die Deutsche Nation*.[128] Heidegger emphatically rejects, however, the racial and biological underpinnings of Nazi ideology – what he dubs "vulgar" National Socialism – and "the brainless appeal of Hitler's *Mein Kampf*." In its stead, Heidegger envisions a "spiritual National Socialism," which nevertheless does not represent an "improved" or "authentic" version of its vulgar cousin, let alone

---

[125] Heidegger, *Being and Truth*, p. 73.
[126] Heidegger, *Being and Truth*, p. 72.
[127] Heidegger, *Ponderings VII–XI*, p. 319.
[128] Heidegger as well as National Socialism thus subscribed in their respective ways to the apocalyptic imagination of German culture; see Vondung, *The Apocalypse in Germany*.

provide its theoretical foundation, but would instead outline the contours of another – secret – Germany and "the metaphysics of Dasein" in an expansive "meta-politics of the historical people." As Heidegger reflects: "*National Socialism* is not a ready-made eternal truth come down from heaven – taken in that way, it is an aberration and foolishness […] it must itself become in becoming and must configure the future – i.e., it must itself, as a formation, recede in favor of the future."[129] Despite this distancing from "vulgar Nationalism Socialism," Heidegger steadfastly retains, in fact more intensely, the coupling of the question, and hence fate, of Germanness with the question, and hence fate, of the enemy. As with the "vulgar National Socialism" he rejected, Heidegger's attitude toward his historical situation remained thoroughly imbued with a heady rhetoric of conflict and operative paranoia, self-induced, regarding the enemy; the realization of a genuine Germany to come hinged on identifying *who* is the genuine enemy and combatting them. Placed against the backdrop of the Great War, the confrontational logic of wartime, albeit duly transfigured, becomes internalized during the 1930s into the topography of Heidegger's thinking. As Heidegger writes:

> What is still decisive is whether the spiritual-historical outward reach and basic attunements are so originary and at the same time so clear that they compel a productive recreation of Dasein –; and the presupposition for it is that National Socialism remains a *struggle* – in the condition of having to accomplish itself not merely "spreading" and "increasing" and asserting. Where *stands the enemy*, and how is he *formed*? In what direction the attack? With what weapons?[130]

This "spiritual transformation" of National Socialism into a quest in the history of Being is conjoined with a renewed assessment of German Idealism during the 1930s. As Heidegger remarks in 1939, "For the Germans, and thus for the history of the West, German Idealism is *a history that has not yet happened*, in whose domain historiological erudition has nothing to seek, because it could never find anything there."[131] Rather than abandon or overcome German Idealism, Heidegger views the legacy of German Idealism as in need of reactualization and eschatological fulfillment in its historical mission of commencing another beginning for the West.[132] The metaphysics of German Idealism remains unthought as to

---

[129] Heidegger, *Ponderings VII–XI*, p. 84.
[130] Heidegger, *Ponderings II–VI*, p. 104.
[131] Heidegger, *Ponderings XII–XV*, p. 9.
[132] Heidegger, *The Metaphysics of German Idealism*, p. 7 ff.

its "Germanness." *Deutschheit*, however, should not be vulgarized into "a folkloristic [*volkskundliche*] tracing back of this philosophy to a certain tribe [*Volkstum*] [...]." As Heidegger remarks, "the essence of the German is determined from there only as the very own capacity [*das ureigene Vermögen*] for a genuine metaphysical experience of thinking: an original experience of beginning essence of Being (*Seyns*) as *phusis*."[133] In contrast to *Deutschtum*, and in particular the National Socialist veneration of *Deutschtum* with its adherence to an ideology of "blood and soil," Heidegger's *Deutschheit* does not signify a "folkloric restoration" of nationality or "some dubious greatness of an even more dubious patriotism full of noise."[134] *Deutschheit*, for Heidegger, names "the Fatherland of Being [*Seyn*] itself" and "the historical Dasein of a people" rooted in the earth.[135] In this frame of mind, the struggle for *Deutschheit* seeks to achieve what remained unfinished with the First World War. The "spiritual conquest" of the war would thus amount to the spiritual conquest of *Deutschheit*. Heidegger's thinking, in other words, is not traumatized by a war that did occur, but rather with a Great War that did *not* occur, and indeed has yet to occur with greater urgency and ontological purchase.[136] Arguably, Heidegger is therefore not "brutalized" by what has happened, but by what has not happened, and it is this "not having happened" that his thinking struggles against and struggles for in breaching an ontological front for it having to happen now: "the hour of our [German] history has struck."[137]

As with other interwar thinkers, Heidegger understands there to be a constitutive relation between "historicity" and "struggle," but unlike his contemporaries, Heidegger displaces the defining aspects of *Kriegsideologie* – "German Freedom," *Kampf ums Dasein*, Germany's *Sonderweg* – from notions of culture, "worldview," and race. Heidegger's idiosyncratic, bellicose conception of historical Dasein and Germanness radicalizes, in transplanting, elements of *Kriegsideologie* into a historical ontology of struggle, where Heidegger's preferred word *polemos* is incessantly crossed out as signifying "war," even as its endorsed signification

---

[133] Heidegger, *Ponderings XII–XV*, p. 9.
[134] Heidegger, *Ponderings XII–XV*, p. 9.
[135] Heidegger, *Hölderlin's Hymns*, p. 108.
[136] Heidegger, *Ponderings VII–XI*, p. 231. As Heidegger states: "We have undergone a global economic *plight* and still stand within it (unemployment), we are held in a *plight* relative to history and the state (Versailles), we have long experienced the concatenation of these plights – but we still sense nothing of the *spiritual plight of Dasein* – and the fact that for *this latter* we are still not ready as regards experience and suffering, i.e., still not great enough for it: precisely that is the *greatest plight*"; *Ponderings II–VI*, p. 109.
[137] Heidegger, *Hölderlin's Hymns*.

of "conflict" or "decisive struggle" remains haunted by the Great War.[138] In the lecture course *Nietzsches metaphysische Grundstellung im abendländischen Denken* (1937), Heidegger amplifies and sharpens his view, first stated in his 1915 "War-Triduum" reflections, that Nietzsche "saw the event coming that we call the world-war."[139] From a Nietzschean vantage point, as Heidegger states in 1937, the "world war" represents a decisive confrontation with modern Nihilism and the age of the "Last Men." Interpreted in planetary terms within the topography of Heidegger's "history of Being," the inconclusiveness of the "world-war" means not merely that the struggle against Nihilism and the "Last Men" remains unfinished, but that what is at stake remains unfathomed; and hence, the spiritual struggle of the Great War, transformed into a titanic struggle over the truth of Being, must continue. Hence the alignment of Heidegger's intense engagement with Nietzsche's thinking (along with Hölderlin's poetry) and the challenge of Nihilism during the late 1930s (and early 1940s) with the double specter of a Great War that remains unfinished and a titanic struggle yet to come. In this time of interwar, as Heidegger writes in his 1936 lecture "Hölderlin and the Essence of Poetry," "it is the age of the gods that have fled *and* of the gods that are coming." The First World War gave witness to the definitive flight of the gods. As Heidegger observes,

> in this happening [the world-war] and all what followed it, the Christian God was taken by friend and enemy in the same way and claimed to be the figure and domain of the doctrine of the Second Coming; all fight in the name of the morality and reason; all fight for democracy and socialism and progress and culture. Is there a clearer sign of the reign of these shadows of the dead gods?[140]

The ideals of infinite progress and happiness for the majority, socialism and "morality of conscience" – all of these Nietzsche unmasked as trappings of a "moral god" undergoing its many deaths. These idols are but shadows of gods long perished, and yet these god husks nonetheless remain, insofar as they were invoked by various factions to legitimate their respective cause during the world war. In this Nietzschean sense, the struggle against nihilism is an epic struggle against the shadows of dead gods who still reign in the age of "the Last Men." As Heidegger remarks: "Nietzsche also knew

---

[138] As Losurdo observes: "The influence of Kriegsideologie continues to be felt, though reshaped and transformed and, in a certain sense, even radicalized"; *Heidegger and the Ideology of War*, p. 55.
[139] M. Heidegger, *Nietzsches metaphysische Grundstellung im abendländischen Denken* (Frankfurt: Vittorio Klostermann, 1986), GA 44, p. 188.
[140] Heidegger, *Nietzsches metaphysische Grundstellung im abendländischen Denken*, p. 189.

that the struggle against these shadows must first demand its own forces and victories in order to come to the point that man no longer drifts in these concealments and obscurations." However, "this victory arises only from a struggle [*Kampf*], and for this struggle it requires not only the fighters [*Kämpfer*], but at the same time a clear knowledge of the opponent and the field of battle."[141]

The Most Extreme Enmity

Heidegger's ponderings on the destiny of *Deutschheit* advocate the imperative of an existential struggle against a privileged enemy for the sake of the self-appointed election of the German people in its *Seynsgeshichtliches* responsibility and burden. Arriving at the "decision for" and "decisiveness of" this "other beginning" must occur in the crucible of a creative struggle (*schöpferischer Kampf*) that transcends the oppositional logic of a clash among cultures or worldviews, and, by the same token, surpasses a dialectical confrontation in which opposing positions could be reconciled or indeed measured against one another. What Heidegger dubs "the confrontation of the other beginning [*die Auseinandersetzung des anderen Anfangs*]" cannot be understood in terms of "adversity [*Gegnerschaft*]," as with Carl von Clausewitz's celebrated definition of war, where each belligerent is equal to the other in the pursuit of the political by other, bellicose means, or as with Hegel's conception of the struggle for recognition, where conflict is pitched in a dialectical tension of reciprocity. The enemy in Heidegger's ontological sights, against which his thinking envisions itself in titanic struggle, is an enemy without equal but likewise without actual relatability and hence encounter, enmeshed, in other words, in a spectral confrontation without encounter. This distinctive rhetoric of Heideggerian *polemos* is aligned with the dynamic of "another beginning," not as the renewal of a faltered beginning that once was, nor as a new beginning plotted along the direction of an alternative to a forlorn beginning in search of completion. The eschatological arc of Heidegger's thinking is, in this sense, apophatic (or "kenomatic"); it is an eschatology without an eschaton; namely, without a redemptive figure (as with Christ) or utopic content (as with the Nazi fantasy of a Third Reich).[142] As Heidegger writes in *Contributions to Philosophy*: "The other beginning

---

[141] Heidegger, *Nietzsches metaphysische Grundstellung im abendländischen Denken*, p. 189.
[142] Wolfe, *Heidegger's Eschatology*. For the term "kenomatic," Cyril O'Regan, *Theology and the Spaces of the Apocalyptic* (Milwaukee, WI: Marquette University Press, 2009).

is not the opposite direction to the first but stands as other outside of the opposite and the immediate comparability."[143] This "outside" or "beyond" the beginning and hence development of Western metaphysics sets Heidegger's own approach to "beginning again" along an orthogonal line of thinking that seeks to bisect the heritage of Western thought from the outside, all the while severing its linkages to its forlorn origins from within. Heidegger's return to the "unthought" of the archaic origins of Western thought reaches into the obscure reaches of a beginning from the outside, as the "inside," as it were, of a reaching toward the outside – the other beginning – of thinking. In this regard, the absence, indeed refusal, of identifying a redemptive figure or determinate content (or form) for the future to come – "the gods who are coming" – allows Heidegger's thinking to exercise (upon itself as well) a force of interruption and postponement for a future that, on the one hand, transcends (and transfigures) the devastated present while at the same time, on the other hand, perpetually inhibiting its arrival, and hence closure.

Mirrored within this inside–outside contortion of obscured beginnings and foreboding remembrance of another beginning is the spectral figure of the "Great enemy." The configuration of Heidegger's "creative struggle" hinges on a paradoxical inversion: The ghosts against which mundane opponents in the war struggle ("friends and enemies") – a war that remains philosophically unfinished – must be unveiled as ghosts of "dead gods" (Socialism, Capitalism, etc.) through the revelation of an ontologically privileged enemy, who, given its spectral presence, endangers the possibility of "another beginning." Heidegger considers that the mundane oppositional logic and political-cultural conflict structuring the discourse of the First World War misses the genuine significance and stakes of the struggle at hand. The thinker as "fighter" (*Kämpfer*), as the one who questions in extremis, is neither the guardian of the polis nor the keeper of morality, but the solitary visionary capable of unveiling the true enemy against Being, thus discovering where the genuine struggle needs to take place, in which contemporary history finds itself unknowingly, fighting, as it does, against shadows. As Heidegger writes:

> Entrusted to *philosophy*, the thinker stands in opposition to an *enemy* (the distorted essence of beings, which belies itself in coming to be), an enemy that, without ever abandoning its malevolence, shows itself as *appertaining* to what the thinker must radically *befriend* (the essence of Being [*Seyn*]) [...] Indigenousness in the homeland is an unconditioned one, because it is rooted in the spatiotemporal field of Being [*Seyn*].[144]

---

[143] M. Heidegger, *Beiträge zur Philosophie* (Frankfurt: Vittorio Klostermann, 1989), GA 65, p. 187.
[144] Heidegger, *Ponderings II–VI*, p. 344.

If "essential thinking, by its very character is inestimable," and thus "not translatable into our ordinary pursuit of things," by the same token, albeit inversely, the "Great enemy" of essential thinking must likewise "not be translatable into our ordinary pursuit of things." What is at stake in confronting this untranslatable "Great enemy" is nothing less than the truth of the Being. This enemy must therefore be found at all costs. Who, then, "appertains" to *Deutschheit* while malevolently residing outside, and indeed standing eternally foreign to, the indigeneity of *Deutschheit*? Who is the great pretender to Being?

On the stage of these considerations, Heidegger's notorious anti-Semitism flashes onto the scene, illuminating in its disturbing darkness the apocalyptic topography of his thinking in its titanic struggle for "another beginning" in the history of Being.[145] The infrequency and sketchiness of Heidegger's anti-Semitic pronouncements belie the significance of their import for his embattled thinking. Expressed in a handful of "ponderings," Heidegger's regenerative anti-Semitism, by which is to be understood how the regeneration of the world, historical existence, and Germanness from the planetary nihilism hinges on struggling against "the most extreme enmity" of so-called "world-Judaism," cannot be detached from a broader spectrum of distress with Bolshevism, Americanism, and Catholicism.[146] As Heidegger writes:

> Even the thought of an understanding [*Verständigung*] with England, in the sense of a division of the imperialistic "franchises," does not touch the essence of the historical process which England is now playing out to the end within Americanism and Bolshevism and thus at the same time within the roll of world-Judaism. The question of the role of *world-Judaism* is not a racial question, but a metaphysical one, a question that concerns the kind of human existence which in an *utterly unrestrained way* can undertake as a world-historical "task" the uprooting of all beings from being.[147]

Nonetheless, Judaism stands out as the privileged enemy in its antipodal position to Germanness; indeed, as an existential threat against the secret Germany to come. As with the confrontation between *Deutschtum* and *Judentum* during the First World War, this dubious conflict in Heidegger's

---

[145] As Donatella Di Cesare remarks: "The landscape in which the Jew appears in the pages of Heidegger's writings is where the story of Being unfolds"; *Heidegger and the Jews: The Black Notebooks*, trans. M. Baca (London: Polity Press, 2018), p. 65.

[146] For this point, R. Bernasconi, "Another Eisenmenger? On the Alleged Originality of Heidegger's Antisemitism," in *Heidegger's* Black Notebooks: *Responses to Anti-Semitism*, eds. A. Mitchell and P. Trawny (New York: Columbia University Press, 2017): 168–185; p. 181.

[147] Heidegger, *Ponderings XII–XV*, p. 191. For the notion of "regenerative anti-Semitism," Traverso, *The Origins of Nazi Violence*.

thinking draws from an ontological paranoia against Judaism as the "foreign" enemy within. Unlike Bolshevism, the English, and Americanism, each of which represents a mundane (or "ontic") adversity, the so-called "world-conspiracy" of "world-Judaism," in its metaphysical, as opposed to racial or biological, status, represents an enemy beyond any logic of opposition, and hence argument, understanding, or reconciliation. Judaism embodies the metaphysical marrow of modernity itself: technology, calculative reasoning, groundlessness, and homelessness, for what is deemed "essentially Jewish" is the uncanny power of "de-racination," "gigantic calculation," and "machination."[148] Heidegger operates an unsparing excision of Judaism from the historical destiny of Being, even as he insists that Judaism "appertains" to the destiny of Being given its endangerment and inhibition of "another beginning."[149] As Heidegger writes:

> But the occasional increase in the power of Judaism is grounded in the fact that Western metaphysics, especially in its modern evolution, offered a point of attachment for the expansion of an otherwise empty rationality and calculative capacity, and these thereby created for themselves an abode in the "spirit" without ever being able, on their own, to grasp the concealed decisive domains.[150]

Both inside and outside, the specter of Judaism haunts the topography of Heidegger's struggle against the desertification and wasteland of modernity. As Heidegger states: "One of the most concealed forms of the *gigantic*, and perhaps the oldest, is a tenacious facility in calculating, manipulating, and interfering; through this facility the worldlessness of Judaism receives its ground."[151] There is here a logic of spectral doubling: concealed behind the recognizable manifestations of technology, calculative rationality, and so on – indeed, across the entire sweep of the "shadows of dead gods" – there lurks the hidden presence of "Judaism," which, in its "machinational pretension to 'history' entangles all participants [...]."[152] This "gigantic" machination of Judaism, on Heidegger's contorted view, has corrupted – "devastated" – the world. The shadows of the dead gods are zombified, as it were, by the spectrality of Judaism, as the "extreme enemy" who cannot,

---

[148] For a useful inventory of Heidegger's seven typifications of Jews, E. Mendieta, "Metaphysical Anti-Semitism and Worldlessness" in *Heidegger's Black Notebooks*: 36–51; p. 42–44.
[149] Di Cesare argues that Heidegger's anti-Semitism is "metaphysical" and not "being-historical," as proposed by Peter Trawny; *Heidegger and the Jews*, pp. 165–167). Joseph Cohen and Raphael Zagury-Orly suggest instead that Heidegger refuses to grant Judaism a metaphysical essence; *L'Adversaire privilégié* (Paris: Galilée, 2021), p. 68.
[150] Heidegger, *Ponderings XII–XV*, p. 124.
[151] Heidegger, *Ponderings XII–XV*, p. 76.
[152] Heidegger, *Ponderings XII–XV*, p. 104.

strictly speaking, be directly "opposed" (i.e., not inscribed in *Gegnerschaft*), and hence cannot be "combatted" or "fought" by conventional means. As Heidegger writes, "the 'victor' in this 'struggle', which contests goallessness pure and simple and which can therefore only be the caricature of a 'struggle,' is perhaps the greater groundlessness that, not being bound to anything, avails itself of everything (Judaism)."[153] In this revealing thought, Heidegger's own caricatural rendition of Judaism becomes unwittingly betrayed; it is symptomatic of the ways in which the wartime intensification of enmity promoted an intensification of caricature and cliché. In Heidegger's besieged thinking during the 1930s, a pathological shadow boxing plays itself out. Judaism is "concealed" and "spectral" in its conspiracy and struggle "against the truth of Being," and yet Judaism, given its "essence," can only engage in the "caricature of struggle," in contrast to the genuine struggle of Heidegger's own thinking, its firmness and resoluteness. As Heidegger writes:

> War, even if an occasion and form for an always varied heroism, is appalling. *But this is even more appalling*: an a-historical people, blind to its uprootedness, and without the sacrifice of blood and without external destruction, tottering about amid the greatest historiological noise of all its orators and newspaper reporters, meditationlessness counting as reason, and the latter securing its essence in unconditional calculation.[154]

What emerges from such "ponderings" on the "gigantic Machination of Judaism," in its blending of stereotypical anti-Semitic clichés with the earnest rhetoric of struggle for "another beginning," is an entrenched grammar of wartime enmity, as a confrontation without encounter, wedded to an entrenched grammar of philosophical anti-Judaism, as centrally configured around the problem of sacrifice. As Heidegger writes in this 1949 postscript to "What Is Metaphysics":

> All calculation lets what is countable be resolved into something counted that can then be used for subsequent counting. Calculation refuses to let anything appear except what is countable [...] Calculation uses all beings in advance as that which is countable, and uses up what is counted for the purposes of counting [...] That thinking whose thoughts not only cannot be calculated, but are in general determined by that which is other than beings, may be called essential thinking. Instead of calculatively counting on beings by means of being, it expends itself in being for the truth of being. Such thinking responds to the claim of being, through the human being letting historical essence be responsible to the simplicity of a singular

[153] Heidegger, *Ponderings VIII–XI*, p. 75.
[154] Heidegger, *Ponderings XII–XV*, p. 103.

necessity, one that does not necessitate by way of compulsion, but creates the need that fulfils itself in the freedom of sacrifice [...] The sacrifice is that of the human essence expending itself – in a manner removed from all compulsion, because it arises from the abyss of freedom – for the preservation of the truth of being for beings. In sacrifice there occurs [*ereignet sich*] the concealed thanks that alone pays homage to the grace that being has bestowed upon the human essence in thinking, so that human beings may, in their relation to being, assume the guardianship of being.[155]

Judaism embodies the planetary dominance of "calculative thinking," but what underlies this troubling "calculative thinking," thus sealing the bond with Judaism in Heidegger's mind, is the ontological significance of sacrifice, the rejection of which defines the essence of Judaism. In a manner that harkens back to Hegel's philosophical anti-Semitism, Judaism ignores and inhibits the truth of sacrifice, which, in turn, allows for the resolution of the truth of Being (or "Spirit" for Hegel).[156] Only the one, whether the individual or the people, who gives themselves, and hence exposes themselves, to the truth of sacrifice can facilitate, without mastering or possession, the eschatological finality of Being. But unlike Hegel, for whom the truth of sacrifice, ignored by "the Spirit of Judaism," opens onto the dialectical resolution of Spirit through the figure of Christ (and hence love), Heidegger's characterization of Judaism as either feigning or failing to adhere to sacrifice has passed beyond the framework of an opposition with Christianity, even as it retains a fundamental opposition to the "people of Hölderlin." Claimed by Heidegger (in echo of Hölderlin's prophetic sayings) as the "elected people" in the history of the truth of Being, Germany (or "Germanness") must struggle against Judaism as the adversary, whose own claim to election becomes subverted and exposed as machinations against the truth of sacrifice.[157]

The devastation of the modern world and abandonment of Being can only be "overcome" through a "sacrifice" that would inaugurate "another beginning" and restitution of "historical Dasein" to the homeland of Being.

---

[155] M. Heidegger, *Pathmarks*, ed. W. McNeill (Cambridge, UK: Cambridge University Press, 1998), p. 235–236.

[156] G. W. Hegel, "The Spirit of Christianity and Its Fate," in *Early Theological Writings* (Philadelphia: University of Pennsylvania Press, 1971). For an analysis of Hegel's anti-Semitism, see J. Cohen and R. Zagury-Orly, "Abraham. The Settling Foreigner," in *The Trace of God: Derrida and Religion*, eds. E. Baring and P. E. Gordon (New York, Fordham University Press, 2014): 132–150.

[157] In this regard, Heidegger's anti-Semitism exhibits, albeit denuded of its Christian content and form, an abiding opposition between Protestantism, as the "chosen people" (with Luther as the true Elijah and "Prophet of Germany" – as he was lionized by Melanchthon) and Judaism. For this configuration of Luther's anti-Semitism, L. Roper, *Living I Was Your Plague: Martin Luther's World and Legacy* (Princeton, NJ: Princeton University Press, 2021), pp. 156–165.

It is the "solitude of the sacrificed victim [*der Einsamkeit des Opfers*]" that escapes any calculative rationality or instrumentalization. As Heidegger observes: "If in the human domain the acquisition of beings amid beings requires a sacrifice such as the one of a war, then, what will the appropriation of a world require of humans?"[158] It is not only that war demands sacrifice; war *is* the decisive "sacrifice" that reveals the other beginning, opens the vista of the homeland, and exposes Dasein to the truth of Being. War, in this ontological sense, is the sacrificial event of appropriation of Being (*Er-eignis*). Heidegger thus calls upon his German compatriots to struggle (*Kampf*) for their authentic essence by enduring "the truth of Being" against a "gigantic menace" in its most extreme manifestation: the "*Weltlosigkeit des Judentums*," with an emphasis placed on the characterization (that is, caricature) of Judaism as engaged in "combat without sacrifice."[159] Hence the impossibility of genuine adversity even as Judaism stands as the "Great enemy." This caricature of Judaism as "combat without sacrifice," where the reign of calculative reasoning and technological mastery effectively uproots the power of sacrifice, leads Heidegger to a curious statement: "When what is essentially 'Jewish' in the metaphysical sense fights against what is Jewish, the high point of self-destruction [*Selbstvernichtung*] in history has been reached; assuming that the 'Jewish' has everywhere completely seized mastery, so that even the fight against 'the Jewish,' and it above all, falls under its sway."[160] The extirpation of sacrifice and hence abdication of struggle for the truth of Being mark the apogee of the "self-destruction" of the history of Being, thus foreclosing the sacrificial destiny of the German nation in its privileged relation to the truth of Being.[161] By contrast, sacrifice in *polemos*, to which Germany is called, promises a redemptive "cleansing" of the desertification and devastation of the world in the planetary age of technology and calculative machination.

Heidegger's inscription of anti-Semitism into the apocalyptic topography of his *Seynsgeschichtliches Denken* imports stock anti-Semitic tropes that, although in cultural circulation before the war, became intensified and sharpened during the war and, especially, in its catastrophic aftermath. "Intellectualism," "rationalism," "calculative reasoning," and "groundlessness" were proffered as determinations of the "essence" of Judaism, which, in turn, functioned as a cipher for the devastation and ailments of modernity. The confrontation between Germanness and Judaism centers for Heidegger

---

[158] Heidegger, *Ponderings XII–XV*, p. 251.
[159] Heidegger, *Ponderings VII–XI*, p. 96–97.
[160] M. Heidegger, *Anmerkungen I–V*, ed. P. Trawny (Frankfurt: Vittorio Klostermann, 2015), p. 20.
[161] *Ponderings VII–XI*, p. 96.

on the eschatological promise and power of sacrifice. Unlike the adulation of Christ-like sacrifice for the Fatherland during the war, Heidegger at once transposes and transforms in his thinking the Christian image of redemptive suffering with the figure of Christ, whose immanent historical solicitation waits to be eschatologically fulfilled (and hence imitated), into a sacrifice within the history of Being without redemptive figuration. The truth of sacrifice, on this Heideggerian view, does not mimetically reconcile the present with nor preempt the arrival of "the gods to come." On the contrary, the power of sacrifice not only constitutes a power of interruption of the calculative machination and technological rationality of the modern age, but, as significantly, defers the arrival of the gods by force of sacrifice's interruption, as an awakening, of the complacency and fallenness of the present age. This inscription of anti-Semitism into Heidegger's thinking during the 1930s accentuates the apocalyptic contours of an obsession with redemptive suffering that already characterized his lectures on the phenomenology of religious life and, in particular, his interpretation of St. Paul. An emphasis on redemptive sacrifice and suffering went hand in hand with the imperative for a "decision" regarding the truth of Being in terms of what, during the interwar years of eschatological suspense, Heidegger referred to as "the today."

In this apocalyptic envisioning of the "event of truth of Being," there is nonetheless for Heidegger nothing comparable to a Christ figure or, indeed, utopic model or content. His distinctive eschatological thinking is characterized instead by its vigilance against fulfillment or closure. With this redemption without redeemer, there issues the appeal to an unnamable "savior," for gods who cannot yet be named, thus leaving the redemptive breach open, not even to be fulfilled by Christianity, let alone secular modernity. Heidegger is waiting for the "new gods" to save us from ourselves in the aftermath of a war that proved metaphysically "undecisive" under the lingering shadows of "dead gods." Given this titanic confrontation between "the devastation of machination," embodied with Judaism, and the secret Germany to come, as the homeland for the "truth of Being," Heidegger's anti-Semitism evinces its own implicit form of Gnostic Marcionism.[162] However, rather than being a radical disjunction between the fallenness of creation (and hence the God of the Old Testament) and the redemptive alien

---

[162] Hans Jonas was not wrong to suspect in Heidegger a novel expression of Gnostic thinking, and this plays itself on the stage of the confrontation between Germany and Judaism, as the titanic struggle over being. Jonas identifies a Gnostic dimension in *Being and Time* with Dasein's *Verfallenheit* and *Geworfenheit*. See H. Jonas, "Gnosticism, Existentialism, and Nihilism," in *The Gnostic Religion: The Message of the Alien God and the Beginnings of Christianity* (Boston, MA: Beacon Press, 2001): 320–340.

God to come (announced in the gospel of the New Testament), Heidegger's *Seyngeschichtliches Denken* aligns the disjunction between the "wasteland of modernity" and the redemptive anticipation of "the gods to come" along the axis of a radical disjunction between "Judaism" and "Germanness," centered on the truth of sacrifice: Judaism as incapable of sacrifice and the Germans as the people of sacrifice for the "truth of Being" and their own earthly ground – *Fatherland* in the two conjoined senses Heidegger reads in Hölderlin: the land of Being in the Heimat of Germany.

Stones for Bread

Increasingly during the late 1930s and into the Second World War, Heidegger's thinking becomes self-radicalized in its embattled and emboldened pursuit of a titanic struggle as the spiritual continuation of the First World War: "thus a wasteland corresponds to the emptiness will be reached, and this wasteland entirely spreads round about itself the semblance of a factually unprecedented fullness." As Heidegger ponders against the horizon of the gathering storms of yet another conflagration:

> If now a second world war should enter the human horizon, then it seems as if once again the *genuine decision* could not be calculated, for such a decision by no means concerns war versus peace, democracy versus authoritarianism, Bolshevism versus Christian culture, but rather: *meditation* and the search for the inceptual appropriation of being versus the *illusion* of the definitive anthropomorphizing of uprooted humanity.[163]

The reign of "unconditional power," the "unconditionality of machination," "world-imperialism" and the "self-annihilation of humanity" were increasingly unfolding before Heidegger's helpless eyes.[164] Heidegger, without explicitly naming it as such, extends in his thinking the First World War into a Second Thirty Years' War.[165] With the outbreak of the Second World War, Heidegger perceived with greater urgency and acuity that "the future will have to be called by the [...] term *brutalitas* [...]."[166] As he writes:

> Is the war an essential convulsion of Western humanity? This second world war is no more that than was the first, with which it belongs together. The second world war, however, is bringing about a new order of the "earth," i.e., a new order of this technological-organized human space [...] the new

---

[163] Heidegger, *Ponderings XII–XV*, p. 149.
[164] Heidegger, *Ponderings XII–XV*, pp. 143, 136, 187, 145.
[165] Losurdo, *Heidegger and the Ideology of War*, p. 234.
[166] Heidegger, *Ponderings XII–XV*, p. 308.

order is the decisive victory of "power" as the essence of being and thus is the onset of the unfolding of this essence into the extreme consummation: machination."[167]

And yet: "German blood will be in vain unless the spiritual decision of Western history is ventured out of the concealed spirit of the West for the sake of the preserved spirit of Europe and is attained by struggle in long meditation."[168]

In his 1941–2 lectures on Parmenides, Heidegger intensifies his struggle against nihilism – extensively discussed in his engagement with Nietzsche – and the "desertification" of the modern world. As he writes: "Therefore it could be that an invisible cloud of forgetting itself, the oblivion of Being, hangs over the whole sphere of the earth and its humanity" and that "it could also be that at an appropriate time an experience precisely of this oblivion of Being might arise—arise as a need, and so be necessary."[169] Repeating a dominant motif from his search for another beginning during the 1930s, this primordial experience of truth as *aletheia* can only be gained "by struggle" in that "unconcealedness is wrested from concealment, in a conflict with it." Heidegger cautions, however, that "conflict" (*polemos*) "means something other than mere quarrel and fight, other than blind discord, other than 'war,' and other than 'competition' as well."[170] In a recapitulation of a part of his lectures that Heidegger did not include in their delivery, he argues that "modern man" presumptively asserts itself as the foundation of beings as a whole and, in this regard, suggests that "the other beginning" does not entail "the impossible task of repeating the first beginning in the sense of renewal of the Greek world and its transformation into the here and now." It demands instead a "confrontation and dialogue with the beginning," as deployed in these lectures with Parmenides, so as to "perceive the voice of the disposition and determination of the future." This voice can only be heard, and hence thought and responded to, in an experience of "suffering in which the essential otherness of beings reveals itself in opposition to the tried and usual." As Heidegger continues, "the highest form of suffering is dying one's death as a sacrifice for the preservation of the truth of being," and this sacrifice is deemed "the purest experience of the voice of Being," only then to wonder:

---

[167] Heidegger, *Ponderings XII–XV*, p. 152.
[168] Heidegger, *Ponderings XII–XV*, p. 178.
[169] M. Heidegger, *Parmenides*, trans. A. Schuwer and R. Rojewicz (Bloomington: Indiana University Press, 1992), p. 28.
[170] Heidegger, *Parmenides*, p. 17.

What if German humanity is that historical humanity which, like the Greek, is called upon to poetize and think, and what if this German humanity must first perceive the voice of Being! Then must not the sacrifices be as many as the causes immediately eliciting them, since sacrifice has *in itself* an essence all its own and does not require goals and uses!¹⁷¹

This devotion to sacrifice as "the power of being" is reflected in two letters of consolation written by Heidegger to the grieving mother and fiancée of Alfred Franz, who studied with Heidegger and Bruno Bauch in Freiburg, and who died in Russia in the early months of Operation Barbarossa.[172] In Heidegger's letter to his student's fiancée, he honors the "sacrifice" of Franz's young life in terms resonating with his own philosophical ponderings. In his letter of condolence to the mother, he writes that "your fallen son still stands before my eyes as he took leave and said goodbye under the door of our house." Heidegger speaks of his own two sons fighting on the Eastern Front and includes with the letter his essay on Hölderlin's hymn "Wie wenn am Feiertage …" with the handwritten addition: "in memory of Alfred Franz / December 1941, signed Martin Heidegger."[173] Much as in 1934 Heidegger spoke of the redemptive sacrifice of those fallen for the Fatherland of Being in the First World War, he evokes once again a mournful remembrance for the ghosts of a secret Germany's future to come. As he writes to the bereaved:

> For those of us left behind it is difficult to arrive at the knowledge that every one of these many young Germans who sacrifice their life with a still genuine spirit and reverent heart may be experiencing the most beautiful destiny. These men, who are intimately known by only a few friends, will once again awaken the Germans to their innermost calling of spirit and loyalty of heart indirectly and only after a century has passed. This hidden effect is more essential than any academic achievement that we might have expected from those who have fallen, no matter how important – had their lives been determined otherwise.[174]

It is as if Heidegger had never left his post in 1918, looking at those who are resolutely going to Hell, those faces who are going to have died, and, as with the handshake with a young field surgeon in 1916, wanting to deliver "ultimate things," not wanting to fail in giving bread rather than stones to ghosts in fact made of stone.

---

[171] Heidegger, *Parmenides*, p. 167.
[172] Both letters are published in R. Mehring, *Heideggers Überlieferungsgeschick* (Würzburg: Königshausen & Neumann, 1992), pp. 90–92.
[173] Mehring, *Heideggers Überlieferungsgeschick*, p. 94.
[174] For this English translation, Bambach, *Heidegger's Roots*, p. 311 (translation slightly modified). See Mehring, *Heideggers Überlieferungsgeschick*, p. 91.

CHAPTER 10

The Tragedy of the Person
Edmund Husserl at War

"Fichte Speaks to Us!"

In late 1917, with the war having taken its grim toll on the student population drawn to the service of the Fatherland, after the collapse of General von Falkenhayn's intended breakthrough at Verdun and the equally calamitous struggle on the Somme in 1916, with an increasingly deteriorating economic situation at the home front, resumption of unrestricted submarine warfare, and entry of the United States into the war, Edmund Husserl delivered three lectures on "Fichte's Ideal of Humanity" at the University of Freiburg.[1] The initiative for these lectures – "emergency wartime seminars" – came directly from the military High Command, most likely at the personal request of General Erich von Gündell, who had studied under Husserl in Göttingen before the war and was Commander General of the Reserve Corps (Fifth Army), in which Husserl's two sons fought.[2] These lectures are unique among Husserl's writings, not only because of the exceptional circumstances of their composition, but as significantly for their focus on Fichte, whose importance for Husserl's thinking could never have been imagined from the breakthrough works of *The Logical Investigations* and *Ideen I*. These lectures were first delivered from November 8 to 17 to an audience of soldiers (many were university students at the outbreak of the war) returning home from the front, many of whom would soon return to the trenches. Husserl repeated these lectures

---

[1] E. Husserl, "Fichte's Menschheitsideal," in *Aufsätze und Vorträge 1911–1921*, eds. H. R. Sepp and T. Nenon (Dordrecht: Martinus Nijhoff, 1987), Hua XXV. English translation: "Fichte's ideal of Humanity," trans. J. Hart, *Husserl Studies* Vol. 12 (1995): 111–133.

[2] As Husserl writes to his brother Heinrich (October 4, 1914): "I received today a four-page letter from my 'student' his Excellence von Gündell, who retired last year and is now the commanding general of an Army Corps in France. A remarkable intelligence, a superior personality, the nature of a leader, as one immediately recognizes. We must have confidence in such men and hope that they can pull through what we are aiming for. What a tremendous achievement, what courageous sacrifice, day by day"; E. Husserl, *Briefwechsel* (Dordrecht: Springer Verlag, 1994), IX, p. 291.

twice to a wider audience in 1918: on January 14 and 16 a few months before the Ludendorff Offensive, or so-called *Kaiserschlacht*, and on November 7 and 9 against the backdrop of the Kiel Mutiny that expedited the end of the war and set into motion the German Revolution. On April 22, 1918, Husserl received a medal of service for his contribution to the war. He was given a second medal of commendation on July 9, 1918.

Whereas Husserl had remained philosophically silent since the outbreak of the war, he decided to engage himself in the war with these lectures at the least propitious moment, when the philosophical promise for the German Spirit proclaimed in 1914–15 had since, for many, become obscured from relevance. As Rudolf Eucken, a vigorous exponent of *Kriegsphilosophie*, recalled in his *Lebenserinnerungen*, he himself experienced "a certain reversal of feeling in October 1916," even if the dimming prospects for a German victory did not lead to a complete abatement of his wartime support.[3] Militarily as well as spiritually, 1916–17 marked a dramatic turning point in the war. Intellectuals and academics, who once openly supported the war effort by argumentative means, began to distance themselves in public and advocate for overtures of peace.[4] Among the most prominent of those who had shared in the *Augusterlebnis* of national solidarity in 1914 was Max Weber, whose articles in 1917 on the failures of political leadership incurred censorship due to his critique of the Kaiser and German military authorities.[5] Ernst Troeltsch, one of the most energetic voices along with Eucken during the spiritual mobilization of 1914, called in 1917 for an emancipation of politics from the militarism of "struggle for existence at all costs" and urged for a "demobilization of intellectuals."[6]

By contrast, all was seemingly not lost for Husserl. In a letter to Dietrich Mahnke in January 1917, Husserl closes with the thought: "we are genuinely called to victory and I hope that we will be worthy of it!"[7] In a letter of March 26, 1918, Malvine Husserl writes to their daughter, Elizabeth:

> And what do you think of these great events on the Western Front, the greatest in this tremendous war? Daddy is completely beside himself and

---

[3] R. Eucken, *Lebenserinnerungen* (Leipzig: Koehler Verlag, 1921), p. 100. For Eucken's wartime writings, de Warren, "Rudolf Eucken."

[4] On the "Ideenwende 1916/1917" among German intellectuals, see Flasch, *Die geistige Mobilmachung*, pp. 279–289.

[5] R. Stromberg, "Max Weber and World War I: Culture and Politics," *Dalhousie Review*, Vol. 59, No. 2 (1979): 350–357; p. 352.

[6] Flasch, *Die geistige Mobilmachung*, p. 285 ff; E. Troeltsch, *Der innere Zusammenhang der politischen Forderungen*, in *Von deutscher Volkskraft* (Gotha, 1918). Troeltsch's call was not received without censure, see Hans Volkelt's polemical response, *Demobilisierung der Geister*.

[7] Husserl, *Briefwechsel*, III, p. 408.

sees a complete victory as finally completely in our hands. We'll now see what a genius can do: the Western front, one always says, is frozen, there's nothing there that can be done about it. And our enemies can't also really do anything [...] And now Hindenburg goes to work, and look how it's going, the breakthrough will be achieved in 3 days.⁸

Two days later, on March 28, Husserl remarks in a letter to Martin Heidegger that "hopefully the war will not last longer after the wonderful victories on the Western Front."⁹ This manifest optimism regarding the war's outcome is reflected in the opening and closing paragraphs of his Fichte Lectures, where Husserl displays an unusual rhetorical prowess. With a rousing exhortation of the bellicose Spirit of 1914, Husserl recalls the German people's "struggle for survival" a century earlier, speaks of "need and death" as "today's teachers," characterizes the war as an attempt to "annihilate Germany's strength and thereby kill the fruitful living, working, and creating for the German people," and finally wonders: "Has there ever been in all of history a greater fate imposed upon a people? A harder test?"¹⁰ In his concluding statements, Husserl praises Fichte's "personality" and his *Reden an die deutsche Nation* during the years of Germany's "profound humiliation." In recalling how Fichte steadfastly kept in view the "sublime national idea in its noble form," Husserl's own voice becomes transfigured into a reactivation of Fichte's original philosophical address to the German Nation.

Rare for his otherwise sober writings, these opening and closing moments in Husserl's Fichte Lectures are an impassioned appeal to the historical present in its need for philosophical renewal, comparable in urgency with the opening paragraphs of *The Crisis of the European Sciences*. Whereas in this later work Husserl responds to the crisis of the European Spirit, it is in 1917–18 the crisis of the German Spirit that calls phenomenology to historical awakening and responsibility. If, as Paul Ricoeur suggested, "one can say surely that it was the very tragedy of history which inclined Husserl to think historically," it was not with the political situation in Germany during the 1930s and impending cataclysm of the Second World War but with the original catastrophe of the First World War that "a philosophy of the cogito becomes capable of a philosophy of history."¹¹ Yet it would seem that Husserl arrives at the tragedy of history in his Fichte Lectures as either an afterthought or an anachronism. In the closing act of Germany's

---

⁸ Husserl, *Briefwechsel*, IX, p. 348.
⁹ Husserl, *Briefwechsel*, IV, p. 129.
¹⁰ Husserl, Hua XXV, pp. 268–269, 112.
¹¹ P. Ricoeur, "Husserl and the Sense of History," in *Husserl: An Analysis of His Phenomenology*, trans. E. G. Ballard and L. Embree (Evanston, IL: Northwestern University Press, 1967): 143–174; p. 145.

catastrophe, Husserl addresses his audience in word and deed as the "educator of humanity," but unlike the euphoric days of 1914, in which much of this rhetoric was forged for those who are going to have died, Husserl speaks in 1917–18 to those who have already gone and died, returning from the war spiritually deadened, as philosophical ghosts of 1914.[12] One can only imagine what it must have been like to hear such declarations, these spirited words of struggle and struggling words of spirit, a few days before November 11, 1918. Of Fichte's ideal, indeed, of *any* ideal, what could still be heard during these final days of humanity – to whom and for whom was Husserl speaking?

"Two Souls Reside in My Breast"

In Erich Maria Remarque's iconic novel *All Quiet on the Western Front*, Paul returns on leave from the front line to visit his old university and enters a lecture hall during Professor Kantorek's declaration to his audience: "there is no other duty now than to save the Fatherland!" Upon seeing Paul enter, Professor Kantorek extends his hand in welcome and exclaims to his former student: "you've come at the right moment!" Paul is urged to share his stories of heroic deeds, but describes instead, much to Kantorek's consternation, the front-line experience without any nobility of spirit. Prompted a second time by Kantorek, Paul exclaims in anger: "I heard you in here, it's the same old stuff, making more iron men […] you still think that it's beautiful and sweet to die for your country, don't you!" Paul's indignation accuses his professors of filling the minds of his lost generation with the old lie, *dulce et decorum est, pro patria mori*. As he bitterly remarks: "We used to think you knew, but with the first bombardment, we knew better."

In 1917–18, Husserl was not a Professor Kantorek. Whereas Kantorek represents the academic who became spiritually mobilized at the outbreak of war, supporting the war with "the same old stuff," Husserl by contrast remained in 1914 publicly silent and philosophically unengaged.[13] When Husserl does come to speak in 1917–18, the incongruity of his timing is striking: He in part repeats "the same old stuff," but addresses an audience

---

[12] "Those who going to have died" – the expression is taken from Geoff Dyer's *The Missing of the Somme* (New York: Vintage, 1994).
[13] With one qualification: although Husserl was not a signatory to the Manifesto of 93, he did sign "Die Erklärung der Hochschullehrer des Deutschen Reiches" on October 16, 1914. For the Manifesto signed by 93 German intellectuals and academics, "An die Kulturwelt!," see J. von Ungern-Sternberg and W. von Ungern-Sternberg, *Der Aufruf 'An die Kulturwelt!' Das Manifesto der 93 und die Anfänge der Kriegspropaganda im Ersten Weltkrieg* (Frankfurt: Peter Lang, 2013).

that, as with Paul in *All Quiet on the Western Front*, must have known better. He arrives too late with words already long spent. Nothing is more central for understanding the impact of the First World War on Husserl's phenomenological thinking than this *lateness* of his entry into the war, which cannot be separated from his preceding silence and the circumstances that inclined him to break his philosophical quietude. The belatedness of Husserl's awakening to history and the form it takes as an interest in Fichte pose, moreover, the question of whether Husserl's "emergency lectures" are a submission of his thinking to the exigency of the war (in which case they might be discounted as an aberration under duress) or whether, on the contrary, Husserl's engagement with Fichte in this time of war represents a substantial and, indeed, transformative event within the development of his phenomenological thinking.

As with other members of the academic elite, Husserl embraced the onset of war in a festive spirit of enthusiasm and promise. As he writes to his brother Heinrich on August 8, 1914: "What excitement—what a great time!"[14] Husserl evokes the "tremendous mobilization" sweeping Göttingen and its sublime atmosphere of solidarity and sacrifice. He declares: "These are tremendous experiences. Everything is filled with the spirit of pure love for the Fatherland and the joy of sacrifice."[15] Husserl defends his German nation against accusations of militarism provoked by the destruction of Leuven and shelling of Rheims Cathedral. As he sarcastically remarks:

> That's the effect of "militarism," that's the effect of the war which is for us not the war of soldiers and armies removed from the people, but a war of the people, a war in which men from every family fight, in which every family has its dead, its wounded, its sick, but also on the other hand, its fighting heroes.[16]

The righteousness of the German cause is proclaimed to be unquestionable, much as the prospect of victory is deemed certain: "This Germany is invincible!" Husserl writes to his brother on August 17. In letters from 1914 and after, Husserl's perception of the war mirrors the tropes of *Kriegsphilosophie* and a spiritual image of Germany's destiny. As Husserl writes: "This spirit, this violence of the will, no power in the world can resist today, much as in 1813–1814!"[17]

---

[14] Husserl, *Briefwechsel*, IX, p. 288.
[15] Husserl, *Briefwechsel*, IX, p. 288.
[16] Husserl, *Briefwechsel*, IX, p. 518.
[17] Husserl, *Briefwechsel*, IX, p. 289.

Despite this privately expressed national solidarity, bolstered by the entry of his two sons into the war as volunteers, Husserl remained as to his philosophical persona rigorously devoted to the pursuit of his transcendental phenomenology. The year 1913 was auspicious for Husserl with the publication of *Ideen I* (his second major publication since the *Logical Investigations* in 1900/1) and its transcendental reformulation of phenomenology. Embroiled in controversies surrounding this contentious turn among his students and emboldened to extend the reach of his phenomenological reformation of philosophical thinking for the twentieth century, Husserl had very much come of age philosophically by the time of war. The years following *Ideen I* witnessed an intensive expansion and deepening of his thinking: engaged rereading of Kant and increased (critical as well as sympathetic) attention to Neo-Kantianism; work on the manuscripts of *Ideen II* and *Ideen III*; lecture courses on the history of philosophy and "Nature and Spirit"; and continued struggle with the "most difficult of all phenomenological problems," inner time consciousness, in the Bernau Manuscripts. As Husserl would later recall in a letter to Adolf Grimme in 1918, despite intermittent bouts of exhaustion, illness, and depression (also not untypical for him prior to the war), the war years proved to be extremely productive.[18]

A few years before the war, the essay "Philosophy as a Rigorous Science" (1911) in the journal *Logos* first introduced Husserl's critical reform of philosophy to a wider academic and intellectual audience.[19] Although Husserl conceived his phenomenological enterprise as critically addressing foundational questions of knowledge, his provocative call to restore the centrality of reason was equally responsive to the cultural crisis of modernity. As he states: "The spiritual need of our time has, in fact, become unbearable."[20] As with *The Crisis of the European Sciences*, Husserl already understands in 1911 the spiritual crisis of modernity as a philosophical crisis of reason.

---

[18] As Husserl writes to Grimme in 1918: "I worked a great deal and am here in Freiburg as productive as during my best years in Göttingen"; *Briefwechsel*, III, p. 82. In an earlier letter in 1917, Husserl reports: "these [my writings at the time] are very good, despite the war"; *Briefwechsel*, III, p. 34.

[19] Edited by Heinrich Rickert and founded by five graduate students from Russia and Germany, the journal served as the "chief organ" for the promotion of *Kulturphilosophie*. Its editorial board included Max Weber, Georg Simmel, Heinrich Wölfflin, and other prominent intellectuals and academics, including Husserl. See J. M. Krois, "*Kulturphilosophie* and Modernism," in *Weimar Thought: A Contested Legacy*, eds. P. Gordon and J. McCormick (Princeton, NJ: Princeton University Press, 2013): 101–114; p. 103. Despite its interdisciplinary and cultural profile, the journal was still perceived as "too academic." Lukács' "Sunday Circle" rejected an invitation to establish an affiliation between their own progressive journal *A Szellem* and *Logos*. See Gluck, *Georg Lukács and His Generation*, p. 20.

[20] E. Husserl, "Philosophy as Rigorous Science," trans. P. McCormick, in *Husserl: Shorter Works*, eds. P. McCormick and F. Elliston (Notre Dame, IN: University of Notre Dame Press, 1981): 166–197; p. 193.

Social and cultural manifestations of modernity's waywardness mask the genuine depth of crisis and the veritable form philosophical reflection must take in response. With the demise of German Idealism and triumph of the natural sciences, European culture increasingly succumbed to a fatigue with reason as well as a falsification of reason. Husserl characterizes the nineteenth century as a parting of the ways between an orientation toward the world shaped by a heightened historical (self)-consciousness and an orientation toward the world shaped by the natural sciences. This rupture between the human sciences and the natural sciences reflected a profound loss of unity and direction within the project of reason itself, which, for Husserl, defined the trajectory of Europe since its Greek inception.

For Husserl, historicism and *Weltanschauungsphilosophie* represent the abdication of a rigorous conception of reason.[21] As a deflationary reaction to Hegel's speculative Idealism, *Weltanschauungsphilosophie*, in the exemplary form promoted by Wilhelm Dilthey, is symptomatic of the dissolution of reason and its universal forms of valid knowledge into changing patterns of historical consciousness. *Weltanschauungsphilosophie* reflects a widespread cultural fatigue with the demands of reason. On the other hand, Husserl recognizes a subtle falsification of reason with the emergence of the natural sciences. As he continues to stress in *The Crisis of the European Sciences*, European rationality finds itself in crisis; it is not the crisis of a failure, but rather the crisis of a success, namely, of the modern natural sciences, whose theoretical validity and significance for human existence are inviolable for Husserl, even as the natural sciences have nonetheless become, paradoxically by virtue of their own success, philosophically obscure and obscuring.[22] As Husserl writes: "There is, perhaps, in all modern life no more powerfully, more irresistibly progressing idea than that of science. Nothing will hinder its victorious advance."[23] And yet, the paradox of scientific progress is that the natural sciences unwittingly produce a falsification of reason by inhibiting transcendental questioning, and hence critical elaboration, of their own meaning and possibility. The natural sciences, and the naturalism that they spawn, remain philosophically *naive* with respect to their own theoretical accomplishment. As Husserl notes, "naturalism sets out with a firm determination to realize the ideal of a rigorously scientific reform of philosophy," but generates instead "absurdities" and "falsifications" that erode a basic confidence in reason, without which the project of the modern natural sciences

---

[21] For an account of German historicism, see F. Beiser, *The German Historicist Tradition* (Oxford: Oxford University Press, 2011).
[22] For the expression "crisis of success," J. Dodd, *Crisis and Reflection*, (Dordrecht: Springer, 2004).
[23] Husserl, "Philosophy as Rigorous Science," p. 170.

would never have been so boldly undertaken in the first place. Whereas naturalism amounts to dogmaticism with its naive assumption of an ontological divide between "mind" and "world," "subject" and "object," historicism and *Weltanschauungsphilosophie* embody a modern relativism with its consequent skepticism. The tragedy that defines the nineteenth century is the tragedy of reason: Reason has become philosophically incomprehensible, not despite its success (as manifest in the natural sciences) but because of it.

Husserl's critical diagnosis is not purely intellectual. On Husserl's understanding, reason is a drive guided by the idea of systematic unity and an apodictic form of knowledge, the perfected realization of which resides "at infinity." While historicism and *Weltanschauungsphilosophie* attest to a weakening of the drive to systematic foundations of knowledge, naturalism falsifies the idea of knowledge itself. This *ethical* failure of the will to know is mutually reinforced by reason's deception regarding its proper ends, or idea. The opposition between *Weltanschauungsphilosophie* and naturalism is thus only apparent from Husserl's transcendental vantage point. Each mutually reinforces the other in their shared obliviousness to reason. Husserl's proposed reform of philosophy is motivated by the theoretical *and* ethical promise of reason, which once again must become a force in the world in grounding how we know and who we are. At issue is not only the transcendental constitution of knowledge, but as significantly the transcendental conditions for the meaningfulness of knowledge for human life. As Husserl writes:

> Would that it were only theoretical lack of clarity regarding the senses of "reality" investigated in the natural and humanistic sciences that disturbed our peace [...] far more than this, it is the most radical emergency of *life* [*Lebensnot*] that afflicts us, a need [*Not*] that leaves no aspect of our lives untouched.[24]

This pursuit of reason's meaningfulness for human existence cannot merely take the form of an argument, method, and system called "phenomenology." Husserl's reenvisioning of the Idea of Reason and reinvigoration of the passion for Reason underpin his attempt to reconstitute confidence in the possibility of reason as the most radical and authentic orientation of human life in the world.[25] This institution of trust in the possibility of reason, in a theoretical as well as ethical sense, Husserl

---

[24] Husserl, "Philosophy as Rigorous Science," p. 193 (translation modified).
[25] Husserl, "Philosophy as Rigorous Science," p. 169 (translation modified). As Husserl writes: "Only such a criticism [his proposed radical critique of naturalism and historicism] is able to preserve intact the confidence in the possibility of a scientific philosophy, a confidence threatened by the absurd consequences of a naturalism build upon empirical sciences."

identifies with the revolutionary origin of philosophy in its Platonic-Socratic form. As Husserl remarks in his 1919–20 lectures on "Introduction to Philosophy" regarding Socrates' "ethical reform" against the "frivolous game of the Sophists": "His most lasting effect was the manner by which he re-established confidence in the possibility of an objectively valid knowledge. In him, the pure drive towards truth was renewed, which is carried by the ethics of commitment to absolute values."[26] Husserl does not call upon his times to resuscitate "Minervas" from "the silent museum of history," nor give birth himself to a "Minerva springing forth complete and full-panoplied from the head of some creative genius."[27] His retrieval of an original idea of philosophy is an act of remembrance that institutes a rupture with the present in order to open a new future. Phenomenology is this philosophical remembrance of the future. As Husserl declares: "I do not say philosophy is an imperfect science; I say simply that it is not yet a science at all."[28] Genuine philosophy, as the project of a rigorous science, has yet to begin.

In 1911, Husserl's ethical directive was, however, not yet fully in possession of an articulated conception of "humanity," "culture," and "history."[29] Nonetheless, this ethical directive was imbued with a sense of historical urgency for humanity. As Husserl states: "It is certain that we cannot wait. We have to take a position, we must rouse ourselves to harmonize the disharmonies in our attitude to reality—to the reality of life, which has significance for us and in which we should have significance."[30] This imperative placed Husserl's thinking in an elective community with other prominent philosophical voices, and not surprisingly, he recognizes in Eucken's philosophy a complementary way "to discover the primordial life that constitutes itself in the experiential world" and "the possibility of a new attitude completely opposed to that of naturalism [...] from an intuition of the becoming and self-development of the spiritual life of mankind."[31]

Even as Husserl addressed "the unbearable spiritual crisis" in 1911, with the outbreak of a war that was experienced as an "absolute situation" in which one could not remain spiritually indifferent or unengaged, Husserl

---

[26] E. Husserl, *Einleitung in die Philosophie. Vorlesungen 1916–1920*, ed. H. Jacobs, Materialien Band IX (Dordrecht: Springer Verlag, 2012), p. 25.
[27] Husserl, "Philosophy as Rigorous Science," p. 167.
[28] Husserl, "Philosophy as Rigorous Science," p. 167.
[29] F. Dastur, *Husserl. Des mathématiques à l'histoire* (Paris: PUF, 1995), p. 102 ff.
[30] Husserl, "Philosophy as Rigorous Science," p. 193 (translation modified).
[31] E. Husserl, "Phenomenology and Rudolf Eucken," trans. F. Elliston and T. Plantinga, in *Husserl: Shorter Works*, p. 353.

prefers neither to speak nor to act philosophically. While colleagues such as Eucken (with whom Husserl enjoyed a close familial relationship), Max Scheler (whom Husserl distrusted), and Paul Natorp (whom he respected) joined in the chorus of spiritual mobilization, Husserl abstained from taking a public stance in 1914–16.[32] This silence did not stem from any lack of personal patriotism or inhibition to share in Germany's historical destiny. Husserl's philosophical silence contrasts sharply, in fact, with his vocal support of the war in letters to family, colleagues, and students, even after the waning of his own *Augusterlebnis* of 1914. As Husserl writes in 1915 to Hugo Münsterberg:

> Our splendid soldiers out in the field—my two sons, like all able-bodied students in Göttingen, are in it too—are resisting the enemy in the mud of the trenches, under unspeakable hardships, no day without being under fire, no night in a bed, the wet clothes never changed, in the midst of ghastly impressions, surrounded by the bodies of the dead; and when they press forward they rush on with ringing song. They have gone out to fight this war in the Fichtean spirit as a truly sacred war, and to offer themselves with full hearts as a sacrifice for the Fatherland.[33]

Husserl's commitment to this "sacred war" was thus an investment of his own flesh and blood, but this emotional investment was not matched – at this time – by philosophical investment, as was the case with Eucken and Natorp, whose sons were also serving in the field. This discrepancy was not lost on Husserl. As he writes to Natorp in 1916:

> That your powerful nature is able to react, not only as father, but also as patriot and philosopher, to these heavy and profound experiences during this unhealthy war with fruitful work and blessed public statements, this gives me great pleasure to hear. I can regrettably report nothing so glorious about myself.[34]

Husserl admires Natorp for remaining both productive philosophically in a time of war as well as productive philosophically for the war with his "blessed public statements." Husserl's admiration runs deeper. The war has mobilized every facet of Natorp's life: He reacts to the war as father, patriot, *and* philosopher. Unlike Natorp, however, "regrettably nothing

---

[32] On the close relationship between the families of Eucken and Husserl, see T. Vongehr, "*Euckens sind wieder da, verstehende und so wertvolle Freunde* – Die Freundschaft der Husserls zu Walter und Edith Eucken in den letzten Freiburger Jahren," in *Phänomenologie und die Ordnung der Wirtschaft. Edmund Husserl – Rudolf Eucken – Walter Eucken – Michel Foucault*, eds. H. Gander, N. Goldschmid, and U. Dathe (Würzburg: Ergon Verlag, 2009): 3–18.

[33] H. Münsterberg, *The Peace and America* (New York, 1915), p. 224. Husserl, Hua XXV, pp. 293–294.

[34] Husserl, *Briefwechsel*, v, p. 123.

The Tragedy of the Person   377

so glorious" can be reported of himself, as Husserl candidly admits.[35] That "nothing so glorious" can be said of himself attests to an inner schism between Husserl as engaged patriotic father and Husserl as disengaged rigorous philosopher. Until 1917–18, the father of phenomenology remained detached from the father of sons offering themselves "for the Fatherland with full hearts."[36] Of Husserl the philosopher, nothing becomes offered to the Fatherland and nothing of what now befalls history calls on phenomenology "to take a stand." This disjunction between the dedicated father of phenomenology and the devoted father of two sons (his daughter Elli served as a medical volunteer with the Red Cross) set the stage for the unfolding drama of the war's impact on him, as if, to echo Goethe, two souls were housed in Husserl, each wrestling for mastery over the other during a time when only the tragedy of history could be master.

"I Did Not Write Any War-Writings"

Aside from his two sons, many of Husserl's students fought and died in the war, and Husserl maintained regular contact with them through letters.[37] The war was never far from his horizon of vision.[38] Although there is no

---

[35] Natorp's exemplary engagement in the war is further valued by Husserl in a 1918 letter in which he expresses gratitude for receiving a copy of *Deutscher Weltberuf. Geschichtsphilosophische Richtlinien*. Although flattery can never be discounted in Husserl's correspondence with his colleagues, Husserl remarks that he cannot remember the last time when he had been so struck by a "new philosophical work" that he had to set aside his own philosophical work in order to "sink fully" into Natorp's thinking. As he writes: "My own work, which I have so passionately pursued without interruption these past years, is as if forgotten" (*Briefwechsel*, v, pp. 136–137).

[36] In a letter to Husserl of March 29, 1916, Natorp reports that "his second son was right at the beginning of the war severely wounded with a gunshot to the head, and it's a miracle that he hasn't lost his life. Paralysis on the right side remains, the bullet sits firmly in the back of his head" (Husserl, *Briefwechsel*, v, p. 121). Rickert's son was killed at the front in 1915.

[37] A significant number of Husserl's students fought in the war: Fritz Kaufmann, Johannes Daubert, Arnold Metzger, Dietrich Mahnke, Kurt Lewin, Hans Lipps, Siegfried Hamburger, Georg Hübener, Hermann Ritzel (killed in 1915 in Galicia), Adolf Reinach (killed in 1917 in Flanders), Fritz Frankfurther (killed in 1914 in Flanders), and Rudolf Clemens (killed in 1914 in Flanders). See de Warren and Vongehr, *Philosophers at the Front*.

[38] In a letter to Husserl in 1915, Reinach offers a small portrait of his life at the front: "Since about 7 weeks, I am with two 'assault guns,' which are under the command of my brother. That these are assault guns means that we only have to go into action in the moment when it matters, but otherwise we must behave quietly like mice – such guns are placed very much in advance […] That he [Scheler] leaves the Yearbook in the lurch is not surprising from previous experiences. It is for a horror, dear Professor, to know that you are harassed during such a great time with so vile and petty things […] I've announced lectures for the next semester – somewhat at random and with a soft heart. Since I will indeed not give them. May God soon give us victory and final peace that we all desire from our hearts deeply." Reinach was killed at Diksmuide, Belgium, on November 16, 1917. For Reinach's reflections on "foreboding" written during his wartime service, see K. Baltzer-Jaray, "Reinach's Phenomenology of Foreboding: Battlefield Notes, 1916–1917," in

evidence that Husserl encouraged his students to volunteer on philosophical grounds, he expressed admiration for the writings of *Kriegsphilosophie*, and was especially taken by his student Dietrich Mahnke's *Der Wille zur Ewigkeit*. As Husserl writes to Mahnke: "I love this small book and would like to see it in the hands of many others and see it have an effect on the hearts of many others."[39] Mahnke's "meditations of a German warrior on the meaning of spiritual life" offer a testament to the renewal of philosophical reflection, and specifically Husserl's method of *Wesenschau* (intuition of essences), in the crucible of his front-line experience. Although Mahnke observes that "it is often said that war silences philosophy," his own experience of the front provoked an awakening to the genuine meaning of "indestructible ideals" and "the will for eternity." This philosophical awakening occurred with his first baptism of fire, during a bombardment where each shell "could have your name of it." That Husserl might have been taken by such a testimonial is suggested by the mirroring of these ideas in his Fichte Lectures, where he speaks of "ideas and ideals on the march again" and of death as the "great reminder of eternity." For all his affection for *Der Wille zur Ewigkeit*, Husserl could be just as cautious about an idealizing war discourse, as he informs Mahnke with respect to his other book, *Die unsichtbare Königsreich des deutschen Idealismus* (1920). As Husserl remarks:

> The worst enemy of this text, I'll say this pre-emptively, is the title, and surely this title has already harmed you with the editor. People whom you want to reach, in whom the passion for authenticity lives in a time in which everything inauthentic is clothed in the language of idealistic sway want to hear nothing more than a sobering language.[40]

Husserl's view of philosophical war writings was thus not uniformly approving, and Scheler's popular *Der Genius des Krieges und der Deutsche Krieg* appears to have been especially unwelcomed. As Adolf Reinach remarks in a letter to Husserl:

> One of his [Scheler's] essays on the 'genius of war' has come into my hands, which in his sloppy, undisciplined and boastful manner made a very repulsive impression on me. Something as un-German is hard to imagine.[41]

Early Phenomenology: Metaphysics, Ethics, and the Philosophy of Religion, eds. B. Harding and M. Kelly (London: Bloomsbury, 2016): 67–86. This collection also includes an English translation of Reinach's "Phenomenology of Foreboding/Foreseeing."

[39] Husserl, *Briefwechsel*, III, pp. 414–415.
[40] Husserl, *Briefwechsel*, III, p. 423.
[41] In a letter to Grimme (April 5, 1918), Husserl speaks of Scheler as a "genius of reproductivity and secondary originality" and "a sophist." Grimme reviewed Scheler's *Krieg und Aufbau*.

This contrast between Husserl's approval of *Der Wille zur Ewigkeit* and disapproval of *Der Genius des Krieges und der Deutsche Krieg* highlights an inner consistency between his idea of philosophy and his image of the philosopher. The manner of thinking in *Der Wille zur Ewigkeit* resonated with Husserl, for Mahnke did not regard the war philosophically through the lens of any common form of *Weltanschauungsphilosophie*, but sought instead to elevate the "needs of life" expressed in *Weltanschauungsphilosophie* to the clarity of a rigorous science armed with an existential purchase for human existence (specifically, for German soldiers serving in the field).[42] By contrast, Scheler's war writing and, undoubtedly, even more irritatingly for Husserl Scheler's public personality fall within the category of "worldly wisdom" and "unscientific profundity" that Husserl rejected in his critique of *Weltanschauungsphilosophie*. As Husserl explains:

> *Weltanschauung* philosophy teaches the way of wisdom: personality directs itself to personality. As a teacher in the style of such a philosophy, then, he alone may direct himself to a wider public who is called thereto because of a particularly significant character and characteristic wisdom – or he may be called as the servant of lofty practical interests, religious, ethical, legal, etc. Science, however, is impersonal [...] What he contributes increases a treasure of eternal validities that must prove a blessing to humanity. And as we saw above, this is true to an extraordinarily high degree of philosophical science.[43]

The genuine philosopher makes no claim to worldly profundity; he is not, in this respect, a "personality." Animated by the infinite task of reason, the drive, or passion (Husserl speaks in his letters of Platonic *eros*), does not belong to the philosopher, but rather, the philosopher belongs to the passion of reason itself. The philosopher lives for the sake of an afterlife, not, however, as the personal immortality of the hereafter, nor for the unending glory of the moment, but as a life entirely dedicated to future

---

[42] As Mahnke writes in his dedication to Husserl: "You, too, the master of eidetic intuition, do not fail to realize that the needs of life require a '*Weltanschauungsphilosophie*' besides a 'rigorous science.' The highest goal of such a *Weltanschauung* is not the purity and depth of truth, but rather the purity and depth of human existence." Husserl, *Briefwechsel*, III, p. 83.

[43] Husserl, "Philosophy as Rigorous Science," p. 195 (translation modified). This aversion to philosophical visibility in the form of journals and conferences is a frequent theme in Husserl's letters and reflects his dedication to the "impersonality" of genuine philosophical, i.e., scientific, research. As Husserl writes to Rickert (January 25, 1910) in response to the invitation to contribute to the journal *Logos*: "Im Ganzen habe ich einen wahren Horror vor allem, was philosophische Zeitschrift heißt, nämlich in Hinblick auf unsere (zumal die deutsche) Zeitschriftenliteratur. Wenn ich die neue erschienenen Hefte durchblättere, schäme ich mich regelmäßig: was sich da als 'wissenschaftliche Arbeit' ausgiebt"; *Briefwechsel*, V, p. 169.

generations and the promise of reason – "the infinite task" of philosophy. The responsibility of the philosopher is to "increase the treasure of eternal validities" and "lead humanity to a condition of blessedness." Even as the philosopher's "impersonality" stands at the service of humankind, it is not the task of the philosopher to lead humankind. It is the task of the philosopher to *awaken* humankind to its most genuine vocation, namely, the pursuit of a life in truth as founded in and guided by reason. The philosopher should not be the charismatic leader who shapes worlds, nor the great personality who gives rise to worlds, nor the prophet who envisions worlds to come. The philosopher should remain discrete with his ambition to complete the noble temple, to echo Fichte, that others have had to leave behind and that he himself must inevitably leave behind to others as well, extended one step farther toward finality.[44] This impersonal toil of the philosopher for a community and a project greater than himself does not damn him to anonymity. On the contrary, Husserl speaks in letters of his philosophical *daimonion*, and so conceives of his philosophical vocation as absolutely singular, namely, as the singularity of a passion for him alone to bear, even as he bears it for others, indeed, for all humanity.

It is through the lens of this constitutive impersonality of the philosopher that Husserl interpreted his own philosophical silence during the war and, moreover, retrospectively understood his Fichte Lectures as *not* an engagement in the war in the manner of *Kriegsphilosophie*. Husserl's fine distinction between the charismatic "leader of humanity" and the impersonal "servant of humanity" comes to the fore once again. As he confides to Arnold Metzger in 1919:

> That is not my task: I am not called to become the leader [*zum Führer*] of a struggling humanity for "blessed life" – in the passionate drive of the war-years I had to recognize this, my *daimonion* had warned me. Deliberately and decisively, I live purely as a scientific philosopher. I therefore did not write any war-writings, I would have seen this as pretentious philosophical histrionics. Not because the truth and science are valid for me as the highest value. On the contrary: "the intellect serves the will," and so I [am] also the servant of a practical shaper of life, of a leader of humanity.

---

[44] As Fichte writes in *Some Lectures Concerning the Scholar's Vocation*: "Where [past generations] had to stop, I can build further. I can bring nearer to completion that noble temple they had to leave unfinished." Husserl adopts Fichte's notion of the devotion to humankind as a devotion to the future of humanity, the afterlife: "My labors will help determine the course of future generations and the history of nations yet to come [...] My life and destiny do not matter at all, but infinitely depends on the results of my life." *Fichte: Early Philosophical Writings*, trans. D. Breazeale (Ithaca, NY: Cornell University Press, 1988): 144–184; pp. 168, 175.

Pro Patria Mori

This self-interpreted consistency between his idea of philosophy and his philosophical conduct during the war was not, however, without an inner tension. This tension appears clearly in the very letter in which Husserl expresses his sympathies for *Der Wille zur Ewigkeit*. After praising Mahnke's war writing, he observes:

> On the whole, it [*Der Wille zur Ewigkeit*] corresponds in the style of its thinking with my own convictions, but there are still differences that I cannot at this time express. I am struggling with my destiny, which has saddled me with so many problems and, as I believe, enduring and valuable insights, but more than I can shape into mature publications.[45]

The shift of attention in these remarks from Mahnke's *Der Wille zur Ewigkeit* to Husserl's own "destiny" is revealing of a dynamic that generally defined Husserl's relationship toward the philosophical writings of others, including, in this context, war writings. While Husserl acknowledges certain affinities between Mahnke's thinking in his war writing and his own as yet unspoken views, he in the same breath admits that he is pressed for time, and hence unable to take the time to express himself on the differences between their views. Husserl thus recognizes Mahnke's writing as a source of inspiration, but the force of this inspiration rebounds back on himself in turning his attention to his own singular destiny. That destiny, as Husserl seamlessly transitions in this letter, is his own phenomenological enterprise ("a very great science"), which, as he explains to Mahnke, appears incomparably greater than can be seen from his writings. Husserl worries that he might not have enough fortitude for the realization of his phenomenological destiny, for what he needs more than anything else is time. During this time of war, he lacks "spiritual freshness" and quietude of the soul.[46] The urgency that presses upon Husserl is his own destiny. The urgency of time is here not the war, but his own, as measured by an infinite task shouldered by a finite life. It is, in other words, not the destiny of the German nation in this time of war, but Husserl's own philosophical destiny that defines the center of his philosophical gravity.

This tension can be characterized in terms of contrasting outward-facing and inward-facing orientations: outward towards the wartime engagement of his fellow philosophers, which Husserl either praises (Mahnke, Natorp) or dismisses (Scheler), and inward toward his own destiny – "the very great

---

[45] Husserl, *Briefwechsel*, III, pp. 414–415.
[46] Husserl, *Briefwechsel*, III, pp. 414–415.

science of phenomenology." It is this inward orientation that establishes the axis around which Husserl's life and world gravitate; everything that occurs to Husserl from the outside becomes leveraged inside. The drama of the war unfolds within the drama of his philosophical struggle with his own destiny. It is only when the war intrudes within this intimate drama of the soul that Husserl's destiny becomes engaged with the tragedy of history, that the outward becomes inward and the inward becomes outward. In a revealing letter to his student Fritz Kaufmann, Husserl writes in 1915:

> The war with its deeply troubling events has made me closed in upon myself. It will be incredibly difficult for me to come out of myself and to express myself even on those issues in which I have taken a lively share. Indeed, these are especially the things that are hardest for me. I have lost through death every month many people close to me, younger and older friends in rapid succession. Then there were health problems, but almost all with their psychological causes. As a result, I lost again the continuity of my scientific life-thread. If I cannot work fruitfully, if I can no longer understand myself, if I read my manuscripts, but cannot put them into intuitions, I'm in the worst of situations.[47]

The collision of these two *dramatis personæ* within Husserl's soul would occur soon after this letter of 1915, when Husserl found himself in the worst kind of situation in which the tragedy of history became very much his own. On March 8, 1916, Husserl's youngest son was killed while leading an assault on Fort Vaux at Verdun. As recorded in their letters, Wolfgang's death affected the family grievously, catching them in the midst of their transition to Freiburg, where Husserl had been appointed as successor to Rickert's chair. As Husserl writes to Natorp:

> The loss of this child affected our family deeply [...] His field-trunk was returned to us in these days, including his last literary company: Horace, Thucydides, Goethes' *Faust* with *Urfaust*, Schillers' poems and dramas, Mörike, etc. Also *Biblia Hebraica*, the Bible: German barbarians! He went to his death with joy.

In Malvine Husserl's letter to their elder son Gerhard, her profound grief is palpable:

> Papa has sent you as an Easter greetings Rilke's *Book of Hours* and I sent you a cake and a sausage. Hopefully everything will arrive safely in your hands and will make you happy [...] Yesterday I finally decided to unpack Wolfgang's trunk and backpack. I cannot express to you how lovingly he kept everything. Can one ever over-come the loss of such a human being?

---

[47] Husserl, *Briefwechsel*, III, p. 340.

His books, which he always took with him, speak well of him: Thucydides, Horace, the New Testament, *Biblia Hebraica*, Mörike, Goethe's and Heine's poems, *Faust*. And with that all kinds of military books.

These two letters of Edmund and Malvine reveal a poignant contrast in attitudes toward the death of their beloved son. While Husserl speaks to his colleague of his son's beautiful death for the Fatherland, Malvine confides to her surviving son the inconsolability of a mother's loss. Husserl's grief, however, would find intimate expression in a moving note found among his papers:

> Regarding Wolfgang's gravesite according to the communications of Lt. Lehrer: In the grave of our Wolfgang is also buried Sgt. Feldmann. Nearby, about 6 meters East is Lt. Ladenburg. Directly next to Wolfgang's grave is the grave of Lt. Rothe. Very near is a mass grave in which 21 Germans and some French are buried.[48]

Of the many gruesome novelties of the war, the absence of corpses and impossibility of locating the place of death introduced new complexities to the rituals of mourning and remembrance for the war dead. In Husserl's note, one feels the need to come close to the dead, to know the details – where it occurred, how it happened – in a word, to *see* the circumstances of death, not just any death, but *this* death, his boy Wolfgang. Husserl's note begins with one soldier, his son, with a proper name and biography, and extends to include a comrade, perhaps friend, and a few meters away another comrade, and then another, and next to the grave of Wolfgang yet another, and nearby a mass grave, not only of Germans but of Germans and French, and so on to infinity. The expanding concentric circles of the horror of war consume what is nearest and dearest, starting from home, engulfing in their grip worlds beyond home, to the enemy, effacing any lines of demarcation between friend and foe. All are buried with each other in the same, nameless grave. The singular absoluteness of death seamlessly blends into the anonymous absolute of being-killing.

Teleological Optimism

One can easily imagine the impression made upon Husserl's audience in 1917–18 by the opening of "Fichte's Ideal of Humanity." Husserl begins with "the strange image" of the development of German spiritual life since "the time of the Reformation to the time of Goethe." As he observes:

---

[48] This sparse information was culled from reports from Wolfgang's comrades and made available to Husserl through General Gündell.

> From the barren steppes with scarcely any elevation in the terrain there rises up individual mountain giants, isolated great spirits: Copernicus, Kepler, and after a long pause, Leibniz. There then towers all at once a huge mountain range of great minds: Lessing, Herder, Winckelmann, Wilhelm von Humboldt; and in literature the sublime summits of Goethe and Schiller; and in philosophy the genius of Kant, and from there is awakened the philosophy of German Idealism which in and of itself is a mighty line of mountains with many hardly accessible peaks.[49]

The strangeness of this image resides less in its metaphor of geological creation than in the narrative of an abrupt obscuring of the "sublime summits" of the German Spirit. As Husserl reflects: "It is a significant fact that a chief part of the eternal content of these great minds [...] brought about its effect on our spiritual life and that it all at once was completely disconnected." As he continues: "it is as if a thick fog descended on the once so radiant glacier heights and hid them from modern humanity. All at once in the middle of the nineteenth century there died away the momentum of spiritual life which came forth from these great idealists and which spread throughout the world and seemed to signify a transformation of world culture."[50] This evocation of the oblivion of German Idealism sets the stage for Husserl's call for the renewal of the spirit of German Idealism, and more specifically Fichte's Ideal of Humanity.

Whereas in "Philosophy as Rigorous Science" Husserl had roundly dismissed German Idealism with the culminating figure of Hegel, in these opening statements to his Fichte Lectures Husserl allies himself with an emergent interest in German Idealism among Neo-Kantianism at the turn of the century. As Husserl remarks, the increasing discontent of modern life has motivated "in smaller circles" a new attitude toward German Idealism. With the outbreak of the war and this "heavy fate for our nation, which goes beyond all comprehension," the imperative to recuperate the "ideal sources of power that once were opened up out of the deepest depths of the soul and that already earlier had proved their saving power" has become urgent. As Husserl reminds his audience, "a century earlier our German people battled for survival," and during this time of challenge the German nation was saved "through the power of the new spirit of German Idealism and its flag-bearer of those days, Fichte." Likewise, when "need and death are today's teachers," when "Ideas and Ideals are on the march again," and when "death has again won back its holy primal right [as] the

---

[49] Husserl, Hua XXV, p. 269/111.
[50] Husserl, Hua XXV, p. 269/111.

great reminder of eternity," the time is ripe once again to develop "organs of vision for German Idealism" and "to esteem that particular individual among the bearers of this philosophy," Fichte.⁵¹ As Husserl announces: "It is of him, of his new shaping of the Ideals of a genuine humanity out of the deepest sources of his philosophy, that I want here to speak."⁵²

Such dramatic words of summoning could have been spoken in 1914 and indeed *were* spoken in 1914, albeit not by Husserl himself, but by leading figures within the spiritual mobilization of German philosophy. If such an incantation of Fichte could bestow in 1914–15 "consolation and strengthening of soul," Husserl's channeling of this same war spirit in 1917–18 would seem far less propitious, at once more urgent, and yet more forlorn. This peculiarity of timing is refracted in the peculiarity of the lectures themselves. Husserl's shrill war rhetoric dominates the opening and closing sections of his lectures. On the face it, Husserl's lectures would appear to enter seamlessly into the chorus of *Kriegsphilosophie*. This outward-facing address to the historical present in its time of crisis is coupled, however, with an inward-facing reflection on Fichte's Ideal of Humanity, which, when considered in abstraction from Husserl's opening and closing exhortations, bears few internal traces of the historical context of its performance. The three main lectures on Fichte's Ideal of Humanity are sober and measured in addressing "the things themselves," namely, the development of Fichte's ethical and religious thinking in his "popular writings."

This dual composition of outward-facing and inward-facing orientations is joined by a further element of rhetorical sophistication. Husserl begins his lectures by addressing the historical tragedy of the war befalling Germany. This philosophical speech act takes the form of speaking *about* Fichte. As becomes evident from how Fichte is invoked when "need and death are today's educators," this act of speaking about Fichte means to channel Fichte as speaking *to us*. As Husserl declares at the end of his lectures, "the Fichte of the War of Liberation still speaks to us." Husserl's own voice becomes the medium through which Fichte can continue speaking to the present and, in this sense, become reactivated in the present. Within the form of this double performance, the lectures arrive at a critical moment when Husserl switches his mode of address and now begins to

---

⁵¹ This understanding of the war as producing a renewed awakening for German Idealism was widespread among war philosophers. As Karl Joël writes in *Neue Weltkultur* (Leipzig: Kurt Wolff Verlag, 1915), "Das Wiedererwachen des alten Deutschen Idealismus [ist] das grösste Schauspiel dieses Krieges" (p. 87).
⁵² Husserl, Hua XXV, p. 269/112.

speak *for himself.* This transition is signaled with the phrasing "we would put it this way" and occurs at the decisive juncture of his presentation of Fichte's critique of Kant ethical formalism. In turning to speak for himself, Husserl invokes his own nascent concept of "absolute values." Such a concept does not, strictly speaking, find any direct equivalence in Fichte. It is a concept, however, that would occupy center stage in the transfiguration of Husserl's ethical thinking after the war during the 1920s and 1930s, the inception of which can be witnessed in these wartime lectures.

This shift in mode of address, when Husserl comes to speak for himself through Fichte (after having Fichte speak through him), reveals a phenomenological interest in Fichte that is neither simply reactive nor reducible to the immediate circumstances of the war. Even as Husserl, on the one hand, repeats "the same old stuff" of Fichte as the "philosopher of the War of Liberation," he, on the other hand, engages Fichte philosophically, stripped, as it were, of any historical circumstance or cultural personality. Husserl tacitly operates a phenomenological suspension of Fichte's *weltanschauuliche* image in order to mine a "scientific" depth of insight. Although Husserl acknowledges the theoretical underpinning of Fichte's popular ethical-religious writings in the *Wissenschaftslehre*, he nonetheless encourages his audience to neutralize Fichte's own "theoretical constructions." As Husserl states: "Someone raised as a theoretician in the spirit of rigorous science will find almost unendurable the many demanding acrobatics of his *Wissenschaftslehre*."[53] And yet, "behind the logical violence that he imposes on us there lies a deeper meaning, an abundance of great intuitions."[54] It is this "deeper meaning" and "fullness of still immature intuitions" that Husserl seeks to extract. It is here that the "true force" of Fichte's thinking resides. Looking back to his wartime lectures in 1921, Husserl explains to Mahnke the underlying aim of these lectures. As he remarks: "The synthesis of Fichte and Plato's doctrine of *eros* I presented in my Fichte lectures (war lectures) and these are thoughts that have animated me since a decade and a half, however I do not see in these something final. My philosophy of religion remains too little developed and I am still in the 'anteroom of truth.'"[55]

---

[53] Husserl, Hua XXV, p. 269.
[54] Husserl, Hua XXV, p. 270.
[55] Husserl, *Briefwechsel*, III, p. 429. Husserl's interest in Fichte reaches back to the years immediately after the breakthrough work of the *Logical Investigations*. As Husserl, moreover, writes to Rickert in 1915: "So I feel in the last decade closely connected with the leaders of the German idealist school, we struggle as [compatriots] against the naturalism of our times as our common enemy." As he further remarks: "Only as I went my own wearisome way, climbing from below, did I find myself,

Within his cursory treatment of Fichte's thinking from *Die Bestimmung des Menschen* to *Die Anweisung zum seligen Leben* and *Die Reden an die deutsche Nation*, Husserl in his second lecture emphasizes a number of "great intuitions." Each of these Fichtean intuitions would become further transfigured in Husserl's thinking during the 1920s and 1930s. If Husserl developed an ahistorical conception of reason in *The Logical Investigations* and *Ideen I*, he now discovers in Fichte the teleological and historical dimension of reason. Reason possesses its own transcendental history. This historical dimension of reason is centered on the dynamic character of reason in pursuit of its own self-realization, as directed toward the fulfillment of its Idea. This discovery of the constitutive dimension of historicity in the development of reason is connected to Husserl's emphasis on the radicalization of Kant's transcendental idealism in Fichte. As Husserl remarks: "Here Fichte, stimulated by Kant's doctrine, seizes upon a thought of great daring through which he grounds a completely new type of world-interpretation and through which he places himself in opposition to the natural understanding of the world. And he does this in a way which is not easily surpassed."[56] The passage from Kant to Fichte takes the form of a passage to the primarily ethical significance of transcendental idealism. As Husserl argues, transcendental idealism is not merely a theoretical philosophical position. More significantly, the theoretical argument of transcendental idealism is inseparable from what Husserl labels "teleological optimism." Indeed, it was Fichte's "activist optimism" that asserted itself in the face of the "humiliating catastrophe" of 1806. As Husserl writes: "But Fichte's activist optimism—and every teleological idealism is theoretical and practical optimism—is not disheartened."[57] This form of transcendental optimism reflects a teleological ideal of reason in conjunction with absolute values as the foundation for a nonformalist ethics. With this argument for the centrality of teleological optimism in its theoretical and practical significance, Husserl endorses Fichte's conception of the person

---

without noticing it, in the Idealist terrain. And then I was in a position to grasp the greatness and eternal significance of German Idealism [*das Grosse und ewig Bedeutsame im deutschen Idealismus*] underneath the layers of all conceptual romanticism (understandably, Fichte attracts me in increasing measure)"; Husserl, *Briefwechsel*, v, p. 178.

[56] Husserl, Hua XXV, p. 274/117.

[57] Husserl, Hua XXV, p. 282/123. This philosophical dedication to transcendental idealism in time of war is silently self-descriptive of Husserl's own experience of the war. As he confided to Felix Kaufmann in 1919: "I sought to save myself through a deepening into my philosophical work as I struggled in all these years of war with the struggle of spiritual self-preservation." ["Ich suchte mich durch Vertiefung in die philosophische Arbeit zu retten, wie ich denn in all den Kriegsjahren diesen Kampf um die geistige Selbsterhaltung kämpfe."] *Briefwechsel*, III, p. 343.

as constituting themselves in actions and deeds. As Husserl writes, "the subject is eo ipso its history and its having of a development," one that progresses from "action to action" such that "it belongs to the essence of acting that it be directed by a goal."[58] As Husserl begins to explore in his research on inner time consciousness in the Bernau Manuscripts (1917–18), the life of consciousness is essentially constituted as self-temporalization. Husserl discovers the genetic unfolding of consciousness in transcendental terms.[59] This genetic conception of consciousness is, among other factors, shaped by Husserl's Fichtean-inspired conception of the ethical person as striving toward self-unification under the *telos* of the "highest ethical goal."

In his third lecture, Husserl underlines the importance of Fichte's critique of Kant's formalist ethics and his introduction of a distinction between morality (*Sittlichkeit*) and a higher morality (*Moralität*). As Husserl notes: "Actually Fichte recognized in such considerations, even though they did not reach a final precision, the basic deficiency in the Kantian as well as his own earlier ethics; thus his distinctions are of permanent value."[60] Fichte's critique of Kant's ethics took issue with the universal and abstract from of the categorical imperative. Whereas Kant's notion of duty is "negative" insofar as it addresses the rational will in abstraction from the concreteness and individuality of the person, Fichte proposes a "positive" notion of duty that speaks to the "heart" and singularity of the ethical person in her striving to achieve "the spiritual prime of life." Whereas Kant's formal imperative can apply to everyone, Fichte's positive ethical ought is a universal form of duty based on the love of concrete individuals. As Husserl writes in a manner that reveals the intervention of his own thinking: "We would put it in this way: The formalist ethics, in its enthusiasm for formal generality always to do one's duty, is lacking any determination of positive absolute values which as practical goals could fulfill the one striving with love and so confer on his acting a positive blessedness, i.e., the realization of Ideals with contents." As Husserl specifies, "what effects this, however, is not a formal general and empty command of duty but rather it is a positive love of eternal values which offers to duty its specific content on each occasion."[61] In the midst of war, with Fichte as his guide, Husserl's ethical

---

[58] Husserl, Hua XXV, p. 275/117.
[59] Natorp's 1912 *Allgemeine Psychologie* equally played a considerable role in the formation of Husserl's genetic phenomenology. For Husserl's analyses of inner time consciousness, N. de Warren, *Husserl and the Promise of Time: Subjectivity in Transcendental Phenomenology* (Cambridge, UK: Cambridge University Press, 2009).
[60] Husserl, Hua XXV, p. 126.
[61] E. Husserl, *Vorlesungen über Bedeutungslehre Sommersemester 1908*, ed. U. Panzer (Dordrecht: Springer, 1986), Hua XXVI, pp. 287, 126.

thinking begins to be transformed from an "ethics of reason," which had defined his sustained interest in axiology and practical ethics before the war (largely under the shadow of Franz Brentano's approach to ethics), to an "ethics of the heart."[62]

The Heroism of Reason against the Contingencies of Life

In the aftermath of the war, Husserl was not alone in facing Europe's uncertain future and rife conflicts in his defeated nation, even as the devotion to his philosophical mission remained, despite bouts of despair during the war, unbroken. Even during the twilight year of 1918, Husserl could still muster the courage and conviction to declare in a letter to Adolf Grimme: "I am absolutely certain that a new age is about to begin for philosophy." Not that Husserl continued to uphold his phenomenological vision in denial of the original catastrophe of the twentieth century. On the contrary, as Husserl writes to Winthrop Bell in 1920: "this war represents the most profound Fall of humanity [...] all valid ideas have been revealed as lacking in authenticity."[63] The war, Husserl writes in another letter, has exposed the ethical and religious "misery of humanity," but likewise, a "hunger for ideals" has become more pronounced. Insisting on his phenomenological enterprise as a "source of salvation for our times," Husserl gingerly admits that his philosophical optimism "will at first appear strange and alienating" to many of his contemporaries.[64] The challenge to renew philosophy in the aftermath of the war was further compounded, as Husserl recognizes, by the enduring after-effects of wartime propaganda and the spiritual mobilization of philosophy. As Husserl notes, the postwar intellectual atmosphere is characterized by "an aversion to idealistic activity" as a direct consequence of the inflated war rhetoric of intellectuals and academics. Given that the war shattered confidence in the idea of philosophy and, indeed, the need for a rigorous reformation of philosophical thinking, who would, and *could*, still believe in what has become despondently decried as the unveiled lie of Reason?

---

[62] For this distinction in the evolution of Husserl's ethics, U. Melle, "Edmund Husserl: From Reason to Love," in *Phenomenological Approaches to Moral Philosophy*, eds. J. Drummond and L. Embree (Dordrecht: Springer, 2002): 229–248; and N. de Warren, "Husserl and Phenomenological Ethics," in *The Cambridge History of Moral Philosophy*, eds. S. Golob and J. Timmerman (Cambridge, UK: Cambridge University Press, 2017): 562–576.
[63] Husserl, *Briefwechsel*, III, p. 12, letter August 11, 1920.
[64] Husserl, XXV, p. 97.

Rather than losing confidence in the project of reason and its phenomenological realization, Husserl's postwar devotion to his phenomenological enterprise, widened in its scope to reflect on history and ethics, makes it seem as if Husserl counter-mobilized the war, as it were, in leveraging the spiritual catastrophe of his times into the propitious occasion for a radicalized transformation of his call for philosophy as a transcendental idealism. As Husserl announces in a series of articles written in the early 1920s for the Japanese journal *Kaizo* (literally: "Renewal"), Reason must become *heroic* in the face of humanity's misery.[65] This transfiguration of Husserl's thinking is characterized by a revealing change in how he speaks of own vocation. In the years after *The Logical Investigations*, Husserl privately speaks of phenomenological philosophy in his letters as a "life-task" (*Lebensaufgabe*). In 1916 – the year of Wolfgang's death – Husserl begins to speak of his "life-mission" (*Lebensmission*) and increasingly refers to the "destiny" as well as "burden" of his quest to usher forth a "genuine humanity" and achieve "blessed life." Phenomenology becomes emphatically understood as a means for the renewal of humanity in its awakening to its historical and cosmopolitan promise as a transcendental humanism.[66]

In his *Kaizo* essays, Husserl's call for renewal reaffirms his argument that a scientific philosophy, in the form developed through his transcendental phenomenology, must be based on the rigorous method of research into essences. The aim of phenomenological inquiry is to arrive at a priori knowledge and eidetic insights over the entire spectrum of possible experience. As with his earliest statement of the systematic plan of his phenomenological enterprise, Husserl proposes three parallel directions of inquiry in the spheres of "logical, valuing, and practical reason." In the three spheres of knowledge, value, and action, Husserl outlines the possibility of a phenomenological critique of reason based on, for each respective dimension of human experience, an analysis of the constitutive structures of intentionality, or, in other words, of how consciousness, in its transcendental operations, allows for the world to manifest itself in different registers of sense (as knowable, valuable, beautiful, etc.). Unlike his prewar formulations, Husserl calls upon his phenomenology of reason to achieve what he calls the "rational science of humankind." This emphasis

---

[65] Only three of the five articles were in fact published in 1923–4; E. Husserl, *Aufsätze und Vorträge (1922–1937)*, eds. T. Nenon and H. R. Sepp (Dordrecht: Springer Verlag, 1987), Hua XXVII.
[66] For the cosmopolitan dimension of Husserl's *Cartesian Meditations*, N. de Warren, "La radicalité de la raison. Le cartésianisme de la phénoménologie husserlienne," *Descartes et la phénoménologie*, eds. C. Riquier and D. Pradelle (Paris: L'Harmattan, 2018): 113–129.

on the cultivation of humanity in the *Kaizo* essays reflects the salience of the ethical, social, and historical dimensions of phenomenological thinking. In fact, the *Kaizo* essays contain the first expression of this new reach and centrality of ethics for Husserl's thinking. In its envisioned form, a phenomenological ethics operates on three levels of analysis: individual, community, humanity. Each level is defined by a teleological drive toward the ideal of achieving an ethical life: as an individual person, as a member of a community, as belonging to humankind. Modeled on the contours of Fichte's thinking, the ethical person is conceived as a task guided by the idea of renewal, which stands as the "highest theme of ethics" for an individual, their community, and humanity as such. This drive toward an ethical life (at each level) has the dynamic of a struggle, yet it is not a struggle for existence, but rather a struggle to achieve a "blessed life." In the striving of self-realization toward "blessedness," an ethical person responds to the call of their vocation – another indication of Fichte's enduring imprint on Husserl's thinking. The pursuit of an ethical life hinges on the cultivation of one's life according to a vocation and corresponding order of ethical values, duties, and norms. The vocation of reason represents the highest vocation of humanity and hence the final *telos* of the history of humanity, in which the world-historical vocation of Europe plays a central role, with all the attendant problematic issues that Husserl's Eurocentrism carries. However, as Husserl would elaborate at greater length and with greater urgency on the eve of a second world war in *The Crisis of the European Sciences*, Europe is neither a geography, a nation-state, a "worldview," or a national culture. Europe is an Idea imbued with "revolutionary potential for all other cultures."[67] This revolutionary potential for humanity resides in nothing less than the demand for the radicalism of a life dedicated to reason in its theoretical, practical, and axiological manifestations, to lead a life, in other words, *in* truth.

Husserl's teleological optimism and call for cultural renewal through a reinvigorated heroism of Reason in his *Kaizo* articles – hallmarks of a classic idea of philosophy that seemingly could no longer be maintained after the war – contrasts, however, with another Husserl, in tension with the outward presentation of his thinking in publications and university lecture courses, where a shattering of confidence in the possibility of a blessed life coupled with the personal loss of his son marbles what can be called Husserl's *unwritten* ethics; namely, a searching and unfinished,

---

[67] Husserl, Hua XXVII, p. 71.

indeed fragmentary, reflection on ethics that Husserl never published and, significantly, rarely allowed for outward-directed glimpses. There is an intimacy to these manuscripts, commonly referred to as Husserl's "Freiburg Late Ethics," both personal and philosophical. It is, therefore, not fortuitous that Husserl's significant transformation from an "ethics of reason" to an "ethics of the heart," but also an increased concern with ethics (as well as with social ontology and collective intentionality) along with questions of religious bearing, occurred during the war. Husserl's postwar research manuscripts on ethics bear witness to an existential coming to terms with how to retain confidence in the heroism of reason, as the pursuit of an ethical life, in a world racked by contingency and uncertainty. In the depths of his subterranean ethics, sketched and scrawled in his intimate research manuscripts, there emerges an existential Husserl, the likes of which remained, and remains, unsuspected.

In a set of reflections from a 1923 manuscript, Husserl's signature idea of the "natural attitude," namely, the pervasive and taken-for-granted – unquestioned – thereness of the world, its unimpeachable presence, undergoes a consequential recalibration in view of increased attention to the value-laden texture of our everyday experiences. Husserl considers that the practical attitude of our "mind or soul" (*das Gemüt*) underlying our common experience of the world is oriented toward "the future good" in terms of our hopes and fears. We are naturally inclined to hope for future good and fear that it might not come to pass. This default disposition concerning the intended success of our actions and lives reflects the values that our actions would either attain or sustain. Despite this assumed optimism, Husserl underlines "a general uncertainty of life" shadowing our projects. The possibility of the world not going our way, of the world disrupting our intentions, goals, and values – in short, of the world disabusing us of what, or who, we care for and what, or who, we value – haunts our world experience in a nonspecifiable and pervasive manner. The restlessness of life stems from its openness to "an infinite empire of contingencies," but also reflects the fragility of our bodies, our intellect, and our memories, all of which are liable to fail us, due to sickness, accidents, or aging.[68] The world's manifestation, testified in experience, is regulated in nonarbitrary ways: We never expect the back side of a three-dimensional object to go missing, colors to float without material support, books to have feelings, and so on. We can be surprised about events occurring in the world, but

---

[68] E. Husserl, *Grenzprobleme der Phänomenologie. Analysen des Unbewusstseins und der Instinkte*, eds. R. Sowa and T. Vongehr (Dordrecht: Springer, 2014), Hua XLII, p. 300.

never by the occurrence of the world as such, since whatever occurs in the world must happen within a minimal infrastructure of sense (that the event occurs in time, that the event is causally relatable to other events, and so on) in order to *be* a possible experience for us. Husserl's recognition of *eine allgemeine Unsicherheit des Lebens* does not, therefore, contravene the general thesis of the natural attitude, that experiences of the world occur within a minimal structure of stability and constancy, or what Husserl referred to as the "original belief" (*Urdoxa*), or "perceptual faith," of the natural attitude. But, whereas the *Urdoxa* of the natural attitude from the accentuation of perceptual experience refers to an assuredness in the "there is" of the world – that the world is there to be discovered – the general insecurity of life refers to the restlessness of life with regard to oneself, not in terms of the existence of the world, nor of the existence of the self, but of the meaningfulness of one's own existence, the enduring importance of what we care about, value, and aspire to be. This general insecurity of life is not a motivated belief that emerges from past experiences (i.e., "once bitten, twice shy"), nor does it designate a psychological or cognitive state (neurosis, for example). It designates instead the "facticity" of life, understood in Husserl's sense of the prefix *Ur*, as an *Urdoxa* of uncertainty. Unlike the general thesis of the natural attitude, however, this original uncertainty does not pertain to the thesis of the world, the "thereness" of the world, that the world is *da*. The general insecurity of life is intrinsically self-regarding, of how we deal with and dispose of ourselves in the world; that is, with the meaningfulness of our life as such.

Set within the frame of the world's uncertainty, Husserl elaborates in his ethical manuscripts in the 1920s and 1930s a conception of the person as a "concrete life" that is self-directed and self-responsible, and in this sense self-constituted, in reciprocal relations with other persons, yet always pursuing one's own individual life under the idea of oneself "in a Kantian sense." A person possesses not only a sense of guiding and shaping their life as an unfinished whole; a person likewise possesses a sense of leading, or aspiring to lead, a certain "type of life," and thus, that they are leading a life in a determinate way rather than a life just having them. In pursuing a certain kind of life and style of being in the world, a person's life understands itself as "satisfied" and "accomplished" (or lack thereof) in its purposiveness – whatever that purposiveness might be for each of us individually. What animates a rational life is its aspirational and valuing dynamic as reflected in an attitude toward life as something to be accomplished, and in this sense *to be had*, or claimed, rather than as pregiven. Life strives, for Husserl, not only to accomplish itself in valued ways; it strives to sustain itself in elevated ways of valuing.[69] A person, however, is not only a valuing subject for whom the world is laden and textured with values. A person is also self-valuing, not just in terms of valuing their own life, measured in terms of satisfaction or dissatisfaction with the kind of life they aspire to have, but, as significantly, as valuing themselves as a person for whom values are important. This valuing of life for itself does not transpire in isolation given the interweaving of one's life with the lives of others. This self-referential valuing of life is bound with the lives of others, and hence inseparable from participatory valuing within a community, extending ultimately, for Husserl, to "the life of humanity." Yet, we value life not in general terms, we value, and thus strive, to become a certain kind of person in relation to others: a husband, a friend, and so on. As Husserl writes, "I cannot value my life without valuing the interwoven lives of others."

On Husserl's thinking, the highest end of life is neither happiness nor the maximization of individual freedom, but what he terms "blessedness" (*Glückseligkeit*). Complex in its different nuances of meaning, blessedness is not merely happiness in the eudemonic sense of flourishing, but the ethical worthiness of happiness, along with unmistakable religious overtones of a life devoted to the highest values of love. We are fundamentally valuing beings, and value ourselves as valuing beings, and strive to realize not just morally right actions, but a life worth living. Striving to attain (and sustain oneself in) "blessedness" requires a constant process of self-renewal and critical self-reflection, as well as framing a view of one's life as a whole in terms of the field of practical possibilities and capacities that are available for oneself. A life stands under the categorial imperative to will what is "best possible for oneself," given one's capacities and circumstances. Striving to attain a blessed life is not solely defined by the disposition of reason, goodwill, and moral judgments, but involves self-assessment and self-cultivation of one's available possibilities and capacities. The emphasis is on leading an ethical life rather than merely conducting oneself morally. Following Fichte, it is not from respect for the moral law but from the uptake of a value, moved by its affective experience, that a person becomes disposed to act for the sake of a moral imperative; it is for the sake of the value expressed and realized through a moral imperative that one acts ethically. This entails, moreover, a decision to be the kind of person for whom such and such values are meaningful, not only "externally," as it were, but internally; that is, as integral to becoming the person I aspire to

---

[69] Hua XLII, p. 301.

be. One must care to (want to) be an ethical person in order to determine one's actions freely, from oneself, in the name of moral duties and norms. Formal ethics, in other words, presupposes the value at stake with a moral imperative as well as the value of moral norms for life, not life or humanity in general, but *my life*, and the kind of person I want to become.

"Let the World Be Hell!"

With this unfolding of a material ethics of value centered around the cultivation, or *Bildung*, of individual personhood, Husserl sharpens his concern with reconciling the heroism of reason, as the pursuit of a life in (ethical) truth or blessedness, with the fragility of the world. As Husserl wonders: "what if life were valueless, when life could not become good through me, when it would lay beyond my power to give value to my life?" Indeed: "What if my free will were nothing but a ball under the sway of blind forces, and which gave me the illusion of free action?" These questions do not represent a statement of the traditional problem of free will (determination vs. indetermination), since Husserl's concern lies elsewhere, not with a metaphysical problem of freedom, but with the existential threat posed by the contingency of the world to the importance of what we care about and hence pursue as valuable in our lives. The form of "causality" implied in Husserl's concern must be understood phenomenologically in terms of "motivation" regarding the affectivity of value. That the will is "good in itself" and predisposed to act according to moral imperatives, from respect for the law itself, proves insufficient, since the decision to determine one's conduct ethically must first of all be grounded in the uptake of (ethical) values. I must not only know what I ought to do. I must first and foremost become moved (affected by a value) toward choosing to do what I ought to do. Through the affordance of value, I become vested in conducting myself according to moral norms; only through the uptake of value in my life do I care to become an ethical person and conduct myself in an ethically correct and norm-directed manner.

With this argument for the basis of ethical conduct in the uptake of value and, correlatively, the traction of freedom, as autonomy, in both a responsiveness to experienced values and responsibility for those values (and oneself as a person who values), Husserl confronts head on *the impossibility* of achieving an ethical life. If ethical conduct is not (merely) based on formal lawfulness, but dependent on the subtending uptake of value, this introduces a salience of contingency into the pursuit of an ethical life. Let us accept, Husserl entertains, that I am able to decide upon my actions, formulate my intentions and projects, and determine my will – in short, that I exist within a field of practical possibilities geared toward my capacities ("what is best possible for me to do"). Granting these felicitous conditions, Husserl nonetheless wonders: "How would it be if all human beings, whom I love, would die, if the wonderful treasures of art and science would go under, if humanity, in which I live, would fall into a devasted degeneracy and the Good, that I effect, in me, in others, would become infinitely small."[70] As Husserl asks himself: "Can I live in a 'meaningless' world?" During the 1920s, these were not simply academic questions or theoretical problems in search of argumentative solutions. The answer to these anxieties – for Husserl – is "clear." If I were, as he remarks, a performance machine (*Leistungsmachine*), constructed to perform ethical acts and thus bring about "value" and, most significantly, enduring value in the world, and if this machine were programmed to attain values as its goals; then, he observes, this machine would also have to possess, if it were more than a formal ethical machine but a concrete life, the idea of the possibility of the impossibility of its aims. What would motivate me to act if I could not exclude the possibility of the meaninglessness of the world? For Husserl, it belongs to the disposition of reason in an ethical life to envision a possible world in which its own ethical striving would be thwarted and subverted by the world itself.

How can I act if I cannot exclude the possibility of the impossibility of the meaningfulness of ethical life? With this grave question, Husserl recasts the methodological operation of the imaginative destruction of the world – the phenomenological *epoché* or suspension of the general thesis of the world for the purpose of a transcendental elucidation of the constitutive structures of intentionality – into an imaginative *ethical* destruction of the world. Throughout the late Freiburg manuscripts on ethics, Husserl varies the scenarios of world catastrophe; we can thus speak of an eidetic variation of the apocalypse through which Husserl seeks to reveal the unshakeable grounds for the possibility of an ethical life in defiance of the world and yet for the sake of the world. This ethical recasting of the imaginative destruction of the world leverages the "general uncertainty of life" for the purpose of clarifying the conditions under which the pursuit, attainment, and sustaining of ethical life not just "are" possible but *endure* as possible despite the vicissitudes of the world. As Husserl specifies the thrust of his reflections: The world is regulated according to natural and eidetic laws; humanity can determine itself rationally; there is a history of intellectual progress; we have developed a culture of learning and knowledge such that

---

[70] Hua XLII, p. 307.

life becomes elevated and enhanced in terms of its value and meaning; we have science and art; and thus, despite the specter of a meaningless world, hope would still seem to prevail. Those outside of us might look down upon the importance of what and who we care for and say: "How wonderful for these souls!" And yet, as Husserl writes: "Is the whole world only there for us and for this time and for this humanity in transience? Are we not but an accidental speck of green in the desert of the world?"[71]

Let us assume, Husserl proposes, that the world is meaningless, that human progress and ethical values amount to naught: "What can therefore be said to all of this? [*Was ist schließlich zu all dem zu sagen?*]" Faced with this specter of an ethically barren and voided world, what is there left to say? But as Husserl now wonders, "what, then, would we say to a mother who lovingly cares for her child?" Where do our cares, and their continuing importance for our lives, stand in a world of canceled meaningfulness? In this stunning argumentative turn, Husserl brings onto the stage of his reflections the figure of the mother and her love for her child. Let the mother *know* that the world is meaningless, "that tomorrow a flood shall devastate the world" and "drown all values." Even if this mother could still convince herself that this end of days is empirically improbable, there is no eidetic necessity against the possibility of an ethical "nonworld," or *Unwelt*. For Husserl, there is no eidetic necessity that the world *must* exist let alone that it *should* be hospitable to us – for the life of our values and the values of our lives. And yet, were the world on the brink of annihilation, it stands "a thousand times more certain" for the mother that she should never abandon her child, that she should continue to care for and love her child, nurture their intellectual and spiritual growth. Even if a mother knew for certain that tomorrow would bring the end of the world, she would still insist on caring for and loving her child, or else betray her responsibility – to herself and her child – as well as her responsibility for the value of loving were she to abandon her child and neglect her duties. The value of caring for her child, as an "absolute value," is immune from the vicissitudes of the world and, indeed, guards against the vicissitudes of the world. For, as Husserl emphasizes, absolute values *transcend* the relativity of the world in their immanence, or intimacy, for the person who defines themselves according to those values in relation to themselves and to others. To love one's child until and *beyond* the end of the world seems, in one sense, to be "irrational." It does not banish the possibility of the meaningless of the world (that the child could die, for example), yet

---

[71] Hua XLII, p. 309.

it nonetheless triumphs over this possibility without the proclamation of any definitive victory. On the other hand, to love one's child absolutely is rational, since the commitment to "being a good mother" places a person in a normative space of reasons and duties. As Husserl declares, speaking as it were for the mother at the end of the world: "Let the world be hell […] I nonetheless resist this 'hell' and do my 'duty.'"[72] This resistance against the hell of the world stands on the immoveable ground of "faith" or "belief" (*Glaube*). Though the world shall move, here I stand, for I can do no other.

The Tragedy of Love

Wolfgang's death was not only an event in the life of Husserl as father and husband. It was also an event in the life of Husserl as philosopher. In numerous manuscripts on ethical and religious questions during the 1920s and 1930s, the example of a mother's love for her son repeatedly serves as a nodal point, indeed, a center of gravity, for Husserl's unwritten ethics. Among other functions, a mother's love for her child exemplifies the notion of absolute values, which emerged in Husserl's reflections in the wake of the war. Husserl distinguishes between general objective values and individual subjective values, or "absolute values." With both, Husserl is committed to the argument that ethical judgments of what I ought to do must be based on the apprehension of a corresponding and underpinning value. Ethical conduct cannot be equated with the lawfulness of action, and hence defined in merely formal terms, but must be grounded in the material givenness of a value; that is, value as the content of experience. Husserl avoids the slippery slope toward the psychologization of values, since values are structured in an a priori manner. Husserl's nonformal ethics of value and personhood represents one of three ways of world disclosing: knowledge, valuing, and acting. Objective values underpin norms and duties that are objective and universal: valid equally for all rational ethical persons. Such values are "higher" or "lower" relative to each other. When an objective value enters in conflict with another (along with corresponding duties), conflicts of this type can be resolved by appealing to their relative position within a rank ordering such that a higher value absorbs a lower value.

In contrast to objective values, with absolute subjective values Husserl does not reproduce in his own manner a distinction between "objective" and "subjective" values, where the latter would be equated with heteronomy or empirical motivations of the subject. On the contrary, absolute

---

[72] Hua XLII, p. 311.

values reveal a dimension of subjectivity other than what had classically been understood as "subjective," namely, not as opposed to "objectivity." The difference between "objective" and "absolute subjective values" does not correspond to two regions or modes of being ("the world" or "consciousness"). This difference refers instead to two different orders of "oughts." Objective values are keyed to norms and duties that are valid intersubjectively for all (rational) persons and, in this sense, can be said to be universal. Absolute values are tethered instead to a personal vocation; an absolute value "calls" on a person "to be" thus and so. It does not prescribe or illuminate a particular action or conduct, but calls upon a certain manner of being, for instance, to be a mother. The uptake of absolute values thus takes the form of responding to the call of an associated vocation, namely, to become the *kind* of person who has invested themselves in shaping their lives, in thinking and in action, according to an absolute value. Conversely, failing to heed the call of vocation represents a failure of oneself and abdication of both responsiveness to an absolute value and responsibility toward who one *ought to be*. The mother stands under the absolute imperative of motherly love – to care for her child, to provide for their development, and so on – in opening a life space (and time) bound by corresponding duties and norms. Although based on an affective experience ("love"), a mother must herself decide to become a good mother and hence decide to devote herself to the value of caring for her child. In this sense, "to be a good mother" is a project of *Selbstbildung* in response to the call of the value itself and, in this, uptake of one's personal vocation. An ethical person constitutes themselves in responsiveness and responsibility: responsiveness to the values, that is, to what one cares about; and responsibility for oneself and one's child. A person is thus not just affected by a value. One is called to be a certain kind of person – one is called, as it were, to be me – to bear those values, and realize them, and thus, in this manner, to realize myself as I am in relation to others and the world.

Absolute subjective values are quixotically subjective *and* absolute. A mother's love for her child cannot be weighed against another mother's love, even though each mother can be said to love their individual child "absolutely." The absolute, as singular, cannot be declinated as either "universal" or "particular." In the same vein, the basis of ethics in absolute values escapes an opposition between reason and love: Love for the child cannot enter into comparison with another's love for their child and hence enter into conflict with other intersubjective objective values. Moreover, love for a child is both "irrational" and "rational," insofar as the uptake of an absolute value places a person in a space of normative conduct and reasoning.

Husserl's ethical manuscripts on ethics reveal an untiring effort to resolve these apparently paradoxical relations between reason and love as well as the subjectivity of the subject (their vocation) and absolute values. As Husserl recognizes: "Among the persons in my environment, my child is the 'closest' to me, and therein is contained an irrationality of the absolute 'ought.'" However, despite this irrationality, each person in their ethical striving and self-constitution stands answerable to others as well as to themselves, hence demanding self-reflection and calibration of norms and duties. How can a plurality of absolute singular ethical persons enter into a community of ethical agents under a common measure of justice and "harmonization" of decisions, actions, and consequences? In struggling conceptually to reconcile his reflections on "absolute values" with the demands of reason, Husserl discovers, almost despite himself, *another* more intimate scene of conflict, at once personal and phenomenological. For if absolute values among a plurality of individuals cannot, strictly speaking, enter in conflict and comparison with each other within the life of an individual, there emerges, given the plurality of absolute values to which a person is affected and called by, what Husserl calls "the tragedy of personal conflict."[73] At the heart of an ethics of love is the tragedy of ethics as exemplified by the irresolvable conflict between a mother's love for her son and a mother's love for the Fatherland. As Husserl notes: "Mother-child, mother-fatherland. The beloved child – the beloved fatherland."[74] There is here a haunting of Husserl's thinking by the death of his son. Who is here speaking, Husserl the father of a son who has gone to die or the father of phenomenology? The tragedy of the person is to be caught without end between an inconsolable death of the beloved without *dulce et decorum* and the "beautiful death" of the beloved *pro patria mori*. This conflict between two souls, set within the contingency of the world, is inscribed in the German word *Opfer*, meaning both "sacrifice" and "victim," such that each sacrifice becomes a victim, and each victim becomes a sacrifice, with neither, nor us, resting in peace. What, then, remains for the possibility of a blessed life given this intolerable oscillation at the heart of love? It is a question that, as attested by his unfinished ethics, Husserl himself took to the grave.

---

[73] Hua XLII, p. 351.
[74] Hua XLII, p. 347.

Bibliography

Adler, J. *Johann Wolfgang Goethe* (London: Reaktion Books, 2020)
Adorno, T., Benjamin, W., Block, E., Brecht, B., and Lukács, G. *Aesthetics and Politics* (London: Verso Press, 2007)
Albert, C., ed. *Deutscher Klassiker im Nationalsozialismus: Schiller, Kleist, Hölderlin* (Stuttgart: J. B. Metzler, 1994)
Almond, P. *Rudolf Otto: An Introduction to His Philosophical Theology* (Chapel Hill: University of North Carolina Press, 1984)
Altmann, W. *Martin Heidegger and the First World War: Being and Time as Funeral Oration* (Lexington, KY: Lexington Books, 2012)
Aly, G. *Why the Germans? Why the Jews? Envy, Race Hatred, and the Prehistory of the Holocaust*, trans. J. Chase (New York: Picador, 2011)
Anderson, R., and Cissna, K. (eds.), *The Martin Buber – Carl Rogers Dialogue. A New Transcript with Commentary.* (Albany: State University of New York Press, 1997).
Arato, A., and Breines, P. *The Young Lukacs and the Origins of Western Marxism* (London: Pluto Press, 1979)
Arendt, H. *The Human Condition* (Chicago: University of Chicago Press, 2018)
Aschheim, S. *The Nietzsche Legacy in Germany, 1890–1990* (Berkeley: University of California Press, 1994)
Askani, H.-C. "Schöpfung der Welt und Grammatik der Sprache. Zum Verhältnis von philosophischem Gedanken und biblischem Text im Stern der Erlösung," in *Rosenzweig als Leser: Kontextuelle Kommentare zum "Stern der Erlosung,"* ed. M. Brasser (Tübingen: Max Niemeyer Verlag, 2004): 411–428
Assmann, A. *Arbeit am nationalen Gedächtnis* (Frankfurt: Campus Verlag, 1993)
Audoin-Rouzeau, S., and Becker, A. *14–18: Retrouver la guerre* (Paris: Gallimard, 2000)
Baehr, P. "The 'Iron Cage' and the 'Shell as Hard as Steel': Parsons, Weber, and the Stahlhartes Gehäuse Metaphor in the Protestant Ethic and the Spirit of Capitalism," *History and Theory*, Vol. 40, No. 2 (May 2001): 153–169
Bahr, H. *Kriegssegen* (Munich: Delphin Verlag, 1915)
Bahr, H. "Über Ernst Cassirer," *Die neue Rundschau*, Vol. xxviii, No. 10 (1917): 1483–1499
Ball, H. *Critique of the German Intelligentsia*, trans. B. Harris (New York: Columbia University Press, 1993)

Ball, H. *Flight Out of Time: A Dada Diary*, trans. A. Raimes (Berkeley: University of California Press, 1996)
Baltzer-Jaray, K. "Reinach's Phenomenology of Foreboding: Battlefield Notes, 1916–1917," in *Early Phenomenology. Metaphysics, Ethics, and the Philosophy of Religion*, eds. B. Harding and M. Kelly (London: Bloomsbury, 2016): 67–86
Bambach, C. *Heidegger's Roots: Nietzsche, National Socialism, and the Greeks* (Ithaca, NY: Cornell University Press, 2003)
Barash, J. "Ernst Cassirer, Martin Heidegger, and the Legacy of Davos," *History and Theory*, Vol. 51, No. 3 (2012): 436–450
Barash, J. *Martin Heidegger and the Problem of Historical Meaning* (New York: Fordham, 2003)
Barash, J. "Der Ort der Religion bei Ernst Cassirer," in *Die Gegenwärtigkeit deutsch-jüdischen Denkens*, eds. A. Noor and J. Matveev (Munich: Fink Verlag, 2011): 383–394
Barth, K. *The Epistle to the Romans*, trans. E. Hoskins (London: Oxford University Press, 1965)
Barth, K. *A Unique Time of God: Karl Barth's WWI Sermons*, trans. W. Klempa (Louisville, KY: Westminster John Knox Press, 2016)
Bauch, B. "Brief an Frau Dr. Ripke-Kühn," *Der Panther*, Vol. 4, No. 6 (1916): 742–746
Bayer, T. *Cassirer's Metaphysics of Symbolic Forms* (New Haven, CT: Yale University Press, 2001)
Becker, A. *Oubliés de la grand guerre* (Paris: Éditions Noêsis, 1998)
Beiser, F. *The Genesis of Neo-Kantianism, 1796–1880* (Oxford: Oxford University Press, 2017)
Beiser, F. *The German Historicist Tradition* (Oxford: Oxford University Press, 2011)
Benjamin, M. *Rosenzweig's Bible: Reinventing Scripture for Jewish Modernity* (Cambridge, UK: Cambridge University Press, 2009)
Benner, M. "Between Hermann Cohen and Karl Marx: The Jewish Dimension of Kurt Eisner's Revolution in Bavaria, 1918–19," *Modern Judaism – A Journal of Jewish Ideas and Experience*, Vol. 40, No. 1 (2020): 17–36
Bensussan, G. "Rosenzweig and War. A Question of 'Point of View': Between Creation, Revelation, and Redemption," *New Centennial Review*, Vol. 13, No. 1 (2013): 115–136
Bergman, S. H. *Dialogical Philosophy from Kierkegaard to Buber*, trans. A. Gersten (Albany: State University of New York, 1991)
Berkowitz, R. *The Gift of Science: Leibniz and the Modern Legal Tradition* (New York: Fordham University Press, 2010)
Bernasconi, R. "Another Eisenmenger? On the Alleged Originality of Heidegger's Antisemitism," in *Heidegger's Black Notebooks: Responses to Anti-Semitism*, eds. A. Mitchell and P. Trawny (New York: Columbia University Press, 2017): 168–185
von Bernhardi, F. *Deutschland und der Nächste Krieg* (Berlin: J. G. Cotta, 1911)
Bessel, R. *Nazism and War* (New York: Modern Library, 2004)

Bielik-Robson, A. "Dreams of Matter. Ernst Bloch on Religion as Organized Matter," *Revue internationale de philosophie*, Vol. 3, No. 289 (2019): 333–360
Bielik-Robson, A. *Jewish Cryptotheologies of Late Modernity: Philosophical Marranos* (London: Routledge, 2014)
Biemel, W. and Saner, H. (eds.), *Martin Heidegger – Karl Jaspers: Briefwechsel 1920–1963* (Frankfurt: Vittorio Klostermann, 1990)
Bloch, E. "Aktualität und Utopie zu Lukács' Geschichte und Klassenbewusstsein" (1923) in *Philosophische Aufsätze zur objektiven Phantasie: Gesamtausgabe 10* (Frankfurt: Suhrkamp Verlag, 1969): 598–621, GA 10
Bloch, E. *Heritage of Our Times* (London: Polity Press, 1991)
Bloch, E. *Philosophische Aufsätze zur objektiven Phantasie* (Frankfurt: Suhrkamp, 1985)
Bloch, E. *The Principle of Hope*, trans. N. Plaice and S. Plaice (Cambridge, MA: MIT Press, 1995)
Bloch, E. *The Spirit of Utopia*, trans. A. Nassar (Stanford, CA: Stanford University Press, 2000)
Bloch, E. *Tagträume vom aufrechten Gang. Sechs Interviews mit Ernst Bloch* (Frankfurt: Editions Suhrkamp, 1977)
Bloy, L. *Jeanne d'Arc et l'Allemagne* (Paris: Mercure de France, 1915)
Blumenfeld, J. *All Things Are Nothing to Me: The Unique Philosophy of Max Stirner* (London: Zero Books, 2018)
Blumenberg, H. "Der Parteibeitrag," in *Die Verführbarkeit des Philosophen* (Frankfurt: Suhrkamp Verlag, 2000): 100–106
Böhm, M. "Vom jüdisch-deutschen Geist," *Preussische Jahrbücher*, Vol. 162 (1915): 404–420.
Bouretz, P. *Witnesses for the Future. Philosophy and Messianism*, trans. M. Smit (Baltimore, MD: Johns Hopkins University Press, 2010)
Braudel, F. *Grammaire des civilisations* (Paris: Flammarion, 2008)
Bridgewater, P. *The German Poets of the First World War* (New York: St. Martin's Press, 1985)
Brody, S. H. "Reason, Revelation, and Election: Hermann Cohen and Michael Wyschogrod," *Toronto Journal for Jewish Thought*, Vol. 1 (2010): 299–321.
Brun, N. *Vom Kulturkritiker zum "Kulturkrieger." Paul Natorps Weg in den "Krieg der Geister"* (Würzburg: Köningshausen & Neumann, 2007).
Buber, M. *Between Man and Man* (New York: Martino Fine Books, 2014)
Buber, M. *I and Thou*, trans. W. Kaufmann (New York: Touchstone Books, 1970)
Buber, M. *On Judaism*, ed. N. Glatzer (New York: Schocken Books, 1995)
Buber, M. *Meetings: Autobiographical Fragments* (London: Routledge, 2002)
van Buren, J. *The Young Heidegger: Rumor of the Hidden King* (Indiana: Indiana University Press, 1994)
Canfora, L. *1914* (Palermo: Sellerio Editore, 2006)
Casper, B. "Franz Rosenzweig. Die Herausforderung zu einer neuen Zukunft" in *Rosenzweig als Leser: Kontextuelle Kommentare zum "Stern der Erlosung"*, ed. M. Brasser (Tübingen: Max Niemeyer Verlag, 2004): 209–222

Cassirer, E. *Descartes: Lehre-Persönlichkeit-Wirkung* (Hamburg: Felix Meiner Verlag, 1995)
Cassirer, E. *An Essay on Man* (New Haven, CT: Yale University Press, 2021)
Cassirer, E. *Freiheit und Form. Studien zur Deutschen Geistesgeschichte* (Darmstadt: Wissenschaftliche Buchgesellschaft, 1975)
Cassirer, E. *Gesammelte Werke. Aufsätze und kleine Schriften 1922–1926*, ed. J. Clemens (Hamburg: Felix Meiner Verlag, 2003)
Cassirer, E. "Judaism and the Modern Political Myth," in *Nachgelassene Manuskripte und Texte. Zu Philosophie und Politik*, eds. J. M. Krois and C. Möckel (Hamburg: Felix Meiner Verlag, 2008): 267–276
Cassirer, E. *The Logic of the Cultural Sciences*, trans. S. G. Lofts (New Haven, CT: Yale University Press, 2000)
Cassirer, E. *Nachgelassene Manuscripte und Texte*, 18 (Hamburg: Felix Meiner Verlag, 2009)
Cassirer, E. *The Philosophy of the Enlightenment*, trans. F. Koellen and J. Pettegrove (Boston, MA: Beacon Press, 1966)
Cassirer, E. *The Philosophy of Symbolic Forms*, iv, trans. J. M. Krois (New Haven, CT: Yale University Press, 1996)
Cassirer, E. "The Technique of Our Modern Political Myths," in *Symbol, Myth, and Culture: Essays and Lectures of Ernst Cassirer, 1935–1945* (New Haven, CT: Yale University Press, 1979): 246
Cassirer, E. *The Warburg Years (1919–1933)*, trans. S. G. Lofts (New Haven, CT: Yale University Press, 2013)
Cassirer, E. "Zur Logik des Symbolbegriffs," in *Wesen und Wirkung des Symbolbegriffs* (Darmstadt: Wissenschaftliche Buchgesellschaft, 1956): 145–175
Cassirer, T. *Mein Leben mit Ernst Cassirer* (Hamburg: Meiner Verlag, 2003)
Chapoutot, J. *Le meurtre de Weimar* (Paris: PUF, 2010)
Chaubet, F. *Paul Desjardins et les Décadees de Pontigny* (Villeneuve d'Ascq: Septentrion, 2009)
Chiaromonte, N. *The Paradox of History* (Philadelphia: University of Pennsylvania Press, 1985)
Cohen, H. *Deutschtum und Judentum* (Giessen: Alfred Töpelmann, 1915)
Cohen, H. *Judische Schriften* (Berlin: C. A. Schwetschke, 1924)
Cohen, H. *Kleinere Schriften VI. 1916–1918*, ed. H. Holzhey (Hildesheim: Olms, 2002)
Cohen, J., and Zagury-Orly, R. "Abraham. The Settling Foreigner," in *The Trace of God. Derrida and Religion*, eds. E. Baring and P. E. Gordon (New York: Fordham University Press, 2014): 132–150
Cohen, J., and Zagury-Orly, R. *L'Adversaire privilege* (Paris: Galilée, 2021)
Cohn, N. *Warrant for Genocide: The Myth of the Jewish World Conspiracy and the Protocols of the Elders of Zion* (New York: Harper and Row, 1967)
Congdon, L. *Exile and Social Thought: Hungarian Intellectuals in Germany and Austria, 1919–1933* (Princeton, NJ: Princeton University Press, 2014)
Congdon, L. *The Young Lukács* (Charlottesville: University of North Carolina Press, 1983)

Coyne, R. "Bearers of Transcendence. Simmel and Heidegger on Death and Immortality," *Human Studies*, Vol. 41, No. 1 (2018): 59–78
Crowe, B. *Heidegger's Phenomenology of Religion* (Bloomington: Indiana University Press, 2008)
Curthoys, N. *The Legacy of Liberal Judaism. Ernst Cassirer and Hannah Arendt's Hidden Conversation* (New York: Berghahn Books, 2013)
Dagan, H. "The Motif of Blood and Procreation in Franz Rosenzweig," *AJS Review* Vol. 26, No. 2 (2002): 241–249.
Dannemann, R. *Das Prinzip Verdinglichung: Studie Zur Philosophie Georg Lukács'* (Frankfurt: Sendler, 1987)
Dannemann, R., and Meyzaud, M. (eds.), *Hundert Jahre "transzendentale Obdachlosigkeit." Georg Lukács' "Theorie des Romans" neu gelesen* (Bielefeld: Aisthesis Verlag, 2018).
Dastur, F. *Husserl. Des mathématiques à l'histoire* (Paris: PUF, 1995)
Davis, Z. "The Values of War and Peace: Max Scheler's Political Transformations," *Symposium*, Vol. 16, No. 2 (2012): 128–149.
Dennis, D. *Beethoven in German Politics, 1870–1989* (New Haven, CT: Yale University Press, 1996)
Derrida, J. Interpretations at War: Kant, the Jew, the German," *New Literary History. Institutions of Interpretation*, Vol. 22, No. 1 (1991): 39–95.
Di Cesare, D. *Heidegger and the Jews: The Black Notebooks*, trans. M. Baca (London: Polity Press, 2018)
Didi-Huberman G. *Atlas, or the Anxious Gay Science*, trans. S. Lillis (Chicago: University of Chicago Press, 2018).
Ditmar, R. (ed.), *Der Langemarck-Mythos in Dichtung und Unterricht* (Luchterhand: Neuwied, 1992).
Dodd, J. *Crisis and Reflection* (Dordrecht: Springer, 2004)
Dupont, C. *Phenomenology in French Philosophy: Early Encounters* (Dordrecht: Springer Verlag, 2014)
Dussort, H. *L'École de Marbourg* (Paris: PUF, 1963)
Dyer, G. *The Missing of the Somme* (New York: Vintage, 1994)
Eksteins, M. *Rites of Spring: The Great War and the Birth of the Modern Age* (Boston, MA: Houghton Mifflin, 1989)
Eucken, R. *Lebenserinnerungen* (Leipzig: Koehler Verlag, 1921)
Evard, J.-L. "La philosophie de la vie part en guerre," in *Georg Simmel face à la guerre* (Paris: Éditions Rue d'Ulm, 2015): 92–119
Faber, R. *Political Demonology: On Modern Marcionism*, eds. T. Feiler and M. Mayo (Eugene: Cascade Books, 2017)
Farias, V. *Heidegger and Nazism* (Philadelphia, PA: Temple University, 1989)
Farrenkopft, J. *Prophet of Decline: Spengler on World History and Politics* (Baton Rouge: Louisiana State University Press, 2001)
Feenberg, A. *Lukács, Marx, and the Sources of Critical Theory* (London: Rowman & Littlefield, 1981)
Feenberg, A. *The Philosophy of Praxis: Marx, Lukács, and the Frankfurt School* (London: Verso, 2014)

Feenberg, A. "Post-Utopian Marxism: Lukács and the Dilemmas of Organization," in *Confronting Mass Democracy and Industrial Technology*, ed. J. McCormick (Durham, NC: Duke University Press, 2002): 45–69

Ferrari, M. *Ernst Cassirer. Stationen einer philosophischen Biographie* (Hamburg: Felix Meiner Verlag, 2003)

Flasch, K. *Die geistige Mobilmachung. Die deutschen Intellektuellen und der Erste Weltkrieg. Ein Versuch* (Berlin: Alexander Fest Verlag, 2000)

Franzen, W. "Die Sehnsucht nach Härte und Schwere: Über ein zum NS-Engagment disponierendes Motiv in Heideggers Vorlesung 'Die Grundbegriffe der Metaphysik' von 1929/30," in *Heidegger und die praktische Philosophie*, ed. O. Pöggeler (Frankfurt: Suhrkamp, 1988): 78–82.

Friedländer, S. "Die politischen Veränderung der Kriegszeit," in *Deutsches Judentum in Krieg und Revolution 1916–1923*, ed. W. Mosse (Tübingen: J. C. B. Mohr, 1971): 27–67.

Friedman, M. *Martin Buber's Life and Work* (New York: E. P. Dutton, 1981)

Friedman, M. *A Parting of the Ways: Carnap, Cassirer, and Heidegger* (Chicago: University of Chicago Press, 2000)

Frisby, D. *Fragments of Modernity: Theories of Modernity in the Work of Simmel, Kracauer and Benjamin* (Cambridge, MA: MIT Press, 1986)

Frisby, D. *Georg Simmel* (London: Routledge, 2002)

Fussell, P. *The Great War and Modern Memory* (Oxford: Oxford University Press, 1975)

Gadamer, H.-G. *Philosophical Hermeneutics*, trans. D. Linge (Berkeley: University of California Press, 1976)

Gaehtgens, T. *Reims on Fire: War and Reconciliation between France and Germany* (Los Angeles: Getty Research Institute, 2018)

Galli, B. "Rosenzweig's Response to Hermann Cohen's 'Deutschtum und Judentum," *Shofar*, Vol. 14, No. 4 (1996): 60–78

Gasman, D. "Ernst Haeckel and the German Monist League," in *The Scientific Origins of National Socialism* (London: Routledge, 2017): 1–30

Gassen, K., and Landmann, M. (eds.), *Buch des Dankes an Georg Simmel* (Berlin: Duncker & Humblot, 1958)

Gawronsky, D. "Ernst Cassirer: His Life and Work," in *The Philosophy of Ernst Cassirer* (The Library of Living Philosophers), ed. P. A. Schlipp (Evanston, IL: Open Court, 1949): 1–38

Glatzer, N., and Mendes-Flohr, P. (eds.), *The Letters of Martin Buber* (Syracuse, NY: Syracuse University Press, 1996)

Gluck, M. *Georg Lukács and His Generation 1900–1918* (Cambridge, MA: Harvard University Press, 1985)

von Goethe, J. W. *Scientific Studies*, trans. D. Miller (Princeton, NJ: Princeton University Press, 1995)

Goldmann, L. "The Aesthetics of the Young Lukacs," *New Hungarian Quarterly*, Vol. XIII, No. 47 (1972): 129–135

Goldmann, L. *Lukács and Heidegger: Towards a New Philosophy*, trans. W. Boelhower (London: Routledge & Kegan Paul, 1977)

Goodstein, E. *Georg Simmel and the Disciplinary Imaginary* (Stanford, CA: Stanford University Press, 2017)
Gordon, P. *Continental Divide: Heidegger, Cassirer, Davos* (Cambridge, MA: Harvard University Press, 2010)
Gordon, P. *Rosenzweig and Heidegger: Between Judaism and German Philosophy* (Berkeley: University of California Press, 2003)
Grady, T. *A Deadly Legacy: German Jews and the Great War* (New Haven, CT: Yale University Press, 2017)
Haag, J. "Othmar Spann and the Quest for a 'True State'," *Austrian History Yearbook*, Vol. 12, No. 1 (1976): 227–250
Habermas, J. "Die deutschen Mandarine," in *Philosophische-Politische Profile* (Frankfurt: Suhrkamp, 1987): 458–469
Habermas, J. "Ernst Bloch – A Marxist Romantic," *Salmagundi*, Vo l. 10/11 (1969–1970): 311–325
Haeckel, E. "England's Blood-Guilt in the World War," *Open Court*, Vol. 10 (1914): Article 2.
Hafner, S. *Defying Hitler: A Memoir*, trans. O. Pretzel (London, Picador, 2002)
Hammer, K. *Deutsche Kriegstheologie* (Munich: Kösel-Verlag, 1971)
von Hartmann, E. *Die Phänomenologie des sittlichen Bewusstseins* (Berlin: Duncker, 1879)
Hartmutt, R. *Emil Lask als Lehrer von Georg Lukács. Zur Form ihres Gegenstandsbegriffs* (Bonn: Bouvier, 1975)
Haupt, G. *Socialism and the Great War: The Collapse of the Second International* (Oxford: Clarendon Press, 1972)
Heidegger, M. *Anmerkungen I–V*, ed. P. Trawny (Frankfurt: Vittorio Klostermann, 2015)
Heidegger, M. *Beiträge zur Philosophie* (Frankfurt: Vittorio Klostermann, 1989)
Heidegger, M. *Contributions to Philosophy*, trans. P. Emad (Bloomington: Indiana University Press, 2000)
Heidegger, M. *The Fundamental Concepts of Metaphysics*, trans. W. McNeill and N. Walker (Bloomington: Indiana University Press, 1995)
Heidegger, M. *Grundprobleme der Phänomenologie (1919/20)* (Frankfurt: Vittorio Klosermann, 1993)
Heidegger, M. *Hölderlin's Hymns "Germania" and "The Rhine,"* trans. W. McNeill and J. Ireland (Bloomington: Indiana University Press, 2014)
Heidegger, M. *Kant and the Problem of Metaphysics* (Bloomington: Indiana University Press, 1990)
Heidegger, M. *Letters to his Wife 1915–1970*, trans. R. Glasgow (London: Polity Press, 2010)
Heidegger, M. *The Metaphysical Foundations of Logic*, trans. M. Heim (Bloomington: Indiana University Press, 1984)
Heidegger, M. *The Metaphysics of German Idealism*, trans. I. Moore and R. Therezo (London: Polity Press, 2021)
Heidegger, M. *Nature, History, State 1933–1935*, trans. G. Fried and R. Polt (London: Bloomsbury, 2015)

Heidegger, M. *Nietzsches metaphysische Grundstellung im abendländischen Denken*, (Frankfurt: Vittorio Klostermann, 1986)
Heidegger, M. *Parmenides*, trans. A. Schuwer and R. Rojewicz (Bloomington: Indiana University Press, 1992)
Heidegger, M. *Pathmarks*, ed. W. McNeill (Cambridge, UK: Cambridge University Press, 1998)
Heidegger, M. *Ponderings II–IV. Black Notebooks 1931–1938*, trans. R. Rojcewicz (Bloomington: Indiana University Press, 2016)
Heidegger, M. *Ponderings VII–XI. Black Notebooks 1938–1939*, trans. R. Rojcewicz (Bloomington: Indiana University Press, 2014)
Heidegger, M. *Ponderings XII–XV. Black Notebooks 1939–1941*, trans. R. Rojcewicz (Bloomington: Indiana University Press, 2014)
Heidegger, M. and Blochmann, E. *Briefwechsel 1918–1969* (Marbach: Deutsche Schillergesellschaft, 1989)
Heidegger, M., and Löwith, K. *Correspondence: 1919–1973*, trans. J. Assaiante and S. Ewegen (London: Rowman and Littlefield, 2021)
Heine, H. *On the History of Religion and Philosophy in Germany*, ed. T. Pinkard (Cambridge, UK: Cambridge University Press, 2007)
Helle, H. J. *Messages from Georg Simmel* (Leiden: Brill, 2012)
Heller, A. "Georg Lukács and Irma Seidler," *New German Critique*, Vol. 18 (1979): 74–106
von Hellingrath, N. *Hölderlin. Zwei Vorträge* (Munich: Hugo Bruckmann, 1922)
Hegel, G. W. *The Phenomenology of Spirit*, trans. A. V. Miller (Oxford: Oxford University Press, 1977)
Hegel, G. W. "The Spirit of Christianity and Its Fate," in *Early Theological Writings*, trans. T. M. Knox (Philadelphia: University of Pennsylvania Press, 1971): 182–301
Herdt, J. *Forming Humanity: Redeeming the German Bildung Tradition* (Chicago: University of Chicago Press, 2019)
Herf, J. *Reactionary Modernism* (Cambridge, UK: Cambridge University Press, 1984)
Herskowitz, D. *Heidegger and His Jewish Reception* (Cambridge, UK: Cambridge University Press, 2021)
Herzfeld, W. *Rosenzweig, "Mitteleuropa" und der Erste Weltkrieg: Rosenzweigs Politische Ideen im Zeitgeschichtlichen Kontext* (Freiburg: Karl Albert Verlag, 2013)
Hesse, H. *If This War Goes On … Reflections on War and Politics*, trans. R. Manheim (Edinburgh: Canongate Press, 2018)
Hoeres, P. *Krieg der Philosophen: Die deutsche und britische Philosophie im Ersten Weltkrieg* (Paderborn: Ferdinand Schöningh Verlag, 2004)
Hollander, D. *Ethics Out of Law: Hermann Cohen and the "Neighbor"* (Toronto: University of Toronto Press, 2021)
Hollier, D. *Against Architecture: The Writings of George Bataille* (Cambridge, MA: MIT Press, 1989)
Holste, C. *Der Forte-Kreis (1910–1915): Rekonstruktion eines utopischen Versuchs* (Stuttgart: M & P, 1992)

Holzhey, H. *Der Marburger Neukantianismus in Quellen: Zeugnisse kritischer Lektüre, Briefe der Marburger, Dokumente zur Philosophiepolitik der Schule* (Basel: Schwabe, 1986)

Honigsheim, P. *The Unknown Max Weber*, trans. J. A. Beegle (New Brunswick, NJ: Transaction Publishers, 2003)

Horwitz, R. *Buber's Way to I and Thou: The Development of Martin Buber's Thought and His Religion as Presence Lectures* (Heidelberg: Verlag Lambert Schneider, 1979)

Hudson, W. *The Marxist Philosophy of Ernst Bloch* (London: Wayne Hudson, 1992)

Hughes, D., and Dinardo, R. *Imperial Germany and War: 1871–1918* (Kansas: University of Kansas Press, 2018)

Husserl, E. *Aufsätze und Vorträge 1911–1921*, eds. H. R. Sepp and T. Nenon (Dordrecht: Springer Verlag, 1987), Hua XXV

Husserl, E. *Briefwechsel* (Dordrecht: Springer Verlag, 1994)

Husserl, E. "Fichte's Ideal of Humanity," trans. J. Hart, *Husserl Studies*, Vol. 12 (1995): 111–133

Husserll, E. "Fichte's *Menschheitsideal*," in *Aufsätze und Vorträge 1911–1921*, eds. H. R. Sepp and T. Nenon (Dordrecht: Springer Verlag, 1987): 267–293

Husserl, E. "Philosophy as Rigorous Science," trans. P. McCormick, in *Husserl. Shorter Works*, eds. P. McCormick and F. Elliston (Notre Dame, IN: University of Notre Dame Press, 1981): 166–197

Jameson, F. *Marxism and Form* (Princeton, NJ: Princeton University Press, 1971)

Jameson, F. *Valences of the Dialectic* (London: Verso, 2009)

Jenkins, P. *The Great and Holy War* (New York: HarperCollins, 2014)

Joas, H. "Kriegsideologien. Der Erste Weltkrieg im Spiegel der zeitgenössischen Sozialwissenschaften," *Leviathan*, Vol. 23, No. 3 (1995): 336–350

Joas, H., and Knöbl, W. *Kriegsverdrängung. Ein Problem in der Geschichte der Sozialtheorie* (Frankfurt: Suhrkamp, 2008)

Johnson, C. *Memory, Metaphor, and Aby Warburg's Atlas of Images* (Ithaca, NY: Cornell University Press, 2012)

Joll, J. *The Second International 1889–1914* (London: Weidenfeld and Nicolson, 1955)

Jonas, H. "Gnosticism, Existentialism, and Nihilism," in *The Gnostic Religion. The Message of the Alien God and the Beginnings of Christianity* (Boston, MA: Beacon Press, 2001): 320–340

Kadarkay, A. (ed.) *The Lukács Reader* (London: Blackwell Publishers, 1995)

Kaegi, D. "Davos und davor," in *Cassirer – Heidegger. 70 Jahre Davoser Disputation*, eds. D. Kaegi, and E. Rudolph (Hamburg: Meiner Verlag, 2002): 67–105

Kavoulakos, K. *Georg Lukács's Philosophy of Praxis* (London: Bloomsbury, 2018)

Keagan, J. *The Face of Battle* (London: Penguin, 1976)

Keck, T. R. *Kant and Socialism* (Ann Arbor: University of Michigan, 1975)

Kern, S. *The Culture of Time and Space 1880–1918* (Cambridge, MA: Harvard University Press, 1983)

Kiesel, T. *The Genesis of Heidegger's* Being and Time (Berkeley: University of California Press, 1993)

Kiesel, T., and Sheehan, T. (eds. and trans.) *Becoming Heidegger: On the Trail of His Early Occasional Writings, 1910–1927* (Evanston, IL: Northwestern University Press, 2007)

Kindermann, H. *Das Goethebild des 20. Jahrhunderts* (Darmstadt: WBG, 1966)

Kjellén, R. *Die Idee von 1914* (Leipzig: G. Hirzel, 1915)

Klibansky, R. "Erinnerungen an Ernst Cassirer," *Internationale Zeitschrift für Philosophie*, Vol. 2 (1999): 275–288

Knowles, A. *Heidegger's Fascist Affinities: A Politics of Silence* (Stanford, CA: Stanford University Press, 2019)

Kohn, H. *Martin Buber. Sein Werk und seine Zeit* (Wiesbaden: Fourier Verlag, 1979)

Köhnke, K. C. *Der junge Simmel: In Theorienbeziehungen und sozialen Bewegungen* (Frankfurt: Suhrkamp, 1996)

Köhnke, K. C. *The Rise of Neo-Kantianism: German Academic Philosophy between Idealism and Positivism*, trans. R. J. Hollingdale (Cambridge, UK: Cambridge University Press, 1991)

Kolakowski, L. *Main Currents of Marxism*, III, trans. P. S. Falla (Oxford: Oxford University Press, 1981)

Korstvedt, B. *Listening for Utopia in Ernst Bloch's Musical Philosophy* (Cambridge, UK: Cambridge University Press, 2010)

Kracauer, S. "Vom Erleben des Krieges," *Preussisches Jahrbuch*, Vol. 158, No. 3 (July–September 1915): 11–22

Královcová, M. "Emil Lederer: On the Sociology of World War" *Central European Papers*, Vol. 2, No. 2 (2014): 51–57

Kramer, A. *Dynamic of Destruction: Culture and Mass Killing in the First World War* (Oxford: Oxford University Press, 2007)

Kreienbock, J. "Franz Rosenzweig's Mitteleuropa as a New Levante," in *Personal Narratives, Peripheral Theatres: Essays on the Great War (1914–18)*, eds. A. Barker, M. E. Pereira, M. T. Cortez, P. A. Pereira, and O. Martins (Dordrecht: Springer, 2018): 185–200

Krieger, L. *The German Idea of Freedom: A History of a Political Tradition* (Boston, MA: Beacon Press, 1957)

Krois, J.-M. "Cassirer's Critique of Heidegger" *Philosophy & Rhetoric*, Vol. 16, No. 3 (1983): 147–159

Krois, J.-M. "*Kulturphilosophie* and Modernism," in *Weimar Thought: A Contested Legacy*, eds. P. Gordon and J. McCormick (Princeton, NJ: Princeton University Press, 2013): 101–114

Krois, J-M. "Urworte: Cassirer als Goethe-Interpret," in *Kulturkritik nach Ernst Cassirer*, eds. E. Rudolph and B.-O. Küpers (Hamburg: Felix Meiner Verlag, 1995): 297–324

Krois, J.-M. "Why Did Cassirer and Heidegger Not Debate in Davos?" in *Symbolic Forms and Cultural Studies: Ernst Cassirer's Theory of Culture*, eds. Cyrus Hamlin and John Michael Krois (New Haven, CT: Yale University Press, 2008): 242–262

Kundera, M. *The Art of the* Novel, trans. L. Asher (New York: Harper Perennial, 1986)

Lang, K. *Chaos and Cosmos: On the Image in Aesthetics and History* (Ithaca, NY: Cornell University Press, 2006)
Lanzer, B. *God Interrupted* (Princeton, NJ: Princeton University Press, 2008)
Leck, R. *Georg Simmel and Avant-Garde Sociology* (London: Humanity Books, 2000)
Lederer, E. *Kapitalismus, Klassenstruktur und Probleme der Demokratie in Deutschland 1910–1940* (Göttingen: Vandenhoeck & Ruprecht, 1979)
Levine, E. *Dreamland of Humanists: Warburg, Cassirer, Panofsky, and the Hamburg School* (Chicago: University of Chicago Press, 2013)
Lindau, H. "Rezension," *Kant-Studien*, Vol. XXII (1918): 125–134
van der Linden, H. *Kantian Ethics and Socialism* (Indianapolis: Hackett Publishing, 1988)
Lipkes, J. *Rehearsals: The German Army in Belgium, August 1914* (Leuven: Leuven University Press, 2007)
Lipton, D. *Ernst Cassirer: The Dilemma of a Liberal Intellectual in Germany, 1914–1933* (Buffalo, NY: University of Toronto Press, 1974)
Lizardo, O. "The Resilience of Life: On Simmel's Last Testament," *Contemporary Sociology*, Vol. 41, No. 3 (2012): 302–304
Losurdo, D. *Heidegger and the Ideology of War: Community, Death, and the West*, trans. M. Morris and J. Morris (New York: Humanity Books, 2001)
Löwith, K. *From Hegel to Nietzsche*, trans. D. Green (New York: Columbia University Press, 1964)
Löwith, K. *Martin Heidegger and European Nihilism*, trans. G. Steiner (New York: Columbia University Press, 1995)
Löwith, K. *My Life in Germany Before and After 1933*, trans. E. King (Champaign, IL: University of Illinois Press, 1994)
Löwy, M. *Georg Lukács – From Romanticism to Bolshevism*, trans. P. Camiller (London: NLB, 1979)
Lübbe, H. *Politische Philosophie in Deutschland* (Darmstadt: DTV, 1985)
Lublinski, S. *Die Bilanz der Moderne* (Tübingen: Niemeyer, 1974)
Luft, S. *The Space of Culture* (Oxford: Oxford University Press, 2015)
Lukács, G. *Briefwechsel 1902–1917* (Stuttgart: J. B. Metzler, 1982)
Lukács, G. *The Destruction of Reason*, trans. P. Palmer (London: Verso, 2021)
Lukács, G. "Die deutschen Intellektuellen und der Krieg," *Text + Kritik*, Vol. 39, No. 40 (1973): 65–69
Lukács, G. *Gelebtes Denken* (Frankfurt: Suhrkamp, 1981)
Lukács, G. G. *Goethe and His Age*, trans. R. Anchor (London: Merlin Press, 1968)
Lukács, G. *Selected Correspondence 1902–1920*, trans. J. Marcus and Z. Tar (New York: Columbia University Press, 1986)
Lukács, G. *Tactics and Ethics 1919–1929* (London: Verso Press, 2014)
Lukács, G. *Tailism and the Dialectic*, trans. E. Leslie (London: Verso, 2000)
Lukács, G. *The Theory of the Novel*, trans. A. Bostock (Cambridge, MA: MIT Press, 1971)
Mann, T. *Reflections on a Nonpolitical Man*, trans. W. Morris (New York: New York Review Books, 2021): 491–506

Marcuse, L. *Mein zwanzigstes Jahrhundert* (Zürich: Diogenes, 1975)
Márkus, G. "Life and the Soul: The Young Lukács and the Problem of Culture," in *Lukács Revalued*, ed. A. Heller (Oxford: Basil Blackwell, 1983): 177–190
Markus, J. *Georg Lukacs and Thomas Mann: A Study in the Sociology of Literature* (Amherst: University of Massachusetts Press, 1988)
Masing-Deling, I. *Abolishing Death: A Salvation Myth of Russian Twentieth-Century Literature* (Stanford, CA: Stanford University Press, 1992)
McElheny, J., and Burgin, C. (eds.) *Glass! Love!! Perpetual Motion!!! A Paul Scheerbart Reader* (Chicago: University of Chicago Press, 2014)
Mehring, R. *Heideggers Überlieferungsgeschick* (Würzburg: Königshausen & Neumann, 1992)
Melle, U. "Edmund Husserl: From Reason to Love," in *Phenomenological Approaches to Moral Philosophy*, eds. J. Drummond and L. Embree (Dordrecht: Springer, 2002): 229–248
Mendes-Flohr, P. *From Mysticism to Dialogue: Martin Buber's Transformation of German Social Thought* (Detroit, MI: Wayne State University Press, 1989)
Mendes-Flohr, P. *German Jews: A Dual Identity* (New Haven, CT: Yale University Press, 1999)
Mendes-Flohr, P. *Martin Buber: A Life of Faith and Dissent* (New Haven, CT: Yale University Press, 2019)
Mendieta, E. "Metaphysical Anti-Semitism and Worldlessness" in *Heidegger's Black Notebooks: Responses to Anti-Semitism*, eds. A. Mitchell and P. Trawny (New York: Columbia University Press, 2017): 36–51
Merleau-Ponty, M. *Adventures of the Dialectic*, trans. J. Bien (Evanston, IL: Northwestern University Press, 1973)
Mészáros, I. *Beyond Capital: Toward a Theory of Transition* (New York: Monthly Review Press, 2010)
Meyer, M. "Jüdische Wissenschaft und jüdische Identität," in *Wissenschaft des Judentums*, ed. J. Carlebach (Darmstadt: Wissenschaftlich Buchgesellschaft, 1992): 3–20
Meyer, T. *Kulturphilosophie in gefährlicher Zeit: Zum Werk Ernst Cassirers* (Hamburg: Meiner Verlag, 2007)
Mierendorff, C. "Wortkunst / Von der Novelle zum Roman" (1920), in *Prosa des Expressionismus*, ed. F. Martini (Stuttgart: Reclam, 1970): 194–197
Moebius, S. "Georg Simmel's Political Thought: Socialism and Nietzschean Aristocratism," *Journal of Classical Sociology* (2021): 1–43
Moll, S. *The Arch-Heretic Marcion* (Tübingen: Mohr Siebeck, 2010)
Mommsen, W. *Bürgerliche Kultur und künstlerische Avantgarde. Kultur und Politik im deutschen Kaiserreich 1870–1919* (Frankfurt: Propyläen, 1994)
Mosès, S. *The Angel of History. Rosenzweig, Benjamin, Scholem*, trans. B. Harshav (Stanford, CA: Stanford University Press, 2008)
Mosse, G. "Jewish Emancipation: Between *Bildung* and Respectability," in *Jewish Response to German Culture*, ed. J. Reinharz and W. Schatzberg (Hannover, NH: University of New England Press, 1985): 1–16

Mosse, G. *Fallen Soldiers: Reshaping the Memory of the World Wars* (Oxford: Oxford University Press, 1990)
Mosse, W., ed. *Deutsches Judentum in Krieg und Revolution 1916–1923* (Tübingen: J. C. B. Mohr, 1971)
Moyhan, G. *Ernst Cassirer and the Critical Science of Germany: 1889–1919* (London: Anthem Press, 2013)
Müller, H.-P. *Krise und Kritik. Klassiker der soziologischen Zeitdiagnose* (Berlin: Suhrkamp, 2021)
Münkler, H. *Der Grosse Krieg. Die Welt 1914–1918* (Berlin: Rowohlt Taschenbuch 2015)
Münsterberg, H. *The Peace and America* (New York, 1915)
Munz, R. "Ob's nach dem Krieg schön zu leben sein wird?" Franz Rosenzweig und Ludwig Wittgensteins Schreiben im 1. Weltkrieg. *Freiburger Zeitschrift für Philosophie und Theologie*, Vol. 45, No. 3 (2012): 480–505
Nahma, P. *Hermann Cohen and the Crisis of Liberalism: The Enchantment of the Public Sphere* (Bloomington, IN: Indiana University Press, 2019)
Naumann, B. "Styles of Change: Ernst Cassirer's Philosophical Writing," in *Symbolic Forms and Cultural Studies. Ernst Cassirer's Theory of Culture*, eds. C. Hamlin and J-M Krois (Berlin: Walter de Gruyter, 2008): 78–96
Naumann, F. *Central Europe*, trans. C. Meredith (New York: A. A. Knopf, 1917)
Negel, J., and Pinggéra, K., eds. *Urkatastophe. Die Erfahrung des Krieges 1914–1918 im Spiegel zeitgenössischer Theologie* (Freiburg: Verlag Herder, 2016)
Neske, G. and Kettering, E. *Martin Heidegger and National Socialism: Questions and Answers*, trans. L. Harries (New York: Paragon Press, 1990)
Nolan, M. *The Invented Mirror: Mythologizing the Enemy in France and Germany, 1898–1914* (New York: Berghahn Books, 2004)
Nordmann, S. *Du Singulier à l'universel. Essai sur la philosophie réligieuse de Hermann Cohen* (Paris: Vrin, 2007)
O'Regan, C. *Theology and the Spaces of the Apocalyptic* (Milwaukee, WI: Marquette University Press, 2009)
Ott, H. *Martin Heidegger. A Political Life*, trans. A. Blunden (New York: Basic Books, 1993)
Ott, M. "Something's Missing. A Study of the Dialectic of Utopia in the Theories of Adorno and Bloch," *Heathwood Journal of Critical Theory: Power, Violence and Non-Violence*, Vol. 1, No. 1 (2015): 133–173
Penslar, D. *Jews and the Military: A History* (Princeton, NJ: Princeton University Press, 2013)
Petitdemange, G. "Hegel et Rosenzweig, la différance se faisant," *Cahiers de la Nuit suveillée. Franz Rosenzweig*, Vol. 1 (1982): 157–170
Peukert, D. *The Weimar Republic* (New York: Hill & Wang, 1992)
Philonenko, A. *L'École de Marbourg: Cohen, Natorp, Cassirer* (Paris: J. Vrin, 1989)
Pick, D. *War Machine: The Rationalisation of Slaughter in the Modern Age* (New Haven, CT: Yale University Press, 1996)

Plenge, J. *1789 und 1914. Die symbolischen Jahre in der Geschichte des politischen Geistes* (Berlin: J. Springer, 1916)
Pollock, B. *Franz Rosenzweig and the Systematic Task of Philosophy* (Cambridge, UK: Cambridge University Press, 2009)
Pollock, B. *Franz Rosenzweig's Conversions: World Denial and World Redemption* (Bloomington: Indiana University Press, 2014)
Polt, R. *Time and Trauma: Thinking through Heidegger in the Thirties* (London: Rowman & Littlefield, 2019)
Poole, W. S. *The Great War and the Origins of Modern Horror* (Berkeley, CA: Counterpoint Press, 2020).
Poorthuis, M. "The Forte-Kreis. A Utopian Attempt to Spiritual Leadership over Europe," *Religion and Theology*, Vol. 24, No. 1–2 (2017): 32–53
Prost, A. and Winter, J. *Penser la grande guerre* (Paris: Gallimard, 2004)
Pulzer, P. *Jews and the German State: The Political History of a Minority, 1848–1933* (Detroit, MI: Wayne State University Press, 2003)
Pyyhtinen, O. "Life, Death and Individuation: Simmel on the Problem of Life Itself," *Theory, Culture & Society*, Vol. 29 No. 7–8 (2012): 78–100
Rabinbach, A. *In the Shadow of Catastrophe: German Intellectuals between Apocalypse and Enlightenment* (Berkeley: University of California Press, 1997)
Radkau, J. *Max Weber: A Biography*, trans. P. Camiller (Cambridge, UK: Polity Press, 2009)
Reed, T. J. *Light in Germany: Scenes from an Unknown Enlightenment* (Chicago: University of Chicago Press, 2013)
Rentsch, T. *Das Sein und der Tod* (Munich: Piper Verlag, 1989)
Renz, U. Cassirer's Enlightenment: On Philosophy and the 'Denkform' of Reason," *British Journal for the History of Philosophy*, Vol. 28, No. 3 (2020): 636–652
Ricoeur, P. "Husserl and the Sense of History," in *Husserl: An Analysis of His Phenomenology*, trans. E. G. Ballard and L. Embree (Evanston, IL: Northwestern University Press, 1967): 143–174
Riedel, M. *Metaphysik des Irgendwie: Georg Simmel als Philosoph* (Freiburg: Alber Verlag, 2021)
Ringer, F. *The Decline of the German Mandarins: The German Academic Community, 1890–1933* (London: Wesleyan University Press, 1969)
Roper, L. *Living I Was Your Plague: Martin Luther's World and Legacy* (Princeton, NJ: Princeton University Press, 2021)
Rosenstock-Huessy, E. *Judaism despite Christianity: The 1916 Wartime Correspondence between Eugen Rosenstock-Huessy and Franz Rosenzweig*, ed. E. Rosenstock-Huessy (Chicago: University of Chicago Press, 2011)
Rosenwald, L. "On the Reception of Buber and Rosenzweig's Bible," *Prooftexts*, Vol. 15, No. 2 (1994): 141–165
Rosenzweig, F. *Die "Gritli"-Briefe. Briefe an Margrit Rosenstock-Huessy*, eds. I. Rühle and R. Mayer (Tübingen: Bilam Verlag, 2002)
Rosenzweig, F. *Der Mensch und sein Werk. Gesammelte Schriften, I/2* (The Hague: Martinus Nijhoff, 1979)

Rosenzweig, F. *Philosophical and Theological Writings*, trans. P. Franks and M. Morgan (Indianapolis: Hackett Publishing, 2000)
Rudolph, E. "From Culture to Politics: The 'Aufhebung' of Ethics in Ernst Cassirer's Political Philosophy in Comparison with the 'Political Theology' of Ernst Kantorowicz," in *Symbolic Forms and Cultural Studies* (New Haven, CT: Yale University Press, 2004): 117–126
Rupnow, D. *Judenforschung im Dritten Reich. Wissenschaft zwischen Politik, Propaganda und Ideologie* (Baden-Baden: Nomos, 2011)
Safranski, R. *Martin Heidegger: Between Good and Evil*, trans. E. Osers (Cambridge, MA: Harvard University Press, 1999)
Saman, M. "Constructions of Goethe versus Constructions of Kant in German Intellectual Culture, 1900–1925," *Goethe Yearbook*, Vol. 21, (2014): 157–189
Savinkov, B. *Pale Horse*, trans. M. Katz (Pittsburgh, PA: University of Pittsburgh Press, 2019)
Scheler, M. *Formalism in Ethics and Non-Formal Ethics of Values*, trans. M. Frings (Evanston, IL: Northwestern University Press, 1973)
Scheler, M. *The Human Place in the Cosmos*, trans. E. Kelly (Evanston, IL: Northwestern University Press, 2009)
Scheler, M. *The Nature of Sympathy*, trans. W. Stark (London: Routledge, 2008)
Scheler, M. *On the Eternal in Man*, trans. B. Noble (New Brunswick, NJ: Transaction Publishers, 2010)
Scheler, M. *Politisch-Pädagogische Schriften*, IV (Bern: Francke Verlag, 1982)
Scheler, M. *Ressentiment*, trans. W. Holdheim (Milwaukee, WI: Marquette University Press, 1994)
Scheler, M. *Schriften aus dem Nachlass: Zur Ethik und Erkenntnislehre* (Bern: Francke Verlag, 1957)
Scheler, M. *Schriften aus dem Nachlaß: Philosophie und Geschichte*, ed. M. Frings (Bonn: Bouvier, 1990)
Scheler, M. *Selected Philosophical Papers*, trans. D. Lachterman (Evanston, IL: Northwestern University Press, 1973)
Schelling, F. W. J. *Philosophy of Revelation (1841–42)*, trans. K. Ottmann (Washington, DC: Spring Publications, 2020)
Schmitt, C. *Roman Catholicism and Political Form*, trans. G. L. Lumen (New York: Praeger, 1996)
Schneck, S. *Persons and Polis: Max Scheler's Personalism as Political Theory* (Albany: State University of New York, 1987)
Scholem, G. "What Is Judaism?" in *On the Possibility of Jewish Mysticism in Our Time and Other Essays*, trans. J. Chipman (Philadelphia, PA: Jewish Publication Society, 1997): 102–116
Schubbach, A. *Die Genese des Symbolischen: Zu den Anfängen von Ernst Cassirers Kulturphilosophie* (Hamburg: Felix Meiner Verlag, 2016)
Schwarzchild, S. "Germanism and Judaism – Herman Cohen's Normative Paradigm of the German-Jewish Symbiosis," in *Jews and Germans from 1860 to 1933*, ed. D. Bronsen (Heidelberg: Carl Winter Verlag, 1979): 129–172

Sebestyen, V. *Lenin: The Man, the Dictator, and the Master of Terror* (New York: Vintage Books, 2017)

Sheehan, T. "Heidegger's Lehrjahre," in *The Collegium Phaenomelogicum: The First Ten Years*, eds. John C. Sallis, Giuseppina Moneta, and Jacques Taminiaux (Dordrecht: Kluwer, 1988): 77–137

Siebers, J. "Noch Nicht," in *Bloch-Wörterbuch. Leitbegriffe der Philosophie Ernst Blochs*, eds. B. Dietschy, D. Zeilinger, and R. Zimmermann (Berlin: De Gruyter, 2012): 403–408

Sieg, U. *Jüdische Intellekuelle im Ersten Weltkrieg* (Berlin: Akademie Verlag, 2001)

Simmel, G. *Briefe 1912–1918. Jugendbriefe*, eds. O. Rammstedt and A. Rammstedt (Frankfurt: Suhrkamp, 2008)

Simmel, G. "The Metropolis and Modern Life," in *On Individuality and Social Forms*, ed. D. Levine (Chicago, IL: University of Chicago Press, 1971): 294–323

Simmel, G. "Henri Bergson," in *Aufsätze und Abhandlungen 1909–1918*, Band II (Frankfurt: Suhrkamp Verlag, 2000): 53–69, GA 13.

Simmel, G. "On Death in Art," in *Aufsätze und Abhandlungen 1909–1918*, Band II (Frankfurt: Suhrkamp Verlag, 2000): 123–132, GA 13

Simmel, G. *On Individuality and Social Forms*, ed. D. Levine (Chicago, IL: University of Chicago Press, 1971)

Simmel, G. "The Metropolis and Modern Life," in *On Individuality and Social Forms*, ed. D. Levine (Chicago, IL: University of Chicago Press, 1971): 324–339

Simmel, G. *Rembrandt: An Essay in the Philosophy of Art*, trans. A. Scott and H. Staubman (London: Routledge, 2005)

Simmel, G. *Schopenhauer and Nietzsche* (Urbana: University of Illinois Press, 1991)

Simmel, G. *Soziologie* (Frankfurt: Suhrkamp Verlag 2018), GA 11

Simmel, G. *The View of Life*, trans. J. Andrews and D. Levine (Chicago, IL: University of Chicago Press, 2010)

Sluga, H. *Heidegger's Crisis: Philosophy and Politics in Nazi Germany* (Cambridge, MA: Harvard University Press, 1993)

Smith, B. "Bela Zalai und die Metaphysik des reinen Seins," *Brentano Studien. Internationales Jahrbuch der Franz Brentano Forschung*, Vol. 5, (1994): 59–68

Spader, P. *Scheler's Personalism: Its Logic, Development, and Promise* (New York: Fordham University Press, 2002)

Später, J. *Kracauer: A Biography*, trans. D. Steuer (London: Polity Press, 2020)

Staude, J. R. *Max Scheler 1874–1928: An Intellectual Portrait* (New York: Free Press, 1967)

Stoetzler, M. *The State, the Nation & the Jews: Liberalism and the Antisemitism Dispute in Bismarck's Germany* (Lincoln: University of Nebraska, 2008)

Stoll, M. *Aufbruch der deutschen Nation 1914–1933*, (Bamberg: Buchners Verlag, 1935)

Streubel, C. *Lenore Kühn (1878–1955): neue Nationalistin und verspätete Bildungsbürgerin* (Berlin: Trafo Verlag, 2007)

Stromberg, R. "Max Weber and World War I: Culture and Politics," *Dalhousie Review*, Vo. 59, No. 2 (1979): 350–357

Susman, M. *Die Geistige Gestalt Georg Simmels* (Tübingen: J. C. B. Mohr, 1959)

Symons, S. *More Than Life: Georg Simmel and Walter Benjamin on Art* (Evanston, IL: Northwestern University Press, 2017)

Szabados, B. "Georg Lukács in Heidelberg: A Crossroad between the Academic and Political Career," *Filozofia*, Vol. 75, No. 1 (2020): 51–64

Tacik, P. "Ernst Bloch as a Non-Simultaneous Jewish Marxist," *Religions*, Vol. 9, No. 11 (2018): 346. https://doi.org/10.3390/rel9110346

Tarr, Z. "A Note on Weber and Lukács," *International Journal of Politics, Culture, and Society*, Vol. 3, No. 1 (1989): 131–139

Taubes, J. "Theodicy and Theology: A Philosophical Analysis of Karl Barth's Dialectical Theology" in *From Cult to Culture* (Stanford, CA: Stanford University Press, 2010): 177–194

Theunissen, M. *The Other: Studies in the Social Ontology of Husserl, Heidegger, Sartre, and Buber*, trans. C. Macann (Cambridge, MA: MIT Press, 1986)

Thimme, F., ed. *Vom inneren Frieden des Deutschen Volkes. Ein Buch gegenseitigen Verstehens und Vertrauens* (Leipzig: Hirzel Verlag, 1916)

Tilitzki, C. *Die Deutsche Universitätsphilosophie in der Weimarer Republik und im Dritten Reich* (Berlin: Walter de Gruyter, 2002)

Toller, E. *Plays One*, trans. A. R. Pearlman (London: Oberon Books, 2000)

Traverso, E. *The Origins of Nazi Violence*, trans. J. Lloyd (New York: New Press, 2003)

Trejo-Mathys, J. "Neo-Kantianism and the Philosophy of Law: Its Value and Actuality," in *New Approaches to Neo-Kantianism*, ed. N. de Warren and A. Staiti (Cambridge, UK: Cambridge University Press, 2015): 147–170

Troeltsch, E. *Der Kulturkrieg* (Berlin: Sehmanns, 1915)

Troeltsch, E. *Schriften zur Politik (1914–1918)* (Berlin: Walter de Gruyter, 2002)

Ullrich, A. "'Nun sind wir gezeichnet' – Jüdische Soldaten und die 'Judenzählung,'" in *Krieg! 1914–1918 Juden zwischen den Fronten*, ed. U. Sieg (Berlin: Hentrich&Hentrich, 2014): 217–238

von Ungern-Sternberg, J. and von Ungern-Sternberg, W. *Der Aufruf "An die Kulturwelt!" Das Manifesto der 93 und die Anfänge der Kriegspropaganda im Ersten Weltkrieg* (Frankfurt: Peter Lang, 2013)

Unruh, K. *Langemarck, Legende und Wirklichkeit* (Koblenz: Bernhard & Graefe, 1986)

Vattel, M. "Nationality, State and Global Constitutionalism in Hermann Cohen's Wartime Writings," in *100 Years of European Philosophy since the Great War*, ed. M. Sharpe, R. Jeffs, and J. Reynolds (Dordrecht: Springer, 2017): 43–63

Verene, D. P. *The Origins of the Philosophy of Symbolic Forms* (Evanston, IL: Northwestern University Press, 2011)

Verhey, J. *The Spirit of 1914: Militarism, Myth and Mobilization in Germany* (Cambridge, UK: Cambridge University Press, 2000)

Volkelt, H. *Demobilisierung der Geister. Eine Auseinandersetzung vornehmlich mit Ernst Troeltsch* (Munich: Beck'sche Verlagsbuchhandlung, 1918)

Vondung, K. *The Apocalypse in Germany*, trans. S. Ricks, (Columbia: University of Missouri Press, 2000)

Vongehr, T. "*Euckens sind wieder da, verstehende und so wertvolle Freunde* – Die Freundschaft der Husserls zu Walter und Edith Eucken in den letzten Freiburger Jahren," in *Phänomenologie und die Ordnung der Wirtschaft. Edmund Husserl - Rudolf Eucken - Walter Eucken - Michel Foucault*, eds. H. Gander, N. Goldschmid, and U. Dathe, (Würzburg: Ergon Verlag, 2009): 3–18

de Warren, N. "Husserl and Phenomenological Ethics," in *The Cambridge History of Moral Philosophy*, eds. S. Golob and J. Timmerman (Cambridge, UK: Cambridge University Press, 2017): 562–576

de Warren, N. *Husserl and the Promise of Time: Subjectivity in Transcendental Phenomenology* (Cambridge, UK: Cambridge University Press, 2009)

de Warren, N. "La radicalité de la raison. Le cartésianisme de la phénoménologie husserlienne," in *Descartes et la phénoménologie*, eds. C. Riquier and D. Pradelle (Paris: L'Harmattan, 2018): 35–53

de Warren, N. "*Eine Reise um die Welt*: Cassirer's Cosmological Phenomenology," in *New Approaches to Neo-Kantianism*, eds. N. de Warren and A. Staiti (Cambridge, UK: Cambridge University Press, 2015): 82–108

de Warren, N. "Rudolf Eucken: Philosophicus Teutonicus (1913–1914)," in *The Intellectual Responses to the First World War*, eds. S. Posman, C. Van Dijck, and M. Demoor (Eastbourne: Sussex Academic Press, 2017): 44–64

de Warren, N. "Skepticism on Violence and Vigilance on Peace," *Graduate Faculty Philosophy Journal*, Vol. 41, No. 1 (2020): 279–317

de Warren, N. "Spirit in the Age of Technical Production," in *Interpreting Cassirer*, ed. S. Truwant (Cambridge: Cambridge University Press, 2020): 109–129

de Warren, N., and Vongehr, T., eds. *Philosophers at the Front. Phenomenology and the First World War*, (Leuven: Leuven University Press, 2017)

Watier, P. "Georg Simmel et la guerre," in *Kultur und Krieg. Die Rolle der Intellektuellen, Künstler und Schriftsteller im Ersten Weltkrieg*, ed. W. Mommsen (Berlin: Walter de Gruyter Oldenbourg, 2015): 31–48

Weber, M. *Charisma and Disenchantment: The Vocation Lectures*, eds. P. Reitter and C. Wellmon (New York: New York Review of Books, 2020)

Weber, M. *Max Weber: A Biography*, trans. H. Zohn (London: Wiley, 1975)

Weidner, D. "Das Absolut des Krieges: Max Schelers Kriegsdenken und die Rhetorik des Äußersten," in *Texturen des Krieges. Körper, Schriften und der erste Weltkrieg*, ed. G. Shahar (Göttingen: Wallstein Verlag, 2015): 85–114

Welch, D. *Germany and Propaganda in World War I* (London: I. B. Taurus, 2014)

Wellbery, D. "The Imagination of Freedom: Goethe and Hegel as Contemporaries," in *Goethe's Ghosts: Reading and the Persistence of Literature*, eds. S. Richter and R. Block (London: Camden House, 2014): 271–239

Westerman, R. "The Irrational Act: Traces of Kierkegaard in Lukács's Revolutionary Subject," *Studies in East European Thought*, Vol. 67, No. 3/4 (2015): 229–247

Westerman, R. *Lukács's Phenomenology of Capitalism* (London: Palgrave Macmillan, 2019)

Wiedenbach, H. *Die Bedeutung der Nationalität für Hermann Cohen* (Hildesheim: Olms, 1997)

Wolfe, J. *Heidegger's Eschatology* (Oxford: Oxford University Press, 2013)
Wolin, R. *Heidegger's Children* (Princeton, NJ: Princeton University Press, 2015)
Wolin, R., ed. *The Heidegger Controversy: A Critical Reader*, (Cambridge, MA: MIT Press, 1992)
Wolin, R. "Notes on the Early Aesthetics of Lukács, Bloch, and Benjamin," *Berkeley Journal of Sociology*, Vol. 26 (1981): 89–109
Wolin, R. *The Politics of Being: The Political Thought of Martin Heidegger* (New York: Columbia University Press, 1990)
Wundt, W. *Die Nationen und ihre Philosophie: ein Kapitel zum Weltkrieg*, Leipzig: Alfred Kroner Verlag, 1915)
Zaborowski, H. *Eine Frage von Irre und Schuld? Martin Heidegger und der Nationalsozialismus* (Frankfurt: Fischer Verlag, 2010)
Zac, S. *La Philosophie réligieuse de Hermann Cohen* (Paris: Vrin, 1984)
Zimmermann, M. "A Road Not Taken – Friedrich Naumann's Attempt at a Modern German Nationalism," *Journal of Contemporary History*, Vol. 17, No. 4 (1982): 689–708
Žižek, S. *Lenin: The Day after the Revolution* (London: Verso, 2017)
Zudeick, P. *Hintern des Teufels: Ernst Bloch – Leben und Werk* (Zurich: Elster Verlag, 1987)

Index

absolute life, 198
absolute values, 398, 400
abstract Idealism, 204
Aby Warburg, 296
Adolf Grimme, 389
Adolf Harnack, 14
Adolf Hitler, 333, 349
Adolf Reinach, 226, 378
Adolf von Harnack, 48, 56, 110
aesthetics, 166, 196, 198
"Albert Schweitzer as Critic
 of Nineteenth-Century Ethics," 279
aletheia, 337, 365
Alfred Franz, 366
All Quiet on the Western Front, 370–371
Alois Riehl, 14
Alsace-Lorraine, 117
America, 124
an old pitcher, 161
Anna Lesznai, 208
Anselm Reust, 189
anti-Semitism, 56, 272, 333, 358, 361, 363
anti-utopia, 180
Archduke Franz Ferdinand, 12
"*Archiv für Sozialwissenschaft und
 Sozialpolitik*," 191
Aristotle, 131
Arnold Metzger, 51, 380
artwork, 164
Augusterlebnis, 368
authenticity, 144
autonomy, 25, 173
autonomy of thinking, 279

Baal Shem, 185
Bartmann Krug, 161
Basisphänomene, 308
Bavarian Revolution, 155
Bavarian Soviet Republic, 86
Beethoven, 167, 169
Beethoven's "Ode to Joy," 169
Befreiungskrieg (1813), 281

Being and Time, 323, 331, 337, 344
being-in-the-world, 322
Béla Balázs, 190
Béla Zalai, 191
Berlin, 316
Bildung, 284, 286
Bildungsbürgetum, 49
biopolitics, 183
Bismarck, 187, 241
Black Notebooks, 337
blessedness, 394
Bolshevism, 208, 210
"Bolshevism as an Ethical Problem," 210
Boris Savinkov, 193
Briefe über die ästhetische Beziehung, 286
Briefe über die Vaterlandsliebe, 286
Bruno Bauch, 62, 333
brutalitas, 364

calculative machination, 362
"Call to Socialism," 86
"Cannä und Gorlice," 240
capitalism, 65, 154, 201
Carl Schmitt, 36
Carl von Clausewitz, 33, 72, 356
Categorical Imperative, 150
Catholicism, 36, 37, 57, 321
Chancellor Bethmann-Hollweg, 238
Christ, 184
Christian idea of love, 29
Christian Wolff, 285
Christian worldview, 315
Christianity, 231, 234, 243, 266
Clara Zetkin, 188
collective person, 29
commandment of love, 79
commemoration, 343
commodification, 214
commodity, 216, 217
commodity-structure, 217
Communist Party, 223
contingency of human existence, 140

Contributions to Philosophy, 341, 356
cosmopolitan humanism, 289
cosmopolitanism, 59, 60
Crime and Punishment, 211
Crisis of the European Sciences., 369
crisis theology, 108
Critique of Practical Reason, 285
Critique of Pure Reason, 293
Critique of the German Intelligentsia, 17
cultural pluralism, 287

Dadaism, 159
Daniel: Dialogues on Realization, 107
Das Ego und sein Eigentum, 98, 104
Das Kapital, 214, 216
"Das Kriegstridiuum in Messkirch," 314
Dasein, 321, 347
Davos Switzerland, 330
death, 129, 135, 137, 180, 183, 250, 253, 345
Decameron, 189
Der Blaue Reiter, 155, 164
Der Genius des Krieges und der Deutsche Krieg, 15, 30, 378
Der Jude, 51
Der Krieg, 17
Der Wille zur Ewigkeit, 378, 381
Deutscher Weltberuf. Geschichtsphilosophische Richtlinien, 277
Deutschheit, 354
"Deutschlands innere Wandlung", 120
Deutschtum, 238
Deutschtum and Judentum, 55
Deutschtum und Judentum, 53, 61, 62, 333
dialogical relationality, 261
Dicthung und Erlebnis, 98
Die Anweisung zum seligen Leben, 387
Die Bestimmung des Menschen, 387
Die Bilanz der Moderne, 187
"Die Dialektik des deutschen Geistes," 120
"Die Idee der Religion bei Lessing und Mendelssohn," 289
"Die Idee des Friedens und der Pazifismus," 21
"Die Idee Europa," 120, 124
"Die Idee von 1914," 277
"Die Juden und das Wirtschaftsleben," 51
"Die Krisis der Kultur," 120
Die Nationen und ihre Philosophie: ein Kapitel zum Weltkrieg, 277
Die Reden an die deutsche Nation, 387
Die unsichtbare Königreich des deutschen Idealismus, 378
Die Ursachen des Deutschenhasses, 35
Dietrich Mahnke, 12, 226, 368, 378
Dietrich von Hildebrand, 16
Ding an sich, 162

disenchantment of the world, 100
Don Quixote, 202
Dostoevsky, 191, 200, 205

Edmund Husserl, 12, 22, 51, 160, 291, 318
Eduard von Hartmann, 33
Einstein's Theory of Relativity, 294
Elfriede Heidegger, 313
Else von Stritzky, 153
Emil Lask, 191, 226
Emil Lederer, 158, 192
Erich Gutkind, 84
Erich Maria Remarque's, 370
Erkenntnistheorie nebst den Grenzfragen der Logik und Denkpsychologie, 297
Ernst Bloch, 209
Ernst Cassirer, 73, 330
Ernst Jünger, 226
Ernst Toller, 155
Ernst Troeltsch, 47, 56, 134, 368
essence of the war, 19
Eternal Thou, 89, 107, 109, 111, 113
eternal values, 388
ethical obligations, 27
ethical socialism, 21
Ethics of the Pure Will, 63
Eugen Rosenstock, 227, 232
Europa und America, 124
Europe, 391
Expressionism, 164

factical life, 321
Faust, 207, 275
Ferdinand Ebner, 88
Fichte, 48, 54, 194, 277, 287, 289, 369, 384
Florens Christian Rang, 84
form of objectivity, 216
Formalism in Ethics and Non-Formal Ethics of Values, 20
Forte Kreis, 84
Foundations of Natural Right, 287
Franco-Prussian War, 117
Franz Brentano, 291, 320
Franz Rosenzweig, 39, 73, 88
Franz Werfel, 114
Frederick the Great, 286
Frederick van Eeden, 84
Freedom, 24, 173, 278, 282, 286, 287, 299, 395
Freie Jüdisches Lehrhaus, 88, 248
Freiheit und Form Studien zur Deutschen Geistesgeschichte, 275, 336
French Revolution, 287
Friedrich Dahlmann, 243
Friedrich Gogarten, 39

Friedrich Meinecke, 232
Friedrich Naumann, 239
Friedrich Schlegel, 290
Friedrich Thimme, 52
Friedrich von Bernhardi, 32
Fritz Kaufmann, 382
Fritz Ringer, 17
Fünf Gesänge, August 1914, 18

"*Gedächtniskranz auf Paul Scheerbarts Grab,*" 189
General Erich von Gündell, 367
General von Falkenhayn's, 367
General von Gneisenau, 72
General von Scharnhorst, 72
Georg Heym, 17
Georg Simmel, 15, 157, 190, 307, 321
Georges Bataille, 13
Gerhart Hauptmann, 12
German Enlightenment, 275
German Humanism, 288, 290
German Idealism, 66, 156, 199, 214, 219, 307, 384
German militarism, 72
German Socialist Party, 49
German spirit, 278, 282, 290, 384
German-Jewish *Bildungsbürgertum.*, 273
Gertrud Oppenheim, 242, 247
Geschichtsphilosophie. Eine Kriegsvorlesung, 277
Gesinnungsmilitarismus, 16, 19, 32
Globus
    Studien zur weltgeschichtlichen Raumlehre, 243
Gnosticism, 111, 183
God, 24, 27, 31, 43, 46, 58, 67, 71, 75, 78, 89, 108, 112, 123, 125, 140, 184, 202, 229, 235, 252, 256, 262, 307
Goethe, 94, 132, 148, 238, 275, 292, 307, 308, 383
Golo Mann, 335
Grand Duke Sergei Aleksandrovich, 194
Grigory Zinoviev, 186
Grundzüge des gegenwärtigen Zeitalters, 288
Guido von List, 56
Gustav Landauer, 84, 102, 155, 187
Gustav Radbruch, 158, 194
György Lukács, 156

H. H. Asquith, 12
Hannah Arendt, 323
Hans Blüher, 335
Hans Blumenberg, 330
Hans Delbrück, 48
Hans Ehrenberg, 228, 236
Harald Høffding, 119
Harvard University, 272
Hebbel, 212
Hegel, 127, 173, 179, 208, 232, 282, 288, 299
Hegel and the State, 231, 241, 244

Heidelberg Aesthetics, 198
Heidelberg Philosophy of Art, 198
Heinrich Heine, 40
Heinrich Rickert, 135
Heinrich von Treitschke, 32, 243, 289
Helene Stöcker, 157
Henri Bergson, 130
Henri Borel, 84
Henrich von Treitschke, 335
Heraclitus, 349
Heritage of the Times, 156
Hermann Bahr, 16, 281
Hermann Cohen, 228, 234, 277, 332
Hermann Cohen's, 53
Hermann Graf von Keyserling, 115, 125
Hermann Hesse, 170
Heuberger Volksblatt, 314
History and Class Consciousness, 209, 212, 219, 220
Hochschule für die Wissenschaft des Judentums, 234
Hölderlin, 289, 317, 341, 355
Holy Roman Empire, 243, 244
homo absconditus, 182
homo symbolicus, 307
hope, 154, 172, 175, 181, 184
Hugo Ball, 17, 36
Hugo Liepmann, 118
Hugo Münsterberg, 376
humanism, 71, 223
humanity, 40, 45, 65, 67, 380, 391
hyper-individualism, 126

I and Thou, 68, 87, 113, 149
Idee und Gestalt, 292
Ideen I, 372, 387
I–It relation, 89, 90
immortality, 135
imputed class consciousness, 221
instrumentality rationality, 105
intentional feelings, 22
interactive reciprocity, 222
intuition of essences, 19, 378
intuitionism, 15
inwardness, 164, 171, 178
Irma Seidler, 199
I–Thou relation, 89, 92, 95, 96, 105, 112

J. S. Bach, 167
Jahrbuch für Philosophie und phänomenologische Forschung, 20
Jean Jaures, 188
Jelena Grabenko, 193
Joan of Arc, 13
John the Baptist, 196

Judaism, 52, 55, 59, 75, 79, 231, 234, 235, 266
Judaism and Christianity, 58–61
Judentum, 277, 289, 358
Julius Langbehn, 56
Jürgen Habermas, 330

kairos, 18, 319
Kaiser Wilhelm II, 14
Kaizo articles, 325, 391
Kampf um das Dasein, 48, 354
Kant, 54, 63, 72, 145, 164, 172, 179, 279, 291, 293, 306, 313, 331
Kantian ethics, 21, 388
Kantian Thoughts in German Militarism, 71
Kants Leben und Lehre, 293
Karl Barth, 39, 108
Karl Jaspers, 158, 194, 201, 339, 342
Karl Kautsky, 188
Karl Liebknecht, 188, 194
Karl Löwith, 226, 322
Kiel Mutiny, 368
Kierkegaard, 197
Konflikt der modernen Kultur, 126
Krieg und Aufbau, 20, 37
Kriegsideologie, 354
Kriegsphilosophie, 32, 192, 193, 212, 276, 288, 333, 378, 385
Kriegspresseamt, 273
Kriegstheologie, 109
Krisis der Kultur, 125
Kulturkampf, 49
Kurt Eisner, 102, 155, 170
Kurt Hiller, 157

language, 295
Law of Moses, 79
Law of the Individual, 147
Lehranstalt für die Wissenschaft des Judentums, 276
Leibniz, 283, 285
Lenin, 223
Leopold von Ranke, 289
Lessing, 235
Leuven, 371
life, 129, 197, 203, 305, 309, 393
Lodewijk Hermen Grondijs, 13
Logical Investigations, 372
love, 24
love and hate, 23
Ludendorff Offensive, 368
Luther, 72, 283, 321

Machtstaat, 64–69, 284
Malvine Husserl, 368
Mammonism, 123, 124

Marburg Neo-Kantianism, 53, 272, 337
Marcion, 110
The Gospel of the Alien God, 110
Marcionism, 184, 233, 363
Margarete Susman, 117, 118, 157, 127
Margrit Rosenstock, 227, 228, 241
Marianne Weber, 116, 190
Martin Buber, 39, 226
Martin Heidegger, 36, 239, 369
Marx, 180
Marxism, 156, 178, 207
Maurice Merleau-Ponty, 213, 221
Max Brod, 16
Max Scheler, 319, 376
Max Stirner, 98, 104
Max Weber, 15, 99, 116, 154, 190, 201, 280, 368
Mein Kampf, 352
messianic peace, 70
messianic prophetism, 58
messianic theory of knowledge, 230
messianism, 70, 182
metaphysics of Dasein, 331
mimetic violence, 246
Mitteleuropa, 239
modern culture, 124
modern society, 97, 218
modernity, 127
Moeller van de Bruck, 56
"Money and Modern Culture," 121
monotheism, 60, 65
moral autonomy, 286
moral norms, 395
Moral und Politik, 21
mother's love for her child, 399
mourning, 347
Mozart, 167
multiplicity of worlds, 134
Munich *Räterepublik*, 155
music, 168
mysterium tremendum, 113
mysticism, 83, 112

Nathan the Wise, 61, 235
National Socialism, 342, 346, 349
Nationalism, 286, 289
nation-state, 64
natural attitude, 392
Nebenmensch, 75
necro-politics, 182, 183
Neo-Kantianism, 199, 272, 313, 320, 332, 333, 372
"New Levante," 240
New Testament, 111
new thinking, 229
Nietzsche, 355

Nihilism, 355
Ninon de l'Enclos, 197
Nobel Prize, 272
Norbert von Hellingrath, 317
not yet consciousness, 174

objective values, 398
October Revolution of 1917, 207
Ökumene. Zur Geschichte der geschichtlichen Welt, 243
Old Testament, 74, 110
"On Poverty of Spirit," 200
On the Eternal in Man, 39, 42, 43, 111
On the Several Senses of Being in Aristotle, 320
ontology of art, 199
ontology of war, 246
Ordo Amoris, 21–33
original belief (*Urdoxa*), 393
Oswald Spengler, 104, 155
Othmar Spann, 332

pacificism, 194
Pale Horse, 193, 206, 208
pantheism, 41
Parmenides, 127, 365
parousia, 319
Paul Desjardins, 42
Paul Ernst, 190
Paul Lagarde, 56, 98
Paul Natorp, 53, 274, 376
Paul Ricoeur, 369
Paul Scheerbart, 189
peace, 45, 80–82
perpetual peace, 73
person, 23, 24, 27, 399
personal salvation, 25
personal vocation, 399
phenomenology of utopic spirit, 167, 183
"Philosophy as a Rigorous Science," 372, 384
Philosophy of Hope, 177
"Philosophy of the Symbolic," 291
planetary age of technology, 362
Plato, 30, 66, 69, 100, 196
Plato's cave, 101
Platonism, 68, 70
polarity, 293
polemos, 352, 356, 365
political terrorism, 207
Poul Bjerre, 84
praxis, 221, 222
Protestantism, 57, 232, 321
psychologism, 320
pure monotheism, 67, 70, 74
purposiveness without purpose, 149

Rainer Maria Rilke, 17
Realpolitik, 33
reason, 288
Rechtstaat, 64
reciprocal interaction, 132, 142–143
Rede an die Deutsche Nation, 48, 287, 369
reification, 214, 216, 218
Reims Cathedral, 12
Religion of Reason Out of the Sources of Judaism, 62, 65, 234
Religion within the Boundaries of Mere Reason, 63
Rembrandt, 135
repentance, 38
responsibility, 380, 395, 397
ressentiment, 37, 38
revolution, 86
revolutionary praxis, 215
Rheims Cathedral, 371
Rilke, 151
Romain Rolland, 12
Roman Rolland, 84
romanticism, 205
Rosa Luxemburg, 159, 189
Rudolf Ehrenberg, 239
Rudolf Eucken, 53, 98, 272, 277, 368
Rudolf Hallo, 232
Rudolf Kjellén, 243, 244, 281
Rudolf Otto, 39, 108
Russian Revolution, 193

Sabine Lepsius, 116
sacrifice, 277, 344, 361, 362, 366
salvation, 180
Samuel Lublinski, 187
Schelling, 244
Schiller, 283
Schopenhauer, 168
Second International, 208, 213
Second Morocco Crisis, 86
self-cultivation, 286
Selma Lagerlöf, 232
Seynsgeschichtliches Denken, 339, 341, 350, 364
Siegfried Kracauer, 281
Sir Arthur Evans, 12
Sittlichkeit, 57, 63, 65, 77, 80, 173, 206, 219, 242, 388
situation, 129
Social Darwinism, 32
socialism, 187
Soul and Form, 190, 196, 212
spirit, 299, 303, 311
spiritual solidarity, 29
Stalinism, 225
State and Revolution, 189

Index 425

Stefan Georg, 158
Straßburg, 117
striving, 23
struggle, 349
subjectivity, 306
suffering, 76
symbolic forms, 295–300

"Tactics and Ethics," 211
Talcott Parson, 99
teleology, 135
temporality, 130
Ten Commandments, 79
the Absolute, 163, 169, 173, 184
the Apocalypse, 177
the bourgeois, 214
The Brothers Karamazov, 206
the Crisis of the European Sciences, 373, 391
The Critique of the Power of Judgment, 294
The Downfall of the West, 104, 155
The Epistle to the Romans, 108
The Fundamental Concepts of Metaphysics, 338
"The German Intellectuals and the War," 192
the Good, 66, 78
"the Great enemy," 357, 358
the Holy, 29
The Human Place in the Cosmos, 15, 44
"The Idea of Perpetual Peace and Pacifism," 45
The Idea of the Holy, 108
the inconstruable question, 176
the individual, 143, 148
"*The Jews and Economic Life*," 334
the lived present, 174–178
The Logical Investigations, 387, 390
the metaphysics of Dasein, 353
The Metaphysics of Tragedy, 196
The Miracles of the Antichrist, 232
The Myth of the State, 274, 278, 283, 305
the Old Testament, 180, 235
"The Origin of the World of Art," 346
the person, 394
The Philosophy of Money, 123
The Philosophy of Symbolic Forms, 291, 296, 300, 304, 331
the proletarian class, 216–220
the proletariat, 210
The prophets, 67
the question of the sense of Being, 326
The Religion of Reason from the Sources of Judaism, 73
the Second International, 187, 224
The Second Morocco Crisis, 187
"The Social Ideal in Plato and the Prophets," 65
the Spirit of 1914, 280, 281

The Spirit of Utopia, 160, 182, 209
The Star of Redemption, 229, 254
"The Style of the Prophets," 58
The Theory of the Novel, 189, 201
the Thou, 75
The tragedy of the person, 400
the Urzelle letter, 227, 231
The View of Life, 116, 120, 127–128, 307, 322
"The Vocation of the Politician," 99
"The Vocation of the Scholar," 99
the We-problem, 178
the will, 395
"*The Word and the Spiritual Realities,*" 88
Theodor Däubler, 84
Theodor Lessing, 16
Theory of the Novel, 202
Third Reich, 356
Thomas Mann, 48, 192, 280
Thomas Münzer als Theologe der Revolution, 153, 209
Thoughts in Wartime, 48
Tolstoy, 205
Toni Cassirer, 272, 332
total mobilization, 281
totality, 214
tragedy of culture, 196
transcendence of life, 129
transcendental consciousness, 321
transcendental homelessness, 202, 206
truth, 134, 298
tzimtzum, 95

Über das Eigentümliche des deutschen Geistes, 60
Ulrich von Wiliamowitz-Moellendorff, 48
Umsturz der Werte, 15
University of Freiburg, 320
utopia, 160
utopic impulse, 177

value essences, 22
values, 22
Verdun, 119, 275, 312, 316, 382
Victor Hugo, 189
violence, 32
Vladimir Lenin, 186, 188
Volksgemeinschaft, 193, 343, 351
"Vom Begriff der Nation," 333
Vom inneren Frieden des Deutschen Volkes, 52
Vorbilder und Führer, 21

Wagner, 167
war, 31, 34, 40, 346
Warburg Library, 295

Weimar Classicism, 272, 296
Weimar Humanism, 275
Weimar liberalism, 285
Weltanschauungsphilosophie, 373, 374, 379
Weltbürgertum und Nationalstaat, 242
Werner Sombart, 15, 51, 335
Western metaphysics, 322
Wilhelm Dilthey, 98, 197, 321

Wilhelm von Humboldt, 275
Wilhelm Wundt, 277
world, 133
world philosophy, 290
world understanding, 297

Zionism, 62
"Zur Soziologie des Weltkriegs," 193

For EU product safety concerns, contact us at Calle de José Abascal, 56–1°, 28003 Madrid, Spain or eugpsr@cambridge.org.

www.ingramcontent.com/pod-product-compliance
Ingram Content Group UK Ltd.
Pitfield, Milton Keynes, MK11 3LW, UK
UKHW021930030226

467659UK00020B/754